MW00835289

THE GRAPHIC STANDARDS GUIDE TO ARCHITECTURAL FINISHES

THE GRAPHIC STANDARDS GUIDE TO ARCHITECTURAL FINISHES

Using MASTERSPEC® to Evaluate, Select, and Specify Materials

ARCOM

The American Institute of Architects

Editor

Elena M. S. Garrison, AIA, CCS, CSI

JOHN WILEY & SONS, INC.

This book is printed on acid-free paper.

Text © 2002, The American Institute of Architects. Illustrations © 2002, John Wiley & Sons, Inc. All rights reserved.

Published by John Wiley & Sons, Inc., Hoboken, New Jersey
Published simultaneously in Canada

No part of this publication may be reproduced, stored in a retrieval system, or transmitted in any form or by any means, electronic, mechanical, photocopying, recording, scanning, or otherwise, except as permitted under Section 107 or 108 of the 1976 United States Copyright Act, without either the prior written permission of the Publisher, or authorization through payment of the appropriate per-copy fee to the Copyright Clearance Center, Inc., 222 Rosewood Drive, Danvers, MA 01923, (978) 750-8400, fax (978) 750-4470, or on the web at www.copyright.com. Requests to the Publisher for permission should be addressed to the Permissions Department, John Wiley & Sons, Inc., 111 River Street, Hoboken, NJ 07030, (201) 748-6011, fax (201) 748-6008, e-mail: permcoordinator@wiley.com.

Limit of Liability/Disclaimer of Warranty: While the publisher and author have used their best efforts in preparing this book, they make no representations or warranties with respect to the accuracy or completeness of the contents of this book and specifically disclaim any implied warranties of merchantability or fitness for a particular purpose. No warranty may be created or extended by sales representatives or written sales materials. The advice and strategies contained herein may not be suitable for your situation. You should consult with a professional where appropriate. Neither the publisher nor author shall be liable for any loss of profit or any other commercial damages, including but not limited to special, incidental, consequential, or other damages.

For general information on our other products and services or for technical support, please contact our Customer Care Department within the United States at 800-762-2974, outside the United States at (317) 572-3993 or fax (317) 572-4002.

Wiley also publishes its books in a variety of electronic formats. Some content that appears in print may not be available in electronic books.

Library of Congress Cataloging-in-Publication Data:

The graphic standards guide to architectural finishes : using Masterspec(R) to evaluate, select, and specify materials / ARCOM, American Institute of Architects.
    p. cm.
  ISBN 0-471-22766-8 (alk. paper)
  1. Flooring—Standards. 2. Ceilings—Standards. 3. Paneling—Standards. 4. Paint—Standards. 5. Drywall—Standards. 6. Masterspec. I. ARCOM. II. American Institute of Architects.

  TH2521 .G69 2002
  721'.021'8—dc21   2002005725

Printed in the United States of America
10 9 8 7 6 5 4 3 2

PREFACE

The purpose of this book is to facilitate a more complete understanding of the issues relevant to evaluating, selecting, and specifying finish materials and to empower architects and designers to make informed choices for their projects.

When preparing drawings, architects refer to *Architectural Graphic Standards* for guidance. When selecting materials and products and when writing specifications, they turn to MASTERSPEC®, a product of the American Institute of Architects (AIA) published by ARCOM. By combining the invaluable resources of *Architectural Graphic Standards* and MASTERSPEC, this book efficiently assists an architect who is preparing a project's construction documents.

MASTERSPEC has long been the building construction industry standard for master specifications. Associated with each master specification section are supporting documents, which include a cover, evaluations, a drawing coordination checklist, and a specification coordination checklist. Evaluations in sections for finishes are the basis of this book.

A primary goal in producing this book is to make architects who are in early stages of the design process more aware of the information in MASTERSPEC evaluations, especially those architects who may not typically prepare specifications. Keeping this reference handy during the early design phases of a project will enable the project designer to ask suppliers and manufacturers educated questions, to make better initial product and system choices, and to successfully integrate these choices into the drawings and the specifications.

MASTERSPEC evaluations are the industry's only source of comprehensive information on product selection and specification. To produce them, ARCOM writers researched and integrated information from consensus standards, industry standards, model codes, industry organizations, manufacturers' product literature, and technical publications.

Evaluations were abridged for this book. Manufacturer listings and product tables were deleted because their data frequently change. This information, along with the master specification text and the coordination checklists, is available only in a complete MASTERSPEC section.

In keeping with *Architectural Graphic Standards* and MASTERSPEC, this book is organized according to the 1995 edition of *MasterFormat*™ published by the Construction Specifications Institute. The chapter numbers identify the *MasterFormat* divisions to which the content relates; chapter numbers and titles correspond to *MasterFormat* five-digit numbers and titles for specification sections.

As with any ambitious undertaking, this book is the product of collaboration. The staff at John Wiley & Sons, Inc. assembled this work; each participant can be proud of its eloquence. A special thanks to my counterpart at John Wiley & Sons, Inc., Julie Trelstad, Senior Editor, Architecture. Julie's vision and persistence were essential to making this book a reality; it is a pleasure to work with her and to count her as a friend.

For the graphic content of this book, we are indebted to the dedicated AIA members and other building construction experts who originally contributed the graphics to *Architectural Graphic Standards,* which now illustrate this work. The contributors' names appear on the acknowledgments pages at the back of this volume.

For the written content, we are indebted to the two AIA committees charged with guiding and reviewing the MASTERSPEC evaluations used in this book: the MASTERSPEC Architectural Review Committee (MARC) and the MASTERSPEC Interiors Review Committee (MIRC). Those who serve on these committees unselfishly volunteer their time to share experience and wisdom so that others might learn and benefit.

For completing the exacting task of associating the graphics from *Architectural Graphic Standards* with the text from MASTERSPEC and editing the annotations of the graphics, I am profoundly grateful to MARC members Philip W. Kabza, AIA, CCS, CSI; David Metzger, FAIA, CSI (current MARC chair); and E. Leo Scott, CDT, CSI, for sharing their time and wisdom.

Every ARCOM staff member helped prepare this book. To my fellow writers, your expertise and the vastness of our collective technical knowledge are astounding. To our editorial staff, thank you for your support, guidance, and unwavering dedication to clear, concise, correct use of the language. To our technical and production staff, thank you for working your magic on the documents to reformat them for this book. Finally, to Edward F. (Ted) Smith, D. Arch., FAIA, CSI, President of ARCOM, thank you for fostering ARCOM's culture of integrity and cooperation and encouraging all of us to find new ways to serve the building construction industry.

ELENA M.S. GARRISON, AIA, CCS, CSI
Senior Architectural Specification Writer
ARCOM Master Systems
Alexandria, Virginia

FOREWORD

The American Institute of Architects (AIA) and ARCOM, publishers of the MASTERSPEC® master specification system for the AIA, are pleased to join with John Wiley & Sons, Inc. in presenting this publication for the building design and construction community. This book combines information from two of the AIA's most valuable resources, *Architectural Graphic Standards* and MASTERSPEC. Both support this nation's building design standards and represent the best architectural practice.

This book, for the first time, integrates graphic representations for finish materials from *Architectural Graphic Standards* with MASTERSPEC's technical information on evaluating, selecting, and specifying finish materials. Each page and each detail assist in the building design process, from product evaluation and selection through construction and evaluation of in-service use.

Every practicing architect is indebted to the founding authors of *Architectural Graphic Standards,* Charles George Ramsey, AIA, and Harold Reeve Sleeper, FAIA, for their creation of this indispensable work in 1932. We recognize the dedicated professionals who have contributed graphics to *Architectural Graphic Standards* to keep it current and vital through its ten editions.

In 1969, the AIA produced the first family of MASTERSPEC specification sections under the direction of John H. Schruben, FAIA. His efforts and the subsequent contributions of Roscoe Reeves, Jr., FAIA, CSI, who was the Director of Architectural Specifications for the AIA and now serves in this capacity for ARCOM, have made MASTERSPEC an essential tool of the profession. We must also acknowledge the immeasurable contributions of the professionals who have served on the MASTERSPEC Architectural Review Committee (MARC), MASTERSPEC Engineering Review Committee (MERC), and MASTERSPEC Interiors Review Committee (MIRC). Committee members give unselfishly and creatively to MASTERSPEC. The building design and construction industry benefits from their knowledge and expertise.

We would also like to express gratitude to those individuals who combined the information in *Architectural Graphic Standards* and MASTERSPEC to produce this volume. For ARCOM, Elena M.S. Garrison, AIA, CCS, CSI, coordinated the selection of MASTERSPEC text and the integration of *Architectural Graphic Standards* graphics. Members of MARC matched the graphics to the MASTERSPEC text. These committed professionals are Philip W. Kabza, AIA, CCS, CSI; David Metzger, FAIA, CSI, the current MARC chair; and E. Leo Scott, CDT, CSI.

To all of the people associated with this unique project, we offer the words of Eliel Saarinen, FAIA: "Always design a thing by considering it in its next larger context — a chair in a room, a room in a house, a house in an environment, an environment in a city plan." By combining two distinctly different and valuable resources, information from each will address its next larger context and will inform and empower professionals to do the same.

NORMAN L. KOONCE, FAIA
Executive Vice President/CEO
The American Institute of Architects
Washington, D.C.

EDWARD F. (Ted) SMITH, D. ARCH., FAIA, CSI
President of ARCOM
Salt Lake City, UT
Alexandria, Virginia

CONTENTS

05511 METAL STAIRS

This chapter discusses straight-run, steel-framed stairs with metal-pan, abrasive-coating-finished formed-metal, metal plate, and steel-bar grating treads. It includes preassembled metal stairs for commercial applications, industrial stairs, and steel-framed ornamental stairs. It also includes steel tube railings for preassembled metal stairs.

This chapter does not discuss alternating tread stairs, spiral stairs, or handrails and railings other than those made from steel tube.

GENERAL COMMENTS

Steel-framed stairs information is covered in the National Association of Architectural Metal Manufacturers (NAAMM) publication NAAMM AMP 510, *Metal Stairs Manual.* NAAMM AMP 510 contains information on typical metal stair construction, as well as many photographs and drawings of more elaborate ornamental metal stairs. NAAMM AMP 510 also contains structural design information for metal-pan stairs, metal floor plate stairs, and metal railings. For structural design information for metal bar-grating stairs, see NAAMM MBG 531, *Metal Bar Grating Manual for Steel, Stainless Steel, and Aluminum Gratings and Stair Treads.* Refer to applicable building codes and accessibility standards to determine requirements for egress widths, structural performance, fire-resistance rating of enclosing walls, and accessibility by people with disabilities (fig. 1).

Metal stairs generally fall into one of three categories: preassembled metal stairs, industrial metal stairs, or ornamental metal stairs. Preassembled metal stairs, which usually have concrete-filled metal-pan treads, are used for commercial, institutional, light industrial, and multifamily residential occupancies (fig. 2). Industrial metal stairs are for more heavy-duty applications than preassembled metal stairs, and usually have steel floor plate or bar grating treads. Ornamental metal stairs are often of unique designs and are finished with highly decorative materials, such as marble, glass, ornamental metals, and so on.

PREASSEMBLED METAL STAIRS

Preassembled stairs offer faster erection, lower erection costs, and both improved and safer access to upper floors during construction (fig. 3). They are made by manufacturers that specialize in metal stairs and by local iron and steel fabricators. They are available either as multistory self-supporting units erected in advance of structural framing or as single-story or single-flight units installed as structural framing or wall and floor construction progresses. Consult manufacturers and local fabricators to determine limitations of these types of units if either is required or permitted as an option.

Preassembled metal stairs are usually specified with performance requirements so the manufacturer can design them based on its standard methods of construction. Performance criteria should always be accompanied by requirements for submitting structural calculations, and detailed shop drawings prepared by a qualified professional engineer who is legally authorized to practice in the jurisdiction where the project is located. In certain jurisdictions, however, authorities may require the engineer of record to prepare the drawings and calculations for fabrications supporting structural loads, or to approve them even when they are signed and sealed by another engineer legally authorized to practice in the jurisdiction where the project is located.

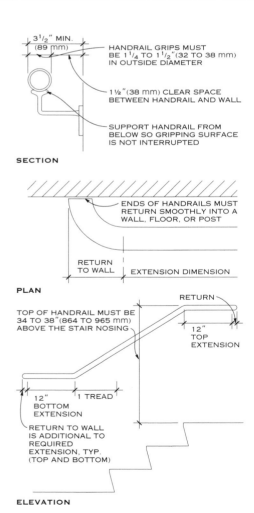

Figure 1. Typical accessibility requirements for steel tube handrail

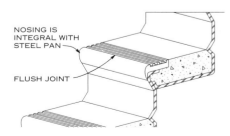

Figure 2. Preassembled stair with concrete-filled steel pan

1

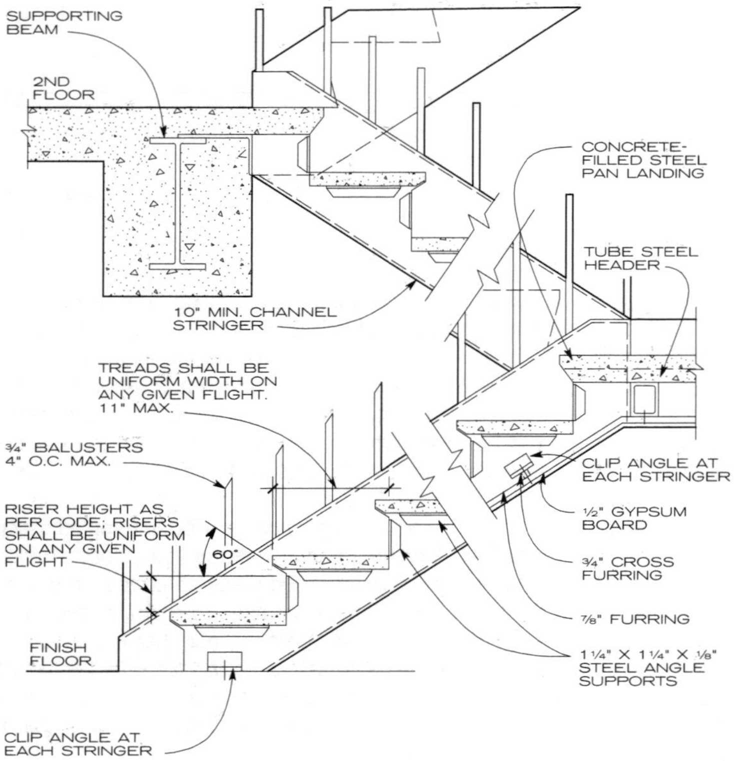

SUPPORTING BEAM
2ND FLOOR
CONCRETE-FILLED STEEL PAN LANDING
TUBE STEEL HEADER
10" MIN. CHANNEL STRINGER
TREADS SHALL BE UNIFORM WIDTH ON ANY GIVEN FLIGHT. 11" MAX.
3/4" BALUSTERS 4" O.C. MAX.
CLIP ANGLE AT EACH STRINGER
RISER HEIGHT AS PER CODE; RISERS SHALL BE UNIFORM ON ANY GIVEN FLIGHT
60°
1/2" GYPSUM BOARD
3/4" CROSS FURRING
7/8" FURRING
FINISH FLOOR
1 1/4" X 1 1/4" X 1/8" STEEL ANGLE SUPPORTS
CLIP ANGLE AT EACH STRINGER

Figure 3. Preassembled metal stairs with pan-type stair construction

STRINGER
PLATFORM
CARRIER PLATE
RUN
CHANNEL
2 1/2" X 3/16" (STEEL)
3" X 3/16" (ALUMINUM)
RISER
OVERLAP
1 3/4" (STEEL)
2 1/4" (ALUMINUM)
7/16" DIA. HOLES IN STRINGER

Figure 5. Industrial metal stairs

Precast concrete treads eliminate the inconvenience of pouring the treads on-site and offer smooth subtreads that are usable by workers without a temporary filler. Since the treads need not be installed until finishing operations are nearly complete, the treads are not vulnerable to job-site damage. Epoxy-filled treads are a lightweight alternative to prefilled concrete treads and have a more finished appearance.

Abrasive-coating-finished formed-metal stairs offer an economical alternative to metal-pan stairs. They require no finishing operations other than painting, but may not feel as solid under foot as metal-pan stairs. With this type of stair and with epoxy-filled metal-pan stairs, some protection is often required to prevent damage during construction.

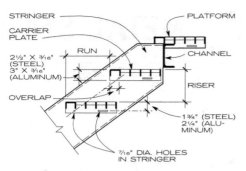

Steel tube railings are standard with most preassembled metal stair manufacturers. Where stairs are primarily utilitarian, and appearance is not critical, performance requirements, together with a general description of the desired railing configuration, are often sufficient, with few or no details on the drawings. Where appearance is more important, delete railing descriptions and show railings on the drawings together with notes for component dimensions, spacing, and so on (fig. 4).

INDUSTRIAL METAL STAIRS

Industrial stairs are usually fabricated by local iron and steel fabricators rather than by metal stair manufacturers (fig. 5). They are usually designed by the project's structural engineer and fully detailed on the drawings rather than being specified with performance requirements. Railings are usually made from steel pipe, bars, or structural shapes, and are also detailed on the drawings.

Steel floor plate treads have traditionally been used in the diamond pattern to provide some measure of slip resistance (fig. 6). Alternatives can be specified along with performance requirements for slip resistance. It should be noted, however, that no test method can totally predict slip resistance; foreign materials and lubricants can increase slipping, and no test adequately incorporates all directional forces involved in walking and all materials used for shoe soles. Other factors to consider in selecting slip-resistant surfacing are its profile, which can increase slip resistance by cutting through lubricants and foreign matter, and its durability.

12" EXTENSION
4" SPHERE MUST NOT PASS THROUGH AT ANY POINT
HANDRAIL
42"
34" TO 38"
1 1/4" TO 1 1/2"
1 1/4"
1 1/4" AT 5 1/8" O.C.
FIELD WELD
CONCRETE-FILLED PAN
CHANNEL STRINGER (TOE OUT)
1 1/2"
1 1/4"
1 1/4"-1 1/2"
5 3/4"
5 1/8"
5 1/2"
WELD
COVER PLATE
1 1/4"-1 1/2" HANDRAIL
TREAD WIDTH AND 12" EXTENSION
CONCRETE
FINISH FLOOR
CLIP ANGLE WITH ANCHOR BOLT EACH STRINGER

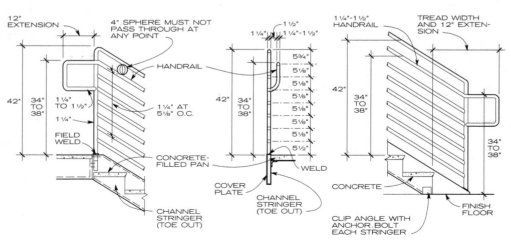

Figure 4. Steel tube railings

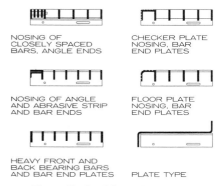

NOSING OF
CLOSELY SPACED
BARS, ANGLE ENDS

CHECKER PLATE
NOSING, BAR
END PLATES

NOSING OF ANGLE
AND ABRASIVE STRIP
AND BAR ENDS

FLOOR PLATE
NOSING, BAR
END PLATES

HEAVY FRONT AND
BACK BEARING BARS
AND BAR END PLATES

PLATE TYPE

Figure 6. Steel floor plate treads

Metal bar gratings are specified by NAAMM standards and the NAAMM-recommended marking system.

ORNAMENTAL METAL STAIRS

Ornamental stairs are often designed with a steel supporting structure and finished with wood, stone, tile, ornamental metal, or another decorative finish. The supporting structure may be left exposed, and painted, or may be completely enclosed by finish materials. In either case, the steel supporting structure can be specified in Division 5, "Metals," with the finishes specified in Division 9, "Finishes." Ornamental metal stairs are usually fabricated by local ironworks, but may also be made by companies specializing in decorative and custom railings.

DESIGN AND DETAILING

Where appearance is important, it is necessary to provide adequate details and other graphic information on the drawings and not try to substitute written requirements that do not define complex relationships and details. Stairs and railings are perfect examples of building components where visual considerations, coupled with complex geometrical relationships, can involve a multitude of conditions. Only proper graphical development reveals all conditions and determines the appropriate specification and drawing requirements.

If appearance is important, the architect will probably not want to relinquish control of aesthetic details to the fabricator. Where appearance is not important, and the manufacturer's standard methods are acceptable, details can be kept to a minimum, and performance specifications with limited descriptive requirements can be used to ensure the most economical solution.

REFERENCES

Publication dates cited here were current at the time of this writing. Publications are revised periodically, and revisions may have occurred before this book was published.

National Association of Architectural Metal Manufacturers

NAAMM AMP 510-92: Metal Stairs Manual

NAAMM MBG 531-93: Metal Bar Grating Manual for Steel, Stainless Steel, and Aluminum Gratings and Stair Tread

06402 **INTERIOR ARCHITECTURAL WOODWORK**

This chapter discusses fabricated wood products for use on the interior of the building. Architectural woodwork is distinguished from other forms of wood construction in that it is manufactured in a woodworking plant and complies with standards of quality for materials and workmanship. It includes items of woodwork permanently attached to the building and exposed to view. Architectural woodwork generally involves items custom-fabricated for an individual project, as opposed to mass-produced moldings or furniture. Woodwork can be specified to be shop- or field-finished.

This chapter also discusses flush wood paneling for transparent finish; it is often considered woodwork. For stile and rail paneling, board paneling, flush paneling for opaque finish, and plastic laminate flush paneling refer to the Chapter 06420, Paneling.

This chapter does not discuss wood doors, wood windows, manufactured casework of stock design, wood furniture, or wood pews or benches. Wood doors are included in Chapters 08211, Flush Wood Doors and 08212, Stile and Rail Wood Doors. Manufactured casework, wood furniture, and wood pews and benches should be specified in Division 12, "Furnishings." As mentioned above, finish carpentry is also not included, although no universal definition exists that states where woodwork ends and finish carpentry begins.

ARCHITECTURAL WOODWORK STANDARDS

Woodworking Standards

Construction as described here is specified to comply with either the Architectural Woodwork Institute (AWI) or Woodwork Institute of California (WIC) standard. The location of the project determines, in part, which standard to reference. Except for projects located in California, Nevada, and Oregon, the standard to reference is the one published by AWI. For California, Nevada, or Oregon, either standard can be used.

Grade of Woodwork

For the most part, both woodworking standards were developed for designating quality by using three separate grades: Premium, Custom, and Economy. WIC, however, also includes Laboratory grade for casework. Although requirements for the same grade are not identical for different categories, the following criteria apply:

- **Premium** requires the highest grade of materials and workmanship recognized in either woodworking standard. Premium grade might be specified for woodwork throughout a building, but it should not be specified indiscriminately. Usually, Premium should be specified for selected areas or for items that have particular architectural significance.
- **Custom** is the predominant grade and requires a reasonable level of quality in both materials and workmanship. It is for typical commercial and institutional work.

- **Economy** is the lowest acceptable grade in both material and workmanship requirements, and is for work where price outweighs quality considerations.
- **Laboratory** is available with WIC-referenced casework, and is for items in chemistry or hard-acid areas that require additional protection. WIC also includes requirements for laboratory tops fabricated from several materials. See WIC's *Manual of Millwork* for explanations and choices for grade and other characteristics.

Substantial cost differences exist among the different grades, wood species, and finishes. Transparent-finished woodwork is more expensive than woodwork with an opaque finish, but the amount depends not only on the species and the cut of wood selected but also on the kind of transparent finish required.

Determination of quality grade should be based on a careful study of design role, function, location, and finish of each woodwork item. If this results in specifying several grades for the same job, the drawings or the specifications must indicate the locations and extent of each grade for a given category of woodwork. For most projects, woodwork will be of one grade, Custom. Premium and Custom grades differ primarily in appearance; where the appearance must be very high-quality, Premium grade is used. Custom and Economy grades may also differ in sturdiness, so the service life of the woodwork must be considered if Economy grade is chosen. Economy grade also does not have the appearance of Custom grade, so Economy should be used only where appearance is insignificant or at least not as significant as cost.

A Monumental grade does not exist in either woodworking standard, but some architects feel there should be such a grade. This belief is apparently shared by some woodworkers who, like architects, feel that the current requirements for Premium grade allow the woodworker too many options in the choice of materials and construction and do not represent the highest level of quality attainable by woodworkers. Several methods are available that try to obtain a higher level of quality than that produced by specifying Premium grade. One such method is the prequalification of woodworkers before bidding, which may be based on work previously completed. Although this is no guarantee that they will continue to perform at the same level, past performance is often an indicator of future performance. Thoroughly research the woodworking firms selected if this procedure is used. Verify that they have not had significant changes in personnel, large increases in workload, or financial difficulties since earning their good reputation.

Another method that attempts to raise the level of quality is the mockup. The problem with this method is that the woodworker may build a mockup that is no better than Premium grade. Still, a mockup does give the owner and the architect a sample of what they are getting before the job is complete, and it does provide a standard for enforcing a level of quality. Mockups can also be required before bidding to identify qualified woodworking firms. A woodworker could also be hired to build the mockup before the bidding, and the bidding could then be based on the premise that the contract work would match the mockup, but most projects do not have the time or budget to allow this procedure.

A third method for raising quality is to increase requirements, eliminate options, tighten tolerances, and so on. This method works for some aspects of woodworking but, unless directly related to results, may unduly restrict the woodworker without ensuring higher quality. This method does not work where expected results cannot be quantified, such as the appearance of the finish, the matching of veneer and solid stock, and so on; nevertheless, it is the basis of the distinction between the various grades established by the woodworking standards.

For interior transparent-finished woodwork, flush doors, matched paneling, and cabinets are often the most important work from a visual standpoint. When this is the case, frames, trim, and ornamental items should match these items. However, there is usually no way to achieve a perfect match between veneered items, plywood, and solid-lumber items. Logs with the best grain character are selected for veneer slicing, leaving less-distinguished logs for sawing into lumber. The direction of the cut for sawing lumber is also not the same from one piece to the next, nor necessarily the same as for slicing, even though specified to be the same. For example, rift sawing and cutting cover a range of cutting methods and grain angles. The architect is usually forced to accept a reasonably good color match and a similar grain character. A high-quality woodworker can provide near-perfect matching, but such matching is impossible, or nearly so, to specify. For work where only perfect matching is acceptable, a mockup should be a must, or samples should be used to define a minimum level of match.

Moisture and associated shrinkage problems must be recognized as serious considerations for achieving successful woodwork. Both woodworking standards include requirements for optimum moisture content of the wood (based on the relative humidity range). Because AWI covers a broad area, it has divided the United States and Canada into four geographical regions. Refer to the AWI standard for these locations and the corresponding requirements, and confirm that the humidity levels given correspond to local conditions before specifying a moisture content range. If they do not, consult the project's mechanical engineer and woodworkers familiar with conditions in the project area, and insert specific requirements into the specification.

Remember that for the woodwork to be at its best, humidity must be controlled within specific limits after installation. In some parts of the United States, this means that humidification will be needed in the winter, or joints will open up and tolerances will be lost. It is pointless to specify furniture-quality woodwork, then not provide the humidification necessary for maintaining that quality. Excessive indoor humidity during cold weather can result in condensation within exterior walls, so exterior walls must be designed to control the transmission of vapor produced by humidification or humidification based on an analysis of vapor-transmission characteristics of exterior walls.

VENEER SPECIES SELECTION

Numerous options are available for specifying veneer species, but a lack of knowledge about wood veneers and the available options can result in unpleasant surprises when the finished woodwork arrives. See Table 1 for an overview of general characteristics of common veneer species.

Natural birch is often specified without either the architect or the owner fully realizing that this means the veneers may contain both heartwood and sapwood, which may vary considerably in color. Birch sapwood is an off-white to light-yellow color; heartwood may be a creamy tan or a reddish brown and may be much darker than sapwood. The distribution of heartwood is not controlled by any standards, so it may appear as stripes in flat-sliced veneers or as blotches in rotary-cut veneers. The pattern can be irregular, regardless of the cut, and the appearance can be gaudy. If natu-ral birch is specified, woodwork cannot be rejected because of the irregular variations in color that are likely to occur. Staining can reduce the contrast but will not eliminate it entirely. Shading (a term for selectively staining the sapwood to try to match the heartwood) can also be specified to reduce the contrast, but its cost may not be justifiable. This contrast in appearance can be eliminated by specifying white birch (all sapwood) or red birch (all heartwood) rather than natural birch.

White and red maple, and white and brown ash similarly distinguish sapwood from heartwood, although white and brown ash distinguish the sapwood of one species group from the heartwood of another species group. Ash is an underutilized species that provides veneers of fine appearance at a modest price. White ash is a very light-colored, open-grained wood that can be used with a clear finish for a blond effect or can be stained. If the blond effect is desired, specify a type of clear finish (such as lacquer) that is water-white; the slightest bit of yellow in the finish will show up on a wood as light in color as white ash. Brown ash shows more variation in color than white ash and is often used for paneling, where a more figured appearance is desired.

Oak veneers usually contain little sapwood, and heartwood is not as easily distinguished from sapwood as it is in birch. For these reasons, oak is not usually specified as all heartwood or all sapwood. The difference between white and red oak is one of species, not cut. White oak is light tan to grayish brown in color, while red oak is pinkish tan to red-brown or brown. Red-oak veneers are also less expensive than white oak. Plain-sliced red-oak veneers are less expensive than plain-sliced white birch, and are a good choice for inexpensive, good-quality woodwork. Oak veneers, besides being plain sliced, are frequently quartered or rift cut for a straight-grain appearance. Since quarter cutting and rift cutting require larger logs, the veneers are more expensive and usually narrower. Rift-cut oak is similar to quartered oak, but the amount and size of ray fleck, which some people find objectionable and which does not take stain well, are less for rift-cut veneers than for quartered veneers. If unsure which cut is desired, look at finished samples to see the grain pattern and the effect that ray fleck has on the appearance of the veneer; consider having the client review the samples for concurrence.

VENEER CUT

Veneers may be rotary cut, rift cut (usually applies only to oak), plain sliced (also called flat sliced), quarter sliced, or half-round sliced (fig. 1). Rotary cutting minimizes waste but results in a grain pattern that does not resemble any cut of lumber and is often very irregular. Plain slicing and half-round cutting can produce pleasing grain patterns, with the ring width increasing from the center to the edge and with a "cathedral grain" effect produced by the natural taper of the log. Quarter slicing and rift slicing (cutting) produce a straight grain and more evenly spaced rings than plain slicing or half-round cutting. Half-round cutting, which is not illustrated, involves reversing a half-log flitch on a lathe (placing the saw cut made at the middle of the log on the outside and the bark side of the log near the center of the lathe) and usually offsetting the flitch away from the center of the lathe to increase the radius of the cut. This process allows a lathe to be used instead of a slicer and produces leaves that are similar to those produced by flat slicing but slightly wider due to the curvature of the cut. Refer to Table 2 for common face veneer patterns.

VENEER MATCHING

Book matching readily comes to mind when discussing veneer matching: laying out the leaves like an open book so pairs of adjacent leaves are nearly mirror images (fig. 2). From one pair of veneer leaves to the next,

Table 1

GENERAL CHARACTERISTICS OF WOOD VENEER SPECIES

SPECIES		WIDTH TO (IN.)	LENGTH (FT)	FLITCH SIZE	COST[1]	AVAILABILITY
Mahogany	Plain sliced Honduras mahogany	18	12	Large	Moderate	Good
	Quartered Honduras mahogany	12	12	Large	High	Moderate
	Plain sliced African mahogany	18	12	Large	Moderate	Moderate
	Quartered African mahogany	12	12	Large	High	Good
Ash	Plain sliced American white ash	12	10	Medium	Moderate	Good
	Quartered American white ash	8	12	Small	High	Good
	Quartered or plain sliced European ash	6, 10	10	Medium	High	Limited
Anegre	Quartered or plain sliced anegre	6, 12	12	Large	High	Good
Avodire	Quartered avodire	10	10	Large	High	Limited
Cherry	Plain sliced American cherry	12	11	Medium	Moderate	Good
	Quartered American cherry	4	10	Very small	High	Moderate
Birch	Rotary cut birch (natural)	48	10	Large	Low	Good
	Rotary cut birch (select red or white)	36	10	Medium	Moderate	Moderate
	Plain sliced birch (natural)	10	10	Small	Moderate	Limited
	Plain sliced birch (select red or white)	5	10	Small	High	Limited
Butternut	Plain sliced butternut	12	10	Medium	High	Limited
Makore	Quartered or plain sliced makore	6, 12	12	Large	High	Good
Maple	Pl. sl. (half round) American maple	12	10	Medium	Moderate	Good[2]
	Rotary bird's-eye maple	20	10	Medium	Very high	Good
Oak	Plain sliced English brown oak	12	10	Medium	Very high	Limited
	Quartered English brown oak	10	10	Medium	Very high	Limited
	Plain sliced American red oak	16	12	Large	Moderate	Good
	Quartered American red oak	8	10	Small	Moderate	Good
	Rift sliced American red oak	10	10	Medium	Moderate	Good
	Comb grain rift American red oak	8	10	Small	Very high	Limited
	Plain sliced American white oak	16	12	Medium	Moderate	Good
	Quartered American white oak	8	10	Small	Moderate	Good
	Rift sliced American white oak	8	10	Medium	High	Good
	Comb grain rift American white oak	8	10	Small	Very high	Limited
Hickory or Pecan	Plain sliced American hickory or pecan	12	10	Small	Moderate	Good
Sapele	Quartered or plain sliced sapele	6, 12	12	Large	High	Good
Sycamore	Plain sliced English sycamore	10	10	Medium	Very high	Limited
	Quartered English sycamore	6	10	Medium	Very high	Limited
Teak	Plain sliced teak	16	12	Large	Very high	Limited[3]
	Quartered teak	12	12	Medium	Very high	Limited[3]
Walnut	Plain sliced American walnut	12	12	Medium	Moderate	Good
	Quarter sliced American walnut	6	10	Very small	High	Rare

[1]Cost reflects raw veneer costs weighted for waste or yield characteristics and degree of labor difficulty.

[2]Seasonal factors may affect availability.

[3]Availability of blond teak is very rare.

NOTE

When quartered or plain sliced are listed on the same line, the width dimensions are listed with quartered first and plain sliced second.

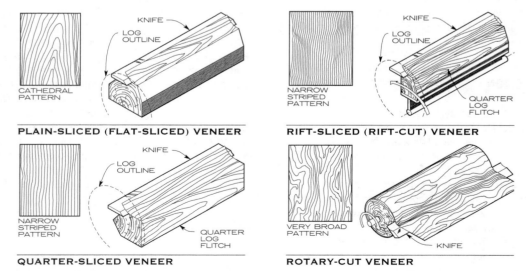

PLAIN-SLICED (FLAT-SLICED) VENEER

RIFT-SLICED (RIFT-CUT) VENEER

QUARTER-SLICED VENEER

ROTARY-CUT VENEER

Figure 1. Veneer cuts

Table 2

COMMON FACE VENEER PATTERNS OF SELECTED COMMERCIAL SPECIES

PRIMARY COMMERCIAL HARDWOOD SPECIES	FACE VENEER PATTERNS[1]			
	PLAIN SLICED (FLAT CUT)	QUARTER CUT	RIFT CUT AND COMB GRAIN	ROTARY CUT
Ash	Yes	Yes	—	Yes
Birch	Yes	—	—	Yes
Cherry	Yes	Yes	—	Yes
Hickory	Yes	—	—	Yes
Lauan	—	Yes	—	Yes
Mahogany (African)	Yes	Yes	—	Yes
Mahogany (Honduras)	Yes	Yes	—	Yes
Maple	Yes	Yes	—	Yes
Meranti	—	Yes	—	Yes
Oak (red)	Yes	Yes	Yes	Yes
Oak (white)	Yes	Yes	Yes	Yes
Pecan	Yes	—	—	Yes
Walnut (black)	Yes	Yes	—	Yes
Yellow poplar	Yes	—	—	Yes
Typical methods of cutting[2]	Plain slicing or half-round on rotary lathe	Quarter slicing	Offset quarter on rotary lathe	Rotary lathe

[1] The headings above refer to the face veneer pattern, not to the method of cutting. Face veneer patterns other than those listed are obtainable by special order.

[2] The method of cutting for a given face veneer pattern shall be at mill option unless otherwise specified by the buyer in an explicit manner to avoid the possibility of misunderstanding. For example, plain-sliced veneer cut on a vertical slicer or plain-sliced veneer cut on a half-round rotary lathe could be specified.

some matching is lost in the progression through the log, but the effect can still be stunning. When looking at a pair of book-matched veneers, the inside surface of one and the outside surface of the other is shown. This view causes some differences in color and sheen between the two leaves, which is called *barber poling.* For this reason, it is preferable to use slip matching with straight-grain veneers, such as quarter sliced or rift cut, or with fairly symmetrical plain-sliced veneers. Sanding and stain color can also affect the appearance of barber poling.

Running match requires all veneer leaves to be from the same flitch and in sequence, which means that they must be either book or slip matched. The width of the running-matched leaves can vary, and the piece trimmed from one edge of the panel can be used to start the next panel. Balance matching also requires a book or slip match and that all veneer leaves be the same width, which results in some trimming waste and an increase in cost. Center-balance matching requires an even number of veneer leaves, all the same width and from the same flitch, which further increases the waste and cost over running or balance match. For maximum economy, random matching, which is really no matching, can be specified so the woodworker can make the most efficient use of the veneer log—veneer leaves can even be from different logs. Random matching can use any number of leaves from any number of flitches with no regard for color or grain; it is used only in Economy grade woodwork.

FIRE-RETARDANT TREATMENT

Usually, small amounts of architectural woodwork (10 percent of the wall surface) are permitted for most occupancies and spaces without regard to flame spread. However, for many applications where woodwork

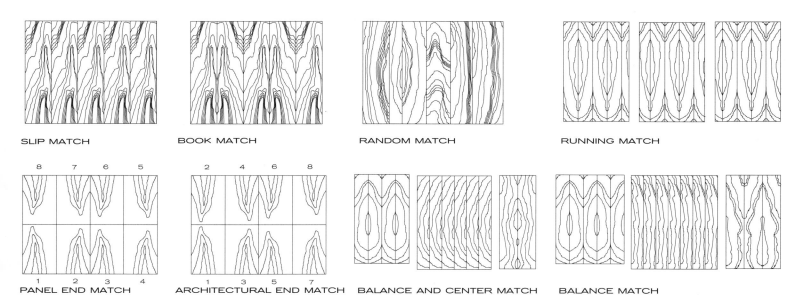

SLIP MATCH   BOOK MATCH   RANDOM MATCH   RUNNING MATCH

PANEL END MATCH   ARCHITECTURAL END MATCH   BALANCE AND CENTER MATCH   BALANCE MATCH

Figure 2. Veneer match types

(of any type) is extensive, flame-spread considerations may require treatment of all or part of the woodwork. Using fire-retardant wood limits choices for materials, thicknesses, treatments, and finishes, particularly transparent finishes.

Specifying fire-retardant treatment of architectural woodwork is complicated because American Wood-Preservers' Association (AWPA) treatment standards (AWPA C20 for lumber, AWPA C27 for plywood) are intended for structural materials used as exceptions to requirements for noncombustible materials. These standards are not intended for use where limits on flame spread of finishes and trim are the goal. Code requirements differ for wood used as a structural element or backing of finish and that exposed as finish or trim. To qualify as fire retardant for structural and backing uses, a material must have a flame-spread index of 25 or less when the test period is extended to 30 minutes, with no evidence of significant progressive combustion. To qualify as finish and trim, materials need only be subjected to a 10-minute test period; flame-spread requirements will depend on the code in effect, size and height of building, use group of building (business, assembly, residential, etc.), location and function of room or space where finish and trim occur, and whether a fire-suppression system is provided. For typical locations where fire-retardant-treated woodwork is specified, most codes require a flame-spread index of either 25 or less or 75 or less.

Fire-retardant-treated lumber is only available in a limited number of species for two reasons. First, penetration of the fire-retardant chemicals varies according to species, requiring each one to be tested individually; and second, testing costs limit available species to those for which a substantial market exists. There even exist certain untreatable species: those for which retention of chemicals is inadequate to achieve the desired test results or which require incising the lumber, a process unsuitable for woodwork. Where woodwork is to be milled after treatment, only western red cedar, red oak, or yellow poplar can be used, and only licensed plants can do the milling. For this reason, it is better to mill the woodwork before treating and to take extra precautions to ensure that the treatment process does not stain or mar the exposed surfaces of the woodwork.

Fire-retardant formulations, commonly used to treat architectural woodwork, are organic-resin type, low-hygroscopic type, and nonpressure-treatment type. The organic-resin formulation qualifies as an exterior type in AWPA C20 (lumber) or AWPA C27 (plywood). An exterior type in these standards produces treated lumber that shows no increase in flame spread when subjected to a standard rain test, ASTM D 2898, Method A. In the treatment of architectural woodwork, particularly hardwoods, this type is often favored because it is unaffected by exposure to moisture or high humidity and, depending on the wood species and product source, can be milled after treatment. Being able to mill woods after treatment allows for the removal of surface imperfections, such as raised grain and sticker marks, caused by the treatment process. Light sanding will also remove raised grain and surface stains.

The low-hygroscopic formulation is referred to as Interior Type A in AWPA standards. It was developed to overcome the problems that often resulted from using the older formulation, now removed from AWPA standards. Though both formulations are water-soluble, the older, conventional type often developed unsightly surface blooming when exposed to moisture and high humidity. The newer, low-hygroscopic type eliminates surface residues and is less expensive than the organic-resin type. Wood treated with the low-hygroscopic formulation cannot be milled after treatment. Always verify availability of a given species before specifying that it be treated.

A nonpressure-treatment process should be less harmful to the woodwork and less expensive to apply. Since the process does not take long, does not require heat or pressure, and does not require kiln drying, there is less ten-dency for the wood to warp or mark, and staining is slight. This treatment is listed by Intertek Testing Services (ITS) for both Class A and Class B finishes for some species of wood and presumably could be applied to wood products supplied by the woodworker to the treatment shop.

Regardless of which formulation is used, all have a darkening effect, particularly in light-colored wood species. Compare treated and untreated samples before deciding which species and finish to use, particularly where matching treated and untreated wood is expected.

Wood-veneered panel products with fire-retardant properties usually consist of treated cores with untreated face veneers. Consequently, the appearance of these panels does not pose the same problems as fire-retardant-treated lumber. Selection of untreated face veneers is limited to those species and thicknesses whose surface-burning characteristics comply with code or other requirements. Where the face veneer is ⅛-inch (0.9-mm) thick or less and does not pose a greater fire hazard than paper, its surface-burning characteristics are generally not regulated by the model codes, provided the veneer is applied directly to substrates that are either noncombustible or of fire-retardant wood that complies with code requirements.

Fire-retardant particleboard and fire-retardant medium-density fiberboard, as well as pressure-treated plywood, have superior qualities as substrates for veneers and plastic laminates. The physical properties of fire-retardant particleboard are not, however, the same as for nonfire-retardant particleboard.

Although both fire-retardant particleboard and fiberboard have a flame-spread index less than 25, neither meets model code requirements for fire-retardant-treated wood and, therefore, they do not qualify as substrates for the exception to flame-spread requirements discussed in the previous paragraph. They have to be tested for flame spread as a veneered panel to be acceptable to the model codes. Surface-burning characteristics of wood are related to their densities, and this is the way veneered, treated panel products are classified in Underwriter Laboratories' (UL's) *Building Materials Directory*. Because surface-burning characteristics increase in direct relation to density, wood for veneers has to be within certain density limits for the required flame-spread index.

FORMALDEHYDE EMISSION LEVELS OF PANEL PRODUCTS

Formaldehyde is a natural component of wood products, but some wood glues, and wood products made with them, contain significantly higher amounts of this chemical than does wood alone. Limits on formaldehyde emissions from wood panel products are now included in the standards in which these materials are specified. For particleboard, the maximum emission level is the same as that required in the Housing and Urban Development (HUD) regulation 24 CFR, Section 3280.308, which controls formaldehyde emissions for particleboard and plywood for manufactured housing. For medium-density fiberboard, which is not regulated by HUD, the emission level is the same but the loading ratio is lower, since fiberboard is intended as a component of cabinets and furniture, not as a material for constructing manufactured housing. It should be understood that HUD regulations apply to manufactured housing, not to applications such as those discussed here.

Particleboard made with phenol-formaldehyde, which emits far less formaldehyde, is available by designating "exterior glue" at an increase in cost of about 30 percent. Medium-density fiberboard made without the addition of formaldehyde is also available. Hardboard uses much less resin than medium-density fiberboard, and phenolic resins rather than urea-formaldehyde, so it does not emit a significant amount of formaldehyde.

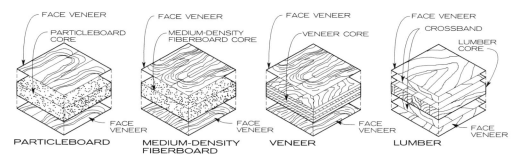

Figure 3. Hardwood plywood core types

Hardwood plywood is also covered by HUD regulations and by HPVA HP-1, published by the Hardwood Plywood & Veneer Association (HPVA). For plywood wall paneling, formaldehyde emission is limited to two-thirds of that allowed for particleboard but is measured at a higher loading ratio (fig. 3). Limits for industrial panels (unfinished multi-ply products with decorative face veneers and various cores) and reconstituted-wood wall panels (panel products made with strands, wafers, particles, or fibers of wood) are the same as for particleboard. According to the American Plywood Association (APA), softwood plywood is not involved because it is made with phenolic glues, which emit far less formaldehyde.

The Occupational Safety and Health Administration's (OSHA's) rules limit formaldehyde emissions of panel products in the workplace. OSHA attempted to require labeling of each formaldehyde-containing product as a potential cancer hazard; although the attempt was not accepted by the Office of Management and Budget, it may be in the future. The Environmental Protection Agency (EPA) is still in the process of investigating the safety of formaldehyde and could decide to implement rules governing the use of products containing this chemical.

Other regulations by federal agencies, including the EPA, the Consumer Products Safety Commission, and OSHA, may be enacted in the future. Moreover, local regulations that are more stringent than those specified in the voluntary standards may be in effect. For more information on formaldehyde emissions of wood products, see the American Institute of Architects (AIA) *Environmental Resource Guide Subscription*, especially the chapters on particleboard and plywood.

FACTORY FINISHING

Prefinishing interior woodwork in the plant or finishing shop is generally limited to items for which a minimum of handling, cutting, fitting, and adjusting is needed during installation, such as cabinets, doors, paneling, and other woodwork near these items. According to AWI, factory finishing is usually chosen for high-quality work where superior appearance and performance of the finish are desired. Factory finishing may also be used to minimize fieldwork, to comply with OSHA regulations, or to reduce volatile organic compound (VOC) emissions. For Economy-grade work, shop-applied finishes that cost less than field-applied finishes are available, and may be used, especially when they are standard with the finishing shop and quantities are too small for efficient jobsite painting. Field finishing is advantageous when woodwork requires extensive fitting at the project site.

Shop finishing or priming serves to seal the woodwork against moisture absorption and helps prevent dirt and foreign substances from penetrating the wood and staining it. Shop priming also makes it easier to clean the woodwork before final finishing. If woodwork is primed or finished in the shop, it should also be backprimed to seal concealed surfaces against moisture penetration during periods of high humidity. Although this does not completely prevent fluctuations in moisture content and the attendant swelling and shrinking, it will delay or lessen this effect; and the more complete and less permeable the seal, the more it will moderate swelling and shrinking. AWI only requires backpriming for factory-finished moldings, factory-finished paneling, and Premium-grade factory-finished cabinets. WIC requires backpriming surfaces that abut walls, ceilings, and so on, on all shop-finished woodwork, but only for Premium or Custom grade. For the little that it costs, backpriming should be specified for all woodwork, regardless of where it is finished.

CABINET HARDWARE

Cabinet hardware can be specified in several ways (Table 3, figs. 4, 5). A schedule listing each cabinet and the items of hardware required for it can be prepared. Specifiers can refer to Builders Hardware Manufacturers Association (BHMA) numbers and standards or use specific manufacturers' names and product designations. For those desiring to list manufacturers' names and product designations, WIC's Manual of Millwork, Supplement No. 1 to Sections 14 and 15, contains a list of products that they consider acceptable.

Table 3
HARDWARE HINGES

HINGE TYPE	BUTT	PIVOT	WRAPAROUND	EUROPEAN STYLE
Applications	Conventional flush with face frame	Reveal overlay, flush overlay	Conventional reveal overlay	Conventional flush without face frame, reveal overlay, flush overlay
Strength	High	Moderate	Very high	High moderate
Concealed when closed	No	Semi	No	Yes
Requires mortising	Yes	Usually	Occasionally	Yes
Cost of hinge	Low	Low	Moderate	High moderate
Ease of installation	Moderate	Moderate	Easy	Very easy
Adjusted easily after installation	No	No	No	Yes
Remarks	Door requires hardwood edge	Door requires hardwood edge	Exposed knuckle and hinge body	Specify degree of opening; no catch required on self-closing styles

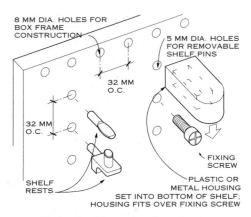

Figure 4. 32 mm box frame system

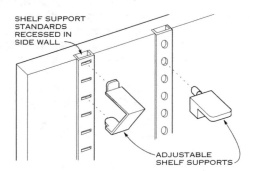

Figure 5. Shelf standards and supports

Because of the quality of work involved in architectural woodwork, it is advisable to specify that cabinet hardware be furnished and installed by the cabinet fabricator to ensure a single point of responsibility. This requirement minimizes problems with coordination and delivery and with potential damage to finish and materials if hardware is supplied and installed in the field by others. Pivot hinges, if used, should be installed in the field because of their tendency to shift during the setting and fitting of cabinets.

Specifying finishes for hardware may be a problem where casework involves products from different manufacturers, such as exposed hinges from one and pulls from another. This is especially true if finishes for both are expected to match but are classified in Category B or C per BHMA A156.18. Category B finishes are not identical when applied to different alloys and forms of base material and when supplied by different manufacturers. Category C finishes are nonuniform by nature (such as a blackened, brushed brass) and vary greatly when supplied by different manufacturers. If uniform appearance is important, specify that hardware with these types of finishes be supplied by the same manufacturer.

ENVIRONMENTAL CONSIDERATIONS

Architectural woodwork is produced primarily from renewable resources (wood and wood products), although glues, plastic laminates, and finishes used in woodwork are, at least in part, made from petroleum and coal-tar products. For this reason, and because the amount of nonrenewable resources consumed by the woodworking industry is small compared to our consumption of these resources as a whole, there is no need to dwell on this aspect of woodwork's environmental impact. Instead, the effects of timber harvesting should be looked at more closely.

Architectural woodwork uses many varieties of both hardwood and softwood, as well as wood products derived from both. The consumption of many species encourages the timber industry to produce a variety of species, which leads away from the monoculture of the tree farm and promotes biological diversity. The large logs used for face-veneer production require a longer growth period to produce the timber necessary, which leads away from even-age stands and promotes biological diversity. Because hardwood species reseed a forest if allowed to, and need shade to become established, hardwood production does not rely on clear-cutting as does softwood production. For these reasons, the hardwood forest supports a wider variety of wildlife than the pine plantation, even though the tree farm supports more deer and rabbits with its abundance of young trees and undergrowth. In specifying architectural woodwork, give some thought to using seldom-used or unusual veneer species to promote diversity, in both buildings and the forest.

Tropical species, on the other hand, are not generally being replanted as they are harvested. Much tropical timber is harvested simply to get it out of the way so the land can be used for agriculture. Selection of veneer species does little to stop the clearing of land for farming, but the careful use of tropical hardwoods may encourage conservation and the replanting of some species. Conscience must also guide selecting tropical veneers to ensure the speed of the extinction process is not increased for some exotic species. Under the Convention on International Trade in Endangered Species (CITES), plants and animals are listed as being in danger of extinction (Category I) or requiring controls to avoid being threatened with extinction (Category II). Unfortunately, it is sometimes difficult to identify the lumber or veneer of these species since the wood may be sold under a name that includes similar, nonthreatened species or those that are not even remotely related and come from a different continent. Most species listed are, however, traded under a name unique to them, so verify that an endangered species is not involved when using any woods named.

Brazilian rosewood (also called *jacaranda* or *palisander*), alerce (South American redwood), and the monkey puzzle tree (sometimes sold along with similar species under the name parana pine) are listed as Category I species along with several lesser-known woods not generally in demand for woodwork. Afrormosia (kokrodua, African teak), Caribbean mahogany (Cuban mahogany), Mexican mahogany (Pacific coast mahogany), lignum vitae, Brazilian padauk (macawood, cristobol, granadillo), and red sandalwood (redsanders) are listed as Category II species. Honduras mahogany (big leaf mahogany) is listed as a Category III species for Costa Rica, but it is unrestricted if it is from other countries.

Category I species cannot be harvested and require special permits to ship unless they are plantation grown, but existing stocks (veneers and logs) are available and are excepted from CITES regulations. Categories II and III species can be harvested, but they are regulated by a permit system. That system requires an export permit issued by the exporting country certifying that the wood was legally obtained and that its export will not be detrimental to the survival of the species. Generally speaking, management of Categories II and III species should restrict harvest to a sustainable level that may force prices up and redirect demand toward other species. It should be noted that there are species with names similar to those listed that are not restricted, such as African mahogany, East Indian rosewood (and many other varieties of rosewood), African padauk, Andaman padauk, Burmese padauk, and true sandalwood. For more information on this subject, see the AIA's *Environmental Resource Guide Subscription: TOPIC.I-6005, Tropical Woods.* For a complete list of scientific and common names of species listed by CITES, see 50 CFR, Section 23.23, which can be viewed at and downloaded from www.access.gpo.gov/nara/cfr/cfr-retrieve.html#page1.

Sustainable forestry is the ultimate answer to preventing the extinction of timber species and the ecosystems that include them. To this end, the Forest Partnership has compiled a database of wood species, called *Woods of the World,* with information about their technical properties and sustainability, as well as color pictures of the wood.

REFERENCES

Publication dates cited here were current at the time of this writing. Publications are revised periodically, and revisions may have occurred before this book was published.

ASTM International

ASTM D 2898-94(Reapproved 1999): Test Methods for Accelerated Weathering of Fire-Retardant-Treated Wood for Fire Testing

American Wood-Preservers' Association

AWPA C20-96: Structural Lumber – Fire-Retardant Treatment by Pressure Processes

AWPA C27-96: Plywood-Fire-Retardant Treatment by Pressure Processes

The American Institute of Architects

Environmental Resource Guide Subscription: *TOPIC.I-6005, Tropical Woods,* 1992.

Architectural Woodwork Institute

Architectural Woodwork Quality Standards, 7th ed., version 1.0, 1997.

Builders Hardware Manufacturers Association

BHMA A156.18-1993: Materials and Finishes

Code of Federal Regulations

24 CFR—Housing And Urban Development, Chapter XX—Office Of Assistant Secretary For Housing—Federal Housing Commissioner, Department Of Housing And Urban Development, Part 3280—Manufactured Home Construction And Safety Standards, Subpart D—Body And Frame Construction Requirements, Section 3280.308 — Formaldehyde emission controls for certain wood products, 2001.

50 CFR — Wildlife And Fisheries, Chapter I — United States Fish And Wildlife Service, Department Of The Interior, Part 23 — Endangered Species Convention, Subpart C—Appendices I, II and III to the Convention on International Trade in Endangered Species of Wild Fauna and Flora, Section 23.23 — Species listed in Appendices I, II, and III, 2000.

Forest Partnership, Inc.

Woods of the World, version 2.5, 1997.

Hardwood Plywood & Veneer Association

HPVA HP-1-1994: Hardwood and Decorative Plywood

Underwriters Laboratories Inc.

Building Materials Directory, published annually.

Woodwork Institute of California

Manual of Millwork, 1995.

WEB SITES

Architectural Woodwork Institute: www.awinet.org

Forest Partnership, Inc.: www.forestworld.com

SmartWood: www.smartwood.org

Wood & Wood Products Red Book Online: www.podi.com/redbook

Woodworking at Woodweb: www.woodweb.com

World Timber Network: www.transport.com/~lege/wtn2.html

06420 PANELING

This chapter discusses custom-manufactured paneling, which includes board paneling, flush wood paneling, laminate-clad paneling, and stile and rail paneling.

This chapter does not discuss stock-manufactured wood paneling and plywood sidings used as interior paneling.

WOOD-PANELING CHARACTERISTICS

This discussion covers custom-fabricated paneling that may involve complex drawing and specification requirements. Choices that seem minor may have significant effects on appearance and cost. Chapter 06402, Interior Architectural Woodwork, has additional information about paneling materials, finishing, and construction.

Standards

Commercial and product standards for stock paneling are inadequate for custom-paneling materials, and do not cover custom-millwork fabrication. Standards developed by the Architectural Woodwork Institute (AWI) and the Woodwork Institute of California (WIC) are widely recognized. They are the basis for the custom-fabricated paneling. The location of the project determines, in part, which standard to reference. Except for projects located in California, Nevada, and Oregon, the standard to reference is the one published by AWI. For California, Nevada, or Oregon, either standard can be used.

BOARD PANELING

Board paneling is included with other types of woodwork in referenced woodworking standards. In the AWI standards, it is included as part of "Standing and Running Trim"; in the WIC standards, it can be found as part of "Miscellaneous Interior Millwork." Because board paneling can take so many forms, and can even be combined with plywood panels, it is difficult to develop universal specification requirements. One example requirement is for fabricating individual boards, which assumes that random-length pieces are unacceptable; otherwise, require end-matched (machined) boards that can be of random length. Additional requirements could be included, such as color and grain matching, in adjoining boards. Usually, requirements for the assembly of boards into panel units assume that details showing backing materials and attachment methods are on the drawings.

FLUSH WOOD PANELING

Premanufactured sets of sequence-matched panels are produced and warehoused by some major panel product manufacturers. These sets can be seen at selected locations, usually at the shop or in large metropolitan areas. Panel construction and the quality of the face veneers and matching are similar to those commonly used in custom-fabricated paneling, but stock sets do not offer the same unlimited possibilities in custom fabrication. Stock sets are generally less expensive than custom-fabricated panels,

and their greatest advantage is availability. Long delays in fabrication are avoided, and stock sets can be seen and judged as a finished product.

As stock items, premanufactured sets are produced in standard sizes, not in exact custom sizes. Although sequence-matched from one flitch or similar flitches, they cannot be matched to other elements, such as doors and casework. The number of panels in a set is limited, moreover, to the size of the log from which the flitch was cut. Usually, smaller logs are used for stock panels. If they can conveniently be inspected by the architect (and possibly the owner), premanufactured sets offer a good solution under the following conditions:

- Wall areas fall within the limits of available panel sets (in total area and height).
- Blueprint match with doors, cabinets, and so on, is not required.
- Some sacrifice of sequence is acceptable at corners.
- Elaborate or extensive fabrication of flush joints, exposed edges, and exterior corners is not required.

If these limitations are unacceptable, specify custom panels. Do not assume that acceptable premanufactured sets are available; investigate the available range and be prepared to accept one of several comparable sets, unless preselected choices can be reserved until the contractor can purchase them.

Shop finishing of premanufactured sets is recommended. Unfinished panels are subject to moisture pickup and damage by soiling and handling.

Flush Paneling Standards

AWI standards have more extensive requirements for flush paneling than WIC standards. For sophisticated veneer selection and matching, additional requirements must be added to both standards. WIC standards tend to treat this type of paneling as plywood that can be bought from existing stock, rather than as an item requiring extensive fabrication. AWI standards include an elaborate, separate chapter titled "Wood Paneling." WIC standards, by contrast, consider paneling as one item in a catchall section titled "Miscellaneous Interior Millwork," and most of the requirements cover stile and rail paneling, with no particular fabrication requirements for flush paneling.

Flush Wood Paneling for Opaque Finish

Custom-fabricated, flush wood paneling usually involves fine hardwood veneers that are finished with a transparent coating. However, fine quality opaque finishes can be specified. Quality depends on the level of fabrication required for joints, exterior corners, and so on. The selection of face species is minor, the main criterion being good paint-holding qualities with resistance to feathering and indentation.

Flush Wood Paneling for Transparent Finish

Custom fabrication of panels for transparent finish involves the most expensive and complex selections in the entire paneling field; hence, it is usually specified only for the most important areas.

Special, uniform-size sequence or blueprint matching is available under AWI standards only in Premium grade. WIC standards include data on sequence matching only as general information, not as specific requirements. Although fabrication requirements derived from AWI standards are feasible only with the thicker panels required under AWI Premium grade, they are equally applicable under WIC standards as long as ¾-inch- (19-mm-) thick paneling is specified.

STILE AND RAIL PANELING

This type of paneling is usually custom-fabricated to exact sizes and profiles and is detailed on the drawings, but it is also available with prefabricated panels made to standard sizes (fig. 1). The basic unit frame consists of solid-wood stiles and rails with infills of relatively small panels.

Panels may be raised or flat and set in simple or elaborately profiled frames. Panel material may be limited to panel products (AWI Premium grade) or solid lumber, in either single-width boards or glued-for-width panels (AWI Custom grade), or it may be laminated or veneered (all WIC grades). The material may not be critical if the paneling is to be painted, but if a transparent finish is required, and the selected species has a strong figure, it may greatly affect appearance.

Both AWI and WIC standards set minimum grades for solid wood and plywood components. Fabrication requirements also differ in AWI and WIC standards. Review the standards to ensure that the grade and other requirements specified will give the quality desired.

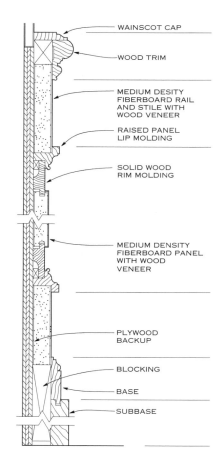

Figure 1. Section-wainscot stile and rail paneling

WAINSCOT CAP

WOOD TRIM

MEDIUM DESITY FIBERBOARD RAIL AND STILE WITH WOOD VENEER

RAISED PANEL LIP MOLDING

SOLID WOOD RIM MOLDING

MEDIUM DENSITY FIBERBOARD PANEL WITH WOOD VENEER

PLYWOOD BACKUP

BLOCKING

BASE

SUBBASE

HARDWOOD FACE VENEERS

Several factors, including species and cut, quality, and types of matching, affect the selection of face veneers for paneling. Selecting stock paneling is a simple matter. If ordinary, prefinished paneling is required, the choice is made after examining representative samples. Flitch-matched stock sets can be examined in the warehouse, where the entire set can be seen.

A less-direct approach for selecting stock paneling involves naming the species and cut and specifying a minimum quality of veneer, based on HPVA HP-1, developed by the Hardwood Plywood & Veneer Association (HPVA). This approach ensures nothing more than submitting panels of the specified species and cut with minimum defects. Book or slip matching of the individual leaves of veneer can also be specified for stock paneling to produce a match of grain or color between adjoining leaves of veneer (fig. 2). The arrangement of veneer leaves on the panel face involves another level of matching, based on the size and number of pieces. However, only the most common match, called running match, is usually available on stock panels. Running match does not restrict the size or number of leaves, and if one leaf is not completely used on a panel face, the surplus starts the next panel. This arrangement results in the least waste, thus is the most economical. Although running match would seem to provide a continuous sequence match, the result is not the same: adjoining pieces may be from different flitches (from different logs), or imperfections may require cutting out and discarding portions or entire pieces of veneer, thus interrupting the sequence.

Sequence matching requires high-quality veneers cut from one log or flitch. The flitch must contain enough veneer not only for the area of paneling but for the trimming required to eliminate defects and still maintain an exact match of grain and color. If the arrangement on the panel face is balance or center-balance matched, as well as book or slip matched, more waste is involved. Custom fabrication of panels to exact sizes to fit a given space also affects sequence matching. This overall sizing can involve uniform spacing of veneer leaves in a given stretch, and placement of remainders at corners and at openings (over and at jambs of doors, windows, etc.). Blueprint match requires specified matches to be continuous on the faces of other wood elements, such as doors and casework. Sophisticated matching arrangements may have a veneer waste factor as high as 4:1; that is, only one-fourth of the flitch may be usable. If the area of the available flitches is inadequate, a similar second flitch cut from another log must be selected, and the joint between the two flitches (which never match) must be located in a corner or other interruption of the paneling.

Vertical and horizontal matching may be required. This may be as simple as matching a transom panel with a door to achieve a continuous vertical grain and color effect, or it may be more complex. Rows of panels separated by a chair rail, picture mold, or reveal may require continuous matching (vertically adjacent veneers are a continuation of the same leaf) or end matching (vertically adjacent veneers are from the same flitch but reversed end for end to produce a vertical book matching, or mirror image). If the paneling is more than 10 feet (3 m) in height, veneer selection is limited to flitches from larger logs, and the cost increases. Flitches up to 16-feet (5-m) long may be available, but heights above 12 feet (3.7 m) usually require vertical matching in addition to the other matches. This creates the effect of two parallel horizontal rows of sequence-matched paneling, all from one flitch or similar flitches.

It is also possible to alternate pieces of veneer in sequence from one end of the wall to the other so the figure created by the grain is largest, or highest, at the center of a wall, and diminishes or tapers toward both ends. However, as veneer strips alternate from the centerline of the wall, a slight

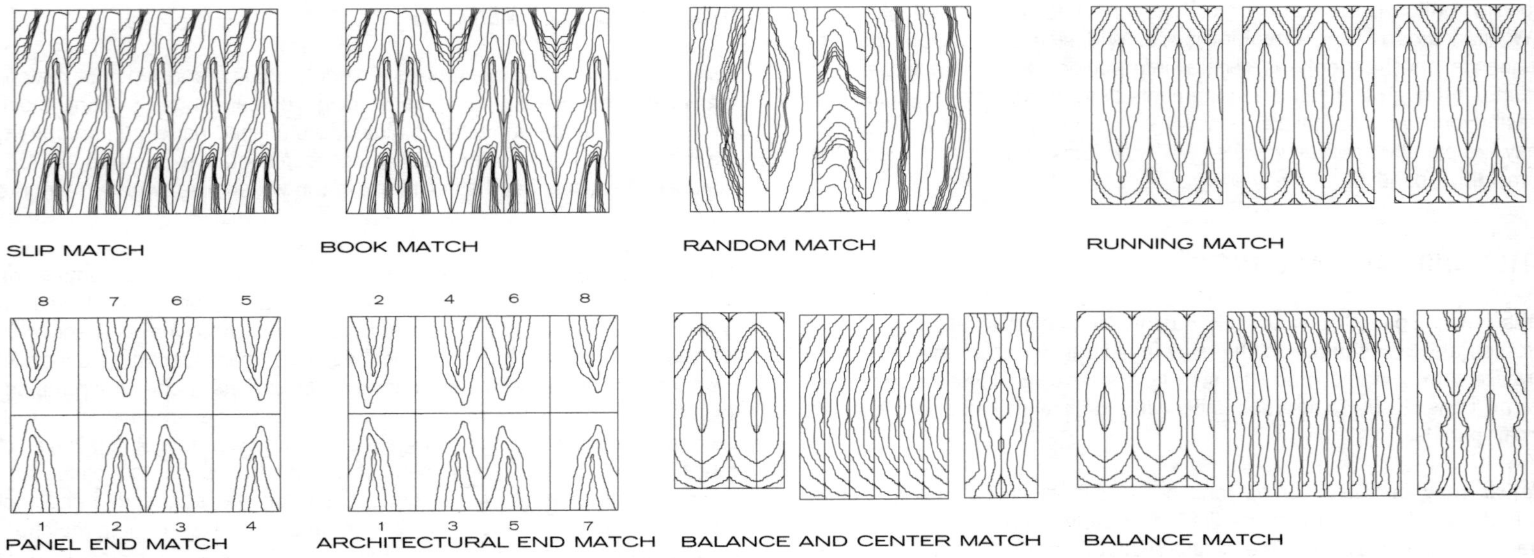

SLIP MATCH

BOOK MATCH

RANDOM MATCH

RUNNING MATCH

PANEL END MATCH

ARCHITECTURAL END MATCH

BALANCE AND CENTER MATCH

BALANCE MATCH

Figure 2. Veneer match types

8-PIECE SUNBURST

BOX MATCH

PARQUET MATCH

REVERSE OR END
GRAIN BOX

HERRINGBONE

SWING MATCH

DIAMOND

REVERSE DIAMOND

SKETCH FACE

NOTE

During specification, use both names and illustrations to
define the desired effect, as names vary by region for these
matching techniques.

Figure 3. Special wood veneer matching options

slippage or mismatch of veneer-figure occurs. Other special matching includes patterns that form figures based on the orientation of the wood grain. Examples are box, diamond, and sketch-face matching (fig. 3).

The almost limitless combinations of species, cuts, and matching possible in custom fabrication of flush wood paneling, and the high cost and visual importance of such work, have led to the practice of the architect's preselecting veneer flitches. This is the only possible way to pick flitches with a particular color and figure range. Nature does not grow uniform trees, and selection based on the most carefully written description may not have the desired effect. Natural variation also dictates inspecting the entire flitch, not just a few representative samples, if unexpected and unacceptable color and grain surprises are to be avoided.

If flitches are preselected and reserved, the number and source of flitches must be indicated. Actual yield of a given flitch is difficult to estimate, and the estimates of the flitch supplier and the panel fabricator frequently differ. If flitches are selected by the architect from flitch samples submitted after bidding, a price allowance is mandatory to control selection. Price allowances must be realistic and must anticipate the selection of additional flitches for adequate yield. For sources of veneers, view the *Wood & Wood Products* Red Book Online Web site, given at the end of this chapter.

LAMINATE-CLAD PANELING

High-pressure decorative laminates are available in many colors, patterns, and finishes. Each manufacturer offers products that differ in one or more of these characteristics from those of competitors. Certain finishes can be specified in nonproprietary terms by referencing the surface-finish designations implemented by the National Electrical Manufacturers Association (NEMA) in NEMA LD 3, which are measured in terms of gloss level. However, textured finishes that cannot be characterized by any available standard test have to be described in proprietary or semiproprietary terms.

Laminate thickness can be specified by referencing NEMA LD 3 grade designations. To specify manufacturers' products that do not comply exactly with NEMA requirements, describe those qualities that are different. Heavily textured laminates may not meet NEMA performance requirements for wear resistance because of resulting variability in thickness of the surface sheet. Before specifying heavily textured laminates, obtain test data that indicate actual performance from manufacturers.

Custom colors and textures are available only as a negotiated product with a particular manufacturer. Custom colors are not feasible in small quantities, and some colors may not be feasible at all. Custom patterns are even more restricted and costly.

Surface-burning characteristics of plastic-laminate paneling are determined by testing an assembly of face laminate, adhesives, core material, and backing-grade laminate. Using a fire-rated laminate is generally not enough to achieve low flame-spread indexes without also using a certain type of adhesive and a core material with fire-retardant properties. No requirements for surface-burning characteristics or test methods are included in NEMA LD 3 for fire-rated plastic laminates. These requirements must be inserted in the project specification to fit the project.

Door matching is easier with wood-grain-patterned, plastic-laminate paneling than with wood veneers. The door manufacturer can use the same manufactured sheet as the paneling fabricator, ensuring that flush doors match the paneling. This is much simpler and less risky than having two fabricators share a sequence-matched wood flitch.

Adhesive type and performance, with the exception of fire-retardant qualities, are covered in the referenced woodworking quality standards.

However, for special applications, it may be necessary to specify the adhesive. Otherwise, adhesive selection should be the fabricator's responsibility.

FIRE-RETARDANT PANELING

Treated wood products are significantly more expensive than untreated products. Some formulations used in fire-retardant treatment make cutting and fastening more difficult and affect the appearance. Chapter 06402, Interior Architectural Woodwork, contains a more comprehensive commentary on fire-retardant-treated materials.

For guidance on face-veneer selection, consult AWI literature and the literature of various panel manufacturers. The densities of available species are listed according to surface-burning characteristics (flame-spread and smoke-developed indexes).

Consult governing codes and local authorities having jurisdiction to verify acceptance of panels with treated cores.

FORMALDEHYDE EMISSION LEVELS OF PANEL PRODUCTS

Chapter 06402, Interior Architectural Woodwork, contains information on formaldehyde emissions from panel products.

SHOP FINISHING

Chapter 06402, Interior Architectural Woodwork, contains information on shop finishing of paneling.

ENVIRONMENTAL CONSIDERATIONS

Chapter 06402, Interior Architectural Woodwork, contains information on environmental considerations relating to paneling.

REFERENCES

Publication dates cited here were current at the time of this writing. Publications are revised periodically, and revisions may have occurred before this book was published.

Architectural Woodwork Institute
Architectural Woodwork Quality Standards, 7th ed., version 1.0, 1997.

Hardwood Plywood & Veneer Association
HPVA HP-1-1994: Hardwood and Decorative Plywood

National Electrical Manufacturers Association
NEMA LD 3-95: High-Pressure Decorative Laminates

Woodwork Institute of California
Manual of Millwork, 1995.

WEB SITES

Architectural Woodwork Institute: www.awinet.org
Forest Partnership, Inc.: www.forestworld.com
SmartWood: www.smartwood.org
Wood & Wood Products Red Book Online: www.podi.com/redbook
Woodworking at Woodweb: www.woodweb.com
World Timber Network: www.transport.com/~lege/wtn2.html

08110 STEEL DOORS AND FRAMES

This chapter discusses standard steel doors and frames fabricated to comply with ANSI A250.8 and with established Steel Door Institute standards.

This chapter does not discuss custom hollow-metal work specified in Division 5, "Metals."

GENERAL COMMENTS

The Steel Door Institute (SDI) publishes the basic reference standard for steel doors and frames, SDI 100, *Recommended Specifications for Standard Steel Doors and Frames*, which was recently updated, approved as an ANSI standard, and redesignated ANSI A250.8. First published in 1980 as a guide, it was recognized as an American National Standard in 1985. Although revised and improved, the general scope of the document has not changed. In this discussion, the standard will henceforth be referred to as ANSI A250.8.

It is useful to acquire a copy of the latest version of ANSI A250.8 before specifying steel doors and frames. The *SDI Fact File* is also useful; contact SDI to order a copy. Obtain catalogs from door and frame manufacturers whose products will be specified.

The line between standard and custom hollow-metal work has blurred over time. Most hollow-metal door and frame manufacturers can also now produce products traditionally considered custom.

PRODUCT CHARACTERISTICS

Door Models

Full-flush doors do not have visible seams on their faces (fig. 1). Seamless and stile and rail doors do not have visible seams on their sur-

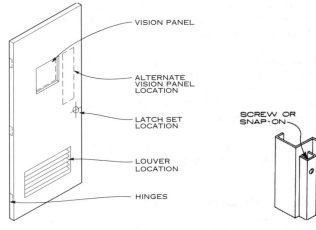

Figure 2. Vision or louvered door   **Figure 3.** Removable glazing bead

faces or along their vertical edges. Doors are available with louvers or with openings for glass with stops (figs. 2, 3) furnished; they can be fabricated as Dutch doors and in many other designs, as illustrated in SDI 108. Six different methods of internal construction are listed in ANSI A250.8.

Frames are available as either welded construction or knock-down units. Welded set-up frames may have mitered or butted corners with welded and finished frame faces. (Continuous welded corners are not needed or recommended.) Knock-down units have mechanical joints between the header and jambs for field assembly (fig. 4). Drywall slip-on frames are designed for installation after gypsum board partitions are erected (fig. 5). Drywall frame corners may have mitered or butt joints, and may be designed to be screwed together, snap-locked, or slip-fitted, but they cannot be welded. Several common wall conditions with various frames and anchors are indicated in SDI 111A.

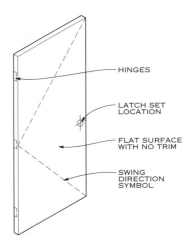

Figure 1. Typical flush door sizes and characteristics

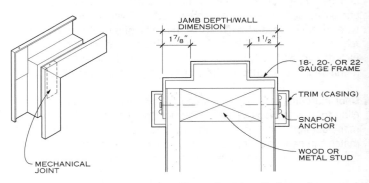

Figure 4. Knock-down frame   **Figure 5.** Drywall slip-on frame

PRODUCT SELECTION CONSIDERATIONS

Metal Thickness

The hollow-metal industry continues to use the term gage to indicate sheet metal thickness although, according to the ASTM standard specifications for these products, sheet metals are only produced in decimal or fractional thicknesses. ASTM A 480/A 480M, *Specification for General Requirements for Flat-Rolled Stainless Steel and Heat-Resisting Steel Plate, Sheet, and Strip*, includes the following statement in Section 4, Ordering Information: "Thickness shall be ordered to decimal or fractional thickness. The use of the gage number is discouraged as being an archaic term of limited usefulness not having a general agreement on meaning." ANSI A250.8 includes not only the gage numbers but the equivalent minimum thicknesses of uncoated steel sheet in both IP and SI units, and the same figures for metallic-coated steel sheet thicknesses, whether the coating is applied by the hot-dip or electrolytic process. The standard explains that the gage numbers and equivalent minimum thicknesses were derived from figures published by Underwriters Laboratories (UL) in its *General Reference Guide No. 1 for Field Representatives*, which was not meant for public use but to enable inspectors to verify the metal thickness of a door skin by using a micrometer.

Uncoated and Metallic-Coated Steel Sheet Thicknesses

ASTM A 568/A 568M, which contains the general requirements for hot- and cold-rolled uncoated steel sheet, allows purchasers to specify minimum or nominal thickness. If minimum thickness is specified, the standard over- and under-thickness tolerances listed in ASTM A 568/A 568M tables are applied only as over-thickness tolerances, and are doubled. This method of applying tolerances can also be invoked for hot-dip metallic-coated steel sheet, but only if it is specified by minimum base metal thickness. Otherwise, over- and under-thickness tolerances in ASTM A 924/A 924M are applied to the total thickness, including both base metal and coating.

Level And Model Table

This table relates the thickness of the steel-face sheet to the door thickness and the SDI Level and Model. If warranted by conditions, specify exterior doors from metallic-coated, galvanized or galvannealed steel sheet.

Table 1
MINIMUM STEEL SHEET THICKNESSES FOR DOOR FACES

SDI Level	SDI Model Designation	MSG No.	Minimum Face Sheet Thickness	Door Thickness
1	Model 1: Full Flush	20	0.032" (0.8 mm)	1⅜" (34.9 mm)
1	Model 2: Seamless	20	0.032" (0.8 mm)	1⅜" (34.9 mm)
1	Model 1: Full Flush	20	0.032" (0.8 mm)	1¾" (44.4 mm)
1	Model 2: Seamless	20	0.032" (0.8 mm)	1¾" (44.4 mm)
2	Model 1: Full Flush	18	0.042" (1.0 mm)	1¾" (44.4 mm)
2	Model 2: Seamless	18	0.042" (1.0 mm)	1¾" (44.4 mm)
3	Model 1: Full Flush	16	0.053" (1.3 mm)	1¾" (44.4 mm)
3	Model 2: Seamless	16	0.053" (1.3 mm)	1¾" (44.4 mm)
3	Model 3: Stile and Rail	16	0.053" (1.3 mm)[1]	1¾" (44.4 mm)
4	Model 1: Full Flush	14	0.067" (1.7 mm)	1¾" (44.4 mm)
4	Model 2: Seamless	14	0.067" (1.7 mm)	1¾" (44.4 mm)

Note
[1]Center panels of stile and rail doors are 0.042 inch (1.0 mm) thick.
Key
Level 1 Standard-Duty Level C according to ANSI A250.4
Level 2 Heavy-Duty Level B according to ANSI A250.4
Level 3 Extra-Heavy-Duty Level A according to ANSI A250.4
Level 4 Maximum-Duty Level A according to ANSI A250.4

Metal Thickness Equivalent Table

This table lists some popular sheet-metal gage equivalents in IP and SI thicknesses.

Table 2
SDI GAGE EQUIVALENT IN INCHES AND MILLIMETERS

Uncoated Steel Sheet											
MSG	7	8	10	12	14	16	18	20	22	24	26	28
INCH	0.167	0.152	0.123	0.093	0.067	0.053	0.042	0.032	0.026	0.020	0.016	0.013
MM	4.2	3.8	3.1	2.3	1.6	1.3	1.0	0.8	0.5	0.5	0.4	0.3

Steel Sheet

Both hot- and cold-rolled steel sheet are commonly used to fabricate doors, frames, and accessories. Door faces should always be made of cold-rolled steel sheet because its surface is smoother than hot-rolled steel, and it is easier to form, weld, and paint. Frames may be made of hot- or cold-rolled steel, but the surface appearance of hot-rolled steel is generally inferior.

Metallic-coated steel sheet is used for improved corrosion resistance. A metallic coating may be applied by either the hot-dip or electrolytic process. For metallic coatings applied by the hot-dip process, the term *galvanized* refers only to steel that has been zinc-coated; the term *galvannealed* refers only to steel that has been zinc-iron-alloy-coated. The latter type of coating is imprecisely referred to in ANSI A250.8 as the alloyed type of hot-dip zinc coating. Electrolytically coated sheets have a thinner zinc coating than the sheets coated by the hot-dip process. ANSI A250.8 includes electrolytically deposited zinc coating for anchors and accessories only, not for door faces or frames. For exterior locations, galvannealed steel sheet provides better corrosion resistance, especially if the atmosphere is corrosive, and has better paint-holding qualities than galvanized steel sheet. ANSI A250.8 establishes a minimum coating weight of A40 (Z120); if a heavier coating is required, verify its availability with manufacturers.

Fabrication

Steel doors can be constructed with internal steel stiffeners placed between two face sheets or with face sheets laminated to several core materials such as impregnated paper honeycomb, plastic foam, or structural mineral blocking (figs. 6-10). The steel-stiffened core construction has been used for many years; it produces a strong, long-lasting door.

Thermal and Acoustical Doors

Thermal and acoustical properties of doors can be improved by packing spaces between steel stiffeners with insulating material. The best possible

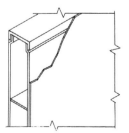

Figure 6. Flush door closer reinforcement

Figure 7. Flush door core

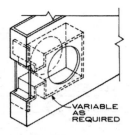

Figure 8. Lock reinforcement

Figure 9. Hinge reinforcement

Figure 10. Flush door bottom and edge construction

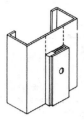

Figure 11. Adjustable sound stop gasketing

insulation, however, uses special construction that isolates the two faces of the door. In general, the best thermal insulation is laminated construction with plastic foam as the core material. Door and frame assemblies with the highest sound transmission class (STC) ratings not only require excellent gasketing or seals on all four edges (fig. 11), but may also require special hinges, lead sheet, and a special composite construction.

PRODUCT STANDARDS

Door Classification

Levels and models are classified according to the latest edition of ANSI A250.8, where the term *level* replaces the term *grade,* which was used in the previous edition of SDI 100 as the designation for identifying door requirements relative to steel thicknesses of face sheets. Performance-level designations identify test-response characteristics for physical performance as listed here:

Level 1 and Physical Performance Level C for Standard-Duty Doors, 1⅜- and 1¾-Inches (34.9- and 44.4-mm) Thick
• Model 1: Full flush
• Model 2: Seamless

Level 2 and Physical Performance Level B for Heavy-Duty Doors, 1¾-Inches (44.4-mm) Thick
• Model 1: Full flush
• Model 2: Seamless

Level 3 and Physical Performance Level A for Extra-Heavy-Duty Doors, 1¾-Inches (44.4-mm) Thick
• Model 1: Full flush
• Model 2: Seamless
• Model 3: Stile and rail

Level 4 and Physical Performance Level A for Maximum-Duty Doors, 1¾-Inches (44.4-mm) Thick
• Model 1: Full flush
• Model 2: Seamless

ANSI A250.4

Physical-endurance tests for steel doors in ANSI A250.4 include swing testing and twist testing of a representative specimen of production doors and frames. During a swing test, with latching, a Level A door is subjected to 1,000,000 cycles, a Level B door is subjected to 500,000 cycles, and a Level C door is subjected to 250,000 cycles. A twist test consists of clamping the door in a test frame and applying loads; deflections are measured and the door is examined to determine the effects of the test. Certain acceptance criteria must be met for each level of door.

Door Sizes

Doors are manufactured in the following standard opening sizes for each door thickness:

• 1⅜-inches (34.9-mm) thick
  Heights: 80, 84, and 86 inches (2032, 2134, and 2184 mm)
• 1¾-inches (44.4-mm) thick
  Heights: 80, 84, 86, 94, and 96 inches (2032, 2134, 2184, 2388, and 2438 mm)
• Widths: 24, 28, 30, 32, 34, 36, 40, 42, 44, 46, and 48 inches (610, 711, 762, 813, 864, 914, 1016, 1067, 1118, 1168, and 1219 mm)

APPLICATION CONSIDERATIONS

Door Usage Guide

SDI 108, which had not been updated when this book was written, includes criteria in tabular form for the selection and usage of doors. The following information summarizes the criteria based on input from SDI representatives:

• **Level 1:** Doors for interior use in residences, dormitories, and hotels; office buildings and other commercial structures; and closets in most buildings
• **Level 2:** Doors for entrances to apartments and hotels, stairwells, toilet rooms, hospital patient and operating rooms, and school classrooms
• **Level 3:** Entrance and stairwell doors in most buildings, in commercial and industrial buildings and schools, except closets, and in hospital kitchens
• **Level 4:** Doors for high-traffic entrances and stairwells in commercial and industrial buildings, and entrances requiring increased security

Frame-material thickness is governed by the level of door installed in the frame, with options for each level except Level 2. Selection of options may be based on many factors, including security needs, width of opening, whether the door is for interior or exterior use, expected frequency of use, and severity of service, availability, and cost.

Finishes

Standard steel doors and frames are usually furnished primed for field painting, but they can be factory-finished by most manufacturers. Other available finishes include vinyl overlays, plastic laminates, wood veneers, and textured metal laminations.

Louvers

Several louvered door types are listed in SDI 106 and ANSI A250.7. SDI 111C shows eight common designs that are available from most manufacturers. Of the sightproof louvers, the inverted-V blade offers the most free area, about 55 percent. Louvers with inverted-Y blades offer more strength than louvers with Z or inverted-V blades, but their free area is only about 30 percent. Fire-rated automatic louvers use fusible links to close movable blades in fires. Lightproof louvers employ baffles to prevent light transmission, but their free area is only about 20 percent. Pierced louvers, which are generally slits cut in the door faces and bent inward, also have a low free area, about 20 percent, because more or closer slits would weaken the door. Adjustable blade louvers have almost 40 percent free area when open, and are used where the airflow must be varied. Grilles are normally associated with air conditioning, and will allow diffused air to pass through the door without causing a high-velocity airflow pattern.

Fire-Rated Automatic Door Louvers

According to NFPA 80 published by the National Fire Protection Association (NFPA), fire-rated doors can be equipped with automatic louvers only if the doors are not exits or if the louvers would allow passage of products of combustion that would jeopardize using exits before actuating louvers. UL's Building Materials Directory advises consulting authorities having jurisdiction before installing door louvers in fire-rated doors.

Fire-Rated Assemblies

NFPA 80 is the standard referenced in building codes for regulating the installation and maintenance of assemblies and devices used to protect openings and walls, floors, and ceilings against the spread of fire and smoke within, into, and out of buildings (fig. 12). Specific requirements for the degree of protection needed are typically covered in building codes of authorities having jurisdiction. Where fire-door assembly sizes exceed those that can be labeled, the building official may give permission to use such oversize assemblies for a given application. Such permission normally requires obtaining an inspection certificate from an agency that is acceptable to the building official, indicating that the oversize assembly's design, materials, and construction are identical to those required for labeled units. Oversize fire-rated doors are not covered in ANSI A250.8.

In exit enclosures, building codes usually require that fire-rated door assemblies have labels denoting the fire-protection rating by time period or letter designation, or both, and the maximum temperature rise allowed on the unexposed face of the door after 30 minutes of fire exposure; this temperature-rise limit is 450°F (250°C). Labels may also indicate other

maximum temperature rises of 250° or 650°F (139° or 360°C). If the temperature rise is not indicated on the label, the temperature rise for the door is in excess of 650°F (360°C) at the end of 30 minutes of fire exposure.

Astragals are used to limit the passage of fire, smoke, light, and sound at the meeting stiles of pairs of doors. Astragals are required by NFPA 80 for fire-rated doors labeled for more than one-and-one-half hours. Other labeled fire-rated doors may not require astragals to obtain their rating. Astragals for controlling sound and light or that are not required to obtain a fire rating are usually specified in the Division 8 door hardware section.

ASSEMBLY CHARACTERISTICS

Cores

Doors are available with the following types of internal construction (not all manufacturers provide all cores specified):

- **Honeycomb:** Resin-impregnated kraft/paper with cells perpendicular to both faces
- **Polyurethane:** Foamed-in-place or rigid board
- **Polystyrene:** Rigid-molded, expanded-foam board
- **Stiffeners:** Not less than 0.026-inch (0.66-mm) steel; 6 inches (150 mm) o.c. vertically with insulation or sound deadener (fig. 13)
- **Continuous Truss Form:** Not less than 0.013-inch (0.33-mm) steel; 3 inches (75 mm) o.c. vertically and horizontally
- **Mineral-Fiber Board:** For labeled doors if a temperature-rise limit is required

Hardware Location

Recommended locations for hardware on standard steel doors and frames differ from those recommended for custom steel doors and frames, notably for hinges, knobs or levers, exit device crossbars, and strikes (figs. 14-17). Hardware locations are established for standard steel doors and frames in Table V, "Hardware Locations," in ANSI A250.8 and in the Door and Hardware Institute's *Recommended Locations for Architectural Hardware for Standard Steel Doors and Frames.* In 1990, the deadlock strike location was lowered to 48 inches (1219 mm) to comply with requirements of the Americans with Disabilities Act. Mutes are located across from the hinges on single doors and about 6 inches (150 mm) from the center of the head of the frame on double doors.

FACTORY MUTUAL   1 1/2 HOUR RATED FIRE DOOR
MINIMUM LATCH THROW 1/2 INCH
FM   FM - XXXXXXX
APPROVED   TESTED IN ACCORDANCE WITH ASTM E512   OAK BROOK, IL
FMF

DOOR LABEL

FACTORY MUTUAL   FIRE DOOR FRAME
FM   FM - XXXXXXX
APPROVED   TESTED IN ACCORDANCE WITH ASTM E512   OAK BROOK, IL
FMF

FRAME LABEL

NOTE

Various agencies test and rate fire door and window units and assemblies. Manufacturers locate metal labels in accessible but concealed locations (the hinge edge of doors, for example); these labels must remain in place, unpainted, uncovered, and unaltered.

Figure 12. Testing labels

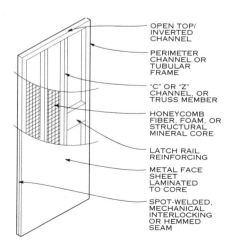

OPEN TOP/
INVERTED
CHANNEL

PERIMETER
CHANNEL OR
TUBULAR
FRAME

"C" OR "Z"
CHANNEL, OR
TRUSS MEMBER

HONEYCOMB
FIBER, FOAM, OR
STRUCTURAL
MINERAL CORE

LATCH RAIL
REINFORCING

METAL FACE
SHEET
LAMINATED
TO CORE

SPOT-WELDED,
MECHANICAL
INTERLOCKING
OR HEMMED
SEAM

Figure 13. Hollow metal door with stiffened core

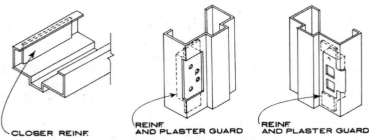

Figure 14. Frame head **Figure 15.** Hinge cut-out **Figure 16.** Strike cut-out

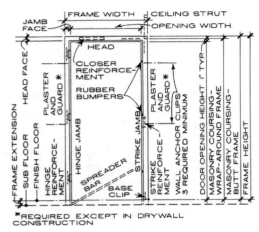

Figure 17. Standard steel frame

Figure 18. Weather stripping

Figure 19. Weather stripping

ENERGY CONSIDERATIONS

The amount of heat transferred through the building's exterior doors will generally be influenced more by air leakage than by thermal conductance through the door. Air leakage occurs when the door is opened, and from airflow through cracks between the door and frame. Weather stripping and improved insulation are effective only when the door is closed, and weather stripping produces a more dramatic effect than insulation (figs. 18, 19). For example, a well-fitted door without weather stripping can have an air-leakage rate of 6 cfm/linear foot (0.863 L/s per linear m) at a pressure differential of 1.57 lb/sq. ft. (75 Pa). Weather stripping can reduce this rate to as low as 0.35 cfm/linear foot (0.050 L/s per linear m). For a 36-by-84-inch (914-by-2134-mm) door that has 240 linear inches (6096 linear mm) of crack, with a temperature differential of 70°F (39°C), infiltration loss would be 9072 BTU (9572 kJ) per hour for a nonweather-stripped door versus 529 BTU (558 kJ) per hour for a weather-stripped door. Heat loss of a door with 0.040 U factor is 588 BTU (620 kJ) per hour. Therefore, efficient weather stripping reduces energy loss much better than the thermal resistance of the door.

DOOR SCHEDULE

When only a single unit or unit size is required on a particular project, a schedule is not necessary. However, when several units of varying sizes, materials, characteristics, and locations are required on a given project, as is usually the case with doors, a schedule is preferred. This schedule could appear in the specifications or on the drawings. Usually, this schedule should appear on the drawings because doors or frames may be specified in several specification sections. Do not duplicate schedule information on both the drawings and specifications. Refer to SDI 111D, *Recommended Door, Frame, and Hardware Schedule for Standard Steel Doors and Frames,* for another example of a schedule that could be placed on the drawings or in the specifications.

Table 3
DOOR SCHEDULE

OPENING NO.	LABEL	DOORS						FRAMES					HARDWARE SET NO.	REMARKS
		DESIGNATION	MAT'L	QTY	NOMINAL SIZE			DESIGNATION	MAT'L	DETAILS				
					WIDE	HIGH	THICK			JAMB	HEAD	SILL		

Key
MAT'L: Material such as steel, metallic-coated steel, wood, and so on
QTY: Number of doors in the opening—single, pair, and so on
DOORS NOMINAL SIZE: Frame opening size
LABEL: Could apply to other than steel doors
For SDI door levels and models; material, sheet metal thicknesses, and finishes; door thickness and core; fire ratings; and so on, see Division 8 specification section.

REFERENCES

Publication dates cited here were current at the time of this writing. Publications are revised periodically, and revisions may have occurred before this book was published.

American National Standards Institute

ANSI A250.4-1994: Test Procedure and Acceptance Criteria for Physical Endurance for Steel Doors and Hardware Reinforcings

ANSI A250.7-1997: Nomenclature for Standard Steel Doors and Frames

ANSI A250.8-1998: Recommended Specifications for Standard Steel Doors and Frames

ASTM International

ASTM A 480/A 480M-99a: Specification for General Requirements for Flat-Rolled Stainless Steel and Heat-Resisting Steel Plate, Sheet, and Strip

ASTM A 568/A 568M-98: Specification for Steel, Sheet, Carbon, and High-Strength, Low-Alloy, Hot-Rolled and Cold-Rolled, General Requirements for

ASTM A 924/A 924M-99: Specification for General Requirements for Steel Sheet, Metallic-Coated by the Hot-Dip Process

Door and Hardware Institute

Recommended Locations for Architectural Hardware for Standard Steel Doors and Frames, 1990.

National Fire Protection Association

NFPA 80-95: Fire Doors and Fire Windows

Steel Door Institute

SDI 106-99: Recommended Standard Door Type Nomenclature

SDI 108-90: Recommended Selection and Usage Guide for Standard Steel Doors

SDI 111 Series (111A-111F): Recommended Details, Steel Doors and Frames

SDI Fact File, 1994.

08211 FLUSH WOOD DOORS

This chapter discusses fire-rated and nonfire-rated architectural flush wood doors. Both solid- and hollow-core units are covered, including those with face panels of wood veneer, medium-density overlay, plastic laminate, and hardboard.

This chapter does not discuss special-function solid-core doors, such as sound-retardant, lead-lined, bullet-resistant, and electromagnetic-shielding doors.

QUALITY STANDARDS

Three quality standards can be referenced for flush wood doors: NWWDA I.S.1-A, *Architectural Wood Flush Doors* (now published by the Window & Door Manufacturers Association, WDMA); the Architectural Woodwork Institute's (AWI) *Architectural Woodwork Quality Standards Illustrated*; and the Woodwork Institute of California's (WIC) *Manual of Millwork*. AWI's and WIC's standards for flush wood doors are similar to NWWDA I.S.1-A but are more restrictive in some instances.

Face-veneer grades for all three standards are based on the Hardwood Plywood & Veneer Association (HPVA) publication HPVA HP-1, *American National Standard for Hardwood and Decorative Plywood*, so the grades are similar but not identical. For critical applications, compare all three quality standards before selecting one as the basis for specifications. AWI and WIC require Premium grade doors to have balance-matched, Grade AA face veneers; however, NWWDA I.S.1-A requires only running-matched, Grade A veneers, with balance matching, and Grade AA specified as options, if desired. These requirements are points of controversy among the three associations: AWI and WIC contend that only balance matching and the highest-grade veneer should be used for the highest-grade door, while WDMA claims that for most applications, the differences would not be noticed, and that the use of running-matched, Grade A veneers is more environmentally acceptable. Balance matching requires all veneer leaves on a door face to be the same width; running matching allows the full width of each leaf to be used and allows narrow remainders to be used at the edges, thus wasting less of the flitch. For Grade AA, veneers are allowed fewer minor defects, and veneer leaves must be wider than for Grade A. Grade AA veneers use less of the log than Grade A because more leaves are rejected, thus requiring more trees to produce the same amount of usable veneer. Use of Grade AA veneers may also require larger and, consequently, older trees than Grade A veneers, increasing the pressure to harvest old-growth forests.

AWI's section on flush wood doors is otherwise similar to NWWDA I.S.1-A but has some significant differences. NWWDA I.S.1-A allows top and bottom rails to be solid wood or medium-density fiberboard, but AWI requires top and bottom rails to be hardwood. NWWDA I.S.1-A requires face veneers to be at least 1/50-inch (0.5-mm) thick and edge-glued only for Premium and Custom grades; AWI requires this minimum thickness and edge gluing for all grades. AWI also does not allow hardboard to be used as face material for Custom and Premium grades and does not recognize plastic-laminate-faced, hollow-core doors.

WIC's section on flush doors differs in some ways from NWWDA I.S.1-A: It contains no Economy grade doors and requires that stiles and rails be bonded to cores. It also does not allow the use of fiberboard for top and bottom rails in Premium grade doors. WIC also requires a 1/8-inch (3.2-mm) thickness for hardboard faces, which must be tempered for exterior doors, and imposes additional requirements for grain matching and for moldings and edges.

CONSTRUCTION

Because there are several aspects of door construction, each of which has multiple options for materials and assembly, many kinds of flush wood doors are available. By analyzing the options one category at a time, the advantages and disadvantages of each can be determined.

Hollow versus Solid Core

Solid-core doors are heavier and generally stronger; they transmit and reflect less sound energy, and usually cost more. Because a solid core is more rigid and can better resist the stresses developed in the faces, solid-core doors are less prone to warping. Institutional hollow-core doors, with heavier stiles and rails and with additional blocking, have increased strength and resistance to warping but may cost as much as some solid-core doors (fig. 1). Some manufacturers do not make hollow-core doors, and some may quote jobs on the basis of substituting particleboard-core doors for hollow-core doors. Hollow-core doors are best suited for light-duty use, such as closet doors and some residential applications.

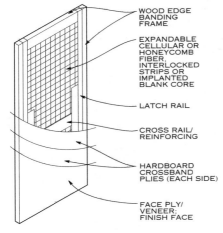

Figure 1. Wood hollow core door

Bonded versus Nonbonded Core

With a bonded core, the stiles and rails are glued to the core material, and the whole assembly is sanded as a unit before the faces are applied. This process ensures that all components making up the core at least start off with the same thickness, which reduces telegraphing of the core. With a nonbonded core, the components are allowed to vary as much as plus or minus 0.005 inch (0.13 mm) from the thickness specified. This variance can lead to as much as 0.01-inch (0.25-mm) difference in thickness between adjacent components, which can telegraph through the faces noticeably. Nonbonded cores are less expensive than bonded cores because fewer operations are required and the door manufacturer does not have to invest in machinery to sand the entire door core as a unit.

Solid Cores

Core material is another variable in the solid-core construction formula. Wood blocks (staves) are one option for solid cores; they are available either glued together as a unit or assembled loosely and secured in place as the faces are glued on (fig. 2). A nonglued-block core cannot have stiles and rails bonded to it and be sanded as a unit before veneering.

Particleboard has, for the most part, replaced wood blocks as a core material, because it costs less. Moreover, particleboard cores are less prone to warping and telegraphing in interior installations; however, they do not have the screw-holding capacity of wood-block cores. Full-threaded screws can be used to improve fastening capacity, as can through-bolting, solid-wood blocking, or using a higher grade of particleboard. Because particleboard is not as strong as solid wood, adequate clearance must be provided between adjacent cutouts and mortises; consult door manufacturers' catalogs for recommendations. Particleboard cores are not suitable for unprotected exterior applications because they absorb moisture readily and swell severely when wet.

Structural composite lumber, sometimes called *laminated-strand* lumber, made from aspen or yellow poplar strands approximately 1-inch (25-mm) wide and 12-inches (300-mm) long and bonded with a waterproof adhesive, is offered by most door manufacturers as an alternative to wood-block cores. Structural composite lumber is water-resistant and is often considered to have better screw-holding capacity than wood blocks and to be stiffer, stronger, and more dimensionally stable than lumber. These qualities seem to give laminated-strand lumber many of the advantages of both

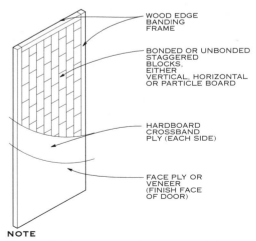

WOOD EDGE BANDING FRAME

BONDED OR UNBONDED STAGGERED BLOCKS, EITHER VERTICAL, HORIZONTAL OR PARTICLE BOARD

HARDBOARD CROSSBAND PLY (EACH SIDE)

FACE PLY OR VENEER (FINISH FACE OF DOOR)

NOTE

For bonded blocks, stave core is the most economical and widely used. Other materials include particleboard (heavier, more soundproof, economical) and mineral composition (lighter, difficult cutouts and detailing, lower screw strength).

Figure 2. Wood solid core door

wood-block cores and particleboard. It is also a positive response to some environmental concerns because aspen and yellow poplar are pioneer species, which are often considered "weed trees," rather than species of old-growth forests, and are somewhat underused.

Structural composite lumber and particleboard cores are heavier than wood-block cores because they contain more glue. This additional weight may decrease sound transmission, but not significantly if the door frame is not gasketed. Extra weight also makes the door more difficult to hang, and increases the force on the hinge screws.

Mineral cores, rather than wood-block or particleboard cores, are used for most fire doors. Mineral cores are made from a material consisting primarily of gypsum, which is soft and unsuitable for fastening hardware. For this reason, unless hardware is through-bolted (usually with sex bolts), special blocking that has been approved for use in fire-rated doors must be included at all hardware locations. Blocking is usually made of a high-density mineral product with a treated-plywood core. Special stiles are made of laminated materials, often including hardboard and plastic laminate, to better retain hinge screws and to eliminate the need for surface-mounted hinges with through bolts.

Plies

The number of plies is another area where door construction varies. Wood-veneer-faced, solid-core doors are usually constructed of five or seven plies.

Five-ply doors are constructed by gluing a crossband and a face veneer to each side of the core. The assembled door is then cured in a hot press; the heat removes moisture from the glue and causes it to cure faster. Temperature, pressure, and time are controlled in the hot press, and the bond is completely cured when the door comes out of the press, allowing it to be further processed immediately.

Seven-ply doors are assembled from a core and two door skins, which are essentially sheets of three-ply plywood. The door skins are adhered to the core in a cold press with a glue that does not need direct heat to cure. In cold pressing, the door components and glue are at the ambient temperature of the factory during pressing. Pressure and time are controlled to the extent necessary to achieve a partial bond during the pressing operation. On removal from the press, the glue requires further curing (four to eight hours) before additional processing can be done. Cold pressing is considered an uncontrolled operation because the bond is not complete when the door comes out of the press.

Cold pressing requires less expensive equipment than hot pressing and is more suitable for a smaller, less-capitalized manufacturer. To avoid investing in the equipment required to make door skins, most seven-ply door manufacturers buy their door skins from companies that specialize in door skins and plywood.

In the past, hot-press glues were vastly superior to cold-press glues, which made five-ply doors superior to seven-ply doors. Glue technology has improved, however, and some cold-press glues can now comply with Type I bonding requirements. Five-ply doors are still better than most seven-ply doors because most seven-ply doors are made with a nonbonded core, while five-ply doors are typically made with a bonded core. To ensure that doors with nonbonded cores are not substituted, exercise caution if specifying bonded, seven-ply, particleboard doors.

Some door skins for seven-ply doors have remarkably thin face veneers. Some are so thin that they must immediately be glued to a door skin as they come from the slicer, producing a four-ply door skin and a nine-ply door.

Because these veneers are moist when they come from the slicer, they tend to shrink and develop splits as the glue cures. Also, because they are so thin, the veneers can easily be sanded completely through. They do, however, conserve the decorative face-veneer log and reduce the cost of doors made from exotic species. All three referenced standards require face veneers of at least ½₀-inch (0.5-mm) thickness (except for Economy grade in NWWDA I.S.1-A) to preclude sand-through, so these door skins cannot be used on a seven-ply door that complies with these standards, except in Economy grade.

If blueprint-matched panels and doors are specified, five-ply doors should be used because premanufactured door skins are not generally custom-made. For other special veneer matching, such as matching all the door faces in a given room, five-ply doors may also be required. Consult door manufacturers whose products will be specified to determine availability of special matching if required.

Door Faces

Face materials for opaque finishes include wood veneers and wood-based products. Only closed-grain hardwood and medium-density overlay (MDO) may be used for doors of Custom and Premium grades. MDO, a resin-treated, kraft-paper sheet that is applied either to hardwood face veneers or directly to crossbands, provides a superior surface for paint. Its main advantages are an absence of knots and patches and a resistance to grain raising and moisture. The AWI standard states that MDO-faced doors should be specified for severe exposure conditions. Some manufacturers may be unwilling to provide warranties for their exterior doors unless the doors are constructed with MDO faces; others will not provide warranties for any exterior doors.

Hardboard is used with three-ply construction for interior doors that are to be painted. NWWDA I.S.1-A allows hardboard faces for opaque finishes in Custom and Economy grades, whereas AWI allows hardboard only for opaque finishes in Economy grade under the catchall provision of "Mill Option." If low cost is a major consideration, hardboard is a good choice for opaque-finished doors; it takes and holds paint well and has no grain or pores to show through the paint.

Plastic-laminate-faced doors are made as three- or five-ply doors, either with the faces glued directly to the core or with crossbands. All three standards require crossbands for plastic-laminate-faced doors with wood-stave cores to prevent telegraphing of the core; AWI and WIC require both particleboard and wood-stave cores to be bonded to stiles and rails for plastic-laminate-faced doors. NWWDA I.S.1-A requires crossbands with wood-stave cores, but does not require bonded cores with either particleboard or wood-stave cores if crossbands are used. Crossbands are not used with the thicker Grade HSH plastic laminate, which increases door cost considerably. Crossbands can add strength to plastic-laminate doors but they also add cost. AWI does not recognize plastic-laminate-faced, hollow-core doors, although NWWDA I.S.1-A does, and AWI does not recommend plastic-laminate-faced doors for exterior applications. Although plastic-laminate doors do not have the fine woodwork look of wood-veneered doors, their good appearance will frequently outlast that of the wood door.

FIRE DOORS

Fire-rated flush wood doors are available with 1½-hour, 1-hour, ¾-hour, ½-hour, and ⅓-hour rating labels (fig. 3). Intertek Testing Services (ITS) and Underwriters Laboratories (UL) predominate as the testing and inspecting agencies that provide labeling service for wood door assemblies. Doors are tested as part of an assembly that includes both the frame and hardware. For an assembly to comply with labeling requirements, each component must be approved for use with other components. This compliance limits such items as the location and type of hardware, methods and materials for fastening

DOOR LABEL

FRAME LABEL

NOTE

Various agencies test and rate fire door assemblies. Manufacturers locate metal labels in accessible but concealed locations (the hinge edge of doors, for example); these labels must remain in place, unpainted, uncovered, and unaltered.

Figure 3. Testing labels

hardware to the door, size and location of vision panels, sizes of doors; and so on (fig 4). Both AWI and NWWDA I.S.1-A state that cutouts for vision panels and louvers must be at least 6 inches (152 mm) from the edges of the door and from other cutouts, and both standards suggest that a 10-inch (254-mm) margin between the edge of the door and the edge of a cutout in the area of the lock be used for fire-rated doors. For a further explanation of these and other considerations, refer to 1300-G-18 in the AWI standard.

Positive-Pressure Fire Testing

Fire doors have historically been tested on a furnace with the fire side ventilated so it is at or near atmospheric pressure, like the other side of the door. During a building fire, the expanding hot gases and smoke created by the fire increase the pressure in the fire area. This rise in pressure can cause smoke, hot gases, and flames to be expelled around the edges of a fire door, subjecting the door edges and the safe side of the door to higher temperatures. Positive-pressure fire testing models this condition, and door edges with intumescent seals are one method of coping with this effect. Intumescent edges expand when subjected to the heat of the escaping flames and hot gases and seal the door perimeter with an insulating char.

The pressure on the fire side of the door can be alleviated in several ways. The building's ventilation systems may help relieve the fire pressure, and smoke exhaust systems will definitely help. Fires ventilate themselves by causing glass breakage and by burning through the building structure to reach the open atmosphere. Firefighters mimic this behavior: They ventilate fires by cutting holes in the structure and by breaking out windows. Stair pressurization systems and many smoke-control systems counterbalance the fire pressure by increasing air pressure on the safe side of the door. For these reasons, positive-pressure testing may often model unlikely worst-case scenarios rather than typical fire conditions.

The 1997 Uniform Building Code (UBC) and the final draft of the new International Building Code (IBC) require positive-pressure fire testing, which is an accepted test method in some other countries. The latest version of the National Fire Protection Association (NFPA) publication NFPA 252 does not specify the test pressure; if that fire test is required, specify either positive or atmospheric pressure. UL has developed a positive-pressure test, UL 10C, which is similar to its atmospheric pressure test, UL 10B, and is based on the same requirements as those contained in the UBC and the final draft of the IBC. The ASTM standard test method that was formerly referenced by model building codes has been withdrawn.

Fire-rated wood door frames are specified in Division 6.

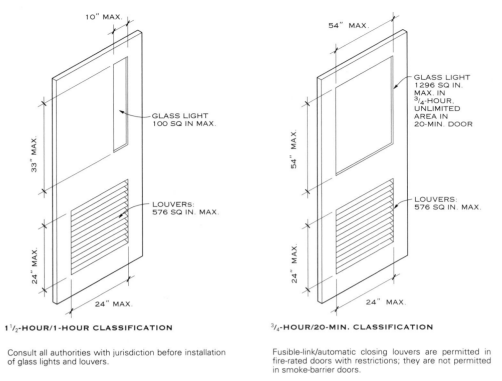

1¹/₂-HOUR/1-HOUR CLASSIFICATION

Consult all authorities with jurisdiction before installation of glass lights and louvers.

³/₄-HOUR/20-MIN. CLASSIFICATION

Fusible-link/automatic closing louvers are permitted in fire-rated doors with restrictions; they are not permitted in smoke-barrier doors.

Figure 4.

APPEARANCE FACTORS

Veneer Matching

Face veneers may be rotary cut, rift cut (oak only), plain sliced (flat sliced), quarter sliced, or half-round sliced (fig. 5). The veneer leaves may then be arranged to produce certain matching effects (fig. 6). Book matching readily comes to mind when discussing veneer matching, laying out the leaves like an open book so adjacent leaves are nearly mirror images. When going from one pair of veneer leaves to the next, some of the matching is lost when progressing through the log, but the effect can still be stunning. When looking at a pair of book-matched veneers, the inside surface of one and the outside surface of the other is shown. This view causes some differences between the two leaves in color and sheen; the differences are called *barber poling*. For this reason, slip matching is preferred with straight-grain veneers such as quarter sliced or rift cut, or with fairly symmetrical plain-sliced veneers. Sanding and stain color can also affect the appearance of barber poling.

Running matching requires all veneer leaves to be from the same flitch and in sequence, but the width of the leaves can vary and the piece trimmed from one edge of the door face can be used to start the next door face. Balance matching additionally requires that all veneer leaves be the same width, which results in some trimming waste and an increase in cost. Center balance matching requires an even number of veneer leaves, all the same width, from the same flitch, and further increases the waste and cost over running matching or balance matching (fig. 7).

For maximum economy, random matching, which is really no matching, can be specified so the door (or door skin) manufacturer can use the veneer log most efficiently—veneer leaves can even be from different logs (fig. 8). Random matching can use any number of leaves from any number of flitches with no regard for color or grain. Pleasing match is similar

to random match except that sharp color contrast at the joints between leaves is not allowed. Pleasing match is a good choice for Economy grade doors with Grade B veneers because it costs slightly more than random match and can greatly improve appearance.

Vertical edges are required to be of the same wood species as the face veneer for Premium grade in all three of the referenced standards and to be of a compatible species for Custom grade. Neither of these requirements ensures a color match, but they do ensure some degree of uniformity. Premium grade does not allow visible joints in the vertical edges; custom grade allows visible joints in the hinge edge. For additional information on edge requirements, especially for critical applications, refer to the applicable quality standard.

Species Selection

Numerous options are available for specifying face veneers for flush wood doors, but a lack of knowledge about wood veneers and the available options can result in unpleasant surprises when the doors arrive on the jobsite. The term natural birch is often used in specifications without either the architect or the owner fully realizing that this term means the veneers may contain both heartwood and sapwood, whose colors may vary considerably. Birch sapwood is an off-white to light-yellow color, whereas heartwood may be a creamy tan or a reddish brown that is much darker than sapwood. The distribution of heartwood is not controlled by any of the standards, so it may appear as stripes in flat-sliced veneers or as blotches in rotary-cut veneers. The pattern can be very irregular, regardless of the type of cut, and the appearance can be gaudy. If natural birch is specified, doors cannot be rejected because of the irregular variations in color. Staining can reduce but not entirely eliminate the contrast. If the contrast in appearance is unacceptable, specify white birch (all sapwood) or red birch (all heartwood) rather than natural birch. White and red maple and white and brown ash similarly distinguish sapwood from heartwood.

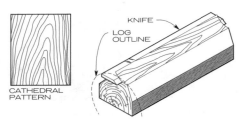

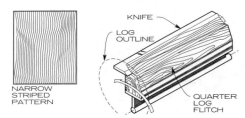

Slicing is done parallel to a line through the center of the log. A combination of cathedral and straight-grain patterns results, with a natural progression of pattern from leaf to leaf.

PLAIN-SLICED (FLAT-SLICED) VENEER

Rift veneers are produced most often in red and white oak, rarely in other species. The cutting is done slightly off the radius lines, minimizing the "flake" associated with quarter slicing.

RIFT-SLICED (RIFT-CUT) VENEER

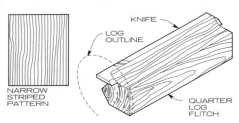

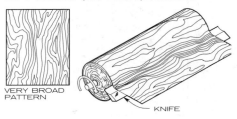

Quarter slicing is roughly parallel to a radius line through the log segment. In many species the individual leaves are narrow as a result. A series of stripes is produced, varying in density and thickness among species. "Flake" is a characterisitc of this slicing method in red and white oak.

QUARTER-SLICED VENEER

To create rotary-cut veneers, the log is center mounted on a lathe and "peeled" along the path of the growth rings, like unwinding a roll of paper. This provides a bold, random appearance. Rotary-cut veneers vary in width, and matching at veneer joints is extremely difficult.

ROTARY-CUT VENEER

Figure 5.

Oak veneers usually contain little sapwood, and heartwood is not as easily distinguished from sapwood in oak as it is in birch. For these reasons, oak is not specified as all heartwood or all sapwood. The difference between white and red oak is one of species, not cut. White oak is light tan to grayish brown in color; red oak is pinkish tan to red-brown or brown. Red-oak veneers are also less expensive than white oak. Plain-sliced red-oak veneers are less expensive than plain-sliced white birch and are a good choice for inexpensive, good-quality doors. Oak veneers, as well as being plain sliced, are frequently quartered or rift cut for a straight-grain appearance. Rift-cut oak is similar to quartered oak, but the amount and size of ray fleck, which some people find objectionable and which does not take stain well, are less in rift-cut veneers than in quartered veneers. If unsure which cut is wanted, look at finished samples to see the grain pattern and the effect that ray fleck has on the appearance of the veneer; also, consider having the client review the samples for concurrence. Quarter- and rift-cut veneers are more expensive than plain-sliced veneers because large, clear, straight logs must be used.

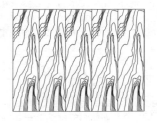

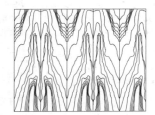

SLIP MATCH

BOOK MATCH

RANDOM MATCH

Figure 6.

Figure 8.

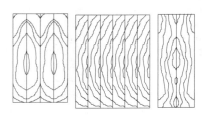

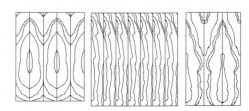

RUNNING MATCH

BALANCE AND CENTER MATCH

BALANCE MATCH

Figure 7.

Finishes

Factory finishes offer many advantages over field-applied finishes, especially for transparent finishes. Factory finishing is done in a temperature- and humidity-controlled, dust-free environment using equipment that can quickly and evenly apply and then heat-cure the finish. Factory-finished doors require care to protect the finish, but field finishing also requires care to protect the doors. Doors that are to receive field-applied transparent finishes must be protected from sunlight to avoid uneven photooxidation (darkening) of the wood. Proper field finishing requires that the doors be block-sanded with 120- to 180-grit sandpaper to remove scratches, scuffs, compression marks (burnishes), raised grain, and other blemishes. Staining should be done with the doors in a horizontal position, so the doors should be finished before being hung. With field-finished doors, care must be exercised while the finish is wet to protect it from damage; as with factory-finished doors, once the finishing is complete, care must be exercised to avoid damaging the finish.

Choices of factory finishes for flush wood doors were once limited to the standard systems offered by door manufacturers. Now, some manufacturers provide finishes complying with the various AWI systems, particularly where transparent finishes are required. First consideration should still be given to manufacturers' standard systems, where differences between them and a given AWI system for appearance and performance are minimal, and where insisting on a special finish would result in additional cost. Before specifying finishes, verify their availability with manufacturers. Manufacturers usually have a setup charge for factory finishing. For standard finishes on an order of only 10 or 15 doors, the setup charge is so low that factory finishing costs about the same as field finishing; however, for larger orders, factory finishing costs less than field finishing.

NWWDA I.S.1-A lists several finish systems and gives useful information on their applicability, but does not specify the number of coats and sealers or sanding requirements, so it is better to reference one of the woodworking standards for finishes rather than the NWWDA (WDMA) standard. However, any finish system, no matter how thoroughly specified, still depends on the skill and judgment of the applicator for the quality of its appearance. For this reason, it is always best to see samples of manufacturers' finish systems before specifying them.

OTHER OPTIONS

Shop Priming

Although flush wood doors are moisture-controlled during manufacture, they are subject to absorption of moisture and subsequent drying and shrinkage during handling and storage at the site before field finishing. Shop priming slows moisture absorption and provides some protection against soiling, scuffing, scratching, and burnishing.

Louvers

Door manufacturers will install various types of louvers at the factory; this may be desirable, particularly where doors are specified with a factory finish.

Cutouts

Cutouts within doors for light openings, louvers, and hardware must be located in such a way that they do not reduce stiles and rails beyond certain minimum widths, or occur too close together. If these minimums are violated, the manufacturer will not warrant the door.

Stiles and Rails

Wider stiles and rails may be available from manufacturers if needed to accommodate finish hardware requirements. Either insert special widths in the specifications or indicate in the schedules and on the drawings.

Factory Fitting and Machining

Most manufacturers are equipped to fit doors to frames and to machine for hardware. Although factory fitting and machining costs much less than performing this work in the field, the additional coordination may increase costs. Still, factory fitting and machining offer factory precision and coordinated installation, usually at no more than a small premium. Fire-rated doors must generally be factory fitted and machined because of the narrow stiles and rails, which have little tolerance for trimming. Plastic-laminate-faced doors with plastic-laminate edges and factory-finished doors must be factory fitted and machined. Some contractors prefer factory-prepared doors because the manufacturer bears the financial responsibility for doors that do not fit.

Door Beveling

The common specification requirement for beveling doors ⅛ inch in 2 inches (3½ degrees), which is also the standard bevel for locksets, is based on AWI requirements for prefitting flush wood doors. For extra-narrow doors and doors thicker than 1¾ inches (44 mm), there may be a need to change the bevel. The amount of bevel needed to produce the same edge clearance in the opening door as exists for the door in the closed position can be calculated from the formula $B = (H (T)/2W$, where B stands for bevel, H for hinge width (in the open position), T for door thickness, and W for door width. Generally, unit locksets are only available with the standard bevel; cylindrical locksets are available with either flat or standard bevel; mortise locksets are available with bevels adjustable from flat to standard.

SPECIAL DOORS

Flush wood doors can be constructed to reduce sound transmission, to resist bullet penetration, or to provide X-ray or electromagnetic shielding. Sound-retardant doors are rated as to their Sound Transmission Class (STC) per ASTM E 90, and are generally constructed of two faces separated by either an unfilled airspace or a space filled with a sound-dampening compound that acts to prevent the two faces from vibrating in unison. These doors are generally furnished as a package that includes special stops, gaskets, and automatic bottom seals because their capability to reduce sound transmission depends on having tight perimeter seals. To be effective, sound-retardant doors must be installed in wall and frame construction that is equally effective in reducing sound transmission.

Bullet-resistant doors incorporate a bullet-resistant layer within the core, usually an aramid fiber and epoxy composite. To specify bullet-resistant doors, require performance based on appropriate test methods for bullet resistance; do not specify the core material. X-ray-shielding doors have one or more continuous sheets of lead from edge to edge, either at the center of the core or between the core and the crossbands or door skins. The thickness of the lead must be specified. Electromagnetic-shielding doors are manufactured with wire mesh in the center of the core or between the core and the crossbands or door skins. Grounding is accomplished with a connection through the hinges to the frame; the connection must be specified and coordinated with the hinges.

WARRANTIES

Most major manufacturers will provide a limited warranty for specific types of doors and installations. These warranties vary for door construction and door use among manufacturers. There is no industry consensus for duration of warranties; hollow-core doors for interior installations may be warranted for one, two, or five years; solid-core doors are usually warranted for the life of the installation. Warranties for exterior installations vary from no warranty to a warranty of up to five years.

The limitations of individual manufacturers' warranties are another concern. These limitations can range from a simple refund of the original purchase (which avoids the added cost of markups by the subcontractor or contractor, as well as installation and finishing costs) to the manufacturer's option to repair or replace without installation or finishing to some manufacturers who will repair or replace, including installation and factory finishing. There may also be limitations and exclusions based on sizes and types of doors and installation practices.

Where warranty terms are a major consideration, consult manufacturers to determine what they offer and perhaps limit the contractor to those manufacturers known to offer suitable warranties.

ENVIRONMENTAL CONSIDERATIONS

Flush wood doors are primarily manufactured from renewable resources (wood products), except for adhesives and finishes made from petrochemicals, and require less energy to manufacture than metal doors. For interior doors, this embodied energy is the only energy-conservation concern. Exterior flush wood doors with solid cores are more effective insulators than uninsulated hollow-metal doors. This advantage is, however, reversed if the metal door has a polyurethane foam core. Flush wood doors also have a natural thermal break, which, though it saves little energy, prevents frost and condensation problems. Except for Residential grade doors, hollow-metal doors are not available with a thermal break. Heat losses and gains from door openings, however, are small compared to those from windows and walls, and air infiltration is generally the major contributor, not conduction through the door.

Veneer species selection is another area of environmental concern. Some tropical timber species that have traditionally been used for furniture, paneling, doors, and other fine woodwork are becoming threatened with extinction as tropical forests are cleared and not replanted. The threat to tropical forests is mostly caused by clearing for agriculture, not by cutting for timber, and many of the threatened species are not well known for their use as timber. Still, actions can help or hinder this situation, and accelerating the extinction process should be avoided. Brazilian rosewood is on the endangered species list, and African cherry, afrormosia, lignum vitae, and several species of tropical American mahogany are regulated in an effort to prevent their becoming endangered. Existing veneers of endangered species can be used, but as they are consumed, pressure may increase to create illegal trade.

Many domestic hardwood species are readily available, including some that produce strikingly attractive veneers. Cherry, American black walnut, pecan, and butternut provide fine veneers, and brown ash, figured hard maple, red gum, or hickory can also provide fine veneers that are out of the ordinary. Red and white oak, white ash, and American elm also produce fine-quality veneers. The use of less well-known tropical species that are not endangered may also be environmentally desirable because it may encourage sustainable forestry. The database *Woods of the World,* version 2.5, listed in the References below, provides information for many lesser-known tropical hardwoods that are not endangered.

Veneer grade and match may also cause environmental concerns because practices that waste more of the flitch require more harvesting of trees. For a discussion of this subject, see the paragraph on face-veneer grades under Quality Standards in this chapter.

All door core materials use fast-growing, low-density wood species that are typically farmed or removed as weeds from hardwood stands. None require cutting old-growth stands, so environmental implications are not generally associated with decisions about core type.

REFERENCES

Publication dates cited here were current at the time of this writing. Publications are revised periodically, and revisions may have occurred before this book was published.

ASTM International

ASTM E 90: Test Method for Laboratory Measurement of Airborne Sound Transmission Loss of Building Partitions

Architectural Woodwork Institute

Architectural Woodwork Quality Standards Illustrated, 7th ed., version 1.0, 1997.

Forest Partnership, Inc.

Woods of the World, version 2.5, 1997.

Hardwood Plywood & Veneer Association

HPVA HP-1-1994: Hardwood and Decorative Plywood

International Conference of Building Officials

UBC Standard 7-2-1997: Fire Tests of Door Assemblies

National Fire Protection Association

NFPA 252-95: Fire Tests of Door Assemblies

Underwriters Laboratories Inc.

UL 10C-98: Positive Pressure Fire Tests of Door Assemblies

Window & Door Manufacturers Association (formerly, National Wood Window and Door Association)

NWWDA I.S.1-A-97: Architectural Wood Flush Doors

Woodwork Institute of California

Manual of Millwork, 1998.

WEB SITES

Architectural Woodwork Institute: www.awinet.org

Hardwood Plywood & Veneer Association: www.erols.com/hpva/

Window & Door Manufacturers Association (formerly, National Wood Window and Door Association): www.nwwda.org

Woodwork Institute of California: www.wicnet.org

08212 STILE AND RAIL WOOD DOORS

<hr>

This chapter discusses *stile and rail doors made from lumber, wood veneers, and wood composites including plywood, particleboard, fiberboard, and laminated-strand lumber. Doors of special design and construction, which may include custom-made doors, are often specified along with doors of stock design and construction. Fire-rated doors with wood-veneered and -edged mineral-core stiles, rails, and panels are also included.*

This chapter does not describe *doors fabricated with molded hardboard faces to have the appearance of stile and rail doors, which are really a variation of hollow-core, flush wood doors; and other doors that are not actually assembled as stiles, rails, and panels. Prehung units and wood door frames also are not included.*

QUALITY STANDARD FOR STOCK DOORS

Window & Door Manufacturers Association (WDMA) publication WDMA I.S.6, *Industry Standard for Wood Stile and Rail Doors,* was developed "to establish nationally recognized specification requirements for interior and exterior wood stile and rail doors." Both hardwood and softwood doors are covered in the standard. Despite this and the capability of some WDMA members to produce both softwood and hardwood doors in special sizes and designs, the standard is often assumed to apply to doors that are manufacturers' standard products.

Deciding which standard to reference will depend on whether the panel designs, door sizes, and material requirements in WDMA I.S.6 are acceptable for the project and on whether the increased control that Architectural Woodwork Institute (AWI) and the Woodwork Institute of California (WIC) standards give over the quality of construction and details of moldings, stiles, rails, and panels is needed. Generally, specifying stile and rail doors to comply with either the AWI or WIC standard affords both greater quality control and freedom in design but may also carry greater risk if details and specifications are inadequate to prevent warpage in excess of specified tolerances or other unsatisfactory performance. Warpage and unsatisfactory performance could be caused by detailing inadequate stile and rail widths or requiring stiles and rails to be constructed of solid hardwood lumber when veneered construction would have been more appropriate (fig. 1, 2).

Two door grades are in WDMA I.S.6: Premium or Select, which is intended for a natural or stain finish—that is, transparent finish; and Standard, which is intended for an opaque finish. The only difference between the two grades is in the material qualities, summarized below:

• WDMA Premium or Select grade prohibits mixing wood species within the door. It also requires veneers to meet the requirements of the Hardwood Plywood and Veneer Association (HPVA) Industry Standard DFV-1, with appearance characteristics based on HPVA HP-1, *American*

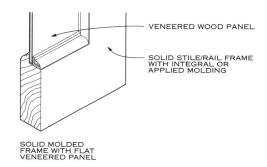

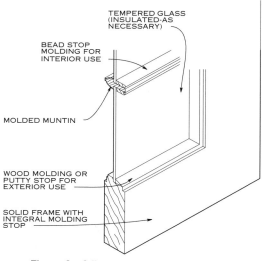

Figure 1. Typical beveled raised panel door

Figure 2. Stile and rail door details

National Standard for Hardwood and Decorative Plywood, and exposed wood surfaces to be without defects that affect the appearance, except for "bright sap, light brown stain and light red kiln burn, mineral streak or carefully repaired pitch or bark defects."

- WDMA Standard grade calls for all exposed wood surfaces to be sound, with defects and discoloration permitted provided "a surface suitable for opaque finish is presented." Exposed finger joints and mixing species are permitted.

Both grades allow veneered construction with no requirement for minimum thickness of face veneers. Both grades also allow the use of wood composites and nonwood substrates, according to the standard, provided they meet "the same performance criteria for solid wood components." The standard, however, gives no performance criteria for solid wood components.

Fabrication and warp tolerances are the same for both grades, but, unlike AWI and WIC standards, requirements for smoothness of exposed surfaces or tightness of joints are not in WDMA I.S.6. The method for measuring warp is similar to that described in the commentary below for the AWI standard, except that doors more than 42 by 84 inches (1067 by 2134 mm) are not covered.

Common designs and layouts (fig. 3) are organized into the following groups:

- 1⅜ Interior Panel Doors
- 1¾ Front Entrance Doors (Exterior)
- 1¾ and 1⅜ Entrance Doors (Exterior)
- French Doors
- Combination Doors
- Side Lights
- Bifold Doors
- 8'-0" High Doors
- Louver Doors
- 1¾ Thermal (Insulated-Glass) Doors (Exterior)
- Screen Doors

Within each group are numerically designated, standard panel designs; standard nominal door sizes; minimum widths of stiles, rails, and other door members; and minimum panel thicknesses. While the names of the groups indicate the intended use, there are exceptions, such as 1⅜ Interior Panel Doors, which may also be specified for exterior use. These exceptions are explained in footnotes in the standard.

Minimum panel thickness varies among design groups. A minimum thickness of ⁷⁄₁₆ inch (11.1 mm) is required for the raised panels of 1⅜ Interior Panel Doors, 1¾ Front Entrance Doors (Exterior), Bifold Doors, and Louver Doors. This thickness is increased to ⅞ inch (22.2 mm) for 1¾ Thermal (Insulated-Glass) Doors (Exterior). Minimum flat panel thickness is ¼ inch (6.4 mm) for 1⅜ Interior Panel Doors and 1¾ and 1⅜ Entrance Doors (Exterior), which are the only two groups where minimum dimensions for flat panels are included.

QUALITY STANDARDS FOR SPECIAL DOORS

AWI's *Architectural Woodwork Quality Standards* establish requirements for qualities of materials and workmanship that are more stringent than WDMA I.S.6.

Permissible defects in lumber are limited by the AWI standard depending on board size and grade. Defects and veneer-matching characteristics applicable to hardwood veneers are specified by reference to grades established by HPVA. Additional grain- and color-matching requirements for Premium and Custom grades are in the AWI standard. Requirements for both opaque and transparent finished doors are in all three grades. Cores for veneered stiles and rails may be lumber, particleboard, or medium-density fiberboard, and cores for veneered panels may also be particleboard or fiberboard. Panels for opaque finish may be fiberboard or medium-density overlay.

The AWI standard includes minimums for thicknesses of door members and face veneers for stiles and rails for Premium and Custom grade doors, but it does not set any requirements for the widths of stiles and rails. The minimum raised panel thickness required by the AWI standard is ¾ inch (19 mm) for Premium and Custom grade 1⅜ inch (35-mm) doors, and 1⅛ inches (29 mm) for 1¾ inch (44-mm) doors.

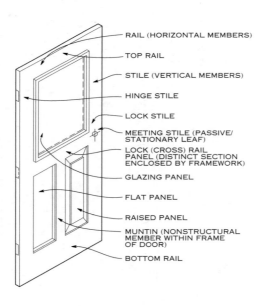

RAIL (HORIZONTAL MEMBERS)
TOP RAIL
STILE (VERTICAL MEMBERS)
HINGE STILE
LOCK STILE
MEETING STILE (PASSIVE/STATIONARY LEAF)
LOCK (CROSS) RAIL
PANEL (DISTINCT SECTION ENCLOSED BY FRAMEWORK)
GLAZING PANEL
FLAT PANEL
RAISED PANEL
MUNTIN (NONSTRUCTURAL MEMBER WITHIN FRAME OF DOOR)
BOTTOM RAIL

TYPICAL COMPONENTS

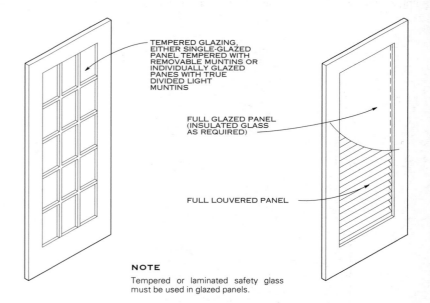

TEMPERED GLAZING, EITHER SINGLE-GLAZED PANEL TEMPERED WITH REMOVABLE MUNTINS OR INDIVIDUALLY GLAZED PANES WITH TRUE DIVIDED LIGHT MUNTINS

FULL GLAZED PANEL (INSULATED GLASS AS REQUIRED)

FULL LOUVERED PANEL

NOTE
Tempered or laminated safety glass must be used in glazed panels.

FRENCH DOOR   **GLAZED/LOUVERED DOOR**

Figure 3. Stile and rail door types

The minimum flat panel thickness is ⅜ inch (10 mm) for Custom and Premium grade 1-3/8-inch (35-mm) doors, and ½ inch (13 mm) for 1¾ inch (44-mm) doors. Veneers for stiles and rails of Premium and Custom grades must be ¹⁄₁₆ inch (1.6 mm) thick, but veneers for panels need only be "of sufficient thickness to preclude sand-through, show-through of core, and glue bleed."

Profiles of moldings (sticking) at the perimeter of panels are the woodworker's option unless indicated on the Drawings. However, only a profile that can be coped without a feather edge is allowed.

Tests are included to measure compliance with minimum requirements for smoothness of exposed surfaces and for tightness and flushness of joints, with these being more stringent for Premium grade doors than for Custom grade. The maximum warp allowed is ¼ inch (6 mm) for either 1⅜- or 1¾-inch (35- or 44-mm) doors. Warp is measured from a straight edge or taut string across a door's concave face to the door face. For 1⅜-inch (35-mm) doors that are 36 by 84 inches (900 by 2100 mm) or smaller, and for 1¾-inch (44-mm) or thicker doors that are 42 by 84 inches (1060 by 2100 mm) or smaller, warp is measured in any position (horizontally, diagonally, or vertically) across the full height and width of the door. For 1¾-inch (44-mm) doors larger than 42 by 84 inches (1060 by 2100 mm), the measurement is taken across any 42-by-84-inch (1060-by-2100-mm) section. Included in the standard is a recommendation against using 1⅜-inch (35-mm) doors for sizes in excess of 36 by 84 inches (900 by 2100 mm).

WIC's *Manual of Millwork* recognizes both stile and rail doors of stock design and construction, which are required to comply with WDMA I.S.6; and stile and rail doors of special design and construction, which are required to comply with WIC established requirements. In some respects, the WIC manual goes into greater detail than the AWI standard; but in others, it is not as detailed. For example, WIC lists minimum stile and rail widths, which are different for exterior and interior doors. No tests or requirements are included, however, for smoothness or for tightness of joints. WIC does not allow the use of particleboard or fiberboard cores for stiles and rails, and allows fiberboard to be used only for opaque-finished panels. WIC requires ¹⁄₁₆-inch- (1.6-mm) thick face veneers on stiles and rails but specifies no minimum for panels.

Useful advice on stile and rail door construction can be found in WIC's Technical Bulletin 405R in "Section 2-General Information" of the WIC standard. While stating that stile and rail doors are still one of the most dependable types of doors, WIC recommends that only certain species of softwoods are suitable for solid stile and rail construction and that most hardwoods are not (mahogany is one exception). The reason offered is that most hardwoods warp and twist regardless of conditions. The same generally applies to panel construction, whether raised or flat. WIC further advises on the adverse effect on door strength that could result if stile and rail widths are too narrow for the door size or for hardware cutouts and large openings.

FIRE-RATED STILE AND RAIL DOORS

According to product literature, stile and rail doors are available with fire ratings of up to 60 minutes for 1¾-inch (44-mm) doors and up to 90 minutes for 2¼-inch (57-mm) doors. Fire-rated doors with a 20-minute rating have been available for several years and are not substantially different from other stile and rail doors, except that the panels have to be thick enough to sustain the fire test for 20 minutes, the same as solid flush wood doors. Fire-rated stile and rail doors with ratings of 45 to 90 minutes use a mineral product similar to that used for reinforcements in flush wood fire doors for the core of the stiles and rails. The cores of the panels for 45- to 90-minute-rated doors are mineral products similar to that used for the cores of flush wood fire doors. Fire-rated stile and rail doors are available with either flat panels or raised panels.

OTHER OPTIONS

Shop Priming

While wood doors are moisture-controlled during manufacture, they are subject to absorption of moisture and subsequent drying and shrinkage during handling and storage at the site before field finishing. Shop priming slows moisture absorption and protects doors against soiling, scuffing, scratching, and burnishing. Shop priming is available from many stile and rail door manufacturers, especially for opaque-finished doors.

Factory Finishing, Prefitting, and Premachining

Unlike its flush wood door standard, no mention is made of factory finishing or premachining in WDMA I.S.6. Prefitting is addressed only by stating that it may be specified on the order and that it is subject to a tolerance of ±¹⁄₃₂ inch (±0.8 mm). In AWI and WIC standards, there are general provisions for factory finishing of architectural woodwork, which provide a good basis for specifying factory finishing of doors. Specifiers should, however, verify the availability of these finishes with manufacturers selected and their appropriateness for a particular project. Both AWI and WIC specify standard prefitting along with tolerances for prefitting. AWI also specifies tolerances for premachining that, if not available from the factory, could be done in a woodworking shop.

Door Beveling

Beveling doors ⅛ inch in 2 inches (3½ degrees) which is also the standard bevel for locksets, is included in AWI requirements for prefitting flush wood doors. For extra-narrow doors and doors thicker than 1¾ inches (44 mm), there may be a need to change the bevel. The amount of bevel needed to produce the same edge clearance in the opening door as exists for the door in the closed position can be calculated from the formula $B = (H \times T)/2W$ in which B stands for bevel, H for hinge width, T for door thickness, and W for door width. Generally, unit locksets are only available with standard bevel, cylindrical locksets with either flat or standard bevel, and mortise locksets with bevels adjustable from flat to standard.

Glazing

Glazing materials in doors should be safety glass products, which are usually specified in the Division 8, "Doors and Windows," section that specifies glazing. Many manufacturers offer doors glazed with decorative glass products, including leaded beveled glass, etched glass, and sand-carved glass. These products are exempt from the safety glazing requirements of the 1996 BOCA Code and the Consumer Product Safety Commission regulations.

Carving

Carved doors are covered in WDMA I.S.6. It includes three panel designs within 1¾ Front Entrance Doors (Exterior) that show different panel arrangements with one or more panels represented as carved. Because of the many designs available and possible, the only practical way to specify carved doors is by naming products of specific manufacturers or, for custom doors, by providing full-scale details.

ENVIRONMENTAL CONSIDERATIONS

Stile and rail wood doors are manufactured primarily from renewable resources (wood products), aside from adhesives and finishes made from petrochemicals, and require less energy to manufacture than metal doors. Many stile and rail wood doors are made from wood products with applied veneers rather than solid lumber. Using veneer not only avoids the warping of solid hardwood components but also helps avoid the use of old-growth, softwood lumber. One wood product being used for stile and rail doors is a laminated-strand lumber, which is made from aspen strands bonded with a waterproof adhesive. It often considered to be stiffer, stronger, and more dimensionally stable than lumber, yet has a better screw-holding capacity than other wood composite products. It also is a positive response to some environmental concerns, since aspen is an underutilized pioneer species.

Wood species can be a major environmental concern. Some tropical timber species that have traditionally been used for furniture, paneling, doors, and other fine woodwork are becoming threatened as tropical forests are cleared and not replanted. Most of the pressure on tropical forests is the result of clearing for agriculture, not cutting for timber; and many of the threatened and endangered species are not well known as timber species. Still, specifying threatened species can contribute to this problem. Brazilian rosewood is on the endangered species list; and African cherry, afrormosia, lignum vitae, and several species of tropical American mahogany are reg-

ulated in an effort to prevent them from becoming endangered. Existing lumber and veneers of endangered species can be used, but as they are consumed, pressure may increase to create illegal trade.

REFERENCES

Publication dates cited here were current at the time of this writing. Publications are revised periodically, and revisions may have occurred before this book was published.

Architectural Woodwork Institute

Architectural Woodwork Quality Standards, Guide Specifications, and Quality Certification Program, 6th ed., version 1.1, 1994.

Hardwood Plywood and Veneer Association

HPVA HP-1-1994: American National Standard for Hardwood and Decorative Plywood

Window & Door Manufacturers Association

NWWDA I.S.4-81: Water-Repellent Preservative Treatment for Millwork

WDMA I.S.6-97: Industry Standard for Wood Stile and Rail Doors

Woodwork Institute of California

Manual of Millwork, 1995.

This chapter describes *wall and ceiling access doors and frames fabricated from prime-painted steel sheet, metallic-coated steel sheet, and stainless-steel sheet panels that are installed in masonry, concrete, gypsum board, plaster, veneer plaster, ceramic tile, and acoustical tile surfaces. This chapter also discusses floor doors.*

This chapter does not discuss *roof hatches, chute doors, or duct access doors.*

GENERAL COMMENTS

Many access door manufacturers also produce duct access doors. Duct access doors are not specifed in Division 8. If they are required, they should be specified in a Division 15, "Mechanical" section.

An access door and frame assembly described as "with exposed trim" has a frame with an exposed flange that surrounds and is flush with the door (fig. 1). This assembly is used in masonry and tile walls and can be installed in existing construction and in any type of surface after the surface is finished. The term *trimless frame* describes a frame that is attached to gypsum board with a gypsum board bead that is concealed with a compound when the gypsum board joints are finished. A trimless frame is secured to plaster with an expanded metal lath embedded in the plaster. In either case, the frame is concealed when the door is closed.

Floor doors are also called *pit, vault,* and *sidewalk doors* or *hatches* (fig. 2). Special applications include airport vault, fire-rated, security, odor-control, and flood-tight doors. Floor doors are fabricated from steel (prime coated or galvanized), aluminum, and stainless steel with numerous options. Exterior applications usually have a perimeter drain channel and a drainage coupling. Manufacturers list this coupling as "1½ inches" but, because it is a pipe fitting, referring to the size using the nominal pipe size (NPS) or the corresponding dimension nominal (DN) metric size, which is NPS 1½ (DN 40), is correct. Most building codes require a commercial floor load rating to support a 300-lbf/sq. ft. (14.4-kN/sq. m) live load. Floor doors for commercial applications usually require at least a pedestrian loading of 300 lbf/sq. ft. (14.4 kN/sq. m). Most manufacturers also offer doors with a pedestrian loading of 150 lbf/sq. ft. (7.2 kN/sq. m) for residential applications, fabricated in the same materials as doors for commercial applications.

H20 loading doors are suitable for areas driven over by cars, trucks, or buses, and can be installed directly in roadways. H20 loading doors are available in all materials except aluminum. Only H20 loading without-impact doors are available in aluminum. *Without impact* is an industry term used to refer to aluminum doors that are not suitable for use in highways or roadways. They are suitable, however, for use in roadway shoulders, parking lots, driveways, sidewalks, and other surfaces that infrequently must support car and truck traffic that does not exceed 20 mph (8.9 m/s).

When a floor door is tested to comply with the requirements in American Association of State Highway and Transportation Officials (AASHTO) H-20, the "H" represents the gross weight in tons of the vehicle; "20" is 20 tons or 40,000 lbf (178 kN). The test is based on a concentrated wheel load of 40 percent of the gross weight, or 16,000 lbf (71 kN).

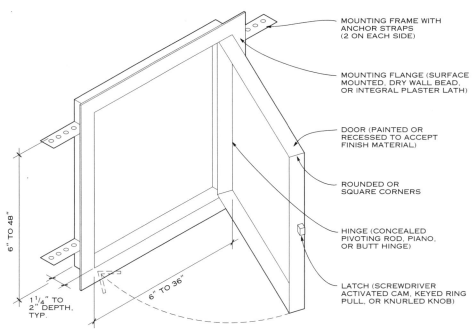

MOUNTING FRAME WITH ANCHOR STRAPS (2 ON EACH SIDE)

MOUNTING FLANGE (SURFACE MOUNTED, DRY WALL BEAD, OR INTEGRAL PLASTER LATH)

DOOR (PAINTED OR RECESSED TO ACCEPT FINISH MATERIAL)

ROUNDED OR SQUARE CORNERS

HINGE (CONCEALED PIVOTING ROD, PIANO, OR BUTT HINGE)

LATCH (SCREWDRIVER ACTIVATED CAM, KEYED RING PULL, OR KNURLED KNOB)

6" TO 48"

6" TO 36"

1¼" TO 2" DEPTH, TYP.

Figure 1. Wall or ceiling access door with exposed trim

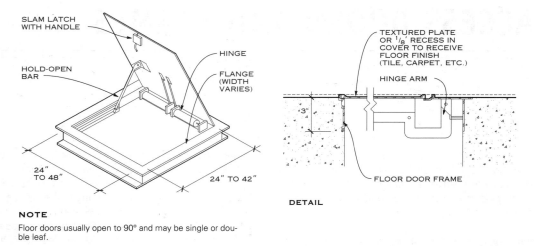

Figure 2. Floor door

Aircraft loading doors are designed per Federal Aviation Administration (FAA) specifications for wheel-loading requirements for currently licensed commercial aircraft and for new, larger aircraft not yet in production. Aircraft loading doors are produced by a limited number of manufacturers.

Recessed floor doors for carpet, tile, and other flooring materials are available, fabricated from aluminum and steel; they are used primarily for residential applications. A few recessed floor doors for commercial applications are listed in some manufacturers' catalogs; however, most manufacturers can provide floor doors with loading capacity to support a pedestrian loading of 300 lbf/sq. ft. (14.4 kN/sq. m) for commercial applications.

PRODUCT CHARACTERISTICS

Access door sheet metal thickness may vary slightly among manufacturers that produce units for the same purpose. Unless units are fire-rated, and a specific thickness is required to achieve the rating, a slight thickness variation should not affect the performance. Hinges may also vary, but if fire-rated units are not involved or hinge appearance is not objectionable, this should not affect the performance. Rounded door corners on access doors are available from some manufacturers.

Floor doors can be either nonwatertight with extruded-aluminum angle frame or watertight with extruded-aluminum gutter frame with NPS 1½ (DN 40) drainage coupling.

PRODUCT SELECTION CONSIDERATIONS

ASTM A 591/A 591M specifies electrolytic zinc-coating requirements for steel sheet. The heaviest zinc coating required by ASTM A 591/A 591M is 0.16 oz./sq. ft. (48 g/sq. m) for Class C. Classes B and A provide progressively less zinc weight. Electrolytic zinc coatings are much lighter than hot-dip coatings and offer less corrosion resistance. For practical purposes, the thickness of electrolytic zinc-coated steel is the same as for uncoated steel sheet.

Stainless steel may be selected for its appearance, durability, or corrosion resistance. For wet areas or areas susceptible to corrosion, stainless-steel access doors may be required. The initial cost of stainless-steel doors is usually much higher than steel or metallic-coated steel doors.

The thickness of steel, metallic-coated steel, and stainless-steel sheet indicated in specifications should be the nominal thickness expressed in decimal form. The steel sheet industry is replacing the customary gage number with the decimal thickness. Nevertheless, some access door manufacturers still use gages to indicate steel sheet thicknesses, despite the steel industry's recommendations that steel sheet be ordered by decimal thickness. The thicknesses of uncoated steel sheet and their equivalent gages are given here; they are based on the decimal thicknesses for uncoated hot- and cold-rolled steel sheets listed as miscellaneous data by the American Institute of Steel Construction (AISC) in various versions of the *Manual of Steel Construction*. Thicknesses have been rounded to three decimals to be consistent with current SI (metric) practices. Manufacturers that specify thicknesses in their product data by using gage are not necessarily referring to the equivalent decimal thicknesses listed here:

0.135 inch (3.4 mm) = 10 gage
0.105 inch (2.7 mm) = 12 gage
0.075 inch (1.9 mm) = 14 gage
0.060 inch (1.5 mm) = 16 gage
0.048 inch (1.2 mm) = 18 gage
0.036 inch (0.9 mm) = 20 gage
0.018 inch (0.45 mm) = 26 gage

The thickness specified for metallic-coated steel represents the uncoated thickness. According to ASTM A 653/A 653M, galvanized coating thickness may be estimated by using 1 oz./sq. ft. (305 g/sq. m) equal to 1.7 mils (0.043 mm); therefore, approximately 0.0015 inch (0.038 mm) can be added to the thickness of uncoated steel sheet for ASTM A 653/A 653M, G90 coated steel, and approximately 0.001 inch (0.025 mm) to the thickness for G60 coated steel.

Single-leaf floor door sizes range from about 24 inches (610 mm) square to a rectangle of 36 by 48 inches (914 by 1219 mm) or 42 inches (1067 mm) square. Double-leaf doors may be as small as or smaller than 36 inches (914 mm) square and as large as or larger than 72 inches (1829 mm) square. When the size required exceeds 12 sq. ft. (1.1 sq. m), a single door may be difficult to handle. Floor door size may be limited by the force required to open or close the door. A door larger than the manufacturer's recommended size may require special authorization from the manufacturer.

The following five questions should be answered when specifying floor doors:

1. **Material:** Will the door be made of aluminum, steel, galvanized steel, or stainless steel?
2. **Loading Requirements:** What load does the door need to hold or withstand?
3. **Water Tightness:** How much water will the floor door need to contend with: none, normal rainfall, or a standing head of water? Odor control may need to be considered and plumbing may be required.
4. **Locks:** What type of locking mechanism should be used? A staple for a padlock is the most basic locking device, but because it may protrude above the surface of the door, a staple could be a tripping hazard. A recessed hasp is similar to a staple that is recessed in a box with a lid. A snap lock with a removable outside handle and an inside release handle is the most popular; it is an easy-to-use, positive-latching slam lock usually constructed of all stainless steel. A deadbolt lock is like that found on an ordinary front door to a building or house. Pentahead bolts require a special wrench.
5. **Options:** What type of options are available and which ones are needed?

APPLICATION CONSIDERATIONS

Access doors and frames are available to suit almost any type of wall and ceiling construction. They are adaptable to openings in masonry, concrete, gypsum board assemblies, and plaster, as well as acoustical tile and panel ceilings. Access doors are designed to be as unobtrusive as possible; either they are placed flush with adjacent surfaces and painted to match or they are recessed, with material applied in the recess to match adjacent surfaces (figs. 3, 4).

Many doors can be applied in both walls and ceilings. The type of substrate construction (e.g., masonry, plaster, gypsum board assemblies, etc.) may require a flange or a bead on the frame for anchoring the frame to the substrate. The trimless units with minimal frame exposure and recessed doors are designed to be almost undetectable, or at least not to stand out, by continuing the surface finish with a minimum of interruption. These doors are extensively used in exposed areas in plaster, tile, gypsum board assemblies, and acoustical tile and board.

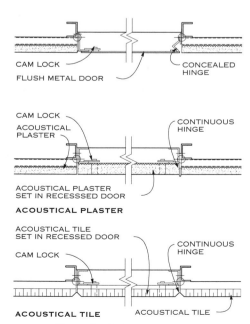

Figure 3. Ceiling access doors

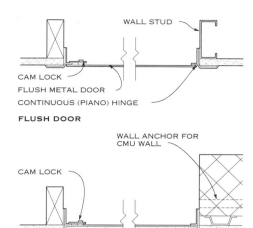

Figure 4. Wall access doors

For special situations, most access door manufacturers can provide glass, plastic, embossed aluminum, or almost any other ornamental metal door panel. Louvered door panels are also available, and doors can be furnished with brass nameplates.

Fire-rated access door assemblies are available from various manufacturers. Units are available in prime-coated steel sheet, metallic-coated steel, and stainless steel. Fire-rated units are classified for openings not exceeding 48-inches (1219-mm) wide by 50-inches (1270-mm) high; they are self-closing and self-latching and have an interior latch release. Every labeled access door will be marked "Access Frame and Fire Door Assembly," with the ratings in hours (e.g., one and one-half, one, or three-fourths) and, when applicable, the class (e.g., B or C) and the maximum degrees of temperature rise for a minimum time (e.g., 30 minutes) (fig. 5).

Time and label requirements for fire-resistance-rated access doors should be identified on the drawings or in the schedules, if using schedules. A maximum temperature rise of 250°F (139°C) at the end of 30 minutes may be required for access doors located in proximity to combustible materials, as determined by authorities having jurisdiction.

The test methods for establishing fire-protection ratings of access doors in walls and ceilings are Uniform Building Code (UBC) Standard 7-2 and the Underwriters Laboratories, Inc. (UL) standards UL 10B for vertical installations and UL 263 for horizontal installations. These are the only methods referenced in the literature of most access door manufacturers that claim to have ceiling access doors with a fire-protection rating from a recognized testing and inspecting agency. It is unclear

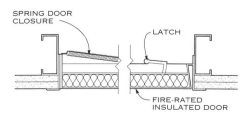

Figure 5. Fire-rated wall access door

whether these test methods are accepted by jurisdictions that have adopted either the Building Officials and Code Administrators International, Inc. (BOCA) National Building Code or the Standard Building Code because neither refers to UBC standards. Intertek Testing Services (ITS) is the only testing and inspecting agency listed by most manufacturers as performing the UBC test on access doors in ceilings. UL does not use the UBC test but indicates in its *Building Materials Directory* that the appropriate test method for rating ceiling access doors is UL 263, which is equivalent to ASTM E 119. UL lists only those access door manufacturers that have obtained fire-protection ratings for walls; it makes no mention of products tested as part of ceiling assemblies. As an example, fire-rated insulated security doors are only approved for wall application; they have not been tested in floors and ceilings. Accordingly, it is important to determine from authorities having jurisdiction as to which test method is required to qualify access doors in fire-resistance-rated ceiling assemblies.

Although some manufacturers describe certain ceiling access doors as fire-resistant or fire-resistive, these products do not have fire-protection ratings from UL or another testing and inspecting agency. The doors are not self-closing or self-latching and do not have an interior latch release. They are made of noncombustible steel with a recessed door filled with the same fire-resistive material as the adjacent fire-rated ceiling. Consult authorities having jurisdiction to verify that such a product is acceptable.

REFERENCES

Publication dates cited here were current at the time of this writing. Publications are revised periodically, and revisions may have occurred before this book was published.

American Association of State Highway and Transportation Officials

AASHTO H-20: Contained in Standard Specifications for Highway Bridges, 16th edition

ASTM International

ASTM A 591/A 591M-98: Specification for Steel Sheet, Electrolytic Zinc-Coated, for Light Coating Mass Applications

ASTM A 653/A 653M-98a: Specification for Steel Sheet, Zinc-Coated (Galvanized) or Zinc-Iron Alloy-Coated (Galvannealed) by the Hot-Dip Process

ASTM E 119-98: Test Methods for Fire Tests of Building Construction and Materials

International Conference of Building Officials

UBC Standard 7.2-1997: Fire Tests of Door Assemblies

Underwriters Laboratories Inc.

UL 10B-97: Fire Tests of Door Assemblies

UL 263-97: Fire Tests of Building Construction and Materials

08351 FOLDING DOORS

This chapter discusses *fire-rated folding doors; nonfire-rated accordion and panel folding doors with vinyl, wood, and other finishes; metal bifold doors; and bifold mirror doors of metal construction. Except for the fire-rated folding doors, these doors are intended primarily for use as visual separation devices and primarily apply to commercial and institutional installations; however, they may accommodate light-commercial and residential construction. A fire-rated folding door provides a fire and smoke barrier for several applications in commercial and institutional installations.*

This chapter does not discuss *sound-rated partitions and fire-resistance-rated operable doors and partitions. The typical sizes and locations of the doors discussed do not require that nonfire-rated units be electrically powered, although such doors are available from some manufacturers.*

GENERAL COMMENTS

Accordion folding doors and panel folding doors are similar or identical to some of the operable and accordion folding partitions often specified in Division 10, "Specialties"; however, the products discussed in this chapter are usually not rated for fire resistance or sound transmission loss, and are typically only available in heights up to 10 feet (3 m).

Because products included in this chapter are smaller, they generally do not need the same degree of structural support that is required for operable panel partitions. A limited degree of acoustical privacy is available from applied sound seal sweeps at the top and bottom of doors, but there is no retractable sound seal at the bottom, as there is with operable panel partitions.

ACCORDION FOLDING DOOR CHARACTERISTICS

Nonfire-rated accordion folding doors have pantograph or X-type hinged frames with a covering on each side (fig. 1). The doors are appropriate for commercial and institutional installations; some may be used in light-commercial and residential construction as a room divider in areas where acoustics and fire ratings are not an issue but where rooms need to be separated for function or to accommodate a small group of people.

The suspension system is influenced by the door's height, weight, travel distance, and stacking method. Although terminology varies among manufacturers, some basic components are consistent throughout the construction of the doors.

The doors are always suspended from a track attached to an overhead support or head of a framed opening. The track is usually made of extruded aluminum or steel, and can be surface- or recess-mounted in the ceiling. If recess-mounted, the unit will normally require a ceiling guard to protect the ceiling surface from being damaged by the door mechanism. The ceiling guard is normally prefinished, but may also be trimmed out with wood if required by the design. The wood material typically is not furnished by the door manufacturer and should therefore be included in a Division 6,

"Wood and Plastics," specification section. Most manufacturers can provide a straight or curved track.

The term *carriers*, plural, is used to describe the tires that are attached to the door and that ride within the track, allowing the door to glide open and closed. These tires are normally made of nylon; large units are required to have ball bearings. The term *carrier*, singular usually refers to a double- or single-wheeled unit; the term *trolley* usually refers to a double-wheeled unit. Before specifying, verify terminology with the manufacturer.

Sweep seals can be found on both sides or on one side of an accordion folding door, depending on the application. Including sweep seals on both sides of the door are an attempt to increase the door's acoustical properties, although a better way to meet acoustical requirements would be to upgrade to an acoustically rated accordion folding door. Sweep seals on one side are often specified to block light. Applications where these characteristics are not an issue do not require sweep seals.

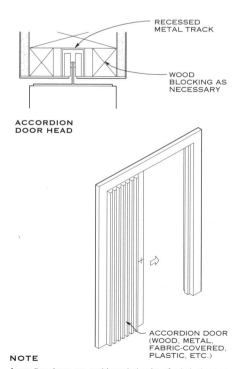

RECESSED METAL TRACK

WOOD BLOCKING AS NECESSARY

ACCORDION DOOR HEAD

ACCORDION DOOR (WOOD, METAL, FABRIC-COVERED, PLASTIC, ETC.)

NOTE

Accordion doors are multipaneled units of relatively narrow wood or fabric that are hinged together. Track-guided hangers/trolleys and optional jamb-side pivots allow the entire assembly to fold together like an accordion. The stacking distance of the panels when open may encroach upon the clear opening dimension or be concealed in a recessed pocket. Sizes vary from traditional doorways to room dividers. Accordion doors require less floor space than swing doors. Refer to codes for egress requirements.

Figure 1. Typical accordion door

The latch is typically operable from both sides, but if the situation demands a keyed lock, it may be operable from one or both sides. Most applications are operable from both sides with a thumb-turn latch. If it is necessary to have a keyed deadlock receive a cylinder, it may be necessary to coordinate with requirements in the Division 8, "Doors and Windows," section that specifies door hardware and lock cylinders.

Configuration of the stacking method will determine where meeting posts are located. Doors can be either single type, stacking at one end of the opening and using a fixed single-jamb post, or center-opening type, stacking at both ends of the opening and using a center meeting post. Meeting posts are free-rolling or they allow the intersection of three and four doors. Consult the manufacturer's literature for information on these types of configurations.

PANEL FOLDING DOOR CHARACTERISTICS

Panel folding doors consist of flat panels finished on both sides and continuously hinged to fold the panels in alternate directions, to form a serpentine configuration in plan view. They are similar to the continuously hinged, operable folding panel partitions specified in Division 10, except for the fire rating, the acoustical rating, and the panel size. Each panel of a folding door is only approximately 4- to 6-inches (100- to 150-mm) wide; operable folding panel partitions are up to 4-feet (1.2-m) wide and 18-feet (5.4-m) high.

Core materials and thicknesses vary among manufacturers. Because acoustics and fire ratings are not involved, the core material is not as important as it is for acoustically rated or fire-rated doors.

The main difference between accordion and panel folding doors, other than configuration, is the hinging mechanism. Instead of pantograph or X-type hinged frames, panel folding doors rely on a system of continuous hinges with seals between each panel. The suspension system and hardware are similar to those of accordion folding doors. Some manufacturers use steel tracks; others use aluminum. Wood molding for the surface-mounted track may be furnished by the panel folding door manufacturer so the wood molding matches the wood facing of the panels.

Typical configuration of panel folding doors allows for a single stack on one end of the opening. If center opening or other configurations are required, verify meeting-post requirements with manufacturers.

BIFOLD DOOR CHARACTERISTICS

Bifold doors are hinged pairs of lightweight doors that are commonly supported with pivots in keepers at stationary jambs and with guide pins in the leading jamb at the overhead track (fig. 2). Floor tracks are also available. Bifold doors are typically available in two- or four-panel units, normally in metal, although wood is commonly used in residential construction.

Metal doors are prefinished in the factory, field-finished, or mirror-faced. Bifold doors are normally used for closet doors in residential-type applications with openings up to 12-feet (3.6-m) wide.

If used in commercial applications, wood bifold doors are typically purchased separately with field-applied hardware. These products are usually specified in Division 8 sections for flush wood or stile and rail wood doors. Wood doors can receive several finishes, including plastic laminate or mirrors.

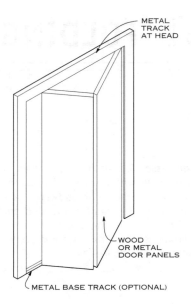

NOTE

Bifold doors are wood or metal door pairs hinged together with pivots at the jamb. Track-guided hangers/trolleys allow the doors to fold against each other when they open. Bifold doors require less floor space than swing doors, but the thickness of the door panels reduces the clear opening.

Figure 2. Typical biofold door

FIRE-RATED FOLDING DOOR CONSIDERATIONS

Fire-rated folding doors must be identical to assemblies tested by manufacturers, complete with all the required components, unless options are permitted by the Underwriters Laboratories Inc. (UL) or Intertek Testing Services (ITS) listing. For listings describing mandatory ratings, components, and allowable options, consult manufacturers and UL's current *Building Materials Directory* or ITS's *Directory of Listed Products*.

Fire-rated folding doors serve as barriers to both fire and smoke. They consist either of a series of unitary panels joined one to another to make a folding door operating on a single track, or of a series of opposing parallel panels, with no interconnections except at lead posts, joined to make an accordion folding door with two facings/covers operating on a dual track.

These doors are electrically operated, automatic- or self-closing, UL- or ITS-listed assemblies, which are top-supported from an overhead track without floor guides, and complete with hardware, seals, track, closing devices, controls, and accessories necessary for the intended operation. Fire-release devices, such as fusible links, electric operators, and electronic and digital controls are available for some products. Depending on the product, the self-closing operation may be initiated by a signal from the fire-alarm system, by power loss, or by melting of the fusible link. Access to operators and controls is required, so coordination with the Division 8 section that specifies access doors and frames is important; verify that fire-rated access panels are specified.

Optional egress opening devices are available for fire-rated folding doors that allow the door to reverse on activation of a push plate on the leading edge of the door. The door will open a predetermined distance and, after a pause to allow egress, will reclose.

Pocket doors may be used to conceal fire-rated folding doors in storage pockets. Pocket doors close openings for, and permit access to, storage pockets. Pocket door swings of less than 180 degrees may affect operational clearances. Fire-rated enclosure construction may be required for pocket door construction to comply with requirements of authorities having jurisdiction. Pocket doors are not typically provided by the fire-rated folding door manufacturer; so if they are specified, pocket doors must be fully coordinated with the fire-rated folding doors to ensure that they do not impede the closing or reversing of the folding door. Also, a pocket door should have a solid core for durability. The door's thickness and covering material are at the discretion of the architect. However, if the total door thickness exceeds 2 inches (50 mm), the pocket depth must be adjusted. A pocket door must be side-hinged with either a reverse-action spring hinge (to hold the door open) or a continuous hinge. A pocket door is typically held closed by a magnetic catch not exerting more than 30 lbf (133 N) of holding force. The total force required to open a pocket cover door cannot exceed 50 lbf (222 N). Consult fire-rated folding door manufacturers for details about both storage pockets and pocket doors and about clearances required for door operation and mounting and for functioning of operators and controls.

Fire-rated folding doors must be installed, complete with all the required components of the manufacturer's fire-resistance-tested and -rated assembly, unless options are permitted by the UL listing, according to installation instructions provided with each assembly. These instructions may include requirements or restrictions for adjacent construction. For example, the required fire rating must be maintained for overhead plenum and wall barrier construction above the fire-rated operable panel partition; or the door may be listed for installation only in masonry walls. Verify limitations with manufacturers and by reviewing installation instructions, and coordinate requirements in the specifications and on the drawings.

The National Fire Protection Association (NFPA) publication NFPA 80, *Fire Doors and Fire Windows,* requires floors extending under doors to be noncombustible or to have special sills. Because special sills are impractical for fire-rated operable panel partitions, floors are required by default to be noncombustible under fire doors installed according to NFPA 80. Combustible floor coverings extending through protected openings with fire ratings of 1 or 1½ hours without sills are also permitted if the coverings are capable of demonstrating a critical radiant flux of not less than 0.22 W/sq. cm. Verify requirements to suit the project.

FINISH SELECTION CONSIDERATIONS

Finishing options are not identical among manufacturers; most offer genuine wood veneers, but available species vary. Besides common species, others such as cherry are available from selected manufacturers.

The appearance of fire-rated folding doors is not an issue because these doors are concealed behind an access door. This access door is usually covered with a finish that blends into the adjacent wall finish, requiring coordination with millwork or access panels or other means of supplying a custom door that conceals the device.

Textile and carpet facings applied to walls have requirements in addition to flame-spread and smoke-developed characteristics according to the three model code organizations and NFPA 101, Life Safety Code. If folding doors are large or prevalent enough to be considered walls by authorities having jurisdiction, they may impose restrictions similar to those for textile facings.

REFERENCES

Publication dates cited here were current at the time of this writing. Publications are revised periodically, and revisions may have occurred before this book was published.

National Fire Protection Association
NFPA 80B99: Fire Doors and Fire Windows

Underwriters Laboratories Inc.
Building Materials Directory, published annually.

Intertek Testing Services
Directory of Listed Products, published annually.

08710 **DOOR HARDWARE**

This chapter discusses hardware applied to doors, formally called finish hardware, builder's hardware, or architectural finish hardware. It covers hardware items essential to the operation, control, and weather stripping of swinging, sliding, and folding wood and metal doors normally provided in a facility. It also addresses electrified door hardware.

This chapter does not discuss how to specify hardware for special doors, which includes detention doors, vault doors, blast-resistant doors, sliding fire doors, entrance doors, automatic-operating doors, sound-rated doors, or other doors of unique application where hardware is normally furnished as part of the door package.

GENERAL COMMENTS

Early planning of door hardware requirements makes specifying door hardware proceed more smoothly. Basic door hardware decisions, such as selecting quality, trim designs, and finishes, and determining code requirements, can be made during design development. Code requirements for fire-rated and smoke doors are complex and are interrelated with other requirements that may affect the design. Determining the owner's requirements for door hardware is also important because many have strong preferences or may need to match existing products, materials, and finishes.

DOOR HARDWARE CONSULTANT

Deciding whether to enlist the help of a door hardware consultant when specifying the door hardware and preparing the door hardware schedule will depend on the specifier's knowledge of door hardware. Even with the help of a door hardware consultant, the specifier must have, or acquire, enough knowledge about door hardware beyond the scope described in this book to verify that the door hardware specified and scheduled suits project requirements for appearance, function, and quality. Although some of this knowledge can be acquired from door hardware catalogs and applicable standards, it should also come from previous experience that has resulted in satisfactory installations. Depending on the complexity of the project and the specifier's knowledge of door hardware, it may prove more efficient and less costly to engage an *architectural hardware consultant* (AHC) to prepare the door hardware sets and to review the specifications.

AHCs must meet Door and Hardware Institute (DHI) qualifications, which includes passing a certification examination and successfully completing an apprenticeship program. AHCs may be self-employed or work for a contract door hardware distributor, an agency representing one or more door hardware manufacturers, or a door hardware manufacturer. One of the services these firms provide is specifications consulting; they often use their own software and specifying system. In most cases, unless the AHC is paid by the architect or owner to prepare the door hardware sets and specifications, compensation comes from sales of door hardware products. This assumes that the contract for supplying the door hardware is negotiated directly with the AHC's company or that the AHC's employer is the successful bidder. In

certain situations, a conflict may occur between project needs and a proprietary specification on which a consultant may earn a commission from the sale. For these reasons, the architect should know of commission arrangements before employing or requesting help from an AHC.

Certified Door Consultant (CDC)

CDC is a new classification of consultant. A CDC must meet certain qualifications, including passing an examination. Many AHCs also become CDCs. CDCs who are not also AHCs may or may not have sufficient door hardware experience; still, their knowledge of doors may be helpful when specifying door hardware.

The owner may also have a security consultant or a business relationship with an access control or burglar alarm dealer who may develop the overall security design of the project. To expedite both the security design process and the development of door hardware requirements, it is a good idea to have the AHC and the security consultant meet early in the project.

METHODS OF SPECIFYING DOOR HARDWARE

Two basic approaches to specifying door hardware are to use *schedules* and *allowances*.

- **Using a door hardware schedule** is the preferred method for specifying door hardware. With this method, it is possible to specify exactly which products and manufacturers to include for each door in a project. This method provides a clear basis for comparing substitutions because function and quality are established.
- **The door hardware allowance** method is used to meet project needs when, for various reasons, it becomes impossible to make final decisions about which products and functions to select. Particularly in retrofit projects, where certain items may be reused based on new usage of the facility, a door hardware allowance postpones these final decisions until all the information is available. An allowance can be included in competitive bidding. The difference between the amount of the allowance and the actual cost is typically resolved by a change order.

Regardless of whether the schedule or an allowance method is used, if a specific door hardware design is preferred or a custom design is required, then that design should be delineated on the drawings. This is particularly common for the design of lever handles and other exposed trim.

Door Hardware Allowance Method

By design, the allowance method postpones decision making on door hardware requirements. The allowance method may be advantageous for those projects of limited scope, or where it is the intent of the owner or architect to control more directly the selection of the door hardware and possibly the supplier. On the other hand, this method also precludes competition and requires including provisions to define the scope of the allowance and additional responsibilities of the contractor. These provisions should be tailored to suit the project.

When specifying by allowance, the specifier should provide sufficient bidding information to enable the contractor to estimate door and frame reinforcements and factory preparation for machining doors and frames. To do this, generic door hardware sets are sometimes included in the specifications.

When determining cash allowances, one of the following two methods is used to establish the allowance amount:

- **Lump sum,** the preferred method, is established by the architect after first selecting prototypical door hardware sets and determining estimated material costs for each set. The architect then assigns door hardware sets to each opening on the drawings, counts the number of each door hardware set, and multiplies these quantities by the unit costs to determine the lump sum.
- **Unit cost** establishes a per-door material cost. The contractor has the responsibility to establish the allowance amount and count the quantities. This is a faster method for the architect but can lead to disagreements on the quantities and the amount of the allowance.

An allowance includes purchase, handling, and delivery, of materials, plus applicable taxes. Typically, the allowance does not include the contractor's overhead and profit. It may or may not include the cost of field installation, which should be clearly stated.

Once the contract has been awarded, the architect must select the quality, function, material, and finish for each type of door hardware required, and determine which types belong in each door hardware set. The next step is to create a door hardware schedule and to present this, along with other contract documents, to the contractor for soliciting bids from qualified door hardware suppliers. The architect reviews the bids and instructs the contractor on which supplier to select. A change order is required to resolve the difference between the bid price and the allowance.

Door Hardware Scheduling Methods

Three methods for scheduling door hardware for door hardware sets are *naming manufacturers' products, referencing Builders Hardware Manufacturers Association (BHMA) standards,* and *describing products.* All three methods can be used to provide enough information to enable a bidder to estimate the labor when a door hardware allowance is specified. It may, however, be necessary to use a combination of these methods, for example, naming a manufacturer's product for electronic door hardware, which has no BHMA standard.

- **Naming manufacturers' products** uses actual product designations to establish the basis of quality and performance, and results in brief materials and fabrication provisions. With this method, the door hardware schedule must be sufficiently complete to establish both the quality and quantity of hardware required for each door. This makes accurate bidding, installation, and inspection of the specified products easier. Custom-designed items may need to be illustrated on the drawings to be completely specified. This scheduling method is the most common because it gives the greatest control over the design and selection of door hardware and trim. Either a proprietary or semiproprietary specification can be developed with this method.
- **Referencing BHMA standards** to specify door hardware results in a specification based on industry-accepted minimum test standards. These standards often allow manufacturers the option of selecting materials; the standards also contain hidden quality choices. Some manufacturers claim that their products exceed the performance requirements of the standards. Because of these considerations, the specifier should be familiar with each standard and should indicate the specific function and quality levels required. Referencing BHMA standards is useful when a clear, concise, and objective description for door hardware

is desired. A list of BHMA standards is included in this chapter. With this method, manufacturers are typically not listed, since the specifier is relying on the standard to establish requirements.

- **Describing products** uses detailed descriptions to establish the material, function, and quality requirements for each item of door hardware. These descriptions include descriptive titles that are used in the door hardware schedule. Descriptions allow the specifier to avoid using manufacturers' proprietary product names.

Sample door hardware schedules that illustrate each of these methods appear later in this chapter.

SPECIFYING HARDWARE FOR SPECIAL DOORS

To review from the beginning of this chapter, special doors include detention doors, vault doors, blast-resistant doors, sliding fire doors, entrance doors, automatic-operating doors, sound-rated doors, and other doors where door hardware is normally furnished as part of the door package. Door hardware for special doors, except cylinders, is typically specified with the door rather than in the general door hardware section, although it some cases it may be preferable to specify it with the rest of the door hardware. Cylinders are often specified with the rest of the hardware so that the keying will match.

Entrance doors are a good example of where door hardware can be specified with either the door or the rest of the door hardware. Many manufacturers furnish door hardware as part of their entrance door packages. Manufacturers have selected these items based on their function, appearance, and past performance. The advantages for the owner of specifying the door hardware with the entrance door are: a single source of responsibility for the door opening, and the confidence that the manufacturer has selected the appropriate door hardware for the product.

Sound-rated door applications require coordination in selecting door hardware for the type of door and frame. The construction surrounding the door should be compatible with the Sound Transmission Class (STC) rating of the door and frame. Sound-rated door assemblies typically include jamb and head gasketing and door bottom components that are tested and furnished as part of the assembly; they should not be specified with door hardware. Properly functioning systems will result in higher-than-normal closing forces, which may require adjustment of closer force to compensate. Lever-handle locksets are recommended since the opening torque may also be higher than normal. Pairs of doors are generally not recommended for sound-rated openings; however, some manufacturers offer a limited number of systems to meet these applications.

Cam hinges may also be appropriate for some sound-rated door applications. These hinges are full-mortise and self-closing; they improve the sealing characteristics along the door bottom by lifting and lowering the door with the swing.

PRODUCT STANDARDS

BHMA has developed industry-accepted standards for most types of door hardware. These standards include cycle, functional, strength, security, and finish test requirements. It is not always easy, however, to determine which standard covers the type of door hardware to be specified. Table 1 summarizes the content of each standard.

BHMA standards implement an alphanumeric system to identify each type of door hardware. In this system, each character in the alphanumeric designation represents a specific material, type, function, or performance

Table 1
BHMA DOOR HARDWARE STANDARDS

Standard Number	Standard Name	Type of Door Hardware Covered by Standard
A156.1	Butts and Hinges	Hinges, pivot hinges, door pivots, rescue hardware
A156.2	Bored and Preassembled Locks & Latches	Bored locks and latches, preassembled locks and latches
A156.3	Exit Devices	Exit devices, flush bolts, removable mullions, coordinators
A156.4	Door Controls-Closers	Door closers, pivots for floor closers
A156.5	Auxiliary Locks & Associated Products	Auxiliary locks, rim locks, cylinders, exit alarms, exit locks, electric strikes, key control systems
A156.6	Architectural Door Trim	Door protection plates, door edgings, push plates, door pulls, push bars, pull bars
A156.7	Template Hinge Dimensions	Dimensions for hinges used on metal doors and frames
A156.8	Door Controls-Overhead Stops and Holders	Overhead stops, overhead holders
A156.12	Interconnected Locks & Latches	Interconnected locks and latches
A156.13	Mortise Locks & Latches	Mortise locks and latches
A156.14	Sliding & Folding Door Hardware	Hardware for horizontal sliding doors, bypassing sliding doors, pocket sliding doors, bifolding doors, multiple folding doors
A156.15	Closer Holder Release Devices	Mechanical and electromagnetic door closers: combined with hold-open devices; combined with releasing devices
A156.16	Auxiliary Hardware	Combination stop and holders, door holders, door stops, door silencers, door guards, garment hooks, garment rods, door knockers, door viewers, identification signs, door bolts, letterbox plates
A156.17	Self Closing Hinges & Pivots	Spring hinges, pivot hinges, dwarf door hinges
A156.18	Materials and Finishes	Finishes on base materials
A156.21	Thresholds	Thresholds, thresholds for closers
A156.22	Door Gasketing Systems	Air-infiltration and smoke-gasketing systems
A156.23	Electromagnetic Locks	Electromagnetic locks
A156.24	Delayed Egress Locks	Products used with conventional exit devices or locks

grade for each door hardware item. Grades 1, 2, and 3 are available; Grade 1 is the best commercial quality, and Grade 3 is residential quality. Each designation is unique, to indicate a specific item and quality of door hardware. To assist specifiers, most manufacturers prepare a cross-reference that compares their products with comparable BHMA designations. To become a member of BHMA, the door hardware manufacturer must have a substantial manufacturing facility in the United States. However, any manufacturer can test to BHMA A156 series standards or indicate that products are comparable to specific BHMA designations.

BHMA also maintains a certification program and directories of certified products. This program is a means for manufacturers to verify compliance with BHMA standards. Participating manufacturers certify compliance with standards by passing a continuing program of tests required in the applicable BHMA standard. An independent testing agency witnesses the tests and conducts random tests of finished products. Currently, the program includes certified directories for locks and latches, door closers, exit devices, and electromagnetic and delayed-egress locks.

HINGE AND PIVOT SELECTION CONSIDERATIONS

Hinge selection includes choosing the kind, size, base metal, finish, hand, type of fasteners, tip style, type, and special features. Most hinge manufacturers' catalogs offer excellent guidelines about which size, number, and quality of hinges to specify based on the frequency of use and the door size. The number of hinges for a door is determined by the height of the door.

Kind of Hinge

The type of door and frame determines the kind of hinge. Kinds include full mortise, half mortise, full surface, swing-clear half mortise, swing-clear half surface, swing-clear full surface, and pivot-reinforced full mortise (fig. 1).

- **Full-mortise, or butt, hinges** are the most common and the least-expensive way to hang side-hinged doors. They are available in two-, three-, and five-barrel, or knuckle, configurations. Two-barrel configurations have fixed pins, making them unusable for doors that extend close to the ceiling because the door must be lifted to remove it from the hinge mounted on the door frame.
- **Swing-clear hinges** are used where a wider clear opening is required, such as for barrier-free applications and for doors that must swing completely clear of the door opening for the passage of wide equipment.
- **Pivot-reinforced hinges** combine a pivot and a butt hinge in an interlocked unit and are used for heavy usage doors, especially with overhead door holders.

Size of Hinge

The door width, thickness, weight, and clearance required determines the size of a hinge. The height is determined by the width and thickness of the door. The width is determined by the thickness of the door and the clearance required. The height is always the first dimension; the width is the second dimension, determined with both leaves in the flat, open position (fig. 2).

Other Hinge Characteristics

Numerous other hinge characteristics must be specified. These are itemized in the following list.

- **Base metal and plating or metallic coating** are determined based on the following factors: atmospheric conditions, the location of the doors (exterior or interior), and special conditions such as chemical laboratories or sewage disposal plants. Nonferrous hinges are recommended for use on exterior doors and on doors in humid areas within the building. Model codes also require that labeled fire doors must hang on steel or stainless-steel antifriction-bearing hinges. This is because nonferrous metals become elastic at lower temperatures than does steel, which could allow the dislocation of the door during a fire.

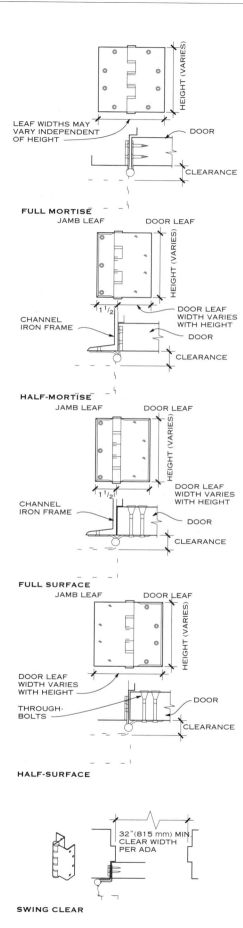

FULL MORTISE

HALF-MORTISE

FULL SURFACE

HALF-SURFACE

SWING CLEAR

Figure 1. Kinds of hinges

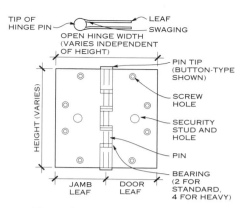

Figure 2. Elements of a hinge

- **Finish** is described in a BHMA standard as the exposed appearance over a base metal. Table 5, later in this chapter, lists the most common finishes.
- **Hand of hinge** is not usually an issue, except for Paumelle and olive-knuckle hinges, which are handed (fig. 3). However, some other types of door hardware may be mounted on only one side of the door, making it necessary to indicate hand. The hand of a door is determined by looking at the door from the outside or the secured side (fig. 4).
- **Fasteners** commonly include both concealed screws and through bolts. Most hinges use screws; however, various types of surface hinges may require through-bolts if the door and frame do not have reinforcing.
- **Tip styles** are numerous, although most are used primarily for residential hinges. Hospital tips, whose barrel ends are sloped, are also available. When used in mental institutions, hospital tips make it difficult for patients to attach rope, wearing apparel, or similar items in attempts to harm themselves (fig. 5).
- **Type of hinge** includes the weight and designation as antifriction (ball bearing) or plain bearing. Type is determined by the frequency of the door operation, door weight, and whether a closer is required. Heavy, high-abuse, and exterior doors are high-frequency installations that require heavyweight, antifriction-bearing hinges; corridor doors are average-frequency installations that require standard-weight, antifriction-bearing hinges; storeroom doors are low-frequency installations that require only plain-bearing hinges. Antifriction hinges should be specified on all doors with door closers.

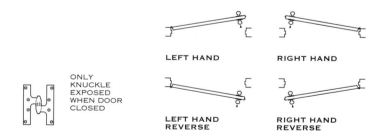

Figure 3. Olive-knuckle hinge

Figure 4. Hands of doors

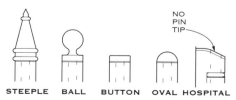

Figure 5. Tip styles

Table 2
HINGE APPLICATIONS

Kind of Hinge	Door Material				Frame Material			
	Wood	Hollow Metal	Mineral Core (Wood)	Aluminum	Wood	Hollow Metal	Channel Iron	Aluminum
Full Mortise	•	•	•		•	•		
Half Mortise	•	•	•				•	
Half Surface	•		•		•	•		
Full Surface		•	•					
Swing Clear, Full Mortise	•	•	•			•		
Swing Clear, Half Mortise	•						•	
Swing Clear, Half Surface			•			•		
Swing Clear, Full Surface			•				•	
Pivot Reinforced, Full Mortise	•	•				•		
Slip In, Full Mortise				•				•

- **Special hinge features** include special swaging, raised barrel, and type of pin. Swaging is a slight offset of the hinge leaf at the barrel, which permits the leaves to come closer together when closed. Raised barrels are used where doors are set deep in a wide frame, and are not available with electrified features. Nonremovable pins are used on exterior doors or other security doors within the building that swing out.
- **Hinge applications** are listed in Table 2.

Special Types of Hinges

Special types of hinges include the following:

- **Electrified hinges** are hinges modified with electrical wiring that transfers power, provides a circuit for monitoring door position, or provides communication for other door hardware. Some electrified hinges contain a concealed switch for activating alarms and other security devices (completing a circuit when the door is open or when the door is closed). Electrified hinges are mounted at the middle hinge location.
- **Spring hinges** are available for single- and double-acting doors (fig. 6). Double-acting spring hinges are used mostly on industrial applications. Single-acting spring hinges match the design of other hinges; however, they do not have adjustments to check the closing speed, so they should be specified with caution in any area where door weight or drafts require more door control. Spring hinges meet the self-closing requirements of labeled fire doors, provided that two hinges are used on each door leaf and that door size and function limitations of codes are followed.
- **Pocket hinges** are full-mortise hinges, designed for use in recessing doors into concealed pockets. These hinges allow the face of doors to be flush with the face of adjacent walls when the doors are fully open. In this position, the hinges are fully concealed.

- **Continuous geared hinges** have been available for many years (fig. 7). The recent trend is toward increased use of heavy-duty continuous geared hinges for high-abuse and special applications. These hinges use two gears to form a rotating joint that extends over the full height of the door and frame, thus distributing the weight of the door over the length of the hinge. The gears are hidden by a continuous cover, which prevents pinched fingers and eliminates privacy gaps. Continuous geared hinges work well in retrofit conditions and are available for labeled fire doors. They are available in extruded aluminum, steel, and stainless steel. As with conventional hinges, continuous geared hinges are available for electrified applications.
- **Pivots** are a hinging device containing a fixed pin and a single point with two knuckles (fig. 8). They are normally specified for aesthetic reasons or where the weight of the door can best be carried on the floor. However, pivots are more costly than typical hinges. They are recommended for oversize, heavy, and commercial and institutional entrance doors. Lead-lined doors, center-pivoted doors, and double-acting doors are typically hung on pivots. Certain floor closers and overhead concealed closers require the use of pivots or include pivots as part of their package. Many of the same selection considerations for hinges also apply to pivots. Electrified pivots are available for power transfer and door-position monitoring.

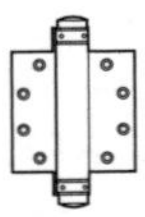

Figure 6. Spring hinge

Figure 7. Continuous geared hinge

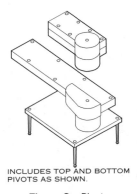

INCLUDES TOP AND BOTTOM PIVOTS AS SHOWN.

Figure 8. Pivots

LOCK AND LATCH SELECTION CONSIDERATIONS

The names assigned to locks were originally selected to identify either the type of construction or the type of installation. Considering the variety of functions, types, designs, styles, sizes, weights, security, and convenience features of locks, it requires substantial experience to fully understand how to select the proper lock for a particular use. Locks that include the lock and the trim are called locksets. The locks most commonly used in all types of construction are described in the following list:

- **Bored locks (cylindrical or tubular)** are installed in a door in two round holes at right angles to each other-one through the face of the door to hold the lock body, and the other in the edge of the door to receive the latch mechanism (fig. 9). When these two are joined, they constitute a complete latching or locking mechanism. Bored locks have the keyway (cylinder) or locking device, such as push or turn buttons, in the knob or lever. They are available in BHMA Grades 1, 2, and 3, and are also known as 4000 Series locks. Commercial backset for a bored lock is 2¾ inches (70 mm), with locks available in high-security and interchange-

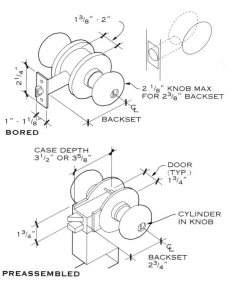

BORED

PREASSEMBLED

NOTE

Installation requires notch cut in lock side of door to suit case size. Complete factory assembly eliminates much adjustment on the job.

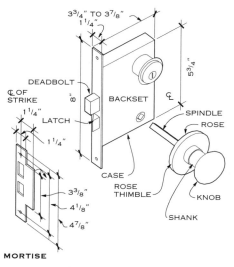

MORTISE

Figure 9. Lock types

able-core cylinders. Many lever-handle designs for bored locks are of cast-zinc construction to reduce the weight of the trim. These trims do not meet BHMA A156.18 finish standards. Cylindrical bored locks are made in a drum style and, because of their heavier construction, are more durable than tubular bored locks. Both styles are equally easy to install, but tubular locks are generally less costly.

- **Preassembled (unit) locks** are installed in a rectangular notch cut into the door edge (fig. 9). This type of lock has all the parts assembled as a unit at the factory and requires little or no assembly to install. Preassembled locks have the cylinder in the knob or lever. These locks are available only in heavy-duty weight, BHMA Grade 1, and are also known as 2000 Series locks.

- **Mortise locks** are installed in a prepared recess (mortise) in a door (fig. 9). The working mechanism is contained in a rectangular-shaped case with appropriate holes into which the required components, cylinder, levers, and turn-piece spindles are attached and threaded to complete the working assembly. For commercial uses, the typical backset is 2¾ inches (70 mm). These locks are available in BHMA Grades 1 and 2, and are also known as 1000 Series locks. The spring tension on lever handles is maintained by additional springs.

- **Interconnected locks** consist of a separate latchbolt or deadlocking latchbolt and a deadbolt that are mechanically interconnected and installed in bored openings in the edge and face of the door. For commercial uses, the typical backset is 2¾ inches (70 mm). These locks are available in BHMA Grades 1, 2, and 3, and are also known as 5000 Series locks.

- **Electromagnetic locks,** also called *mag locks,* are electrically powered locks that lock and unlock by activating an electromagnet coupled to a strike, or armature. The two basic types of electromagnetic locks are direct hold and shear. With direct-hold locks, the lock body and the strike come into direct contact; the mated surfaces resist opening forces when the magnet is engaged. With shear locks, the lock body and the strike are mounted perpendicular to the direction of door travel; they resist opening forces when they are close together and the magnet is engaged. The type of mounting will determine which type to select. Locks are available for surface mounting on or mortising into the header or jamb of the door frame or for mortising into the bottom of the door. Electromagnetic locks are available only in heavy-duty weight, BHMA Grade 1; they are also ranked by the amount of force they resist: 1500 lbf (6673 N), 1000 lbf (4448 N), and 500 lbf (2224 N). Locks with a 1500-lbf (6673-N) ranking are typically used for exterior doors, steel-stiffened high-security doors, and detention doors. Locks with a 1000-lbf (4448-N) ranking are used for typical commercial applications. Locks with a 500-lbf (2224-N) ranking are used for aluminum storefront doors, since the aluminum will give way at approximately 450 lbf (2002 N), and for applications requiring traffic control, such as interior doors. Sometimes, 2000-lbf (8896-N) locks are used for special applications, such as gates. Doors that swing out from the area being protected can use locks with lower strength rankings because an intruder can exert less pulling force against the lock than against a door that can be pushed.

- **Electrified locks** function as either fail-secure or fail-safe. *Fail-secure* means that when the power is off, the lock is locked. *Fail-safe* means that when the power is off, the lock is unlocked. Nonfail-safe is the same as fail-secure. Electrified locks include those in the following list:

  - **Delayed-egress locks** are another type of electromagnetic lock. There are two types: security grade and movement grade. Security-grade locks are activated by an exit device or other door hardware from the secure side of the door, releasing the door after 15 seconds. These locks are often used for exterior doors. Movement-grade locks are activated by the movement of the door, releasing the door after 15 seconds, and are often used for lobby or cross-corridor doors. Either type may be connected to an access control system.

- **Electromechanical locks** are electrically powered, motor- or solenoid-driven locks that can also be operated by a traditional key. Power is supplied through an electrified hinge or a door and frame transfer device. They are available in both mortise and cylindrical designs and can be either fail-secure or fail-safe.

- **Stand-alone electronic locks** are battery-powered, motor-driven, programmable electrified locks. They are available in both mortise and cylindrical designs and can be either fail-secure or fail-safe. Instead of traditional keys, they are controlled by card readers or keypads.

- **Deadbolts** have no spring action and must be manually operated. Deadbolts provide security, with hardened-steel inserts providing a higher level of security. The minimum throw of the bolt beyond the face of the lock should be 1 inch (25 mm). A deadbolt may be specified with certain functions of either mortise or preassembled locks, but cannot be used on required exit doors unless retractable with a single action, such as an interconnected lock. Because deadbolts are not self-latching, they cannot be used alone on labeled fire doors.

Lever-handle trims are the most commonly specified design for locksets because they are interpreted as complying with the Americans with Disabilities Act (ADA), *Accessibility Guidelines for Building and Facilities (ADAAG)* requirements and codes governing accessibility. Lever handles are available for bored, preassembled, and mortise locks. Lever designs are available in solid and tube construction; good-quality lever handles are solid forged brass, or cast bronze or stainless steel; lesser-quality handles are hollow or plastic filled. Two basic vandal-resistant designs developed to prevent damage to the lock mechanism and internal parts are freewheeling, with a clutch that releases if excessive force is applied, and breakaway, which breaks free with excessive force.

Lock function is a critical element when specifying locks, latches, and bolts. Manufacturers generally publish lock function charts, which should be consulted when selecting products.

DOOR BOLT SELECTION CONSIDERATIONS

Door bolts fall into one of two major categories: surface or flush, depending on their installation characteristics. The term bolt is often used to designate any device that fastens a door manually in a secure way.

Surface bolts are simpler to install than flush bolts since they require no mortising, but they provide less security from unauthorized manipulation.

Lever-operated extension flush bolts are widely used for fastening the inactive leaf of a pair of doors, since the flush installation permits its use in the door's edge, and its extension allows it to be conveniently located (fig. 10). Flush bolts are either self-latching or automatic, as described in this list:

- **Self-latching flush bolts** provide latching of the door and frame, and mount on the inactive leaf of a pair of doors. These bolts must be manually released. They are available for labeled fire doors, but they do not meet model code requirements for doors used as a means of egress. A coordinator is also required.
- **Automatic flush bolts** provide both self-latching and self-releasing action, and mount on the inactive leaf of pairs of doors. When used on labeled fire doors or standard pairs of doors, a coordinator is also required. If there is no other operating trim on the inactive leaf, automatic flush bolts are allowed by model codes for doors used as a means of egress.

EXTENSION FLUSH BOLT

Figure 10. Bolt mechanism

The specifier should select strikes suitable not only for the type of bolt involved but also for the conditions at the head and sill. The use of manually operated bolts to secure the inactive leaf of pairs of doors, where the inactive leaf is required as a part of the means of egress, is not allowed by model building codes.

EXIT DEVICE SELECTION CONSIDERATIONS

The primary purpose of exit devices is to protect life safety by providing free egress to occupants. Exit devices consist of a door-latching assembly that incorporates a mechanism that releases the latch when a force is applied in the direction of exit travel. When the latch is released by an actuating bar, this mechanism is called a *panic exit device* or a *fire exit device*. When the latch is released by a push pad or a push bar extending partway across the width of the door, the device is called an exit lock. Testing and listing of exit devices is performed by nationally recognized independent testing and inspecting agencies.

Panic exit devices are for use for a panic hazard (egress) and may be placed on any nonfire-rated door. Based on room occupancy and assembly type or classification, model codes require egress doors to be equipped with panic exit devices. A lockdown feature, called *dogging*, that keeps the bar depressed and latchbolts retracted is also available.

Fire exit devices are for use for a panic hazard (egress) and have also been tested for use on fire-rated doors. They should bear the supplemental label "Fire Exit Hardware" and be self-latching. The self-latching requirement keeps the door closed to prevent the spread of fire. Because fire exit devices must be constantly latched, they must not be able to be manually dogged, which is the ability to hold the latchbolt in the retracted position. However, fire exit devices are available in which the latchbolt is held back by using fail-safe electric latch retraction, which latches when the fire alarm system is activated.

Types of exit devices include rim, mortise, surface vertical rod, and concealed vertical rod, all available in BHMA Grades 1 and 2 (fig. 11). All types except mortise are available for narrow-stile entrance doors.

- **Rim exit devices** have the lock mechanism surface mounted to the door.
- **Mortise exit devices** have the lock mechanism recessed in a cavity in the edge of the door.
- **Vertical-rod exit devices** consist of bolts connected to an actuating bar or rod. The rods may be surface mounted or concealed within the door and may consist of top and bottom rods or top rods only. Because of their projection at the bottom of the door, surface-mounted bottom rods may create obstacles for people with disabilities.

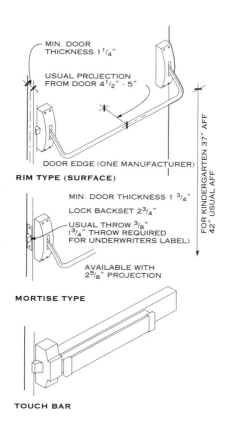

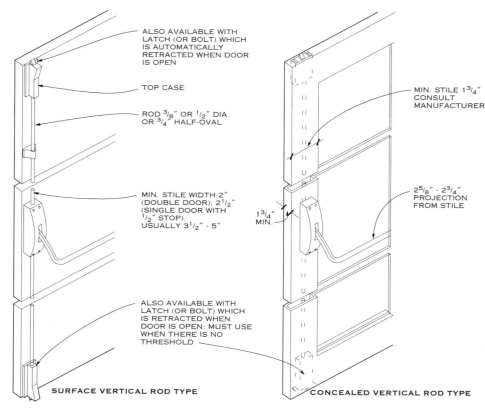

Figure 11. Exit devices

Specifications should indicate the type of actuating bar and desired function, as well as the type of exit device. Table 3 is from ANSI/BHMA A156.3-1994 Standard for Exit Devices, which can be obtained by contacting Builders Hardware Manufacturers Association; 355 Lexington Avenue; New York, NY 10017. A Directory of Exit Devices that certify to this standard can also be obtained by contacting BHMA.

Table 3
EXIT DEVICE FUNCTIONS

BHMA Number	Function Description
01	Exit only, no trim.
02	Entrance by trim when actuating bar is locked down.
03	Entrance by trim when latchbolt is retracted by key. Key removable only when locked.
04	Entrance by trim when latchbolt is retracted by key or set in a retracted position by key.
05	Entrance by thumb piece. Key locks or unlocks thumb piece.
06	Entrance by thumb piece only when released by key. Key removable only when locked.
07	Entrance by thumb piece. Inside key locks or unlocks thumb piece. Outside key retracts latch.
08	Entrance by knob or lever. Key locks or unlocks knob or lever.
09	Entrance by knob or lever only when released by key. Key removable only when locked.
10	Entrance by knob or lever. Inside key locks or unlocks knob or lever. Outside key retracts latch.
11	Entrance by control turn piece. Key locks or unlocks control.
12	Entrance by control turn piece only when released by turning key. Key removable only when locked.
13	Entrance by key or combination lock.

To prevent loss of goods or unwanted use of a door, NFPA 101, published by the National Fire Protection Association (NFPA), now allows exit door hardware with built-in delayed release and internal alarms. These devices allow immediate use of the door if a fire alarm or smoke detector goes off or if power fails, but otherwise sound an alarm and keep the door locked for 15 seconds. The alarm can be turned off temporarily to permit authorized use of the door without sounding the alarm.

CYLINDER AND KEYING SELECTION CONSIDERATIONS

Cylinders contain a tumbler mechanism and a keyway into which a key is inserted to actuate the locking mechanism. Most cylinders contain five, six, or seven pins, although some cylinders have no pins and are designed to receive special electronic keys. High-security cylinders are not available with five pins. Cylinders consist of a housing and a core. Both of these components are available as either interchangeable or removable. *Interchangeable* means that one manufacturer's component will fit into another manufacturer's lock. *Removable* means that a manufacturer's component will fit only into its own lock. Interchangeable and removable cores are removed by a special change key. Interchangeable cores are available from most manufacturers in bored, mortise, deadbolt-type, and auxiliary locks. Many institutional facilities have standardized on the interchangeable-core cylinder because it allows the quick changing of cylinder combinations and helps maintain security and key control.

Construction keying may be advisable. On major projects, it is a recommended practice to specify locks with either construction master-keyed or construction-core cylinders to ensure the security of the final key system. Both of these construction key systems limit the contractor to keys that will function only during the construction period. In most cases, construction keying adds cost to the cylinder and requires additional installation time.

- **Locks with construction master-keyed cylinders** are installed by the contractor. Locks are operable by construction keys until permanent keys are inserted or a partial key is removed, deactivating construction keys.
- **Locks with construction-core cylinders** have a color-coded core inserted into the housing; they are a more secure method for interchangeable-core cylinders. Construction cores are operable only with construction keys and are removed with a special control key. Permanent cores are then installed to activate the owner's permanent keys.

Master keying systems may be necessary. All commercial cylinders are available with additional pins for master keying and grand master keying. The complexity of the level of keying does not generally affect the overall first cost, but it does make a significant difference in the degree of control and security attained. A master key will open several keyed-different doors. The grand master key will open several different master-keyed doors. The larger the number of keys, master keys, and grand master keys passing one door, the lesser the degree of security; moreover, maintenance will become a problem. Most manufacturers offer restricted keyway sections to negate the easy duplication of master and grand master keys. DHI's *Keying Systems and Nomenclature* is an excellent handbook to further explain the concept of master keying.

High-security cylinders are becoming more prevalent due to the increasing concern over key duplication. These cylinders are available in both standard cylinder and removable core. Some high-security cylinders are tested according to Underwriters Laboratories' (UL's) standard for safety UL 437 and are UL listed. UL 437 includes tests for pick resistance, drill resistance, and other physical properties.

Each manufacturer's particular high-security cylinder design is proprietary, and it is impossible to add on to an existing key system with another manufacturer's high-security cylinder. For the manufacturer to ensure the high-security features, some inflexibilities become apparent. Keys may not be readily available and cannot be locally duplicated. It may take more time to replace a key, and the originating manufacturer must provide any addition to an existing key system. Owners have been able to justify the use and additional cost of high-security cylinders by the security and control realized from keys not easily duplicated.

The simpler the design of the keying system, the better it will perform from the standpoint of security and maintenance. The owner and an AHC should always be involved in the selection and design of a project's keying system.

Key control systems are classified as either single-tag or double-tag systems. Single-tag systems consist of a single numerically numbered tag for each key. This system is economical and provides a reasonable level of security. Double-tag systems provide a higher level of security than single-tag systems. They consist of a permanent key, which remains in the key control cabinet, and a temporary key, which is loaned, each with a numerically numbered tag. The permanent key is used only to make duplicate keys.

STRIKE SELECTION CONSIDERATIONS

Lock strikes consist of a metal plate mortised into the jamb of the frame to receive and to hold the projected latchbolt or deadbolt. A strike box, also called a wrought box, installed in back of the strike protects the latchbolt hole from the intrusion of plaster or other foreign material that would prevent the bolt from projecting properly into the strike. BHMA standards covering installation dimensions for locks include dimensions for strikes, and establish uniformity in frame preparation.

Dustproof strikes have a spring-actuated plunger that protects the opening receiving the bolt, thereby keeping out dirt. Locking types are useful for preventing spiked heels from entering the opening. Dustproof strikes are typically used with flush bolts.

Electric strikes are electrified versions of lock strikes that electronically release the strike keeper. They can be rim mounted, semi-rim mounted, mortised in the jamb of the frame, or mortised into the edge of one door of a pair of doors. Because of testing requirements, an electric strike used with an exit device on a pair of labeled fire doors should be recommended by the manufacturers of both door hardware products. When used with a fire exit device, both devices must be tested and listed together and should be recommended by the manufacturers for use as a system. Electric strikes are available as fail-secure and fail-safe. Electric strikes used with fire-rated devices must be nonfail-safe (fail-secure) to ensure that the door latches during a fire.

Monitor strikes are lock strikes that monitor the position of the latch or bolt. The two types are cast strikes with an internal toggle, and dustbox strikes installed under a standard strike. Dustbox strikes cost significantly less than cast strikes. A secondary use of monitor strikes is to initiate delayed egress when an interior latch is withdrawn on doors with delayed-egress locks.

OPERATING TRIM SELECTION CONSIDERATIONS

Operating trim consists of push plates, door pulls, push and pull bars, and push-pull units.

- **Push plates** are surface applied to doors, located where users push to open them. Push plates are available in aluminum, stainless steel, brass, plastic laminate, and rigid plastic.
- **Door pulls** are applied to the face of doors, enabling users to pull open doors. They can be surface applied, through bolted, or mounted back to back. Door pulls may be straight, offset, flush, or drop-ring type. They are available in aluminum, stainless steel, brass, plastic, wood, stone, and ceramics.
- **Push and pull bars** are available in almost any orientation on a door. As their names imply, push bars are used for pushing doors open, and pull bars are used for pulling doors open. They can be surface applied, through bolted, or mounted back to back. Push and pull bars may be a single straight bar, two straight bars, or a combination of joined horizontal and vertical bars. Custom designs are also possible. They are available in aluminum, stainless steel, brass, plastic, wood, stone, and ceramics.
- **Push-pull units** are nonlatching devices that are surface applied to doors to provide both pushing and pulling operation.

Operating trim, because of its prime visual exposure, is frequently given considerable attention by the designer and may be custom designed. Concealment of fasteners and secure attachment to prevent unauthorized removal and loosening are important considerations. Because of constant use, door pulls and push plates should be constructed of suitable materials and properly fastened to the door. Finishes are also critical, with integral finishes more durable than painted or even plated finishes.

CONSIDERATIONS IN SELECTION OF ACCESSORIES FOR PAIRS OF DOORS

Coordinators are used with pairs of doors where the inactive leaf must close and latch first. The pair of doors may or may not have overlapping astragals. The type of inactive-leaf bolts or exit devices determines whether the door will require a coordinator to function or will meet code requirements if fire-rated. An overlapping astragal must not be specified when two vertical-rod exit devices are used on a pair of doors.

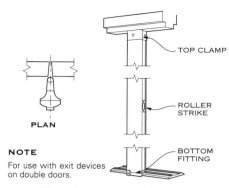

Figure 12. Removable mullion

NOTE
For use with exit devices on double doors.

PLAN

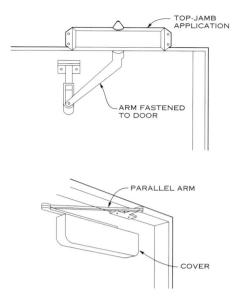

Figure 13. Closers—surface mounted

Removable and fixed mullions provide single-door performance (both leaves active) in double-door openings (fig. 12). They are available in steel and aluminum. Steel mullions are required on labeled pairs of fire doors. Removable and fixed mullions are most often used with rim-type exit devices. Removable mullions are also available with a key-locking feature, which prevents unauthorized removal.

Astragals are used to limit the passage of light, sound, smoke, and fire at the meeting stile of pairs of doors. For doors fire-rated more than 1½ hours, astragals are required by NFPA 80. Other labeled fire-rated doors may or may not require astragals to obtain their rating, depending on how they are tested. For pairs of doors used as a means of egress, most codes do not allow astragals that depend on the opening of one door before the other. This requires split astragals rather than overlapping astragals. Astragals required for a door listing are usually specified with the doors rather than in the door hardware section. Typically, only astragals controlling light and sound are specified in the door hardware section.

DOOR CLOSER SELECTION CONSIDERATIONS

Door closers, when properly installed and adjusted, control doors throughout the opening and closing swings by combining three basic components: (1) a power source to close the door (spring), (2) a checking source to control the rate at which the door closes (hydraulic mechanism), and (3) a connecting component (arm) to transmit the closing force from the frame to the door. The closing speed is controlled by an adjustable valve or valves that control the rate of fluid flow. Door closers are available in three types: surface, overhead concealed in door or frame, and floor concealed, as described in this list:

- **Surface closers** are available in traditional, modern-with-no-cover, and modern-with-cover types (fig. 13). Mounting options include regular arm (closer mounted on the door on its pull side), parallel arm (closer mounted on the door on its push side), and top jamb (closer mounted on frame at head on push side of the door). For top jamb mounting, the frame height should be verified to determine whether a drop bracket is required.
- **Overhead concealed closers** can be mounted in the top of the door or in the head of the frame (fig. 14). For frame-mounted closers, the operating arm can be either exposed or concealed. Concealed arms are connected to a track in the top of the door. Center-pivoted closers for double-acting doors are available concealed in the frame head with pivots furnished as part of the closer. Closers concealed in the top rail of wood doors require precise mortising and blocking in the door and, even then, may cause the veneer to bow. Coordination is important for overhead concealed closers. The height and width of the head frame must

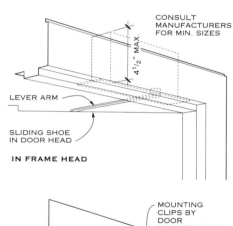

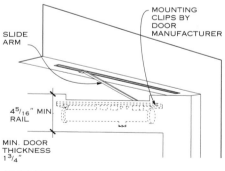

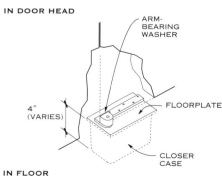

Figure 14. Concealed closers

be large enough to accommodate the closer. Further, if an overhead lock, stop, or holder is required, available space should be verified to accommodate both door hardware items.

- **Floor concealed closers** are recessed into the floor and are available in deep- and narrow-recess versions to accommodate the varying thicknesses of floor slabs (fig. 14). Floor closers are available as single-acting and double-acting for center- and offset-pivoted installations. Floor-concealed closers require the use of floor plates, thresholds, or finish floor materials extending over the closer mechanism. Spindle heights are adjustable to accommodate door undercut and the various thicknesses of finish floor materials. Floor closers are most often specified for aesthetic reasons, on special glass doors, or to carry the weight of heavy doors.

Optional closer features available include adjustable closing speed and hydraulic backcheck, delayed-action closing, and many hold-open functions. The trend in the industry is to specify door closers that are size-adjustable rather than size-specific. The purpose of this is to allow the adjustment of the opening force to meet the variety of opening conditions, such as door weight, accessibility, fire rating, and latching force. The field adjustment of size-adjustable closers is imperative or the door will not function properly.

Hold-open and stop-type arms in a parallel mounting (push side) are available from most manufacturers. Closers should not be used in lieu of door stops to stop doors, unless the hold-open or stop-type arm is specified. This also assumes that backcheck, the control of the door in the opening cycle, is also specified. Model codes do not permit the hold-open feature for fire doors unless electrified and connected to a fire alarm system.

Closer selection depends on the these factors: size and thickness of the door (size of closer and mounting), whether the door is an interior or exterior application, the desired appearance (surface or concealed), the degree of door opening, the function of the closer arm (regular, hold open, positive stop, fusible link, extra-duty, double-egress, swing-free), and special conditions (such as how doors are hung). Floor closers on exterior doors are subject to ice and snow, and should have appropriate cold-resistant seals, hydraulic fluid, and so on.

Electromechanical, electrohydraulic, and pneumatic power-assisted closers are also available to help open doors in both surface and concealed mountings.

PROTECTIVE TRIM UNIT SELECTION CONSIDERATIONS

Protection plates include kick, mop, armor, and stretcher plates and door edge guards. Kick plates (push side) and mop plates (pull side) protect the door from damage by shoes, carts, and cleaning equipment. Armor and stretcher plates and door edge guards protect the door from damage caused by rolling equipment such as food carts and hospital stretchers. Metal plates should be beveled stainless steel, brass, or bronze, and be at least 0.050-inch (1.3-mm) thick. Acrylic, high-impact polyethylene, and laminated plastic at least ⅛-inch (3.2-mm) thick are frequently used.

- **Armor plates** protect the lower half of doors subject to carts, trucks, or rough usage. They are usually applied to the push side of single-acting doors and to both sides of double-acting doors. Standard heights are 36, 40, and 42 inches (914, 1016, and 1067 mm).

- **Kick plates** protect the bottom of the push side of doors subject to foot traffic. Standard heights are 8, 10, and 12 inches (203, 254, and 305 mm).
- **Mop plates** protect the bottom of the pull side of doors that are subject to abuse during floor cleaning. Standard heights are 4 and 6 inches (102 and 152 mm).
- **Stretcher plates** protect doors at specific areas where consistent contact is made by stretchers, service carts, or other equipment. These plates are not designated in BHMA A156.6. Standard heights are 6 and 8 inches (152 and 203 mm). Mounting height depends on the use.

Doors subjected to high abuse, particularly in hospitals and nursing homes, require special considerations when specifying kick, mop, and armor plates and door edging. Exercise care to notch these plates around locksets, deadbolts, bottom rods of exit devices, and door lights and louvers that may conflict. Alternatively, some manufacturers offer protective trim that covers the bottom rod of exit devices. NFPA 80 restricts the maximum height for a kick plate on a labeled fire door to 16 inches (406 mm) above the bottom of the door, unless otherwise listed and labeled.

STOP AND HOLDER SELECTION CONSIDERATIONS

Floor stops are available in varied heights, sizes, and shapes, and for varied functions. They may include a device to hold the door. Door clearances from finished floor, shape of stop, and location in relation to traffic are important considerations. The incorrect location of floor stops can present a tripping hazard (fig. 15).

Wall stops do not constitute a traffic hazard and are located to receive the impact of a knob, pull, or other door hardware. Where stops and bumpers are installed on gypsum wallboard, they should be attached directly to the supporting framing or blocking installed for this purpose. Wall stops are available with hold-open mechanisms. Door-coordinating, roller-type stops should be used where the swinging of two doors through the same area may cause damage to either door.

Floor holders commonly used are the spring-loaded "step-on" type and the lever or "flip-down" type. Neither type acts as a door stop.

Overhead stops and holders may be either concealed or surface mounted. They are available in a variety of optional functions that hold the door at any point up to 110 degrees; these functions include hold-open, built-in hold-open, nonhold-open, and friction hold-open. Where overhead stops and holders are scheduled for doors with overhead closers, verify that the arm and track are not in conflict. Overhead stops and holders may be the only way to stop and control certain doors. Table 4 lists overhead stops and holders by BHMA type.

Electromagnetic holders are used to hold doors open, most commonly fire doors, equipped with self-closing and -latching devices. They are typically connected to the fire alarm system. When the current is cut off, doors close under the control of the closing device. Doors may be released by a manual fire alarm pull, an electric switch, or by smoke and heat detectors. Electromagnetic holders connected to a detection system and using standard fire door hardware may be less of a maintenance problem than the more complicated electromechanical closer-holder detector units. The projection of the holder should exceed the projection of the lock trim so the trim does not impact the wall.

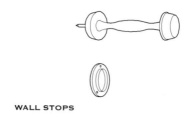

WALL STOPS

FLOOR STOPS

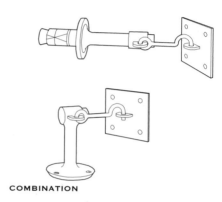

COMBINATION

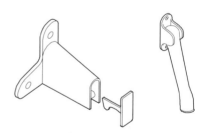

LEVER-TYPE HOLDERS

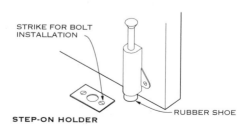

STRIKE FOR BOLT INSTALLATION

RUBBER SHOE

STEP-ON HOLDER

Figure 15. Stops and holders

Table 4
OVERHEAD STOPS AND HOLDERS

BHMA Type	Exterior Doors	Interior Doors
Type 1, Overhead Concealed Slide Holder	•	•
Type 1, Overhead Concealed Slide Stop	•	•
Type 2, Overhead Surface-Mounted Slide Holder	•	•
Type 2, Overhead Surface-Mounted Concealed Slide Stop	•	•
Type 3, Overhead Surface-Mounted Jointed-Arm Holder	•	•
Type 3, Overhead Surface-Mounted Jointed-Arm Stop	•	•
Type 4, Overhead Concealed Friction Slide Holder		•
Type 4, Overhead Concealed Nonfriction Slide Stop		•
Type 4, Overhead Concealed Nonfriction Slide Holder		•
Type 5, Overhead Surface-Mounted Friction Slide Holder		•
Type 5, Overhead Surface-Mounted Nonfriction Slide Stop		•
Type 5, Overhead Surface-Mounted Nonfriction Slide Holder		•
Type 8, Overhead Surface-Mounted Rod Holder	•	•
Type 8, Overhead Surface-Mounted Rod Stop	•	•
Type 9, Overhead Surface-Mounted Jointed-Arm Holder	•	•
Type 9, Overhead Surface-Mounted Cantilever Holder	•	•
Type 9, Overhead Surface-Mounted Cantilever Stop	•	•

DOOR GASKETING SELECTION CONSIDERATIONS

Door gasketing is the new preferred term for weather stripping and seals. It reduces the clearances around a door to decrease the passage of air, smoke, sound, light, or water. It is installed integrally during the manufacturing process of the door or is applied to the door or frame in the field. BHMA standards classify gasketing by location, including perimeter, meeting stile, and bottom of the door.

Gasketing materials include brush, solid neoprene, expanded neoprene, vinyl, silicone rubber, pile, thermoplastic elastomer, thermoplastic urethane, thermoplastic rubber, spring metal, felt, and rubber fabric. For colder climates, silicone rubber stays flexible in temperatures as low as -30°F (-34°C);thermoplastic elastomer stays flexible in temperatures as low as -70°F (-57°C). Housing materials include brass, bronze, aluminum, and stainless steel. Manufacturers' catalogs should be checked before specifying any product.

Perimeter gasketing is applied to the head and jamb of door frames or to the top rail and stiles of doors (fig. 16). It consists of fixed or adjustable materials, typically applied to the frame stop. Materials can be resilient, such as rubber, vinyl, or neoprene, or nonresilient, such as spring metal. Some types are enclosed in a housing or flange.

Meeting stile gasketing is applied to one or both meeting stiles of a pair of doors (fig. 17). It is surface mounted on the meeting edges of doors, or semimortised or mortised into the lock edges of doors. Intumescent products expand to fill the gap between doors in case of fire.

Door bottom gasketing consists of door sweeps and automatic door bottoms (fig. 18). Door sweeps can be surface applied to the bottom face of doors or mounted on the bottom edge of doors. Automatic door bottoms can be surface mounted to the face of doors, or semimortised or mortised to the bottom edge of doors. To be effective, a threshold should be used with door bottoms.

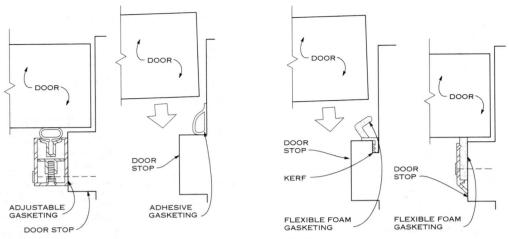

Figure 16. Perimeter gasketing

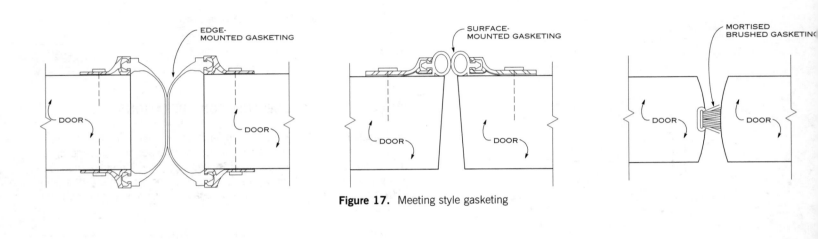

Figure 17. Meeting style gasketing

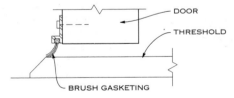

Figure 18. Door bottom gasketing

THRESHOLD SELECTION CONSIDERATIONS

Thresholds are horizontal members installed at the sills of doors (fig. 19). They are available in many shapes and sizes to meet almost any condition. Extruded brass, extruded bronze, and aluminum are typical materials.

Threshold configurations include compressing top, flat or half saddle, interlocking, latching/rabbeted, plate, ramped, and saddle for floor closer. They come in fluted, smooth, and abrasive surface finishes. Some types are designed to comply with requirements for accessibility by people with disabilities (fig. 20).

Thresholds for floor closers require that information about the closer be specified, including closer model number and manufacturer; door opening width between jambs; dimension of offset, if any; door thickness; whether for a single door or a pair of doors and whether single- or double-acting; hand of doors; width and height of threshold; and floor offset and location at the door (fig. 21).

Installation conditions may require different fasteners. The standard fasteners used by most manufacturers are wood screws, therefore, other fasteners such as sheet metal screws or machine screws, should be indicated in the specifications or on the drawings. Also, the standard expansion anchors used by most manufacturers are made from fiber or plastic; if lead or steel anchors are required, they should also be indicated (fig. 22).

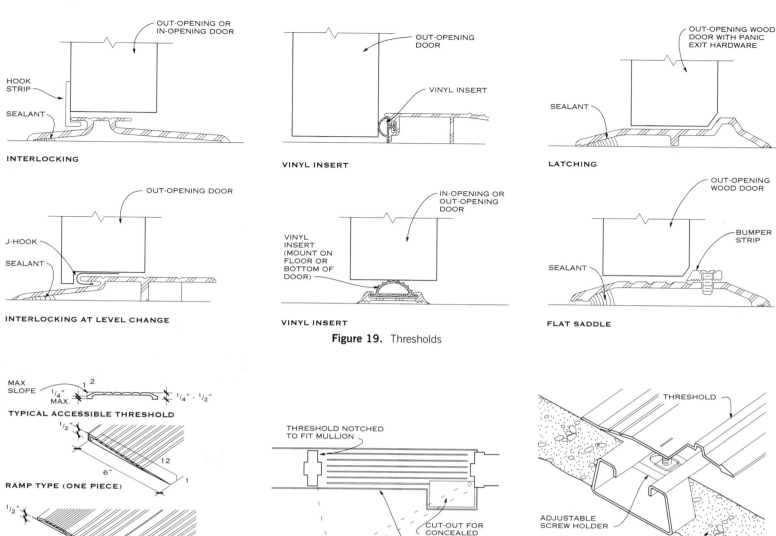

Figure 19. Thresholds

NOTE

Level changes at thresholds up to $^1/_4$ in. (6 mm) may be vertical, without edge treatment. Level changes between $^1/_4$ and $^1/_2$ in. shall be beveled with a slope no greater than 1:2. Abrasive finish recommended for threshold surface. Consult manufacturer for other threshold profiles and textures. ADAAG limits new thresholds to $^1/_2$ in. maximum height except at exterior sliding doors ($^3/_4$ in. maximum

Figure 20. Accessible threshold

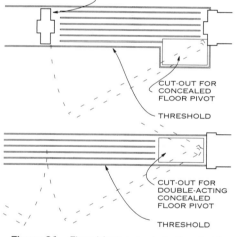

Figure 21. Floor hinge cutouts in threshold

CHANNEL ANCHORAGE IN CONCRETE

NOTES

1. For channel-type threshold anchors, exact location is required at time concrete floor is poured.

2. For installation on wood floors, use wood screws; for masonry floors, use no less than a #10 machine screw and double-cinch anchors for best results. In descending order of holding power, the following may be satisfactory, depending on frequency of use: machine screws with lead anchors, wood screws with lead expansion shields, wood screws with plastic anchors.

Figure 22. Threshold anchorage

SLIDING DOOR HARDWARE SELECTION CONSIDERATIONS

Sliding doors are classified into standard sliding doors, heavy sliding doors, bypassing sliding doors, and pocket sliding doors. BHMA A156.14 defines heavy sliding doors as those weighing more than 240 lb (109 kg).

Standard and heavy sliding doors are typically supported by a wheeled carriage assembly traveling in a wrought-steel box track, or rail, attached to the structure with wrought-steel hangers.

Bypassing sliding doors are supported by wrought-steel or aluminum rails, with or without an integral fascia. BHMA Grades 1 and 2 hangers are available. Grade 1 hangers are rated for doors weighing up to 80 or 120 lb (36 or 54 kg), depending on the configuration. Grade 2 hangers are rated for doors weighing up to 40 lb (18 kg). Grade 1 rails are rated for doors weighing up to 80 lb (36 kg); Grade 2, for doors weighing up to 40 lb (18 kg).

Pocket sliding doors may be either single door or biparting doors. Rails are wrought steel or aluminum, and both are available in BHMA Grades 1 and 2. For single doors, Grade 1 rails support doors weighing up to 120 lb (54 kg); Grade 2 rails support doors weighing up to 60 lb (27 kg). For biparting doors, Grade 1 rails support doors weighing up to 120 lb (54 kg); Grade 2 rails support doors weighing up to 60 lb (27 kg). Pocket doors required to be accessible by people with disabilities usually require slightly different door hardware. These installations should accommodate the need for pulls to remain accessible when the door is open (in the pocket), which may result in a longer track, a door stop on the track, and possibly even a different type of pull.

FOLDING DOOR HARDWARE SELECTION CONSIDERATIONS

Folding doors are classified into bifolding doors and multiple folding doors. Bifolding doors consist of two leaves; a jamb door, and a lead door. Multiple folding doors consist of more than two door leaves.

Folding door rails are either wrought steel or aluminum. Bifolding door rails are available in BHMA Grades 1, 2, and 3; multiple folding door rails are available only in Grades 1 and 2. Grade 1 supports doors of 50 lb (23 kg), Grade 2 supports doors of 30 lb (14 kg), and Grade 3 supports doors of 20 lb (9 kg).

MISCELLANEOUS DOOR HARDWARE SELECTION CONSIDERATIONS

Miscellaneous door hardware, also called *auxiliary door hardware*, includes numerous items: door guards, door stops and holders, door knockers, door silencers, door viewers, coat and garment hooks, roller latches, door bolts, house numbers, and letterbox plates. They are available in several materials and finishes.

FIRE DOOR HARDWARE SELECTION CONSIDERATIONS

The most difficult door hardware applications are egress and fire doors. The model building codes, along with NFPA 80, *Fire Doors and Windows,* and NFPA 101, *Life Safety Code,* are the textbook references for door hardware requirements involving these types of doors. The situation is further complicated by interpretations made by local authorities having jurisdiction. The frame, door, and door hardware must be tested as an assembly to be included on the building material lists of the approved inspecting and testing agencies. Field modification of doors and door hardware will void the label provided by manufacturers for these assemblies, unless performed by someone authorized by the manufacturer to make these modifications.

- **Smoke gasketing** is required by codes for labeled doors in one-hour-rated partitions and smoke barriers. In some jurisdictions, 20-minute-rated doors are considered smoke doors, which must have jamb and head smoke gasketing. Smoke gasketing is not the same as gasketing required for labeled fire doors. Smoke gasketing systems typically include jamb and head gasketing; an automatic door bottom, door sweep, or door shoe; and a threshold. Some types of gasketing, because of inadequate clearances between doors and frames or unbeveled vertical door edges, could cause doors to bind and not function correctly. An astragal is usually required for pairs of doors, as discussed elsewhere in this chapter.
- **Automatic latching devices** engaging the strike must also be provided for swinging fire doors, to ensure that the door remains closed during a fire.
- **A closing device,** such as a closer or spring hinges, must be provided for fire doors. These devices ensure that the door is closed during a fire, preventing spread of the fire.

Surface-mounted door hardware, such as exit devices and closers, require testing as part of the new UL 10C for positive-pressure testing of fire-rated doors.

METAL AND FINISH SELECTION CONSIDERATIONS

Except for a few instances where plastic, wood, and ceramic are used, door hardware is made of metal. Selection of the base metal and finish depends on such factors as use, exposure to elements, and appearance desired. The door hardware in a room should also harmonize in design and finish. Specifying BHMA finish numbers will ensure that the base metal and finish appearance are consistent for door hardware components.

Base metals used in door hardware are brass, bronze, iron, steel, stainless steel, aluminum, and zinc, as described in the following list

- **Brass and bronze** are copper alloys, the greatest portion being copper with smaller amounts of other metals such as lead and zinc. While, technically, a true bronze is a copper alloy that differs from brass in that bronze contains some tin, the term bronze is often used architecturally to describe color rather than element content. Differences in color result from the proportions of the various metals included. Brass and bronze hinges are used in humid environments.
- **Steel** is widely used in butt hinges. Ordinary carbon steel used in door hardware contains not only iron but also portions of other elements such as carbon, manganese, phosphorus, and sulfur. Exposed to the weather, uncoated or unplated carbon steel will rust. Steel's advantage is its strength and low cost.
- **Stainless steel** is a ferrous-metal product that contains a substantial amount of chromium and small quantities of a number of other elements, including nickel. Because it is highly rust-resistant, scratch-resistant, and is easy to maintain, stainless steel is a popular door hardware material. The specifier should note, however, that some imported door hardware products are made with stainless-steel alloys that are less rust-resistant than alloys used by domestic manufacturers.
- **Aluminum** is alloyed with about 4 percent of other elements. Cast, forged, and wrought products are obtained by much the same processes as are other metals. Aluminum is softer and less scratch-resistant than other door hardware metals and is not popular as a door hardware metal. It is used for door closer bodies.
- **Zinc** has long been used in door hardware. As a coating over iron and steel, it resists rust. Many products are made using die-cast zinc as a base metal. Zinc is easily cast, machined, and plated, and it weighs less than other metals and is being supplied on bored, lever-handle locks. Certain plated finishes can wear off to expose the zinc.

The base metals described in the preceding list may be cast, extruded, forged, machined, or wrought, as described here:

- **Cast metal** is produced by pouring or forcing molten alloy into premolded forms. This method results in shapes that can be machined, etched, or carved to yield a variety of designs.
- **Extruded shapes** are produced by forcing or drawing semimolten metal through dies. Designs having linear characteristics are possible. Extruded materials are limited to aluminum and copper alloys, including brass and bronze.
- **Forged metal** is hammered, pressed, or rolled into shape. A smooth, dense product results from this process, the value of which relates to the thickness of the metal. Forged metal is better able to distribute stresses and is stronger than cast or wrought metal.
- **Wrought metal** is rolled into flat sheets or strips. Products are formed by punching or die-cutting the metal into desired forms that may be thick, as in a hinge, or thin, as in a push plate.

Natural finishes take the color of the base metal in the product, and may be either bright or satin. A satin finish is one of low luster. A protective clear coating can be applied to the base metal by an electrostatic process and heat. The preparation given base metals before finishing may consist of cleaning, machining, buffing, and polishing to produce the finished luster. Door hardware finishes vary a great deal in appearance, cost, durability, and availability, as described in the following list:

- **Bright finishes of natural brass and bronze** are produced by buffing the natural metal to a high gloss before applying a clear coating. Satin brass and bronze finishes are obtained by dry buffing or scouring the natural metal and by applying a coating. The coating will break down through use and exposure to the atmosphere, and the finish will discolor. The original finish can be restored by polishing and recoating.

- **Uncoated finishes of brass or bronze** are used where natural oxidation of the entire exposed surface yields the desired result. Factory-oxidized finishes are also available. Oil rubbing of uncoated bronze produces a dark-oxidized finish suitable for some decor. However, oil-rubbed finishes are unstable and difficult to match. This instability is typically seen as bright spots where people have repeatedly handled the door hardware, resulting in a change of appearance.

- **Stainless steel,** unlike brass and bronze, requires no coating because it does not oxidize. Bright finishes are produced by buffing the natural metal to a high gloss. Satin finishes are produced by polishing and then scouring the surface. Both finishes are durable and maintenance-free.

- **Plated finishes** are often used. The most popular are bright chromium and satin chromium. Brass, bronze, chrome, and nickel plating of door hardware is usually applied by an electrolytic process. Oxidizing is also used, especially where designs are ornamental. Finishes on steel hinges can be plated to match other door hardware. A preservative coating may also be applied.

- **Coatings** are used to prevent tarnishing or oxidation of natural and plated brass and bronze finishes. The original color and brightness of the finish can be maintained for an extended period.

- **Anodizing** forms a protective and uniform oxide on aluminum, giving it a hard, tough skin. Several color-anodized finishes, such as black and bronze, are available. Anodic finishes scratch or wear off when subjected to normal door hardware uses.

Finish Standards

The National Institute of Standards and Technology (NIST) was the first to develop standards for finishes used for door hardware. These are generally referred to as United States Standards (e.g., US10B, US26D, etc.). These designations are still used by some manufacturers. More recently, BHMA developed a more complete description of door hardware finish standards. BHMA A156.18, *Materials and Finishes,* gives details of finishes, along with the closest U.S. Standard number equivalent. BHMA A156.18 takes into account the base metal on which the finish is applied, whereas the U.S. Standard does not. BHMA A156.18 also provides appearance equivalents for various base metals.

For example, the BHMA finish number for steel with satin chrome finish is 652; the finish number for the same appearance but with brass base metal is 626. However, in both cases, the U.S. Standard finish number is US26D. Additional appearance equivalents include plated base metals of stainless steel (654), zinc (682), and aluminum (702 and 713). Table 5, excerpted from BHMA A156.18, lists some popular finishes.

Matching the finishes of door hardware to other components of a project may also be required. One method to ensure a close match is to specify the actual metal alloy number to be provided for plated finishes, for example, unified numbering system (UNS) No. C32000 for brass (leaded red brass). This method is more costly than using manufacturer's standard finishes, and may not be available for some types of door hardware. Further, even if the metal alloy of a plated finish matches, if the underlying base metal is not the same, the finished appearance will be slightly different. Whether matching finishes or just referencing BHMA finish numbers, the specifier should verify the actual finish by requesting samples from manufacturers. Matchplate samples for some finishes are also available from BHMA.

Table 5
FINISHES

Description	BHMA Base Metal	BHMA Code	U.S. Standard Number
Primed for painting	Steel	600	P
Bright brass plated, clear coated	Brass	605	3
Satin brass, clear coated	Brass	606	4
Satin brass, blackened, satin relieved, clear coated	Brass	609	5
Bright bronze, clear coated	Bronze	611	9
Satin bronze, clear coated	Bronze	612	10
Oxidized satin bronze, oil rubbed	Bronze	613	10B
Bright nickel plated, clear coated	Brass, bronze	618	14
Satin nickel plated, clear coated	Brass, bronze	619	15
Flat black coated	Brass, bronze	622	19
Light oxidized statuary bronze, clear coated	Bronze	623	20
Dark oxidized statuary bronze, clear coated	Bronze	624	20A
Bright chromium plated over nickel	Brass, bronze	625	26
Satin chromium plated over nickel	Brass, bronze	626	26D
Satin aluminum, clear coated	Aluminum	627	27
Satin aluminum, clear anodized	Aluminum	628	28
Bright stainless steel	Stainless steel	629	32
Satin stainless steel	Stainless steel	630	32D
Bright chromium plated over nickel	Steel	651	26
Satin chromium plated over nickel	Steel	652	26D
Aluminum painted	Any	689	28
Dark bronze painted	Any	690	20
Light bronze painted	Any	691	10
Bright aluminum, uncoated	Aluminum	717	26
Satin aluminum, uncoated	Aluminum	718	27
Dark oxidized bronze, oil rubbed	Architectural bronze	722	10A

ENERGY CONSIDERATIONS

Selection of the proper type and quality of gasketing materials for exterior door openings can have a significant effect on energy savings for any building. The seal should be continuous around the entire perimeter of the door. High-quality closers should also be used on exterior doors to ensure that no door is inadvertently left open.

Thresholds with thermal breaks should be considered for extremely adverse weather conditions. Avoid creating conditions that interfere with the operation of other door hardware. Do not overlook difficulties that people with disabilities might encounter when using the door. Ramped thresholds are useful for these applications. Door gasketing must also be coordinated with door and frame types, since benefits gained through using quality gasketing can be lost if the door does not have similar thermal performance capabilities.

COORDINATING DOOR HARDWARE SCHEDULE WITH DRAWINGS

When using a door hardware schedule, every door in the project should be referenced to its unique door hardware requirements. Several methods can be used to do this; however, only one method should be used on any given project, to avoid errors. Choose from these methods:

- List doors with their corresponding door hardware set in the door hardware schedule in the specifications, but do not include the door hardware set number in the door and frame schedule or on the drawings. This method can be difficult on large projects with many doors.
- Note the door hardware set numbers in the door and frame schedule, but do not list doors and door hardware sets in the specifications or on the drawings.
- Note the door hardware set numbers on the drawings at each opening, but do not list doors and door hardware sets in the specifications or in the door and frame schedule.

The examples that appear later in this chapter assume that door hardware set numbers will be included in the door and frame schedule or on the drawings. The door hardware schedule can be placed in the specifications at the end of the door hardware section, or on the drawings. Do not include schedules or duplicate any of the schedule information on both the drawings and specifications.

SAMPLE DOOR HARDWARE SCHEDULES

The following are three examples of a completed schedule that may be adapted to specify door hardware set requirements. The examples contain the kind of data that would be inserted, and the order in which it should be listed, as recommended by DHI. The specifier must insert appropriate product requirements in the door hardware schedule for each door hardware set required for the project.

- Example 1 names manufacturers' products, using model numbers. Fictitious manufacturers are identified.
- Example 2 references BHMA standards and designations, except where no BHMA standard applies and a fictitious manufacturer and model number are named.
- Example 3 uses the descriptive title specified in the door hardware specification section.

Products of fictitious manufacturers are included in the samples solely to demonstrate how to specify names of products and manufacturers.

DOOR HARDWARE SCHEDULE
(Example 1: Naming Manufacturers' Products)

Hardware Set 1

3	Hinges	TB2714	XYZ Hardware Co.	626
1	Lockset	8205 LNL	ABC Hardware Co.	626
1	Closer	4011 - Regular - Alum	LMN Hardware Co.	689
1	Kick Plate	#48 - 10 x 2 inches L.D.W.		
		(254 x 51 mm L.D.W.)	QRS Hardware Co.	630
1	Wall Stop	407	IJK Hardware Co.	626
1	Set Smoke Seal	5050	NOP Hardware Co.	

Hardware Set 2

1	Electric Hinge	T4B3386 MM x NRP	XYZ Hardware Co.	626
1	Electric Hinge	T4B3386 CC x NRP	XYZ Hardware Co.	626
1	Hinge	T4B3386 x NRP	XYZ Hardware Co.	626
1	Electrified Panic			
	Exit Device	E90075L x FSE x 9992L–M	VW Hardware Co.	626
1	Cylinder	32-0200	MMM Hardware Co.	626
1	Closer	4110 Cush Alum	LMN Hardware Co.	689
1	Kick Plate	#48 - 10 x 2 inches L.D.W.		
		(254 x 51 mm L.D.W.)	MNO Hardware Co.	630
1	Threshold	R50SA x Miter	PQR Hardware Co.	627
1	Weather Stripping	303AV Head and Jamb	PQR Hardware Co.	627
1	Sweep	307AV	PQR Hardware Co.	627
1	Access Control	7183 x 7804 Box	VW Hardware Co.	
1	Relay	7000 (JB7)	VW Hardware Co.	
1	Heater	7801	VW Hardware Co.	
1	Set Communication			
	Cable	7865, 7866, 7868	VW Hardware Co.	
1	Power Supply	MPB-851	VW Hardware Co.	

Access control shall release electrified panic exit device outside trim and shall shunt monitoring hinge. Monitor door position at security panel.

DOOR HARDWARE SCHEDULE
(Example 2: Referencing BHMA Standards)

Hardware Set 1

3	Hinges	A8112	626
1	Lockset	1000 Series, Grade 1 - F04	626
1	Closer	C02011 - PT-4H	689
1	Kick Plate	J102 - 10 x 2 inches L.D.W. (254 x 51 mm L.D.W.)	630
1	Wall Stop	L22101	626
1	Set Smoke Seal	ROE154	

Hardware Set 2

1	Electric Hinge	A2111 x monitoring switch x NRP	626
1	Electric Hinge	A2111 x continuous circuit x NRP	626
1	Hinge	A2111 x NRP	626
1	Electrified Panic	Type 3, Grade 1 - F08 modified (lever trim	
	Exit Device	electronically unlocked)	626
1	Cylinder	E09211A	626
1	Closer	C02021 - PT-4G	689
1	Kick Plate	J102 - 10 x 2 inches L.D.W. (254 x 51 mm L.D.W.)	630
1	Threshold	J38130	627
1	Weather Stripping	R3D165	627
1	Sweep	R3D414	627
1	Access Control	VW Hardware Co. 7183 x 7804	
1	Relay	VW Hardware Co. 7000 (JB7)	
1	Heater	VW Hardware Co. 7801	
1	Set Communication		
	Cable	VW Hardware Co. 7865, 7866, 7868	
1	Power Supply	VW Hardware Co. MPB-851	

Access control shall release electrified panic exit device outside trim and shall shunt monitoring hinge. Monitor door position at security panel.

DOOR HARDWARE SCHEDULE (Example 3: Describing Products)

Hardware Set 1

3	Hinges	Antifriction-bearing, heavyweight, full mortise, steel	626
1	Lockset	Mortise, Grade 1, entry function	626
1	Closer	Surface, modern type with cover, hinge-side mounting, regular arm, adjustable closing force	689
1	Kick Plate	10 inches (254 mm) high x 2 inches (51 mm) less door width	630
1	Wall Stop	Wall bumper, convex	626
1	Set Smoke Seal	Adhesive-backed head and jamb gasket, silicone	

Hardware Set 2

1	Electric Hinge	Antifriction- bearing, heavy weight, full mortise, monitoring switch, nonremovable pin	626
1	Electric Hinge	Antifriction-bearing, heavyweight, full mortise, continuous circuit, nonremovable pin	626
1	Hinge	Antifriction-bearing, heavyweight, full mortise, nonremovable pin	626
1	Electrified Panic Exit Device	Mortise, Grade 1, entrance by lever, lever trim electronically unlocked	626
1	Cylinder	Mortise cylinder, pick resistant, interchangeable core	626
1	Closer	Surface, modern type with cover, parallel arm mounting, regular arm, factory-set dead stop	689
1	Kick Plate	10 inches (254 mm) high x 2 inches (51 mm) less door width	630
1	Threshold	Ramped, fluted top, 1/2-inch (13 mm) rise, aluminum, top plate, mitered corners	627
1	Weather Stripping	Rigid, housed gasket, head and jamb, aluminum, vinyl	627
1	Sweep	Surface mounted, aluminum housing, vinyl	627
1	Access Control	Auxiliary magnetic card reader without keypad, surface mounted in junction box, 24-V dc	
1	Relay	24-V dc, for lock output, mounted in junction box	
1	Heater	24-V dc, factory-installed on mounting plate	
1	Set Communication Cable	Two 10-foot (3.0-m), twisted, shielded pair cables between reader and power supply; 8-inch (200-mm) connector cable to field wiring	
1	Power Supply	24-V dc, box type, isolated, low leakage capacitance	

Access control shall release electrified panic exit device outside trim and shall shunt monitoring hinge. Monitor door position at security panel.

REFERENCES

Publication dates cited here were current at the time of this writing. Publications are revised periodically, and revisions may have occurred before this book was published.

Builders Hardware Manufacturers Association

BHMA A156.1-97: Butts and Hinges (ANSI)

BHMA A156.2-96: Bored and Preassembled Locks & Latches (ANSI)

BHMA A156.3-94: Exit Devices (ANSI)

BHMA A156.4-92: Door Controls-Closers (ANSI)

BHMA A156.5-92: Auxiliary Locks & Associated Products (ANSI)

BHMA A156.6-94: Architectural Door Trim (ANSI)

BHMA A156.7-88: Template Hinge Dimensions (ANSI)

BHMA A156.8-94: Door Controls-Overhead Stops and Holders (ANSI)

BHMA A156.12-92: Interconnected Locks & Latches (ANSI)

BHMA A156.13-94: Mortise Locks & Latches (ANSI)

BHMA A156.14-97: Sliding & Folding Door Hardware (ANSI)

BHMA A156.15-95: Closer Holder Release Devices (ANSI)

BHMA A156.16-89: Auxiliary Hardware (ANSI)

BHMA A156.17-93: Self Closing Hinges & Pivots (ANSI)

BHMA A156.18-93: Materials and Finishes (ANSI)

BHMA A156.21-96: Thresholds (ANSI)

BHMA A156.22-96: Door Gasketing Systems (ANSI)

BHMA A156.23-92: Electromagnetic Locks (ANSI)

BHMA A156.24-92: Delayed Egress Locks (ANSI)

Directory of Certified Door Closers, 1997.

Directory of Certified Electromagnetic & Delayed-Egress Locks, 1997.

Directory of Certified Exit Devices, 1997.

Directory of Certified Locks & Latches, 1997.

Door and Hardware Institute

Keying Systems and Nomenclature, 1989.

National Fire Protection Association

NFPA 80-95: Fire Doors and Fire Windows

Underwriters Laboratories Inc.

UL 10C-98: Positive Pressure Fire Tests of Door Assemblies

UL 437-94: Key Locks

United States Architectural & Transportation Barriers Compliance Board

ADAAG: Accessibility Guidelines for Buildings and Facilities, adopted in 1991; continual revisions.

09210 GYPSUM PLASTER

This chapter discusses gypsum lath and plaster; metal lath, furring, accessories, and support systems; and plastic accessories.

This chapter does not discuss portland cement plaster, stucco, or veneer plaster.

PRODUCT CHARACTERISTICS

Fire-Resistance-Rated Assemblies

Where fire-resistance ratings are required, refer to Underwriters Labratory's (UL's) *Fire Resistance Directory,* another agency's listing, or the Gypsum Association's (GA's) publication GA-600, *Fire Resistance Design Manual,* to select design designations that fit project conditions. Indicate these design designations on the drawings.

For fire-resistant plaster, use the finish-coat plaster originally tested and rated with the base-coat plaster. Usually, fine perlite or sand finish aggregate is used with a perlite base, and only fine vermiculite with a vermiculite base.

Plaster Bases

In addition to metal and gypsum laths (fig. 1), gypsum plaster may be applied directly to surfaces of interior masonry walls and of monolithic concrete that are not part of an exterior wall or roof slab. Gypsum plaster cannot be applied where moisture from condensation or seepage might occur at the bonding plane between plaster and base. Surface conditions and tolerances must comply with specific requirements before direct application of plaster over unit masonry or concrete is acceptable. When total bonding of plaster to a solid base is questionable, use a bonding compound. If a specific form of surface preparation such as bushhammering or etching is required, include it in the specifications. A bonding compound may not be acceptable for fire-rated applications unless it was used in the tested assembly.

Base-Coat Gypsum Plasters

The base coat is a critical element in plaster application, as the resistance of plaster to cracking, impact, fire, and sound transmission is primarily determined by the base coats. When selecting a base coat, consider the surface to which the base coat is to be applied and the type of finish to be supported.

Gypsum base-coat plasters come in three basic types: gypsum ready-mixed plaster, gypsum neat plaster, and gypsum wood-fibered plaster. Gypsum ready-mixed plaster is mixed at the mill with a mineral aggregate; currently, the only aggregate offered by the two major manufacturers is perlite. Gypsum neat plaster requires the addition of aggregate on the job; currently, both major manufacturers offer this product. Gypsum wood-fibered plaster is gypsum neat plaster mixed at the mill with nonstaining wood fibers; currently, only one manufacturer markets this product.

Fibered versus Unfibered Gypsum Plasters

In the past, it was necessary to add fibers (hair or sisal) to scratch coats over metal lath to act as a binder in the formation of mechanical keys and to keep them from breaking off until the plaster had set. However, the two major manufacturers no longer offer gypsum neat plaster with fibers added, on the basis that adequate keying occurs without it.

Base-coat aggregates are added to gypsum plaster to provide dimensional stability and to increase the bulk and coverage of the plaster. Sand, wood fiber, perlite, and vermiculite are common aggregates used in base coats, and the characteristics of each are noted in the following list. Note that these characteristics can be drastically affected by improper gradation or proportioning.

- **Sand** is the most commonly used aggregate because it is economical and widely available. If suitable sand is available, sanded base coats will meet most design requirements, except where higher fire ratings or higher strengths are required or weight reduction is desired.
- **Wood fiber** is a mill-mixed aggregate; it should not be confused with hair or sisal fiber. Wood-fibered base coats provide greater strength and impact resistance than other base coats, hence they should be considered for work that requires greater strength than sanded base coats or for regular work if suitable sand is not available or is too costly. Wood-fibered base coats weigh less than sanded base coats, but more than perlite or vermiculite base coats. Similarly, fire-resistance ratings are greater for wood-fibered base coats than for sanded base coats, but less efficient than for the lightweight aggregates, particularly for ratings of two hours or more. Material costs are slightly higher than for base coats with other aggregates, but labor costs are generally the same as for sanded base coats.
- **Lightweight aggregates** generally produce base coats with higher fire ratings and decreased weight. Strength and hardness will be less than

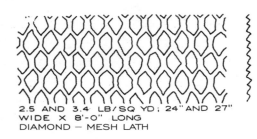

2.5 AND 3.4 LB/SQ YD; 24" AND 27" WIDE X 8'-0" LONG
DIAMOND — MESH LATH

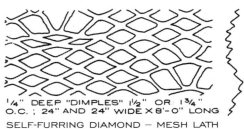

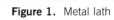

1/4" DEEP "DIMPLES" 1½" OR 1¾" O.C.; 24" AND 24" WIDE X 8'-0" LONG
SELF-FURRING DIAMOND — MESH LATH

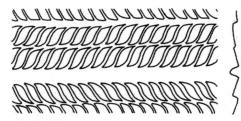

RIB LATH

Figure 1. Metal lath

for sanded or wood-fibered base coats. Lightweight aggregate is not recommended where high Sound Transmission Class (STC) ratings are required.

- **Perlite aggregate** is commonly used for fire-resistance-rated plaster, up through four hours. Most ready-mixed plaster base coats contain perlite aggregate.
- **Vermiculite aggregate** results in the softest plaster base coats. It is similar to perlite in fire-resistance performance and cost.
- **A proprietary, high-strength, base-coat product** is an alternate to wood-fibered gypsum base coat.

Ceiling Suspension Systems

The sizes, spans, and spacings of components included in ASTM and other industry standards are primarily intended to support the weight of lath and gypsum plaster; they are not designed to support heavy, concentrated, mechanical and electrical equipment loads or the weight of workers or vibrational loads (fig. 2). Independently supported platforms and catwalks must be provided for such loading. Using metal deck tabs to hang plaster ceilings should not be allowed. Each ceiling installation should be individually designed to ensure that the suspension system, the anchorage devices from which the ceiling is hung, and the structure itself can safely support the full range of anticipated loads.

Lath and Plaster Partitions

Nonload-bearing studs are the same as those used in gypsum board and veneer plaster construction where the gypsum board is screw attached (figs. 3, 4). These studs are capable of withstanding transverse loads within cer-

tain limitations. If needed for added strength to withstand transverse loads, load-bearing steel or wood studs should be specified separately in a Division 5, "Metals," or Division 6, "Wood and Plastics" section.

Vertical furring can be constructed of cold-rolled steel channels, Z-furring members, and steel studs. Channel studs are also used to construct hollow partitions and solid plaster partitions (as shown in fig. 5). Metal contact furring, in which members are directly attached to masonry, tends to shadow or telegraph. Braced or freestanding furring, in which supporting members do not contact walls, minimizes this problem, eliminates shimming, and provides more cavity space for utilities and insulation.

PRODUCT SELECTION CONSIDERATIONS

Metal Lath

Selecting the best lath for an application depends largely on the supporting members and their spacing. For instance, where studs or ceiling supports are closely spaced, furring may not be required or self-furring lath may be acceptable. On the other hand, using furring may mean using a less costly form of lath and may solve a number of other dimensional problems. Metal lath is readily adaptable to creating unusual plaster shapes, which are not economically feasible in most other materials. However, overall success and economy of such installations depend heavily on the detailer's skill in selecting proper lath and support systems. Major curved support members should be shop-fabricated to template tolerances. Otherwise, unevenness of the supporting structure may not be fully overcome by plaster thickness variations, and resulting work will show imperfections.

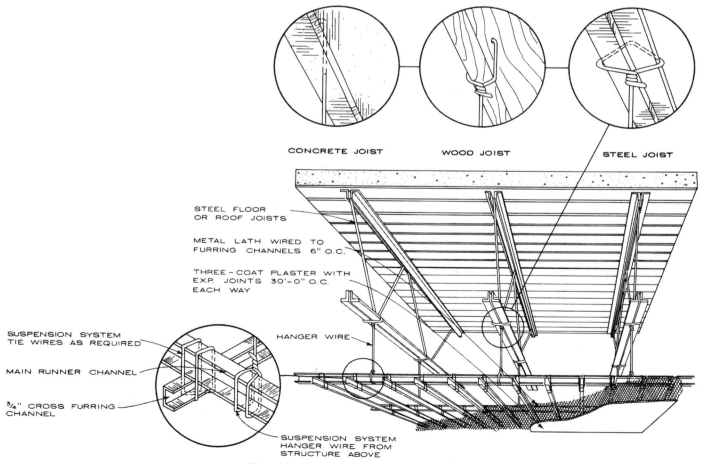

CONCRETE JOIST   WOOD JOIST   STEEL JOIST

STEEL FLOOR
OR ROOF JOISTS

METAL LATH WIRED TO
FURRING CHANNELS 6" O.C.

THREE-COAT PLASTER WITH
EXP. JOINTS 30'-0" O.C.
EACH WAY

HANGER WIRE

SUSPENSION SYSTEM
TIE WIRES AS REQUIRED

MAIN RUNNER CHANNEL

¾" CROSS FURRING
CHANNEL

SUSPENSION SYSTEM
HANGER WIRE FROM
STRUCTURE ABOVE

Figure 2. Suspended lath and plaster ceiling

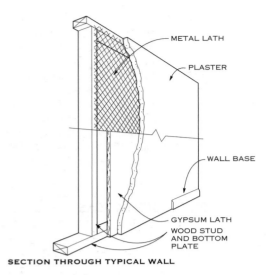

PLANE USING METAL LATH

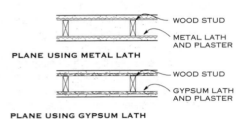

PLANE USING GYPSUM LATH

Figure 3. Wood stud and lath

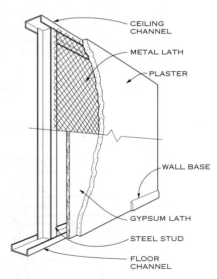

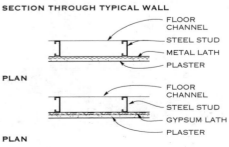

Figure 4. Metal stud and lath

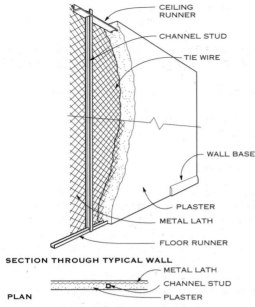

Figure 5. Metal lath/channel stud-plaster

Wire-type lath, either 1½-inch (38-mm) hexagonal woven mesh or 2-by-2-inch (50-by-50-mm) welded-wire lath, is commonly used on wood framing for light-commercial buildings, and residences. Often it is used with integral paper backing where machine-applied plaster requires paper backing.

Accessories

In addition to the standard accessories required for each plaster installation, certain special-purpose moldings may be required, such as window stools, picture moldings, decorative reveals, transitional trim, chair rails, terrazzo bases, and screeds. Some are stock items with certain manufacturers; others have to be custom-fabricated. Standard and selected special-purpose accessories are generally available in galvanized steel and high-impact polyvinyl chloride (PVC). Certain special-purpose moldings are available in coated aluminum.

Gypsum Plaster Selection Criteria

Selecting plaster base- and finish-coat compositions involves the assessment of both appearance and physical performance. Although choosing the method of finishing plaster may be based primarily on appearance, there are also functional considerations; for example, floated or textured finishes on wall surfaces exposed to soiling from frequent hand and body contact may discourage such touching due to the unpleasant feeling of an abrasive surface. Resistance to damage from abrasion and impact is improved by using finish- and base-coat plasters with higher compressive strengths. Because of the increased costs of high-strength plaster both in materials and installation, it may be more economical to limit its use to corridor walls, lobbies, and other high-traffic areas, using lower-strength compositions on ceilings and in low-traffic space.

Gypsum plaster is not recommended for "wet" areas of buildings or for unprotected exterior exposures. That said, it will successfully withstand occasional wetting and mild dampness and can be used in residential bathrooms (but not for shower stalls and around tubs) and for exterior soffits where the exposure is well protected and the climate is not too severe or humid. A common misunderstanding is that using Keene's cement finish will overcome this basic limitation of gypsum plaster.

Gypsum lath consists of a core of gypsum plaster, usually air-entrained and with up to 15 percent fibers by weight, sandwiched between two sheets of fibrous absorbent paper. As plaster sets, some of the dissolved cementitious material is absorbed by suction into the lath, forming crystals in the gypsum core, which interlock with those in the plaster to form a continuous bond. Gypsum lath is not suitable as a base for portland cement or lime plasters, direct paint finishes, or adhesively applied tile. Other considerations for gypsum lath include the following:

- **The rigidity** of the base to which the plaster is applied is an important factor in preventing plaster cracking. Under comparable circumstances, a board lath usually provides higher performance than does a more flexible lath. However, conventional plaster systems are more rigid than veneer plaster systems due to the rigidity of plaster.
- **Exterior walls:** Gypsum lath should not be applied directly to exterior masonry or concrete walls. Interior surfaces of exterior walls should always be furred to provide an air space of at least ¾ inch (19 mm) between the lath and masonry.
- **Types of laths** include regular and Type X, which has a special fire-resistant core.
- **Thicknesses:** Gypsum lath is commonly available in ⅜- and ½-inch (9.5- and 12.7-mm) thicknesses. The recommended spacing for supporting framework is 16 inches (406.4 mm) for ⅜ inch (9.5-mm) lath and 24 inches (609.6 mm) for ½-inch (12.7-mm) lath for the usual ½-inch- (12.7-mm-) thick, two-coat plaster applications. While thicker, three-coat applications may be applied, the economy of gypsum lath is based on combining gypsum lath and thinner plaster.
- **Sheet Widths and Lengths:** Unlike veneer plaster or gypsum board applications where joints between gypsum boards require reinforcing and finish treatment, joints between gypsum lath are covered with relatively thick layers of plaster. As a result, sheet widths and lengths for gypsum lath were developed for ease of application rather than for minimizing the number of joints.

APPLICATION CONSIDERATIONS

Load Isolation

Typical details that should be shown on the drawings are those required to ensure that live building loads, which cause deflections in the building structure, will not be transferred to the metal stud systems, which are non-load-bearing and may buckle if subjected to axial loading. Consult manufacturers' details for methods to prevent load transmission. Abutment at exterior walls, interior shear walls, and columns may also be crucial. In many buildings, the structural surround of a partition section changes (slightly) from a rectangle to a parallelogram between summer and winter, and this movement can seriously damage the partition if adequate isolation is not provided.

Height of Partitions

Determining whether partitions should extend through suspended ceilings to the structural system above is a complex process. Suspended acoustical-unit ceilings are seldom a good support system for the tops of heavy partitions unless designed integrally for that purpose, such as for demountable partitions on a fixed module. Other ceilings are usually structurally adequate or can be made adequate by introducing a minor amount of knee bracing. However, other considerations, such as control of sound transmission and fire resistance, may still dictate an extension of the stud system and some degree of applied finish to the structure above (through the plenum). Nonload-bearing studs are not intended to be used without applied face sheets, and may need to be stabilized with applications of

gypsum board on both faces in the plenum, even where there is no need for resistance to fire or sound transmission.

Attach gypsum lath to framing or furring either directly by conventional fasteners, such as nails, screws, or staples, or indirectly by clips. In either case, each piece of lath should be secured to each framing member. If supports are nailable or can receive screws, direct fastening is the usual method. Clips are available for fastening gypsum lath to metal furring channels and to channel studs with lips. These clips are designed to be springy and hold the lath away from supports, thereby decreasing sound transmission and reducing cracking.

Methods of bonding plaster to ensure the best possible bond to the base include providing mechanical roughness of base (either natural or processed), bonding compounds, or self-furring metal lath or reinforcing mesh secured to the base. Any of these methods forge a total bond between the plaster and the substrate or completely separate them. Ordinarily, smooth concrete will not provide good mechanical bond; sand-blasting, bushhammering, or deep acid etching may be required. Masonry must be level and rough textured to give good bond, and is usually improved by etching.

Troweled finishes are smooth finishes provided by using ready-mixed gypsum finish coats or by mixing gypsum finish-coat plaster (gypsum gauging plaster, high-strength gypsum gauging plaster, or gypsum Keene's cement) with lime putty. Over gypsum base coats without lightweight aggregates, such as sanded gypsum neat plaster and sanded or unsanded gypsum wood-fibered plaster, sand is not incorporated in the mix of troweled finish coats. For base coats with lightweight aggregates, adding specially graded fine aggregate in troweled finish coats is required. Mix designs can be varied to control the hardness of the finish coat. Refer to manufacturers' literature for comparative performance characteristics.

Floated finishes are sand-float finishes provided by mixing gypsum gauging plaster or gypsum Keene's cement with lime putty and job-mixed aggregate. If special textures are required, adjustments to the thickness of the finish coat and to the amount of cementitious material may be required. To control the desired effect of floated and other textured finishes, require the contractor to match the architect's sample and to provide a field-constructed mockup for quality control.

Gypsum Keene's cement is a specially processed gypsum gauging plaster, not a portland-type cement. Regular gypsum gauging plasters are burned in a calciner or kettle to remove about 75 percent of the chemically combined water, while Keene's cement is burned in a kiln to remove almost all of this water, which results in a dense, hard material. Though the density provides a lower rate of water absorption, Keene's cement should not be considered an alternate or a substitute for portland cement plaster in high-humidity areas and should not be applied over portland cement plaster base coats.

REFERENCES

Publication dates cited here were current at the time of this writing. Publications are revised periodically, and revisions may have occurred before this book was published.

Gypsum Association

GA-600-97: Fire Resistance Design Manual

Underwriters Laboratories Inc.

Fire Resistance Directory, published annually.

09215 GYPSUM VENEER PLASTER

This chapter discusses gypsum-based veneer plaster applied on gypsum base panels, unit masonry, or monolithic concrete. This chapter also addresses metal support systems, sound attenuation insulation, and cementitious backer units, because they are often integrated with veneer plaster construction.

This chapter does not discuss conventional gypsum or portland cement plaster systems, which are covered in other Division 9, "Finishes," chapters, or lead lining for veneer plaster partitions.

PRODUCT CHARACTERISTICS

Gypsum veneer plaster systems consist of gypsum-based plaster applied in thin layers of one or two coats over a suitable substrate. Layers are $\frac{1}{16}$- to $\frac{3}{32}$-inch (1.6- to 2.4-mm) thick. Suitable substrates include gypsum base panels, masonry, and monolithic concrete.

One-component systems are defined in ASTM C 843 as consisting of a single plaster material applied directly over an approved base in one coat or in a double-back operation. These systems are suitable for use over gypsum base panels or monolithic concrete substrates. They are not universally recommended for masonry substrates; consult manufacturers for limitations.

Two-component systems are defined in ASTM C 843 as consisting of two separate plaster materials mixed and applied individually as the base and finish coats. These systems are suitable for use over gypsum base panels, unit masonry, or monolithic concrete substrates. Two-component systems provide greater resistance to cracking, fastener pops, joint beading, and joint shadowing than one-component systems and are available with various finish-plaster options.

Veneer plaster compositions vary. Select plasters based on requirements for surface hardness and smoothness. It is more difficult to produce a smooth surface with hard plasters; therefore, they cost more to apply. Conversely, more workable plasters are easier to apply but their finish surface is not as hard. Lime increases plaster workability and coverage but reduces strength and durability.

Conventional plaster systems are more expensive than veneer plaster systems. Veneer plaster systems have lower material costs, are installed more quickly, and dry faster than conventional plaster systems.

Standard gypsum board assemblies are less expensive than veneer plaster assemblies. The difference in cost between the two types of assemblies depends on the level of gypsum board finish and the veneer plaster system required. Gypsum base for veneer plaster costs slightly more than standard gypsum panels. Installed costs for veneer plaster systems, including finishing, generally average about 10 percent more than those for standard gypsum board. Veneer plaster has a harder surface and a more monolithic appearance than standard gypsum board. It is also more resistant to fastener pops, impact, abrasion, and joint beading than standard gypsum board.

Advantages of gypsum veneer plaster include the following:

- Installation is rapid, and the plaster sets and dries quickly.
- Surfaces are abrasion-resistant.
- Surfaces resist fastener pops and cracking.
- Finishes appear similar to conventional plaster finishes and are less expensive to install.
- Architectural features, such as vaulted ceilings, can be installed with a smooth, monolithic appearance more easily than they can be installed with standard gypsum board.
- Sound- and fire-rated assemblies are available.

Limitations of gypsum veneer plaster include the following:

- It is not recommended for exterior use or in areas subject to weather, moisture, or high humidity.
- Surfaces are less rigid than similar conventional plaster systems.
- Compound curves are more difficult to form than with conventional plaster systems.
- Veneer plaster is subject to joint beading and cracking under rapid drying conditions caused by low humidity, high temperatures, or drafts.
- Framing spacing and acceptable partition heights may be reduced from those used for standard gypsum board assemblies because of lower deflection tolerances.
- Ceramic tile cannot be directly applied to gypsum base panels; the surfaces must be plastered first.
- Polyethylene vapor barriers are not recommended for use with veneer plaster assemblies unless spaces are adequately ventilated during application.

Gypsum base panels for veneer plaster have a gypsum core that is surfaced with a specially treated, multilayer paper face. The outer layers of the paper are highly absorptive and draw moisture rapidly and uniformly from the plaster mix so the mix bonds quickly to the panel and does not slide during application. The inner layers are chemically treated and form a barrier that prevents moisture from damaging the gypsum core. The color of the paper surface is blue or blue-gray, which is why gypsum base panels are often called *blue board* in the industry.

- **If the paper face fades** from exposure to light, it can adversely affect the bond between the base panels and one-component-system finish plasters that contain lime. Manufacturers' recommendations for restoring faded paper vary and include treating the surface with a spray-applied alum solution, using a base coat of plaster that does not contain lime, and using a bonding agent.
- **Gypsum plaster lath** is not for use with veneer plasters. This solid gypsum lath is for use with conventional plasters.

Joints between gypsum base panels are reinforced with embedded tape, like those in standard gypsum board assemblies.

- **Joint tape** is either paper or open-mesh, glass-fiber fabric. The Gypsum Association (GA) publication GA-151, *Veneer Plaster*, states that opti-

mum joint strength is not obtained using glass-fiber-fabric tape. Manufacturers' recommendations for joint tape vary.
• **Embedding materials** also vary among manufacturers.

Cementitious backer units are often installed as ceramic tile substrates in areas where the remainder of the space is finished with veneer plaster.

FIRE-RESISTANCE-RATED ASSEMBLIES

Most building codes require tested fire-resistive assemblies with hourly ratings for specified uses. Generally, a limited number of assemblies are described in the code itself. Authorities having jurisdiction often accept design designations of tested assemblies listed by independent agencies on the drawings as evidence of code compliance. Factory Mutual Global's (FMG's) *Approval Guide, Building Materials;* GA-600, *Fire Resistance Design Manual;* Intertek Testing Service's (ITS's) *Directory of Listed Products;* and Underwriters Laboratories' (UL's) *Fire Resistance Directory* are frequently cited sources for fire-resistance ratings.

METAL SUPPORT SYSTEMS

Steel framing for veneer plaster assemblies is generally the same as for standard gypsum board assemblies; however, member sizes or thicknesses may need to increase, and spacings may need to decrease, to satisfy more stringent deflection limits. Manufacturers often recommend limiting the maximum deflection of veneer plaster assemblies to L/360, compared to the recommended maximum deflection of L/240 for standard gypsum board assemblies. If deflection exceeding these recommendations is acceptable, limit the deflection for veneer plaster assemblies to not more than L/240 because greater deflections are likely to cause cracking and other damage to finishes. For tile or similar finishes, verify substrate deflection limits when specifying assembly requirements.

ASTM C 844, *Specification for Application of Gypsum Base to Receive Gypsum Veneer Plaster,* tabulates allowable framing spacing based on the panel thickness and number of layers. The standard states that framing and furring should otherwise comply with ASTM C 754, *Specification for Installation of Steel Framing Members to Receive Screw-Attached Gypsum Panel Products.*

ASTM C 754, Appendix X1, tabulates maximum clear span heights for studs used in standard one- and two-layer gypsum board assemblies when deflection is limited to L/120, L/240, and L/360.

Conventional suspended ceiling and soffit systems have gypsum base panels applied to furring channels (furring members). Cold-rolled channels, steel studs, and hat-shaped rigid or resilient channels are common furring channels. Furring is wire tied to the structure or is supported by carrying channels (main runners) suspended from the structure. ASTM C 754 tabulates requirements for hanger types and sizes, and main runner spans and spacings, but does not state the anticipated deflection limit for the support system. Before selecting member sizes and spacing, determine the desired deflection limit and coordinate the structural support spacing; hanger spacing; main runner size and spacing; and furring member type, size, and spacing accordingly.

Grid suspension systems traditionally were not recommended by manufacturers for use with veneer plaster ceilings. However, recent large, high-profile installations have used them successfully. These manufactured systems of main runners, interlocking cross-furring channels, and wall angles are direct hung and do not employ intermediate carrying channels.

Grid suspension systems may be less-expensive alternatives to conventional indirect suspension systems. Before specifying them, consult manufacturers for recommendations.

Framing that supports doors is subject to stresses generated by door swinging and impact. See GA-600 and manufacturers' literature for recommendations. Standard door framing details may not be adequate for extra-wide, tall, or heavy doors.

STEEL SHEET THICKNESSES

ASTM C 645, *Specification for Nonstructural Steel Framing Members,* requires that sectional properties of framing members be computed according to the requirements in American Iron and Steel Institute's (AISI's) *Specification for the Design of Cold-Formed Steel Structural Members,* 1986 edition (which is not the most recent edition) and 1989 Addendum, and requires a minimum base metal thickness of 0.0179 inch (0.45 mm). According to the AISI specification, the delivered minimum base metal thickness is 95 percent of the design thickness, and the design thickness is uncoated. In product literature, some steel framing member manufacturers list design thicknesses and actual minimum base metal thicknesses, others list design thicknesses only, and still others list minimum base metal thicknesses only.

Specifying steel thickness by gage number is imprecise because steel sheet is ordered by thickness, and the actual thickness offered by manufacturers may differ. Traditional steel gage numbers and the corresponding minimum base metal (uncoated) thicknesses are included in the Table 1.

Cold-formed, 20-gage steel studs used in load-bearing or nonload-bearing, curtain-wall applications (usually specified in a Division 5, "Metals" section) generally have a minimum steel base metal thickness of 0.0329 inch (0.84 mm), which is greater than that indicated for 20-gage "drywall" steel sheet in Table 1. However, some manufacturers, particularly those in the western United States, also provide the 0.0329-inch- (0.84-mm-) thick steel for "drywall" studs.

CORROSION PROTECTION OF STEEL FRAMING

ASTM C 645 and ASTM C 754 include requirements for corrosion resistance of framing members. ASTM C 645, which specifies studs, runners, hat-shaped rigid channels, and grid suspension systems, states "Members shall have a protective coating conforming to Specification A 653/A 653M - G40 (hot-dip galvanized) minimum or shall have a protective coating with an equivalent corrosion resistance." ASTM C 754 includes a similar requirement for cold-rolled channels, and requires galvanized soft-annealed steel wire for ties and hangers. ASTM C 754 states that rod and flat hangers, when specified, can be protected by a zinc coating or another equally rust-inhibiting coating. ASTM C 645 and ASTM C 754 do not advise or

Table 1
STEEL SHEET THICKNESSES

Gage	Minimum Steel Base Metal (Uncoated) Thickness	
	Inch	Millimeter
16	0.0538	1.37
20	0.0312	0.79
22	0.0270	0.69
25	0.0179	0.45

prescribe how to evaluate equivalent corrosion resistance for other types of protective coatings, such as electrolytically deposited zinc coatings or rust-inhibiting paints.

For framing members, manufacturers generally use steel sheets that are zinc or zinc-iron-alloy coated by the coil-coating process; however, painted steel sheet can be used. Some manufacturers cold-reduce (reroll) sheets to decrease their thickness, which may affect the integrity of the zinc coating. ASTM A 653/A 653M specifies steel sheet that is zinc coated (galvanized) or zinc-iron-alloy coated (galvannealed) by the hot-dip process. ASTM A 879 specifies steel sheet with electrolytically deposited zinc coatings. When coating masses are equal, electrolytically deposited zinc and galvannealed coatings provide equivalent corrosion resistance to hot-dip galvanized coatings.

For normal environments, specifying the manufacturer's standard corrosion-resistant zinc coating will promote the most competition while excluding painted framing members.

CRACK CONTROL

Gypsum veneer plaster surfaces will crack if nonload-bearing assemblies are subjected to structural movements. In nonload-bearing assemblies, isolate gypsum base panels from structural elements at all points of contact except floors. Because all structural systems are subject to creep, settlement, deflection, thermal movement, and wind-load strains, consider the effect of these forces on assemblies, and detail isolation requirements on the drawings. Because wood framing is subject to swelling and shrinking, "floating" interior-angle panel application is recommended, particularly for directly attached ceilings. Using resilient channels can also minimize or eliminate wood-framing movement problems.

Deflection tracks used for the top runner in steel-framed partitions accommodate varying amounts of movement. Detail deflection track requirements on the drawings.

Standard generic details for deflection tracks use long-leg tracks and include double-track and channel-braced systems. Where deflection may be great, evaluate the lateral stability of the top-track flanges and consider using a steel channel instead.

- **In double-track systems,** the long-leg track is attached to the overhead structure; a second track, which is fastened to the studs, slides up and down within the long-leg track.
- **In channel-braced systems,** studs are inserted into, but not fastened to, the long-leg track and are laterally braced with a continuous cold-rolled channel near the top of the framing.

Table 2
RECOMMENDED CONTROL JOINT LOCATIONS

Ceilings with perimeter relief	Install control joints in areas exceeding 2,500 sq. ft. (232 sq. m). Space control joints not more than 50 feet (15.2 m) o.c. Install control joints where ceiling framing or furring changes direction.
Ceilings without perimeter relief	Install control joints in areas exceeding 900 sq. ft. (85 sq. m). Space control joints not more than 30 feet (9.1 m) o.c. Install control joints where ceiling framing or furring changes direction.
Partitions and furring	Space control joints not more than 30 feet (9.1 m) o.c. Install control joints in furred assemblies where control joints occur in base exterior wall.

Proprietary deflection tracks are available that reduce the labor associated with typical generic details. Proprietary tracks designed to isolate framing while maintaining the continuity of specific fire-resistance-rated assemblies are also available.

For perimeter relief, if a deflection track is not used, studs are generally cut ½ inch (12.7 mm) short and friction-fit into the top runner.

Locate control joints at natural lines of weakness to prevent cracking. ASTM C 844 requirements for control-joint locations are summarized in Table 2. Show the location of and detail control joints on the drawings. Control joints in fire-resistance-rated construction require rated joint systems and special detailing.

VAPOR CONTROL

Vapor control is difficult because vapor retarders are often penetrated by electrical outlets, joints between panels, and careless installation practices. In cold climates, vapor retarders are placed on the warm interior sides of insulation. For air-conditioned buildings located in climates with high outside temperatures and humidity, the location of the vapor retarder should be determined by a qualified mechanical engineer. Avoid construction that traps moisture within wall cavities. Indicate on the drawings how the continuity of the vapor retarder is to be maintained at transitions to other construction.

Consider the effect of vapor retarders on the drying of the veneer plaster. To avoid drying the plaster too quickly, manufacturers caution that ventilation and air movement should be kept to a minimum level during veneer plaster application and until the plaster is dry. A polyethylene vapor retarder can be used if ventilation measures adequately protect the veneer plaster from thermal shock and air temperature variations. If a polyethylene vapor retarder is desired, it can be specified with veneer plaster assemblies or in the Division 7, "Thermal and Moisture Protection," section that specifies building insulation.

Manufacturers recommend using foil-backed gypsum base panels when a vapor retarder is required at a wall's interior face. Because the foil resists the passage of moisture vapor, foil-backed panels are unsuitable for applications where the backing can trap moisture within the board itself or within the assembly. For example, foil-backed panels are unsuitable substrates for ceramic tile or for use as face layers of a multilayer construction.

As an alternative to foil-backed gypsum base panels, insulation blankets faced on one side with a vapor retarder can be used to provide vapor control in framed exterior walls.

ENVIRONMENTAL CONSIDERATIONS

Recycled paper is used for the facing of gypsum board products. In some areas, companies are recycling gypsum waste from construction sites. Verify the availability of gypsum recycling operations in the project area, and specify requirements for recycling gypsum waste, if applicable.

Gypsum board waste and scraps are used as soil enhancers to control acidity and as mulch.

Products using synthetic gypsum, rather than mined natural gypsum, are available. Manufacturers do not identify products by the type of gypsum used. The availability of each type of gypsum to regional manufacturing plants determines whether a plant uses natural or synthetic gypsum or a combination. Limiting gypsum products to those incorporating only synthetic materials in areas where these materials are not readily available will adversely impact the environment because of the need for transporting the bulky and heavy products.

REFERENCES

Publication dates cited here were current at the time of this writing. Publications are revised periodically, and revisions may have occurred before this book was published.

ASTM International

ASTM A 653/A 653M-98: Specification for Steel Sheet, Zinc-Coated (Galvanized) or Zinc-Iron Alloy-Coated (Galvannealed) by the Hot-Dip Process

ASTM A 879-96: Specification for Steel Sheet, Zinc Coated by the Electrolytic Process for Applications Requiring Designation of the Coating Mass on Each Surface

ASTM C 645-98: Specification for Nonstructural Steel Framing Members

ASTM C 754-97: Specification for Installation of Steel Framing Members to Receive Screw-Attached Gypsum Panel Products

ASTM C 843-96: Specification for Application of Gypsum Veneer Plaster

ASTM C 844-98: Specification for Application of Gypsum Base to Receive Gypsum Veneer Plaster

Factory Mutual Global

Approval Guide, Building Materials, published annually.

Gypsum Association

GA-151-97: Veneer Plaster

GA-600-97: Fire Resistance Design Manual

Intertek Testing Services

Directory of Listed Products, published annually.

Underwriters Laboratories Inc.

Fire Resistance Directory, published annually.

09220 **PORTLAND CEMENT PLASTER**

This chapter discusses portland cement plaster assemblies. These assemblies include metal framing, furring, lath, and accessories; plastic accessories; job-mixed portland cement finish; and factory-prepared finishes such as stucco, acrylic-based, and exposed aggregate.

This chapter does not discuss veneer plaster, gypsum plaster, or gypsum sheathing.

GENERAL COMMENTS

Standards

This chapter discusses ASTM and other recognized industry standards for products and their installation. Adhering to these standards limits an architect's participation in the details of the plasterer's work; regional variations in practices and materials that modify these standards can also be included in specifications. The best sources of information for such variations are regional lathing and plastering bureaus or, if none are available, local plasterers experienced in applying portland cement plaster.

Seismic Considerations

In earthquake areas, additional members, ties and anchors, and closer spacing of supports may be needed. Consult local codes and recognized design manuals for information on these requirements.

Comparative Qualities

Portland cement plaster has provided durable exterior and interior finishes in warm and cold areas for many years. It is relatively hard, strong, and resistant to fire, weather, rot, fungus, and termites, and it does not deteriorate after repeated wetting and drying. In addition, portland cement plaster retains color and is capable of heavy texturing, which provides a wide range of decorative possibilities and low maintenance costs.

PRODUCT CHARACTERISTICS

Smooth-troweled finishes are unsuitable for portland cement plaster. As a very thin concrete slab, it is subject to shrinkage and cracking, effects that are difficult to conceal in smooth finishes and that tend to produce a crazed and patchy appearance. Heavier textures are generally used for exterior applications, but to minimize dirt buildup in urban or industrial environments, lighter textures should be considered.

Integrally colored stucco cannot accept more than 12 percent pigment to the cement used without affecting its strength. This results in pastel colors only. If dark colors are required, use a polymerized or acrylic-based finish coat, such as used with exterior insulation and finish systems, or produce an integral pastel-colored plaster and paint it to the required color. Portland cement plaster can be painted with good results if the proper paints are used. Integral color finishes, in addition to having a lower long-range maintenance, tend to hide surface damage better than painted surfaces.

Fire-Resistant Applications

Portland cement plaster requires a greater thickness than gypsum plaster to produce the same fire-resistance ratings. Higher fire-resistance ratings may also require using lightweight aggregate rather than sand; if this is required, include the aggregate and appropriate mixes in the specifications.

Ceiling Suspension Systems

Using portland cement plaster on ceilings requires appropriate design modification. Industry sources advise that tables for sizing and spacing members included in recognized industry standard publications identify more than adequate structural capacity to carry portland cement plaster.

- **The sizes, spans, and spacings** of components included in the standards are primarily intended to support the weight of lath and plaster; they are not designed to support heavy, concentrated, mechanical and electrical equipment loads, or the weight of workers (fig. 1). Independently supported platforms and catwalks must be provided for such loading.
- **Wire-hanger sizes** included in the the National Association of Architectural Metal Manufacturers (NAAMM) publication ML/SFA 920, *Guide Specifications for Metal Lathing and Furring,* are supposedly based on gypsum plaster ceiling loads of 10 lb/sq. ft. (48.8 kg/sq. m), while ceiling loads imposed by three-coat portland cement plaster may be as much as 14 lb/sq. ft. (68.3 kg/sq. m). Using metal deck tabs to hang plaster ceilings should not be allowed. Each ceiling installation should be individually designed to ensure that the suspension system, the anchorage devices from which the ceiling is hung, and the structure itself can safely support the full range of anticipated loads.

Metal Stud Systems

Nonload-bearing studs are the same as those used in gypsum board and veneer plaster construction, where the gypsum board is screw-attached. These studs are capable of withstanding transverse loads within certain limitations. If needed for added strength to withstand transverse loads, load-bearing steel or wood studs should be specified separately in a Division 5, "Metals," section or Division 6, "Wood and Plastics" section.

Vertical furring can be constructed of not only cold-rolled steel channels but also of steel studs. Channel studs are also used to construct hollow partitions and solid plaster partitions. Metal contact furring, in which members are directly attached to masonry, tends to shadow or telegraph. Braced or freestanding furring, in which supporting members do not contact walls, minimizes this problem, eliminates shimming, and provides more cavity space for utilities and insulation.

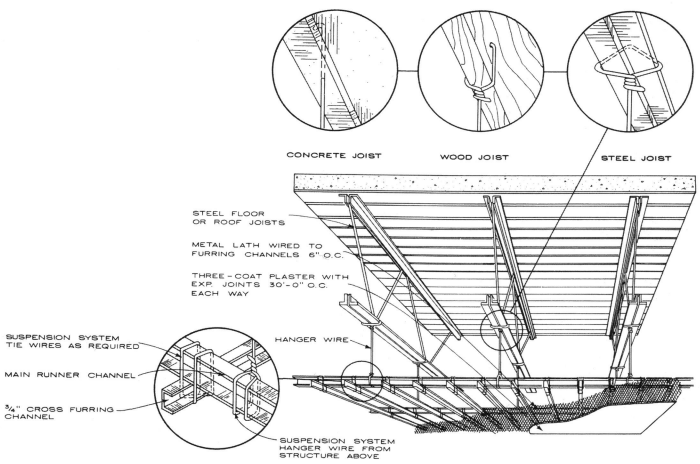

CONCRETE JOIST   WOOD JOIST   STEEL JOIST

STEEL FLOOR OR ROOF JOISTS

METAL LATH WIRED TO FURRING CHANNELS 6" O.C.

THREE - COAT PLASTER WITH EXP. JOINTS 30'-0" O.C. EACH WAY

HANGER WIRE

SUSPENSION SYSTEM TIE WIRES AS REQUIRED

MAIN RUNNER CHANNEL

¾" CROSS FURRING CHANNEL

SUSPENSION SYSTEM HANGER WIRE FROM STRUCTURE ABOVE

Figure 1. Suspended lath and plaster ceiling

PRODUCT SELECTION CONSIDERATIONS

Metal Lath

Selecting the most economical combination of members and spacings for subframing, furring, and lathing (fig. 2) is a complicated process. An experienced technical representative of a major manufacturer should be consulted for work beyond the scope of available literature. Where studs or ceiling supports are closely spaced, furring may not be required. On the other hand, using furring may mean implementing a less costly form of lath and may solve a number of other dimensional problems.

Wire-type lath is used primarily with integral paper backing for exterior work, in wet areas, and where machine-applied plaster requires paper backing.

Accessories

In addition to the standard accessories required for each plaster installation, certain special-purpose moldings may be required, such as window stools, decorative reveals, terrazzo bases, and screeds. Some are stock items with certain manufacturers; others have to be custom-fabricated.

- **Metals:** Accessories may be formed from stainless steel, galvanized steel, and zinc alloy. Certain special-purpose shapes are available in stainless steel.

- **Plastic:** Many standard and special-purpose accessories are also available in high-impact polyvinyl chloride (PVC).

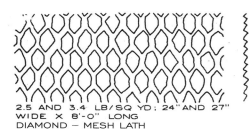

2.5 AND 3.4 LB/SQ YD; 24" AND 27" WIDE X 8'-0" LONG DIAMOND - MESH LATH

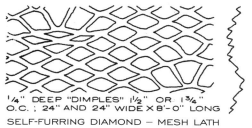

¼" DEEP "DIMPLES" 1½" OR 1¾" O.C.; 24" AND 24" WIDE X 8'-0" LONG SELF-FURRING DIAMOND - MESH LATH

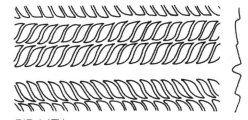

RIB LATH

Figure 2. Metal lath

APPLICATION CONSIDERATIONS

Load Isolation

Typical details that should be shown on the drawings are those required to ensure that live building loads, which cause deflections in the building structure, will not be transferred to the metal stud systems, which are non-load-bearing and may buckle if subjected to axial loading. Consult manufacturers' details for methods to prevent load transmission. Abutment at exterior walls, interior shear walls, and columns may also be crucial. In many buildings, the structural surround of a partition section changes (slightly) from a rectangle to a parallelogram between summer and winter, and this movement can seriously damage the partition if adequate isolation is not provided.

Height of Partitions

Determining whether partitions should extend through suspended ceilings to the structural system above involves considering a number of issues. Suspended acoustical-unit ceilings are seldom a good support system for the tops of heavy partitions unless designed integrally for that purpose, such as for demountable partitions on a fixed module. Other ceilings are usually structurally adequate or can be made adequate by introducing a minor amount of knee bracing. Other considerations, such as control of sound transmission and fire resistance, may, however, dictate an extension of the stud system and some degree of applied finish to the structure above (through the plenum). Nonload-bearing studs are not intended to be used without applied face sheets and may need to be stabilized with applications of gypsum board on both faces in the plenum, even where there is no need for resistance to fire or sound transmission.

Curved Surfaces

Metal lath and plaster are readily adaptable to creating unusual shapes, which are not economically feasible in most other materials. However, overall success and economy of such installations depend heavily on the detailer's skill in selecting proper lath and support systems. Major curved support members should be shop fabricated to template tolerances. Otherwise, unevenness of the supporting structure may not be fully overcome by plaster thickness variations, and resulting work will show imperfections.

Plaster Bases

Portland cement plaster is applied to either a solid or a metal base. The metal base may be applied over open framing or some form of solid backing that is not a suitable substrate for direct bonding of the plaster. Stable and rigid concrete and masonry are the usual solid bases. Bonding to these substrates should not be attempted unless there is little or no doubt that it will be successful for 100 percent of the surface; otherwise, shrinkage will crack the plaster. Gypsum block or lath is not a suitable base for bonding portland cement plaster. Up to certain thickness limitations, reinforcement is usually omitted on bonded plaster applications. In ASTM C 926, unreinforced, bonded, portland cement plaster is generally limited to ⅜-inch (9.5-mm) thickness for horizontal, and ⅝ inch (15.9 mm) for vertical, applications.

Bonding Methods for Solid Bases

Methods to ensure the best possible bond to the base include providing mechanical roughness of base (either natural or processed), dash coat of portland cement grout, bonding agent, bonding additive (acrylic, latex, etc.), proprietary admixtures for first base coat), or self-furring metal lath or reinforcing mesh securely nailed to the base. Do not specify half-hearted methods to achieve bond; only an all-out effort or a complete separation

will do. Ordinarily, smooth concrete will not provide good mechanical bond; sandblasting, bushhammering, or deep acid etching may be required. Masonry must be level and rough-textured to give good bond. A dash coat over etched concrete will ensure good bond but should not be depended on for thick plaster coats, particularly horizontal (ceiling) coats. The same is true of both bond coats and bonding additive on concrete and masonry. The last resort for thick-coat work is self-furring lath thoroughly nailed to the substrate.

Metal bases include expanded-metal lath, woven-wire lath, and welded-wire lath. All three are available with a weather-resistant paper backing that acts as a separator behind the plaster. In this case, the plaster and its metal reinforcement or lath must perform as a thin concrete slab. Total separation must be achieved and lines of weakness must be avoided. Metal bases are applied over open framing or solid backings. The solid backing can be any type of sheathing, masonry, concrete, or old stucco, as long as it is rigid. Control joints must be used at frequent intervals to avoid a buildup of shrinkage stresses, which will crack the plaster at its natural weakest lines. Nailing to the base, in this case, is for support of the independent, thin concrete slab, which is slightly different from self-furring lath in a bonded plaster finish.

Plaster Accessories

For interior work, accessories can be used similarly to gypsum plaster. This same treatment (and the use of metal lath) can also be extended to well-protected exterior work. However, weather-exposed exterior plaster should have a minimum of accessories, and those used should be sufficiently corrosion-resistant to ensure they do not deteriorate and stain the plaster. Cornerbeads are generally not used, and the external corners are reinforced where they are not detailed as control joints.

Zinc is frequently used for exposed accessories. Permanent screeds are avoided, except for a drip-base screed at the bottom edge.

Base-Coat Plaster Mixes

In ASTM C 926, various choices are offered for base-coat mixes for cementitious materials and their proportions, but no advice is given about which to choose for a given application. The Portland Cement Association's (PCA) *Portland Cement Plaster (Stucco) Manual* suggests that "a good rule is to select a mixture with a maximum amount of aggregate-to-cement ratio to reduce shrinkage and cracking." The same publication recommends "for simplicity and economy" selecting the same plaster type for "both scratch- and brown-coat applications" but "proportions should be adjusted to allow for more sand in the brown coat" for three-coat work. Consult experienced plasterers or local lathing and plastering bureaus, if possible, when choosing mix designs. One axiom to remember is: Never add lime or other plasticizers to mixes containing masonry cement or plastic cement because both already contain such materials.

Finish-Coat Plaster Mixes

Where finish is to be painted, finish-coat plaster mixes can be specified in the same manner as for gypsum plastering; however, gypsum finish should never be applied over portland cement base coat. Otherwise, for uniformity of texture and color, factory-prepared finish coats are recommended. Controlling color and texture will be difficult; hence, results are often unsatisfactory unless a sample submittal is required. Finish and color options are endless, and terminology is not standard and can have different meanings to the parties involved. To achieve the most exact control, require the contractor to match the architect's samples that are established before bidding or, in major work, the contractor to install mockup panels at the project site.

Special applications are available. Hard, stable aggregates, such as marble, granite, or ceramic, may be exposed either by impinging into the plaster or by mixing with the plaster and using a retarder and water wash.

Other special applications include handball courts, single-coat proprietary products for spray application to monolithic concrete surfaces, and resurfacing old portland cement plaster or stucco surfaces. Consult industry standards or manufacturers for recommendations on such applications.

Curing portland cement plaster work is quite different from drying gypsum plaster. Each coat must be moisture cured if the whole is to achieve maximum strength and minimum shrinkage. However, it is possible to use the subsequent wet coat of plaster to supply the moisture curing for the preceding coat, and this is commonly done where appearance is not a prime consideration. Better control of the color and texture is achieved if each coat is moisture cured, dried, and subsequently moistened to a uniform moisture content at the time the next coat is applied.

REFERENCES

Publication dates cited here were current at the time of this writing. Publications are revised periodically, and revisions may have occurred before this book was published.

ASTM International

ASTM C 926–90: Specification for Application of Portland Cement-Based Plaster

National Association of Architectural Metal Manufacturers, Metal Lath/Steel Framing Association Division

ML/SFA 920–91: Guide Specifications for Metal Lathing and Furring

Portland Cement Association

Portland Cement Plaster (Stucco) Manual, 1980.

09251 FACTORY-FINISHED GYPSUM BOARD

This chapter discusses vinyl-film-faced gypsum board panels and associated trim.

This chapter does not discuss gypsum board that is prefinished with an applied coating, panels that are part of a demountable partition system, and framing or other systems that support factory-finished gypsum board.

PRODUCT CHARACTERISTICS

Factory-finished gypsum board panels have vinyl-film facings that are durable, easily cleaned, and available in various textured patterns and colors. Manufacturers advertise that factory-finished panels are less expensive to install than conventional gypsum board with a field-applied decorative covering and that they speed completion of interior spaces. Factory-finished panels are also used to reconfigure occupied spaces where dust from gypsum board finishing operations is unacceptable.

Factory-finished gypsum board is suitable for use on interior partitions. It is generally unsuitable for use on ceiling surfaces because end joints are difficult to conceal.

Restrictions for using factory-finished gypsum board panels include the following:

- Do not install panels over foil-backed gypsum board or vapor retarders.
- Do not install panels where direct heat or steam can affect vinyl-film surfaces, where surface temperatures will exceed 125°F (51.7°C), in bathtub and shower areas, and in areas subject to free moisture.
- To prevent mildew and stains, do not apply panels over wet or damp substrates or substrates that may periodically become damp.
- In hot, humid climates, dry air circulation behind panels or other suitable vapor control is required. Where panels abut concrete or masonry, maintain a ⅛-inch (3.2-mm) clearance between panels and these materials to prevent wicking of moisture.
- Adhesives used to apply panels to supports must be compatible. Incompatible adhesives may cause surface stains or delaminate the vinyl facings. The Gypsum Association (GA) publication GA-224, *Recommended Specifications for Installation of Predecorated Gypsum Board,* cautions against using solvent-based adhesives.
- Do not adhesively apply panels directly to exterior masonry or concrete walls.
- Lumber that has been treated with incompatible chemicals can cause surface stains and delaminate the vinyl facings.

Vinyl-film-facing thicknesses vary and are determined by the pattern selected. Manufacturers offer unbacked and fabric-backed vinyl-film facings. For competitive bidding, specify patterns by manufacturers' designations or describe facing types and thicknesses or weights; otherwise, bidders cannot accurately determine material costs. Depending on the quantity required, custom vinyl-film facings can be laminated to gypsum board panels; consult manufacturers for availability.

Color, tone, and pattern variations occur among panels because facing material manufacturers provide a commercial, not a perfect, color match.

Require the installer to lay out panels in each space to minimize the effect of variations.

Panel long edges are usually beveled. Long edges are wrapped with the facing material.

Vapor-permeability ratings for unbacked vinyl-film facings are published by manufacturers. If the unbacked vinyl-film facing functions as a vapor retarder, consider inserting a permeability rating requirement in the specification.

Fire-test-response characteristics of the gypsum board core are generally not affected by the facing material; however, the facing material does affect surface-burning characteristics. Generally, joints between panels must be covered for fire-resistance-rated construction. Assemblies incorporating factory-finished gypsum board panels have been tested according to ASTM E 119 and are listed in Factory Mutual's (FM's) and Underwriters Laboratories' (UL's) publications. Where specific fire-resistance-rated assemblies are required, materials and construction identical to the tested assemblies must be specified and detailed.

Sound transmission class (STC) ratings for assemblies are not affected by panel facings but are affected by standard installation methods, which make sealing cracks and openings difficult. Detail acoustical sealants, if any, on the drawings.

Matching wall coverings are generally required to cover minor areas, unless the entire installation's surface is uninterrupted. Clean-out plugs, service covers, and other penetrations often make it impossible to cut and patch panels to produce an acceptable appearance. Indicate areas of field-applied wall coverings on the drawings.

Factory-finished trim is extruded plastic with laminated facings that match those of panels or is unfaced (fig. 1). Trim is one-piece, slip-on, or push-

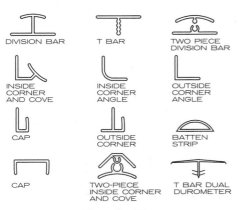

Figure 1. Trim

70

in type, or two-piece, snap-on type. One-piece trim is available for corners, flat joints, exposed edges, and ceiling-to-wall joints. Two-piece trim units have factory-finished plastic coverings held in place by metal retainer clips. They are used at corners and flat joints (battens) and are generally required for fire-resistance-rated assemblies.

Factory-finished exposed fasteners are color-coated, corrosion-resistant steel nails (color pins). Verify their availability to match facing colors and patterns selected. Unlike conventional nails, color pin heads are not set below the panel surface (dimpled) and are driven using a plastic-headed or padded hammer to avoid damaging their finish.

Concealed edge clips for mechanically fastening panels to wood or steel framing are available from some manufacturers. They can be used without surface trim to produce a fine-line joint between square-edged panels; however, the panels must be absolutely flat to prevent lipping at the joints.

REFERENCES

Publication dates cited here were current at the time of this writing. Publications are revised periodically, and revisions may have occurred before this book was published.

ASTM International

ASTM E 119-98: Test Methods for Fire Tests of Building Construction and Materials

Factory Mutual Global

Approval Guide, Building Materials, published annually.

Gypsum Association

GA-224-97: Recommended Specifications for Installation of Predecorated Gypsum Board

Underwriters Laboratories Inc.

Fire Resistance Directory, published annually.

09260 GYPSUM BOARD ASSEMBLIES

This chapter discusses gypsum board assemblies and metal support systems. The chapter also addresses the specification of sound attenuation insulation and cementitious backer units for tile, because they are often components of gypsum board assemblies.

This chapter does not discuss gypsum board panels attached to metal furring members imbedded in plastic insulation, solid and semisolid gypsum board partitions, custom-fabricated anchors for attaching gypsum board to metal decking and other supports, and gypsum sheathing attached to metal framing at exterior walls. Gypsum board shaft-wall assemblies, gypsum veneer plaster assemblies, factory-finished gypsum board panels, and glass-reinforced gypsum fabrications are discussed in other chapters in this book.

GYPSUM BOARD ASSEMBLY CHARACTERISTICS

Steel ceiling suspension systems are designed to carry ceiling dead loads, which, in addition to framing members and ceiling panels, usually include the weight of air diffusers, speakers, and the like. Do not use ceiling suspension systems to support the weight of mechanical and electrical equipment or the weight of above-ceiling maintenance workers; use supports that are independent of ceiling suspension systems to support these loads. Building codes, however, often also require support that is independent of the suspended ceiling for lighting fixtures.

Thermal and acoustical insulation laid on a suspended ceiling can produce a noticeable sag in the ceiling panels if their weight exceeds the support capabilities of the gypsum board or suspension system. Exterior soffit framing must be designed and detailed to resist wind uplift and flutter. If seismic considerations are critical, or if partitions are laterally supported by suspended ceilings, analyze the need for cross-bracing in the plenum. Ceiling framing for cementitious backer units must comply with the unit manufacturer's recommendations.

Partition steel framing is nonload-bearing. It is not designed to support floor or roof loads, but it can support certain transverse loads without exceeding allowable loading stresses or deflection limits. Whether the manufacturer's design criteria or ASTM C 754 structural criteria are used in selecting framing, the components specified must comply with requirements of authorities having jurisdiction and with structural requirements of a particular application.

Framing-member spacing may be based on requirements other than on loading. Spacing limitations for both single- and double-layer gypsum panel applications are tabulated in ASTM C 754 according to the panel thickness. Whether panels are installed vertically or horizontally to partition framing, and perpendicular or parallel to ceiling framing, affects the support spacing requirements. Closer-than-normal spacing improves visual flatness and impact resistance. Placing studs so that flanges point in the same direction, and attaching leading edges or ends of each gypsum board to open (unsupported) edges of stud flanges first also improves visual flatness.

Doorways in gypsum board partitions are subject to stresses generated by door swinging and impact and stresses in the panel itself at the reentrant corners between the door frame head and jambs. See the Gypsum Association (GA) publication GA-600, *Fire Resistance Design Manual,* and manufacturers' literature for recommendations. Standard door framing details may not be adequate for extra-wide or heavy doors.

Double-layer gypsum board applications are stronger and have greater fire and sound-transmission resistance than single-layer applications. Adhesively applying a face layer improves resistance to cracking, sagging, and joint deformation, and minimizes exposed fasteners; on the other hand, doing so may be unacceptable for fire-resistance-rated assemblies.

Mechanical fastening methods for attaching gypsum board to wood supports include single nailing, double nailing, adhesive and nailing, and screw attachment (in order of increasing resistance to fastener popping). Because the electric screw gun is familiar to most installers, screw attachment to wood has become common. Nail-fastening gypsum board to ¾-inch- (19.1-mm-) thick wood furring that is applied across framing is not recommended because when framing flexes under hammer impact, previously driven nails can loosen.

ASTM C 840, *Specification for Application and Finishing of Gypsum Board,* does not require panels to be installed with abutting tapered edges at finished joints. To optimize appearance, specify orienting panels to minimize abutting square edges or abutting square edges and tapered edges at joints.

Laminating gypsum board directly to concrete and masonry in lieu of furring is suitable only for interior locations and certain substrate conditions; see manufacturers' literature and referenced installation standards.

FIRE-RESISTANCE-RATED ASSEMBLIES

Most building codes require tested fire-resistive assemblies with hourly ratings for specified uses. Generally, a limited number of assemblies are described in the codes themselves. Authorities having jurisdiction frequently accept design designations of tested assemblies listed by independent agencies on the drawings as evidence of code compliance. Factory Mutual Global's (FMG's) *Approval Guide, Building Products;* GA-600, *Fire Resistance Design Manual;* Intertek Testing Services' (ITS's) *Directory of Listed Products;* and Underwriters Laboratories' (UL's) *Fire Resistance Directory* are frequently cited sources for fire-resistance ratings.

ACOUSTICAL PARTITIONS

The mitigating affects that assemblies have on airborne sound transmission are indicated by the sound transmission class (STC) ratings for the assemblies that are published by manufacturers. STC ratings do not indi-

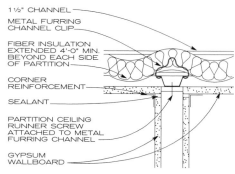

Figure 1. Sound-isolated interrupted ceiling

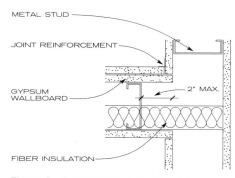

Figure 2. Sound-isolated partition intersection

cate reductions of vibration or impact noise, which is classified by impact insulation class (IIC) ratings according to ASTM E 989. Vibration and impact noise reduction requires dampening and isolation by other means, such as floor coverings and isolation mountings. See figures 1 and 2 for examples of sound-isolated ceiling and partition details.

STC ratings depend on mass, resiliency (or isolation), dampening, and absorption. Multilayer applications contribute mass. Unbalanced gypsum board partitions (a single layer on one face and double layers on the other face) are almost as efficient as double layers applied to both faces, and save material and labor costs. Wood supports are less resilient than steel studs; therefore, they generally transmit more sound. Isolating wood studs by staggering them or using resilient channels increases resistance to sound transmission. Staggering steel studs is not practical because light-gage steel studs are unstable unless panels are applied to both surfaces. Dampening and absorption are provided in sound-rated assemblies by insulation (sound attenuation) blankets in the cavity, which may add 5 or 6 dB to the rating.

A bead of acoustical sealant is required at perimeter edges of panel surfaces on both sides of the assembly. Sealant is also required at gaps and around cutouts in assemblies for outlet boxes and other penetrations and openings behind control joints, unless the control joint manufacturer recommends another way of blocking sound transmission. STC ratings are meaningless if airborne noise can travel through cracks, openings, penetrations, or flanking paths. Eliminating flanking paths requires careful detailing and material selection.

Sound-rated-assembly performance is not as efficient as published ratings, which are based on carefully controlled laboratory conditions. Assume that an assembly's acoustical performance will actually be at least 5 dB below that of its STC rating.

Table 1
STEEL SHEET THICKNESSES

| Gage | Minimum Steel Base Metal (Uncoated) Thickness | |
	Inch	Millimeter
16	0.0538	1.37
20	0.0312	0.79
22	0.0270	0.69
25	0.0179	0.45

STEEL SHEET THICKNESSES

ASTM C 645, *Specification for Nonstructural Steel Framing Members,* requires that sectional properties of framing members be computed according to the requirements in American Iron and Steel Institute's (AISI's) *Specification for the Design of Cold-Formed Steel Structural Members,* 1986 edition, and 1989 Addendum, and requires a minimum base metal thickness of 0.0179 inches (0.45 mm). According to the AISI specification, the delivered minimum base metal thickness is 95 percent of the design thickness, and the design thickness is uncoated. In their product literature, some manufacturers of steel framing members list design thicknesses and actual minimum base metal thicknesses, others list design thicknesses only, and still others list minimum base metal thicknesses only.

Specifying steel thickness by gage number is imprecise because metal sheet is ordered by thickness, and the actual thickness offered by manufacturers may differ. Traditional steel gage numbers and the corresponding minimum base metal (uncoated) thicknesses are included in Table 1.

Cold-formed, 20-gage steel studs used in load-bearing or nonload-bearing curtain-wall applications (usually specified in a Division 5, "Metals," section) generally have a minimum steel base metal thickness of 0.0329 inch (0.84 mm), which is greater than that indicated for 20-gage "drywall" steel sheet in Table 1. However, some manufacturers, particularly in the western United States, also provide the 0.0329-inch- (0.84-mm-) thick steel for "drywall" studs.

STEEL FRAMING MEMBERS

Light-gage steel framing components for screw application of gypsum board come in various shapes, thicknesses, sizes, and finishes. The most commonly used thickness for hat-shaped furring members, studs, and runners complying with ASTM C 645 is 0.0179 inch (0.45 mm). For supporting cementitious backer units, 0.0312-inch- (0.79-mm-) thick studs are recommended. Select the size and thickness of components based on the spacing and span or height of steel supporting members; the type, number, and orientation of panels applied to each face; and the degree of load and impact resistance required.

Stud height and spacing limitations for single- and double-layer gypsum panel applications are tabulated in ASTM C 754 according to maximum deflection and minimum lateral loading requirements. Manufacturers often recommend a deflection limit for gypsum board assemblies of L/240. The deflection that is allowed should never exceed L/120 because deflection greater than L/120 is likely to cause cracking or other damage to gypsum board finishes under normal conditions. Tile finishes applied to gypsum board assemblies may require deflection limits of L/360 or less. Verify specific substrate deflection requirements of tile products specified.

Conventional suspended ceiling and soffit systems have gypsum board panels applied to furring channels (furring members). Cold-rolled channels, steel studs, and hat-shaped rigid or resilient channels are common furring channels. Furring is wire-tied to the structure or is supported by carrying channels (main runners) suspended from the structure.

Grid suspension systems are suitable for interior gypsum board ceilings. These systems consist of main runners, interlocking cross-furring channels, and wall angles; they are direct-hung and do not employ intermediate carrying channels. Grid suspension systems may be a less expensive alternative to conventional indirect suspension systems.

Z-furring members support both gypsum board and thermal insulation. They are not intended to be used without insulation; coordinate their use with requirements specified in Division 7, "Thermal and Moisture Protection," sections. Z-furring members distort when gypsum board is fastened to them; therefore, careful installation is required to produce surfaces that appear flat. Manufacturers advise attaching gypsum board first to the open (unsupported) edges of flanges of Z-furring members. To minimize distortion, avoid using Z-furring with mineral-fiber blanket insulation that easily compresses. Using rigid, plastic insulation boards or higher-density mineral fiber can help decrease distortion.

CORROSION PROTECTION OF STEEL FRAMING

ASTM C 645 and ASTM C 754 include requirements for corrosion resistance of framing members. ASTM C 645, which specifies studs, runners, hat-shaped rigid channels, and grid suspension systems, states "Members shall have a protective coating conforming to Specification A 653/A 653M - G40 (hot-dip galvanized) minimum or shall have a protective coating with an equivalent corrosion resistance." ASTM C 754 includes a similar requirement for cold-rolled channels, and requires galvanized soft-annealed steel wire for ties and hangers. ASTM C 754 states that rod and flat hangers, when specified, can be protected by a zinc coating or another equally rust-inhibiting coating. ASTM C 645 and ASTM C 754 do not prescribe how to evaluate equivalent corrosion resistance for other types of protective coatings, such as electrolytically deposited zinc coatings or rust-inhibiting paints.

For framing members, manufacturers generally use steel sheets that are zinc- or zinc-alloy-coated by the coil-coating process; however, painted steel sheet can be used. Some manufacturers cold-reduce (reroll) sheets to decrease their thickness, which may affect the integrity of the coating. ASTM A 653/A 653M specifies steel sheet that has been zinc coated (galvanized) or zinc-iron-alloy coated (galvannealed) by the hot-dip process. ASTM A 879 specifies steel sheet with electrolytically deposited zinc coatings. When coating masses are equal, electrolytically deposited zinc and galvannealed coatings provide equivalent corrosion resistance to hot-dip galvanized coatings.

For normal environments, components with hot-dip galvanized coatings complying with ASTM A 653/A 653M, G40 (Z120), are readily available. Specifying the manufacturer's standard corrosion-resistant zinc coating will promote the most competition while excluding painted framing members.

For corrosive environments and high-humidity areas, consider requiring a thicker zinc coating on framing members, such as a hot-dip galvanizing coating that complies with ASTM A 653/A 653M, G60 (Z180).

INTERIOR GYPSUM WALLBOARD

Gypsum board panels are available in various thicknesses, edge configurations, lengths, and types. Select thickness and type based on appearance, impact resistance, loading, framing spacing, number of layers, field-applied finish, sound reduction, and fire-resistance requirements.

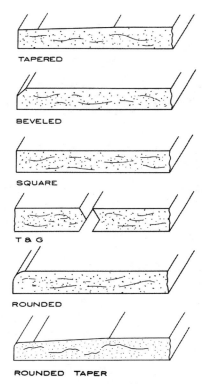

Figure 3. Types of gypsum board edges

Gypsum board edge configuration affects the appearance of the finished assembly. Gypsum panels are available with square edges and with long tapered edges and square returns (fig. 3). Standard, regular-type wallboard is available with long tapered edges and either rounded or beveled returns for prefilling with setting-type joint compound. Treated joints between tapered or prefilled beveled or rounded edges are less noticeable in completed construction than treated joints between square edges. Prefilling beveled or rounded edges increases joint strength, helps minimize joint imperfections, and compensates for temperature and humidity extremes during and after construction. Prefilling joints also increases cost because of the additional labor and joint compound required.

Regular gypsum wallboard is available in ¼-, ⅜-, and ½-inch (6.4-, 9.5-, and 12.7-mm) thicknesses; ½ inch (12.7 mm) is the standard. Use ¼- and ⅜-inch (6.4- and 9.5-mm) thicknesses only for double-layer applications or single-layer applications over existing ceilings and interior partitions.

Type X gypsum wallboard has greater fire resistance than regular gypsum wallboard and is usually ⅝-inch (15.9-mm) thick, but is available in ½-inch (12.7-mm) thickness from some manufacturers. In addition to having enhanced fire-resistive properties, Type X gypsum wallboard is heavier and stronger than regular wallboard, which improves dimensional stability, appearance, and resistance to sound transmission and abuse. Use Type X panels combined with closer frame spacing to improve visual flatness and sag resistance of wall and ceiling assemblies.

Flexible gypsum wallboard with a ¼-inch (6.4-mm) thick, regular-type core is a specialized product designed for double-layer application on tight radius construction.

Sag-resistant gypsum wallboard for ceiling application is available in ½-inch- (12.7-mm-) thick panels and is advertised as having equivalent sag resistance to ⅝-inch- (15.9-mm-) thick, Type X gypsum board. Some

Table 2

TYPES OF GYPSUM PANEL PRODUCTS

DESCRIPTION	THICKNESS (IN.)	WIDTH/EDGE (FT)	STOCK LENGTH (FT)
Regular gypsum wallboard used as a base layer for improving sound control; repair and remodeling with double layer application	1/4	4, square or tapered	8–10
Regular gypsum wallboard used in a double wall system over wood framing; repair and remodeling	3/8	4, square or tapered	8–14
Regular gypsum wallboard for use in single layer construction	1/2, 5/8	4, square or tapered	8–16
Rounded taper edge system offers maximum joint strength and minimizes joint deformity problems	3/8 1/2, 5/8	4, rounded taper	8–16
Type X gypsum wallboard with core containing special additives to give increased fire resistance ratings. Consult manufacturer for approved assemblies	1/2, 5/8	4, tapered, rounded taper, or rounded	8–16
Aluminum foil backed board effective as a vapor barrier for exterior walls and ceilings and as a thermal insulator when foil faces 3/4" minimum air space. Not for use as a tile base or in air conditioned buildings in hot, humid climates (Southern Atlantic and Gulf Coasts)	3/8 1/2, 5/8	4, square or tapered	8–16
Water resistant board for use as a base for ceramic and other nonabsorbant wall tiles in bath and shower areas. Type X core is available	1/2, 5/8	4, tapered	8, 10, 12
Prefinished vinyl surface gypsum board in standard and special colors. Type X core is available	1/2, 5/8	2, 2 1/2, 4, square and beveled	8, 9, 10
Prefinished board available in many colors and textures. See manufacturers' literature	5/16	4, square	8
Coreboard for use to enclose vent shafts and laminated gypsum partitions	1	2, tongue and groove or square	8–12
Shaft wall liner core board type X with gypsum core used to enclose elevator shafts and other vertical chases	1, 2	2, square or beveled	6–16
Sound underlayment gypsum wallboard attached to plywood subfloor acts as a base for any durable floor covering. When used with resiliently attached gypsum panel ceiling, the assembly meets HUD requirements for sound control in multifamily dwellings	3/4	4, square	6–8
Exterior ceiling/soffit panel for use on surfaces with indirect exposure to the weather. Type X core is available	1/2, 5/8	4, rounded taper	8, 12
Sheathing used as underlayment on exterior walls with type X or regular core	1/2	2, tongue and groove	8
	1/2, 5/8	4, square	8, 9, 10

manufacturers recommend using sag-resistant panels on ceilings where water-based textures are applied.

Proprietary, special fire-resistive gypsum wallboard has a special core whose fire resistance is greater than that of standard Type X. For fire-resistance-rated assemblies, proprietary panels from different manufacturers cannot be intermixed because the ratings apply only to assemblies identical in materials and construction to those tested. Besides enhanced fire-resistive properties, proprietary types are heavier and stronger than regular gypsum wallboard, which improves dimensional stability, appearance, and resistance to sound transmission and abuse.

Foil-backed gypsum wallboard has a reflective insulating value where an enclosed air space of at least ¾ inch (19.1 mm) is formed next to the foil. Typically, it is used on exterior walls where the foil provides a vapor retarder; however, the membrane is interrupted at panel joints. Because foil resists passage of moisture vapor, foil-backed gypsum panels are unsuitable for applications where the backing can trap moisture within the board itself or within the assembly. Do not use foil-backed gypsum panels as a base for tile or other highly moisture-resistant wall coverings or for face layers of multi-layer applications. Laminating foil-backed panels is not recommended except for attaching to wood framing with adhesives approved by the manufacturer.

Proprietary abuse-resistant gypsum wallboard is manufactured to have greater resistance to surface indentation from incidental impacts and through-penetration from blunt hard-body impacts than standard, regular and Type X, wallboard. Besides having enhanced abuse-resistance properties, these panels are heavier and stronger than standard wallboard, which improves dimensional stability, appearance, and resistance to sound transmission. ASTM Committee C-11 is developing a separate standard for these products with requirements for flexural strength; humidified deflection; core, end, and edge hardness; and abuse resistance.

Gypsum backing board complying with ASTM C 442 requirements may still be available from some manufacturers, but most have stopped producing it. Standard gypsum board is suitable, and commonly used for, base layers. Producing and stocking backing board, which is only slightly less expensive than standard gypsum board and infrequently used, is unprofitable.

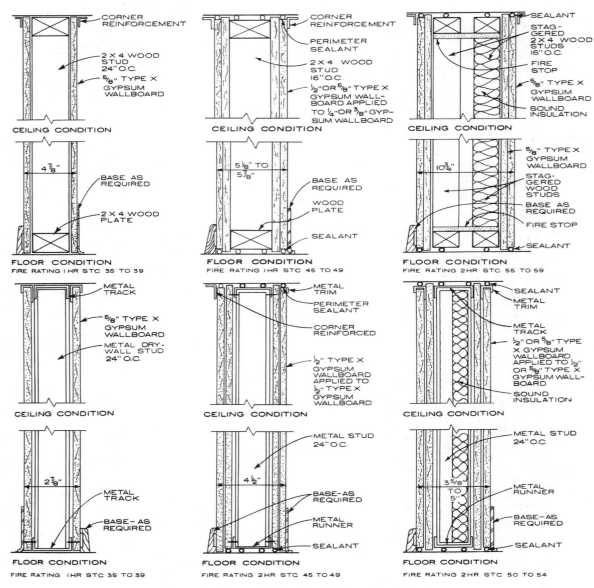

Figure 4. Gypsum wood and metal framed type partitions

GYPSUM PANELS FOR EXTERIOR CEILINGS AND SOFFITS

Exterior gypsum soffit board is a weather- and sag-resistant board designed for exterior soffits and other locations indirectly exposed to the weather. It is available with a ½-inch (12.7-mm) thick, regular type and ⅝-inch (15.9-mm) thick Type X core. It should be painted immediately after the joint compound finish coat has dried; coordinate these requirements with the Division 9 sections that specify painting.

Glass-mat gypsum sheathing board is the generic term for a proprietary product. The manufacturer recommends it as an alternative to exterior gypsum soffit board. It has a gypsum core and a coated glass-fiber mat surface to protect the core from moisture.

Although the gypsum cores of exterior products are water-resistant, they will soften over time when exposed to water. Consider a more expensive, portland-cement-based plaster finish system in lieu of using gypsum products on the exterior.

TILE BACKING PANELS

In areas subject to wetting, water-resistant backing board, glass-mat water-resistant backing panels, and cementitious backer units are suitable tile substrates. Regular gypsum board is a suitable substrate for wall tile not subject to wetting. When panels are substrates for tile, the materials used to finish joints must be compatible with the tile setting beds.

Water-resistant gypsum backing board has a treated core and facings to increase water resistance; however, the gypsum core will soften and deteriorate over time when exposed to moisture. It is intended as a substrate for wall tile with a fused impervious finish (ceramic, plastic, or metal) set in adhesive and can be used in locations, such as tub and shower enclosures, where tile is subject to intermittent wetting. The board itself should not be exposed to direct water flow or used as a substrate in saunas, steam rooms, and communal shower rooms. Neither should it be applied over a vapor retarder. Water-resistant board is paintable.

- ASTM C 840 and GA-216, *Application and Finishing of Gypsum Board: Specifications,* recommend installing water-resistant panels with a ¼-inch (6.4-mm) open space between the panels and other construction or penetrations. Manufacturers recommend treating exposed cut edges with sealant or thinned tile mastic. See manufacturers' literature for product limitations.
- Generally, do not specify water-resistant panels for ceiling applications because they sag. However, ASTM C 840 and GA-216 state that water-resistant backing board may be used on ceilings when framing spacing does not exceed 12 inches (304.8 mm) o.c. for ½-inch- (12.7-mm-) thick panels or 16 inches (406.4 mm) o.c. for ⅝-inch- (15.9-mm-) thick panels.

Glass-mat, water-resistant backing panel is the generic term for a proprietary product. It is an alternative to water-resistant gypsum backing board. It has a gypsum core, which is lighter than cementitious backer units, and a coated glass-fiber mat surface that protects the core from moisture. Although the gypsum core is water-resistant, it will soften and deteriorate over time when exposed to moisture. The manufacturer recommends installing these panels with a ¼-inch (6.4-mm) open space between the panels and other construction or penetrations. Joints must be treated, and cut edges must be sealed against moisture penetration to comply with the manufacturer's installation instructions.

Cementitious backer units have a portland cement core and are surfaced on both sides with glass-fiber-mesh mats. They are intended to serve as the substrate for tile set with adhesives, dry-set mortar, or latex portland cement mortar. According to their manufacturers, products with portland cement cores will not disintegrate or delaminate like gypsum board. These products do not provide a waterproof membrane or a vapor retarder. See manufacturers' literature for other uses for these products.

JOINT COMPOUNDS

Setting-type joint compounds harden by chemical action and do not shrink once set, even before fully drying. Their bond is not affected by high humidity or changes in humidity. Formulations are available with different setting times ranging from 20 minutes to 6 hours. Same-day joint finishing is possible with these compounds because of their setting characteristics. After one coat sets, another coat can be applied without waiting for the previous coat to dry.

- **Setting-type compounds** are available as powders that are job-mixed with water and are generally more expensive than drying-type compounds. They are suitable for filling, smoothing, and finishing interior concrete ceilings, walls, and columns, as well as exterior gypsum soffit panels.
- **Setting-type taping compounds** with long setting times produce the best taped and filled joints because of their high levels of strength and hardness. They are, however, difficult to sand; drying-type or sandable setting-type topping compounds are generally used for finish coats.

Drying-type joint compounds are available ready-mixed and as job-mixed powders. Both products are vinyl-based. As their name suggests, these products harden and bond to surfaces by drying through water evaporation. The compounds shrink until they dry completely, and a minimum of 24 hours is required for drying between coats. Ready-mixed, drying-type compounds are factory-mixed to a smooth, lump-free paste. Job-mixed, drying-type compound powders are mixed with water at the site, generally with electric-powered drill mixers. Packaged, job-mixed joint compound powder can be stored at the site indefinitely and is not susceptible to freezing.

- **Taping compounds** are designed to produce a strong bond between tape and gypsum board. They are also intended as a first fill coat over corner beads, trim accessories, and fasteners; they are harder and more difficult to sand than topping or all-purpose compounds.
- **Topping compounds** generally offer low shrinkage, the best workability, and they are the easiest to sand and finish. They produce the smoothest finish but have less bond strength than taping or all-purpose compounds. They are unsuitable for use as taping compounds or as the first coat over corner beads, trim accessories, and fasteners.
- **All-purpose compounds** are commonly used, as they offer a compromise between the higher bonding strength of taping compounds and the excellent finishing and shrink-resistant characteristics of topping compounds. Lightweight, all-purpose joint compounds have better shrink resistance, are more easily worked, and sand as easily as topping compounds; however, they are softer than other joint compounds.

Consider specifying setting-type taping compounds with multipurpose drying-type compounds for finish coats. This combination produces strong joints that resist cracking. The appearance among various joint compound combinations differs, but is not significant.

GYPSUM BOARD FINISH LEVELS

ASTM C 840 and GA-214, *Recommended Levels of Gypsum Board Finish,* specify finish levels; however, ASTM C 840 requirements, listed here, are more stringent:

- **Level 0:** Taping, finishing, and cornerbeads are not required.
- **Level 1:** At joints and angles, embed tape in joint compound. Panel surfaces must be free of excess joint compound, but tool marks and ridges are acceptable.
- **Level 2:** At joints and angles, embed tape in joint compound and apply one separate coat of joint compound over tape, fastener heads, and flanges of trim accessories. Joint compound applied on the face of the tape when the tape is embedded is considered a separate coat. Panel surfaces must be free of excess joint compound, but tool marks and ridges are acceptable.
- **Level 3:** At joints and angles, embed tape in joint compound and apply two separate coats of joint compound over joints, angles, fastener heads, and flanges of trim accessories. Panel surfaces and joint compound must be smooth and free of tool marks and ridges.
- **Level 4:** At joints and angles, embed tape in joint compound and apply three separate coats of joint compound over joints, angles, fastener heads, and flanges of trim accessories. Panel surfaces and joint compound must be smooth and free of tool marks and ridges.
- **Level 5:** Finish must be equal to Level 4 (embedding coat and three finish coats) plus a skim coat over the entire gypsum board surface. Surfaces must be smooth and free of tool marks and ridges.

Level 5 is considered a high-quality gypsum board finish; it is recommended for areas that will receive glossy paint or that are subject to severe lighting. In lieu of requiring Level 5, consider using a more expensive gypsum veneer plaster for a better, monolithic appearance.

CRACK CONTROL

Gypsum board surfaces will crack if nonload-bearing assemblies are subjected to structural movements. In nonload-bearing assemblies, isolate gypsum board panels from structural elements at all points of contact except floors. Because all structural systems are subject to creep, settlement, deflection, thermal movement, and wind-load strains, consider the effect of

Table 3
RECOMMENDED CONTROL JOINT LOCATIONS

Ceilings	Install control joints in areas exceeding 2,500 sq. ft. (232 sq. m). Space control joints not more than 50 feet (15.2 m) o.c. Install control joints where ceiling framing or furring changes direction.
Partitions and furring	Install control joints in partitions and wall furring runs exceeding 30 feet (9.1 m). Space control joints not more than 30 feet (9.1 m) o.c. Install control joints in furred assemblies where control joints occur in base exterior wall.

these forces on gypsum board assemblies, and detail isolation requirements on the drawings. Because wood framing is subject to swelling and shrinking, "floating" interior-angle gypsum board application is recommended, particularly for directly attached ceilings. Using resilient channels can also minimize or eliminate wood-framing movement problems.

Deflection tracks used for the top runner in steel-framed partitions accommodate varying amounts of movement. Detail deflection track requirements on the drawings.

Standard generic details for deflection tracks use long-leg tracks and include double-track and channel-braced systems. Where deflection may be great, evaluate the lateral stability of the top-track flanges and consider using a steel channel instead.

- **In double-track systems,** the long-leg track is attached to the overhead structure; a second track, which is fastened to the studs, slides up and down within the long-leg track.
- **In channel-braced systems,** studs are inserted into, but not fastened to, the long-leg track and are laterally braced with a continuous cold-rolled channel near the top of the framing.

Proprietary deflection tracks that reduce the labor associated with typical generic details are available. Proprietary tracks designed to isolate framing while maintaining the continuity of specific fire-resistance-rated assemblies are also available.

For perimeter relief, if a deflection track is not used, studs are generally cut ½ inch (12.7 mm) short and friction-fit into the top runner.

Control joints prevent cracks in large areas of gypsum board resulting from dimensional changes caused by temperature and humidity fluctuations (fig. 5). Cracks tend to occur at weak points such as corners of openings. ASTM C 840 requirements for control-joint locations are summarized in Table 3. Show the location of and detail control joints on the drawings. Control joints in fire-resistance-rated construction require rated joint systems and special detailing.

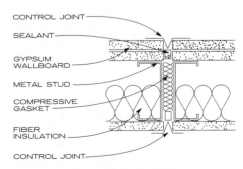

CONTROL JOINT
SEALANT
GYPSUM WALLBOARD
METAL STUD
COMPRESSIVE GASKET
FIBER INSULATION
CONTROL JOINT

Figure 5. Control joint

Do not bridge building expansion joints with gypsum board panels. Set the width of the gaps between gypsum panels to accommodate the calculated movement. To cover gaps, often both board edges are trimmed with metal, and a metal backer strip is attached to only one side; or manufactured covers are specified in a Division 5 section. Sealants or gaskets used to close the gap must be capable of accommodating movement without transferring stresses to gypsum board construction and without failing in adhesion or cohesion.

TEXTURE FINISHES

Decorative and acoustical texture finishes that can be painted or left unpainted are available. The gypsum board installer often applies texture finishes; however, these products can be specified in sections for painting or special coatings. Sometimes, textures are applied using the same topping compound used to finish gypsum wallboard joints. See manufacturers' literature for detailed descriptions of the different products and application methods. Because many variables affect texture finish appearance, requiring a mockup is recommended.

Water-based texture finishes can cause gypsum board ceilings to sag. Some manufacturers recommend sag-resistant ceiling board for areas that will receive texture finishes. Precautions must be taken during texture finish application to ensure moisture does not condense within the gypsum panel.

VAPOR CONTROL

Vapor control is difficult because vapor retarders are often penetrated by electrical outlets, joints between panels, and careless installation practices. In cold climates, vapor retarders are placed on the warm interior sides of walls. For air-conditioned buildings located in climates with high outside temperatures and humidity, the location of the vapor retarder should be determined by a qualified mechanical engineer. Avoid construction that traps moisture within wall cavities. Indicate on the drawings how the continuity of the vapor barrier is to be maintained at transitions to other construction.

Foil-backed gypsum board can be used for vapor control, or a separate polyethylene vapor retarder can be installed. Polyethylene vapor retarders cannot be exposed in plenum areas. For framed, insulated exterior walls, another alternative is to install insulation blankets faced on one side with a vapor retarder.

ENVIRONMENTAL CONSIDERATIONS

Recycled paper is used for the facing of gypsum board products. In some areas, companies are recycling gypsum waste from construction sites. Verify the availability of gypsum recycling operations in the project area, and specify requirements for recycling gypsum waste, if applicable.

Gypsum board waste and scraps are used as soil enhancers, to control acidity, and as mulch.

REFERENCES

Publication dates cited here were current at the time of this writing. Publications are revised periodically, and revisions may have occurred before this book was published.

ASTM International

ASTM A 653/A 653M-97: Specification for Steel Sheet, Zinc-Coated (Galvanized) or Zinc-Iron Alloy-Coated (Galvannealed) by the Hot-Dip Process

ASTM A 879-96: Specification for Steel Sheet, Zinc Coated by the Electrolytic Process for Applications Requiring Designation of the Coating Mass on Each Surface

ASTM C 442/C 442M-99a: Specification for Gypsum Backing Board and Coreboard

ASTM C 645-97: Specification for Nonstructural Steel Framing Members

ASTM C 754-97: Specification for Installation of Steel Framing Members to Receive Screw-Attached Gypsum Panel Products

ASTM C 840-97: Specification for Application and Finishing of Gypsum Board

ASTM E 989-89 (Reapproved 1999): Standard Classification for Determination of Impact Insulation Class (IIC)

Factory Mutual Global

Approval Guide, Building Products, published annually.

Gypsum Association

GA-214-96: Recommended Levels of Gypsum Board Finish

GA-216-96: Application and Finishing of Gypsum Board: Specifications

GA-600-97: Fire Resistance Design Manual

Intertek Testing Services

Directory of Listed Products, published annually.

Underwriters Laboratories Inc.

Fire Resistance Directory, published annually.

This chapter discusses nonload-bearing, steel-framed gypsum board assemblies that provide fire-resistance-rated enclosures for vertical shafts and horizontal enclosures.

The chapter does not discuss requirements for finishing gypsum wall-board, gypsum base for veneer plaster, or cementitious backer units applied as assembly face layers. These requirements are discussed in other chapters of this book.

ASSEMBLY CHARACTERISTICS

Gypsum board shaft-wall assemblies are nonload-bearing alternatives to traditional masonry shaft enclosures. They are used for elevator hoistway, unlined return-air shaft, chase, stair, and horizontal enclosures. Gypsum board shaft-wall assemblies are designed for installation from outside the shaft; they include proprietary gypsum board liner panels set between special-profile steel studs with gypsum wallboard or similar finish panels applied to the studs on room-side surfaces. In stair enclosures, finish panels are also applied on the shaft side. These partitions are inexpensive, lightweight, thin, rapid and easy to install, fire-resistive, and sound-insulating. They are able to resist intermittent air-pressure loads generated by elevator operation and sustained air-pressure loads in unlined return-air shafts.

Testing of assemblies differs among manufacturers. Analyze these differences to determine which assemblies have the structural, acoustical, and fire-resistance characteristics that satisfy project requirements. Compare manufacturers' product data to determine how typical shaft-wall components were tested; select assemblies with the desired performance characteristics; and identify those assemblies on the drawings and in the specifications.

Restrictions for assemblies include the following:

- Elevator hoistway doors and other openings require structural support independent of the shaft-wall assembly.
- Assemblies should not be installed in areas subject to high ambient humidity and temperatures.

Stud profile, thickness, and fabrication requirements differ among manufacturers. Studs are produced by metal framing manufacturers to comply with requirements of each gypsum board shaft-wall manufacturer's system and are available through the shaft-wall manufacturer. Assemblies are fire-response tested as proprietary systems; therefore, the stud type, which is described by its profile, used in one shaft-wall manufacturer's assemblies cannot be substituted for a different type required for another manufacturer's assemblies.

Limiting height and span support capabilities for each stud type differ because of profile and thickness differences. Manufacturers publish system support capabilities based on intermittent and sustained air-pressure loads for elevator hoistways and unlined return-air shafts, respectively, and allowable deflection limits, including L/120, L/240, and L/360. Limiting

Table 1
ELEVATOR SHAFT-PRESSURE RECOMMENDATIONS

ELEVATOR VELOCITY	ONE OR TWO ELEVATORS PER SHAFT	THREE OR MORE ELEVATORS PER SHAFT
0 to 180 fpm (0 to 0.91 m/s)	5 lbf/sq. ft. (0.24 kPa)	5 lbf/sq. ft. (0.24 kPa)
180 to 1000 fpm (0.91 to 5.08 m/s)	7.5 lbf/sq. ft. (0.36 kPa)	5 lbf/sq. ft. (0.24 kPa)
1000 to 1800 fpm (5.08 to 9.14 m/s)	10 lbf/sq. ft. (0.48 kPa)	7.5 lbf/sq. ft. (0.36 kPa)
1800 to 3000 fpm (9.14 to 15.24 m/s)	15 lbf/sq. ft. 7.5 lbf/sq. ft.	(0.72 kPa) (0.36 kPa)

spans for horizontal applications such as duct enclosures are tabulated based on stud size and thickness, the number of layers of gypsum panels on the exposed face, and allowable deflection. Review manufacturers' literature when specifying assembly requirements.

Allowable deflection, rather than bending stress or shear, is often the limiting structural consideration for installations because deflection affects the finishes applied to the assembly and a building occupant's sense of stability. Manufacturers often recommend limiting deflection to L/360 for veneer plaster and L/240 for gypsum board. If deflection exceeding these recommendations is acceptable, limit deflection to not more than L/240 for veneer plaster and L/120 for gypsum board because greater deflections are likely to cause cracking and other damage to finishes. For tile or similar finishes, verify substrate deflection limits when specifying assembly requirements.

For elevator hoistway enclosures, consider intermittent air-pressure loads. As elevators move through the shaft, they subject the enclosure to both positive and negative air pressures and cause flexing in the shaft wall. The intermittent air-pressure load on the shaft walls depends on the number of elevators within a shaft, their velocity, and the clearance between the elevator(s) and the shaft enclosure. United States Gypsum's *System Folder SA-926-USG Cavity Shaft Wall Systems* recommends the elevator-shaft pressures listed in Table 1. These recommendations are based on tests conducted by United States Gypsum in three buildings ranging from 17 to 100 stories high. The elevator manufacturer can calculate loads for a specific installation; however, the first two rows of the table apply to most elevator installations.

FIRE-RESISTANCE RATINGS

Fire-resistance requirements and hourly ratings for shaft walls are established by building codes according to building use group and construction type. Authorities having jurisdiction frequently accept design designations of tested assemblies listed by independent agencies on the drawings as evidence of code compliance. Factory Mutual Global's (FMG's) *Approval Guide, Building Products;* the Gypsum Association (GA) publication GA-600, *Fire Resistance Design Manual;* Intertek Testing Services' (ITS's) *Directory of Listed Products;* and Underwriter Laboratories' (UL's) *Fire*

Table 2
SHAFT WALLS

FIRE RATING	STC	WALL THICKNESS	CONSTRUCTION DESCRIPTION	WALL SECTIONS
1 HOUR	35 TO 39	3 1/8"	1 in. x 24 in. proprietary type X gypsum panels inserted between 2½ in. floor and ceiling J runners with 2½ in. proprietary vented C-H studs between panels. One layer ⅝ in. proprietary type X gypsum wallboard or veneer base applied parallel to studs on side opposite proprietary gypsum panels with 1 in. type S drywall screws spaced 12 in. o.c. in studs and runners. STC estimate based on 1 in. mineral fiber in cavity. (NLB)	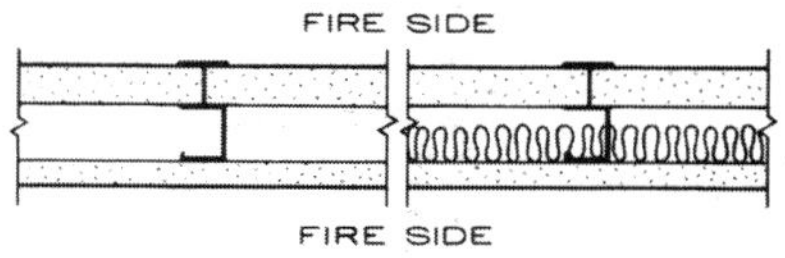 FIRE SIDE / FIRE SIDE
	40 TO 44	2 7/8"	¾ in. x 24 in. proprietary type X gypsum panels inserted between 2¼ in. floor and ceiling track and fitted to proprietary 2¼ in. slotted metal I studs with tab-flange. Face layer ⅝ in. type X gypsum board applied at right angles to studs, with 1 in. type S drywall screws, 12 in. o.c. Sound tested with 1 in. glass fiber friction fit in stud space. (NLB)	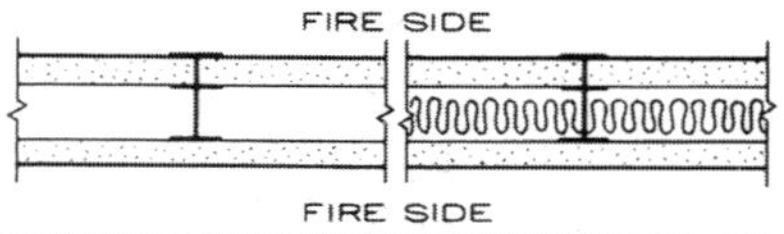 FIRE SIDE / FIRE SIDE
2 HOURS	40 TO 44	3 1/2"	1 in. x 24 in. proprietary type X gypsum panels inserted between 2½ in. floor and ceiling J track with T section of 2½ in. proprietary C-T metal studs between proprietary gypsum panels. Two layers of ½ in. type X gypsum wallboard applied to face of C-T studs. Base layer applied at right angles to studs with 1 in. type S drywall screws 24 in. o.c. and face layer applied at right angles to studs with 1⅝ in. type S drywall screws 8 in. o.c. Stagger joints 24 in. o.c. each layer. (NLB)	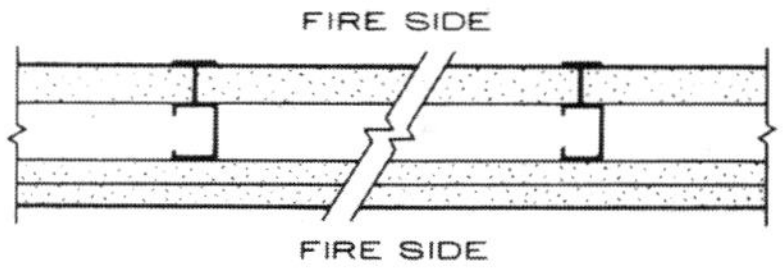 FIRE SIDE / FIRE SIDE
	45 TO 49	3 1/2"	1 in. x 24 in. proprietary type X gypsum panels inserted between 2½ in. floor and ceiling track with tab-flange section of 2½ in. metal I studs between proprietary gypsum panels. One layer of ½ in. proprietary type X gypsum wallboard or veneer base applied at right angles to each side of metal I studs with 1 in. type S drywall screws 12 in. o.c. Sound tested using 1½ in. glass fiber friction fit in stud space. (NLB)	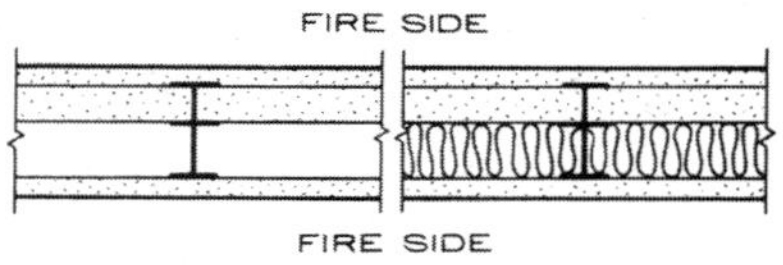 FIRE SIDE / FIRE SIDE
	50 TO 54	4"	1 in. x 24 in. proprietary type X gypsum panels inserted between 2½ in. floor and ceiling track with tab-flange section of 2½ in. metal I studs between proprietary gypsum panels. One layer of ½ in. proprietary type X gypsum wallboard or veneer base applied at right angles to flanges of I studs adjacent to proprietary gypsum panels with 1 in. type S drywall screws 12 in. o.c. Resilient channels spaced 24 in. o.c. horizontally, screw attached to opposite flanges of I studs with ⅜ in. type S screws, one per channel-stud intersection. ½ in. proprietary type X gypsum wallboard or veneer base applied parallel to resilient furring channels with 1 in. type S drywall screws 12 in. o.c. Sound tested using 1 in. glass fiber friction fit in stud space. (NLB)	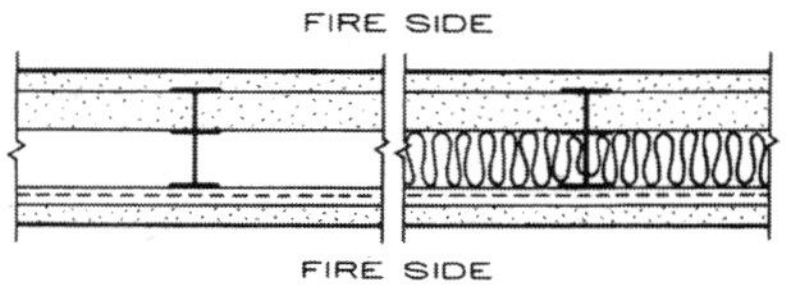 FIRE SIDE / FIRE SIDE
3 HOURS	40 TO 44	4 1/8"	2 in. x 24 in. laminated gypsum board panels installed vertically between floor and ceiling 20 gauge J runners with 25 gauge steel H members between panels. Panels attached at midpoint to 2½ in. leg of J runners with 2⅜ in. type S-12 drywall screws. H studs formed from 20 or 25 gauge 2 in. x 1 in. channels placed back to back and spot welded 24 in. o.c. Base layer ⅝ in. gypsum wallboard or veneer base applied parallel to one side of panels, with 1 in. type S drywall screws 12 in. o.c. to H studs. Rigid furring channels horizontally attached 24 in. o.c. to H studs with 1 in. type S drywall screws. Face layer ⅝ in. gypsum wallboard or veneer base attached at right angles to furring channels with 1 in. type S drywall screws 12 in. o.c. Stagger joints 24 in. o.c. each layer and side. (NLB)	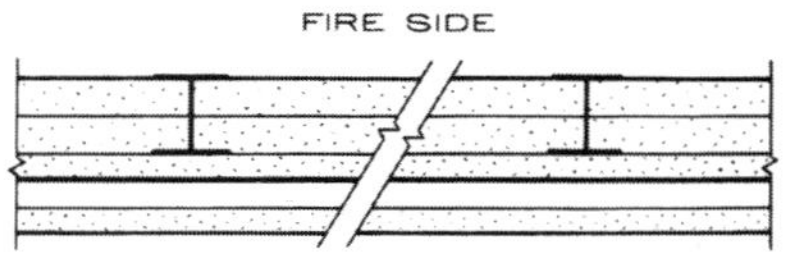 FIRE SIDE / FIRE SIDE
	45 TO 49	5 1/4"	¾ in. x 24 in. proprietary type X gypsum panels inserted between 2¼ in. floor and ceiling tracks and fitted to 2¼ in. slotted metal I studs with tab-flange. First layer ⅝ in. type X gypsum board applied at right angles to studs with 1 in. type S drywall screws 24 in. o.c. Second layer ⅝ in. type X gypsum board applied parallel to studs with 1⅝ in. type S drywall screws 42 in. o.c. starting 12 in. from bottom. Third layer ⅝ in. type X gypsum board applied parallel to studs with 2¼ in. type S drywall screws 24 in. o.c. Resilient channels applied 24 in. o.c. at right angles to studs with 2¼ in. type S drywall screws. Fourth layer ⅝ in. type X gypsum board applied at right angles to resilient channels with 1 in. type S drywall screws 12 in. o.c. Sound tested with 1 in. glass fiber friction fit in stud space. (NLB)	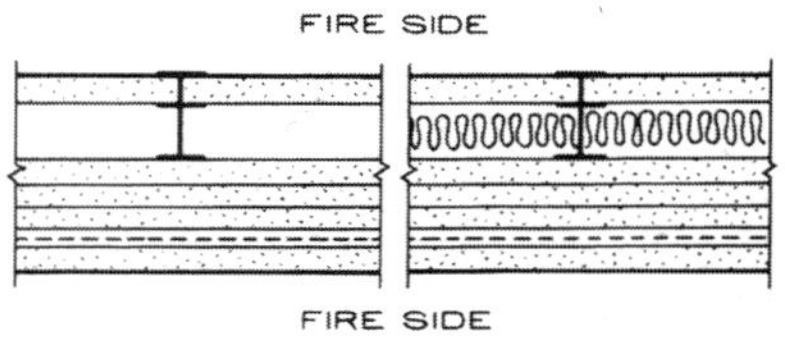 FIRE SIDE / FIRE SIDE

Resistance Directory are frequently cited sources for fire-resistance ratings. Seek specific approval from authorities having jurisdiction before using assemblies that deviate in any way from those that have been fire-response tested and rated by a qualified testing and inspecting agency.

When selecting stud depth and detailing shafts, consider elevator hoistway doors, other doors, elevator call buttons, elevator floor indicators, wiring devices, and other items that must be contained within the assembly without destroying its fire-resistance rating. If a shaft-wall assembly's fire-test performance for penetrations is extrapolated from tests on other assemblies, verification of acceptance of such construction by authorities having jurisdiction may be necessary.

ACOUSTICAL CHARACTERISTICS

Sound Transmission Class (STC) ratings listed in manufacturers' literature and GA-600 provide a way to compare the acoustical performance of different assemblies. STC-rated assemblies cannot be expected to perform as efficiently as their published ratings suggest because ratings are based on carefully controlled laboratory conditions and field conditions are uncontrolled.

Acoustical sealant should be installed where assemblies enclose shafts subject to positive or negative air pressures. Require sealant installation at the system's perimeter and other voids where moving air would cause dust accumulation, noise, or smoke passage.

CRACK CONTROL

Gypsum board and veneer plaster surfaces will crack if nonload-bearing shaft-wall assemblies are subjected to structural movements. Isolate gypsum finish panels from structural elements with sealant installed according to assembly requirements, and detail these joints on the drawings.

Control joints prevent cracks in large areas of gypsum board and veneer plaster resulting from dimensional changes caused by temperature and humidity fluctuations. For partitions, control joints are required at not more than 30 feet (9 m) o.c. vertically and horizontally. ASTM C 840, *Specification for Application and Finishing of Gypsum Board,* and ASTM C 844, *Specification for Application of Gypsum Base to Receive Gypsum Veneer Plaster,* include requirements for control joints. Review these standards or Chapter 09215, Gypsum Veneer Plaster, and Chapter 09260, Gypsum Board Assemblies, for recommendations. Show the location of, and detail control joints on, the drawings. Control joints must have rated joint systems and require special detailing.

Reinforcing at corners of openings in assemblies may be required if control joints are not used or if heavy loads must be supported. Cracks tend to occur at weak points such as corners of openings.

REFERENCES

Publication dates cited here were current at the time of this writing. Publications are revised periodically, and revisions may have occurred before this book was published.

ASTM International

ASTM C 840-97: Specification for Application and Finishing of Gypsum Board

ASTM C 844-98: Specification for Application of Gypsum Base to Receive Gypsum Veneer Plaster

Factory Mutual Global

Approval Guide, Building Products, published annually.

Gypsum Association

GA-600-97: Fire Resistance Design Manual

Intertek Testing Services

Directory of Listed Products, published annually.

Underwriters Laboratories Inc.

Fire Resistance Directory, published annually.

09271 GLASS-REINFORCED GYPSUM FABRICATIONS

This chapter discusses factory-molded products fabricated with glass-reinforced gypsum (GRG), for interior use.

This chapter does not discuss ornamentation fabricated from plastic or fiberglass, or gypsum board products.

PRODUCT CHARACTERISTICS

Glass-reinforced gypsum (GRG) fabrications are lightweight, molded, thin-shelled architectural shapes or ornaments made from gypsum cement reinforced with glass fiber. The terms *fiberglass-reinforced gypsum* (FGRG) and *glass-fiber-reinforced gypsum* (GFRG) are sometimes used to describe these fabrications. Introduced to North America from the United Kingdom in 1977, the GRG industry offers many shapes previously available only in plaster. GRG has all but replaced table-run plaster trim and is often used where traditional ornamental forms are required in gypsum board construction.

Common applications for GRG fabrications include column covers, light coves, barrel vaults, domes, and decorative moldings (see figs. 1, 2 and 3). The products are molded in the manufacturer's plant and shipped to a project site, ready to be installed.

GRG characteristics include high tensile strength and inherent flame resistance—it will not burn, smoke, melt, or generate toxic fumes. GRG fabrications have exceptionally hard, impact-resistant surfaces and are dimensionally stable. Because of the material's surface strength, its shape can be retained with little framing. Support framing requirements are reduced compared to those of most plaster or gypsum board installations. Because it is lightweight, GRG is suitable for ceiling applications or renovations where weight is a factor. Products are easily installed with minimal field labor, using standard gypsum board finishing techniques. Like gypsum board, GRG is not a load-bearing material. However, in some cases, lightweight products such as recessed down lights can be supported. When detailing such attachments, consult GRG manufacturers. Most manufacturers offer a selection of stock designs and provide technical support for custom-designed fabrications.

Composition of GRG is gypsum cement that is reinforced with either glass fiber or glass strands. Gypsum cement is alpha-based (as opposed to beta-based used in gypsum board), which requires less water absorption to produce a workable slurry and yields a high-density, high-strength plaster when hydrated and cured. An E-type glass fiber is used in GRG. Other glass-fiber types are not appropriate for GRG, such as the expensive alkali-resistant glass formulated for reinforced cement.

GRG fabrications are manufactured either by hand-laying layers of continuous glass-fiber mat and gypsum slurry in the mold or by introducing chopped strands of glass into the gypsum slurry as it is sprayed into the mold. The finish face is smooth, resembling a plaster surface. Its backside appearance resembles the inside of a fiberglass boat hull, with glass fibers often visible.

Warping is a common problem with GRG components; however, units can often be repaired on a project site by dampening and reshaping them. To prevent damage, exercise care when storing and handling units. Warping is often caused by one or more of the following factors:

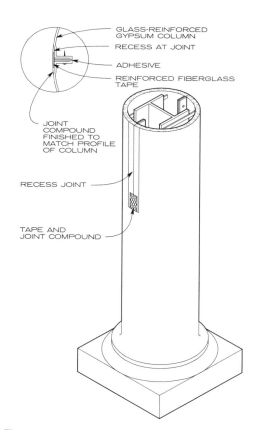

Figure 1. Two-piece glass-reinforced gypsum column

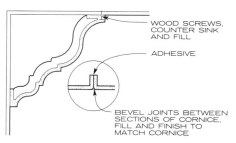

Figure 2. Glass-reinforced gypsum cornice

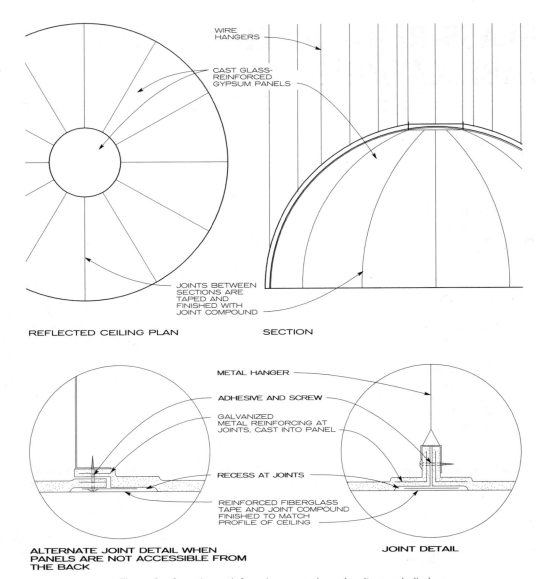

Figure 3. Cast glass-reinforced gypsum dome (vaults are similar)

- **Bad molds:** This is caused by a manufacturing defect.
- **Improper curing:** GRG units should remain in their molds at the manufacturing facility until they are dry.
- **High humidity:** GRG units should remain in their packing crates until they are installed and should not be installed until climatic conditions in the building are maintained at levels indicated for final occupancy.

GRG installation, depending on the size and configuration of units, is similar to gypsum board installation. Butt joints in GRG linear moldings are typically treated with joint compound. Joints for larger pieces—for example, domes—are taped and treated with joint compound. Joint-finishing procedures are the same as those used for gypsum board.

PRODUCT STANDARDS

GRG standard ASTM C 1355/C 1355M, *Specification for Glass Fiber Reinforced Gypsum Composites,* includes requirements for compressive strength, hardness, flexural strength, impact resistance, linear thermal expansion, humidified deflection, and nail pull resistance. First issued in 1996, this standard also includes criteria for GRG materials such as alpha gypsum cement and E-type glass fiber.

Two other GRG standards are ASTM C 1381, *Specification for Molded Glass Fiber Reinforced Gypsum Parts,* and ASTM C 1467/C 1467M, *Specification for the Installation of Molded Glass Fiber Reinforced Gypsum Parts.*

PRODUCT SELECTION CONSIDERATIONS

Cost factors for GRG assemblies are affected by the following design considerations:

- **Amount of detail:** Highly detailed molds are more labor-intensive to build.
- **Tolerances:** Increased precision requires more attention to detailing connections.
- **Number of repetitive pieces:** The more often a mold can be reused, the

greater the cost savings. Where the number of pieces involved is few, it may be more economical to use ornamental plaster to achieve the same effect.

- **Size:** Fabricating, crating, shipping, and installing large pieces require more labor and materials.
- **Surface finish:** Smoother finishes require more labor-intensive fabrication processes.
- **Color:** Pigments will increase the cost.
- **Special reinforcement:** Increased or stronger anchors and supports may be required for large, heavy, or unusually shaped pieces.

Finishes for GRG Units

Similar to other gypsum surfaces, GRG units must be primed before paint can be successfully applied. The priming and painting of GRG units are usually specified in the painting specification sections in Division 9, "Finishes." Some GRG pieces are unsuitable for high-gloss finishes; however, with the proper compounds, sealers, and primers, the GRG surface may be properly prepared to receive high-gloss paint. Consult the GRG manufacturer for fabrication requirements for a high-gloss finish.

REFERENCES

Publication dates cited here were current at the time of this writing. Publications are revised periodically, and revisions may have occurred before this book was published.

ASTM International

ASTM C 1355/C 1355M-96: Specification for Glass Fiber Reinforced Gypsum Composites

ASTM C 1381-97: Specification for Molded Glass Fiber Reinforced Gypsum Parts

ASTM C 1467/C 1467M-00: Specification for the Installation of Molded Glass Fiber Reinforced Gypsum Parts

09310 CERAMIC TILE

This chapter discusses *unglazed and glazed ceramic tile, including ceramic mosaic, quarry, paver, and wall tile; tile setting and grouting materials; accessories; and installation requirements.*

This chapter does not discuss *dimension stone tile, stone paving and flooring, and brick flooring, which are covered in other chapters, nor does it address agglomerate stone tile.*

GENERAL COMMENT

This chapter offers a brief review of different types of ceramic tile and tile-setting and -grouting materials. For more extensive and detailed data, refer to publications listed in the References at the end of this chapter and to manufacturers' literature. And, as necessary, seek the advice of qualified product manufacturers, tile contractors, tile industry associations, and consultants.

TILE CHARACTERISTICS

Tile is defined in American National Standards Institute (ANSI) publication ANSI A137.1 as "a ceramic surfacing unit, usually relatively thin in relation to facial area, made from clay or a mixture of clay and other ceramic materials, called the body of tile, having either a glazed or unglazed face and fired above red heat in the course of manufacture to a temperature sufficiently high to produce specific physical properties and characteristics."

Tile is further classified in the standard as follows, based on water absorption:

- **Impervious tile:** 0.5 percent or less
- **Vitreous tile:** 0.5 to 3.0 percent
- **Semivitreous tile:** 3.0 to 7.0 percent
- **Nonvitreous tile:** More than 7.0 percent

These water-absorption classifications may be useful in specifying tile because water absorption is directly related to stain resistance and may be indirectly related to durability. Lower water absorption generally indicates a denser, more thoroughly fused product and therefore also generally indicates a stronger, more durable product. Water absorption, however, is not directly correlated to strength and durability. Before specifying one or more of these water-absorption classifications, verify that the selected tile will comply with requirements and that the specified classifications do not exclude otherwise acceptable products.

Glaze is the glassy coating on the ceramic body. It may be clear (transparent and colorless or colored) or opaque, and may have a high-gloss, mat, or semimat surface. High-gloss finishes tend to show scratch and wear marks more quickly than mat finishes. Crystalline glazes are manufactured by firing tiles with a heavy-color topping, resulting in a crackled finish as the glaze cools and shrinks. In a second firing, the tiles receive a clear overglaze to produce a smooth finish.

Glaze types are defined in ASTM C 242, *Terminology of Ceramic Whitewares and Related Products.* These definitions are descriptive only; they do not include performance criteria for gloss characteristics that can be specified and verified by testing. A bright glaze, as the name suggests, has a high gloss and can be clear or opaque. Mat glazes can also be clear or opaque but with a low gloss. A semimat glaze has a moderate gloss. Other types of glazes include crystalline (which contains macroscopic crystals) and vellum (a semimat glaze having a satinlike appearance). Glaze should be selected for desired appearance and performance characteristics. However, because ANSI A137.1 does not include criteria for specifying finishes of glazed units either, specifying glaze types by the above terms may not be entirely satisfactory in ensuring that products with the desired finish will be provided. It is preferable to include a list of products that comply with specified characteristics, available from one or more manufacturers.

Unglazed ceramic mosaic tiles are small units with a facial area less than 6 sq. in. (38.7 sq. cm), and are usually ¼- to ⅜-inch (6- to 10-mm) thick. (See figure 1 for typical mosaic tile dimensions.) They are formed by either the dust-pressed or the plastic method. They may be of porcelain or natural clay composition and are available with abrasive content for better slip resistance. Porcelain tiles are impervious; natural clay tiles range from impervious to vitreous. Porcelain units have a hardness rating of 100 or more; natural clay, 50 or more. Because unglazed ceramic tiles are homogenous in composition, with color diffused throughout the tile body, abrasion will not affect their appearance as it would glazed products. High strength and low water absorption make these tiles durable and suitable for use on both exterior and interior horizontal and vertical surfaces, including floors. However, for applications requiring resistance to the effects of freezing or severe weather, only those products that have a history of

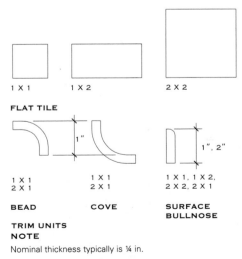

Figure 1. Ceramic mosaic tile

enduring such conditions and have been certified by the tile manufacturer as suitable for the application indicated should be used.

Glazed ceramic mosaic tiles are of the same composition as unglazed units, but have a tinted, glazed finish fused to an untinted body. Glazed units often have a lower coefficient of friction than unglazed units and may be unsuitable for horizontal traffic surfaces. Slip resistance is discussed more fully later in this chapter.

Quarry tiles are unglazed or glazed units with a facial area usually exceeding 6 sq. in. (38.7 sq. cm) and usually are ⅜-, ½-, or ¾-inch (10-, 13-, or 19-mm) thick. (See figures 2 and 3 for typical quarry tile and trim unit sizes.) They are formed by the extrusion process from natural clay or shale. Their water absorption is 5 percent or less, which is midway in the range of water absorption allowed for semivitreous compositions. Quarry tile is virtually unaffected by moisture, acids, oils, or chemicals and is intended for both interior and exterior applications where tile with optimum performance characteristics is needed. As with ceramic mosaic units, where exposure to severe weather and freezing is anticipated, only those products that have demonstrated such capabilities in actual use and are certified by the tile manufacturer for the application indicated should be used. For additional slip resistance, unglazed units are available with an abrasive aggregate embedded in the surface or with a raised pattern stamped into the surface. If glazed units are selected, consider not only their slip resistance but also the durability of the glaze under conditions of anticipated use.

Paver tiles (figs. 4 and 5) are also available both unglazed and glazed. They are manufactured in the same way and of similar materials as ceramic mosaic tiles, but they have a facial area greater than 6 sq. in. (38.7 sq. cm).

Glazed wall tiles (figs. 6 and 7) are units with an impervious glazed finish that is fused to a body that may be nonvitreous but with water absorption not exceeding 20 percent. These tiles are not intended to withstand excessive impact or exposure to freezing and thawing. Because they have limited capability to endure abrasion and impact, their use should be limited to interior vertical and nontraffic horizontal surfaces.

Special-purpose tiles are products with one or more special characteristics, including physical properties and appearance that place them outside the standard tile types already described. These special characteristics may include one or more qualities such as facial size, thickness, shape, color, decoration, method of assembly, or configuration of tile backs and sides. (Figure 8 shows some typical special tile shapes.) More important, special characteristics can refer to resistance to staining, frost, alkalis, acids, thermal shock, physical impact, or coefficient of friction. Although the 1988 revision of ANSI A137.1 included specific test methods for measuring tile properties for freeze-thaw cycling, visible abrasion resistance, static coefficient of friction, moisture expansion, and linear thermal expansion, it did not establish specific performance levels for each property to suit different conditions of use. Specifying special-purpose tiles requires determining the properties of available products and including these properties and the corresponding test methods in the specifications.

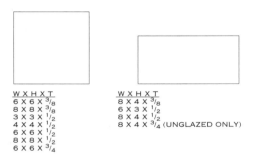

Figure 2. Quarry tile

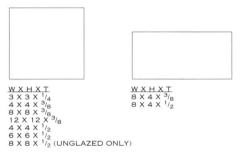

Figure 4. Paver tile

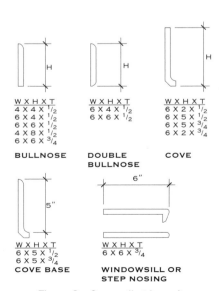

Figure 3. Quarry tile trim units

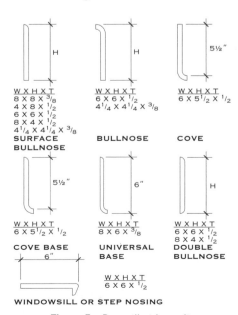

Figure 5. Paver tile trim units

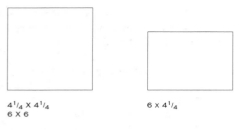

FLAT TILE

NOTE

Nominal thickness typically is $\frac{5}{16}$ in.

Figure 6. Glazed wall tile

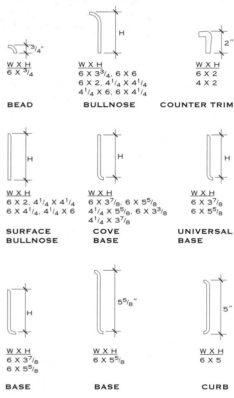

Figure 7. Wall tile trim units

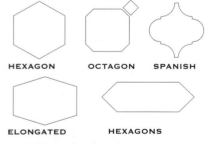

Figure 8. Special tile shapes

Foreign-Made Tiles

More than 50 percent of the ceramic tile sold in the United States is imported. Many suppliers offer both domestic and imported tiles; others are primarily importers. Some imported tiles are tested for compliance with ANSI A137.1, but others are not; these are advertised as complying with foreign standards that differ in many respects from ANSI A137.1. Although imported products may comply with ANSI A137.1, acceptance of foreign products requires understanding foreign standards. An effort is underway to develop an international tile standard.

TILE DIMENSIONS

Manufacturers differ in how they list sizes in their product data. Some list nominal sizes for facial dimensions that are really module sizes (actual facial dimension plus one joint width), but do not always make this clear or even include recommended joint widths. For ceramic mosaic tile and glazed wall tile, the nominal dimension listed in product data is usually the module size. ANSI A137.1 does include lists of nominal facial dimensions for each tile type, but these lists are accompanied by the following caveat: "NOTE: Nominal dimensions are provided for information only and are not a requirement of this standard for grading nor acceptance of tile. Consult manufacturer for actual dimensions."

Once facial dimensions have been included in a specification, they become a requirement of ANSI A137.1, subject to the provisions applicable to dimensional characteristics. If nominal facial dimensions are used in the specifications, the tolerances specified in the standard are ample enough to accommodate a variety of sizes, including those with a tile's actual minor facial dimension plus one joint width.

SLIP RESISTANCE

Tile flooring, like other floor finishes in government buildings and places of interstate commerce, must now meet the standards of the Americans with Disabilities Act (ADA), *Accessibility Guidelines for Buildings and Facilities* (ADAAG). ADAAG requires that newly constructed or altered ground and floor surfaces of accessible routes on sites and in buildings and facilities be "stable, firm, and slip resistant." ADAAG does not specify standards or methods of measurement under scoping or technical provisions. The Appendix to ADAAG does, however, offer recommendations for slip-resistance values derived from research sponsored by the United States Architectural & Transportation Barriers Compliance Board (Access Board). These recommendations are advisory in nature and not mandatory. According to Access Board Bulletin #4, which was first issued in July 1993 and again, with revisions, in April 1994, the recommendations "should not be construed as part of the regulatory requirements for entities covered by Title II and III of the ADA." The bulletin notes that other agencies such as OSHA may impose regulations for slip resistance in the interest of worker safety.

The static coefficients of friction recommended by ADAAG are 0.6 for level floors and 0.8 for ramped surfaces. These values differ from the 0.5 rating recommended by the Ceramic Tile Institute and specified in ASTM D 2047, which is the standard test method for determining the static coefficient of friction for polish-coated floor surfaces as measured by the James Machine, a laboratory device that is not suitable for measuring the static coefficient of friction in the field. ADAAG values are based on a research project sponsored by the Access Board that involved people with disabilities. Their report makes recommendations for static coefficient of friction values and lists the following three testing devices with a commentary on the performance of each:

- **The Horizontal Pull Slipmeter** provided reliable, repeatable results in the laboratory but not in the field.
- **The PTI Drag Sled Tester** performed well but was not commercially available when the report was issued.
- **The NBS-Brungraber Tester** was recommended as the best device currently available.

A comparison of various testers was held at Bucknell University in the summer of 1991. Although the purpose of the comparison was to settle the controversy over which tester should be referenced in standard test methods, this action did not occur.

Measuring the slip resistance of tiles and other walkway surfaces remains a thorny issue. The Access Board acknowledged in Access Board Bulletin #4 that recommendations for static coefficients of friction in the Appendix to ADAAG were not included in the body of ADAAG because they were derived from research involving a small sample size and a unique testing method that produced findings not yet corroborated by other research.

ANSI A137.1 references ASTM C 1028, *Test Method for Determining the Static Coefficient of Friction of Ceramic Tile and Other Like Surfaces by the Horizontal Dynamometer Pull-Meter Method,* as the test method for measuring the coefficient of friction. It does not include minimum criteria for wet and dry values of surfaces considered slip-resistant, but it does include the following note concerning slip-resistance characteristics:

> When coefficient of friction (COF) data are required for a specific project, testing shall conform to ASTM C 1028. However, because area of use and maintenance by the owner of installed tile directly affect coefficient of friction, the COF of the manufactured product shall be as agreed upon by manufacturer and purchaser.

Reaching agreement on definitions for slip resistance, and gaining approval of alternative test methods and testing devices, continues to be difficult. Product manufacturers fear they will be held liable for injuries suffered in falls resulting from conditions over which they have no control, such as poor maintenance practices by owners, exposure to unforeseen surface conditions, or the use of footwear differing from that used during testing. Until all those involved, including manufacturers, owners, pedestrians, design professionals, building officials, and shoe manufacturers, recognize their individual responsibilities concerning this issue, a universally acceptable criterion for slip resistance is unlikely to emerge.

TILE-INSTALLATION MATERIAL CHARACTERISTICS

Tile-installation materials include mortars, adhesives, grouts, cementitious backer units, waterproofing, and crack-suppression membranes. ANSI standards now cover both materials and installation for all these products except crack-suppression membranes.

Load-bearing performance for tile floor installations can be generally predicted by testing according to ASTM C 627, *Test Method for Evaluating Ceramic Floor Tile Installation Systems Using the Robinson-Type Floor Tester.* ASTM C 627 is a pass-fail test for evaluating the load-bearing capabilities of ceramic tile floor installations. It evaluates performance based on the number of tiles and joints damaged during testing, but not other characteristics such as abrasion resistance. Types of damage assessed include chipped, broken, and loose tile, and popped-up, cracked, and powdered grout joints.

The Tile Council of America (TCA) has performed this test on assemblies listed in its *Handbook for Ceramic Tile Installation* and has rated them according to five performance levels: Extra Heavy, Heavy, Moderate, Light, and Residential. Each level is based on the number of cycles using different wheels, loads, load durations, and revolutions that an assembly is subjected to without failing. The TCA rating system was based on testing selected types of tiles over selected substrates using representative setting products and certain TCA installation methods, so similar performance should be expected if the same types of tiles, setting products, and installation methods are used.

TILE-SETTING MATERIALS

General

Tile-setting materials fall into three categories: organic adhesives, cement mortars, and epoxies. Cement mortars include unmodified portland cement mortar, dry-set portland cement mortar, and latex-portland cement mortar. Table 1 lists some of the shear-strength requirements from ANSI standards for these materials and provides a rough comparison of their bonding capabilities. Although the values in the table are minimum values, and the performance of specific products may greatly exceed these requirements, the table generally indicates that organic adhesives are primarily for light-duty use; dry-set and latex-portland cement mortars are for general-duty use; and epoxies are for heavy-duty use.

Organic adhesives are generally water-emulsion latex products, but may include some solvent-release-curing products, although these have largely been eliminated due to VOC regulations. Organic adhesives are generally limited to residential and light-duty commercial applications, and may be advantageous where a degree of flexibility is required, although latex-portland cement mortars that have as much flexibility as most organic adhesives are available.

Portland cement mortar setting methods include both thick- and thin-bed methods. Thick-bed methods use a setting bed, usually of unmodified portland cement mortar, with a bond coat of unmodified portland cement

Table 1
SHEAR-STRENGTH REQUIREMENTS

Setting Material and Standard	Bonded to Glazed Wall Tile	Bonded to Impervious Ceramic Mosaic Tile	Bonded to Quarry Tile
Organic Adhesive, Type I, ANSI A136.1	50 psi (0.34 MPa), same after seven-day water immersion	No requirement	No requirement
Organic Adhesive, Type II, ANSI A136.1	50 psi (0.34 MPa), 20 psi (0.14 MPa) after four cycles of four-hour water immersion	No requirement	No requirement
Dry-Set Portland Cement Mortar, ANSI A118.1	250 psi (1.7 MPa), 150 psi (1.0 MPa) after seven-day water immersion	150 psi (1.0 MPa), 100 psi (0.7 MPa) after seven-day water immersion	100 psi (0.7 MPa)
Latex-Portland Cement Mortar, ANSI A118.4	300 psi (2.1 MPa), 200 psi (1.4 MPa) after seven-day water immersion	200 psi (1.4 MPa), 150 psi (1.0 MPa) after 7-day water immersion, 175 psi (1.2 MPa) after 20 freeze-thaw cycles	150 psi (1.0 MPa), 100 psi (0.7 MPa) after 20 freeze-thaw cycles
Tile-Setting and -Grouting Epoxy and Epoxy Adhesive, ANSI A118.3	No requirement	No requirement	1000 psi (6.9 MPa), 500 psi (3.4 MPa) after four immersion cycles in 72 and 205°F (22 and 96°C) water

mortar, dry-set portland cement mortar, or latex-portland cement mortar. For floors, the setting bed may be placed over a bond breaker to allow the substrate to move independent of the setting bed, in which case the setting bed must be reinforced. Alternatively, the setting bed may be bonded to the substrate, in which case it is generally not reinforced. Advantages of the thick-bed method include allowing some minor leveling to be accomplished in placing the setting bed and allowing the setting bed to be independent of the substrate.

The thick-bed method involves setting the tile on either a plastic setting bed (wet-set method) or a cured setting bed (cured-bed method). ANSI A108.1A specifies installation of ceramic tile by the wet-set method using unmodified portland cement mortar, dry-set portland cement mortar, or latex-portland cement mortar for the bond coat. ANSI A108.1B specifies installation on a cured setting bed, which requires either dry-set or latex-portland cement mortar for the bond coat. ANSI A108.1C allows the contractor the option of using either the wet-set or cured-bed method.

The thin-bed method does not require subfloors to be recessed in order for finished floors to be at similar elevations. On walls, the thin-bed method allows gypsum board or cementitious backer units to be used as substrates rather than metal lath. Another advantage of this method is that it may also save time by eliminating the need for applying multiple layers of setting materials. ANSI A108.5 specifies thin-set methods using dry-set portland cement mortar or latex-portland cement mortar over concrete, cementitious backer units, masonry, gypsum board, and portland cement plaster; ANSI A108.12 specifies the thin-set method for latex-portland cement mortar over exterior-glue plywood.

Waterproofing materials used under a thin-set application must be capable of bonding to the setting bed, because thin-set applications must be bonded to the substrate. ANSI A118.10, *Specifications for Load Bearing, Bonded, Waterproof Membranes for Thin-Set Ceramic Tile and Dimension Stone Installations,* specifies bonded waterproof membranes for thin-set applications and includes both sheet products and fluid-applied products. Sheet products are generally adhered to the substrate with the same thin-set mortar used to install the tile, while fluid-applied products are self-adhering and may be either fabric-reinforced or unreinforced. Some of these products can bridge minor cracks in the substrate without transferring the cracks to the setting bed above. Careful attention to manufacturers' written instructions may be required to ensure crack isolation; and, if crack movement exceeds the products' isolation capability, a flexible sealant-filled joint will be required.

Dry-set portland cement mortars are prepackaged formulations of portland cement, sand, and water-retentive additives. The term *dry-set* means that highly absorptive tile does not need to be soaked before setting because the mortar contains a water-retentive additive. These mortars are suitable for thin-set applications only over substrates that comply with requirements specified in the applicable standards for surface variations, soundness, and rigidity under service. ANSI A118.1, *Specifications for Dry-Set Portland Cement Mortar,* covers only prepackaged products, including fast-setting dry-set mortars and nonsagging dry-set mortars. To qualify as fast-setting, a mortar must attain required shear-bond strength at a much faster rate than normal dry-set mortar. Nonsagging mortars must demonstrate no vertical sag of tile from the original position in the test specimen, as opposed to normal mortar where sag is limited to less than 1/16 inch (1.6 mm).

Latex-portland cement mortars incorporate a polymer in either liquid-latex form or redispersible powder form. Liquid-latex additive is added at the project site to a prepackaged dry-mortar mix that the manufacturer supplies for use with the particular additive. In most cases, the prepackaged

dry-mortar mix is also marketed as a dry-set portland cement mortar. For products in which the polymer is in powder form, only water must be added. Liquid-latex additives can be field mixed with sand and portland cement, but ANSI A118.4, *Specifications for Latex-Portland Cement Mortar,* does not include field-mixed mortars. As with dry-set portland cement mortars, the standard covers two specialized latex-portland cement mortars: fast-setting formulations and nonsagging formulations.

Latex-portland cement mortars for use over exterior-glue plywood are specified in another standard, ANSI A118.11. This standard is based on ANSI A118.4 but has different performance requirements. ANSI A118.11 only requires a 12-week shear strength of 150 psi (1.0 MPa) for quarry tile bonded to plywood, which is the approximate limit placed on this characteristic by the strength of the plywood. ANSI A118.11 does not include the requirements for shear strength after exposure to freeze-thaw cycles that are found in ANSI A118.4. TCA's *Handbook for Ceramic Tile Installation* does not include installation methods that use latex-portland cement mortars with exterior-glue plywood; either organic or water-cleanable epoxy adhesive could also be used for applications where latex-portland cement mortars would be used.

Liquid-latex polymers are either a concentrate that can be diluted with water at the project site according to the latex manufacturer's written instructions or a prediluted product that replaces water entirely for mixing the mortar. The two latex emulsions most commonly used are styrene-butadiene rubber (SBR) and acrylic resin. Although both SBRs and acrylics display excellent bond strengths, low water absorption, and resiliency, acrylics seem to have the edge on these properties. SBRs, however, have a longer history of successful use. Although liquid latexes are generally more water-resistant than redispersible powders, they risk being watered down, or even omitted, unless the mixing operation is observed.

Redispersible powder polymers that are included in prepackaged dry-mortar mixes are either polyvinyl acetate (PVA) or ethylene vinyl acetate (EVA); manufacturers usually describe them as vinyl acetate copolymers. The advantage with redispersible powder polymers is that the architect does not have to watch the workers add them to ensure that the powders are actually in the mix. A disadvantage is that most redispersible powder polymers tend to redisperse when wet, even after the mortar has cured, which eliminates their use for exterior locations and locations exposed to prolonged wetting.

Advantages of latex-portland cement mortars over dry-set mortars include improved adhesion and greater resistance to frost damage, impact, and cracking due to the flexibility of the latex. Latex additives also improve hydration of the cement by retarding evaporation. Exercise care, however, when using latex additives with dry-set mortars, because dry-set mortars contain water-retentive agents, and curing time may be extended excessively by overly retarded evaporation of water. Also, when latex-portland cement mortar is used in locations constantly exposed to moisture, such as swimming pools and shower rooms, ensure that the mortar is allowed to dry thoroughly before exposure to moisture from in-service conditions; if latex-portland cement mortar does not dry thoroughly, the latex may remain emulsified and not develop adequate strength. Drying may take longer than with other mortars because of retarded evaporation. TCA's *Handbook for Ceramic Tile Installation* states that the use of latex additives is required for setting large-unit porcelain-bodied tiles.

Water-cleanable epoxy mortars and adhesives are specified in ANSI A118.3, *Specifications for Chemical Resistant Water Cleanable Tile-Setting and Grouting Epoxy and Water Cleanable Tile-Setting Epoxy Adhesive;* installation methods for these materials are specified in ANSI A108.6. ANSI A118.3 designates these materials as chemical-resistant, water-cleanable, tile-setting and -grouting epoxies and water-cleanable, tile-setting epoxy adhesives. Both are epoxy systems composed essentially of 100 percent solids produced by mixing two or more parts, including an epoxy resin, a hardener, and usually sand or a filler, and both are partly emulsifiable in water after mixing so the residue can be easily cleaned from tile surfaces during installation.

The distinction between chemical-resistant, water-cleanable, tile-setting and -grouting epoxies and water-cleanable, tile-setting epoxy adhesives is that the tile-setting and -grouting epoxies are designed specifically to be chemical-resistant and are formulated for use as grouts and adhesives, whereas the epoxy adhesives are not intended to provide chemical resistance or to serve as grouts. However, all epoxies generally have some degree of chemical resistance. Because ANSI A118.3 does not include specific requirements for chemical resistance and requires both products to comply with the same performance requirements, the difference between the two products may be in name only.

ANSI A118.3 references ASTM C 267, *Test Method for Chemical Resistance of Mortars, Grouts, and Monolithic Surfacings and Polymer Concretes,* for chemical resistance, but requires that chemical concentrations and immersion temperatures be chosen to simulate exposure conditions, and thus they must be designated by the user. If tile-setting materials must be resistant to certain reagents, include descriptions of reagents to which the tile will be exposed in the specifications that include not only the reagents' chemical concentrations and temperatures but also acceptable performance criteria to use in measuring the effects of exposure. In establishing such requirements, request that the owner provide the data, and consult the manufacturers of chemical-resistant products to determine the availability of products with the desired characteristics. For certain severe exposures, it may be necessary to use brick flooring instead of tile; refer to Chapter 09636, Chemical-Resistant Brick Flooring.

Although epoxy mortars, grouts, and adhesives are required to withstand 205°F (96°C) for at least one-half hour, not all will withstand temperatures above 140°F (60°C) for prolonged periods. Some will withstand temperatures up to 350°F (177°C), but products must be carefully selected if this degree of temperature resistance is required. Note that the modified-epoxy emulsion mortar/grout covered by ANSI A118.8 is not at all similar to tile-setting and -grouting epoxies or epoxy adhesives; it is a polymer-modified portland cement product that is only required to provide shear strengths similar to those required for dry-set portland cement mortars. Modified-epoxy emulsion mortars and grouts are not included in any of the methods in TCA's *Handbook for Ceramic Tile Installation.*

Chemical-resistant furan mortars and grouts for ceramic tile are covered by ANSI A118.5 for materials and by ANSI A108.8 for installation. Furan mortars and grouts are produced by combining a furan resin with a powder containing fillers and an acid catalyst. Fillers are either carbon or silica, depending on the chemical-resistant properties required of the mortars and grouts. Epoxy mortars are often used for setting tile that is grouted with furan grouts because the acid catalyst used with furans reacts with the portland cement in concrete, impairing the bond and depleting the catalyst, which keeps the furan from setting properly. If tile is set with furan mortar, it must be applied over a chemical-resistant waterproof membrane, not over concrete.

Furan mortars and grouts will generally withstand temperatures up to 375°F (190°C), and some are available that will withstand continuous exposure up to 430°F (220°C) and intermittent exposure to 475°F (245°C). If the application involves high temperatures, it is best to carefully select products or specify the required temperature resistance because ANSI A118.5 has no requirement for temperature resistance.

WATERPROOFING

Load-bearing, bonded waterproofing membranes specifically designed for use with dry-set or latex-portland cement mortars under ceramic tile include sheet membrane waterproofing; both fabric-reinforced and unreinforced, fluid-applied waterproofing; latex-portland cement mortars; and urethane tile-setting adhesives. The industry standard for these products is ANSI A118.10. These products, along with those intended only to serve as crack-suppression membranes, are probably best specified by naming manufacturers and products, but only after thoroughly investigating their suitability for the substrate and in-service conditions involved. These products can also be used under portland cement mortar (thick-set) installation.

Waterproofing for use under portland cement mortar (thick-set) installation can also be specified in Division 7, "Thermal and Moisture Protection." specification sections.

CRACK-SUPPRESSION MEMBRANES

Crack-suppression membranes are designed to reduce or eliminate transference of minor substrate cracks through tile surfaces. By transferring crack movements in substrates to sealant-filled tile joints, crack-suppression membranes generally eliminate the need to locate sealant-filled tile joints directly over each minor substrate crack. However, crack-suppression membranes should not be considered a substitute for properly placed expansion and control joints.

When selecting a crack-suppression membrane, consider that although the more resilient crack-suppression membranes have greater capability to reduce crack transfer, they provide less support for tile that is subjected to heavy loads. No industry standard currently exists for these products, but ANSI A118.10 is useful for specifying them because it includes requirements that are applicable to crack-suppression membranes. If referencing this standard in the specification for crack-suppression membranes only, it may be desirable to exempt Section M-4.5, "Waterproofness"; Section M-5.4, "7-Day Water Immersion Shear Strength"; and Section M-5.7, "100-Day Water Immersion Shear Strength." Most manufacturers of tile-setting products offer crack-suppression membranes, and they, along with consultants, should be consulted before specifying such products. For thin-set applications, latex-portland cement mortars with their greater flexibility should be used with these products.

CEMENTITIOUS BACKER UNITS

Cementitious backer units are an alternative to water-resistant gypsum board for walls over bathtubs, shower receptors, and similar areas where optimum water resistance is required and where, for cost or other reasons, a panel material is preferred instead of a portland cement mortar bed. Specifications for cementitious backer units are found in ANSI A118.9, and their installation is specified in ANSI A108.11. Among the advantages that cementitious backer units offer over water-resistant gypsum board is that their cut edges and penetrations do not require treatment with a water-resistant adhesive or sealant to prevent deterioration of the backing. TCA's *Handbook for Ceramic Tile Installation* recommends a maximum stud spacing of 16 inches (400 mm) with cementitious backer units and, if metal studs are used, a minimum metal thickness of 0.039 inch (1.0 mm).

GROUTING MATERIALS

Sand-portland cement grouts are mixtures of sand and portland cement that are usually field mixed. Although they are an acceptable grouting material, they are not specified in ANSI A118.6, *Specifications for Standard Cement Grouts for Tile Installation.* Requirements for sand-portland cement grout ingredients and mixing proportions are found in ANSI A108.10.

Standard sanded cement grouts (formerly called *commercial portland cement grouts*) are prepackaged mixes appropriate for joints ⅛ inch (3.2 mm) and wider, as stated in the material description in ANSI A118.6. These grouts are a combination of portland cement, sand, and other ingredients that produce a dense, water-resistant material with uniform color. Many are appropriate for use as polymer-modified sanded grouts when mixed with a latex additive formulated for this purpose.

Standard unsanded grouts (formerly called *dry-set grouts*) are appropriate for joints ⅛ inch (3.2 mm) and narrower. These prepackaged mixtures of portland cement, fillers (which reduce shrinkage), and additives that improve water retentivity are intended for grouting walls and floors. Many, if not all, of these products are also appropriate for use as polymer-modified unsanded grouts when combined with a latex additive formulated for this purpose.

Polymer-modified cement grouts (formerly called *latex-portland cement grouts*) are covered by new standard ANSI A118.7, *Specifications for Polymer Modified Cement Grouts for Tile Installation,* which was created by removing the requirements for these grouts from ANSI A118.6. Because this standard is new, many grout manufacturers do not reference it in their catalogs but continue to cite compliance with ANSI A118.6-1992, Paragraph H-2.4. If a manufacturer's product data references ANSI A118.6-1992 but not specifically Paragraph H-2.4, the grout may not meet the requirements for a polymer-modified cement grout. Polymer-modified cement grouts are prepackaged dry mixes containing portland cement, graded aggregates or fillers, and other ingredients, with either a redispersible powder polymer additive included in the dry mix and requiring only the addition of water at the project site or a latex additive in concentrate or dilute form that is added at the project site. The liquid-latex additives are generally either SBR or acrylic resin, and the redispersible powders are either PVA or EVA, with EVA predominating. Use of polymer-modified cement grouts eliminates the need for damp curing.

Acrylic resins exhibit the best resistance to UV light, are nonyellowing, and have the lowest water-absorption rates, resulting in better stain resistance. They are often the product of choice, particularly for color stability and exterior exposures. Acrylics are available in either concentrated or prediluted form. Typically, acrylic additives that are prediluted and marketed for both mortars and grouts must be further diluted in the field to produce a polymer-modified cement grout. Some manufacturers offer two different prediluted formulations: one for mortar, the other for grout. An advantage of PVA and EVA resins is that, as dry polymers included in prepackaged mixtures, they cannot be overly diluted or left out when no one is watching.

A disadvantage of polymer-modified cement grouts is the increased difficulty of removing grout film from exposed tile faces, particularly those with porous surfaces. To minimize this problem, the grout should be mixed and applied in a manner that produces as little grout residue as possible, and what residue there is should be removed immediately. Allowing grout residue to cure makes cleaning more difficult. Where grout color contrasts markedly with the tile and where tile surfaces are porous and light colored, it may be necessary to precoat exposed tile surfaces with a temporary protective coating or to seal them with a penetrating sealer. Most manufacturers of tile-setting materials offer a grout haze remover for cleaning tile, but this type of product may not be safe for some tiles and should not be considered a substitute for cleaning the tile as it is grouted.

Water-cleanable epoxy grouts, specified in ANSI A118.3, are discussed in the paragraphs above for water-cleanable epoxy mortars and adhesives.

Chemical-resistant furan grouts, specified in ANSI A118.5, are discussed in the paragraphs above for chemical-resistant furan mortar.

Temporary Protective Coatings

Wax or grout release as a temporary protective coating for exposed tile surfaces is necessary with furan grouts and may also be necessary with other grouts such as polymer-modified cement products. Application of a protective temporary coating to quarry and other tile can be done at the factory or in the field by the installer. The tile industry's current recommendation is to leave the choice to installers because they can select the most appropriate coating for project requirements and be responsible for workmanship. Of the two coatings that are often specified, paraffin wax and proprietary grout releases, wax is the only material that will protect all types of tile. However, the use of wax with epoxy-grouted tile is not recommended, particularly if removal of the wax requires using live steam or other methods involving extreme heat that could damage the epoxy grout. Most manufacturers of water-cleanable epoxy grouts also offer a citric-acid-based cleaner for removing hardened grout. Before using one of these cleaners, test it on a sample of the tile and on other surfaces where it will be used.

Silicone-rubber grouts are one-part, chemically curing, silicone-rubber-based elastomeric sealants used for factory-grouted joints within pregrouted sheets of glazed wall tile and for field-grouted joints between the same pregrouted sheets. These grouts are no longer included in ANSI A118.6. The use of pregrouted sheets with silicone-rubber grout reduces installation labor and provides crack-resistant grout joints that are impervious to moisture.

SEALANTS

Elastomeric sealants for expansion, contraction, control, and isolation joints in tile work can be specified with the tile or in a Division 7 section. Deciding where to specify sealants will depend on the size of the project and whether tile contractors likely to be awarded the tile subcontract are qualified to install the sealants in a satisfactory manner.

INSTALLATION CONSIDERATIONS

General

The referenced standards and references listed in this chapter contain information concerning the selection of materials and methods for setting tile to suit various in-service conditions. Because of the variety of tile, setting materials, and grouts available, it is important to follow the recommendations in these references and to seek further advice from qualified sources for specific installations. Figures 9, 10, and 11 illustrate typical tile setting methods.

Substrates

One of the most important factors for satisfactory tile installation is a suitable substrate. Be sure to include in the section in which each substrate is specified the kinds of surface tolerances and finishes required to comply with the limitations of the mortar or adhesive system selected for installing the tile. If attaining the tolerances and surface conditions is unlikely, a full portland cement mortar bed or underlayment may be needed; substrate construction must accommodate, without failure, the weight and thickness that this entails. It is also essential to require that substrates have finish and surface conditions that allow for optimum adhesion of the setting materials selected. Ensure that curing compounds, waxy or oily films, and other surface contaminants are not present on substrates when tile is installed.

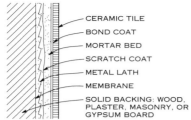

Use over solid backing, over wood or metal studs. Preferred method for showers and tub enclosures. Ideal for remodeling.

CEMENT MORTAR

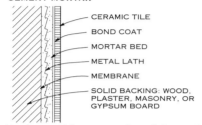

Use for remodeling or on surfaces that present bonding problems. Preferred method of applying tile over gypsum plaster or gypsum board in showers and tub enclosures.

ONE-COAT METHOD

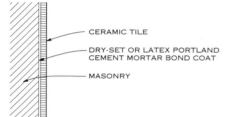

Use over gypsum board, plaster, or other smooth, dimensionally stable surfaces. Use cementitious backer units in wet areas.

DRY-SET MORTAR

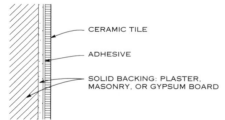

Use over gypsum board, plaster, or other smooth, dimensionally stable surfaces. Use water-resistant gypsum board in wet areas.

ORGANIC ADHESIVE

Use over dry, well-braced studs or furring. Preferred method of installation in showers and tub enclosures.

CEMENT MORTAR

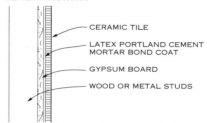

Use in dry interior areas in schools, institutions, and commercial buildings. Do not use in areas where temperatures exceed 125°F.

LATEX - PORTLAND CEMENT MORTAR

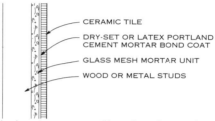

Use in wet areas over well-braced wood or metal studs. Stud spacing not to exceed 16 in. o.c., and metal studs must be 20 gauge or heavier.

DRY-SET MORTAR (CEMENTITIOUS BACKER)

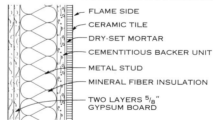

Use where a fire resistance rating of 2 hours is required with tile face exposed to flame. Stud spacing not to exceed 16 in. o.c. and mortar dry-set minimum thickness $3/32$ in.

DRY-SET MORTAR (FIRE-RATED WALL)

Figure 9. Wall tile setting methods

Except for light-duty applications where water exposure is limited, wood products, including plywood, are not considered acceptable tile substrates. For this reason, TCA's *Handbook for Ceramic Tile Installation* includes the following statement:

> Some installation methods and materials are not recognized and may not be suitable in some geographical areas because of local trade practices, climatic conditions or construction methods. Therefore, while every effort has been made to produce accurate guidelines, they should be used only with the independent approval of technically qualified persons.

An application of cementitious backer units or a waterproof membrane over wood construction can help overcome these limitations if the wood floor is stiff enough to provide adequate support for a tile floor.

Expansion, contraction, control, and isolation joints must be provided to attain a satisfactory tile installation, according to recommendations in TCA's *Handbook for Ceramic Tile Installation* and ANSI installation standards. Although requirements for joint spacing and width could be in the specification, their actual locations should be determined by the architect and shown on the drawings (fig. 12). Showing them on the drawings provides direct control over appearance and helps ensure that joints in substrates receiving the tile are properly located. Note that tile installation must include joints directly above joints in substrates. If locations of joints are not shown on the drawings, misunderstandings or claims for change orders may result when attempts are made to work out joint locations with contractors after contracts have been awarded because the installer's interpretation of the extent of joints may differ from the architect's. The importance of providing properly spaced, located, and sized expansion and other sealant-filled joints to allow for tile movement cannot be overemphasized.

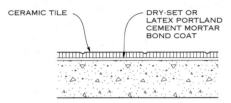

Use over structural floors subject to bending and deflection. Reinforcing mesh mandatory; mortar bed 1 1/4 to 2 in. thick and uniform.

CEMENT MORTAR

Use on level, clean slab-on-grade construction where no bending stresses occur and expansion joints are installed. Scarify existing concrete floors before installing tile.

DRY-SET OR LATEX PORTLAND CEMENT MORTAR

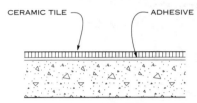

Use where moderate chemical exposure and severe cleaning methods are used, such as in commercial kitchens, dairies, breweries, and food plants.

EPOXY MORTAR AND GROUT

Use over concrete floors in residential construction only. Will not withstand high impact or wheel loads. Not recommended in areas where temperatures exceed 140°F.

ORGANIC OR EPOXY ADHESIVE

Figure 10. Concrete slab tile setting methods

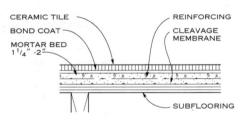

Use over wood floors that are structurally sound and where deflection, including live and dead loads, does not exceed $1/360$ of span.

CEMENT MORTAR

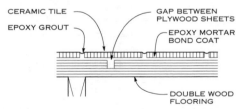

Use in residential, light commercial, and light institutional construction. Recommended where resistance to water, chemicals, or staining is needed.

EPOXY MORTAR AND GROUT

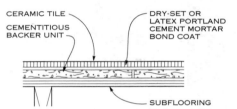

Use in light commercial and residential construction, deflection not to exceed $1/360$, including live and dead loads. Waterproof membrane is required in wet areas.

DRY-SET MORTAR

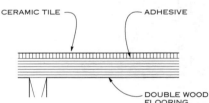

Use over wood or concrete floors in residential construction only. Not recommended for use in wet areas.

ORGANIC ADHESIVE

Figure 11. Wood frame floor tile setting method

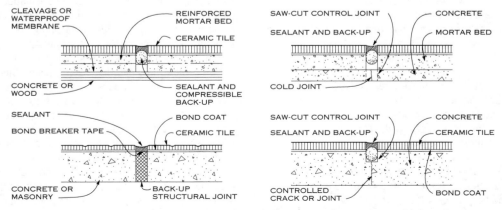

Figure 12. Vertical and horizontal expansion, contraction, and control joints

REFERENCES

Publication dates cited here were current at the time of this writing. Publications are revised periodically, and revisions may have occurred before this book was published.

American National Standards Institute

ANSI A108 Series (A108.1A, .1B, .1C, .4, .5, .6, .8, .9, .10, .11, .12, and .13-1999): Specifications for Installation of Ceramic Tile

ANSI A118.1-1999: Specifications for Dry-Set Portland Cement Mortar

ANSI A118.3-1999: Specifications for Chemical Resistant Water Cleanable Tile-Setting and Grouting Epoxy and Water Cleanable Tile-Setting Epoxy Adhesive

ANSI A118.4-1999: Specifications for Latex-Portland Cement Mortar

ANSI A118.5-1999: Specifications for Chemical Resistant Furan Mortars and Grouts for Tile Installation

ANSI A118.6-1999: Specifications for Standard Cement Grouts for Tile Installation

ANSI A118.7-1999: Specifications for Polymer Modified Cement Grouts for Tile Installation

ANSI A118.8-1999: Specifications for Modified Epoxy Emulsion Mortar/Grout

ANSI A118.9-1999: Test Methods and Specifications for Cementitious Backer Units

ANSI A118.10-1999: Specifications for Load Bearing, Bonded, Waterproof Membranes for Thin-Set Ceramic Tile and Dimension Stone Installations

ANSI A118.11-1999: Specifications for EGP (Exterior Glue Plywood) Latex-Portland Cement Mortar

ANSI A136.1-1999: Organic Adhesives for Installation of Ceramic Tile

ANSI A137.1-1988: Specifications for Ceramic Tile

ASTM International

ASTM C 242-99a: Terminology of Ceramic Whitewares and Related Products

ASTM C 627-93 (reapproved 1999): Test Method for Evaluating Ceramic Floor Tile Installation Systems Using the Robinson-Type Floor Tester

ASTM C 1028-96: Test Method for Determining the Static Coefficient of Friction of Ceramic Tile and Other Like Surfaces by the Horizontal Dynamometer Pull-Meter Method

ASTM D 2047-99: Test Method for Static Coefficient of Friction of Polish-Coated Floor Surfaces as Measured by the James Machine

Tile Council of America, Inc.

Handbook for Ceramic Tile Installation, 2000.

United States Architectural & Transportation Barriers Compliance Board

ADAAG: Accessibility Guidelines for Buildings and Facilities, adopted in 1991; continual revisions.

WEB SITES

Ceramic Tile Distributors Association: www.ctdahome.org

Ceramic Tile Industry Information and Resources: www.ceramic-tile.com

Ceramic Tile Institute of America, Inc.: www.ctioa.org

InfoTile—the Internet Tile Center: www.infotile.com

Tile Council of America, Inc.: www.tileusa.com

09385 DIMENSION STONE TILE

This chapter discusses natural stone tile for flooring, wall facing, and trim for commercial and residential installations. Dimension stone tile is defined as modular units less than ¾-inch (19-mm) thick fabricated from natural stone. Stone thresholds are also covered.

This chapter does not discuss dimension stone that is ¾ inch (19 mm) or more in thickness or that is not in the form of modular units, nor does it cover tile made from stone composites. Stone base in the form of running trim rather than tile also is not addressed.

GENERAL COMMENTS

Most varieties of dimension stone can be cut to form tile; refer to Chapter 09638, Stone Paving and Flooring, for more information about selecting stone for use as flooring when dimension stone tile will be applied to floors. For information on specific manufacturers' tile-setting and grouting products, refer to manufacturers' product literature (fig. 1).

SPECIFYING STONE TILE

For projects that allow proprietary specifications, the most effective way to specify stone tile is to name acceptable sources and varieties of stone. When this method is used, substitute sources (suppliers) will usually be allowed; however, other varieties will generally not be allowed. If this method of specifying is chosen, do not reference ASTM stone standards and classifications in the specifications. If specifications must be nonproprietary, reference the applicable ASTM stone standards and classifications in specifications with several acceptable varieties and sources and consider adding descriptive requirements that will enable stone of undesirable color, texture, and so on, to be rejected.

STONE TILE

Dimension stone tiles have developed as a surfacing material that provides the elegance of natural stone without the cost, weight, or depth of dimension stone slabs. Stone tiles are defined as natural stone units less than ¾-inch (19-mm) thick. Tiles range anywhere in thickness from ¼ to ⅝ inch (6 to 16 mm), depending on the size, finish, and type of stone. As a general rule, smaller tiles can be thinner, since it is easier to get full coverage of setting bed with smaller tiles; they are, therefore, not required to span gaps in the setting bed. Larger tiles also need to be thicker to avoid breakage during handling and beat-in. Tiles with a heavily textured finish, such as a thermal or natural-cleft finish, need to be thicker than tiles with a smooth finish to allow for the depth of the finish. Inexpensive stone will often be made into tiles that are thicker than those made from more expensive stone, since little is gained by making them thinner. Typical finishes and common sizes of dimension stone tiles are listed in Table 1.

Surface-abrasion resistance is important when selecting stone tile for floors. ASTM C 1353, *Test Method for Abrasion Resistance of Dimension Stone by the Taber Abraser,* is used to determine a value for abrasion resist-

Table 1
TYPICAL FINISHES AND COMMON SIZES OF DIMENSION STONE TILES

Stone	Finish	Thickness (in.)	Face Dimension (in.) (max.)
Granite	Polished Honed Thermal	⅜, ½	12 x 12
Marble	Polished Honed	¼, ⅜	12 x 12
Slate	Natural cleft Sand-rubbed	¼, ¾	12 x 12
Flagstone	Natural cleft Semirubbed	½, ¾	12 x 12

ance, H_a, which correlates closely with the values produced by ASTM C 241, *Test Method for Abrasion Resistance of Stone Subjected to Foot Traffic,* which was previously used for this purpose. ASTM C 241 tests are no longer done because the abrasive used for the test is no longer available, but many varieties of stone have been tested by this method and most of the literature on abrasion resistance of stone is based on it. The Marble Institute of America recommends that tiles have a minimum H_a of 10 for floors subject to single-family residential foot traffic, and a minimum H_a of 12 for commercial floors, stairs, or other floors experiencing heavy foot traffic. If different stone types are used within the same floor area, the abrasion-hardness values for the different stone types should be within five of each other. Where stone tile is used on walls, abrasion resistance is not a concern, and combining radically different stones presents no problems.

Combining different finishes of stone tiles for floors also has its problems. If a floor polish or wax is used on polished stone that is adjacent to thermal-finished or other rough-finished stone, the floor polish will invariably get on the rough-finished stone and make it look dirty. Although it is better not to use a floor polish or wax on stone floors, it is unknown whether the owner's staff will use such products. Again, as with abrasion resistance, where stone tile is used on walls, combining different textures poses no problem as long as the thicknesses of the different tiles are compatible.

Slip resistance for stone tile is covered by the recommendations of the Americans with Disabilities Act (ADA), *Accessibility Guidelines for Buildings and Facilities (ADAAG).* ADAAG recommends that designers specify materials for flooring surfaces that have a minimum static coefficient of friction (COF) of 0.6 for level floors and 0.8 for ramped surfaces. Although this is only a recommendation, failure to heed the recommendation could lead to a lawsuit. The Ceramic Tile Institute of America (CTA) recommends a minimum COF of 0.6 as measured by the horizontal dynamometer pull-meter method. Note that stone sealers, waxes, and other applied finishes can affect the COF of a floor surface.

TILE-SETTING MATERIALS

Portland cement mortar consists of portland cement, sand, and water or latex additives, proportioned and mixed at the project site. Specifications for

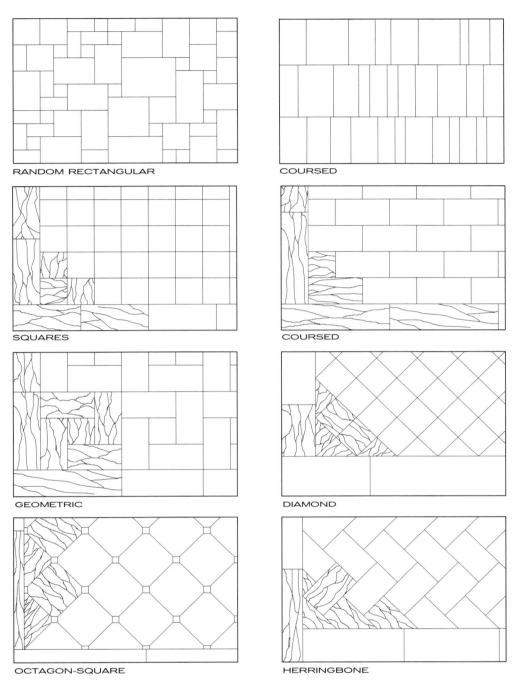

Figure 1. Dimension Stone Tile Patterns

installing tile in the wet-set method with portland cement mortar are covered in American National Standards Institute (ANSI) publication ANSI A108.1A. This method involves tile set on a mortar bed that is still plastic. ANSI A108.1B covers installation of tile on a cured portland cement mortar bed with dry-set or latex-portland cement mortar. ANSI A108.1C gives the contractor the option of using either the wet-set or cured mortar-bed method. Thick-bed methods are suitable for most surfaces, particularly where it is necessary to use the setting bed to produce true sloping or flat surfaces or where a reinforced setting bed is desirable.

Dry-set portland cement mortars are factory-mixed formulations of portland cement, sand, and water-retentive additives to which only water needs to be added at the project site. Intended as a bond coat, not as a setting bed, it is suitable only for thin-set applications over substrates that comply with

requirements specified in the applicable standards for surface variations, soundness, and rigidity under service. ANSI A118.1, which is the material standard for these products, covers only factory-prepared and -packaged products. The water-retentive additives eliminate the need to soak tile. Two specialized mortars covered in this standard are fast-setting dry-set mortars and nonsagging dry-set mortars. To qualify as a fast-setting mortar, a product must obtain the required shear bond strength at a much faster rate than normal dry-set mortar. Nonsagging mortars must demonstrate no vertical sag of tile in the test specimen from the original position, as opposed to normal mortar where sag is limited to less than $\frac{1}{16}$ inch (1.6 mm). The installation standard for dry-set and latex-portland cement mortars is ANSI A108.4.

Latex-portland cement mortars are products incorporating a polymer either in liquid-latex form or as a redispersible powder. Liquid-latex additive is added at the job site to a prepackaged dry-mortar mix that the manufacturer either specifies or supplies for use with the particular additive. In most cases, the prepackaged dry-mortar mix is also marketed as a dry-set portland cement mortar. For products in which the polymer is in the form of a redispersible powder, only water needs to be added. As is the case for dry-set portland cement mortars, the standard covers two specialized latex-portland cement mortars: fast-setting formulations and nonsagging formulations.

Four types of polymers or copolymers are available. Redispersible powders are polyvinyl acetate (PVA) or ethylene vinyl acetate (EVA), with the latter now predominating. Liquid-latex polymer is either a concentrate that can be diluted with water at the project site according to the latex manufacturer's written instructions or a prepackaged, prediluted product that replaces water entirely for mixing the mortar. Two latex emulsions available are styrene butadiene rubber (SBR) and acrylic resin. Both SBRs and acrylics display excellent bond strengths, low water absorption, and resiliency. Of the two, SBRs have the longer history of successful use. Acrylics seem to have the edge over SBRs in the properties listed above.

Advantages of latex-portland cement mortars over dry-set mortars mixed with water include improved adhesion and greater resistance to frost damage, shock, and impact. They also improve hydration of portland cement and sand mixtures for both thin-set mortar and thick-set mortar-bed applications. Exercise care in selecting latex additives with dry-set mortars because the dry-set mortars contain water-retentive agents; the latex additive may or may not. If both have this property, cure will be delayed. The material standard for latex-portland cement mortar is ANSI A118.4. The installation standard is ANSI A108.5.

Water-cleanable epoxy adhesives are covered by ANSI A118.3 for materials and ANSI A108.4 for installation. These products are intended for thin-set application of tile on floors, walls, and counters. They are designed for high bond strength and ease of application. They have better chemical and solvent resistance than organic adhesives.

Organic adhesives include solvent-release-curing products and latex emulsions that are water-cleanable. They have limited applications where some flexibility for the tile facing is required. Organic adhesives are classified as Type I or Type II according to ANSI A136.1. Both types must comply with the same requirements in the standard for physical properties, except for shear strength physical property. Type I products are required to exhibit greater shear strength after immersion in water for seven days than Type II formulations immersed for only four hours

ACCESSORIES

Cementitious backer units are a recommended alternative to water-resistant gypsum board for walls over bathtubs, shower receptors, and similar areas where optimum water resistance of the tile-mortar/adhesive-backing assembly is required and where, for cost or other reasons, a panel material is desired rather than a portland cement mortar bed. Among the advantages that cementitious backer units offer in comparison to water-resistant gypsum board is that cut edges and penetrations in the former do not have to be treated with a water-resistant adhesive or sealant to prevent deterioration of the backing. Cementitious backer units are also used as a substrate for tile with wood-framed floors. For thin-set mortars, they provide a substrate to which the mortar will adhere and are less resilient than plywood.

Waterproofing and crack suppression membranes may be required; refer to Chapter 09310, Ceramic Tile for information.

GROUTS

Commercial portland cement grouts are factory-prepared mixes meant for joints ⅛ inch (3.2 mm) and wider, as stated in the material description in ANSI A118.6, which means that they are sanded grouts. They combine portland cement with other ingredients to produce a dense material that is water-resistant and has uniform color. Many of these products are intended for use as sanded latex-portland cement grouts when mixed with a latex additive formulated for this purpose.

Sand-portland cement grouts are job-site mixtures of sand and portland cement. Although they represent an acceptable grouting material, they cannot be specified by reference to ANSI A118.6 due to uncontrollable quality and mixing conditions of the raw materials.

Dry-set grouts are unsanded grouts intended for joints ⅛ inch (3.2 mm) and narrower. They are also factory-prepared mixtures of portland cement and additives that provide water retentivity and are intended for grouting walls and floors. Many, if not all, of these products are also intended for use as unsanded latex-portland cement grouts when combined with a latex additive formulated for this purpose.

Latex-portland cement grouts are mixtures of any of the three grouts described above with a latex additive added in concentrate or dilute form at the job site or are factory-prepared dry mixes combining portland cement, graded aggregate, and polymer additive in the form of redispersible powder to which only water is added at the project site. The liquid-latex additives are generally either SBR or acrylic resin, and the redispersible powders are either PVA or EVA, with the latter predominating. Using latex-portland cement grouts eliminates the need for damp curing.

- Acrylic resins exhibit the best resistance to ultraviolet radiation, are nonyellowing, and have the lowest water-absorption rates. Therefore, they are the product of choice, particularly where color stability and exterior exposures are involved. Acrylics are available in concentrated or prediluted form. Typically, acrylic additives that are prediluted and marketed for both mortars and grouts have to be further diluted in the field to produce a latex-portland cement grout. In other cases, manufacturers provide two different prediluted formulations: one for mortar, the other for grout.
- One disadvantage of latex-portland cement grouts is the increased difficulty in removing grout film from exposed tile faces, particularly those with porous surfaces. To minimize this problem, the grout should be mixed and applied in a manner that produces as little grout residue as possible, and residue should be removed immediately. Allowing the grout residue to cure makes cleaning more difficult.

REFERENCES

Publication dates cited here were current at the time of this writing. Publications are revised periodically, and revisions may have occurred before this book was published.

American National Standards Institute

ANSI A108.1A-1992: Specifications for Installation of Ceramic Tile in the Wet-Set Method, with Portland Cement Mortar

ANSI A108.1B-1992: Specifications for Installation of Ceramic Tile on a Cured Portland Cement Mortar Bed with Dry-Set or Latex-Portland Cement Mortar

ANSI A108.1C-1992: Specifications for Contractor's Option: Installation of Ceramic Tile in the Wet-Set Method with Portland Cement Mortar or Installation of Ceramic Tile on a Cured Portland Cement Mortar Bed with Dry-Set or Latex-Portland Cement Mortar

ANSI A108.4-1992: Installation of Ceramic Tile with Organic Adhesives or Water-Cleanable Epoxy

ANSI A108.5-1992: Installation of Ceramic Tile with Dry-Set Portland Cement Mortar or Latex Portland Cement Mortar

ANSI A118.1-1992: Specifications for Dry-Set Portland Cement Mortar

ANSI A118.3-1992: Specifications for Chemical Resistant, Water Cleanable Tile Setting and Grouting Epoxy and Water Cleanable Tile Setting Epoxy Adhesive

ANSI A118.4-1992: Specifications for Latex-Portland Cement Mortar

ANSI A118.6-1992: Specifications for Ceramic Tile Grouts

ANSI A136.1-1992: Organic Adhesives for Installation of Ceramic Tile

ASTM International

ASTM C 241-90: Test Method for Abrasion Resistance of Stone Subjected to Foot Traffic

ASTM C 503-96: Specification for Marble Dimension Stone (Exterior)

ASTM C 568-96: Specification for Limestone Dimension Stone

ASTM C 615-96: Specification for Granite Dimension Stone

ASTM C 629-96: Specification for Slate Dimension Stone

ASTM C 1353-96: Test Method for Abrasion Resistance of Dimension Stone by the Taber Abraser

United States Architectural & Transportation Barriers Compliance Board

ADAAG: Accessibility Guidelines for Buildings and Facilities, adopted in 1991; continual revisions.

09400 **TERRAZZO**

This chapter discusses *cast-in-place cementitious, rustic, and resinous (thin-set) terrazzo. It also discusses precast terrazzo.*

This chapter does not discuss *decorative epoxy flooring that is not ground; these systems are discussed in Chapter 09671, Resinous Flooring. It also does not discuss terrazzo tile.*

GENERAL COMMENTS

The National Terrazzo and Mosaic Association (NTMA) defines the following terms in its Terrazzo Ideas & Design Guide:

Terrazzo: Consists of marble, granite, onyx, or glass chips in portland cement, modified portland cement, or resinous matrix. The terrazzo is poured, cured, ground, and polished. Typically used as a finish for floors, stairs, and walls, terrazzo can be poured in place or precast.
Rustic terrazzo: A variation where, in lieu of grinding and polishing, the surface is washed with water or otherwise treated to expose the marble chips. Quartz, quartzite, and riverbed aggregates can also be used.
Matrix: The portland cement and water mix or noncementitious binder that holds the marble chips in place for the terrazzo topping.

Cementitious matrices consist of portland cement, pigments (if required), and water. White cement is color controlled. Gray cement may not be color controlled, which can cause color variations in the matrix.

Resinous matrices include epoxy, polyacrylate-modified cement, and polyester compositions used for thin-set applications. Epoxy matrices are the most commonly used.

Marble chips are the most commonly used aggregate. For commercial purposes, marble includes all calcareous rocks suitable for polishing by grinding; this includes onyx, travertine, and serpentine. To accurately grade chips by size, marble is crushed in a process that substantially eliminates flat or sliverlike chips.

- **Chips are graded** by numbered sizes according to producer standards. The screen sizes of sieves that pass and retain chips determine the grade of the chips. Standard cementitious terrazzo normally uses No. 1 and 2 chips. Venetian cementitious terrazzo uses No. 1, 2, 3, 4, and 5 and sometimes 6, 7, and 8 chips. Thin-set resinous systems, such as epoxy terrazzo, generally use No. 1 and 0 chips for ¼-inch- (6.4-mm-) thick toppings, and No. 1, 2, and 0 chips for ⅜-inch- (9.5-mm-) thick toppings. Standard marble chip grades are listed in Table 1.
- **Hardness** is measured according to ASTM C 241 and indicates the abrasion resistance of the marble.

Exotic aggregates can be used to create special decorative effects with terrazzo. Cementitious terrazzo incorporating exotic aggregates is sometimes called stone terrazzo. Granite or quartz aggregates can be specified for additional wear resistance. Other stones, such as pea gravel and mother-of-pearl, and glass chips may be substituted for marble. Consult NTMA to evaluate how these aggregates affect strength and durability.

Table 1
STANDARD MARBLE CHIP GRADES

Number	Passes Screen	Retained in Screen
0	⅛ inch (3.2 mm)	¹⁄₁₆ inch (1.6 mm)
1	¼ inch (6.4 mm)	⅛ inch (3.2 mm)
2	⅜ inch (9.5 mm)	¼ inch (6.4 mm)
3	½ inch (12.7 mm)	⅜ inch (9.5 mm)
4	⅝ inch (15.9 mm)	½ inch (12.7 mm)
5	¾ inch (19 mm)	⅝ inch (15.9 mm)
6	⅞ inch (22.2 mm)	¾ inch (19 mm)
7	1 inch (25.4 mm)	⅞ inch (22.2 mm)
8	1⅛ inches (28.6 mm)	1 inch (25.4 mm)

Rustic-terrazzo aggregates include marble, quartz, and granite chips and river gravel.

Matrix pigments are powdered, inorganic substances used to color the cementitious terrazzo mix. They are either alkali-resistant mineral or synthetic powders.

Colors and patterns for terrazzo can be specified from NTMA plates to ensure competitive bidding. NTMA provides samples to designers. Custom colors are also available.

Custom patterns, including artwork and logos, can be produced using terrazzo but require an installer with great skill and craftsmanship. Consult NTMA for designers and installers of artistic designs.

INSTALLER CONSIDERATIONS

The installer's (applicator's) competence is critical because terrazzo is fabricated at a project site. Consider requiring an NTMA membership for the installer. To qualify for NTMA contractor membership, an installer's capabilities are reviewed based on the following: submission of names and pertinent information for six installations; manpower information, including training; and financial responsibility statements.

Epoxy terrazzo manufacturers may restrict who can purchase and apply their products. Manufacturers' restrictions on applicators do not necessarily indicate the quality of the manufacturers' products. Minimally, an applicator should be experienced and acceptable to the manufacturer. Some manufacturers endorse applicators' qualifications by licensing or otherwise certifying them to apply the manufacturer's products, but requiring a certified applicator limits the manufacturers that can comply with a specification.

With the owner's consent, consider compiling a list of preapproved installers. Consult NTMA to obtain names of contractor members, and consult epoxy terrazzo manufacturers to obtain the names of acceptable or certified applicators.

CEMENTITIOUS TERRAZZO

NTMA plates for cementitious terrazzo include various standard and Venetian options. Mixes that match standard plates use smaller chips than those that match Venetian plates. Because of the larger aggregates, Venetian terrazzo requires greater minimum topping thicknesses than standard terrazzo.

Sand-cushion cementitious terrazzo (fig. 1) provides the best insurance against cracking and general failures. It consists of a ½-inch (12.7-mm) thick, standard-terrazzo topping or a ¾-inch (19-mm) thick, Venetian-terrazzo topping over a 2½-inch (63.5-mm) thick, reinforced underbed separated from the supporting concrete slab by an isolation membrane over a thin sand bed. Single divider strips inserted into the underbed at 60 inches (1500 mm) o.c. maximum generally control anticipated shrinkage, eliminating the need for control joints.

Bonded cementitious terrazzo (fig. 2) consists of a ½-inch (12.7-mm) thick, standard-terrazzo topping or a ¾-inch (19-mm) thick, Venetian-terrazzo topping over a minimum 1¼-inch (31.8-mm) thick underbed. The underbed is bonded to a concrete substrate. NTMA recommends locating divider and control-joint strips at 96 inches (2400 mm) o.c. maximum, and locating control joints directly over breaks in the concrete substrate.

Monolithic cementitious terrazzo (fig. 3) consists of a ½-inch (12.7-mm) thick, standard-terrazzo topping or a ¾-inch (19-mm) thick, Venetian-terrazzo topping installed directly over a concrete substrate. NTMA recommends locating divider strips at all breaks or saw cuts in the supporting slab.

Cementitious terrazzo over metal deck consists of a ½-inch (12.7-mm) thick, standard-terrazzo topping or a ¾-inch (19-mm) thick, Venetian-terrazzo topping over a minimum 2½-inch (63.5-mm) thick, reinforced-concrete underbed measured from the top of the supporting metal deck. NTMA recommends locating divider strips at 36 inches (900 mm) o.c. maximum and locating them directly above all joist and beam centers.

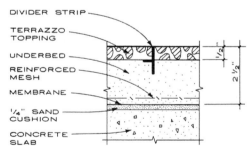

Figure 1. Sand-cushion cementitious terrazzo

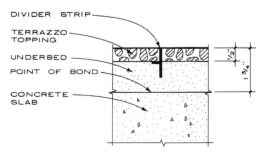

Figure 2. Bonded cementitious terrazzo

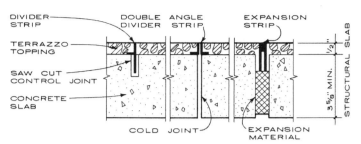

Figure 3. Monolithic cementitious terrazzo

Structural cementitious terrazzo consists of a ½-inch (12.7-mm) thick, standard-terrazzo topping or a ¾-inch (19-mm) thick, Venetian-terrazzo topping and a minimum 4½-inch (114.3-mm) thick, reinforced-concrete slab over a vapor retarder on compacted fill. NTMA recommends locating control-joint strips at 96 inches (2400 mm) o.c. maximum for a minimum 1½-inch (38.1-mm) depth. NTMA also recommends 18-inch (460-mm) long-by-½-inch (12.7-mm) diameter, smooth steel dowels placed at 36 inches (900 mm) o.c. maximum at column lines or breaks in the slab.

Palladiana and mosaic are variations from standard cementitious terrazzo.

- **Palladiana** is produced by setting fractured marble slabs in a mortar bed. Wide, irregular joints between slabs are filled with terrazzo matrix, and the surface is ground like terrazzo.
- **Mosaic** is produced by setting a pattern or design of marble, glass, or tile units into a terrazzo matrix. The surface is either ground or wiped clean, depending on the types of mosaic pieces (tesserae) used and the desired effect.

RUSTIC TERRAZZO

Rustic terrazzo is generally used at exterior locations because ground cementitious or epoxy terrazzo is often too smooth or slippery for this use. NTMA recommends using expansion-joint strips with removable zip-strip tops for sealant installation and using air-entraining agents in exterior rustic-terrazzo underbeds. Further, NTMA recommends locating control-joint strips at 10 feet (3 m) o.c. maximum and over all joints in the substrate. Rustic terrazzo types include the following:

- **Structural rustic terrazzo** consists of a ½- or ¾-inch- (12.7- or 19-mm-) thick topping, depending on the aggregate size, and a minimum 4½-inch (114.3-mm) thick, reinforced-concrete slab over a vapor retarder on compacted fill, similar to structural cementitious terrazzo.
- **Bonded rustic terrazzo** consists of a ½- or ¾-inch- (12.7- or 19-mm-) thick topping, depending on the aggregate size, over a minimum 1¼-inch (31.8-mm) thick underbed, similar to bonded cementitious terrazzo.
- **Monolithic rustic terrazzo** consists of a ½- or ¾-inch- (12.7- or 19-mm-) thick topping, depending on the aggregate size, installed directly over a concrete substrate, similar to monolithic cementitious terrazzo.
- **Unbonded rustic terrazzo** consists of a ½- or ¾-inch- (12.7- or 19-mm-) thick topping, depending on the aggregate size, over a minimum 3½-inch (88.9-mm) thick, reinforced-concrete underbed separated from the supporting concrete slab by an isolation membrane.

EPOXY TERRAZZO

Thin-set, epoxy terrazzo systems (fig. 4) are available in ¼- and ⅜-inch (6.4- and 9.5-mm) thicknesses, depending on the marble-chip sizes used. Manufacturers recommend ⅜-inch- (9.5-mm-) thick toppings in areas

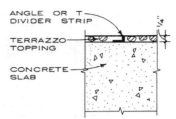

Figure 4. Thin-set epoxy terrazzo

where there are many divider strips because these areas generally require more grinding; the larger thickness prevents topping "grind-through."

NTMA recommends locating divider strips for resinous terrazzo at all breaks or saw cuts in the supporting slab.

Epoxy resin has high bond strength. It is highly resistant to mild acids (but not lactic acid, acetic acid, or strong solutions of other acids), staining, and impact and concentrated-load indentations. It is resistant to alkalis (most cleaning agents) and is suitable for exterior use, but white matrices tend to yellow under UV light. Epoxy-resin terrazzo is available in colors matching NTMA standard and thin-set color plates and in custom colors. If a flexible reinforcing membrane is used, manufacturers claim it has substrate-crack bridging capabilities comparable to sand-cushion cementitious terrazzo.

Flexible reinforcing membranes or substrate crack-isolation systems help prevent cracks from reflecting through the epoxy flooring. Fiberglass scrim reinforcement can be installed in the membrane to maximize tensile strength. The membrane can be installed at cracks only or on the entire substrate surface. Manufacturers often use the same material for waterproofing membranes as for reinforcing membranes. Before specifying requirements for a flexible reinforcing membrane, verify availability and manufacturers' recommendations for selected flooring systems.

Brass divider strips traditionally were not recommended for use with epoxy-resin matrices because the matrices reacted with loose metal granules released from strips during grinding to form a blue stain; however, most epoxy-resin matrices now have inhibitors to prevent this reaction. Still, staining may occur if two-component systems are improperly mixed. Consult resin manufacturers for divider-strip material recommendations.

OTHER THIN-SET TERRAZZO SYSTEMS

Polyacrylate-modified cement terrazzo has high bond strength; is resistant to moisture, snow-melting salts, food, and urine; and is nontoxic and relatively free from objectionable odors under ordinary conditions. Some manufacturers claim it "breathes," and recommend it for use on slabs-on-grade that may be subject to moisture problems. Polyacrylate-modified cement terrazzo has limited movement capability and is available in a limited color range.

Polyester-resin terrazzo's matrix, of the resinous matrices used for terrazzo, has the highest compressive strength and is the most resistant to abrasion, indentation, and burning. It also has the best weathering and stain-resistant characteristics and good chemical resistance, except its resistance to alkaline compounds is only fair. Matrices do not yellow from UV light. Its major disadvantage is that the styrene content of the matrix causes an intense odor during curing, so building occupants, if any, may need to evacuate the area and workers may need to wear respirators. For this reason, polyester-resin terrazzo is recommended only for specialized needs such as pharmaceutical installations. Consult NTMA and manufacturers before specifying polyester-resin terrazzo.

Conductive terrazzo, which is available in epoxy- and polyester-resin matrices, conducts electric charges produced by static within prescribed resistance levels. Carbon black is the matrix's conductive vehicle; therefore, conductive matrices are available only in black. If conductive terrazzo is required for a project, the owner must establish the electrical requirements necessary for the installation.

APPLICATION CONSIDERATIONS

Consult NTMA for substrate recommendations. Terrazzo generally requires a rigid substrate. Monolithic terrazzo systems are the least tolerant of substrate movement, and considerable cracking and bond failures occur when they are used over substrates that move. High-tensile-strength, epoxy-resin matrices are recommended by some manufacturers for use over composite slabs where limited deflection is expected. Consult NTMA if considering the use of terrazzo over a flexible substrate.

Cementitious terrazzo is not recommended for use in areas requiring high resistance to acids, alkalis, or staining, or for severe exposures or constant wetting. Stains that penetrate the matrix are difficult or impossible to remove; therefore, sealing the surface is important. Cementitious terrazzo is generally not recommended for use in toilet rooms, kitchens, and laboratories.

Bonded cementitious and rustic terrazzo can crack from stresses caused by the shrinkage of the concrete substrate. Coordinate requirements with the project's structural engineer.

Epoxy terrazzo is used in installations that require resistance to wetting, food, urine, oils, acids, and mild alkalis. These thin-set systems also contribute less weight and depth to construction than cementitious systems; however, irregularities in the supporting slab will more readily telegraph through the terrazzo surface. Other considerations for epoxy terrazzo include the following:

- It does not bond to concrete substrates contaminated by curing, hardening, and surface-protecting compounds. Areas of concrete with excessive moisture or high surface alkalinity will also create application problems.
- It should not be used over permanent, unvented, metal forms with concrete fill. If metal forms do not allow free evaporation, water vapor can be trapped between the slab and epoxy terrazzo and cause the membrane to delaminate. Adequate drying of residual moisture in concrete poured over permanent, unvented, metal forms requires a prolonged period (possibly years). To further ensure free evaporation, avoid applying paintlike coatings that will inhibit vapor transmissions to the underside of vented metal forms or to concrete where forms have been stripped.
- Moisture from hydrostatic pressure, capillary action, and vapor transmission can cause adhesion failure of epoxy systems installed on slabs-on-grade. These concrete substrates require capillary water barriers (drainage fill), vapor retarders, and effective measures to prevent hydrostatic pressure.
- Concrete substrates must be roughened before applying epoxy terrazzo to ensure that surfaces are clean and free of laitance, oil, grease, curing compounds, or other materials incompatible with resins, and to enhance adhesion of the flooring system. Substrates are roughened by abrasive blasting (shot blasting) or mechanical scarifying. Shot blasting is generally considered the best method for preparing concrete slabs.

Dust from grinding operations can damage unprotected mechanical equipment, and grinding existing installations can damage adjacent surfaces. Specify requirements for protective enclosures if required for the project.

If existing cementitious terrazzo will be refinished, specify requirements using the NTMA Guide Specification recommendations for restoring finishes as a guide.

ACCESSORIES

Divider and control-joint strips are required to control terrazzo cracking; their proper placement often determines an installation's success or failure (figs. 5 and 6). Strips are also used to produce elaborate decorative patterns. Consult NTMA for further information on strips and recommendations for strip locations.

Divider strips define terrazzo panel areas, limit the area of continuous terrazzo surface, and prevent cracks from occurring in the field of panels. Coordinate divider-strip locations with the supporting structural frame. Locate them over each edge of major beams and girders, centered over other beams and joists, and directly over control joints, breaks, and saw cuts in supporting concrete slabs.

Control joints are generally formed by back-to-back angle or straight strips. In monolithic cementitious terrazzo, folded, single-section T-strips are often used. These strips form two angle strips when the vertical leg's top is ground away. Control joints can be filled with elastomeric sealant in lines of known, measurable movement. Prefabricated expansion dividers filled with polyurethane sealant are available. Neoprene-insert expansion strips are no longer recommended by NTMA.

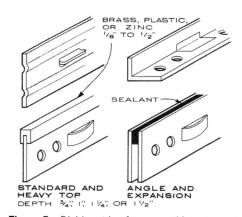

Figure 5. Divider strips for cementitious terrazzo

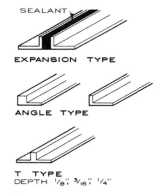

Figure 6. Divider strips for thin-set terrazzo

Consult NTMA for spacing recommendations for divider and control-joint strips. The length of terrazzo panel areas formed by divider or control-joint strips should not exceed twice the panel width.

For exterior applications, brass strips are recommended, but they will require maintenance where de-icing chemicals are used. Do not use white-zinc-alloy strips for exterior applications. Plastic strips are not recommended by strip manufacturers for exterior use.

For conductive terrazzo, consult NTMA and epoxy terrazzo manufacturers for strip recommendations.

Other accessories include the following:

- **Base-bead strips** conceal the unfinished top edge of the terrazzo integral cove base. Base divider strips must conform to the profile of the integral cove base.
- **For stair treads and landings,** nosings can be finished or concealed with nosing strips.
- **Edge-bead strips** are used to conceal the unfinished edges of terrazzo where it terminates at other flooring materials. Edge strips that have recesses to receive resilient flooring are not recommended because grinding operations wear down the recessed edges.
- **Abrasive strips** at ramps, stair treads, and landings increase the slip resistance of the terrazzo surface.

PRECAST TERRAZZO

Precast terrazzo offers the advantages of controlled forming, curing, and surfacing operations. However, edge chipping often occurs unless edges are eased to a ⅛-inch (3.2-mm) radius. Cement grout or elastomeric sealants are generally used to fill joints between units. Epoxy grout, because of its high tensile and bond strengths, may cause cracking of smaller precast units.

If precast units are used with cast-in-place systems, expect color and pattern variations between the two types of terrazzo. Simultaneously field fabricating precast units when installing cast-in-place systems may reduce appearance variations.

The thickness and reinforcement required for precast cementitious terrazzo units are affected by the size of the unit. Consult manufacturers for recommendations

REFERENCES

Publication dates cited here were current at the time of this writing. Publications are revised periodically, and revisions may have occurred before this book was published.

ASTM International

ASTM C 241-90 (reapproved 1997): Test Method for Abrasion Resistance of Stone Subjected to Foot Traffic

National Terrazzo and Mosaic Association, Inc.

Terrazzo Ideas and Design Guide, 1996.

WEB SITE

National Terrazzo and Mosaic Association, Inc.: www.ntma.com

09511 ACOUSTICAL PANEL CEILINGS

This chapter discusses *ceilings consisting of acoustical panels and exposed suspension systems. These include special-use type ceilings for exterior locations, high-temperature and -humidity locations, and clean rooms.*

This chapter does not discuss *acoustical tile and concealed suspension systems, acoustical snap-in metal pans, or linear metal ceilings; these are discussed in Chapter 09512, Acoustical Tile Ceilings, Chapter 09513, Acoustical Snap-in Metal Pan Ceilings, and Chapter 09547, Linear Metal Ceilings. Lay-in or other types of metal pan ceilings with exposed suspension systems are also not covered.*

GENERAL COMMENTS

This chapter addresses the most typical applications of acoustical panel ceilings. ASTM E 1264 is the principal standard referenced for specifying panels discussed here. This standard provides a method only for the generic specification of acoustical panel and tile ceilings; specifications rapidly become proprietary as more constraints for type, pattern, color, size, acoustical properties, light reflectance, and fire-resistance ratings are included. Although a degree of variety is available in patterns, finishes, and levels of performance, the number of generic choices is limited, partly because manufacturers want to maintain unit costs at a competitive level. Code requirements and material limitations also restrict generic choices. Custom-designed and -produced acoustical panels are rarely developed for a single room or even for a single project, although custom colors may be available depending on the manufacturer, product type, and quantities involved. Other materials are usually arranged in combinations for custom-designed work, to achieve an overall acoustical effect and to satisfy other functions related to appearance, light distribution, and fire protection.

The process of fulfilling appearance and performance criteria for a particular application results in reducing the number of products acceptable for a particular application. Ultimately, cost limitations may dictate the choice of two or three viable alternatives. Where acoustical panels represent the predominant ceiling finish of a large project, seemingly small differences in unit costs among products may have a larger impact on overall costs than first recognized. Nevertheless, cost considerations may not totally outweigh design considerations for most projects because of the high visibility of ceiling surfaces. If initial and life-cycle costs are critical to a project, consider consulting manufacturers during design development or earlier phases about installed price ranges.

The semiproprietary specification method accommodates the actual selection process adhered to by most design professionals in choosing acoustical panel ceilings. Although it is possible to specify acoustical panel ceilings based entirely on compliance with performance and descriptive requirements, this method is unlikely to offer adequate control when it comes to appearance or visual uniformity among competing products. The most reasonable approach is to let a project team know that only a limited number of products, whose appearance is acceptable, exist.

Exterior installations of suspended acoustical ceilings require engineering analysis and evaluation of materials and coatings that are beyond the scope of ASTM C 635, *Specification for the Manufacture, Performance, and Testing of Metal Suspension Systems for Acoustical Tile and Lay-in Panel Ceilings;* ASTM C 636, *Practice for Installation of Metal Ceiling Suspension Systems for Acoustical Tile and Lay-in Panels;* and International Conference of Building Officials' (ICBO's) Uniform Building Code (UBC) Standard 25-2, *Metal Suspension Systems for Acoustical Tile and for Lay-In Panel Ceilings,* the commonly used design and installation standards for suspended acoustical ceilings. Accordingly, ASTM C 635 includes the following statement: "While this specification is applicable to the exterior installation of metal suspension systems, the atmospheric conditions and wind loading require additional design attention to ensure safe implementation. For that reason, a specific review and approval should be solicited from the responsible architect and engineer, or both, for any exterior application of metal suspension systems...." Moreover, ASTM C 636 states: "While recommendations from the manufacturer should be solicited, it remains the final responsibility of the architect/engineer to ensure proper application of the materials in question." The majority of the acoustical panels described in this chapter are not suitable for exterior use; some are not suitable for unconditioned interior spaces or for interior spaces with severe or extreme conditions. If exterior installation of an appropriate acoustical panel ceiling is required for a project, specify requirements for engineering analysis, and carefully evaluate materials and coatings.

PRODUCT CLASSIFICATION

ASTM E 1264 includes a designation system to identify the various performance and physical properties of acoustical panels and tiles. These designations, which are explained below, are often included in specifications. Because the designations by themselves tend to be cryptic for those unfamiliar with their meaning or without ready access to ASTM 1264, specifications also often include the corresponding full description of type, form, and pattern.

Type and sometimes form serve to classify the materials and finishes available. Common types are listed here. Not listed are those of cellulose composition (Types I, II, VIII, and X); those that combine 19 metal facings (steel, stainless-steel, and aluminum pan types) with mineral- or glass-fiber-base backing (Types V, VI, and VII); and those with aluminum or steel strip, perforated and nonperforated, and with mineral- or glass-fiber-base backing (Type XIII, Form 1 and Form 2).

- **Type III** – Mineral base with painted finish:
  Form 1 – Nodular
  Form 2 – Water-felted
  Form 3 – Dry-felted
  Form 4 – Cast or molded

- **Type IV** – Mineral base with membrane-faced overlay:
  Form 1 – Nodular
  Form 2 – Water-felted
  Form 3 – Dry-felted
  Form 4 – Cast or molded

- **Type IX** – Mineral base with scrubbable pigmented or clear finish:
  Form 1 – Nodular
  Form 2 – Water-felted
  Form 3 – Dry-felted
  Form 4 – Cast or molded

- **Type XI** – Mineral base with fabric-faced overlay:
  Form 1 – Nodular
  Form 2 – Water-felted
  Form 3 – Dry-felted
  Form 4 – Cast or molded

- **Type XII** – Glass-fiber base with membrane-faced overlay:
  Form 1 – Plastic
  Form 2 – Cloth
  Form 3 – Other

- **Type XIV** – Excelsior bonded with inorganic binders:
  Form 1 – No backing
  Form 2 – Backed with mineral- or glass-fiber-base backing

- **Type XX** – Other types (describe in specifications)

The different forms of mineral-base acoustical panels listed above refer to the following manufacturing processes:

- **Nodular panels** consist of mineral fibers wound into balls, perlite, fillers, and binders, which are mixed into a high-solids slurry, formed into sheets, oven dried, and cut to size. Panels are then given a variety of surface textures, ranging from a fine scale to a natural heavy texture, using fissuring, embossing, and etching processes; painting follows. The nodular substrate and texturing process controls uniformity of surface texture from panel to panel. Nodular products are characterized by an inherently porous, more sound-absorbent mat that does not require acoustical punching to achieve good sound absorption.

- **Water-felted panels** consist of mineral wool, perlite, fillers, and binders, which are mixed to produce a low-consistency slurry that is formed into large sheets. Draining, compacting, drying by convection, and cutting

sheets to size follow. Textures are imparted into panel faces by mechanical means, which can involve fissuring, perforating, or both. The panels are then painted. Water-felted panels typically cost less than the other two forms of panels.

- **Cast or molded panels** consist of mineral fibers, fillers, and binders, which are mixed to produce a pulp that flows into pans lined with foil or paper and sized to form the finished panels. The panels are given the desired surface texture, oven dried, trimmed to final size, and painted. Cast or molded panels are characterized by their natural random texture, high acoustical performance, and the option to have the same color throughout. They cost about the same as nodular panel products.

Pattern designations listed below are for use individually or in combination to describe in broad terms the appearance of acoustical panels. Panel manufacturers are wary of specifications using this method exclusively to select and specify patterns because such classifications allow subjective interpretation and cannot define subtle differences in appearance among various products. These classifications can be used to specify products if the client prohibits the naming of products or manufacturers, and to narrow down the choices available for a given pattern (fig. 1).

Pattern Designation	Pattern Description
A	Perforated, regularly spaced large holes
B	Perforated, randomly spaced large holes
C	Perforated, small holes
D	Fissured
E	Lightly textured
F	Heavily textured
G	Smooth
H	Printed
I	Embossed
J	Embossed-in-register
K	Surface scored
L	Random swirl
Z	Other patterns (describe in specifications)

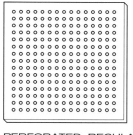

PERFORATED, REGULARLY SPACED HOLES

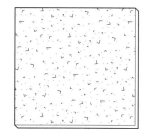

FISSURED

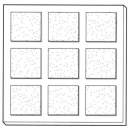

NINE-SQUARE SURFACE SCORED

EMBOSSED DESIGN

TWO-SQUARE, SURFACE SCORED

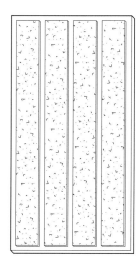

LINEAR, SURFACE SCORED

Figure 1. Acoustical panel patterns

Acoustical performance and other performance ratings include the following:

- **Minimum Noise Reduction Coefficient (NRC):** A single-number rating expressed in increments of 0.05. NRC is derived from values for sound-absorption coefficients determined according to ASTM C 423. NRC gives an estimate of a material's sound-absorption properties. The higher the number, the greater the material's ability to absorb or not otherwise reflect randomly incident sound power. Several manufacturers publish NRCs lower than the bottom limit of 0.40 recognized in the current edition of ASTM E 1264, and some manufacturers express NRC as a range rather than a single-number rating per ASTM C 423, alleging that a difference of less than plus or minus 0.05 is usually undetected by the ear when in spaces with acoustical ceilings. If acoustical performance is critical to a project, request test reports from manufacturers to obtain accurate values at stated test frequencies. Verify that reported values and test frequencies are appropriate for the project.

- **Minimum Articulation Class (AC):** This rating is expressed in increments of 10 and replaces noise isolation class. AC measures the interzone attenuation of ceiling systems in open-plan offices in conjunction with partial-height partitions but without the use of a sound-masking system. The test method used to obtain this rating is ASTM E 1111, which provides for testing ceilings in the laboratory and field. Testing is performed in an area at least 15 by 30 feet (4.5 by 9 m) with a ceiling height of 108 inches (2700 mm). This area has a floor made of concrete or wood weighing at least 4 lb/sq. ft. (20 kg/sq. m) and covered with carpet having an NRC ranging from 0.2 to 0.4; walls having random incidence sound-absorption coefficients of at least 0.9 for all test frequencies; and a space divider 60 inches (1500 mm) high, extending at least 108 inches (2700 mm) from both end walls, that is faced on both sides with sound-absorbing material and having an NRC of 0.80. This test measures sound that is produced by intelligible speech frequencies striking a ceiling surface and reflected at specific angles thought to be typical of open-plan office cubicle partitions having a height of 60 inches (1500 mm). ASTM E 1110 determines AC. According to ASTM E 1264, typical values for AC may range from 150 to 250.

- **Minimum Ceiling Attenuation Class (CAC):** Formerly reported as a range, this rating is now expressed as a single figure per ASTM E 413. ASTM E 1414, which was first adopted in 1992, has replaced the AMA-1-II Test Method for determining CAC per ASTM E 1264. Acoustical ceiling manufacturers have retested their ceilings according to this method, which is designed to measure the sound attenuation properties of suspended ceilings installed with continuous plenum spaces. CAC indicates the degree of sound transmission from adjacent spaces, including the floor above, and from the services in the plenum above. Replaced by CAC, ceiling sound transmission class (CSTC) is no longer referenced.

- **Minimum Light Reflectance (LR) coefficients:** These coefficients are listed in increments of 0.01 by manufacturers. Several manufacturers publish LR coefficients in excess of the top limit of 0.80 recognized in the current edition of ASTM E 1264.

Independent third-party classification (certification) of acoustical ceiling products is a new quality-control development within the industry. The purpose of the classification is to ensure uniformity of products and the accuracy of published values for AC, CAC, and NRC per ASTM test methods and procedures. Underwriters Laboratories (UL) provides in-factory inspection, auditing of testing, and labeling of products. Labels appear on the packaging. The listing of this classification for acoustical properties is part of the "Acoustical Materials (BIYR)" article in UL's *Building Materials Directory*.

ACOUSTICAL CEILING CHARACTERISTICS

Definitions for acoustical panels and tiles are not well understood, causing considerable confusion for design professionals. According to ASTM E 1264, the differences between a panel and a tile are the method of support and the type of suspension system. Acoustical panels are used with exposed suspension systems. Acoustical tiles are used with concealed or semiexposed suspension systems, stapling, or adhesive bonding. Although most tiles are smaller than most panels, the size of the acoustical unit does not determine the type. In recent years, more and more acoustical ceilings have been specified using panels. Many special-use products are available today only in panel form. Some large-sized fiberglass and excelsior units are installed on standard exposed suspension systems, but special edges result in visual concealment of the suspension system. These products are often considered panels used with exposed suspension systems. Alternatively, if concealed suspension systems are interpreted as being concealed to view, these products could be considered tiles.

Light reflectances for most standard products fall within the top range of 0.75 LR or greater. Lower values are typical for some textured, embossed, and scored patterns; nonwhite units; and those covered with fabric. This lower reflectance is not necessarily significant, however, unless the ceiling is depended on as a distributor of ambient illumination. Ceiling light reflectance performance is especially important in buildings with substantial levels of indirect lighting, and in building designs incorporating daylighting. Using daylight as a lighting source often requires directing a portion of the daylight toward the ceiling for subsequent rereflection and diffusion. This strategy may be used to deliver uniform, usable light levels without glare throughout the illuminated space.

Ceiling appearance may be affected by ceiling height, fixture mountings, light intensity, and light direction from daylight and fixture sources. Low-angle-of-incidence light intensifies normal ceiling plane irregularities and may adversely affect installed ceiling appearance. If low-incident light is likely and cannot be minimized or diffused, panels with beveled or stepped edges and suspension systems with butt-edge cross tees often look better than square-edged panels and suspension systems with override cross tees. ASTM C 636 addresses the effect of light on appearance and recommends beveled edges in lieu of square edges, flush- or recessed-mounted lighting fixtures, and tinted glass, blinds, or drapes to diffuse daylight. In areas subject to severe lighting, where ceiling appearance is especially critical, consider including requirements in the specifications for evaluating installed ceiling appearance, including viewing a mockup throughout the range of natural and permanent artificial lighting conditions.

Resistance to humidity varies among acoustical ceiling components. Most regular composition tiles and panels deteriorate when exposed to high humidity or humidity fluctuation. High-density, ceramic ceiling panels are specifically recommended for high-humidity conditions, as are vinyl-film-faced and metal-foil-faced products. Acoustical units designed not to sag in high-temperature, as high as 104°F (40°C), and high-humidity (90 percent to 100 percent relative humidity) conditions, are available. Metal ceiling units (tile, panels, and pan units) are stable, but base metal, protective coatings, and finishes must be selected with care to avoid deterioration. Similar care must be exercised when selecting suspension system components for high-humidity areas, including exterior applications and areas such as saunas, shower rooms, indoor swimming pools, kitchens, dishwashing rooms, laundries, and sterilization rooms. Also, to reduce moisture-related problems, make provisions for ventilating the ceiling plenum.

Fluctuations in percent humidity and other ambient conditions that may affect the state of acoustical ceiling systems can occur in exterior locations exposed to weather, during construction before activating the HVAC system, in buildings that have HVAC systems designed to circulate a high percentage of outside air, and in facilities such as schools, camps, or resorts that experience seasonal or periodical shutdown of HVAC systems.

Humidity-resistant units will withstand wide temperature ranges, as will metal units, if an allowance is made for expansion and contraction.

Other units should not be subjected to extremes. Plastic-film-faced units should not be exposed to temperatures above 140°F (60°C), including temperatures of abutting metal items such as light fixtures and diffusers.

If acoustical ceilings are located in corrosive environments, consider the corrosive agents, their concentration, the extent of exposure (fumes, splash, or immersion), the duration of exposure (continuous, periodic, or infrequent), and critical variables (temperature, pressure, UV light, or potential for contact with destructive agents) and obtain test data and other evidence from manufacturers about which of their products have the necessary stain- and corrosion-resistant properties for such applications. If the data are inconclusive, it may be necessary to subject specific products to testing and to seek the advice of corrosion experts, including metallurgists. The indoor swimming pool is an example of an environment that has led to the failure of stainless-steel components. The chloramines, chlorides, and other corrosive agents present in the atmosphere of an indoor swimming pool have produced stress-corrosion cracking in austenitic stainless-steel components. An alternative metal for hangers and fasteners is a nickel-copper alloy; it has demonstrated resistance to stress-corrosion cracking under low-pH conditions and high-chloride conditions present in the laboratory. Hanger wires and postinstalled fasteners are available in this alloy but at a considerably greater cost than either galvanized steel or stainless-steel components.

Soil resistance affects appearance and life-cycle costs. Soiled units have reduced light reflectance and acoustical performance, are unsightly, may be unhealthy, may or may not be easily cleanable, and are a maintenance problem requiring cleaning, repainting, or replacing. Airborne soil in air supplies can cause soiling of acoustical units.

If sanitation is a concern, membrane-faced units are more sanitary than any other units with an acoustically absorbent finish. If sanitation requirements are less severe, and perforations of surface texture are acceptable, several solutions are possible, including metal-faced units and scrubbable and soil-resistant units with special coatings or membranes. The finish of most acoustical materials is washable (if done carefully) but not scrubbable; refer to the manufacturer's data for definitions and test procedures on this subject. Verify acceptability of specific products with the local authorities that regulate sanitation in a jurisdiction.

Control of particulate matter for clean-room design requires units that do not contribute to particle emission. Unperforated or membrane-faced panels are easily kept clean. They can be combined with a gasketed suspension system and hold-down clips to accommodate typical clean-room designs that are positive pressurized within to keep particles out. Tape may also be used to seal panels to the exposed grid.

Nonmagnetic areas require all-aluminum (available as extruded or light-duty roll-formed) or stainless-steel (available only as intermediate-duty) suspension systems.

Acoustical units with more resistance to abuse than most typically formulated units include metal-faced and plastic-membrane-faced units and some units with an overlay of tough mineral material. One way to judge abuse resistance of composition units is to measure the indentation resistance (structural hardness); ASTM C 367 is the standard for measuring this. A rating of 100 to 150 lbf (445 to 667 N) for a ¼-inch (6.35-mm) penetration of a 2-inch- (50.8-mm-) diameter ball is considered highly abuse-resistant. Other tests can be conducted for friability, sag, linear expansion, and transverse strength if desired, but information on these properties is not routinely published by or available from manufacturers. Abuse-resistant panels are often held in place with retention or hold-down clips for an abuse-resistant ceiling.

Flat, horizontal ceilings, installed as a single plane, as multiple horizontal planes, or as soffits, are the most typical acoustical ceiling configuration. Flat, sloped ceilings are also possible, but panels may need to be shimmed in place or clipped in place. Multidimensional systems allow curved, contoured configurations including arched, barrel vaulted, and undulating. A ceiling system's acoustical and light reflectance performance will be affected by a nonplanar configuration.

Extruded-aluminum edge trim with a variety of finishes, linear configurations, and decorative profiles is available from several manufacturers. Trim may be used to conceal and embellish ceiling perimeters, ceiling height transitions, penetrations, and openings for fixtures. Trim may also be used to form soffits, ceiling surrounds, ceiling clouds, ceiling coffers, light coves, and recessed pockets for blinds, curtains, and drapes. Visual interest can be added to acoustical ceilings with curved edge trim.

Easy access is one of the factors favoring the wide use of lay-in panel systems. Accessible acoustical tile systems are not easily taken apart and reassembled without involving some edge damage. Cemented and stapled tile installations require regular access doors through the substrate, with tile infill for the door faces. Overlaying supplementary insulation on the backs of acoustical ceiling systems interferes with accessibility.

Overall size may be important for appearance and other reasons. Large acoustical panels in an exposed grid suspension system install quickly with less labor. If speed or ease of installation is critical, and a smaller-sized appearance is required for the project, panels scored to simulate smaller units may be selected.

Ceiling Weight

Ordinarily, the only major ceiling weight considerations are those for fire-resistance rated assembles and for wind uplift on lay-in panels. However, there is frequently a close association between CAC and weight. The overall weight of ceiling assemblies, including the lighting fixtures and other items they support, may be of importance in sizing roof structural members.

Establishing Ceiling Plane

Typically, acoustical ceilings are set at heights above finished floors. Because floors are often uneven, aligning and leveling the plane of the ceiling to coordinate with heads of door frames can be difficult, especially if doors are full height. If this is a critical issue, mockups can be used to establish acceptable appearance, or surveys can be required to establish the variation of the floor level in each space, and adjustments can be made to ceiling planes; include requirements in the specifications.

ACOUSTICAL PANELS

The most common modular sizes of acoustical panels are 24 by 24 inches (610 by 610 mm) and 24 by 48 inches (610 by 1220 mm). Hard metric sizes, including 600 by 600 mm and 600 by 1200 mm, are available, subject to a variety of manufacturer-imposed conditions and limitations. Verify availability of hard metric sizes with applicable manufacturers. Also, special sizes and shapes are fabricated for compatibility with manufacturers' integrated ceiling systems. Scored panels of 24 by 48 inches (610 by 1220 mm) provide interesting visuals, such as 6- to 24-inch (150- to 610-mm) squares, linear strips, and cross-etched linear ceilings, to vary and embellish the basic modular appearance of the panels and suspension system while maintaining the advantages of full-size panels.

Surface texture and acoustical pattern provide visual interest and affect acoustical performance. Colored panels with color-compatible suspension systems are available to vary appearance, but white panels provide superior light reflectance.

Common edge treatment and joint details are described and illustrated in ASTM E 1264. Most acoustical panels have square or reveal edges (fig. 2). Panels with these edges are easily placed in the suspension system and pushed upward for removal or access to ceiling plenum. For certain proprietary patterns, the edges are stepped, tapered, rounded, or otherwise formed. For some patterns, the reveal may relate to the depth of scoring or embossing so the plane of the exposed cap on the runner is on the same plane as the face of the scored reveals in the field of the panel. For other narrow-face, box-shaped suspension members, the exposed flange of the runners ends up flush with the face of the panel. Reveal edges are generally selected for their aesthetic value and for disguising the grid. Panels are available with sealed edges if necessary for use in clean rooms and similar applications.

Contrary to definitions in ASTM E 1264, some manufacturers make acoustical units, called *panels,* that are configured for exposed grid on two opposite edges, and kerfed and rabbeted in the factory on the other two opposite edges for concealing the supporting, flat-spline cross members. Another type of unit, also called *panels* by manufacturers, are rabbeted on the back, have beveled edges on the face, and are kerfed on two edges to allow panels to engage runner flanges. When installed, panels with this type of edge totally or partially conceal the grid from view.

Perforated and fissured acoustical panels typically have increased sound absorption and higher NRCs than comparable unperforated panels. Smooth units, with an acoustically transparent surface that is not perforated or fissured, and microperforated units have been developed and may be now available. Both types have significant sound-absorption capabilities and high NRCs.

Thicker panels made of porous materials have increased sound absorption and higher NRCs than comparable thinner panels. For example, mineral-fiber products average an NRC increase of about 0.10 as the thickness of the panel or tile is increased from ½ to ¾ inch (13 to 19 mm).

Foil-backed or back-coated acoustical panels have enhanced sound attenuation and higher CACs and ACs than comparable panels without sound-impervious back treatments because of increased sound blockage and distortion of the angle of reflection, respectively.

Installing thermal or acoustical insulation on the back of suspended acoustical panel ceilings is not recommended by manufacturers. Excessive loading caused by added insulation can cause sagging and unsafe installations. Condensation may occur if ceiling insulation places the dew point inside the plenum. Condensation within the plenum can damage both acoustical units and suspension systems. Uncovered mineral-fiber insulation in the plenum may increase particulate counts in air supplies and contribute to poor indoor air quality. If other considerations require that acoustical or thermal insulation be installed on top of the acoustical ceiling, manufacturers may not warrant installations or they may have weight restrictions, requirements for vapor retarders, and other limitations. Because blanket-insulation rolls span multiple cross tees and contact the backs of acoustical units less frequently, rolls are preferred to batts.

One of the main advantages of lay-in panel ceilings compared to tile ceilings is that they provide easier access to the ceiling plenum. However, ease of removal has a downside: Panels may become displaced because of cleaning (such as pressure cleaning of metal-faced kitchen panels), pressure differences from wind uplift in exterior locations and vestibules, and abuse. Although they slightly restrict access, hold-down clips may be the solution for these applications and may also be needed, with gaskets, to maintain a seal between the panel and the suspension system grid in areas

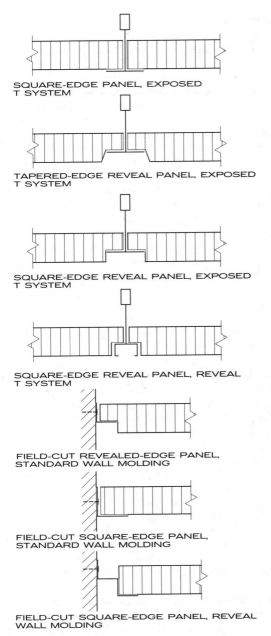

SQUARE-EDGE PANEL, EXPOSED T SYSTEM

TAPERED-EDGE REVEAL PANEL, EXPOSED T SYSTEM

SQUARE-EDGE REVEAL PANEL, EXPOSED T SYSTEM

SQUARE-EDGE REVEAL PANEL, REVEAL T SYSTEM

FIELD-CUT REVEALED-EDGE PANEL, STANDARD WALL MOLDING

FIELD-CUT SQUARE-EDGE PANEL, STANDARD WALL MOLDING

FIELD-CUT SQUARE-EDGE PANEL, REVEAL WALL MOLDING

Figure 2. Edge treatment and joint details

such as clean rooms. In general, fire-resistant ceilings with panels weighing less than 1 lb/sq. ft. (4.89 kg/sq. m) require hold-down clips. The drawings should indicate areas to receive special accessible-type clips. Always use hold-down clips with exterior panel ceilings.

If refinishing is needed, most acoustical units can be repainted—ideally with high hiding power, nonbridging latex paints applied strictly according to the manufacturer's written instructions—without significantly affecting their sound-absorption properties. When painted, units with large surface perforations or fissures lose less acoustical efficiency than finely perforated units. Depending on the burning characteristics of the paint, repainting may modify the flame-spread and smoke-developed indexes of the original product to exceed levels allowed by authorities having jurisdiction. Paint formulations that are classified by UL's *Building Materials Directory* are available.

SUSPENSION SYSTEMS

The industry's strong orientation to ASTM C 635 and its companion standard ASTM C 636 makes it unnecessary for the design professional to reinvent suspension systems and installation specifications for most applications. Except for a brief explanation of structural classification requirements, the content of these two standards will not be repeated or interpreted here. UBC Standard 25-2 is based on these two ASTM standards.

Structural performance of metal suspension systems in ASTM C 635 is divided into three classifications: light, intermediate, and heavy-duty. Light-duty systems can support only the acoustical units themselves, are normally for residential and light-commercial applications. Intermediate-duty systems can support some additional loads, such as those from light fixtures and ceiling diffusers, and are for ordinary commercial structures. Heavy-duty systems have the greatest capacity to support additional loads from light fixtures, ceiling diffusers, and the like. For every application, calculate potential ceiling loads and compare them with the carrying capacities of the systems being considered for selection.

The visible components of exposed suspension systems are formed by interlocking main and cross tees with flanges of various materials, widths, profiles, and finishes into a modular grid (fig. 3). Wide-face, double-web, steel suspension systems are available with either override or butt-edge cross tees. This choice is restricted primarily to nonfire-resistance-rated systems. With the override type, there will be a gap between the faces of panels at their corners and the top edge of the cross-runner flange equal to the thickness of the stepped-up flange of the cross tee. This gap does not occur with the butt-edge cross tee where the top surface of both main and cross runners is on the same plane. The gap that occurs with override cross tees can be visible and exaggerated by lighting conditions. Under conditions such as asymmetric loading, butt-edge cross tees have less torsional resistance compared to similarly dimensioned override cross tees, and single-web tees have less torsional resistance compared to similarly dimensioned override and double-web tees.

Cross-tee end-clip details provide a locked connection that varies among products. Designs include interlocking devices, for example, bayonet-type couplings and clips with hook-on, stake-on, or stab-on ends. Depending on the design of the interlocking device or end-clip detail, some systems are easier to install and remove than others.

Designs with cross-tee end details that accommodate lateral movement and have the strength to resist grid pullout are used for fire-rated systems and to comply with seismic-design requirements. Fire-rated systems have additional expansion-relief capabilities (fig. 4). Not all systems can be used in all seismic zones. Verify a system's seismic capabilities with its manufacturer.

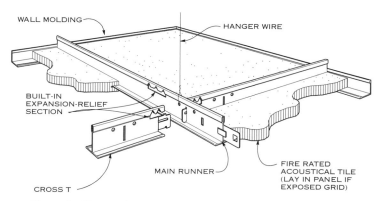

Figure 4. Fire rated suspension system (concealed system shown)

Gypsum-board and plaster-board suspension systems may be suitable for installation of acoustical panel ceilings, especially combination gypsum-board/acoustical ceilings; for exterior applications; and for those ceilings exposed to positive pressure, wind uplift, and severe environments such as wet or humid conditions.

ACOUSTICAL PERFORMANCE CONSIDERATIONS

Acoustics designers strive to create and control the conditions that maximize perception (hearing) of wanted sound, and minimize perception of unwanted sound. Acoustical control can be divided into two broad categories: noise isolation between spaces, and control of sound reflections and reverberations within a space. Acoustical ceilings can accomplish both types of control, within limits; but for optimum performance in one category, performance in the other tends to be sacrificed. Most acoustical ceiling materials are compromises between good sound absorption (which is indicated by NRC and indirectly indicated by AC) and good noise isolation (which is indicated by CAC). NRC measures overall sound absorption. Good sound absorbers are porous and usually lightweight. A ceiling is often the largest and most expedient surface for locating absorbers. If the ceiling area is small in relationship to other room surface proportions, absorptive acoustical ceilings may be supplemented with absorbers on walls and floors. For good noise isolation, it is important not only to select barriers with rated sound-isolation properties but to install them in a manner that does not detract from their sound-insulating properties. By comparing CAC plus NRC ratings of various acoustical ceiling materials, the inverse relationship that usually occurs can be seen. AC measures conversational noise that is reflected (not absorbed) at specific angles off ceilings into adjacent cubicle spaces. Proper selection of the ceiling system requires analyzing the acoustical performance characteristics the ceiling will be expected to fulfill. Some acoustical panel ceilings can be modified to achieve better sound-isolation ability. Impervious facings or backings on some porous products measurably improve sound attenuation ratings.

Acoustical design for conventional closed offices involves selecting ceiling products based on their NRC and CAC. If office partitions extend to the underside of the floor above, and are designed and constructed as barriers with sealed perimeters and penetrations to contain sound within the space and exclude outside sound, the ceiling's sound absorption, expressed as NRC, is the most important variable. In office layouts with partitions that extend to the face of the ceiling, the sound absorption afforded by the ceiling is less important than the capability to attenuate airborne sound from one space to another. As explained earlier, CAC is a measure of the ceiling's capability to reduce sound transmission through the ceiling between adjacent spaces. Overlaid acoustical insulation and plenum barriers consisting of acoustical insulation infilling above ceiling-height partitions may also mitigate noise from spaces with a shared plenum by absorbing sound originating from

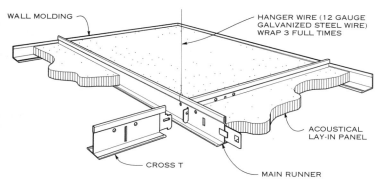

Figure 3. Exposed suspension system

the partitioned spaces and from within the plenum. However, manufacturers' product data usually contain cautions about overlaid insulation; see the preceding discussion of overlaid insulation in this chapter.

Selection of acoustical ceilings for open offices (offices without ceiling-height partitions) involves choosing products based on their NRC and AC ratings. Speech privacy in open-plan office design is attained only by the interaction of several components besides the ceiling, including the space dividers, wall treatments, window treatments, furnishings, background sound-masking system, HVAC system, and positions of the speaker and listener. Because test conditions for AC involve dimensional and geometric constraints and additional materials with specific minimums for sound-blocking and -absorbing densities and NRC performances, using AC as a guide to acoustical ceiling design for projects with dissimilar conditions may be imprecise. ASTM E 1264 cautions that "the addition of hard surfaced elements in the ceiling, such as surface mounted or recessed lighting fixtures can impair the AC rating, depending upon the area of the hard surface and its location relevant to occupants in the space." Diffusers and grilles associated with HVAC systems can also be sources of noise leakage and sound reflection. As noted earlier, ASTM E 1111 measures the interzone attenuation of acoustical ceilings; a ceiling's AC is intended to correlate with the reduction of intelligible speech transmitted between adjacent cubicles. ASTM E 1375 measures the interzone attenuation of furniture panels. ASTM E 1376 measures the effect of flanking or reflections of vertical surfaces. ASTM E 1130 describes a method to objectively measure speech privacy by using the articulation index. For a more detailed discussion of the test methods and the use of ASTM standards in understanding the interactions affecting acoustical performance in an open-plan office, refer to ASTM E 1374, *Guide for Open Office Acoustics and Applicable ASTM Standards.* According to ASTM E 1374, speech privacy is rated confidential when speech may be detected but not understood, and normal or nonintrusive when effort is required to understand it and is judged nondistracting. According to acousticians, an AC between 180 and 200 is usually considered acceptable for normal privacy. Factors to consider in open-plan office design include the following:

- Office size and cubicle layout designed to minimize the exposure to nuisance noise sources, to avoid direct sound fields, and to adequately distance speakers and listeners. ASTM E 1111 tests at a distance of 108 inches (2700 mm). Entrance openings in cubicles should be staggered to prevent direct sound transmission between opposing cubicles.
- Effective cubicle partition heights. According to ASTM E 1374, barrier heights of from 60 to 80 inches (1520 to 2030 mm) are most efficient.
- Sound-masking systems designed to provide nondistracting low-level background sound.
- The ceiling system's tested acoustical performance.
- Acoustical performance of surrounding environments. Densities and NRCs that are equal to or exceed those set by test conditions are beneficial. Cubicle partitions should have an NRC of not less than 0.80 to comply with test condition minimums.

Installation methods affect acoustical performance. Suspended acoustical units are more absorptive than adhesively or mechanically attached tiles because the exposed back surface provides additional adsorptive area and the resultant plenum space absorbs some sound.

A convex or concave acoustical panel ceiling, as compared to a flat ceiling, will significantly alter acoustical performance. Acoustical ceiling manufacturers' reported ratings for sound performance are for flat panels and tiles. Deviating from a flat, horizontal plane ceiling can negate generally acceptable practices for designing acoustical ceilings and influence which of the several available sound criteria are critically important to control within a given space. For example, a concave surface focuses sound energy. If the resulting focused sound is undesirable, the concave ceiling

must be highly sound-absorptive and have a high NRC to lessen the unwanted effect. A convex surface reflectively disperses sound energy and may enhance uniform sound distribution and dissipation.

Consult acoustics specialists to determine the degree of sound control where exacting performance is expected, such as in public-assembly areas, special usage areas such as recording studios, and areas with unusual noise sources.

FIRE-TEST-RESPONSE CHARACTERISTICS

Fire testing of acoustical panel ceilings is performed to determine surface-burning characteristics of acoustical panels and to establish fire-resistance ratings of floor- and roof-ceiling assemblies. It is essential to distinguish between these two types of tests because one relates to the performance of a product as a finish material only, and the other relates to a component of a fire-resistant assembly. The latter involves not only the panels but the suspension systems, the floor or roof structures from which they are hung, and items penetrating the ceiling membrane, including lighting fixtures and air outlets.

Finishes are tested only for flame-spread and smoke-developed indexes per ASTM E 84. The flame-spread index is a measure of surface-burning characteristics only. Associated values indicate the smoke-developed index. Fuel contribution is no longer measured. ASTM E 1264, the Standard Building Code, and the 2000 International Building Code (IBC) refer to Classes A, B, and C materials with a flame-spread index of no more than 25, 75, and 200, respectively. UBC and the BOCA National Building Code refer to Classes I, II, and III materials with an identical classification of values for flame-spread index. According to ASTM E 1264, for Class A materials, the smoke-developed index may not exceed 50. Currently, the three model building codes and the 2000 IBC set 450 as the maximum allowed smoke-developed index for finish materials of Classes I-III or Classes A-C. Most products available in the United States are Class A per ASTM E 1264. Depending on requirements imposed by authorities having jurisdiction related to the presence or absence of active fire-protection systems and the occupancy and use of the space in which the ceilings are located, acoustical panel ceilings must satisfy the requirements of the appropriate classification. Typically, finish materials with flame-spread indexes exceeding 25 are not allowed in unsprinklered exit-access corridors and in vertical exits and passageways. Since its 1996 edition, the BOCA Code also requires ceiling materials that are exposed within an air distribution plenum to have a flame-spread index of no more than 25 and a smoke-developed index of no more than 50. Before selecting acoustical materials, always verify requirements of authorities having jurisdiction so surface-burning characteristics do not exceed the imposed limits.

Fire-resistance ratings are applied to certain types of construction that have endured fire and high temperatures for a given period under test conditions. ASTM E 119 (UBC Standard 7-1, UL 263, and NFPA 251) is the standard test method for measuring the fire-test-response characteristics of various floor-ceiling and roof-ceiling assemblies for purposes of assigning fire-resistance ratings. The rating applies to the entire assembly and not to individual components; because it applies only to the exact construction tested, do not assume that deviations will routinely be accepted by authorities having jurisdiction without obtaining an interpretation. Even minor deviations often require formal approval and should be checked before releasing documents. Tests are time-consuming and expensive, and manufacturers submit only materials that are certain to pass, and then only as components of the more common constructions. The details of each assembly, along with listings of manufacturers, products, and ratings, that may be acceptable to authorities having jurisdiction are found in UL's *Fire*

Resistance Directory, Intertek Testing Services' (ITS's) *Directory of Listed Products,* and other sources.

Selection of a time-rated construction for a suspended acoustical panel ceiling is best made in the early stages of a job and with an awareness of the limitations involved. Each rating designation limits not only the structural system, in combination with basic acoustical and suspension system materials, but requirements for size, thickness, spacing, attachments, and other details. Major limitations include the spacing, size, and protection (covering) of penetrations for lighting, HVAC, and so on. Coordinating finishes may be critical; some manufacturers control panel and tile design for visual compatibility between rated and nonrated products, but some do not. Not all types of construction, such as wood truss structural designs, are rated for assemblies with acoustical ceilings.

Manufacturers of acoustical ceiling materials may designate, by key names, their products that are UL rated for fire-resistant ceilings for use in one or more UL-rated, fire-resistant assemblies.

ENERGY CONSIDERATIONS

Although heat-transfer resistance is normally not a prime consideration in selecting acoustical ceilings, a ceiling system can improve the overall thermal resistance of a ceiling-to-roof assembly. Each panel manufacturer publishes the thermal-insulation properties of its products. However, if the plenum space is used for air distribution or if light fixture ballasts keep it well heated, this may be of little value.

ENVIRONMENTAL CONSIDERATIONS

The American Institute of Architects' *Environmental Resource Guide* includes a material report for acoustical ceiling systems that highlights concerns for waste generation, natural resource depletion, energy consumption, and indoor air quality for Type III and Type IX units and suspension systems.

The recycled content and disposability of acoustical ceiling products are being addressed by manufacturers. Recycled materials may be used to conserve raw materials and reduce waste, consequently affecting the management of natural resources, forest sustainability (paper), energy consumption, landfill capacity, and other environmental concerns. Acoustical ceiling factory waste or other industry waste, which is termed *preconsumer waste,* may be recycled and used to fabricate ceiling components or other products. Defective mineral-fiber panels and slag (a byproduct of steel fabrication) are examples of preconsumer waste used in the manufacture of acoustical ceiling panels. Recycled newspaper, an example of what is termed *postconsumer waste,* is used in the manufacture of acoustical ceiling panels. According to manufacturers, both metal-grid components and acoustical units are being fabricated from recycled materials, as much as 96 percent total recycled content in some instances. Currently, most products contain limited amounts of postconsumer waste. Manufacturers cannot certify the recycled-material content of the components furnished for a specific project; they can only estimate recycled content for overall production. Contact individual manufacturers for information on ceiling reclamation programs, verify the availability of recycling operations in the project area, and specify requirements for recycling existing acoustical ceilings if applicable.

Indoor air quality issues related to acoustical panels include particulate inhalation and irritation to eyes and skin, VOC emissions and absorption, and contamination by biological agents. Panels and tiles with a high content of unconfined or erodible fiber and less-durable, friable binders and

that produce dust when handled and on deterioration represent more potential particulate risk than units without these characteristics. More durable, denser, harder, more abrasion- and impact-resistant panels and tiles and those that are tightly sealed are less likely to release particles. Sensitive environments may have stringent requirements for control of particulate matter in indoor air, VOC emissions, and potential pathogens.

Inhaled mineral fibers have been classified by the International Agency for Research on Cancer as possibly carcinogenic to humans, by the National Toxicology Program as a substance "reasonably anticipated as a carcinogen," and by the American Conference of Governmental Industrial Hygienists as a confirmed animal carcinogen with unknown relevance to humans.

Because they are often porous, many acoustical panels may be sources of and sinks for pollutants and pathogens. They may absorb and emit VOCs and odors and, if wetted or exposed to humid conditions, may serve as a medium for microbial, mold, mildew, and fungal growth. Absorbed gases, moisture, humidity, and the presence of microbiological organisms may also affect the appearance, performance, durability, and serviceability of acoustical panel ceilings.

Antifungal treatments or fungicides to control mold and mildew growth, and antibacterial treatments or biocides to control microbiological pathogens, are added by some manufacturers. Treatments may be added during fabrication and be dispersed throughout the acoustical unit, or they may be applied as coatings to top and face surfaces and perhaps to edges. Surface-applied fungicide and biocide coatings may be paint-based or be applied as topcoats over painted finishes.

SEISMIC CONSIDERATIONS

Acoustical ceilings installed in areas requiring seismic bracing may require bracing designed to applicable building codes. Local codes normally define design forces that must be resisted by architectural components.

For areas that require seismic restraint, the following the installation standards can be included in specifications: ASTM E 580, *Practice for Application of Ceiling Suspension Systems for Acoustical Tile and Lay-in Panels in Areas Requiring Moderate Seismic Restraint;* Ceilings & Interior Systems Construction Association's (CISCA's) *Recommendations for Direct-Hung Acoustical Tile and Lay-in Panel Ceilings-Seismic Zones 0-2;* CISCA's *Guidelines for Seismic Restraint of Direct-Hung Suspended Ceiling Assemblies-Seismic Zones 3 & 4;* and UBC Standard 25-2. Because codes are subject to periodic revision and to interpretation and amendment by local and state authorities having jurisdiction, verify requirements in effect for each project to determine which publications and standards to reference, if any, in the specifications and whether design of seismic restraints by a professional engineer and submission of engineering calculations are required. When dealing with code requirements for seismic loads on suspended ceilings, the design professional must comply with one of the three following alternatives (note that UBC, the BOCA National Building Code, and the Standard Building Code have exceptions to seismic requirements for ceiling components under some conditions):

- Even though there may be no explicit mention of any of the following in the model code in effect for the project, cite one of the following standards as a prescriptive criterion: ASTM E 580, the applicable CISCA standard, or UBC Standard 25-2.
- Design all the ceiling components based on the analytical method in the American Society of Civil Engineer's (ASCE's) publication ASCE 7, *Minimum Design Loads for Buildings and Other Structures,* or on criteria found in the building code in effect for the project.
- Delegate the design of seismic restraints to a professional engineer

engaged by the contractor, citing the analytical method to be used as the basis of design performance criteria. This option requires that the analytical method to be used as the basis of design is well understood by the design professional and that all relevant information is indicated in the contract documents. Examples of criteria that might need to be specified if ASCE 7 is used as the basis of design include seismic-design category or seismic use group, occupancy importance factor, and site classification.

Changes to ASCE 7, which were new in the 1998 edition that was published in January 2000, include reference to CISCA standards and requirements for special inspections during the installation of architectural components in Seismic Design Categories D, E, and F. If special inspections are required for the project, include requirements in the specifications.

NOISE REGULATIONS

Noise regulations may be either source- or ambient-based. Source-based regulations are for a specific noise source such as HVAC equipment. Ambient-based regulations are those that protect hearers from noise pollution regardless of the origin of the pollutant.

The United States Department of Housing and Urban Development (HUD) includes regulatory requirements for acoustics for multifamily residential occupancies in its International One- and Two-Family Dwelling Code. The General Services Administration (GSA) has a requirement for federal courtrooms. Some states and localities mandate requirements for schools. Since the Occupational Safety and Health Act of 1970 (Williams-Steiger) was implemented, protection of workers from permanent and temporary hearing impairment caused by exposure to high noise levels has been required of employers. Acoustical ceilings can contribute to noise-control efforts.

Currently, the United States Architectural & Transportation Barriers Compliance Board is supporting the efforts of the American National Standards Institute (ANSI) and the Acoustical Society of America (ASA) to "develop technical and scoping recommendations for classroom acoustics." According to the board, a draft ANSI/ASA standard for classroom acoustics has been submitted to ANSI for adoption. The board believes that the criteria in this standard should be incorporated into the acoustical requirements of the model building codes and is working toward this goal. Additional information is available at http://www.access-board.gov.

Existing standards that may be useful for designing classroom acoustics include recommendations in the 1999 *ASHRAE HANDBOOK – HVAC Applications* and in ANSI S12.2, *Criteria for Evaluating Room Noise*. Additional information can be accessed at the National Clearinghouse for Educational Facilities, a part of the United States Department of Education's Educational Resources Information Center, at www.edfacilities.org.

REFERENCES

Publication dates cited here were current at the time of this writing. Publications are revised periodically, and revisions may have occurred before this book was published.

The American Institute of Architects
Environmental Resource Guide, 1996 (1997 and 1998 supplements).

American National Standards Institute
ANSI S 12.2-1995 (reapproved 1999): Criteria for Evaluating Room Noise

American Society of Heating, Refrigeration and Air-Conditioning Engineers, Inc.
1999 ASHRAE HANDBOOK — HVAC Applications

ASTM International
ASTM C 367-99: Test Methods for Strength Properties of Prefabricated Architectural Acoustical Tile or Lay-In Ceiling Panels

ASTM C 423-99a: Test Method for Sound Absorption and Sound Absorption Coefficients by the Reverberation Room Method

ASTM C 635-97: Specification for the Manufacture, Performance, and Testing of Metal Suspension Systems for Acoustical Tile and Lay-in Panel Ceilings

ASTM C 636-96: Practice for Installation of Metal Ceiling Suspension Systems for Acoustical Tile and Lay-in Panels

ASTM E 84-99: Test Method for Surface Burning Characteristics of Building Materials

ASTM E 119-98: Test Methods for Fire Tests of Building Construction and Materials

ASTM E 413-87 (reapproved 1999): Classification for Rating Sound Insulation

ASTM E 580-96: Practice for Application of Ceiling Suspension Systems for Acoustical Tile and Lay-in Panels in Areas Requiring Moderate Seismic Restraint

ASTM E 1110-86 (reapproved 1994): Classification for Determination of Articulation Class

ASTM E 1111-92 (reapproved 1996): Test Method for Measuring the Interzone Attenuation of Ceiling Systems

ASTM E 1130-90 (reapproved 1994): Test Method for Objective Measurement of Speech Privacy in Open Offices Using Articulation Index

ASTM E 1264-98: Classification for Acoustical Ceiling Products

ASTM E 1374-93 (reapproved 1998): Guide for Open Office Acoustics and Applicable ASTM Standards

ASTM E 1375-90 (reapproved 1994): Test Method for Measuring the Interzone Attenuation of Furniture Panels Used as Acoustical Barriers

ASTM E 1376-90 (reapproved 1994): Test Method for Measuring the Interzone Attenuation of Sound Reflected by Wall Finishes and Furniture Panels

ASTM E 1414-00: Test Method for Airborne Sound Attenuation Between Rooms Sharing a Common Ceiling Plenum

Ceilings & Interior Systems Construction Association
Guidelines for Seismic Restraint of Direct-Hung Suspended Ceiling Assemblies-Seismic Zones 3 & 4, 1991.

Recommendations for Direct-Hung Acoustical Tile and Lay-in Panel Ceilings-Seismic Zones 0-2, 1991.

International Conference of Building Officials
UBC Standard 25-2-1997: Metal Suspension Systems for Acoustical Tile and for Lay-in Panel Ceilings

Intertek Testing Services
Directory of Listed Products, published annually.

Underwriters Laboratories Inc.
Building Materials Directory, published annually.

Fire Resistance Directory, published annually.

09512 ACOUSTICAL TILE CEILINGS

This chapter discusses ceilings consisting of acoustical tiles and concealed suspension systems.

The chapter does not discuss acoustical panels and exposed suspension systems; these are discussed in Chapter 09511, Acoustical Panel Ceilings, Chapter 09513, Acoustical Snap-in Metal Pan Ceilings, and Chapter 09547, Linear Metal Ceilings. Lay-in or other types of metal pan ceilings with exposed suspension systems are also not covered.

GENERAL COMMENTS

This chapter includes the most typical applications of acoustical tile ceilings. ASTM E 1264 is the principal standard to reference for specifying tiles; note, however, that although this standard provides a method for generically specifying acoustical panel and tile ceilings, specifications rapidly become proprietary as more constraints for type, pattern, color, light reflectance, acoustical properties, size, and fire-resistance ratings are included. Although a degree of variety is available in patterns, finishes, and levels of performance, the number of generic choices is limited, partly because manufacturers want to maintain unit costs at a competitive level. Code requirements and material limitations may also restrict generic choices. Custom-designed and -produced acoustical tiles are rarely developed for a single room or even for a single project, although custom colors may be available depending on the manufacturer, product type, and quantities involved. Other materials are usually arranged in combinations for custom-designed work, to achieve an overall acoustical effect and to satisfy other functions related to appearance, light distribution, and fire protection.

The process of fulfilling appearance and performance criteria for a particular application results in reducing the number of products acceptable for a particular application. Ultimately, cost limitations may dictate the choice of two or three viable alternatives. Typically, acoustical tile ceilings cost more than comparable acoustical panel ceilings. Where acoustical tiles represent the predominant ceiling finish of a large project, seemingly small differences in unit costs among products may have a larger impact on overall costs than first recognized. Nevertheless, cost considerations may not totally outweigh design considerations for most projects because of the high visibility of ceiling surfaces. If initial and life-cycle costs are critical to a project, consider consulting manufacturers during design development or earlier phases about installed price ranges.

The semiproprietary specification method accommodates the actual selection process adhered to by most design professionals in choosing acoustical tile ceilings. Although it is possible to specify acoustical tile ceilings based entirely on compliance with performance and descriptive requirements, this specification method is unlikely to offer adequate control when it comes to appearance or visual uniformity among competing products. The most reasonable approach is to let a project team know that only a limited number of products, whose appearance is acceptable, exist.

PRODUCT CLASSIFICATION

Definitions for acoustical tiles and panels are not well understood, causing considerable confusion for design professionals. ASTM E 1264 includes a designation system for identifying the various performance and physical properties of acoustical tiles and panels. These designations by themselves, however, tend to be cryptic for those unfamiliar with their meaning or without ready access to ASTM E 1264; therefore, they are explained in Chapter 09511.

ACOUSTICAL CEILING CHARACTERISTICS

According to ASTM E 1264, the differences between a tile and a panel are the method of support and the type of suspension system. Acoustical tiles are used with concealed or semiexposed suspension systems (fig. 1), stapling, or adhesive bonding. Acoustical panels are used with exposed suspension systems. Although most tiles are smaller than most panels, the size of the acoustical unit does not determine the type. In recent years, more and more acoustical ceilings have been specified using panels. Many special-use products are available today only in panel form. Some large-sized fiberglass and excelsior units are installed on standard exposed suspension systems, but special edges result in visual concealment of the suspension system. These products are often considered panels used with exposed suspension systems. Alternatively, if concealed suspension systems are interpreted as being concealed to view, these products could be considered tiles. Because many tile products have been discontinued, verify product availability before including them in the specifications.

Extruded-aluminum edge trim with a variety of finishes, linear configurations, and decorative profiles is available from several manufacturers. Trim may be used to conceal and embellish ceiling perimeters, ceiling height transitions, penetrations, and openings for fixtures. Trim may also be used to form soffits, ceiling surrounds, ceiling clouds, ceiling coffers, light coves, and recessed pockets for blinds, curtains, and drapes.

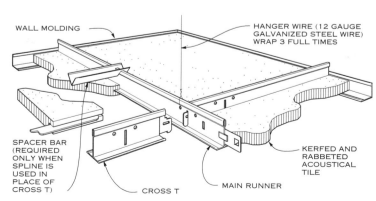

Figure 1. Concealed suspension system

Accessibility is one consideration that has led to using lay-in panel ceilings rather than tile ceilings. Accessible acoustical tile ceilings are not easily taken apart and reassembled without involving some edge damage to tiles. Cemented and stapled tile installations require regular access doors through the substrate, with tile infill for the door faces.

Options available for the type of and locations for access to space above suspended tile ceilings depend on project design constraints and the system and the manufacturer selected. Factors to consider include purpose for access; locations and life cycles of equipment and components requiring adjustment, maintenance, monitoring, repair, or replacement; plenum and room area obstructions; dimensional clearances; correlation to direct-hung or indirect-hung suspension system; and fire-rating and seismic requirements. Nonaccessible systems are uncommon but may be satisfactory where access to plenum space is not needed. Single-tile access may be adequate for small areas and simple tasks where limited access is needed, such as for valve adjustment. Multiple-tile access and subsequent removal of tiles permit access to larger plenum areas for more complex operations. Systems with bipart-opening action are common; those with side-pivot-opening action are available from some manufacturers. Downward- or upward-acting systems are typically available (see figs. 2 and 3). Upward-acting systems require a deeper plenum space than downward-acting systems. Special components allow movement; Z-shaped components are associated with upward action. Downward-acting systems are more expensive than upward-acting systems. Downward-acting systems are activated by manipulating access clip(s), sometimes with special tools; the clips are visible, and the tiles must be marked. Tile edges are frequently damaged

in the process. With either system, especially when large areas are removed, accessed tiles may not align properly after reinstallation, resulting in an uneven ceiling appearance.

Installation methods affect acoustical performance. Suspended acoustical tiles are more sound-absorptive than adhesively or mechanically attached tiles because the exposed back surface provides additional adsorptive area, and the resultant plenum space absorbs some sound.

Other general properties of acoustical tile ceilings are similar to those discussed for acoustical panel ceilings in Chapter 09511.

ACOUSTICAL TILES

The common sizes of acoustical tiles are 12 by 12 inches (305 by 305 mm) and 12 by 24 inches (305 by 610 mm). Hard metric sizes, including 300 by 300 mm and 300 by 600 mm, are available, subject to a variety of manufacturer-imposed conditions and limitations. Verify availability of hard metric sizes with applicable manufacturers.

Tiles with sharp-cut edges make joints less conspicuous, particularly with 12-inch (305-mm) square, directionally textured units, but the industry would rather handle eased and beveled edges, because sharp-edged tiles may fail to conceal joints, may be easily damaged with handling, and may have an unsatisfactory appearance if the light striking the ceiling is unfavorable (i.e., if it strikes at a low angle of incidence). Tiles with eased and beveled edges minimize the low-angle-of-incidence lighting problem and are more durable when handled.

A high quality of workmanship is achievable with square edges, a one-directional pattern, and favorable lighting. With medium-fissured or heavily fissured tiles, it is possible to go back over the completed ceiling and (with a penknife) expand major fissures across each joint to help conceal tile joints in the ceiling. But because this could lead to damaged tiles, it is considered a rather unusual and extreme requirement to specify. A better alternative is to specify tile with an embossed-in-register pattern that extends into adjacent tiles, making joints less visible.

In ASTM E 1264 and in manufacturers' product data, joint details (such as the detail shown in fig. 4) are illustrated, and the terms *kerfed (splined)*, *flanged*, *rabbeted (cut back)*, and *tongue and groove (T & G)* are defined and explained graphically. Sometimes the desired or required profile on all four edges is identical; sometimes not. For example, T & G treatments are usually the same on two adjacent edges, and different (as required for nesting) on the other two adjacent edges. It is impossible to install tile uniformly prepared in this manner in a checkerboard pattern unless half of the shipment has the direction of the pattern oriented differently for the edge profile arrangement. If tile with a directional pattern is selected, include the applicable requirement indicating tile arrangement in the specifications or show it on reflected ceiling plans.

Other general properties of acoustical tiles are the same as those discussed for acoustical panels in Chapter 09511.

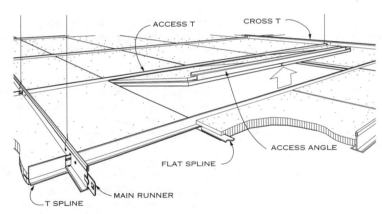

Figure 2. Concealed suspension system – upward access (side pivot shown; end pivot available)

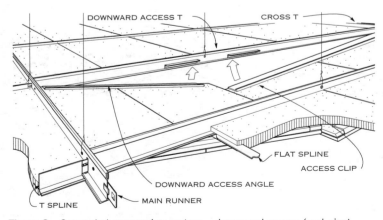

Figure 3. Concealed suspension system – downward access (end pivot shown; side pivot available)

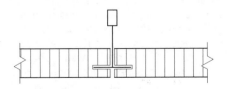

Figure 4. Kerfed edge tile, concealed T system

SUSPENSION SYSTEMS

The industry's strong orientation to ASTM C 635, *Specification for the Manufacture, Performance, and Testing of Metal Suspension Systems for Acoustical Tile and Lay-in Panel Ceilings,* and to its companion standard ASTM C 636, *Practice for Installation of Metal Ceiling Suspension Systems for Acoustical Tile and Lay-in Panels,* makes it unnecessary for the design professional to reinvent suspension systems and installation specifications for most applications. See Chapter 09511, for a brief explanation of structural classification requirements and of requirements for areas needing seismic restraint.

Three types of suspension systems are covered in ASTM C 635: direct-hung, indirect-hung, and furring bar. Direct-hung systems are those in which main runners are hung directly from the structure above. Indirect-hung systems are those in which main runners are attached to carrying channels that are hung from the structure above. Furring-bar systems are those in which tile is laminated to backing boards that are fastened by screws or nails to furring or nailing bars, with the bars clipped to carrying channels hung from the structure above.

DIRECTLY ATTACHED ACOUSTICAL TILE CEILING INSTALLATIONS

Direct attachment of ceiling tiles may be to ceiling surfaces or to furring or backer boards attached to the overhead structure. Substrates subject to significant thermal movement are not suitable for direct attachment.

According to the Ceilings & Interior Systems Construction Association's (CISCA's) *Ceiling Systems Handbook,* adhesive attachment is suitable for "plastered ceilings (either painted or unpainted), plasterboard, gypsum board, hollow masonry blocks" or any other surface "that permits adequate bonding" (fig. 5). According to the same source, "metal plates, plywood, fiber or composition boards are not satisfactory surfaces. Troweled acoustical plaster is also hazardous as a base." Adhesive or *glue-up* installation is not suitable for tile with foil backing. Large tiles, usually those larger than 12 by 24 inches (305 by 610 mm), may not be adequately attached by adhesive alone.

Stapled, nailed, or screwed direct installation methods are not included in CISCA's *Ceiling Systems Handbook.* Manufacturers recommend few products for stapled installation in their product data. Products intended for direct installations are usually for residential use. Staple attachment is suitable for tile with stapling flange (fig. 6). According to manufacturers, tiles may be stapled over gypsum board substrates with a minimum thickness

of ½ inch (12.7 mm), without bumps or ridges. Contact manufacturers for other suitable substrates.

SEISMIC CONSIDERATIONS

Acoustical ceilings installed in areas requiring seismic bracing may require bracing designed to applicable building codes. Local codes normally define design forces that must be resisted by architectural components.

For areas that require seismic restraint, the following installation standards can be included in specifications: ASTM E 580, *Practice for Application of Ceiling Suspension Systems for Acoustical Tile and Lay-in Panels in Areas Requiring Moderate Seismic Restraint;* CISCA's *Recommendations for Direct-Hung Acoustical Tile and Lay-in Panel Ceilings—Seismic Zones 0-2;* CISCA's *Guidelines for Seismic Restraint of Direct-Hung Suspended Ceiling Assemblies—Seismic Zones 3 & 4,* and International Conference of Building Officials' (ICBO's) Uniform Building Code (UBC) Standard 25-2, *Metal Suspension Systems for Acoustical Tile and for Lay-in Panel Ceilings.* Because codes are subject to periodical revision and to interpretation and amendment by local and state authorities having jurisdiction, verify requirements in effect for each project to determine which publications and standards to reference, if any, in the specifications and whether design of seismic restraints by a professional engineer and submission of engineering calculations are required. Note that UBC, the BOCA National Building Code, and the Standard Building Code have exceptions to seismic requirements for ceiling components under some conditions.

OTHER CONSIDERATIONS

Acoustical performance, fire-test-response characteristics, and considerations about energy, the environment, accessibility, and safety/health regulations are discussed in Chapter 09511.

REFERENCES

Publication dates cited here were current at the time of this writing. Publications are revised periodically, and revisions may have occurred before this book was published.

ASTM International

ASTM C 635-97: Specification for the Manufacture, Performance, and Testing of Metal Suspension Systems for Acoustical Tile and Lay-in Panel Ceilings

ASTM C 636-96: Practice for Installation of Metal Ceiling Suspension Systems for Acoustical Tile and Lay-in Panels

ASTM E 580-96: Practice for Application of Ceiling Suspension Systems for Acoustical Tile and Lay-in Panels in Areas Requiring Moderate Seismic Restraint

ASTM E 1264-98: Classification for Acoustical Ceiling Products

Ceilings & Interior Systems Construction Association

Ceiling Systems Handbook, 1999.

Guidelines for Seismic Restraint of Direct-Hung Suspended Ceiling Assemblies—Seismic Zones 3 & 4, 1991.

Recommendations for Direct-Hung Acoustical Tile and Lay-in Panel Ceilings—Seismic Zones 0-2, 1991.

International Conference of Building Officials

UBC Standard 25-2-1997: Metal Suspension Systems for Acoustical Tile and for Lay-in Panel Ceilings

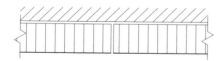

Figure 5. Square-cut tile, adhesive applied

Figure 6. Stapling flange tile, staple attached

This chapter discusses ceilings consisting of acoustical snap-in metal pans and concealed suspension systems. Types of metal pan ceiling units covered include both perforated and nonperforated snap-in steel, stainless steel, or aluminum pans.

This chapter does not discuss mineral-base or glass-fiber-base ceiling acoustical panels or tiles or linear metal ceilings. Also not covered are snap-in metal pan security ceilings and lay-in or other types of metal pan ceilings supported by exposed suspension systems.

GENERAL COMMENTS

Exterior installations of snap-in metal pan ceilings require engineering analysis and evaluation of materials and coatings that are beyond the scope of ASTM C 635, ASTM C 636, and International Conference of Building Officials' (ICBO's) Uniform Building Code (UBC) Standard 25-2, the commonly used design and installation specifications for acoustical ceilings. Accordingly, ASTM C 635 includes the following statement:

> While this specification is applicable to the exterior installation of metal suspension systems, the atmospheric conditions and wind loading require additional design attention to ensure safe implementation. For that reason, a specific review and approval should be solicited from the responsible architect and engineer, or both, for any exterior application of metal suspension systems....

In addition to that statement, ASTM C 636 states: "While recommendations from the manufacturer should be solicited, it remains the final responsibility of the architect/engineer to ensure proper application of the materials in question." Some of the metal pans and suspension systems discussed in this chapter may be suitable for exterior use, in unconditioned interior spaces, and in interior spaces with severe or extreme conditions. Verify the suitability of exterior ceiling installations—for example, soffits and parking garages—with manufacturers; perform engineering analysis or delegate the responsibility to a qualified professional engineer; and carefully evaluate materials and coatings.

Factors to consider when comparing some of the different types of available metal ceilings include the following:

- **Acoustical snap-in metal pan ceilings** are the most secure type of metal ceiling and have a monolithic appearance with a completely concealed grid. According to manufacturers, acoustical snap-in metal pan ceilings are durable and are less likely to be affected by construction operations, access of the plenum, or maintenance servicing of fixtures and equipment located in the plenum or penetrating the ceiling plane than other acoustical ceilings. Detractors emphasize the amount of force required to install and remove snap-in pans and the potential for ceiling system damage when accessing the plenum and replacing pans. Typically, acoustical snap-in metal pan ceilings are the most expensive of the metal ceilings.
- **Acoustical metal pans,** including lay-in, clip-in, and torsion-spring-hinge systems, are suspended by standard tee grids, are typically less

costly than other metal pan ceilings, are ideal for renovation, and are useful if multiple, random, convenient accessibility to the plenum is required. These ceilings are available in a wide range of possible appearances, including exposed or concealed grids.
- **Linear metal ceilings** are often selected, when plenum accessibility is a low priority, for their unique appearance and visually integrated services, for example, light fixtures and air diffusers that are almost invisible and do not disrupt the linear appearance of the ceiling. Usually, these ceilings cost more than acoustical metal pan ceilings but not as much as acoustical snap-in metal pan ceilings. If linear pans are wide, the ceiling may be comparable or more costly than acoustical snap-in metal pan ceilings. Refer to Chapter 09547, Linear Metal Ceilings, for more detailed information.
- **Suspended decorative grids** are economical, distinctive, often self-supporting, and mask but do not enclose the plenum and its contents. They define the ceiling plane and, unlike metal pan ceilings, have the advantage of allowing light fixtures to be placed above, below, or in the ceiling plane. Unlike metal pan ceilings, suspended decorative grids are not designed to be sound absorbers, but they can be used to improve fire safety and can reduce security risks. Refer to Chapter 09580, Suspended Decorative Grids, for more detailed information.

PRODUCT CLASSIFICATION

ASTM E 1264, *Classification for Acoustical Ceiling Products,* includes a designation system for identifying the various performance and physical properties of acoustical panels and tiles. These designations are explained in Chapter 09511, Acoustical Panel Ceilings. Although it is possible to classify snap-in metal ceiling pans according to ASTM E 1264 as Type V, "perforated steel facing (pan) with mineral- or glass-fiber-base backing"; Type VI, "perforated stainless steel facing (pan) with mineral- or glass-fiber-base backing"; Type VII, "perforated aluminum facing (pan) with mineral-base or glass-fiber-base backing"; or Type XX, "other types described as...," manufacturers do not commonly do so. Specifications often reference the ASTM standard to facilitate specifying acoustical, light reflectance, and fire-resistance performance for snap-in metal ceiling pans. Including classification according to ASTM E 1264 may also be useful if a nonproprietary specification is required for the project.

SNAP-IN METAL PAN CEILING CHARACTERISTICS

The two major components of an acoustical snap-in metal ceiling are concealed snap-tee- or snap-bar-grid runners and square or rectangular snap-in panels. Runners are suspended directly by hangers or indirectly by hangers and carriers from the building structure, similar to suspended acoustical ceiling systems. Panels snap in to the matching contour of the bar or tee and are rigidly secured in place. Acoustical qualities of the ceiling are enhanced by adding an acoustically absorbent pad, fabric, or board (fig. 1).

The snap-in metal pan ceilings described in this chapter differ from other types of metal pan ceilings because they are suspended by specially

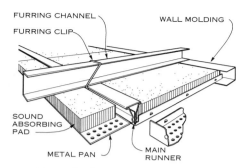

Figure 1. Snap-in metal pan ceiling

designed concealed suspension systems using snap-tee bars or snap bars designed for snap-in installation and retention of the metal pan edges. Other metal pan ceilings may be suspended by the same exposed ceiling suspension systems that are commonly used to suspend lay-in mineral-base and glass-fiber-base acoustical panels, or they may be suspended by another type of specially designed suspension system. Examples of the latter type of metal pan ceilings are hook-in and linear metal ceilings.

Many unique modular unit and grid sizes are available for snap-in metal pan ceilings, and sizes may vary among manufacturers. Metal pans are installed from below the ceiling plane; they snap in and conceal the suspension system to effectively close the ceiling and provide a nearly monolithic appearance. Snap-in metal pans are self-locking and self-locating within their specially designed suspension system. The positive fit of the snap-in design can be supplemented by retention clips to prevent the pans from detaching in the event of impact, wind uplift, or application of other forces. Servicing within the ceiling plenum is by downward action. The plenum can be designed for minimal height and volume because operational clearances are less than those required for upward accessibility. Some systems have access via swing-down pans retained in the grid by springs or other devices. Systems that use hold-down clips to secure pans in place can be accessed through lockable, hinged access panels.

The appearance and design flexibility of metal pan ceilings are enhanced by a wide selection of metal pan sizes, perforation patterns, pan edge profiles, edge joint details, and finishes.

Acoustical metal pan ceilings are primarily used for aesthetic effect, for upscale appearance, where strength is required, where frequent cleaning may be necessary, and where long life with low maintenance is desired. Snap-in metal ceilings are often used where the decorative effect of the ceiling is more important than flexibility or efficiency of the lighting. Metal ceilings are relatively lightweight and available in many colors and finishes. The metal surface makes a better base for coatings than soft, absorbent materials do. Metal components and enclosed insulation pads have no exposed fibers that could pose a risk to interior air and environmental quality. For certain exposures, an uncoated, finished metal is highly desirable for corrosion resistance, sanitation, or the appearance of sanitation.

Metal ceiling pans may be comparatively stable in severe environments, but base metals, protective coatings, and finishes must be selected with care to avoid deterioration. Similar care must be exercised in selecting suspension-system components for unconditioned spaces, exterior environments, and high-moisture, high-humidity areas such as saunas, shower rooms, indoor swimming pools, kitchens, dishwashing rooms, laundries, and sterilization rooms. Also, to reduce moisture-related problems, consider making provisions for ventilating the ceiling plenum. Manufacturers generally make few claims about the durability of finishes, and they do not usually test or warrant protective coatings and finishes.

Metal surfaces are nonporous; do not absorb odors, moisture, dirt, or other substances; and do not support biological growth. Metal pan ceilings are durable, easily cleanable, and seldom require refinishing or replacing for appearance or health reasons.

Light reflectance, as measured by Light Reflectance (LR) coefficients varies widely, from highly reflective mirror finishes to nonwhite paint and anodized colors, depending on the metal, metal finish, and color (if any) selected. Light reflectance and LR are discussed in Chapter 09511. Mirror and other highly reflective finishes can cause unwanted glare.

Coordinated perimeter trim and hold-down clips are available from ceiling system manufacturers. If custom extruded-aluminum edge trim is required for the project, include requirements to that effect in the specifications. Extruded-aluminum or formed-steel edge trim with a variety of finishes, linear configurations, and decorative profiles is available from several manufacturers. Trim may be used to conceal and embellish ceiling perimeters, ceiling height transitions, penetrations, and openings for fixtures. It may also be used to form soffits, ceiling surrounds, ceiling clouds, ceiling coffers, light coves, and recessed pockets for blinds, curtains, and drapes.

Standardized components for traditional-size ceiling modules are economical and widely available. Standard light fixtures, air-distribution diffusers and grilles, speakers, and sprinklers can be integrated into the ceiling system if standardized modules are adhered to. Because snap-in metal pan ceilings are also available in nonstandard modular sizes, take care to coordinate the integration of electrical or mechanical fixtures and equipment with snap-in metal pan ceilings.

SNAP-IN METAL PANS

A wide variety of modular sizes are common for snap-in metal pan ceilings. Hard SI (metric) sizes are available from some manufacturers; verify their availability with applicable manufacturers.

Cold-rolled steel is the least-expensive base metal and provides a flat, smooth base for coatings; but it is less resistant to the corrosive effects of moisture and other substances than are hot-dip galvanized steel, aluminum, and stainless steel. Steel ceiling pans are strong, rigid, and economical. Most are electrogalvanized and suitable for interior use in conditioned spaces with humidity control. Hot-dip galvanized steel pans are available. Galvanized steel sheet may not be completely protected if the carbon core is exposed by the perforating process; protection is based only on final finishing. Aluminum pans are lighter than steel and are often recommended by manufacturers for exterior use if protected by a suitable finish. Stainless-steel pans are strong and rigid, but are costly and more likely to be a custom, rather than a standard, product.

Aluminum and stainless-steel pans can be installed in unconditioned spaces, exterior environments, and applications subject to high moisture and high humidity, with a reduced risk of corrosion or moisture damage when compared to steel. For metal ceiling pans, Types 304 and 430 are the most commonly used stainless-steel alloys. Type 304 austenitic stainless is commonly used for architectural purposes and is usually considered suitable for most rural, moderately polluted urban, and low-humidity and low-temperature coastal environments where corrosion potential is low. Type 430 stainless steel is a chromium grade that contains no nickel; its corrosion resistance to certain substances is lower than for types falling within the 300 Series that contain nickel. The forming characteristics of the 300 Series stainless steels may make them unsuitable for use with some manufacturers' equipment. Verify the availability of stainless-steel alloys with manufacturers and ascertain the limitations of their forming and punching equipment. Refer to Chapter 09511 for a discussion of the available alloys and the potential effects of chloramines, chlorides, and other corrosive agents on stainless steel. It is also important to specify materials for the suspension system that have corrosion-resistant properties consistent with the metal pan ceiling units that the system supports.

To be acoustically effective sound absorbers, metal pan units must be perforated and backed with sound-absorbent material. According to fabricators, square holes in straight or diagonal (staggered) patterns achieve more open area for sound absorption than round holes. Round holes in diagonal patterns, either 45 or 60 degrees, achieve more open area than round holes in straight patterns and do not weaken the pan as straight patterns do. The 60-degree, staggered center, round-hole perforation pattern is popular with manufacturers because it is widely available in a range of sizes and open areas, and it produces a strong pan. Perforation patterns with small holes better absorb sounds in the higher frequency range, while those with larger holes better absorb lower frequencies.

A wide range of perforation-patterned metal pans, with and without non-perforated edge margins, are available. Sizes, spacing, and patterns of perforations and margins can vary extensively. When positioned precisely in modular repeating arrangements, these units can provide a variety of appearances and add considerable visual interest. If a precise uniform appearance is critical, select perforation patterns carefully. Depending on the manufacturing process, the perforation-pattern pitch, and the face dimensions of the metal pan, it may not be possible to have equal side and end margins. Pans with elaborate graphic arrangements of perforated patterns alternating with nonperforated areas or linear strips provide additional visual interest similar to the scoring of mineral-base and glass-fiber-base products, and embellish the basic modular appearance of the pans and suspension system while maintaining the advantages of full-size pans.

Depending on the type of material, thickness of sheet metal, and size of metal pans, practical fabrication methods limit possible metal pan patterns. For example, pans with perforations in excess of 40 to 60 percent open area may distort and not remain flat. If the perforated area has margins on all four sides, or if margins are 1 to 3 inches (25 to 75 mm) wide or more, or are unequal, the potential for distortion increases. Other factors that may contribute to pan distortion include thickness, for example, 0.1116 inch (2.8 mm) or thicker steel; and hardness, for example, stainless-steel 300 Series.

Edge profiles and joint details for snap-in metal pans are limited to square and beveled edges with or without a reveal between pans. Selecting beveled pans from a range of different bevel dimensions and profiles results in a variety of appearances for beveled edge pan ceilings. Similarly, reveal systems can produce reveals of different dimensions.

Finishes for metal pans are varied. Mechanical finishes may be mill, brushed, mirror, natural, satin, or textured. Aluminum and steel may be finished with baked color coatings or powder coatings. Aluminum and steel may also have a metallic finish produced by chemical/mechanical or chemical/mechanical/protective coating processes. Aluminum may be lacquered, anodized, or coated with a high-performance coating. Steel may be bare, electrogalvanized, or hot-dip galvanized before coating, or it may be electroplated.

Factory-punched and -cut openings for fixtures such as canned light fixtures, air diffusers, air grilles, speakers, sprinklers, and others may be possible. Consult manufacturers for details and include applicable requirements in the specifications.

SUSPENSION SYSTEMS

The industry's strong orientation to ASTM C 635, *Specification for the Manufacture, Performance, and Testing of Metal Suspension Systems for Acoustical Tile and Lay-in Panel Ceilings,* and its companion standard, ASTM C 636, *Practice for Installation of Metal Ceiling Suspension Systems for Acoustical Tile and Lay-in Panels,* makes it unnecessary for the design professional to reinvent suspension systems and installation specifications for most applications. See Chapter 09511 for a brief explanation of structural classification requirements and of requirements for areas needing seismic restraint.

Two types of suspension systems applicable to snap-in metal pan ceilings are covered in ASTM C 635: direct hung and indirect hung. Direct-hung systems are those in which main runners are hung directly from the structure above. Indirect-hung systems are those in which main runners are attached to carrying channels that are hung from the structure above.

Indirect-hung systems are commonly available and are used for most installations. These systems are more rigid, more easily leveled if supporting construction is not uniformly level, more familiar to most installers, and easier to install. This type of system accommodates variations in design-load requirements by using wire, strap, rod, angle, or channel hangers, and has greater capacity than direct-hung systems for supporting light fixtures, air-distribution equipment, and other equipment interacting with the ceiling. Spacing of indirect-hung system hangers is more versatile than for direct-hung systems and is more adaptable to variable plenum construction and the presence of interfering obstructions. Because snap-in metal pans must be snapped in place with some force, the rigidity of the indirect-hung system facilitates installation. Most indirect-hung systems combine aluminum components with steel primary support. If dissimilar metals are used in a system, and moisture is present, there is potential for electrolytic corrosion unless metals are separated.

Direct-hung systems are not commonly available. According to manufacturers, advantages of this system are its light weight, all-aluminum components, and, compared to indirect-hung systems, a simplified plenum space that is relatively unencumbered by suspension system components. Some manufacturers may be willing to provide custom-designed direct-hung systems.

Snap-in runners may be one of two types: snap tee or snap bar. Snap-tee runners are commonly available, but they are not as strong as snap-bar runners, and are typically designated "intermediate duty" by manufacturers. Snap-bar runners are typically designated "heavy-duty," have an inverted-V-shaped profile, and are usually recommended for applications requiring greater load-bearing capacity—for example, withstanding wind load at exterior locations.

ACOUSTICAL PERFORMANCE CONSIDERATIONS

Airborne sound can be absorbed within enclosed areas of buildings by metal pan ceilings. The acoustical qualities attainable depend primarily on the characteristics of the sound-absorbent pads or fabric installed in the pans and the perforations in the exposed metal pan surfaces. To determine the best balance for optimum acoustical performance, consider the thickness and density of the sound-absorbent backing; the extent of perforated open areas; the size, shape, and center-to-center distance of holes; and the perforation pattern of the metal pan. These factors must function together without impairing the strength and rigidity of the original sheet metal to support itself without distortion.

Noise Reduction Coefficient (NRC) is discussed in Chapter 09511. Of the parameters for pans listed in the preceding paragraph, the percent of open area (the area of perforations) and the center-to-center distance of perforations have the greatest effect on acoustical performance. Typically, the greater the open area in the pan, the greater the acoustical transparency of the pan and ceiling, and the greater the NRC. If absorption of sound in all frequencies is needed, the degree of acoustical transparency and the efficiency of the absorber are most important. If numerous small perforations are closely spaced, the acoustical transparency of metal pans is maximized. However, densely microperforated sheet, with the greatest number of perforations possible, may not be the best solution for maximizing acoustical performance for ceiling pan applications because of the pan's lack of rigidity and strength, its high fabrication cost, and the tendency of very small perforations to clog. Also, if sound absorption in selected frequencies is needed, other variables become important.

Thick glass- and mineral-wool-fiber acoustical pads are more sound-absorbent than thin pads of the same density, but they cost more and require more space. A 1-inch- (25-mm-) thick glass-fiber absorber effectively absorbs high-frequency sound, but is less effective for low-frequency sound. A 6-inch- (150-mm-) thick glass-fiber pad is an efficient absorber for sound of all frequencies. Wrapped mineral-fiber pads must be installed over a spacer grid to be effective; unwrapped pads do not. However, placing unwrapped pads directly on the back of metal pans may result in a less-than-satisfactory appearance. For best appearance with some perforation patterns, unwrapped pads should be covered with a black facing or coating. Black is usually recommended for pans with perforations exceeding ⅛ inch (3 mm) in diameter in a standard-height ceiling.

A black, nonwoven, acoustically absorbent fabric is often used by manufacturers of acoustical metal pan ceilings in lieu of mineral-fiber pads. The fabric's sound-absorbent efficiency reduces the required thickness of the absorptive backing and saves space. Factory application of the fabric ensures proper positioning and secure placement inside the pan. If fabric is used, less labor is required and installation is simplified. However, acoustical fabric is limited to moderate ratings for NRC. For the highest possible NRCs, pads and accessories must be used.

The presence and size of the air space between the pan and the absorbent backing material or behind the absorbent backing material can affect acoustic performance. The larger the space, the more sound is absorbed. Spacer grids can be incorporated between metal pans and absorbent backing in acoustical metal pan ceilings to provide a uniformly dimensioned, compartmentalized layer of air space. An arrangement of perforated metal, absorbent backing material, air layer, and solid backing may be used to design a tuned-resonance sound absorber that absorbs a selected range of sound frequencies.

Sound-insulating qualities are specified in terms of Ceiling Attenuation Class (CAC) based on laboratory tests performed according to ASTM E 1414. Some manufacturers still use Sound Transmission Class (STC) to rate their ceilings, based on laboratory tests performed according to AMA-1-II, which was an adaptation of ASTM E 90 to suit suspended ceilings and is available from the Ceilings & Interior Systems Construction Association (CISCA). ASTM E 90 is intended only to measure airborne sound transmission loss through building partitions. CAC and STC are both single-number ratings that indicate the effectiveness of a construction assembly, in this case the ceiling, in resisting passage of airborne sound when tested. Sound-pressure level differentials in ⅓-octave bands are measured and single-number CAC or STC ratings are calculated according to ASTM E 413 using sound transmission loss (TL). A high CAC or STC rating indicates better sound isolation performance; a low CAC or STC rating indicates a low resistance to sound transmission.

Ordinarily, sound attenuation through acoustical snap-in metal pan ceilings is poor. The pans themselves transmit sound through the perforations, and the limited mass of absorption material above the pans also offers little resistance to sound transmission. Accordingly, adjacent spaces separated by partitions that stop at the ceiling line instead of extending through the plenum space have almost no acoustical separation unless other measures are taken. The best method for providing acoustical privacy in such situations is to extend the partition through the plenum to the structure above, carefully sealing around all service penetrations. If this option is not elected, the alternative course is to add a continuous, nonperforated layer of sheet metal above the metal pan ceiling to provide a barrier to airborne sound, but the results are apt to be unsatisfactory unless the installation of the supplementary surface is continuous and virtually airtight. These optional sound attenuation panels are usually designed to snap into the pans from above. Unfortunately, unless an additional layer of acoustical absorption is placed above the attenuation material, the plenum space will be acoustically untreated, allowing sound to travel long distances through the plenum without being absorbed. Assemblies consisting of sound attenuation panels and supplementary acoustical insulation can improve sound absorption within the plenum. Absorbers work best if there is a reflective surface to reflect residual, unabsorbed sound back and through the absorber yet again to increase the acoustical absorption.

Because not all combinations of sound-absorbent backing material, pan perforations, spacer grids, air spaces, and sound attenuation panels have been tested, and because manufacturers report the maximum performance possible for only some combinations of components, verify with manufacturers, and correlate components and ratings for acoustical performance of each metal pan assembly specified.

FIRE-TEST-RESPONSE CHARACTERISTICS

If Class A (or Class I) materials per ASTM E 1264 are required, metal pan ceilings are limited to those with flame-spread and smoke-developed indexes of no more than 25 and 50, respectively. Similar or better ratings are available for wrapped, faced, and unwrapped glass- and mineral-wool-fiber acoustical pads and acoustical fabric tested per ASTM E 84. Refer to the Chapter 09511 for a discussion of surface-burning characteristics.

Although acoustical metal pans are categorized as Acoustical Materials (BYIT) in the 1999 edition of Underwriter Laboratories' (UL's) *Fire Resistance Directory,* no systems are listed in it or in the 1999 edition of Intertek Testing Services' (ITS's) *Directory of Listed Products* as being part of fire-rated floor-ceiling or roof-ceiling assemblies.

ENVIRONMENTAL CONSIDERATIONS

Indoor air and environmental quality issues relevant to acoustical pads include particulate inhalation, particulate eye and dermal irritation, VOC emissions and absorption, and contamination by biological agents. Acoustical fabrics and tightly sealed pads are less likely to release particles. Sensitive environments may have stringent requirements for the control of particulate matter in indoor air, VOC emissions, and potential pathogens.

PVC or PE plastic sheet that encloses or covers acoustical insulation makes the backing pads less likely to release loose fibers, less irritating to touch, and easier to handle and install. Microperforations in the sheet vent the insulation and discourage the accumulation of moisture and consequent microbiological growth. Because interior air quality in buildings is a concern, most metal pan ceilings are now installed with backing pads wrapped to prevent the escape of loose fiber.

The absorptive nature of acoustical mineral-fiber pads acts to absorb more than sound. Pads exposed to odors absorb, retain, and outgas odors over time. Pads enclosed by PVC wrappings may be less likely to absorb transitory odors, but over time may absorb lasting odors. Outgassing unpleasant or possibly hazardous gases can be a problem; for example, tobacco smoke absorbed by acoustical pads can linger in a space or building intended to be a smoke-free environment. Detectable odors are not easily eliminated from acoustical pads; therefore, sometimes pads must be replaced.

SEISMIC CONSIDERATIONS

Acoustical (suspended) ceilings installed in areas requiring seismic bracing may require bracing designed to applicable building codes. Local codes normally define design forces that must be resisted by architectural components.

For areas that require seismic restraint, the following installation standards can be included in specifications: ASTM E 580, *Practice for Application of Ceiling Suspension Systems for Acoustical Tile and Lay-in Panels in Areas Requiring Moderate Seismic Restraint;* CISCA's *Recommendations for Direct-Hung Acoustical Tile and Lay-in Panel Ceilings—Seismic Zones 0-2;* CISCA's *Guidelines for Seismic Restraint of Direct-Hung Suspended Ceiling Assemblies—Seismic Zones 3 & 4;* and UBC Standard 25-2, *Metal Suspension Systems for Acoustical Tile and for Lay-in Panel Ceilings.* Because codes are subject to periodic revision and to interpretation and amendment by local and state authorities having jurisdiction, verify requirements in effect for each project to determine which publications and standards to reference, if any, in the specifications; also verify whether the design of seismic restraints by a professional engineer along with submission of engineering calculations is required. When dealing with code requirements for seismic loads on suspended ceilings, the design professional must comply with one of the three following alternatives (note that UBC, the BOCA National Building Code, and the Standard Building Code have exceptions to seismic requirements for ceiling components under some conditions):

- Cite ASTM E 580, the applicable CISCA standard, or UBC Standard 25-2 as a prescriptive criterion, even though there may be no explicit mention of these in the model code in effect for the project.
- Design all the ceiling components based on the analytical method in the American Society of Civil Engineer's (ASCE's) publication ASCE 7, *Minimum Design Loads for Buildings and Other Structures,* or on criteria found in the building code in effect for the project.
- Delegate the design of seismic restraints to a professional engineer engaged by the contractor, citing the analytical method to be used as the basis of design as performance criteria. This option requires that the analytical method to be used as the basis of design is well understood by the design professional and that all relevant criteria are indicated in the contract documents. Examples of criteria that might need to be specified if ASCE 7 is used as the basis of design include seismic-design category or seismic use group, occupancy importance factor, and site classification.

Changes to ASCE 7, which were new to the 1998 edition that was published in January 2000, include reference to CISCA standards and requirements for special inspections during the installation of architectural components in Seismic Design Categories D, E, and F. If special inspections are required for the project, include requirements in the specifications.

REFERENCES

Publication dates cited here were current at the time of this writing. Publications are revised periodically, and revisions may have occurred before this book was published.

ASTM International

ASTM C 635-97: Specification for the Manufacture, Performance, and Testing of Metal Suspension Systems for Acoustical Tile and Lay-in Panel Ceilings

ASTM C 636-96: Practice for Installation of Metal Ceiling Suspension Systems for Acoustical Tile and Lay-in Panels

ASTM E 84-00a: Test Method for Surface Burning Characteristics of Building Materials

ASTM E 90-99: Test Method for Laboratory Measurement of Airborne Sound Transmission Loss of Building Partitions and Elements

ASTM E 413-87 (reapproved 1999): Classification for Rating Sound Insulation

ASTM E 580-96: Practice for Application of Ceiling Suspension Systems for Acoustical Tile and Lay-in Panels in Areas Requiring Moderate Seismic Restraint

ASTM E 1264-98: Classification for Acoustical Ceiling Products

ASTM E 1414-00: Test Method for Airborne Sound Attenuation Between Rooms Sharing a Common Ceiling Plenum

Ceilings & Interior Systems Construction Association

Guidelines for Seismic Restraint of Direct-Hung Suspended Ceiling Assemblies—Seismic Zones 3 & 4, 1991.

Recommendations for Direct-Hung Acoustical Tile and Lay-in Panel Ceilings—Seismic Zones 0-2, 1991.

International Conference of Building Officials

UBC Standard 25-2-1997: Metal Suspension Systems for Acoustical Tile and for Lay-in Panel Ceilings

Intertek Testing Services

Directory of Listed Products, published annually.

Underwriters Laboratories Inc.

Fire Resistance Directory, published annually.

09514 ACOUSTICAL METAL PAN CEILINGS

This chapter discusses *ceilings consisting of lay-in, clip-in, and torsion-spring-hinged acoustical metal pans and standard tee- or slot-grid exposed suspension systems.*

This chapter does not discuss *mineral-base or glass-fiber-base acoustical panels and exposed suspension systems, acoustical tile and concealed suspension systems, acoustical snap-in metal pan ceilings, linear metal ceilings, suspended decorative grid ceilings, or security ceilings; these are discussed in other chapters.*

GENERAL COMMENTS

Exterior installations of acoustical metal pan ceilings require engineering analysis and evaluation of materials and coatings that are beyond the scope of ASTM C 635, ASTM C 636, and International Conference of Building Officials' (ICBO's) Uniform Building Code (UBC) Standard 25-2, the commonly used design and installation specifications for acoustical ceilings. Accordingly, ASTM C 635 includes the following statement:

> While this specification is applicable to the exterior installation of metal suspension systems, the atmospheric conditions and wind loading require additional design attention to ensure safe implementation. For that reason, a specific review and approval should be solicited from the responsible architect and engineer, or both, for any exterior application of metal suspension systems....

ASTM C 636 also states: "While recommendations from the manufacturer should be solicited, it remains the final responsibility of the architect/engineer to ensure proper application of the materials in question." Some of the metal pans and suspension systems discussed in this chapter may be suitable for exterior use, unconditioned interior spaces, and interior spaces with severe or extreme conditions. Verify the suitability of exterior ceiling installations—for example, soffits and parking garages—with manufacturers; perform engineering analysis or delegate the responsibility to a qualified professional engineer; and carefully evaluate materials and coatings. If made from noncorrosive base metals and superior protective finishes, metal ceilings discussed in Chapter 09513, Acoustical Snap-in Metal Pan Ceilings, and Chapter 09547, Linear Metal Ceilings, are more typically recommended for exterior applications than are the types of metal ceilings included in this chapter.

Factors to consider when comparing some of the different types of available metal ceilings include the following:

- **Acoustical metal pans,** including lay-in, clip-in, and torsion-spring-hinged systems, are suspended by standard tee or slot grids, are typically less costly than other metal pan ceilings, are ideal for renovation, and are useful if multiple, random, and convenient accessibility to the plenum is required. These ceilings are available in a wide range of possible appearances including visible, partially visible, or invisible grids.
- **Linear metal ceilings** are often selected, when plenum accessibility is a low priority, for their unique appearance and visually integrated services, for example, light fixtures and air diffusers that are almost invisible and that do not disrupt the linear appearance of the ceiling.

Usually, these ceilings cost more than acoustical metal pan ceilings but not as much as acoustical snap-in metal pan ceilings. However, if linear pans are wide, the cost may be comparable to or higher than for acoustical snap-in metal pan ceilings. See Chapter 09547 for more detailed information.

- **Acoustical snap-in metal pan ceilings** are the most secure type of metal ceiling and have a monolithic appearance with a completely concealed grid. According to manufacturers, acoustical snap-in metal pan ceilings are the most durable ceilings and are less likely to be affected by construction operations, plenum access, or maintenance servicing of fixtures and equipment located in the plenum or penetrating the ceiling plane. Possible disadvantages include the amount of force required to install and remove snap-in pans and the potential for ceiling system damage when accessing the plenum and replacing pans. Suspension systems for acoustical snap-in metal pan ceilings need to be rigid enough to withstand the increased force required for installation. This requirement explains why indirect-hung suspension systems are commonly used with acoustical snap-in metal pan ceilings and why direct-hung suspension systems use channels and angles rather than wire hangers, hanger rods, and flat hangers. Typically, acoustical snap-in metal pan ceilings are the most expensive of the metal ceilings. See Chapter 09513 for more detailed information.
- **Suspended decorative grids** are economical, distinctive, often self-supporting, and mask but do not enclose the plenum and its contents. They define the ceiling plane and, unlike metal pan ceilings, have the advantage of allowing light fixtures to be placed above, below, or in the ceiling plane. Unlike metal pan ceilings, suspended decorative grids are not designed to be sound absorbers, but they can be used to improve fire safety and can reduce security risks. See Chapter 09580, Suspended Decorative Grids, for more detailed information.

PRODUCT CLASSIFICATION

ASTM E 1264, *Classification for Acoustical Ceiling Products,* includes a designation system for identifying the various performance and physical properties of acoustical panels and tiles. These designations are explained in Chapter 09511, Acoustical Panel Ceilings. Although it is possible to classify acoustical metal ceiling pans according to ASTM E 1264 as Type V, "perforated steel facing (pan) with mineral- or glass-fiber-base backing"; Type VI, "perforated stainless steel facing (pan) with mineral- or glass-fiber-base backing"; Type VII, "perforated aluminum facing (pan) with mineral-base or glass-fiber-base backing"; or Type XX, "other types described as...," manufacturers do not commonly do so. Specifications often reference the ASTM standard to facilitate specifying acoustical, light reflectance, and fire-resistance performance for metal ceiling pans. Including classification according to ASTM E 1264 may also be useful if a nonproprietary specification is required for the project.

ACOUSTICAL METAL PAN CEILING CHARACTERISTICS

The major components of acoustical metal pan ceilings are runners and cross-runner grids and square or rectangular metal pans. Runners are suspended directly by wire hangers, like most installations of suspended acoustical ceiling systems. Acoustical qualities of these ceilings are enhanced by adding acoustically absorbent pads, fabrics, or boards.

Acoustical metal pan ceilings in this chapter differ from other types of metal pan ceilings; unlike other metal pan ceilings that are suspended by specially designed suspensions systems, acoustical metal pan ceilings are suspended by the same exposed ceiling suspension systems that are commonly used to suspend lay-in mineral-base and glass-fiber-base acoustical panels. These exposed ceiling suspension systems are often called *standard tee grids;* their design and installation are governed by ASTM C 635, ASTM C 636, and UBC Standard 25-2. Standard slot (bolt and screw) grids are also commonly used with acoustical metal pans and lay-in mineral-base and glass-fiber-base acoustical panels. Modular unit and grid sizes are standard, being dimensioned for common sizes of lay-in mineral-base and glass-fiber-base acoustical panels, with 24 by 24 inches (610 by 610 mm) predominating for metal pan ceilings. These suspension systems have the advantage of being economical, widely available, and familiar to designers and installers for uncomplicated installation (fig. 1).

Lay-in ceilings are the simplest metal pan ceiling systems to install, and they provide easy access to the ceiling plenum. Typically, the main and cross tees or other runners of the suspension system remain exposed; pans are installed from above the grid and supported by main and cross tees. Access is achieved simply by lifting upward. Occasionally, pans are butted together on two parallel edges and hooked on opposite edges to lay in an exposed main tee, to form a one-way-exposed suspension system without cross members. The strength of the metal pan eliminates the need for cross tees, splines, and spacer bars, which are common to similar systems using mineral-base or glass-fiber-base units. Two-way-exposed suspension systems are common for all sized units; one-way-exposed suspension systems frequently involve elongated planks, for example, units spanning corridors.

Other metal pan ceiling systems using standard tee or slot grids totally or partially conceal the suspension grid, are designed to be installed from below the ceiling plane, and are capable of downward access, with or without the use of a special tool. These systems are more secure, more costly, more difficult and labor-intensive to install, and less easy to access than lay-in systems. These systems may be designed to be self-locating and self-leveling. If pan edges are squared and butted, these ceilings have a nearly monolithic, flat, planar appearance. Systems with square- or beveled-edge pans with butted joints are particularly advantageous for renovating ceilings with an existing exposed suspension system that is structurally sound but aesthetically unsatisfactory. If pan edges are separated by a reveal, these ceilings have a modular, three-dimensional appearance. These ceilings are more suitable than lay-in systems for exterior locations, areas subject to wind uplift and pressure differentials, and potential impact forces or vandalism. However, not all systems are recommended for these uses by manufacturers. Verify with manufacturers the appropriateness of each system for the intended use.

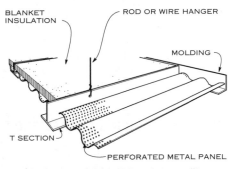

Figure 1. Perforated metal pan ceiling

- **Clip-in or clip-on systems** clip over and conceal or partially conceal the face of the standard tee grid to effectively close the ceiling. Typically, metal pans are held in place by proprietary clips or formed pan edges. This system is less costly than those described below.
- **Clip-in metal pan ceilings with reveals between pans** are designed to attach pans by snapping them into narrow-face steel suspension systems with slotted, box-shaped flanges, rather than with tees. Because this type of grid is typically twice as expensive as standard tee grids, this ceiling is also more expensive than lay-in or clip-in types combined with tee grids. Access to the plenum behind this type of system may be more complex. Using this type of grid flange allows square-edge metal pans to make a reveal-edge ceiling.
- **Torsion-spring-hinged systems** need modified standard tee suspension system grid members that are prepunched or slotted to coordinate with spring hinges that are attached to pans. These systems have swing-down access with pans hanging from the grid by two remaining torsion-spring hinges. This design feature reduces the potential damage to pans and pan finishes during servicing of systems located in the plenum, and is of particular advantage if it is anticipated that frequent access to ceiling plenums will be necessary or if ceilings are difficult to reach, such as very high ceilings.

Metal pans can also fit the openings of decorative grid cells and beams that are discussed in Chapter 09580.

The appearance and design flexibility of metal pan ceilings are enhanced by a wide selection of metal pan perforation patterns, pan edge profiles, edge joint details, and finishes. Also, pans can be paired with a variety of widely available standard suspension system profiles and finishes.

Acoustical metal pan ceilings are primarily used for aesthetic effect, for upscale appearance, where strength is required, where frequent cleaning may be necessary, and where long life with low maintenance is desired. Acoustical metal pan ceilings are often used where the decorative effect of the ceiling is more important than efficiency of the lighting. Metal ceilings are relatively lightweight and available in many colors and finishes. The metal surface makes a better base for coatings than do soft, absorbent materials. Metal components and enclosed insulation pads have no exposed fibers that could pose a risk to interior air and environmental quality. For certain exposures, an uncoated, finished metal is highly desirable for corrosion resistance, sanitation, or the appearance of sanitation.

Metal ceiling pans may be comparatively stable in severe environments, but base metal, protective coatings, and finishes must be selected with care to avoid deterioration. Similar care must be exercised in selecting suspension system components for unconditioned spaces, exterior environments, and high-moisture, high-humidity areas such as saunas, shower rooms, indoor swimming pools, kitchens, dishwashing rooms, laundries, and sterilization rooms. Also, to reduce moisture-related problems, consider making provisions for ventilating the ceiling plenum. Manufacturers generally make few claims about the durability of finishes, and they do not usually test or warrant protective coatings and finishes.

Metal surfaces are nonporous; do not absorb odors, moisture, dirt, or other substances; and do not support biological growth. Metal pan ceilings are durable, easily cleanable, and seldom require refinishing or replacing for appearance or health reasons.

Light reflectance, as measured by Light Reflectance (LR) coefficients, varies widely, from highly reflective mirror finishes to nonwhite paint and anodized colors, depending on the metal, metal finish, and color (if any) selected. Light reflectance and LR are discussed in Chapter 09511. Mirror and other highly reflective finishes can cause unwanted glare.

Coordinated perimeter trim and hold-down clips are available from ceiling system manufacturers. If custom extruded-aluminum edge trim is required for the project, include requirements to that effect in the specifications. Extruded-aluminum or formed-steel edge trim with a variety of finishes, linear configurations, and decorative profiles is available from several manufacturers. Trim may be used to conceal and embellish ceiling perimeters, ceiling height transitions, penetrations, and openings for fixtures. It may also be used to form soffits, ceiling surrounds, ceiling clouds, ceiling coffers, light coves, and recessed pockets for blinds, curtains, and drapes.

Standardized components for traditional-size ceiling modules are economical and widely available. Standard light fixtures, air-distribution diffusers and grilles, speakers, and sprinklers can be integrated into the ceiling system if standardized modules are adhered to. Acoustical metal pan ceiling systems may be designed to have integrated ceiling capability. Some manufacturers offer special fixtures, such as light fixtures and air distribution diffusers and grilles to fit their systems. If electrical or mechanical fixtures and equipment are required for a project, obtain specifications from manufacturers and include appropriate requirements in the project specifications.

Options available for type of and locations for access to spaces above suspended metal pan ceilings depend on project design constraints and the system and manufacturer selected. Factors to consider include the purpose for access; locations and life cycles of the equipment and components requiring adjustment, maintenance, monitoring, repair, or replacement; plenum and room area obstructions; dimensional clearances; correlation to suspension system; and fire-rating and seismic requirements. Accessibility is one consideration that has led to use of lay-in unit ceilings. Most metal pan ceilings are designed for 100 percent access but require some care in handling. Lay-in metal pan ceilings are designed for upward access; clip-in, clip-on, and torsion-spring metal pan ceilings are designed for downward access. Upward-acting systems require a deeper plenum space than downward-acting systems. Downward opening may be activated by manipulating access clips and springs, sometimes with special tools.

ACOUSTICAL METAL PANS

The common modular sizes of acoustical metal pans are 24 by 24 inches (610 by 610 mm) and 24 by 48 inches (610 by 1220 mm). Pans sized 30 by 30 inches (760 by 760 mm) and 30 by 60 inches (760 by 1525 mm) are less commonly available. Lay-in and torsion-spring pans may come in other sizes up to 48 by 48 inches (1220 by 1220 mm). Pans spanning greater distances need to be thicker or have fewer perforations. Hard SI (metric) sizes are available from some manufacturers; verify their availability with manufacturers selected.

Cold-rolled steel is the least-expensive base metal and provides a flat, smooth base for coatings, but it is less resistant to the corrosive effects of moisture and other substances than are hot-dip galvanized steel, aluminum, and stainless steel. Steel ceiling pans are strong, rigid, and economical. Most are electrogalvanized and are suitable for interior use in conditioned spaces with humidity control. Hot-dip galvanized steel pans are available but may not be completely protected if the carbon core is exposed by the perforating process; protection is based only on final finishing.

Aluminum or stainless-steel pans can be installed in unconditioned spaces, exterior environments, and applications subject to high moisture and high humidity, with reduced risk of corrosion or moisture damage when compared to steel. Aluminum pans are lighter than steel. Stainless-steel pans are strong and rigid but are costly and more likely to be a custom, rather than a standard, product. For metal ceiling pans, Types 304 and 430 are the most commonly used stainless-steel alloys. Type 304 austenitic stainless is commonly used for architectural purposes and is usually considered suitable for

most rural, moderately polluted urban, and low-humidity and low-temperature coastal environments where corrosion potential is low. Type 430 stainless steel is a chromium grade that contains no nickel; its corrosion resistance to certain substances is lower than for types falling within the 300 Series that contain nickel. The forming characteristics of the 300 Series stainless steels may make them unsuitable for use with some manufacturers' equipment. Verify the availability of stainless-steel alloys with manufacturers and ascertain the limitations of their forming and punching equipment. Chapter 09511 has a discussion of the available alloys and the potential effect of chloramines, chlorides, and other corrosive agents on stainless steel. It is also important to specify materials for suspension systems that have corrosion-resistant properties consistent with the metal pan ceiling units that the system supports.

To be acoustically effective sound absorbers, metal pan units must be perforated and backed with sound-absorbent material. According to fabricators, square holes in straight or diagonal (staggered) patterns achieve more open area for sound absorption than round holes. Round holes in diagonal patterns, either 45 or 60 degrees, achieve more open area than round holes in straight patterns; and they do not weaken the pan as do straight patterns. The 60-degree, staggered-center, round-hole perforation pattern is popular with manufacturers because it is widely available in a range of sizes and open areas and produces a strong pan. Perforation patterns with small holes better absorb sounds in the higher-frequency range, while those with larger holes better absorb lower frequencies.

A wide range of perforation-patterned metal pans, with and without non-perforated edge margins, is available. Sizes, spacing, and patterns of perforations and margins can vary extensively. When positioned precisely in modular repeating arrangements, these units can provide a variety of appearances and add considerable visual interest. If a precise uniform appearance is critical, select perforation patterns carefully. Depending on the manufacturing process, the perforation-pattern pitch, and the face dimensions of the metal pan, it may not be possible to have equal side and end margins. Pans with elaborate graphic arrangements of perforated patterns alternating with nonperforated areas or linear strips provide additional visual interest similar to the scoring of mineral-base and glass-fiber-base products, and embellish the basic modular appearance of the pans and suspension system, while maintaining the advantages of full-size pans.

Depending on the type of material, thickness of sheet metal, and size of metal pans, practical fabrication methods limit possible metal pan patterns. For example, pans with perforations in excess of 40 to 60 percent open area may distort and not remain flat. The potential for distortion increases if the perforated area has margins on all four sides, if the margins are 1- to 3-inches (25- to 75-mm) wide or more, or if the margins are unequal. Other factors that may contribute to pan distortion include thickness, for example, 0.1116-inch (2.8-mm) or thicker steel, and hardness, for example, stainless-steel 300 Series.

Edge profiles and joint details for metal pans vary widely among products and manufacturers. Edges may be die, press, or roll formed in an assortment of profiles, such as square, beveled, reveal, or stepped-reveal edges, to provide diverse ceiling appearances when pans are installed in various combinations of edge and joint details with grids. Formed edges may also be designed to engage the suspension system for a positive, more secure fit than that afforded by square-edge lay-in pans. Reveal-edge metal pans that fit snugly with faces that protrude beyond the grid, and clip-in-type pans with roll-formed edges, are examples of pans with positive-fit formed edges. Pans with positive fit are easily and accurately positioned and are less likely to be dislodged.

Finishes for metal pans are varied and may be unique (proprietary) to a product or manufacturer. Mechanical finishes may be mill, brushed, mirror, natural, satin, or textured. Aluminum and steel may be finished with baked color coatings or powder coatings. Aluminum and steel may also have a metallic finish produced by chemical/mechanical or chemical/mechanical/protective coating processes. Aluminum may be lacquered, anodized, or coated with a high-performance coating. Steel may be bare, electrogalvanized, or hot-dip galvanized before coating, or it may be electroplated.

Many manufacturers provide custom pan sizes, edge profiles, perforation patterns, and finishes for use in standard or custom suspension systems. Verify the availability of custom options with manufacturers selected.

Factory-punched and -cut openings for fixtures such as canned light fixtures, air diffusers, air grilles, speakers, sprinklers, and others are possible. Consult manufacturers for details and include applicable requirements in the specifications.

SUSPENSION SYSTEMS

The industry's strong orientation to ASTM C 635, *Specification for the Manufacture, Performance, and Testing of Metal Suspension Systems for Acoustical Tile and Lay-in Panel Ceilings,* and to its companion standard ASTM C 636, *Practice for Installation of Metal Ceiling Suspension Systems for Acoustical Tile and Lay-in Panels,* makes it unnecessary for the design professional to reinvent suspension systems and installation specifications for most applications. UBC Standard 25-2, *Metal Suspension Systems for Acoustical Tile and for Lay-in Panel Ceilings,* is based on the two ASTM standards. Refer to Chapter 09511 for a brief explanation of structural classification requirements and of requirements for areas needing seismic restraint.

Standard configurations of $^{15}/_{16}$- and $^{9}/_{16}$-inch (24- and 15-mm), exposed, direct-hung ceiling suspension systems support laid- or clipped-in metal pans. Other-than-tee profiles may be allowed, for example, slotted, box-shaped reveal (bolt or screw slot), for a different type of system or look. See Chapter 09511 for additional information about exposed, direct-hung ceiling suspension systems.

Wide-face, double-web, steel suspension systems are available with either override or butt-edge cross tees. This choice is restricted primarily to nonfire-resistance-rated systems. With the override type, there will be a gap between panel faces at their corners and the top edge of the cross-runner flange equal to the thickness of the stepped-up flange of the cross tee. This gap does not occur with the butt-edge cross tee where the top surface of both main and cross runners is on the same plane. The gap resulting from override (stepped) end condition of cross runners may be especially noticeable when combined with metal pans and may compromise a monolithic, flat, planar ceiling appearance. A few manufacturers fabricate pans with edges slightly recessed so metal pans are flush with the bottom of butt-edge cross-tee grids (flush reveal with grid). However, when compared to override tees, butt-edge tees have less torsional resistance under conditions such as asymmetric loading.

ACOUSTICAL PERFORMANCE CONSIDERATIONS

Airborne sound can be absorbed within enclosed areas of buildings by metal pan ceilings. The acoustical qualities attainable depend primarily on the characteristics of the sound-absorbent pads or fabric installed in the pans and the perforations in the exposed metal pan surfaces. To determine the best balance for optimum acoustical performance, consider the thickness and density of the sound-absorbent backing; the extent of perforated open areas; the size, shape, and center-to-center distance of holes; and the

perforation pattern of the metal pan. These factors must function together without impairing the strength and rigidity of the original sheet metal to support itself without distortion.

Noise Reduction Coefficient (NRC) is discussed in Chapter 09511. Of the parameters for pans listed in the preceding paragraph, the percent open area (the area of perforations) and the center-to-center distance of perforations have the greatest effect on acoustical performance. Typically, the greater the open area in the pan, the greater the acoustical transparency of the pan and ceiling, and the greater the NRC. If absorption of sound in all frequencies is needed, the degree of acoustical transparency and the efficiency of the absorber are most important. If numerous small perforations are closely spaced, the acoustical transparency of metal pans is maximized. However, densely microperforated sheet, with the greatest number of perforations possible, may not be the best solution for maximizing acoustical performance for ceiling pan applications because of the pan's lack of rigidity and strength, its high fabrication cost, and the tendency of very small perforations to clog. Also, if sound absorption in selected frequencies is needed, other variables become important.

Thick glass-fiber and mineral-wool-fiber acoustical pads are more sound-absorbent than thin pads of the same density, but they cost more and require more space. A 1-inch- (25-mm-) thick glass-fiber absorber effectively absorbs high-frequency sound but is less effective for low-frequency sound. A 6-inch- (150-mm-) thick glass-fiber pad is an efficient absorber for sound of all frequencies. Wrapped mineral-fiber pads must be installed over a spacer grid to be effective; unwrapped pads do not. However, placing unwrapped pads directly on the back of metal pans may result in a less-than-satisfactory appearance. For best appearance with some perforation patterns, unwrapped pads should be covered with a black facing or coating. Black is usually recommended for pans with perforations exceeding ⅛ inch (3 mm) in diameter in a standard-height ceiling.

A black, nonwoven, acoustically absorbent fabric is often used by manufacturers of acoustical metal pan ceilings in lieu of mineral-fiber pads. The fabric's sound-absorbent efficiency reduces the required thickness of the absorptive backing and saves space. Factory application of the fabric ensures proper positioning and secure placement inside the pan. If fabric is used, less labor is required and installation is simplified. However, acoustical fabric is limited to moderate ratings for NRC. For the highest possible NRCs, pads and accessories must be used.

The presence and size of the air space between the pan and the absorbent backing material or behind the absorbent backing material can affect acoustic performance. The larger the space, the more sound is absorbed. Spacer grids can be incorporated between metal pans and absorbent backing in acoustical metal pan ceilings to provide a uniformly dimensioned, compartmentalized layer of air space. An arrangement of perforated metal, absorbent backing material, air layer, and solid backing may be used to design a tuned-resonance sound absorber that absorbs a selected range of sound frequencies.

Sound-insulating qualities are specified in terms of Ceiling Attenuation Class (CAC) based on laboratory tests performed according to ASTM E 1414. Some manufacturers still use Sound Transmission Class (STC) to rate their ceilings, based on laboratory tests performed according to AMA-1-II, which was an adaptation of ASTM E 90 to suit suspended ceilings and is available from the Ceilings & Interior Systems Construction Association (CISCA). ASTM E 90 is intended only to measure airborne sound transmission loss through building partitions. CAC and STC are both single-number ratings that indicate the effectiveness of a construction assembly, in this case the ceiling, in resisting passage of airborne sound when tested. Sound-pressure level differentials in ⅓-octave bands are measured, and single-number

CAC or STC ratings are calculated according to ASTM E 413 using sound transmission loss (TL). A high CAC or STC rating indicates better sound isolation performance; a low CAC or STC rating indicates a low resistance to sound transmission.

Ordinarily, sound attenuation through acoustical metal pan ceilings is poor. The panels themselves transmit sound through the perforations, and the limited mass of absorption material above the pans also offers little resistance to sound transmission. Accordingly, adjacent spaces separated by partitions that stop at the ceiling line instead of extending through the plenum space have almost no acoustical separation unless other measures are taken. The best method for providing acoustical privacy in such situations is to extend the partition through the plenum to the structure above, carefully sealing around all service penetrations. If this option is not elected, the alternative course is to add a continuous, nonperforated layer of sheet metal above the metal pan ceiling to provide a barrier to airborne sound, but the results are apt to be unsatisfactory unless the installation of the supplementary surface is continuous and virtually airtight. These optional sound attenuation panels are usually designed to snap into the pans from above. Unfortunately, unless an additional layer of acoustical absorption is placed above the attenuation material, the plenum space will be acoustically untreated, allowing sound to travel long distances through the plenum without being absorbed. Assemblies consisting of sound attenuation panels and supplementary acoustical insulation can improve sound absorption within the plenum. Absorbers work best if there is a reflective surface to reflect residual, unabsorbed sound back and through the absorber yet again to increase the absorption. Torsion-spring-hinged ceiling systems cannot be fitted with sound attenuation panels.

Because not all combinations of sound-absorbent backing material, pan perforations, spacer grids, air spaces, and sound attenuation panels have been tested, and because manufacturers report the maximum performance possible for only some combinations of components, verify with manufacturers, and coordinate components and ratings for acoustical performance of each metal pan assembly specified.

FIRE-TEST-RESPONSE CHARACTERISTICS

If Class A (or Class I) materials per ASTM E 1264 are required, metal pan ceilings are limited to those with flame-spread and smoke-developed indexes of no more than 25 and 50, respectively. Similar or better ratings are available for wrapped, faced, and unwrapped glass- and mineral-wool-fiber acoustical pads and acoustical fabric tested per ASTM E 84. Refer to Chapter 09511 for a discussion of surface-burning characteristics.

Although acoustical metal pans are categorized as Acoustical Materials (BYIT) in the 1999 edition of Underwriters Laboratories' (UL's) *Fire Resistance Directory,* no systems are listed in it or in the 1999 edition of Intertek Testing Services' (ITS's) *Directory of Listed Products* as being part of fire-rated floor-ceiling or roof-ceiling assemblies. Many fire-resistance-rated suspension systems are widely available and can be combined with metal pans.

ENVIRONMENTAL CONSIDERATIONS

Indoor air and environmental quality issues relevant to acoustical pads include particulate inhalation, particulate eye and dermal irritation, VOC emissions and absorption, and contamination by biological agents. Acoustical fabrics and tightly sealed pads are less likely to release particles. Sensitive environments may have stringent requirements for the control of particulate matter in indoor air, VOC emissions, and potential pathogens.

PVC or PE plastic sheet enclosing or covering acoustical insulation makes the backing pads less likely to release loose fibers, less irritating to touch, and easier to handle and install. Microperforations in the sheet vent the insulation and discourage the accumulation of moisture and consequent microbiological growth. Because interior air quality in buildings is a concern, most metal pan ceilings are now installed with backing pads wrapped to prevent the escape of loose fiber.

The absorptive nature of acoustical mineral-fiber pads acts to absorb more than sound. Pads exposed to odors absorb, retain, and outgas odors over time. Pads enclosed by PVC wrappings may be less likely to absorb transitory odors, but over time may absorb lasting odors. Outgassing unpleasant or possibly hazardous gases can be a problem; for example, tobacco smoke absorbed by acoustical pads can linger in a space or building intended to be a smoke-free environment. Detectable odors are not easily eliminated from acoustical pads, therefore, sometimes pads must be replaced.

SEISMIC CONSIDERATIONS

Acoustical (suspended) ceilings installed in areas requiring seismic bracing may require bracing designed to applicable building codes. Local codes normally define design forces that must be resisted by architectural components.

For areas that require seismic restraint, the following installation standards can be included in specifications: ASTM E 580, *Practice for Application of Ceiling Suspension Systems for Acoustical Tile and Lay-in Panels in Areas Requiring Moderate Seismic Restraint;* CISCA's *Recommendations for Direct-Hung Acoustical Tile and Lay-in Panel Ceilings—Seismic Zones 0-2;* CISCA's *Guidelines for Seismic Restraint of Direct-Hung Suspended Ceiling Assemblies—Seismic Zones 3 & 4;* and UBC Standard 25-2. Because codes are subject to periodic revision and to interpretation and amendment by local and state authorities having jurisdiction, verify requirements in effect for each project to determine which publications and standards to reference, if any, in the specifications; also verify whether the design of seismic restraints by a professional engineer along with submission of engineering calculations is required. When dealing with code requirements for seismic loads on suspended ceilings, the design professional must comply with one of the three following alternatives (note that IBC, UBC, the BOCA National Building Code, and the Standard Building Code have exceptions to seismic requirements for ceiling components under some conditions):

- Cite ASTM E 580, the applicable CISCA standard, or UBC Standard 25-2 as a prescriptive criterion, even though there may be no explicit mention of these in the model code in effect for the project.
- Design all the ceiling components based on the analytical method in the American Society of Civil Engineer's (ASCE's) publication ASCE 7, *Minimum Design Loads for Buildings and Other Structures,* or on criteria found in the building code in effect for the project.
- Delegate the design of seismic restraints to a professional engineer engaged by the contractor, citing the analytical method to be used as the basis of design as performance criteria. This option requires that the analytical method to be used as the basis of design is well understood by the design professional and that all relevant criteria are indicated in the contract documents. Examples of criteria that might need to be specified if ASCE 7 is used as the basis of design include seismic-design category or seismic use group, occupancy importance factor, and site classification.

Changes to ASCE 7, which are new to the 1998 edition that was published in January 2000, include reference to CISCA standards and requirements for special inspections during the installation of architectural components in Seismic Design Categories D, E, and F. If special inspections are required for the project, include requirements in the specifications.

REFERENCES

Publication dates cited here were current at the time of this writing. Publications are revised periodically, and revisions may have occurred before this book was published.

ASTM International

ASTM C 635-00: Specification for the Manufacture, Performance, and Testing of Metal Suspension Systems for Acoustical Tile and Lay-in Panel Ceilings

ASTM C 636-96: Practice for Installation of Metal Ceiling Suspension Systems for Acoustical Tile and Lay-in Panels

ASTM E 84-00a: Test Method for Surface Burning Characteristics of Building Materials

ASTM E 90-99: Test Method for Laboratory Measurement of Airborne Sound Transmission Loss of Building Partitions and Elements

ASTM E 413-87 (reapproved 1999): Classification for Rating Sound Insulation

ASTM E 580-96: Practice for Application of Ceiling Suspension Systems for Acoustical Tile and Lay-in Panels in Areas Requiring Moderate Seismic Restraint

ASTM E 1264-98: Classification for Acoustical Ceiling Products

ASTM E 1414-00: Test Method for Airborne Sound Attenuation Between Rooms Sharing a Common Ceiling Plenum

Ceilings & Interior Systems Construction Association

Guidelines for Seismic Restraint of Direct-Hung Suspended Ceiling Assemblies—Seismic Zones 3 & 4, 1991.

Recommendations for Direct-Hung Acoustical Tile and Lay-in Panel Ceilings—Seismic Zones 0-2, 1991.

International Conference of Building Officials

UBC Standard 25-2-1997: Metal Suspension Systems for Acoustical Tile and for Lay-in Panel Ceilings

Intertek Testing Services

Directory of Listed Products, published annually.

Underwriters Laboratories Inc.

Fire Resistance Directory, published annually.

09547 LINEAR METAL CEILINGS

This chapter discusses strip, decorative, linear metal ceilings.

This chapter does not discuss ceilings consisting of suspension systems and mineral-base or glass-fiber-base acoustical panels or tiles, or snap-in metal pan ceilings; these are discussed in Chapter 09511, Acoustical Panel Ceilings, Chapter 09512, Acoustical Tile Ceilings, and Chapter 09513, Acoustical Snap-in Metal Pan Ceilings. This chapter also does not cover ceilings integrated with lighting and air-distribution systems or linear metal baffles.

GENERAL COMMENTS

Exterior installations of linear metal ceilings require engineering analysis and evaluation of materials and coatings that are beyond the scope of ASTM C 635, ASTM C 636, and International Conference of Building Officials' (ICBO's) Uniform Building Code (UBC) Standard 25-2, the commonly used design and installation specifications for acoustical ceilings (fig. 1). Accordingly, ASTM C 635 includes the following statement:

> While this specification is applicable to the exterior installation of metal suspension systems, the atmospheric conditions and wind loading require additional design attention to ensure safe implementation. For that reason, a specific review and approval should be solicited from the responsible architect and engineer, or both, for any exterior application of metal suspension systems....

In addition to that statement, ASTM C 636 states: "While recommendations from the manufacturer should be solicited, it remains the final responsibility of the architect/engineer to ensure proper application of the materials in question." Some of the metal pans and suspension systems discussed in this chapter may be suitable for exterior use, in unconditioned interior spaces, and in interior spaces with severe or extreme conditions.

Verify the suitability of exterior ceiling installations, for example, soffits and parking garages, with manufacturers; perform engineering analysis or delegate the responsibility to a qualified professional engineer; and carefully evaluate materials and coatings.

Factors to consider when comparing some of the different types of available metal ceilings include the following:

- **Linear metal ceilings** are often selected, when plenum accessibility is a low priority, for their unique appearance and visually integrated services, for example, light fixtures and air diffusers that are almost invisible and do not disrupt the linear appearance of the ceiling. Usually, these ceilings cost more than acoustical metal pan ceilings but not as much as acoustical snap-in metal pan ceilings. If linear pans are wide, the ceiling may be comparable or more costly than acoustical snap-in metal pan ceilings.
- **Acoustical metal pans,** including lay-in, clip-in, and torsion-spring-hinge systems, are suspended by standard tee grids, are typically less costly than other metal pan ceilings, are ideal for renovation, and are useful if multiple, random, convenient accessibility to the plenum is required. These ceilings are available in a wide range of possible appearances, including exposed or concealed grids.
- **Acoustical snap-in metal pan ceilings** are the most secure type of metal ceiling and have a monolithic appearance with a completely concealed grid. According to manufacturers, acoustical snap-in metal pan ceilings are the most durable ceilings and are less likely to be affected by construction operations, access to the plenum, maintenance servicing of fixtures and equipment located in the plenum, or penetrating the ceiling plane. Detractors emphasize the amount of force required to install and remove snap-in pans and the potential for ceiling system damage when accessing the plenum and replacing pans. Typically, acoustical snap-in metal pan ceilings are the most expensive of the metal ceilings. Refer to Chapter 09513 for more detailed information.

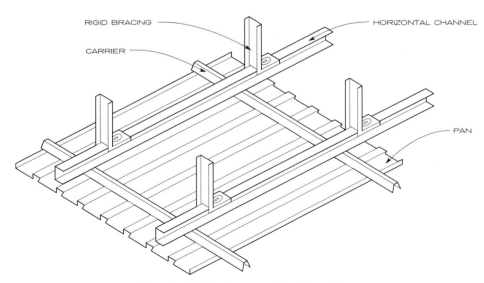

Figure 1. Exterior linear metal ceiling system

- **Suspended decorative grids** are economical, distinctive, often self-supporting, and mask but do not enclose the plenum and its contents. They define the ceiling plane and, unlike metal pan ceilings, have the advantage of allowing light fixtures to be placed above, below, or in the ceiling plane. Unlike metal pan ceilings, suspended decorative grids are not designed to be sound absorbers, but they can be used to improve fire safety and can reduce security risks. Refer to Chapter 09580, Suspended Decorative Grids, for more detailed information.

PRODUCT CLASSIFICATION

ASTM E 1264, *Classification for Acoustical Ceiling Products,* includes a designation system for identifying the various performance and physical properties of acoustical panels and tiles. These designations are explained in Chapter 09511. Although it is possible to classify linear metal ceiling pans according to ASTM E 1264 as Type XIII, "aluminum or steel strip with mineral or glass fiber base backing," or Type XX, "other types described as...," manufacturers do not commonly do so. Specifications often reference the ASTM standard to facilitate specifying acoustical, light reflectance, and fire-resistance performance for linear metal ceiling pans. Including classifications according to ASTM E 1264 may also be useful if a nonproprietary specification is required to for the project.

LINEAR METAL CEILING CHARACTERISTICS

The two major components of a linear metal ceiling are carriers and snap-on linear pans. Carriers are suspended by wires from the building structure, similar to suspended acoustical ceiling systems. Pans snap on to the matching contour of the carrier and are rigidly secured in place. Acoustical qualities of the ceiling are enhanced by adding an acoustically absorbent pad, fabric, or board (fig. 2).

The linear metal ceilings discussed in this chapter differ from other types of metal pan ceilings primarily because they are continuous, narrow, linear strips rather than square or wide rectangular shapes delineated by a two-way grid pattern, and because they are suspended by specially designed concealed or semiconcealed suspension systems. Other metal pan ceilings may be suspended by the same exposed ceiling suspension systems that are commonly used to suspend lay-in mineral-fiber- and glass-fiber-base acoustical panels, or they may be suspended by another type of specially designed suspension system. Examples of the latter type of metal pan ceilings are hook-in and snap-in metal pan ceilings.

Linear metal pans are installed from below the ceiling plane. When formed with integral recessed edges or installed with filler strips, they can conceal the suspension system and effectively close the ceiling. Because linear metal pans lock securely and permanently into their specially designed

suspension system, servicing within the ceiling plenum is limited to access panels with upward or downward action.

The appearance and design flexibility of linear metal ceilings are enhanced by a wide selection of metal pan widths, pan edge profiles, accessory trim profiles, edge joint details, finishes, and components with matching or contrasting colors.

Linear metal ceilings are primarily used for aesthetic effect, for upscale appearance, where strength is required, where frequent cleaning may be necessary, and where long life with low maintenance is desired (fig. 3). Linear metal ceilings are often used where the decorative effect of the ceiling is more important than flexibility or efficiency of the lighting. Metal ceilings are relatively lightweight and available in many colors and finishes. The metal surface makes a better base for coatings than soft, absorbent materials. Metal components and enclosed insulation pads have no exposed fibers that could pose a risk to interior air and environmental quality. For certain exposures, an uncoated, finished metal is highly desirable for corrosion resistance, sanitation, or the appearance of sanitation.

Linear metal ceiling pans may be comparatively stable in severe environments, but base metal, protective coatings, and finishes must be selected with care to avoid deterioration. Similar care must be exercised in selecting suspension system components for unconditioned spaces, exterior environments, and high-moisture, high-humidity areas such as saunas, shower rooms, indoor swimming pools, kitchens, dishwashing rooms, laundries, and sterilization rooms. Also, to reduce moisture-related problems, consider making provisions for ventilating the ceiling plenum. Manufacturers generally make few claims about the durability of finishes, and they do not usually test or warrant protective coatings and finishes.

Metal surfaces are nonporous; do not absorb odors, moisture, dirt, or other substances; and do not support biological growth. Linear metal ceilings are durable, easily cleanable, and seldom require refinishing or replacing for appearance or health reasons.

Light reflectance, as measured by Light Reflectance (LR) coefficients, is not usually reported by linear metal ceiling manufacturers in their product literature. Exposed finishes and the presence or absence of filler strips affect LR. Consult manufacturers if LRs are important, and verify assemblies and ratings.

Coordinated perimeter trim is available from ceiling system manufacturers, including wall angle and channel profiles; exposed, floating perimeter channels; and perimeter end caps. Other accessories include pan splices, filler strips, hold-down clips, and access doors. If custom extruded-aluminum edge trim is required for the project, include requirements to that effect in the specifications. Extruded-aluminum or formed-steel edge trim with a variety of finishes, linear configurations, and decorative profiles is available from several manufacturers. Trim may be used to conceal and embellish ceiling perimeters, ceiling height transitions, penetrations, and openings for fixtures. It may also be used to form soffits, ceiling surrounds, ceiling clouds, ceiling coffers, light coves, and recessed pockets for blinds, curtains, and drapes.

Linear metal ceilings may be designed to have integrated ceiling capability. Some manufacturers offer special fixtures, such as light fixtures and air-distribution diffusers and grilles to fit their systems. If integrated electrical or mechanical fixtures and equipment are required for a project, obtain specifications from manufacturers, consult with the project's mechanical and electrical engineers, and include requirements in the project specifications.

Curved linear metal ceilings assembled with curved carriers or curved pans are available.

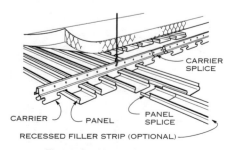

Figure 2. Linear metal ceiling

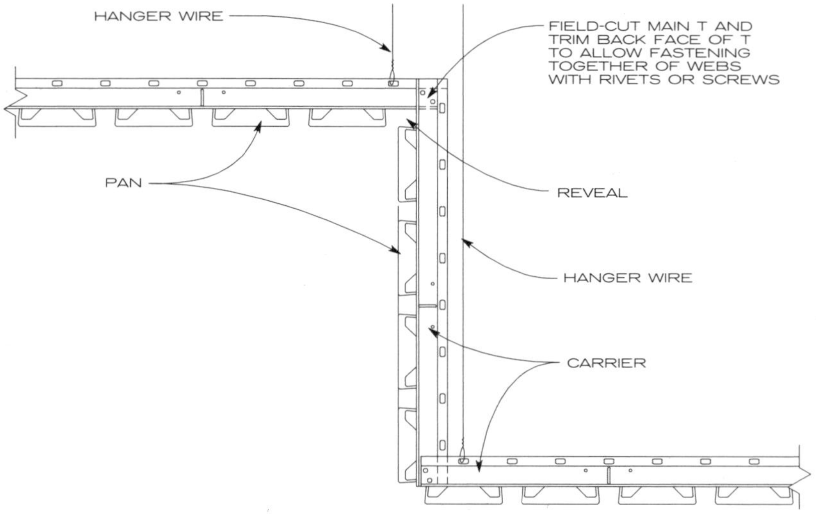

Figure 3. Linear metal ceiling system

LINEAR METAL PANS

Common linear metal pan modules are strips that repeat in uniformly dimensioned rows, from 2 to 6 inches (50 to 150 mm) wide. Less common are wider pans up to 8 or 12 inches (200 or 300 mm). The modular dimension is the unit repeat pattern, which includes any gap between pans. Hard SI (metric) sizes are available from some manufacturers. Verify the availability of hard SI (metric) sizes with applicable manufacturers.

Cold-rolled steel is the least-expensive base metal; it provides a flat, smooth base for coatings, but it is less resistant to the corrosive effects of moisture and other substances than are aluminum and stainless steel. Metal ceiling pans made from steel are strong, rigid, and economical. Most steel pans are electrogalvanized and suitable for interior use in conditioned spaces with humidity control. Aluminum pans are lighter than steel and are often recommended by manufacturers for exterior use if protected by a suitable finish. Stainless-steel pans are also strong and rigid, but they are costly and more likely to be a custom, rather than a standard, product.

Aluminum and stainless-steel pans can be installed in unconditioned spaces, exterior environments, and applications subject to high moisture and high humidity, with a reduced risk of corrosion or moisture damage when compared to steel. For metal ceiling pans, Types 304 and 430 are the most commonly used stainless-steel alloys. Type 304 austenitic stainless is commonly used for architectural purposes and is usually considered suitable for most rural, moderately polluted urban, and low-humidity and low-temperature coastal environments where corrosion potential is low. Type 430 stainless steel is a chromium grade that contains no nickel; its corrosion resistance to certain substances is lower than for types falling within the 300 Series that contain nickel. The forming characteristics of the 300 Series stainless steels may make them unsuitable for use with some manufacturers' equipment. Verify the availability of stainless-steel alloys with manufacturers and ascertain the limitations of their forming and punching equipment. See Chapter 09511 for a discussion of the available alloys and the potential effects of chloramines, chlorides, and other corrosive agents on stainless steel. It is also important to specify materials for the suspension system that have corrosion-resistant properties consistent with the metal pan ceiling units that the system supports.

Edge profiles for linear metal pans are limited to rounded, square, or beveled edges. Joint details depend on whether there is a reveal between pans or whether pan profiles provide an integral recessed reveal. Filler strips and integral recessed reveals fill gaps between pans, increase the apparent pan width, and reduce sound transmission to other spaces. Filler strips can be flush, recessed, or a distinct profile, for example, V-shaped.

Finishes for metal pans are varied. Mechanical finishes may be mill, brushed, mirror, natural, satin, or textured. Aluminum and steel may be finished with baked color coatings. Aluminum and steel may also have a metallic finish produced by chemical/mechanical or chemical/mechanical/protective coating processes. Aluminum may be lacquered, anodized, or coated with a high-performance coating. Steel may be bare, electrogalvanized, or hot-dip galvanized before coating, or it may be electroplated.

SUSPENSION SYSTEMS

Carriers are either concealed or semiconcealed by the strips of linear metal pans. Besides standard carriers running perpendicular to linear metal pans, the following variations are available:

- **Renovation carriers** attach to existing 24-by-48-inch (600-by-1200-mm) ceiling grid T-bars. Using an existing grid and other components that are in sound condition eliminates the cost of tearing out the old and purchasing and installing new components. These ceiling systems can also be directly mounted to walls.
- **Carriers** are available to adapt linear metal ceilings to irregularly shaped contours and out-of-square conditions.
- **Expansion carriers** are used if the ceiling size does not comply with the standard nominal 4-inch (100-mm) increment. Expansion carriers can increase the centerline-to-centerline dimension by approximately ⅛ inch (3.2 mm) per pan. The additional nominal amount is imperceptible and does not interfere with the ceiling's visual impact.
- **Flexible radius carriers** are available to create custom radius applications and are compatible with standard carriers. If used in curves or slopes, the radius should be supported by structural members or braces. These carriers can also be used to create pan patterns.
- **Stabilizer bars** snap into slots located every 4 inches (100 mm) along the carriers and may be used to increase the strength and rigidity of the carrier system, to speed pan attachment, and to simplify ceiling installation by eliminating the need to tie carriers in place.

ACOUSTICAL PERFORMANCE CONSIDERATIONS

Airborne sound can be absorbed within enclosed areas of buildings by linear metal ceilings. The acoustical qualities attainable depend primarily on the characteristics of the sound-absorbent pads or fabric installed in the pans or over the pans, the perforations in the exposed metal pan surfaces, and the presence and characteristics or absence of filler strips. To determine the best balance for optimum acoustical performance, consider the thickness and density of the sound-absorbent backing; the extent of perforated open areas; the size, shape, and center-to-center distance of holes; and the perforation pattern of the metal pan. These factors must function together without impairing the strength and rigidity of the original sheet metal to support itself without distortion. Typically, fewer perforation pattern choices and only smaller perforation patterns are available for linear metal pans compared to square or rectangular metal pans. Perforation patterns with small holes better absorb higher sound frequencies; those with larger holes better absorb low frequencies.

The Noise Reduction Coefficient (NRC) is discussed in Chapter 09511. Of the parameters for pans listed in the preceding paragraph, the percent open area (the area of perforations) and the center-to-center distance of perforations have the greatest effect on acoustical performance. Typically, the greater the open area in the pan, the greater the acoustical transparency of the pan and ceiling, and the greater the NRC. If absorption of sound in all frequencies is needed, the degree of acoustical transparency and the efficiency of the absorber are most important. If numerous small perforations are closely spaced, the acoustical transparency of metal pans is maximized. However, densely microperforated sheet, with the greatest number of perforations possible, may not be the best solution for maximizing acoustical performance for ceiling pan applications because of the pan's lack of rigidity and strength, its high fabrication cost, and tendency of very small perforations to clog. Also, if sound absorption in selected frequencies is needed, other variables become important.

Thick glass- and mineral-wool-fiber acoustical pads are more sound-absorbent than thin pads of the same density, but cost more and require more space. A 1-inch- (25-mm-) thick glass-fiber absorber effectively absorbs high-frequency sound but is less effective for low-frequency sound. A 6-inch- (150-mm-) thick glass-fiber pad is an efficient absorber for sound of all frequencies.

A black, nonwoven, acoustically absorbent fabric is often used by manufacturers of acoustical metal pan ceilings in lieu of mineral-wool-fiber pads. The fabric's sound-absorbent efficiency reduces the required thickness of the absorptive backing and saves space. Factory application of the fabric ensures proper positioning and secure placement inside the pan. If fabric is used, less labor is required and installation is simplified. However, acoustical fabric is limited to moderate ratings for NRC. For the highest possible NRCs, pads and accessories must be used.

Ordinarily, sound attenuation through linear metal ceilings is poor. Sound is transmitted through the pan perforations and the voids between pans. The limited mass of absorbent material above the pans also offers little resistance to sound transmission. Using nonperforated panels and filler strips can decrease sound transmission to other spaces but does little to absorb sound originating within the space. Adjacent spaces separated by partitions that stop at the ceiling line instead of extending through the plenum space have almost no acoustical separation unless other measures are taken. The best method for providing acoustical privacy in such cases is to extend the partition through the plenum to the structure above, carefully sealing around all service penetrations.

Because not all combinations of sound-absorbent backing material, pan perforations, spacer grids, air spaces, and sound attenuation panels have been tested, and because manufacturers report the maximum performance possible for only some combinations of components, verify with manufacturers and correlate components and ratings for acoustical performance of each metal pan assembly specified.

FIRE-TEST-RESPONSE CHARACTERISTICS

If Class A (or Class I) materials per ASTM E 1264 are required, linear metal ceilings are limited to those with flame-spread and smoke-developed indexes of no more than 25 and 50, respectively. Similar or better ratings are available for wrapped, faced, and unwrapped glass- and mineral-fiber acoustical pads and acoustical fabric tested per ASTM E 84. Refer to Chapter 09511 for a discussion of surface-burning characteristics.

Fire-resistance-rated assemblies consisting of a linear metal ceiling installed over an acoustical ceiling are available from some manufacturers.

ENVIRONMENTAL CONSIDERATIONS

Indoor air and environmental quality issues relevant to acoustical pads include particulate inhalation, particulate eye and dermal irritation, VOC emissions and absorption, and contamination by biological agents. Acoustical fabrics and tightly sealed pads are less likely to release particles. Sensitive environments may have stringent requirements for the control of particulate matter in indoor air, VOC emissions, and potential pathogens.

PVC or PE plastic sheet that encloses or covers acoustical insulation makes the backing pads less likely to release loose fibers, less irritating to touch, and easier to handle and install. Microperforations in the sheet vent the insulation and discourage the accumulation of moisture and consequent microbiological growth. Because interior air quality in buildings is a concern, most metal pan ceilings are now installed with backing pads wrapped to prevent the escape of loose fiber.

The absorptive nature of acoustical mineral-fiber pads acts to absorb more than sound. Pads exposed to odors absorb, retain, and outgas odors over time. Pads enclosed by PVC wrappings may be less likely to absorb transitory odors, but over time may absorb lasting odors. Outgassing unpleasant or possibly hazardous gases can be a problem; for example, tobacco smoke absorbed by acoustical pads can linger in a space or building intended to be a smoke-free environment. Detectable odors are not easily eliminated from acoustical pads, and sometimes pads must be replaced.

SEISMIC CONSIDERATIONS

Acoustical (suspended) ceilings installed in areas requiring seismic bracing may require bracing designed to applicable building codes. Local codes normally define design forces that must be resisted by architectural components.

For areas that require seismic restraint, the following installation standards can be included in specifications: ASTM E 580, *Practice for Application of Ceiling Suspension Systems for Acoustical Tile and Lay-in Panels in Areas Requiring Moderate Seismic Restraint;* Ceilings & Interior Systems Construction Association's (CISCA's) *Recommendations for Direct-Hung Acoustical Tile and Lay-in Panel Ceilings—Seismic Zones 0-2;* CISCA's *Guidelines for Seismic Restraint of Direct-Hung Suspended Ceiling Assemblies—Seismic Zones 3 & 4;* and UBC Standard 25-2, *Metal Suspension Systems for Acoustical Tile and for Lay-in Panel Ceilings.* Because codes are subject to periodic revision and to interpretation and amendment by local and state authorities having jurisdiction, verify requirements in effect for each project to determine which publications and standards to reference, if any, in the specifications and whether the design of seismic restraints by a professional engineer along with submission of engineering calculations is required. When dealing with code requirements for seismic loads on suspended ceilings, the design professional must comply with one of the three following alternatives (note that UBC, the BOCA National Building Code, and the Standard Building Code have exceptions to seismic requirements for ceiling components under some conditions):

- Cite ASTM E 580, the applicable CISCA standard, or UBC Standard 25-2 as a prescriptive criterion, even though there may be no explicit mention of these in the model code in effect for the project.
- Design all the ceiling components based on the analytical method in the American Society of Civil Engineer's (ASCE's) publication ASCE 7, *Minimum Design Loads for Buildings and Other Structures,* or on criteria found in the building code in effect for the project.
- Delegate the design of seismic restraints to a professional engineer engaged by the contractor, citing the analytical method to be used as the basis of design as performance criteria. This option requires that the analytical method to be used as the basis of design is well understood by the design professional and all relevant criteria are indicated in the contract documents. Examples of criteria that might need to be specified if ASCE 7 is used as the basis of design include seismic-design category or seismic use group, occupancy importance factor, and site classification.

Changes to ASCE 7, which were new to the 1998 edition that was published in January 2000, include reference to CISCA standards and requirements for special inspections during the installation of architectural components in Seismic Design Categories D, E, and F. If special inspections are required for the project, include requirements in the specifications.

REFERENCES

Publication dates cited here were current at the time of this writing. Publications are revised periodically, and revisions may have occurred before this book was published.

ASTM International

ASTM C 635-97: Specification for the Manufacture, Performance, and Testing of Metal Suspension Systems for Acoustical Tile and Lay-in Panel Ceilings

ASTM C 636-96: Practice for Installation of Metal Ceiling Suspension Systems for Acoustical Tile and Lay-in Panels

ASTM E 84-00a: Test Method for Surface Burning Characteristics of Building Materials

ASTM E 580-96: Practice for Application of Ceiling Suspension Systems for Acoustical Tile and Lay-in Panels in Areas Requiring Moderate Seismic Restraint

ASTM E 1264-98: Classification for Acoustical Ceiling Products

Ceilings & Interior Systems Construction Association

Guidelines for Seismic Restraint of Direct-Hung Suspended Ceiling Assemblies—Seismic Zones 3 & 4, 1991.

Recommendations for Direct-Hung Acoustical Tile and Lay-in Panel Ceilings—Seismic Zones 0-2, 1991.

International Conference of Building Officials

UBC Standard 25-2-1997: Metal Suspension Systems for Acoustical Tile and for Lay-in Panel Ceilings

09549 SECURITY CEILING SYSTEMS

This chapter discusses downward-locking-panel and security-plank security ceiling systems, including ceiling panels and suspension systems. Panel types include both perforated and nonperforated units made of steel, galvanized steel, stainless steel, and aluminum.

This chapter does not discuss steel-plate or hollow-metal security ceiling systems.

GENERAL COMMENTS

High levels of noise are common in detention facilities because of the use of hard surfaces such as steel, masonry, and concrete necessary to achieve required security performance. These materials reflect sound rather than absorb it. American Correctional Association standards indicate that appropriate noise-level standards are 45 dBA at night and 70 dBA for inmate housing areas in the daytime. Security ceiling systems are one method of providing acoustical absorption to control noise levels in these facilities.

The selection, design, and specification of security ceiling systems are influenced by many factors. Specific factors to consider include the following:

- **Security finish versus security barrier:** Security finishes can effectively prevent concealment of contraband and can withstand significant levels of abuse. Snap-in-pan and downward-locking-panel security ceiling systems are security finishes. Security-plank and composite security ceiling systems are security barriers that prevent escape and concealment of contraband.
- **Supervised versus unsupervised areas:** The amount of supervision in a particular area may be the most important criterion in the selection of security ceiling systems. Supervised areas (e.g., dayrooms) can have less-secure ceiling systems, such as snap-in-pan or downward-locking-panel security ceiling systems, because guards are observing inmates' actions. Areas such as cells and other indirectly supervised areas need more secure ceiling systems, such as security-plank or composite systems.
- **Ceiling height:** Ceilings that are within reach of inmates are more susceptible to abuse than those that are not. This level of accessibility is an important factor in the selection of security ceiling systems.
- **Classification of inmates:** Although there is no objective classification of inmates, the terms *minimum, medium,* and *maximum* are often used. Minimum to medium security areas are often provided with snap-in-pan or downward-locking-panel security ceiling systems. Maximum security areas commonly have security-plank or composite security ceiling systems.
- **Duration of stay:** Security ceiling systems subject to long periods of inmate abuse must be more durable than those that are not, meaning that the ceiling panel must be thicker. Areas housing short-term stays (e.g., a temporary holding cell) might have 0.0528- or 0.0428-inch- (1.35- or 1.1-mm-) thick panels; areas housing long-term stays might have 0.0677-inch- (1.7-mm-) thick panels.
- **Moisture:** Areas subject to moisture, such as showers and kitchens, may require the use of steel that has been metallic coated by the hot-dip process or stainless-steel components capable of withstanding this type of environment. Nonperforated panels may also be required to reduce moisture transfer.

PRODUCT CHARACTERISTICS

Types of security ceiling systems include the following, generally listed from least to most secure:

- **Snap-in-pan security ceiling systems** are security finishes rather than security barriers. They consist of metal pan panels supported by a heavy-duty, concealed suspension system, both of which are heavy-duty versions of commercial systems. Security is achieved by tying the corners of the metal pan panels to the suspension system with concealed wire clips. Panels are typically 24 by 24 inches (610 by 610 mm) and fabricated from 0.0329-inch- (0.85-mm-) thick or lighter steel or aluminum. Access to the space above the ceiling is through hinged, keyed access doors or by leaving some panels unsecure by eliminating the wire tire. The system accepts recessed light fixtures and diffusers.
- **Downward-locking-panel security ceiling systems** are security finishes rather than security barriers. They consist of metal pan panels supported by a heavy-duty, exposed suspension system, both of which are heavy-duty versions of commercial systems. The panels are held in place by locking the panel edges under the rectangular bulb of the suspension runners. Vertical compression struts spaced at 48 inches (1220 mm) o.c. prevent uplift. Panels are typically 24 by 24 and 24 by 48 inches (610 by 610 and 610 by 1220 mm) and fabricated from 0.0428- or 0.0329-inch- (1.1- or 0.85-mm-) thick steel or 0.040-inch- (1.0-mm-) thick aluminum. Access to the space above the ceiling is through hinged, keyed access doors or by removable ceiling panels that are fastened to the suspension grid with security fasteners. The system accepts lay-in troffer light fixtures and diffusers without modifying the ceiling.
- **Security-plank security ceiling systems** are security barriers. They consist of long metal panels that can span up to 16 feet (4.9 m), although typical spans are 8 to 12 feet (2.4 to 3.7 m). Panels are supported on perimeter wall angles or channels. When the size of the ceiling exceeds the panel's capacity for spanning it using a single panel, a special exposed suspension system is used. Panels interlock with adjacent panels and are typically held in place by security fasteners or welds, although rivets or concealed hardware may also be used. Panels are typically 12, 18, or 24 inches (305, 457, or 610 mm) wide, with custom lengths as necessary to span the space, and are fabricated from 0.0966- to 0.0329-inch- (2.5- to 0.85-mm-) thick steel in single- or double-layer configurations; 0.0677- or 0.0528-inch- (1.7- or 1.35-mm-) thick, single-layer configurations are typical. Access to the space above the ceiling is generally through downward-acting, keyed access doors that are either factory or field installed. The system accepts recessed security light fixtures and diffusers.

When security-plank security ceiling systems are designed to receive a steel backer sheet, they can serve as a structural floor for the space above, in which case they are often called composite systems. These types of panels may bear on masonry walls and be welded to a metal cap plate or they may be supported by a special suspension system. Composite security ceiling systems typically do not have access doors. Light fixtures and diffusers used with this system are corner or wall mounted, surface mounted, or recessed if the system is modified and provided with C-shaped closures.

Both security-plank and composite security ceiling systems are primed for field painting because the panels are typically welded during installation.

Airborne sound can be absorbed within enclosed areas by perforated security ceiling systems. The absorption values that are obtainable depend on the sound-absorption pad installed in above-the-ceiling panels and on the size and frequency of perforations in the exposed ceiling panel itself. Wrapped sound-absorptive pads must be installed over a spacer grid to be effective, but unwrapped pads do not. However, resting unwrapped sound-absorptive pads directly on the back of ceiling panels may result in a less-than-satisfactory appearance, and unwrapped pads must be covered with a black coating. Because interior air quality in buildings is a concern, most security ceiling systems are now installed with insulation pads wrapped to prevent the escape of loose fibers.

Ordinarily, sound attenuation through security ceiling systems is poor. The ceiling panels themselves transmit sound through the perforations, and the limited mass of absorption material above the panels also offers little resistance to sound transmission. Accordingly, adjacent spaces separated by partitions that stop at the ceiling line, instead of extending through the plenum space, have almost no acoustical separation unless other measures are taken. The best method for providing acoustical privacy in such situations is to extend the partition through the plenum to the structure above, carefully sealing around all service penetrations. This method also provides additional security. If this option is not elected, the alternative is to add a continuous, nonperforated backer plate above the ceiling panels to provide a barrier to airborne sound waves. An additional layer of sound absorption should be placed above the backer plate to acoustically treat the plenum space and to prevent sound from traveling long distances through the plenum without being absorbed.

The variations in pattern and size are limited for security ceiling panels when compared to mineral-based acoustical ceiling units. To be acoustically effective, panels must be perforated and backed with sound-absorptive pads. Size, spacing, and pattern of perforations can vary extensively.

Because all combinations of pads, ceiling panel perforations, spacer grids, and backer plates have not been tested, and because manufacturers report the maximum performance possible for selected combinations of compo-

nents, verify with the manufacturer which ceiling components are required to achieve the needed acoustical performance values for each ceiling panel assembly specified.

Cold-rolled steel is the least-expensive base metal for security ceiling panels; it provides a flat, smooth base for coatings, but it is less resistant to the corrosive effects of moisture and other substances than steel sheet that is metallic coated by the hot-dip process (galvanized or galvannealed), aluminum sheet, or stainless-steel sheet. It is also important to specify suspension system materials whose corrosion-resistant properties are consistent with the ceiling panels that the system supports.

Two types of suspension systems, direct hung and indirect hung, which are applicable to downward-locking-panel security ceiling systems, are covered in ASTM C 635. Direct-hung systems are those in which main runners are hung directly from the structure above. Indirect-hung systems are those in which main runners are attached to carrying channels that are hung from the structure above.

SEISMIC CONSIDERATIONS

Products installed in areas requiring seismic bracing must have bracing designed to applicable building codes. Local codes normally define design forces that must be resisted. Seismic restraints should be designed by a professional engineer.

SECURITY FASTENERS

Detention and security facilities require fasteners that cannot be manipulated without the use of special tools. Security fasteners meet this requirement and come in several drive systems and configurations.

REFERENCES

Publication dates cited here were current at the time of this writing. Publications are revised periodically, and revisions may have occurred before this book was published.

ASTM International

ASTM C 635-97: Specification for the Manufacture, Performance, and Testing of Metal Suspension Systems for Acoustical Tile and Lay-in Panel Ceilings

09580 SUSPENDED DECORATIVE GRIDS

This chapter discusses open-cell grid, plenum mask ceiling systems.

This chapter does not discuss linear metal or acoustical ceilings or suspension systems. These are addressed in the following chapters: Chapter 09511, Acoustical Panel Ceilings; Chapter 09512, Acoustical Tile Ceilings; Chapter 09513, Acoustical Snap-in Metal Pan Ceilings; and Chapter 09547, Linear Metal Ceilings. This chapter also does not discuss ceilings integrated with lighting and air-distribution systems or wood-suspended decorative grids.

GENERAL COMMENTS

Factors to consider when comparing some of the different types of available metal ceilings include the following:

- **Suspended decorative grids** are economical, distinctive, often self-supporting, and they mask but do not enclose the plenum and its contents. They define the ceiling plane and, unlike metal pan ceilings, have the advantage of allowing light fixtures to be placed above, below, or in the ceiling plane. Unlike metal pan ceilings, suspended decorative grids are not designed to be sound absorbers, but they can be used to improve fire safety and can reduce security risks.
- **Acoustical metal pans,** including lay-in, clip-in, and torsion-spring-hinge systems, are suspended by standard tee grids, are typically less costly than other metal pan ceilings, are ideal for renovation, and are useful if multiple, random, convenient accessibility to the plenum is required. These ceilings are available in a wide range of possible appearances, including exposed or concealed grid.
- **Linear metal ceilings** are often selected, when plenum accessibility is a low priority, for their unique appearance and visually integrated services, for example, light fixtures and air diffusers that are almost invisible and do not disrupt the linear appearance of the ceiling. Typically, these ceilings cost more than acoustical metal pan ceilings but not as much as acoustical snap-in metal pan ceilings. If linear pans are wide, the ceiling may be comparable or more costly than acoustical snap-in metal pan ceilings. Refer to Chapter 09547 for more detailed information.
- **Acoustical snap-in metal pan ceilings** are the most secure type of metal ceiling and have a monolithic appearance with a completely concealed grid. According to manufacturers, acoustical snap-in metal pan ceilings are the most durable ceilings and are less likely to be affected by construction operations, accessing the plenum, maintenance servicing of fixtures and equipment located in the plenum, or penetrating the ceiling plane. Detractors emphasize the amount of force required to install and remove snap-in pans and the potential for ceiling system damage when accessing the plenum and replacing pans. Typically, acoustical snap-in metal pan ceilings are the most expensive of the metal ceilings. Refer to Chapter 09513 for more detailed information.

SUSPENDED DECORATIVE GRID CEILING CHARACTERISTICS

Suspended decorative grids are open-cell systems that define the ceiling plane while masking the ceiling plenum and its contents. These grids do not enclose the plenum space. They are often suspended at a considerable distance from the structural ceiling to define a more comfortable ceiling height. Different combinations of cell depth and cell size may be used to emphasize or deemphasize the demarcation of the ceiling plane and its degree of openness. A decorative grid system's masking capability may be described by the *shielding angle,* that is, the angle that describes the sightline that allows a person to view into the plenum area through a cell. Greater shielding angles restrict more of the view into the plenum area. Small cells have greater shielding angles than large cells.

Suspended decorative grids are usually self-supporting when attached to structural support, but they may be suspended by the same exposed ceiling suspension systems that are commonly used to suspend lay-in mineral-base and glass-fiber-base acoustical panels, called *standard tee grid suspension systems.* Special decorative covers are available for the webs of suspension members. Because such systems are installed with a standard tee grid, standard lighting and conditioned air fixtures and grilles are compatible. Moreover, these ceiling systems are economical and easy to install and remove for 100 percent accessibility to the ceiling plenum. If the suspension system grid is not made by the same manufacturer as the cell system, a potential problem is matching the color and appearance of the finish. If these products are selected, include requirements for the appropriate suspension system and color matching in the specifications.

The appearance and design flexibility of suspended decorative grid ceilings is enhanced by a wide selection of dimensions, scales, and patterns for frames and cells; distinctive combinations of frame and cell components; and the availability of a variety of finishes.

Suspended decorative grid ceilings are primarily used for aesthetic effect, dramatic appearance, space definition, and freedom of placing lighting fixtures, conditioned air fixtures and grilles, and sprinklers in, above, or below the ceiling plane. In Europe, suspended decorative grid ceilings are promoted as a safety feature. Fire safety is improved by allowing easy detection of and access to fire occurring in the plenum. In case of fire, smoke can freely rise to the plenum space and decrease the rate of accumulation in occupied spaces, consequently increasing escape time. Smoke management systems can also extract smoke above the grid plane. Sprinklers can be located above the ceiling plane and help suppress fire throughout the space. Security is improved by making hidden contraband and unwanted items more visible and easily detected above suspended decorative grids than above accessible, monolithic, barrier-type suspended ceilings.

Suspended decorative grids generally consist of right-angled grids, arranged in various patterns, suspended from above. Grids are typically formed by U-shaped profiles roll formed from sheet metal, with various dimensions for grids and profiles and a range of capabilities for obscuring overhead views and controlling sightlines. Systems consisting of profiles with widths of 1 inch (25 mm) or more are generally called *beams* or *frames* by manufacturers. Beam grids may be used to form large-scale patterns with a significant percentage of free area. They may also be used in combination with cell grids having profiles and patterns of smaller dimensions, to function as supporting frames. Systems consisting of profiles with widths of less than 1 inch (25 mm) are generally called *cells* by manufacturers. Ceiling grids may consist of beams, of cells, of combinations of beams and cells, or of combinations of different-sized beams or cells. Bilevel combinations cross profiles with different heights so the bottom of the grid is defined by intersects on two different planes. Aluminum components are more available than steel components, especially for cell grids.

Cells and beams with U-shaped profiles with the top edge return flange turned inward are stronger and more rigid than those with simple U-shaped profiles.

Suspended decorative grids may be comparatively stable in severe environments, but base metal, protective coatings, and finishes must be selected with care to avoid deterioration. Similar care must be exercised in selecting suspension system components for unconditioned spaces, exterior environments, and high-moisture, high-humidity areas such as saunas, shower rooms, indoor swimming pools, kitchens, dishwashing rooms, laundries, and sterilization rooms. Manufacturers typically make few claims about the durability of finishes; nor do they commonly test or warrant protective coatings and finishes.

Metal surfaces are nonporous; do not absorb odors, moisture, dirt, or other substances; and do not support biological growth. Because of the sizable extent of their exposed surface areas, suspended decorative grids may be more difficult to keep clean than other types of metal ceilings, but they are durable and seldom require refinishing or replacing for appearance or health reasons.

Common finishes are baked color coatings and metallic finishes produced by mechanical/chemical or mechanical/chemical/protective coating processes.

Coordinated perimeter trim, including wall angle and channel profiles; exposed, floating perimeter channels; and perimeter end caps are available from ceiling system manufacturers for terminations, penetrations, and intersections at walls and other ceiling materials. Suspension system web covers and cell infill panels for incandescent lighting and sprinklers may be available to suit the system. If custom extruded-aluminum edge trim is required for a project, include requirements in the specification. Extruded-aluminum or formed-steel edge trim with a variety of finishes, linear configurations, and decorative profiles is available from several manufacturers.

Some ceiling systems provide support for banners; low-voltage, bare-wire lighting systems; neon lights; fiber-optic lighting systems; and air grilles, air diffusers, or other fixtures. For other systems, alternate support for fixtures must be provided. Verify load-bearing capacity of each system with the manufacturer.

Installation is quick and usually free from involvement with lighting, air-handling, and sprinkler systems. Beams and other carriers are designed to accept cell members at regular intervals.

SEISMIC CONSIDERATIONS

Suspended ceilings installed in areas requiring seismic bracing may require bracing designed to applicable building codes. Local codes normally define design forces that must be resisted by architectural components.

For areas that require seismic restraint, the following installation standards are usually referenced in specifications: ASTM E 580, *Practice for Application of Ceiling Suspension Systems for Acoustical Tile and Lay-in Panels in Areas Requiring Moderate Seismic Restraint;* Ceilings & Interior

Systems Construction Association's (CISCA's) *Recommendations for Direct-Hung Acoustical Tile and Lay-in Panel Ceilings—Seismic Zones 0-2;* CISCA's *Guidelines for Seismic Restraint of Direct-Hung Suspended Ceiling Assemblies—Seismic Zones 3 & 4;* and International Conference of Building Officials' (ICBO's) Uniform Buildng Code (UBC) Standard 25-2, *Metal Suspension Systems for Acoustical Tile and for Lay-in Panel Ceilings.* Because codes are subject to periodic revision and to interpretation and amendment by local and state authorities having jurisdiction, verify requirements in effect for each project to determine which publications and standards to reference, if any, in the specifications and whether the design of seismic restraints by a professional engineer along with submission of engineering calculations is required. When dealing with code requirements for seismic loads from suspended ceilings, the design professional must comply with one of the three following alternatives (note that UBC, the BOCA National Building Code, and the Standard Building Code have exceptions, under some conditions, to seismic requirements for ceiling components):

- Cite ASTM E 580, the applicable CISCA standard, or UBC Standard 25-2 as a prescriptive criterion, even though there may be no explicit mention of these in the model code in effect for the project.
- Design all the ceiling components based on the analytical method in American Society of Civil Engineers' (ASCE's) publication ASCE 7, *Minimum Design Loads for Buildings and Other Structures,* or on criteria found in the building code in effect for the project.
- Delegate the design of seismic restraints to a professional engineer engaged by the contractor, citing the analytical method to be used as the basis of design as performance criteria. This option requires that the analytical method to be used as the basis of design is well understood by the design professional and that all relevant criteria are indicated in the contract documents. Examples of criteria that might need to be specified if ASCE 7 is used as the basis of design include seismic-design category or seismic use group, occupancy importance factor, and site classification.

Changes to ASCE 7, new to the 1998 edition, which was published in January 2000, include reference to CISCA standards and requirements for special inspections during the installation of architectural components in Seismic Design Categories D, E, and F. If special inspections are required for the project, include requirements in the specifications.

REFERENCES

Publication dates cited here were current at the time of this writing. Publications are revised periodically, and revisions may have occurred before this book was published.

ASTM International

ASTM E 580-96: Practice for Application of Ceiling Suspension Systems for Acoustical Tile and Lay-in Panels in Areas Requiring Moderate Seismic Restraint

Ceilings & Interior Systems Construction Association

Guidelines for Seismic Restraint of Direct-Hung Suspended Ceiling Assemblies—Seismic Zones 3 & 4, 1991.

Recommendations for Direct-Hung Acoustical Tile and Lay-in Panel Ceilings—Seismic Zones 0-2, 1991.

International Conference of Building Officials

UBC Standard 25-2-1997: Metal Suspension Systems for Acoustical Tile and for Lay-in Panel Ceilings

09621 **FLUID-APPLIED ATHLETIC FLOORING**

This chapter discusses polyurethane floorings that are intended for use in athletic-activity areas and are homogenous or installed over resilient underlayment.

This chapter does not discuss resinous floorings for decorative, general-use, and high-performance applications; they are specified in Chapter 09671, Resinous Flooring.

PRODUCT CHARACTERISTICS

Fluid-applied, athletic-flooring systems are inexpensive alternatives to traditional, maple, gymnasium flooring. Sometimes these products are used with maple flooring in areas normally concealed from public view, such as under bleachers or in corridors leading to locker rooms. Fluid-applied flooring is either homogenous polyurethane or polyurethane installed over a resilient, rubber, base-mat underlayment.

Polyurethane formulations used for athletic flooring are self-leveling, thermosetting, noncellular (solid), resins that are slurry (fluid) applied to produce nonporous, seamless surfaces. They conform to substrate contours, may reflect surface irregularities, and will flow if surfaces are not level. Therefore, proper substrate preparation is essential.

Mercury is a catalyzing agent in some polyurethane formulations. Other formulations that do not use mercury as a catalyst are often called *zero-mercury formulations*. Homogenous systems are available in mercury-catalyzed and zero-mercury formulations. The resins used in base-mat systems are usually only available in zero-mercury formulations.

- **Mercury-catalyzed formulations** cure faster than zero-mercury formulations of the same thickness and are affected less by high temperatures and humidity. The thicknesses of polyurethane used in homogenous systems are generally greater than those of base-mat systems, which is why homogenous systems are often mercury catalyzed.
- **Mercury is a hazardous material.** According to manufacturers' representatives, catalyzing agents are approximately 6 percent of formulations, and mercury, if any, makes up approximately $\frac{1}{100}$ of this percentage. Even with this little mercury, mercury-catalyzed formulations generally are categorized as hazardous materials when tested. This classification affects disposal of excess materials and how the flooring is disposed of after its useful life. In the United States, hazardous materials cannot be disposed of in a landfill because materials such as mercury can contaminate ground water. Consequently, old polyurethane floors that contain mercury are often removed and disposed of in other countries that have less-stringent environmental regulation, or they are resurfaced or covered with other flooring.

Resilient, rubber, base mats are manufactured roll-goods made from granulated rubber set in polyurethane binder. Base mats are adhesively applied to concrete substrates.

Surfaces are primed or sealed before applying the polyurethane. In homogenous systems, concrete substrates are primed. In base-mat systems, the base mat is sealed with a polyurethane sealer.

Topcoats are also polyurethane; they are generally applied by a squeegee or roller. Topcoat appearance characteristics vary among products. Consult manufacturers' literature and samples to decide similarities and differences among products.

APPLICATION CONSIDERATIONS

A trained, experienced installer (applicator) is essential to a successful fluid-applied, athletic floor. The installer must know how to prepare substrates, including how to treat cracks, joints, and penetrations; how to mix and apply the system components within each component's working time; and how to apply components to reduce surface imperfections. Most manufacturers provide some way to ensure that installers are competent, usually by approving, training, or certifying them or by having their own employees install the products.

Air-quality concerns may affect product selection. Local VOC restrictions may limit available products. Verify VOC requirements of authorities having jurisdiction and the availability of suitable formulations with manufacturers. Installations in occupied buildings may require additional ventilation provisions or formulations that reduce odors during application and curing; consult manufacturers for recommendations.

Substrate conditions and preparation are critical. A clean, dry, neutral-pH substrate is required.

- **Moisture** from hydrostatic pressure, capillary action, and vapor transmission can cause adhesion failure of flooring systems installed on slabs-on-grade. Protect slabs-on-grade from subsurface moisture by appropriate grading and drainage, a capillary water barrier of porous drainage fill, and a membrane vapor retarder.
- **Concrete-slab substrates must be dry.** Temperature, relative humidity, and ventilation affect concrete drying time. A slab allowed to dry from only one side generally takes 30 days for every 1 inch (25.4 mm) of thickness to dry adequately.
- **Before applying flooring,** concrete substrates are mechanically cleaned, by abrasive blasting (shot blasting) or disc sanding, to ensure that surfaces are clean and free of laitance, oil, grease, curing compounds, or other materials incompatible with flooring system resins or adhesives.

Environmental conditions during installation are critical. Generally, manufacturers recommend a minimum ambient temperature between 55 and 65°F (13 and 18°C) and less than 50 percent relative humidity.

SPECIFYING METHODS

Generic specifications are feasible for fluid-applied, athletic-flooring systems common to several manufacturers. However, physical properties of components vary among systems, so naming the specific products that are acceptable is more precise. Some manufacturers may have more than one system that meets generic requirements. Some systems may also be unique to a manufacturer or be patented and, therefore, result in proprietary specifications.

FIRE-TEST-RESPONSE CHARACTERISTICS

Some manufacturers report fire-test-response characteristics for their products, although flooring material is exempt from fire-test-response requirements in most building codes. However, under some circumstances and in some jurisdictions, flooring materials are required to meet certain fire-test-response criteria.

The National Fire Protection Association (NFPA) publication NFPA 101, *Life Safety Code,* requires that flooring in exits and in access to exits meets critical radiant flux (CRF) limitations in certain occupancies. NFPA 101 does not regulate interior floor finishes based on smoke developed. Authorities having jurisdiction may impose other restrictions. Before including requirements for fire-test-response characteristics in a specification for fluid-applied, athletic flooring, verify applicable requirements of authorities having jurisdiction.

CRF is established by the flooring radiant panel test, ASTM E 648. The test measures the tendency of flooring to spread flames when installed in a corridor and exposed to the flames and hot gases from an adjacent room fire. The higher the CRF value, the more resistant the material is to flame spread. Consequently, the NFPA 101, Class I requirement of 0.45 W/sq. cm or greater is more stringent than the Class II requirement of 0.22 W/sq. cm or greater.

Specific optical smoke density is established by testing according to ASTM E 662. The traditional test for flame spread and smoke developed is ASTM E 84, which requires placing the test material on the ceiling of the test tunnel in an upside-down position. Since this test procedure does not relate to the conditions that flooring is likely to encounter in a real fire, the ratings are of limited use. Although flooring products are tested according to ASTM E 84, many manufacturers report smoke developed as the specific optical density according to ASTM E 662.

MEASURING ASSEMBLY PERFORMANCE

United States standards currently do not exist for measuring athletic-flooring performance. Some manufacturers reference a German Institute for Standardization (DIN) standard developed at the *Otto-Graf Institut* in Stuttgart.

Requiring DIN certification generally results in a proprietary specification. Before including requirements for DIN certification in a specification, determine which characteristics are important for an installation. Although

assemblies may not meet all requirements of the standard, they may meet the criteria important for the installation.

The DIN standard includes test procedures and criteria for the following:

- **Shock absorption or force reduction:** This test requires that a minimum of 53 percent of a load be absorbed by the floor assembly and that 47 percent be returned to the body. However, higher shock absorption is generally recommended for aerobic activities to decrease fatigue. Conversely, high-percentage shock absorption creates a wider depression from impacts, which is undesirable for basketball.
- **Ball bounce:** This test measures the rebound of a ball from the assembly compared with a rigid, concrete floor. A minimum of 90 percent rebound is required. High rebound percentage improves ball control.
- **Vertical and area deflection:** This test measures the depression (trough or shockwave) created by an athlete landing on the floor. The shock is measured at 20 inches (500 mm) from the point of impact and cannot exceed 15 percent of the load. Excessive area deflection or shock causes improper ball bounce and may accelerate fatigue in nearby athletes.
- **Surface friction:** This test measures a floor's sliding behavior as the quotient of vertical force applied by a shoe to the horizontal force needed to move the shoe across the floor. To pass, this coefficient of friction (COF) must be between 0.5 and 0.7. If the COF is high, athletes' feet may tend to stick on the floor, causing strain to feet and leg muscles and ligaments.
- **Rolling load:** This test measures the flooring assembly's ability to withstand the effects of a 300-lb (136-kg) load placed on a rolling cart with a single wheel in the center. It is used to predict the flooring's behavior when subjected to loads imposed by items such as portable equipment and telescoping bleachers.

REFERENCES

Publication dates cited here were current at the time of this writing. Publications are revised periodically, and revisions may have occurred before this book was published.

ASTM International

ASTM E 84-99: Test Method for Surface Burning Characteristics of Building Materials

ASTM E 648-99: Test Method for Critical Radiant Flux of Floor-Covering Systems Using a Radiant Heat Energy Source

ASTM E 662-97: Test Method for Specific Optical Density of Smoke Generated by Solid Materials

09622 RESILIENT ATHLETIC FLOORING

This chapter discusses rubber, vinyl, and thermoplastic-rubber-blend floor coverings in interlocking-tile or roll form that are designed for use in athletic-activity or support areas.

This chapter does not discuss general- and other special-use resilient floorings, fluid-applied athletic flooring, and wood athletic-flooring assemblies. These products are discussed in other chapters.

PRODUCT SELECTION CONSIDERATIONS

Various specialized resilient floorings in tile and roll form are offered for use in areas where athletic activities occur. The type selected for an installation depends on activity, budget, and code requirements. Before selecting athletic floorings, contact manufacturers for recommendations.

Each athletic activity has its own requirements. For example, aerobic exercise requires flooring that absorbs impact to prevent shin splints and that returns enough energy to users' legs to prevent excessive muscle fatigue. The floor must provide enough traction to minimize slipping, while not grabbing shoes and restricting intentional sliding movements. For basketball and volleyball, shock absorption and ball bounce are critical characteristics. Floors adjacent to ice-skating rinks must resist damage from skate blades and must drain water. Locker rooms and shops near activity areas must resist damage from cleats or spikes.

Rubber tile and sheet vinyl floorings are inexpensive alternatives to traditional maple gymnasium flooring. Sometimes these products are used with maple flooring in areas normally concealed from public view, such as under bleachers or in corridors leading to locker rooms.

Some manufacturers report fire-test-response characteristics for their products, although flooring material is exempt from fire-test-response requirements in model building codes unless it is installed in an exit-access corridor and the flooring is judged to present an unusual hazard. Under these circumstances, flooring materials are generally required to meet critical radiant flux (CRF) limitations.

The National Fire Protection Association (NFPA) publication NFPA 101, *Life Safety Code,* requires that flooring in exits and in access to exits meet CRF limitations in certain occupancies. NFPA 101 does not regulate interior floor finishes based on smoke developed.

CRF is established by the flooring radiant panel test, ASTM E 648. The test measures the tendency of flooring installed in a corridor to spread flames when exposed to the flames and hot gases from an adjacent room fire. The higher the CRF value, the more resistant the material is to flame spread. Consequently, the NFPA 101, Class I requirement of 0.45 W/sq. cm or greater is more stringent than the Class II requirement of 0.22 W/sq. cm or greater.

Specific optical smoke density is established by testing according to ASTM E 662. The traditional test for flame spread and smoke developed is ASTM E 84, which requires placing the test material on the ceiling of the test tunnel in an upside-down position. Since this test procedure does not simulate the conditions that flooring is likely to encounter in a real fire, the ratings are of limited use. Although flooring products are tested according to ASTM E 84, many manufacturers report smoke developed as the specific optical density according to ASTM E 662.

Authorities having jurisdiction may impose other fire-test-response restrictions on flooring. Before specifying requirements for fire-test-response characteristics for resilient athletic flooring, verify applicable requirements of authorities having jurisdiction.

PRODUCT CHARACTERISTICS

Resilient athletic flooring is made from rubber, recycled rubber, polypropylene, vinyl, recycled vinyl, or thermoplastic rubber-and-vinyl blends. Solid-surface tiles are rubber, recycled rubber, or recycled vinyl. These tiles are free-lay type, interlocked with male-female connections, or they are adhesively applied. Free-lay tiles are available with beveled border tiles to transition to adjacent, lower flooring surfaces. Polypropylene is used for free-lay, suspended tiles. The backs of suspended tiles are formed so only portions of their surface periodically contact the substrate, which increases resiliency. Roll goods are generally vinyl and are used as free-lay mats or runners or adhesively applied with welded seams. For vinyl sheet flooring, seams are heat welded or chemically (adhesively) welded.

Plastics are generally more resistant to fading than rubber. Consider fade resistance if the flooring will be subjected to direct sunlight.

Rubber products are available with a range of resilience characteristics. Increasing the thickness and reducing the durometer hardness of the rubber makes it more resilient. The resilience of vinyl products varies with the backing used. Backings are generally foam.

Rubber-strip tile, because of its carpetlike surface, is required by United States law to pass the 16 (Code of Federal Regulations) CFR 1630 (DOC FF-1-70) methenamine pill test, which measures a carpet's capability to ignite from a flaming methenamine tablet and spread the flame across the floor. Manufacturers' literature states that rubber-strip tile passes DOC FF-1-70.

For applications requiring ventilation under the flooring, manufacturers recommend suspended, polypropylene tile or open geometric-grid tiles made from various plastics, such as polyethylene and vinyl, or from thermoplastic rubber blends. Open geometric grids also allow water to drain from the walking surface.

Table 1 shows typical indoor athletic-activity and support areas and the types of products that manufacturers generally recommend for use in these spaces.

MEASURING FLOORING PERFORMANCE

United States standards currently do not exist for measuring athletic-flooring performance. Standardizing the measurement of criteria such as fatigue reduction and injury reduction has been hampered by myriad variables

Table 1
RESILIENT FLOORING RECOMMENDED FOR ATHLETIC-ACTIVITY AREAS

Indoor Athletic-Activity or Support Area	Product							
	Rubber Tile, Free Lay	Rubber or Vinyl Tile, Adhered	Rubber-Strip Tile, Adhered	Rubber or Vinyl Mats, Movable	Polypropylene Tile, Suspended	Plastic or Thermoplastic Rubber, Open Geometric-Grid Tile, Free Lay	Vinyl Sheet, Adhered with Welded Seams	Rubber Sheet Flooring
Aerobic Studios	•				•	•		
Basketball Courts		•			•		•	
Cleats, Areas Subject to		•		•				
Dance Studios	•				•			
Golf Spikes, Areas Subject to		•	•	•				
Ice Skates, Areas Subject to		•		•				
Locker Rooms						•		•
Recreation/ Multiuse Gyms	•	•			•		•	
Roller Hockey Rinks		•			•			
Running Tracks							•	•
Indoor Soccer Courts					•			
Swimming Pool Decks						•	•*	
Tennis Courts						•	•	
Volleyball Courts					•		•	
Weight Rooms	•	•						

*Note: Only products with slip-resistance properties that are enhanced by abrasive grit embedded in the surface are recommended.

that cause fatigue and injury. Manufacturers use various methods to establish product performance for these criteria, as well as more objective criteria, such as shock absorbency, ball bounce, static load limit, and coefficients of friction. To evaluate the performance of different types of products, consider surveying installations similar to those proposed that have been in service for a reasonable time period.

GAME LINES

Game lines can be painted on vinyl and rubber sheet flooring, as well as on some open geometric-grid tiles. For other tile products, varying the color of tiles can define activity areas or add visual interest.

ENVIRONMENTAL CONSIDERATIONS

Recycled rubber and vinyl are used to produce smooth and nondirectional textured tiles. Contact manufacturers to verify the extent of recycled materials used in products and whether materials are recycled postconsumer waste or manufacturing waste.

Recycled truck and bus tires are used to produce rubber-strip tile. These tiles have a close-nap, carpetlike surface made from rubber-fabric strips bonded to a flexible dry-adhesive backing. The backing reacts with separate adhesives applied to the substrate to form the tile-to-substrate bond.

VOC restrictions of authorities having jurisdiction may affect the selection of installation adhesives for adhered flooring. Specifications can place responsibility on the flooring manufacturers for selecting appropriate adhesives for substrates and conditions indicated. If specific adhesive requirements or VOC restrictions are included in the specifications, verify requirements of authorities having jurisdiction. If odor and indoor-air quality during installation and curing are concerns, consult manufacturers for recommendations.

REFERENCES

Publication dates cited here were current at the time of this writing. Publications are revised periodically, and revisions may have occurred before this book was published.

ASTM International

ASTM E 84-99: Test Method for Surface Burning Characteristics of Building Materials

ASTM E 648-99: Test Method for Critical Radiant Flux of Floor-Covering Systems Using a Radiant Heat Energy Source

ASTM E 662-97: Test Method for Specific Optical Density of Smoke Generated by Solid Materials

Code of Federal Regulations

16 CFR 1630 (7-1-97 Edition): Standard for the Surface Flammability of Carpets and Rugs (DOC FF-1-70)

09635 BRICK FLOORING

This chapter discusses brick flooring for interior applications subject to pedestrian and light vehicular traffic. Three setting methods discussed are loose-laid brick flooring with sand-filled, hand-tight joints; thick-set mortared brick flooring, with or without grouted joints; and thin-set mortared brick flooring, also with or without grouted joints.

This chapter does not discuss chemical-resistant brick flooring, brick or concrete pavers for exterior applications, or quarry and paver tile. Chemical-resistant brick flooring is covered in Chapter 09636, Chemical-Resistant Brick Flooring.

GENERAL COMMENTS

This chapter is a brief review of the characteristics of brick flooring products and setting methods suitable for interior applications. Unlike brick paving on the exterior, brick flooring is usually not required to withstand the destructive effects of freezing and thawing. However, resistance to such effects is one good indication of a brick flooring product's durability, even if not exposed to freezing temperatures.

BRICK PAVERS

Pedestrian and light-traffic paving brick generally supports pedestrian and light vehicular traffic in applications such as patios, walkways, floors, plazas, and driveways. In ASTM C 902, brick is classified into three weather classes, three traffic types, and three applications. Weather classes and traffic types are distinguished from one another by physical requirements that relate to performance under various weather and traffic exposures. The three applications are differentiated according to unit dimensional tolerances, extent of corner and edge chippage, and warpage, since these qualities affect installation with different joint treatments and patterns. These classifications and their applicability to various uses are summarized below.

Weather resistance is evaluated according to physical properties, such as compressive strength, cold-water absorption, and saturation coefficient. For Class SX units, limits are placed on all three properties; for Class MX and Class NX units, there are no limits for saturation coefficient; and for Class NX units, there are no limits for cold-water absorption.

- **Class SX** is for uses where water-saturated brick is exposed to freezing.
- **Class MX** is for exterior uses where brick is not exposed to freezing.
- **Class NX** is for interior uses where brick will be sealed, waxed, or otherwise coated.

The following exceptions apply to the physical property requirements of ASTM C 902 for weather classes:

- Compliance with the requirement for saturation coefficient is not needed if the average cold-water absorption is less than 6 percent.
- Compliance with requirements for cold-water absorption and saturation coefficient is not needed if a sample of five bricks undergoes a freeze-thaw test (described in ASTM C 67) for 50 cycles without breakage or more than 0.5 percent loss in dry weight of any single unit. Survival of a five-brick sample, after undergoing 15 cycles of a sulfate-soundness test (Sections 4, 5, and 8 of ASTM C 88) without visible damage, is an alternative to the freeze-thaw test.
- Another exception in ASTM C 902 applies to molded brick, which is further defined in the standard as "soft mud, semi-dry pressed, and dry pressed brick." Under this exception, the maximum absorption value for Class SX brick is changed from 8 to 16 percent for an average of five bricks and from 11 to 18 percent for single units. Compressive strength is also reduced from 8000 to 4000 psi (55.2 to 27.6 MPa) for an average of five bricks and from 7000 to 3500 psi (48.3 to 24.1 MPa) for single units.
- Compliance with physical properties is waived if the manufacturer submits information acceptable to the specifier that demonstrates satisfactory performance of its products under similar environmental and application conditions. Note 2 in ASTM C 902 explains this exception by stating that "resistance of brick to weathering cannot be predicted with complete assurance at the present state of knowledge. There is no known test that can predict weathering resistance with complete accuracy....The best indication of brick durability is its service experience record."

Traffic performance of pedestrian and light-traffic paving brick is evaluated by its abrasion resistance. Two alternatives provided for measuring this characteristic are abrasion index and volume abrasion loss. Abrasion index is calculated by dividing the brick's cold-water absorption value by its compressive strength and then multiplying that by 100. Volume abrasion loss is determined by testing per ASTM C 418, but with changes in procedures for type of sand, test duration, rate of sand flow, condition of brick, and method of determining volume loss.

- **Type I** is for exposure to extensive abrasion, such as driveways and entrances to public and commercial buildings.
- **Type II** is for exposure to intermediate traffic, such as exterior walkways and floors in restaurants and stores.
- **Type III** is for exposure to low traffic, such as floors and patios in single-family homes.

Three applications are as follows:

- **PS** is for general use where units are installed either with mortar- or grout-filled joints between units in any pattern or without mortar joints, but only in a running or other bond pattern that does not require units manufactured to close dimensional tolerances. The dimensional tolerance for this category is plus or minus ⅛ inch (3.2 mm) for dimensions of 3 inches (76 mm) or less, ³⁄₁₆ inch (4.7 mm) for 3 to 4 inches (76 to 102 mm), ¼ inch (6.4 mm) for 5 to 8 inches (127 to 203 mm), and ⁵⁄₁₆ inch (7.9 mm) for dimensions more than 8 inches (203 mm). Chippage limits are ⁵⁄₁₆ inch (7.9 mm) for edges and ½ inch (12.7 mm) for corners, with no single unit having an aggregate length of chips exceeding 10 percent of the perimeter of exposed face. Warpage (distortion) tolerances for this application are ³⁄₃₂ inch (2.4 mm) for units 8 inches (203 mm) and less, ⅛ inch (3.2 mm) for units 8 to 12 inches (203 to 305 mm), and ⁵⁄₃₂ inch (4.0 mm) for units 12 to 16 inches (305 to 406 mm).

- **PX** is for installations without mortar joints between units that require minimal dimensional variations because of special bond patterns or other special construction conditions. Compared to Application PS, dimensional tolerances are halved, and chippage at edges is ¼ and ⅜ inch (6.4 and 9.5 mm) at corners. Warpage (distortion) tolerances for this application are ¹⁄₁₆ inch (1.6 mm) for units 8 inches (203 mm) and less, ³⁄₃₂ inch (2.4 mm) for units 8 to 12 inches (203 to 305 mm), and ⅛ inch (3.2 mm) for units 12 to 16 inches (305 to 406 mm).
- **PA** is for units selected for certain appearance characteristics stemming from variations in color, texture, and size. No limitations on dimensional tolerance or warpage are imposed for this category, and edge and corner chippage requirements must be specified.

SLIP RESISTANCE

No slip-resistance requirement is included in ASTM C 902, but a note is provided indicating that this property should be considered when selecting brick and that future editions of the standard may include a suitable requirement. Specifications, however, can contain a provision based on a recommendation in the appendix to the Americans with Disabilities Act (ADA), *Accessibility Guidelines for Buildings and Facilities (ADAAG)*. The ADAAG appendix suggests a minimum value of 0.6 for the static coefficient of friction for level surfaces and 0.8 for ramps. Unfortunately, the appendix does not specify the test method to be used to determine the value, and the several test methods that are available give widely varying results. One test method that can be referenced in specifications is ASTM C 1028, which is for "ceramic tile and other like surfaces" and gives values that seem appropriate to the 0.6 and 0.8 requirements.

Coefficient of friction is not a simple, inherent property of a floor material; it depends on shoe material and the condition of the floor's surface. Contaminants (such as water, soil, mud, oils, etc.) and coatings (such as floor polishes) can greatly alter the value for a floor material. For this reason, a slip-resistance requirement might be specified for the floor wax applied over the brick flooring, such as a static coefficient of friction of at least 0.5 when tested according to ASTM D 2047. This requirement is based on test procedures and criteria for floor polishes developed at Underwriters Laboratories (UL) in the 1940s and supported by experience since then. Some authorities claim that the presence of contaminants, rather than the static coefficient of friction of the floor material, is the primary cause of most slipping accidents. However, designers cannot control contaminants; they can only anticipate them and try to get a coefficient of friction high enough to make up for their presence.

The slip-resistance requirement for floor polishes referenced previously is an industry standard that is easily met by many products, so no harm is done by including it in specifications. Specifying slip-resistance requirements for brick, such as static coefficients of friction of at least 0.6 where used on level surfaces and 0.8 where used on ramps when tested according to ASTM C 1028, however, will definitely limit selection; some argue that it is overly cautious. The specifier has to decide whether ADAAG has established a reasonable standard of care and whether to include the slip-resistance requirement in a specification.

INSTALLATION METHODS

Various installation methods are shown in figures 1 through 4. For reinforced brick, see figure 5 and Table 1.

Loose-laid applications are commonly chosen for exterior brick paving, but can also be used for interiors. They must, however, be sealed to prevent moisture and dirt from penetrating hand-tight joints.

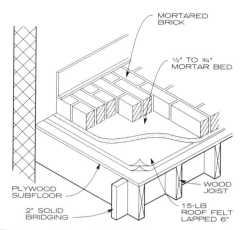

Figure 1. Mortared brick flooring on wood framing

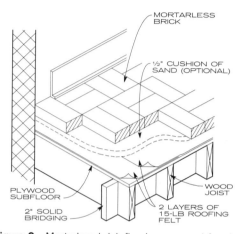

Figure 2. Mortarless brick flooring on wood framing

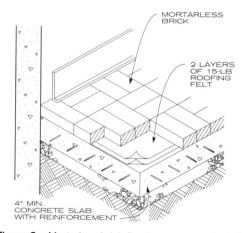

Figure 3. Morterless brick flooring on concrete slabs

Thick-set mortared applications include several methods ranging from brick wet-set in a workable mortar bed to brick set on a cured mortar bed. With either application, the dry mortar ingredients for the cement-paste bond coat, setting bed, bond coat, or any combination can be mixed with water alone or with a latex additive in the form of a water emulsion substituted for part or all of the gaging water. Brick can be installed in a thick-set mortar bed by the bricklayer's or tilesetter's method. With the

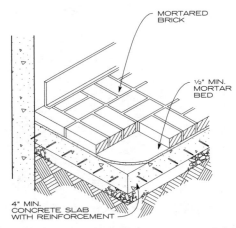

Figure 4. Mortared brick flooring on concrete slab

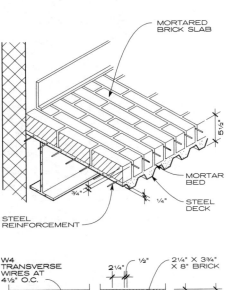

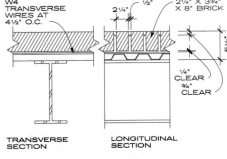

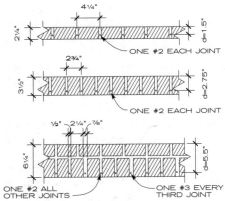

Figure 5. Reinforced brick flooring

Table 1.
REINFORCED BRICK MASONRY SLABS

LIVE LOAD (PSF)	MAXIMUM CLEAR SPAN		
	$t =2\,^1/_4$ IN. 1 #2 EACH JOINT	$t =3\,^1/_2$ IN. 1 #2 EACH JOINT	$t =6\,^1/_4$ IN. 1 #3 EVERY 3RD JOINT 1 #2 OTHER JOINTS
30	6'- 10"	10'- 5"	14'- 5"
40	6'- 3"	9'- 9"	13'- 8"
50	5'- 10"	9'- 2"	13'- 1"
100	4'- 6"	7'- 3"	10'- 11"
250	1'- 10"	5'- 0"	7'- 10"

NOTES

1. Design parameters for the table above: The compressive strength average of the brick is 8000 psi. The mortar is type M (1:$^1/_4$:3), portland cement:lime:sand. Reinforcement steel is ASTM A 82, f_s = 20,000 psi. A simple span loading condition was assumed.

$$M = \frac{wl^2}{8}$$

2. All mortar joints are $^1/_2$ in. thick for the slabs shown, except as noted.

bricklayer's method, mortar is spread on the sides of the brick as it is set, eliminating the need to grout joints after the brick has been laid. With the tilesetter's method, the brick is set with spaced joints grouted after the brick has been laid.

A thick-set mortar bed can accommodate limited unevenness and rough subfloor surfaces and can be used to create a slope to drains. It also allows the installation of a cleavage membrane to separate the setting bed from the subfloor, which, according to American National Standards Institute (ANSI) tile installation standards and the Tile Council of America's (TCA's) *Handbook for Ceramic Tile Installation,* should be used for structural slabs subject to bending and deflection. Assuming that good practices for tile installation also apply to brick flooring, bonded thick-set setting beds should be limited to applications over slabs-on-grade, to slabs where deflection does not exceed $^1/_{360}$ of the span, and to well-cured slabs of a limited area. Installing brick flooring in a workable mortar bed, as opposed to installing it on a cured mortar bed, also allows for adjustment for variations in brick dimensions when bricks are tamped and beat into place.

Latex additives provide better adhesion between the brick and the setting bed and more flexibility than portland cement mortars without latex additives. However, Brick Institute of America (BIA) Technical Notes 14A advises that brick should be tested for compatibility with such mortars because not all bricks perform well with latex-portland cement mortar. Because there are many latex-additive formulations, the latex-additive manufacturer's written instructions should be followed for materials and proportions used to produce mortar. Formulations containing separate retarders should be avoided. For more information on latex mortars and grouts containing latex additives, see Chapter 09310, Ceramic Tile.

Major disadvantages of thick-set setting beds include a greater overall thickness of floor construction, the additional dead load that the structure must be designed to support, coordination problems associated with varying the top of slab elevations needed to accommodate differing floor finishes, and increased material and labor costs. Where floors are sloped for drainage or other purposes, these slopes should usually be built into the subfloor, not created by varying the setting-bed thickness.

Thin-set mortar bed applications require closer control over subfloor tolerances and surface finishes than do thick-set applications. Specify the qualities required for the subfloor in the specification sections that specify the subfloor construction. For both bonded thick-set and thin-set applications, curing agents or sealers should not be applied to concrete subfloors.

Joint treatments for brick set in either thick-set or thin-set mortar beds include both grout-filled and hand-tight joints where a dry mixture of portland cement and sand is swept into the joints and set by fogging with water. Grout can be a job-mixed portland cement and aggregate mixture either pigmented or with color achieved by using natural color or white cement and white or colored aggregates; grout can also be a packaged formulation incorporating pigments. Where grout colors cannot be obtained by selecting cement and aggregates, the packaged grout products provide better color uniformity than pigments added to job-mixed sand and cement grout. Latex additives in grout enhance color retention and stain resistance. They also lessen the need for damp curing under dry conditions.

REFERENCES

Publication dates cited here were current at the time of this writing. Publications are revised periodically, and revisions may have occurred before this book was published.

American National Standards Institute

ANSI A108 Series (A108.1A, .1B, .1C, .4, .5, .6, .8, .9, .10, and .11-1992): Specifications for Installation of Ceramic Tile

ASTM International

ASTM C 67-97: Test Methods of Sampling and Testing Brick and Structural Clay Tile

ASTM C 88-99: Test Method for Soundness of Aggregates by Use of Sodium Sulfate or Magnesium Sulfate

ASTM C 418-98: Test Method for Abrasion Resistance of Concrete by Sandblasting

ASTM C 902-95: Specification for Pedestrian and Light-Traffic Paving Brick

ASTM C 1028-89: Test Method for Determining the Static Coefficient of Friction of Ceramic Tile and Other Like Surfaces by the Horizontal Dynamometer Pull-Meter Method

ASTM D 2047-82 (reapproved 1988): Test Method for Static Coefficient of Friction of Polish-Coated Floor Surfaces as Measured by the James Machine

Brick Institute of America.

Technical Notes 14A: Brick Floors and Pavements-Part II, Revised 1993.

Tile Council of America

Handbook for Ceramic Tile Installation, 1995.

United States Architectural & Transportation Barriers Compliance Board

ADAAG: Accessibility Guidelines for Buildings and Facilities, adopted in 1991; continual revisions.

WEB SITE

Brick Institute of America: www.bia.org

09636 CHEMICAL-RESISTANT BRICK FLOORING

This chapter discusses *chemical-resistant brick flooring installed with mortars, grouts, and setting beds that offer varying degrees of chemical protection.*

This chapter does not discuss *chemical-resistant carbon brick, chemical-setting silicate mortars, or exterior brick paving; or brick flooring used primarily for aesthetic reasons.*

GENERAL COMMENTS

The brick and setting materials covered in this chapter include special flooring products and installation methods that have varying resistance to chemicals, absorption, and mechanical and thermal shock. Chemical-resistant brick is characterized by low water- absorption rates (typically from 1 to 7 percent) that result from higher kiln temperatures than those used in making standard paving and interior floor brick.

Chemical-resistant brick flooring is used for sanitary and industrial applications. Besides thermal and mechanical shock resistance required for both applications, the sanitary floor requires resistance to degradation from spilled food products and chemical cleaning agents. Mild and less-severe chemical environments include floors in food processing (manufacturing and preparation), food serving, and dairy product processing. Spaces within these facilities require cleanup and sterilization areas that also extend to public toilets and employee toilet and change rooms. Brick and tile floors in these spaces require additional attention to design details to minimize bacterial growth and to control contaminants.

The industrial floor must often resist aggressive chemicals used in manufacturing processes, such as in the chemical and metalworking industries. Severe chemical exposure can be complicated in some industrial brick floor applications, such as metal manufacturing plants, where extremely corrosive acids in liquid and gas forms are used or created in the production process. If the facility falls in this exposure category, then the owner should seek expert advise from a corrosion specialist accredited by the National Association of Corrosion Engineers.

FLOOR BRICK

Chemical-resistant brick is included in two ASTM specifications: ASTM C 279 for chemical-resistant masonry units, which includes both brick and tile, and ASTM C 410 for industrial floor brick.

ASTM C 279 for chemical-resistant masonry units includes both brick and tile produced as kiln-fired solid units from clay, shale, or a mixture of both. Brick for a specific application may be selected from three performance categories, Types I, II, and III, listed in Table 1 in the standard. Warpage tolerances (Table 2 in the standard) indicate a maximum permissible warpage by face size, based on sampling methods in ASTM C 67. Applications suitable for the three types are described in the standard as follows:

- **Type I:** For use where low absorption and high acid resistance are not major factors.

- **Type II:** For use where lower absorption and higher acid resistance are required.
- **Type III:** For use where minimum absorption and maximum acid resistance are required.

Note that the standard's only requirement for chemical resistance is based on resistance to boiling sulfuric acid. While this may serve as a good general indicator of chemical resistance, it may be necessary to verify the suitability of units when severe exposure to other chemicals is anticipated.

ASTM C 410 is limited to industrial floor brick and does not include quarry tile. Industrial floor brick may be manufactured from clay, shale, or mixtures of both, and are classified by the standard into four types. Differing industrial applications and end uses have diverse requirements for physical properties and chemical resistance, which requires different types of floor brick to meet these needs. Applications suitable for the four types are described in the standard as follows:

- **Type T:** For use where a high degree of resistance to thermal and mechanical shock is required but low absorption is not.
- **Type H:** For use where resistance to chemicals and thermal shock are service factors but where low absorption is not required.
- **Type M:** For use where low absorption is required. Brick of this type are normally characterized by limited mechanical (impact) shock resistance but are often highly resistant to abrasion.
- **Type L:** For use where minimal absorption and a high degree of chemical resistance are required. Brick of this type are normally characterized by very limited thermal and limited mechanical (impact) shock resistance but are highly resistant to abrasion.

Note that the standard does not have actual requirements for thermal or mechanical shock or abrasion resistance and that its requirement for chemical resistance is based solely on resistance to boiling sulfuric acid. For conditions anticipated to be severe, it may be necessary to verify the suitability of units to the applications. Also note that the chemical resistance and water-absorption requirements for Types H and L are similar to those of ASTM C 279 for Types I and III, respectively.

Brick colors produced from shale are limited for the kinds of brick covered in this chapter, with red being the predominant color available. Chemical-resistant brick can also be made with fireclay, which produces beige bricks.

Traffic surfaces of floor brick include a smooth surface and several textures intended to improve slip resistance when wet or otherwise coated with a slippery substance. Many slip-resistant surfaces increase cleaning difficulty. Scored surfaces are more vulnerable to wear, chippage, and build-up of dirt and corrosive substances than surfaces incorporating an abrasive aggregate. The abrasive aggregate may, however, be vulnerable to certain chemicals. Vertical-fiber brick, which may no longer be available, is difficult to clean, particularly where oil or greasy conditions exist.

Floor brick thickness is typically 1¾₁₆, 1⅜, or 1½ inches (30, 35, or 38 mm) where only foot and forklift traffic is expected. Where heavy truck traffic is expected, 2¼-inch (57-mm) thickness is typically used; and where severe physical abuse is anticipated, 3¾- or 4½-inch (95- or 114-mm) thickness is used. Thicker units provide increased resistance to thermal shock and increased thermal protection to waterproofing membranes, as well as the capability to withstand higher loads. Shipping costs for thicker units will be more than for thinner units, but material and installation costs may not be much higher.

Base and trim units are produced from the same material as flooring units by most manufacturers. Available base units include the turn-up type with a pitched edge at vertical surfaces, which is usually selected where the floor is installed against existing walls.

MORTAR AND GROUT

Setting bed and joints are often different materials in order to optimize floor system properties and costs. For less-severe exposures, hydraulic-cement setting beds and resin-grouted joints may be adequate but are generally not recommended by chemical-resistant mortar and grout manufacturers. For food-processing plants, where the severity of attack is minimal to moderate, epoxy-mortar setting beds are often used with furan resin-grouted joints.

Hydraulic-cement mortars (portland cements) generally have inadequate or borderline resistance to most chemicals. ASTM C 398, Table 1, shows the relative resistance of each form of hydraulic cement (i.e., portland cement, portland blast-furnace slag cement, and calcium aluminate cement) to various aqueous solutions. Relative resistance is rated in Table 1 by the following: N—*not recommended,* G—*generally recommended,* and L—*limited use.* If hydraulic cement mortar does not provide the degree of chemical resistance required for a given application, other more chemical-resistant materials, including underlayments and membranes, should be considered.

Resin mortars include furan-, epoxy-, phenolic-, polyester-, and vinyl-ester-based formulations. Resin grouts include epoxy- and furan-based formulations. ASTM C 395 specifies physical properties for chemical-resistant resin mortars but sets no requirements for chemical resistance. This standard notes that the chemical resistance of these mortars is best determined by ASTM C 267, which is a test method, not a specification. When using these mortars, either specify a mortar type or manufacturer's brand known to provide the required chemical resistance, or specify the chemical resistance that is required based on testing according to ASTM C 267. Generally, epoxy and furan resin mortars are used for typical applications; formulations containing phenolic, polyester, and vinyl-ester resins are limited to special applications. Installation practices for chemical-resistant resin mortars are listed in ASTM C 399.

Chemical resistance is affected by the choice of filler, which can be silica, carbon, or a carbon-silica blend. The practice for use is in ASTM C 397. Carbon fillers are required where resistance to strong alkaline or acid-fluoride chemicals is needed.

While resin mortars combined with industrial brick provide a relatively impervious floor, the joints are vulnerable to movement that could cause cracks to develop (particularly under thermal shock), and the brick can become saturated if exposed to liquids for a long time.

Furan mortars are based on furfuryl alcohol and are resistant to a range of chemicals including nonoxidizing acids, alkalis, salts, gases, oils, greases, detergents, and most solvents at temperatures of up to 375°F (190°C). Certain formulations are capable of resisting temperatures as high as 430°F (220°C) for continuous exposure and 475°F (245°C) for intermittent exposure.

Using a carbon filler in place of the more common silica filler increases resistance to hydrofluoric acid, fluoride salts, and strong hot alkalis. Furan mortars are thermally sensitive during installation, and the temperature range in installation areas must be carefully controlled. Batches must be mixed in small quantities and used within 20 minutes, and may require cooling in hot weather.

Staining of brick by furan mortar during installation can be a severe problem unless exposed brick surfaces are coated with a temporary paraffin wax protective coating that is removed after the mortar is cured.

Unlike epoxies, furan mortar will not develop a good chemical bond with concrete because of a reaction with the chemical hardening agent. This causes depletion of the hardening agent and prevents the contact surfaces from curing. It can be resolved by applying a barrier coating or a membrane, which allows the mortar to cure, but no effective bond will develop with the substrate except for that obtained from the mechanical adhesion with surface irregularities. For similar reasons, furan mortar does not adhere to metal.

Epoxy mortars possess not only excellent physical and mechanical properties but also offer excellent resistance to nonoxidizing acids and alkalis. Their resistance to solvents, however, is not outstanding. Epoxy formulations are available to resist temperatures through 140°F (60°C) for continuous exposure and up to 212°F (100°C) for intermittent exposure.

Unlike furan, epoxies can be applied directly to concrete. They also adhere well to most surfaces and shrink little on hardening. These qualities may be particularly important in food plants where the severity of attack on joints is typically low and the major concern is preventing ingredients from falling through fine cracks or joint openings and fermenting below the brick flooring.

Epoxy resins are not resistant to oxidizing agents. They are resistant to acetic acid to about 10 percent concentration, which is higher than most vinegars found in food plants. Epoxies are available with carbon fillers. Joints filled with epoxy mortars or grouts should not be subjected to hot water or steam jet cleaning, as either can have an eroding effect.

For food-plant floors, the system often selected uses an epoxy mortar for the setting bed and either a furan mortar or grout for joints, depending on whether the bricklayer's or tilesetter's installation method is used. For vertical applications, such as walls and cove bases, only mortars are feasible because grout would flow out of joints. Epoxies are available in water-cleanable formulations that do not require prewaxing the face of the brick.

Polyester mortars have a more limited resistance range than furan mortars, and set shrinkage is greater than with other resin-based products. Though seldom used in flooring, their high resistance to mild oxidizing agents, such as chlorine dioxide and other bleaches, provides good protection for linings of bleaching vessels, particularly in the pulp and paper industry. Vinyl-ester mortars have similar chemical resistance and uses as polyester mortars but are not as rigid. Vinyl-ester grouts are often used with brick set in epoxy or cement mortar for floors in food-and-beverage plants, where the grout's resistance to cleaning products that contain bleach is required.

Sulfur mortars are hot-melt materials, specified in ASTM C 287, with chemical resistance determined by testing according to ASTM C 267. Sulfur mortars have limited resistance to most oils and petroleum derivatives. When carbon filled, they provide protection against nonoxidizing acids and nitric-hydrofluoric acid. Sulfur mortar has low heat resistance; that is, above 190°F (88°C) it will crumble and fall out; and its resistance to alkaline, polysulfide solutions and many organic solvents, phenol-related organic chemicals, and aromatic compounds and solvents is poor.

The appearance of sulfur-mortar installations is always rough and unattractive because of overpour at joints. Cutting, scraping, or hot-iron trimming of joints is neither practical nor cost-effective. Excess mortar is normally left to wear away with use unless it projects enough to be a tripping hazard, in which case it is chipped back until it is flush with the rest of the floor. Sulfur-mortar joints are used in extreme exposures of cleaning stainless steel in nitric-hydrofluoric-acid pickling vessels.

ACCESSORY MATERIALS

The most common protective membrane is a ¼-inch- (6.4-mm-) thick, fabric-reinforced, hot-applied asphaltic underlayment. This membrane offers a corrosion-resistant barrier to liquids other than strong solvents; it also acts as a permanently resilient cushion between the concrete subfloor and the setting bed.

Other types of membranes may be required for specific subfloor protection. Membranes must be placed on concrete subfloors with a positive slope, minimum ¼ inch per foot (1:50), for drainage to internal or perimeter drains.

Concrete slabs on grade and elevated concrete floor construction that are potentially subject to severe attack should be protected by a membrane. The floor finish is the chemical-resistant flooring (the brick and resin mortar) that protects the membrane.

Expansion joints in chemical-resistant floors are typically sealed with flexible epoxies, urethane, urethane-asphalt copolymer, polysulfide, or silicone sealants. Before selecting a sealant, the potential choices should be tested for chemical resistance, compatibility with mortars and grouts, adhesion, compression, and resistance to anticipated traffic conditions. Silicones should not be used in submerged conditions, since they would lose adhesion. In sanitary applications, the backer rod should be closed-cell or semirigid polyethylene construction, to minimize the potential for absorption.

PRODUCT SELECTION CONSIDERATIONS

Determine the chemical severity and nature of the corrosive conditions anticipated by obtaining information on the chemical agent or combination of agents that will contact the flooring. The form (liquid, dry solid, wet solid, dry gas, moist gas), concentration, temperature or temperature range, condition (stationary or flowing), and duration of exposure (intermittent or continuous) for the various chemical agents must be known before selecting suitable materials. Obtain this information in writing from a knowledgeable person within the owner's organization or from a consultant whose recommendations are approved by the owner. Where more than one corrosive material is anticipated, the documentation should be explicit about each location involved.

The owner's data must include areas exposed to cleaning compounds, especially those with a solvent base. Cleaning practices are frequently overlooked, and floor surfaces capable of performing well under normal conditions may fail prematurely due to maintenance procedures.

The availability of special materials and experienced mechanics to install the products should be considered, in addition to chemical resistance, appearance, and material costs.

The physical and mechanical properties of the flooring system, including the resistance to abrasion and thermal and mechanical shock, must be taken into account when selecting brick flooring, mortar, grouts, and expansion-joint materials.

Where food and pharmaceutical products are handled or manufactured, the spaces with brick flooring and synthetic-resin-based mortars and grouts typically require product approval of mortars and grouts by the Food and Drug Administration, and approval of state and local health authorities.

In remodeling and expanding existing facilities, choose chemical-resistant materials that do not emit toxic vapors or obnoxious odors. Some epoxy and phenolic formulations may cause severe reactions on contact. Occupied schools, hospitals, food plants, restaurants, and similar facilities are examples of situations where special precautions are required to protect occupants from the effects of such systems during installation.

INSTALLATION METHODS

Before detailing or specifying chemical-resistant brick flooring, the architect should collect data from the owner on the type of in-service exposures involved, then determine, with manufacturers' advice, the brick type, setting bed, joint, and expansion-joint materials that will provide optimum resistance to the expected conditions.

The typical subfloor for chemical-resistant brick flooring is reinforced cast-in-place concrete. The type of concrete finish and surface preparation must be compatible with the protective membrane or setting bed. This could vary from a wood float finish for one type of membrane to a single-pass steel trowel finish for another. With an epoxy or polyester setting bed, a wood float finish, without depressions, is generally required. Do not use air-entraining agents, curing compounds, or other concrete additives that may interfere with the bond of the setting system selected. Most chemical-resistant brick floorings require control of liquids to internal or perimeter drains; therefore, the flooring and subfloor require a minimum slope of ¼ inch per foot (1:50).

Internal drains must have weep holes in the body section that intersect and receive the membrane, and the tops of drains need to be set ⅛ inch (3 mm) below the surface of the floor. Selecting proper floor drains for above-grade slabs in wet conditions cannot be overemphasized. Additionally, above-grade watertight concrete slab joints must be provided with continuous waterstops and seals that will not deteriorate under anticipated chemical conditions.

The use of bricks with scored or grooved backs have created some controversy among manufacturers of resin setting-bed materials. Deeply scored or grooved backs increase the possibility of creating voids in the setting bed. Voids can trap corrosive, organic, or odor-causing liquids and bacteria, which can lead to costly floor repairs. Buttering and filling the grooved backs of these units can help prevent this condition, and buttering is typically required to improve bond for thick, grooved and thin, nongrooved floor tile units.

A continuous base should be considered for above-grade floors to contain liquid spillage. Cove bases are offered in two different shapes, square top and round top. Select the former where recessing the exposed face of the base with the finished surface of the wall above is possible, and the latter where recessing it is impossible.

Sanitary-type base selection is typically governed by local or state health requirements that may allow only the flush or recessed type. Stretcher units and trim shapes are available for wall surfaces, pit and trench linings, double-coved curbs.

The industrial floor system uses a chemical-resistant membrane to protect the subfloor from strong corrosive exposure and to provide moisture protection. Common applications are meat-packing facilities and dairies. Positive floor drainage is required for both the subfloor and floor surface. The asphaltic primer and hot-laid membrane products are not roofing asphalt, nor should they be applied by a roofing or water-protection installer, but by the mason or tilesetter. Brick is laid immediately after the membrane cools. Chemical-resistant mortar is used to set the brick either by buttering the sides and back of each brick (bricklayer's method) or by placing the units in the mortar bed without filled joints and then grout-filling the vertical joints after setting (tilesetter's method).

In the food-plant floor system, the bricks are typically set in an epoxy-resin-based mortar directly on the floor slab. Either the bricklayer's or tilesetter's method can be used with head joints filled with epoxy resin or furan mortar or grout. No chemical-resistant membrane is used in this system; however, where moisture penetration is a concern, require a membrane that will function as a water-protection membrane separate from the chemical-resistant floor system.

Expansion joints for most applications are ⅝-inch (16-mm) wide, spaced at 20 feet (6 m) o.c., which allows for about ¼ inch (6 mm) of movement. Expansion joints are required at vertical intersections, curbs, and perimeter walls, and directly above subfloor expansion and control joints.

Details for expansion joints require that mortar is completely removed to the base of supporting concrete slab. The inside face of intersecting joints and surfaces must be mortared or grouted full with straight edges and without voids. A continuous backer rod must be installed to support the sealant without allowing the sealant to adhere to the backer rod.

REFERENCES

Publication dates cited here were current at the time of this writing. Publications are revised periodically, and revisions may have occurred before this book was published.

ASTM International

ASTM C 67-99a: Test Methods for Sampling and Testing Brick and Structural Clay Tile

ASTM C 267-97: Test Methods for Chemical Resistance of Mortars, Grouts, and Monolithic Surfacings and Polymer Concretes

ASTM C 279-88 (reapproved 1995): Specification for Chemical-Resistant Masonry Units

ASTM C 287-93a: Specification for Chemical-Resistant Sulfur Mortar

ASTM C 395-95: Specification for Chemical-Resistant Resin Mortars

ASTM C 397-94: Practice for Use of Chemically Setting Chemical-Resistant Silicate and Silica Mortars

ASTM C 398-93: Practice for Use of Hydraulic Cement Mortars in Chemical-Resistant Masonry

ASTM C 399-93: Practice for Use of Chemical-Resistant Resin Mortars

ASTM C 410-60 (reapproved 1992): Specification for Industrial Floor Brick

09638 STONE PAVING AND FLOORING

This chapter discusses dimension stone paving and flooring installed on a thick, mortar setting bed.

The chapter does not discuss dimension stone tile for interior flooring and stone facing on vertical surfaces, which are included in Chapter 09385, Dimension Stone Tile. Rough stone pavers (cobblestones), which are usually specified in a section in Division 2, "Site Construction," and stone paving set in an aggregate setting bed also are not covered here.

GENERAL COMMENTS

Selecting dimension stone for paving and flooring is, for the most part, based on color, texture, finish, durability, and water absorption. In this chapter, the terms *paving* and *flooring* refer, respectively, to exterior and interior installations. Associated with surface durability and finish is slip resistance, which is difficult to define but is discussed later in this chapter. A polished finish is suitable for flooring, although a honed finish may be more appropriate where heavy traffic would wear or abrade a polished surface. A polished or honed finish may be suitable for paving or flooring that is usually dry; paving or flooring that is subject to frequent wetting may need a rougher finish for better slip resistance.

Combining different varieties of stone and different finishes seems to be in fashion, but should not be done indiscriminately. Combining stone varieties with different abrasion resistance, such as a hard granite with a softer stone, will result in one wearing faster than the other. The lesser worn of the two stone varieties will emphasize the wear of the other; when refinishing becomes necessary, it will be complicated by the fact that the two stone varieties may require different refinishing techniques. For best results, where contrast is desired, use varieties that do not differ in abrasion-resistance value by more than five points and that, preferably, are from the same stone group.

Combining different finishes also has its problems. If a floor polish or wax is used on polished stone that is adjacent to thermal-finished or other rough-finished stone, the floor polish will invariably get on the rough-finished stone and make it look dirty. Even if a floor polish or wax is not specified or recommended initially, the owner's maintenance staff might use such products eventually. Also, when the polished floor requires refinishing, it will be difficult to avoid damaging the rough-finished stone with the grinding and polishing equipment. For paving, combining a honed finish with a thermal finish is not a problem because waxing and refinishing are generally not done.

Abrasion resistance, which is a stone's capability to resist wear, and absorption, which relates to a stone's capability to resist soiling and staining as well as the effects of weather, should be considered when selecting a stone variety for paving or flooring. A history of successful use in a similar environment and application is also a good indicator of a stone's suitability for a particular project. The visual qualities (color, texture, and finish) of stone for a specific project are usually best determined by selecting from available choices offered by a reputable source. Local fabricators and suppliers are usually helpful in finding suitable varieties.

CHARACTERISTICS OF DIMENSION STONE

Dimension stone is defined in ASTM C 119, *Terminology Relating to Natural Building Stones,* as "natural stone that has been selected, trimmed, or cut to specified or indicated shapes or sizes, with or without one or more mechanically dressed surfaces." *Cut stone* is defined as "stone fabricated to specific dimensions." Dimension stone is further classified as thin stone if less than 2-inches (51-mm) thick and is often called *cubic stone* if thickness is 2 inches (51 mm) or more.

Geologists classify stone based on chemical composition, structure, and method of formation. Although this type of classification is helpful in understanding the nature of the material, it has limited value to architects or others whose primary interest is in using stone as a building material. There are many geological classifications of stone, each separated by subtle distinctions. At the other extreme is the classification of stone by common names, which are vague and ill-defined but at least widely recognized.

ASTM C 119 begins with common name classifications for the principal stones, including those intended for building construction, and provides definitions for the classifications. Unfortunately, many of these classifications are not always well understood by the quarriers, fabricators, and others in the stone trade. This misunderstanding occurs partly because ASTM definitions are based on common names, which are associated with the common-usage meanings of these terms, and partly because ASTM C 119 definitions are not exact. ASTM C 119 classifies dimension stone into six groups: granite, limestone, marble, quartz-based dimension stone, slate, and other stone.

GRANITE

Granite is defined in ASTM C 119 as "visibly granular, igneous rock ranging in color from pink to light or dark gray and consisting mostly of quartz and feldspars, accompanied by one or more dark minerals. The texture is typically homogeneous but may be gneissic or porphyritic. Some dark granular igneous rocks, though not geologically granite, are included in the definition." Gneissic texture refers to an arrangement of crystals somewhat separated into alternating layers of different minerals or mineral groups. Porphyritic texture refers to an arrangement of large crystals of one mineral with the spaces between them filled with smaller crystals of other minerals. Geologists limit the term *granite* to crystalline plutonic rocks (igneous rocks that formed beneath the earth's surface) with 20 to 60 percent quartz, 20 to 80 percent feldspar (with at least 35 percent of the feldspar being alkali feldspar), and no more than 20 percent dark minerals. The commercial term *granite* includes rocks containing other proportions of these ingredients and is referred to by geologists as granodiorite, syenite, monzonite, diorite, gabbro, foyaite, essexite, diabase, picrite, and gneiss (pronounced "nice").

The National Building Granite Quarries Association (NBGQA) classifies domestic granites offered by association members according to color and grain characteristics, but specifying them by these terms alone is not usually adequate and selection is best controlled by specifying one or more

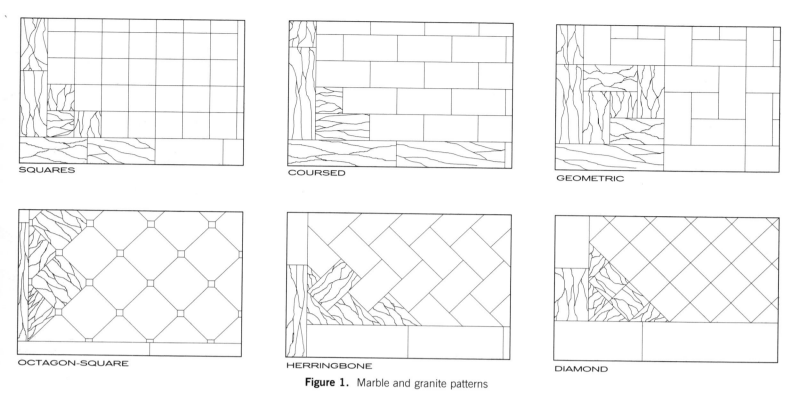

Figure 1. Marble and granite patterns

sources. To maximize competition while retaining control of the appearance, investigate as many stone sources as possible and name all that are found acceptable in the specifications. An alternative procedure is to specify that the stone must match the architect's sample and be submitted for approval before bidding.

All varieties of granite make good stone paving and flooring. Granite has high compressive strength, good abrasion resistance, and low absorption. It is available in many finishes, including polished, honed, and thermal. Polished granite is very resistant to wear, including scratching and dulling of the finish; however, such wear will usually occur given enough time. Doormats help retain the polished finish by removing abrasives, such as sand, from the feet of those who walk on the stone floor. Waxes and polishes can also protect the finish, but removing and renewing them may cause more abrasion than would occur without their use. Remember that although the polished finish on granite lasts longer than a polished finish on marble or other stone, it is not permanent. Also, be aware that because

granite is so much harder than marble, regrinding and repolishing a granite floor can be more difficult and expensive than repolishing a marble floor.

Some rough fieldstone that is not a true granite, but is physically similar, is suitable for use as paving if it has a reasonably high compressive strength, a suitable abrasion resistance, and a low water absorption. Much of this stone is a highly metamorphosed schist (also called a *gneiss*), which still retains some schistocity (tendency to split) that enables it to be split into flagstones. It usually varies in color and is available as a mixture of split-face stone (stone with a clean, newly split face) and seam-face stone (stone that has been split along a dry seam where it is usually stained brown by iron oxides). Some of this stone, especially when quarried near the surface or near fissures in the quarry, can be too soft to be used for paving or flooring, but testing or a history of previous successful use can determine whether a particular source provides suitable material. With some of this stone, it may be necessary to cull out the softer material when it is quarried or installed.

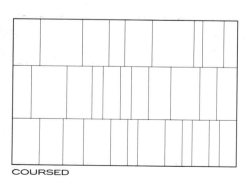

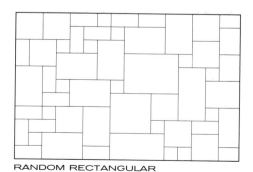

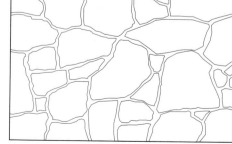

Figure 2. Flagstone and slate patterns

LIMESTONE

ASTM C 119 defines *limestone,* as a group, as "a rock of sedimentary origin composed principally of calcium carbonate (the mineral calcite), or the double carbonate of calcium and magnesium (the mineral dolomite), or a combination of these two minerals."

ASTM C 568 further classifies limestone dimension stone into three categories based on density and other physical properties: Classifications I (Low-Density), II (Medium-Density), and III (High-Density). The classifications are arbitrarily defined and do not necessarily signify a difference in quality or durability, although a higher classification indicates a stronger, less porous stone. Indiana limestone and most other calcitic limestones used as dimension stone are Classification II; dolomitic limestones are Classification III or at the high end of Classification II.

Oolitic limestone, such as Indiana limestone, consists of calcite-cemented calcareous rock formed from precipitated lime, shell fragments, and shells and is practically noncrystalline. Oolites are spheroidal particles formed from shell fragments or sand grains that are coated in concentric layers with precipitated lime. Oolitic limestone is primarily made of small oolites cemented together with precipitated lime.

Dolomitic limestone is somewhat crystalline and stronger than oolitic limestone. Dolomite forms when magnesium-bearing water, such as seawater, replaces the calcium in calcitic limestone with magnesium. This magnesium replacement (dolomitization) can occur during the formation of the limestone or afterward. When the dolomitization takes place after the limestone is already formed, textural characteristics, such as stratification and fossils, are obliterated; the crystals formed are larger; and the stone is more porous. Dolomitic limestone can usually be polished and then marketed commercially as marble.

For flooring applications, dolomitic limestone with a honed finish is frequently used, as is oolitic limestone with a smooth-machined finish. For dolomitic limestone flooring, a honed finish is usually preferred to a polished finish because it does not generally show wear. For paving applications, split-face limestone is used as is smooth-machined or honed material. Soft, low-density limestones, such as shell limestones, are generally not used for paving or flooring because they are subject to excessive wear.

MARBLE

Marble, **as a group, is defined in ASTM C 119** as comprising "a variety of compositional and textural types, ranging from pure carbonate to rocks containing very little carbonate that are classed commercially as marble (for example, serpentine marble)" and "must be capable of taking a polish." ASTM C 503 classifies marble dimension stone into four categories: I Calcite, II Dolomite, III Serpentine, and IV Travertine. Each category is assigned a minimum density value under physical requirements. ASTM C 503 refers to ASTM C 119 for definitions of calcite, dolomite, serpentine, and travertine marble, but ASTM C 119 uses five categories: marble, limestone marble, onyx marble, serpentine marble, and travertine marble.

The Marble Institute of America (MIA) classifies marble varieties for soundness according to fabrication characteristics, as demonstrated from experience, and not on each stone's physical properties. The four classifications listed here are quoted from MIA's *Dimensional Stone-Design Manual IV:*

- **Group A:** Sound marbles with uniform and favorable working qualities; containing no geological flaws or voids.
- **Group B:** Marbles similar in character to the preceding group, but with

less favorable working qualities; may have natural faults; a limited amount of waxing, sticking, and filling may be required.

- **Group C:** Marbles with some variations in working qualities; geological flaws, voids, veins, and lines of separation are common. It is standard practice to repair these variations by one or more of several methods-waxing, sticking, filling, or cementing. Liners and other forms of reinforcement are used when necessary.
- **Group D:** Marbles similar to the preceding group, but containing larger proportion of natural faults, maximum variations in working qualities, and requiring more of the same methods of finishing. This group comprises many of the highly colored marbles prized for their decorative values.

Marble is frequently used for stone flooring and occasionally for stone paving. As with dolomitic limestone, a honed finish is usually preferred for marble pavements and floors to avoid showing wear, although a polished finish is often used on floors. Note that ASTM C 503 is for exterior marble (no standard currently exists for interior marble) and that many varieties of marble in commercial use will not comply with this standard. For flooring, it is not critical that marble comply with ASTM C 503; and for exterior use, where stone is exposed to freezing and thawing, even compliance with the standard will not guarantee durability. Refer to the discussion of stone durability in this chapter for information on testing for resistance to freezing and thawing.

Green marble, which is usually serpentine and not actually marble according to geologists, has a tendency to warp when exposed to moisture. For this reason, it should not be used for flooring in wet or damp areas or in areas where it will become wet. It should also not be set in a portland cement mortar, rather in a setting material that does not contain water, such as a water-cleanable epoxy adhesive or epoxy mortar. The owner's maintenance staff should be instructed not to allow water to stand on the floor when green marble is being cleaned.

QUARTZ-BASED STONE

ASTM C 119 does not define quartz-based stone as a group; it defines three subdivisions. From the three definitions, one can ascertain that quartz-based stone is "sedimentary rock composed mostly of mineral and rock fragments within the sand range (from 0.06 to 2 mm) cemented or bonded to a greater or lesser degree by various materials including silica, iron oxides, carbonates, or clay." It is classified as sandstone, quartzitic sandstone, or quartzite, depending on the percentage of silica and the degree of metamorphosis, both generally affect the degree of bonding between the particles. ASTM C 616 gives requirements for each of the three classifications of quartz-based stone, defining each of them further.

Bluestone and Tennessee quartzite are frequently used as flagstone for paving and for rustic interior flooring. They are typically used with a natural-cleft (or split-face) finish, gaged (ground down to a standard nominal thickness) or not. Both are available with a honed finish, squared and cut to size, squared but random-sized, or random-sized and shaped for use in a polygonal pattern. Most other quartz-based stones are too soft to be used as paving or flooring, but some suitable quartzites are found in various regions of the United States. Before specifying, verify that proposed stone varieties have a history of successful use in the project's area, and consult quarries or distributors to determine availability of varieties, finishes, and patterns.

SLATE

Slate **is defined in ASTM C 119** as "microcrystalline metamorphic rock most commonly derived from shale and composed mostly of micas, chlorite, and quartz. The micaceous minerals have a subparallel orientation and thus impart strong cleavage to the rock which allows the latter to be split into thin but tough sheets."

Slate finishes frequently used for paving and flooring are honed, sand-rubbed (roughly smoothed), or natural-cleft. Often, natural-cleft slate is sand rubbed on the backside and gaged for easier installation. For thin-set application, the stone must be gaged. Better results will be obtained if the slate is also gaged for thick-set application. For interior application, slate need not be unfading, but specifying unfading will result in a more durable material. Similarly, specifying exterior grade for interior use will also ensure a higher degree of durability. Specifying exterior grade and unfading quality limits competition and may also limit color selection. Be sure that the selected or desired variety of slate has the qualities that are listed as requirements in the specification before naming the variety.

STONE DURABILITY

Stone is a natural product that is subject to wide variations in physical properties, even when obtained from a single quarry. Physical properties for each of the major stone groups are often established in specifications by reference to applicable ASTM standards. These standards include minimum requirements for the physical properties of each stone group or classification of that stone group. Properties measured by referenced ASTM test methods include water absorption, density, compressive strength, modulus of rupture, abrasion resistance and, sometimes, flexural strength. Except for requirements for abrasion resistance, having these properties comply with the minimum requirements of these ASTM standards is not always critical for durability of stone paving or flooring. For exterior applications, where exposure to freezing and thawing is expected, compliance with applicable ASTM standards will not guarantee durability.

Freezing and thawing cycles can damage stone paving that is naturally vulnerable to such damage due to its permeability, inelasticity, or low compressive strength, or that becomes vulnerable because of the effects of fabrication or conditions after installation. Thermal finishing and bushhammering produce microfractures in the surface of the stone that allow water to be absorbed. If this water is subjected to freezing, surface damage results; for nonabsorbent stone, this damage is limited in depth to approximately that of the microfractures. For more absorbent stone, damage from freeze-thaw weathering can occur when the microfractures become saturated and, through repeated freezing and thawing, progressively deeper. Stone durability also depends on compressive strength because a high compressive strength can help resist the forces of freezing water if the stone is saturated.

Testing for resistance to weathering can also be valuable. Freeze-thaw resistance can be evaluated using a procedure similar to that in ASTM C 666, the freeze-thaw test in ASTM C 67, or by some suitable variation of the sulfate soundness test in ASTM C 88. ASTM C 217 testing can provide useful information about the effects of an acidic environment.

In his book *Stone in Architecture,* Erhard M. Winkler maintains that wet-to-dry strength ratios are indicative of a stone's durability. Wet-to-dry strength ratios can be calculated for compressive strength, flexural strength, or modulus of rupture. For modulus of rupture, Winkler indicates that a wet-to-dry ratio of 70 percent represents good durability and that 80 percent represents excellent durability.

Local experience, however, is the best measure of the durability of a proposed stone. If the stone has been used successfully for similar applications in the project area over a suitable period of time, then it should perform well for the project. If the proposed stone has experienced failures, they should be investigated to determine whether the project's circumstances are significantly different before deciding to use it.

SLIP RESISTANCE

Slip resistance is an area of controversy that affects stone paving and flooring, just as it affects other hard flooring materials. The appendix to the Americans with Disabilities Act (ADA), *Accessibility Guidelines for Buildings and Facilities (ADAAG)* recommends, but does not require, that designers specify materials for flooring surfaces that have a minimum static coefficient of friction of 0.6 for level floors and 0.8 for ramped surfaces; it does not, however, indicate a test method. These values are based on the findings of a research project, sponsored by the United States Architectural & Transportation Barriers Compliance Board (Access Board), that conducted tests involving people with disabilities. The values differ from the 0.5 rating recommended by the Ceramic Tile Institute of America (CTIOA) and specified in ASTM D 2047 which is the standard test method for determining the static coefficient of friction for polish-coated floor surfaces as measured by the James Machine.

A series of tests conducted by Cold Spring Granite, in 1988, provided some interesting information about static coefficients of friction for granite floors. The tests involved four varieties of granite in three finishes (polished, honed, and thermal) that were tested both wet and dry using a horizontal dynamometer pull-meter with each of three shoe sole materials (leather, rubber, and Neolite). Two types of samples were tested: those with no cleaning or treatment and those cleaned with a commercially available floor stripper. The following conclusions can be drawn from the results:

- In general, slip resistance varies more among the different shoe sole materials than among the different stone varieties.
- A thermal finish provides better slip resistance than a polished or honed finish, regardless of stone variety, shoe sole material, or floor condition (wet versus dry). To get a static coefficient of friction of 0.8, a thermal finish must be used, and only certain stone varieties provide that high a value even with a thermal finish.
- On average, a honed finish provides better slip resistance than a polished finish. When tested wet, a honed finish provides better slip resistance than a polished finish tested with the same stone and shoe sole material.
- When tested dry, with rubber or Neolite shoe sole material, a polished finish generally provides better slip resistance than a honed finish. With leather shoe sole material, a honed finish typically provides better slip resistance than a polished finish.
- None of the stone varieties tested provides a static coefficient of friction of 0.5 or higher for all test conditions using either a polished or a honed finish.
- Cleaning typically improves slip resistance.

The various test methods for determining static coefficient of friction also produce different values for the same floor material and finish.

INSTALLATION METHODS

Stone paving and flooring must be installed on a sound structural substrate (fig. 3). Although stone flooring is not subject to the same extreme environmental conditions as stone paving, a durable, thick, mortar setting bed that can resist minor building or substrate movement is still critical to long-term service life. Dimension stone paving and flooring installations for most commercial applications use the thick, reinforced or unreinforced mortar bed over a reinforced-concrete slab. Stone flooring on suspended structures of cast-in-place concrete or composite construction may be impractical because of material thickness and load requirements, but are possible.

Steel framing and wood framing are acceptable substrates for stone paving and flooring only if stiff enough to limit deflection to that which the

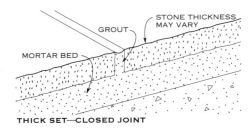

THICK SET—CLOSED JOINT

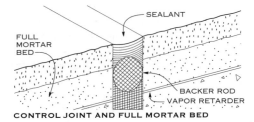

CONTROL JOINT AND FULL MORTAR BED

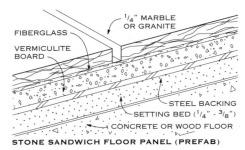

STONE SANDWICH FLOOR PANEL (PREFAB)

Figure 3. Stone flooring

stone can tolerate, usually about 1/720 of the span. Installation over a cleavage membrane would be appropriate for wood framing, but installation of a reinforced setting bed directly on metal deck could be used with steel framing. It is usually more practical, however, to use stone tile, such as that discussed in Chapter 09385, Dimension Stone Tile, with construction other than concrete slabs-on-grade.

A vapor retarder is generally recommended with stone paving, either as a part of the substrate construction or beneath a reinforced setting bed, to prevent water from migrating up into the stone from below and carrying with it dissolved materials that can stain the stone. Although nothing can prevent dissolved materials in the setting bed from getting into the stone, a polyethylene cleavage membrane will prevent dissolved materials in the concrete substrate from staining the stone.

Unit thicknesses for stone paving and flooring range from 3/4 to 2 inches (19 to 50 mm), with face areas up to 48 inches (1200 mm) square, depending on specific stone characteristics. For specific stone size requirements and limitations, consult both fabricators and installers. To achieve a high bond, each floor unit must be cleaned by washing, wetted but not drenched, and the bed side coated with a slurry of portland cement and water (or portland cement and latex emulsion), then immediately set in place. Suggested flooring details can be found in the Marble Institute of America's *Dimension Stone-Design Manual IV.*

Latex additives used in the setting bed and grout have become more and more popular because they generally increase flexural strength of mortar and improve curing by retarding the evaporation of mix water. The stone

industry is now referencing the same American National Standards Institute (ANSI) standards developed for tile setting and grouting materials, but these still do not include a standard for latex additives that are mixed with portland cement and sand at the job site.

Dry-set grouts are mixtures of portland cement and water-retentive additives. They are unsanded and are suitable for joints up to 1/8 inch (3 mm) wide. For larger joints, a sanded grout, such as a commercial portland cement grout, must be used because the sand will reduce shrinkage and help minimize cracking. Sanded grouts should be avoided for polished stone because the sand will scratch the stone as the grout smears are wiped from the surface. Sand from the grout will also come loose as the floor is walked on and will contribute to additional scratching. This problem is more severe with marble, which is much softer than sand, than it is with granite, which has about the same hardness as sand. If large joints are required in polished stone floors, sanded grouts must be used and the inevitable scratching accepted.

Ground-in-place floors were the rule rather than the exception in the recent past. Now they seem to be the exception, but are occasionally still used. Although grinding-in-place eliminates lippage, it does have several disadvantages. First, all the stone used in the floor must be of similar hardness and be otherwise compatible because it will all be ground at the same time. Second, the stone must usually be finished with a fine, honed finish, although a polished finish is sometimes used. Third, skilled and knowledgeable mechanics must be found who are capable of doing this type of stone setting and grinding. Fourth, the process is messy, noisy, and expensive.

To produce a ground-in-place floor, the stone is set in a regular, thick bed but without grouted joints. As the stone units are placed, their edges are wiped with a thin coat of neat cement paste, then the units are tightly butted to the adjoining units, which produces the smallest possible joint and requires accurate fabrication and fitting. If normal grout joints were used, they would be ground deeper than the stone, resulting in unevenness and possible damage to grinding equipment, and would be discolored by the process.

Grinding a floor, as in grinding slabs in the production shop, involves about five separate grinding operations with abrasives ranging in size from 60 to 1,200 grit. The abrasives are usually in the form of ceramic-bonded silicon carbide "bricks" or diamond-impregnated metal or plastic disks. The grinding process uses water to cool the abrasives, to eliminate airborne dust, and to remove the grinding waste. The polishing may simply be an extremely fine grinding operation with a 4,500-grit diamond, or it may be the traditional method, which uses a tin-oxide slurry on a felt buff. For granite, aluminum-oxide polishing powder is often added; for marble, a small amount of oxalic acid added to the polishing medium often produces a higher polish.

STONE SEALERS AND FLOOR POLISHES

Using sealers and polishes on stone paving and flooring is somewhat controversial because of the range of products used for this purpose and the range of results produced. Sealers can prevent moisture penetration and attendant staining, but may require periodic reapplication, which can result in an undesirable buildup. Sealers containing oils may oxidize over time, changing the appearance of the stone, and may cause dirt to adhere to the floor. Sealers used on stone paving may retard moisture evaporation and thereby cause more damage than they prevent. On the positive side, polishes can protect stone from moisture and dirt, increase slip resistance, and help conceal scratches. For these reasons, it is best to use only floor treatments that have been successfully used on stone floors over a reasonable length of time.

REFERENCES

Publication dates cited here were current at the time of this writing. Publications are revised periodically, and revisions may have occurred before this book was published.

ASTM International

ASTM C 67-99a: Test Methods for Sampling and Testing Brick and Structural Clay Tile

ASTM C 88-99a: Test Method for Soundness of Aggregates by Use of Sodium Sulfate or Magnesium Sulfate

ASTM C 119-99: Terminology Relating to Dimension Stone

ASTM C 215-97: Test Method for Fundamental Transverse, Longitudinal, and Torsional Frequencies of Concrete Specimens

ASTM C 217-94 (reapproved 1999): Test Method for Weather Resistance of Slate

ASTM C 503-99: Specification for Marble Dimension Stone (Exterior)

ASTM C 568-99: Specification for Limestone Dimension Stone

ASTM C 616-99: Specification for Quartz-Based Dimension Stone

ASTM C 666-97: Test Method for Resistance of Concrete to Rapid Freezing and Thawing

ASTM D 2047-99: Test Method for Static Coefficient of Friction of Polish-Coated Floor Surfaces as Measured by the James Machine

Marble Institute of America

Dimensional Stone-Design Manual IV, 1991.

United States Architectural & Transportation Barriers Compliance Board

ADAAG: Accessibility Guidelines for Buildings and Facilities, adopted in 1991; continual revisions.

BOOK

Winkler, Erhard M. *Stone in Architecture.* Berlin: Springer-Verlag, 1994.

WEB SITES

Canadian Stone Association: www.stone.ca

Indiana Limestone Institute of America, Inc.: www.iliai.com

Italian Trade Commission: www.marblefromitaly.com

National Building Granite Quarries Association, Inc.: www.nbgqa.com

Stone World and *Contemporary Stone & Tile Design*: www.stoneworld.com

09640 WOOD FLOORING

This chapter discusses solid- and engineered-wood flooring that is either factory or site finished.

This chapter does not discuss resiliently mounted wood flooring systems used in athletic facilities, which are covered in Chapter 09644, Wood Athletic-Flooring Assemblies.

GENERAL COMMENTS

Technical, installation, and maintenance information for wood flooring is available from associations that represent manufacturers, distributors, dealers, and contractors. Contact the organizations listed below for literature. The Maple Flooring Manufacturers Association and the National Oak Flooring Manufacturers Association provide literature free of charge to specifiers.

- **Maple Flooring Manufacturers Association (MFMA)**
  60 Revere Drive, Suite #500
  Northbrook, IL 60062
  (847) 480-9138

- **National Oak Flooring Manufacturers Association (NOFMA)**
  P.O. Box 3009
  Memphis, TN 38173-0009
  (901) 526-5016

- **National Wood Flooring Association (NWFA)**
  Kirkland Building, 11046 Manchester Road
  St. Louis, MO 63122
  (800) 422-4556; (314) 821-8654

PRODUCT CHARACTERISTICS

Wood flooring is either solid or engineered wood and is available as strip, plank, and parquet flooring.

- **Solid-wood flooring** is commonly available in various hard- and soft-wood species. Because it is very susceptible to the effects of moisture, it is generally unsuitable for below-grade applications. Solid wood can be refinished many times (figs. 1, 2, 3).

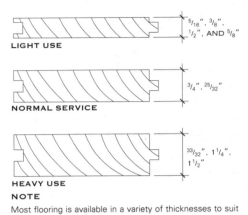

Figure 2. Solid wood flooring thicknesses

- **Engineered-wood flooring** is made up of surface veneers, generally hardwood, laminated to one or more supporting plies that add strength and dimensional stability. Engineered-wood flooring is less susceptible to the effects of moisture than solid wood and can be used in below-grade applications.
- **Strip flooring** is 1½- to 2¼-inches (38- to 57-mm) wide and usually comes in random lengths
- **Plank flooring** is 3- to 8-inches (76- to 203-mm) wide and usually comes in random lengths.
- **Parquet** means a patterned floor (fig. 4).

  Parquet strips or planks are regular-length boards arranged in a pattern, such as a herringbone.

  Solid-wood parquet blocks or squares are "tiles" made of up individual wood pieces that are factory assembled and adhered to a removable paper facing or cotton-mesh backing. They are not necessarily square or regular in dimension.

  Engineered-wood parquet tiles simulate solid-wood parquet blocks using face veneers of one or more wood species laminated to supporting plies.

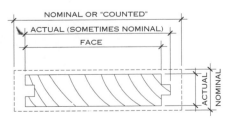

NOTE

Cross-sectional dimensioning systems vary among species, patterns, and manufacturers. Trade organizations provide percentage multipliers for computing coverage.

Figure 1. Solid wood flooring cross-sectional dimensions

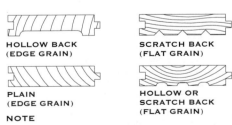

NOTE

The underside of flooring boards may be patterned and often contains more defects than are allowed in the top face. Grain is often mixed in any given run of boards. Edge grain is also called vertical grain.

Figure 3. Solid wood flooring characteristics

NOTE

Many patterns are available; consult manufacturers' design manuals.

Figure 4. Parquet floor patterns

PRODUCT SELECTION CONSIDERATIONS

Flooring is a highly visible building finish that receives significant wear and abuse and impacts on the safety and comfort of occupants. It is subject to abrasion, water, dirt, and cleaning agents. When selecting wood flooring products and finishes, consider the following:

- Amount and type of daily pedestrian traffic
- Abrasiveness of local soils
- Vehicular traffic (carts, wheelchairs, etc.)
- Exposure to moisture and fluctuations in relative humidity
- Exposure to stains and reagents
- Exposure to sunlight through glass; ultraviolet (UV) light may cause color changes
- Exposure to in-service damage such as scratches, indentations, and gouges
- Anticipated type and frequency of maintenance and its effect on appearance and slip resistance
- Appearance expectations

The durability of wood flooring depends on the wood species and the finish selected.

- **Evaluate the density and wear resistance** of wood species being considered for flooring. Hardwoods commonly used for millwork, such as mahogany and poplar, may not be dense enough to provide a durable floor. Many species of softwood, such as redwood, cedar, and white pine, are also not dense enough for use as flooring. Comparing the hardness of woods suggests their relative densities and resistance to wear.
- **The hardness of a wood species** is its capability to resist indentation, wear, and marring. The Forest Products Laboratory (FPL), a unit of the research organization of the Forest Service, U.S. Department of Agriculture, reports side hardnesses of species. Side hardness values are the average pounds of pressure required to embed a 0.444-inch- (11-mm-) diameter steel ball one-half its diameter into the wood with the load applied perpendicular to the grain. Values are the average of radial and tangential penetrations. These values are sometimes called the *Janka hardness* of wood. Table 1 shows the average side hardnesses of domestic and imported species in a dry state according to FPL's *Wood Engineering Handbook,* second edition, and manufacturer's technical data, respectively.
- **Finishes protect wood** from wear, dirt, oxidation, and moisture. NWFA's literature lists the following finish types:

    Wax finishes over penetrating stains are the least-durable finishes available. Generally, they are unsuitable for commercial applications. These finishes are the most susceptible to water damage and require buffing and periodic rewaxing. Wax finishes are factory or site applied.

    Surface finishes over penetrating stains are durable and require little maintenance. Oil-modified and water-based polyurethanes are used most. Shellacs, manufactured and natural varnishes, and lacquers are rarely used. Epoxy-ester finishes are very durable and are recommended for gym floors. Moisture-cured urethanes and acid-curing formaldehyde finishes are also very durable but are difficult to apply and have a high VOC content. Generally, water-based finishes are clear and nonyellowing and leave the wood with the most natural appearance. Solvent- and oil-based finishes tend to yellow with age and change the appearance of stained or natural wood. Surface finishes are factory or site applied. Factory-applied urethane finishes are generally cured by exposure to UV light, which is why they are called UV urethanes.

Acrylic-impregnated finishes are the most durable. For these finishes, the wood is saturated with chemicals that polymerize into solid acrylic. Because the chemical reaction occurs throughout the thickness of the wood, it increases the density, hardness, and wear resistance of the wood flooring product. Acrylic seals the wood against moisture and, therefore, increases dimensional stability. Acrylic-impregnated finishes are factory applied.

MFMA authorizes an independent testing agency to test floor-finish products for sports and other surfaces. Test results provide floor finish comparison and selection data. Contact MFMA for a list of tested floor finishes.

The species, grade, and cut of solid wood affect the appearance, durability, and dimensional stability of the flooring surface.

Table 1
AVERAGE SIDE HARDNESS OF WOODS

Wood Species	Side Hardness Load Perpendicular to the Grain
Ash, White	1320 lbf (5870 N)
Beech, American	1300 lbf (5780 N)
Birch, Yellow	1260 lbf (5600 N)
Cherry, African*	1110 lbf (4900 N)
Cherry, Black	950 lbf (4230 N)
Cherry, Brazilian*	2280 lbf (10 140 N)
Maple, Black	1180 lbf (5248 N)
Maple, Hard	1450 lbf (6450 N)
Oak, Northern Red	1290 lbf (5740 N)
Oak, Red Southern	1060 lbf (4720 N)
Oak, White	1360 lbf (6050 N)
Pecan	1820 lbf (8100 N)
Pine, Eastern White	380 lbf (1690 N)
Pine, Southern Yellow (loblolly and shortleaf)	690 lbf (3070 N)
Pine, Heart (longleaf)	870 lbf (3870 N)
Walnut, African*	1290 lbf (5740 N)
Walnut, Black	1010 lbf (4490 N)
Walnut, Brazilian*	3680 lbf (16 370 N)
Walnut, Peruvian*	1080 lbf (4800 N)

*Imported wood species

Table 2
STANDARD GRADING RULES FOR SOLID-WOOD FLOORING

Organization	Species	Cut	Grade	
			Name	**Description**
Maple Flooring Manufacturers Association	Unfinished Hard Maple	Edge Grain (No grain requirements if edge grain is not specified.)	Competition Grade (First Grade)	Face practically defect-free.
			Standard Grade (Second & Better Grade)	Admits tight knots and slight imperfections.
			Multipurpose Grade (Third Grade)	Admits knots and defects.
			Third & Better Grade	Combination of First, Second, and Third grades.
National Oak Flooring Manufacturers Association	Unfinished Oak	Plain Sawn Quarter Sawn Rift Sawn Quarter/Rift Sawn	Clear	Face practically clear; color not considered.
			Select	Admits small knots and other minor imperfections.
			No. 1 Common	Varying wood characteristics permitted.
			No. 2 Common	Sound natural variations permitted.
	Unfinished Beech, Birch, & Hard Maple	—	First Grade	Practically free of face defects; varying color is not a defect.
			Second Grade	Varying wood characteristics permitted.
			Third Grade	Serviceable.
			Second & Better	Combination of First and Second grades.
			Third & Better	Combination of Second and Third grades.
	Unfinished Hard White Maple	—	First Grade Hard White Maple	Selected for uniform ivory white color.
	Unfinished Red Beech & Birch	—	First Grade Red Beech & Birch	Special grade selected for color.
	Unfinished Hickory/Pecan	—	First Grade	Practically free of face defects; mixed color.
			First Grade Red	Practically free of face defects; 95% heartwood.
			First Grade White	Practically free of face defects; 95% bright sapwood.
			Second Grade	Varying wood characteristics permitted.
			Second Grade Red	Varying wood characteristics permitted; 85% heartwood.
			Third Grade	Serviceable for flooring.
			Third & Better	Combination of First, Second, and Third grades.
	Unfinished Ash	—	Clear	Practically free of face defects.
			Select	Admits tight sound knots and minor defects.
			No. 1 Common	Varying wood characteristics permitted.
			No. 2 Common	Serviceable for flooring.
	Prefinished Oak	—	Prime Grade	Selected for appearance; color variations permitted.
			Standard Grade	Containing sound wood variations that can be filled and acceptably finished.
			Standard & Better	Combination of Standard and Prime grades
			Tavern Grade	Serviceable for flooring
			Tavern & Better	Combination of Prime, Standard, and Tavern grades.
Southern Pine Inspection Bureau			B & B Flooring	Best quality, generally clear, only minor defects permitted.
			C Flooring	Choice quality, reasonably clear, minor defects in most pieces.
			C & Better Flooring	Combination of B & B and C flooring grades.
			D Flooring	Good quality, admits some major defects.
			No. 2 Flooring	Utility value; major defects permitted that require cutting.
			No. 3 Flooring	Recommended for subflooring, sheathing, or lathing.
West Coast Lumber Inspection Bureau	Unfinished Douglas Fir, Western Hemlock, Western Red Cedar, White Fir, & Sitka Spruce	Vertical Grain Flat Grain Mixed Grain	C & BTR - Flooring	Sound, good appearance; only minor imperfections permitted.
			D - Flooring	Serviceable; some pieces may have one or more serious defects.
			E - Flooring	Recommended for subflooring, sheathing and similar uses.

- **Standardized grading rules for solid-wood strip and plank flooring** vary for wood species and among industry organizations. There are no standard grading rules for certain woods that are infrequently used for flooring or for recycled and imported woods. Some manufacturers establish their own grading systems, using the same or similar terms as those used by industry organizations' grading standards. Table 2 summarizes the grading rules commonly used for domestic solid-wood strip and plank flooring.
- **Sizes of solid-wood strip and plank** vary with grade and species. Not all face sizes or thicknesses are available in every grade or in every species. Consult manufacturers or suppliers for available dimensions.
- **The cut of solid-wood flooring** affects its appearance, durability, and dimensional stability.

The spring growth of wood (springwood) that forms woods' characteristic grain patterns is less dense than its summer growth (summerwood).

Moisture absorption and emission causes wood to expand and contract. Generally, the most significant dimensional change occurs parallel to the grain (tangentially). The dimensional change across the grain (radially) is about one-half that of the tangential change, and the change along the grain (longitudinally) is slight.

A cut that produces grain perpendicular to the board face minimizes the distance between growth rings on the face and exposes the least amount of the softer springwood. Therefore, this is the most durable cut. It is also the most dimensionally stable because the maximum shrinkage and swelling occur across the board's thickness rather than across its face width.

Plain sawing logs produces about 80 percent of the boards with the grain running across the board face and 20 percent with the grain running perpendicular. Therefore, if the grain or annular rings run across the width of a board, the board's cut is called *plain* or *flat sawn*. When a plain-sawn cut is specified, some boards are usually vertically grained.

Quarter sawing logs produces boards that are primarily vertically grained. Therefore, if the grain runs at right angles to the face or across the thickness, the cut of a hardwood board is called *quartered* or *quarter sawn*. The cut of a softwood board is called *vertical* or *edge grain*. Because quarter sawing lumber produces narrower boards and more waste than plain sawing, saw mills generally cull boards with vertical grain from plain-sawn lumber to provide vertically grained boards and charge more for them.

Rift sawing logs produces boards with characteristics similar to quarter sawing; however, it creates more waste than quarter sawing and is generally more expensive. Because rift sawing reduces the number of cuts parallel to a log's medullary rays, it reduces the flake effect common to quartered oak.

Among the hardwoods commonly used for flooring, only oak is generally available quartered or rift sawn. For increased dimensional stability, manufacturers of solid-wood parquet flooring gang-rip plain-sawn boards through their thicknesses. The ripped pieces of plain-sawn boards are turned and become thinner quartered parquet blocks.

The Hardwood Plywood and Veneer Association (HPVA) publishes ANSI/HPVA LF, *Laminated Wood Flooring*. This standard establishes requirements for grade of plies, moisture content, machining, bond line (delamination resistance), construction (ply assembly), formaldehyde emissions for products made with urea-formaldehyde or melamine-formaldehyde adhesives or surface coatings, and finish of engineered-wood flooring. Veneers for the face ply can be of one or more species. Common species used include pecan, hard maple, red oak, white oak, birch, ash, beech, black walnut, southern pine, and black cherry. Face Grades established by the standard are Prime (practically clear with minor imperfections) and

Character (sound wood variations and a greater allowable level of imperfections than Prime). Veneers are rotary cut, sliced, or sawed from a log, bolt, or flitch. Sawed veneers are the most durable and look the most like traditional solid-wood flooring products.

APPLICATION CONSIDERATIONS

Controlling the moisture content of wood is critical both before and after installation. Wood is hygroscopic, meaning it changes dimensionally with the absorption or release of moisture. Swelling and shrinking varies with the wood species, cut, and type of flooring. Because engineered products' cross-ply construction adds dimensional stability, moisture control for engineered-wood flooring is less critical than for solid-wood flooring.

Manufacturers kiln-dry wood flooring so it will behave predictably. During transit, delivery, and storage, it must be protected from moisture. Before installation, wood flooring must stabilize at (acclimatize to) the temperature and relative humidity of space in which it will be installed. After installation, and even after finishing, fluctuations in environmental conditions cause shrinking and swelling.

Wood flooring installations must accommodate movement. An expansion space is required at the perimeter of the installation. For larger installations, more expansion provisions may be required (fig. 5).

Concrete slab substrates must be dry and protected from subsurface moisture by appropriate grading and drainage, a capillary water barrier of porous drainage materials, and a membrane vapor retarder. Temperature, relative humidity, and ventilation affect concrete drying time. A slab allowed to dry from only one side generally takes 30 days for every 1 inch (25.4 mm) of thickness to dry adequately (fig. 6).

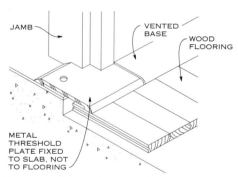

Figure 5. Expansion plate at doorway joint with dissimilar construction

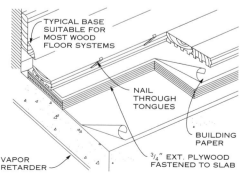

Figure 6. Wood flooring over plywood underlayment on concrete slab

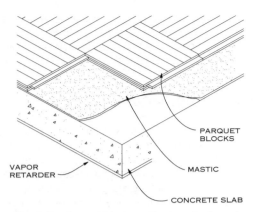

Figure 7. Parquet blocks, adhesive attachment

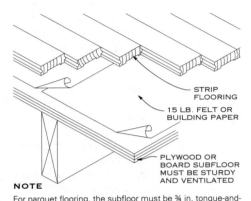

NOTE

For parquet flooring, the subfloor must be ¾ in. tongue-and-groove plywood, minimum, with mastic over it.

Figure 8. Wood flooring over wood-framed subfloor

For adhesive attachment to concrete, slabs must be clean and free of curing compounds, sealers, hardeners, and other materials that may interfere with an adhesive bond (fig. 7).

Spaces below wood flooring must be dry and well ventilated. Cross-ventilate crawl spaces and cover the ground with a polyethylene vapor retarder. If solid-wood flooring is installed over wood sleepers on a concrete slab, NOFMA recommends covering the sleepers with a polyethylene vapor retarder and making provisions for ventilating the airspaces between sleepers (fig. 8).

TROPICAL WOODS

Tropical moist forests, including rainforests and seasonal or monsoon forests, provide the hardwoods generally called *tropical woods*. The destruction of rainforests is an important environmental issue. More than half the plant and animal species on Earth are found in tropical rainforests concentrated mainly in the South American Amazon Basin, Africa's Congo Basin, and Southeast Asia.

Land-use changes, not the timber industry, are the major cause of rainforest destruction, according to most reports. Some organizations assert that boycotting the use of tropical woods may accelerate the destruction of rainforests because it devalues the timber as a resource and encourages changes in land use to those uses that immediately profit the local human population. Organizations concerned with preserving rainforests generally also have social agendas. They encourage responsible, sustainable forestry-management practices and timber production as a means of providing for a region's human population. If desired, verify that forestry operations of suppliers to imported wood product manufacturers are certified by a reputable organization.

SPECIFYING METHODS

Generic specifications are feasible for unfinished, solid-wood strip and plank flooring covered by standard grading rules (see Table 2). Standard grading rules do not apply to woods less commonly used for flooring, to antique woods, and to imported woods. For these products, specify acceptable manufacturers or specify that the grade and cut match a representative sample.

Name acceptable products in the wood flooring specification to identify wood flooring that cannot be categorized with precision, such as wood flooring that is parquet block, factory finished, or engineered. For competitive pricing, name several acceptable products.

REFERENCES

Publication dates cited here were current at the time of this writing. Publications are revised periodically, and revisions may have occurred before this book was published.

Forest Products Laboratory
Wood Engineering Handbook, 2nd ed., 1990.

Hardwood Plywood and Veneer Association
ANSI/HPVA LF 1996: Laminated Wood Flooring

Maple Flooring Manufacturers Association
MFMA Grading Rules for Hard Maple (Acer saccharum), 1995.

National Oak Flooring Manufacturers Association
NOFMA Official Grading Rules, 1997.

Southern Pine Inspection Bureau
Standard Grading Rules for Southern Pine Lumber, 1994.

West Coast Lumber Inspection Bureau
WCLIB No. 17-1/1/96: Grading Rules for West Coast Lumber

This chapter discusses *hard maple, finish flooring and subflooring assem-blies designed for use as athletic playing or exercising surfaces. Subflooring systems include those with enhanced shock-absorbing properties.*

This chapter does not discuss *synthetic athletic flooring, portable and per-manent dance flooring, and standard wood flooring traditionally installed in residential and commercial applications. Standard wood flooring is dis-cussed in Chapter 09640, Wood Flooring.*

PRODUCT CHARACTERISTICS

Wood-flooring surfaces for athletic-flooring assemblies are usually hard maple (Acer saccharum). Hard maple is close grained, hard fibered, light in color, and durable. Oak flooring is available from some manufacturers in engineered-strip (laminated) or parquet-block form. Generally, these oak sys-tems are less expensive than typical maple systems and are used for aerobic and other exercise surfaces in floating systems installed over foam blocks.

Subfloor systems for athletic-flooring assemblies are provided by the floor-surface manufacturer, unlike traditional wood flooring used for decorative purposes. Subfloor systems have various shock-absorbing, energy-rebound-ing, and sound-deadening characteristics. Structural floor systems are generally concrete slabs. Common subfloor systems include the following:

• **Floating systems** use resilient pads of rubber, neoprene, or PVC; or foam underlayment.

  Resilient pads isolate athletic-flooring assemblies from the supporting slab and allow ventilation. Pads are mechanically attached to wood panels, sleepers, or sleepers supporting panels. Tongue-and-groove, wood, strip flooring is mechanically fastened to the panels or sleepers using barbed cleats or staples. In some systems, square-edged par-quet strips are applied to panels with mastic. Various pads are available for different applications. Some manufacturers suggest using harder pads under bleachers. Include specific pad requirements in the specifications (fig. 1, 2).

  Foam underlayment isolates the athletic-flooring assemblies from the

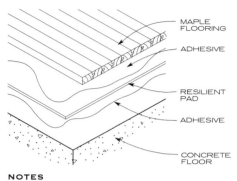

MAPLE FLOORING
ADHESIVE
RESILIENT PAD
ADHESIVE
CONCRETE FLOOR

NOTES
1. Lowest cost
2. Easy to install
3. Suitable for multipurpose applications
4. Use where floor performance is not critical

Figure 2. Mastic applied system

supporting slab but does not provide ventilation space (fig. 2). In ven-tilated systems, two layers of side-spaced board subflooring, laid in opposite directions, accommodate underfloor ventilation. Tongue-and-groove, wood, strip flooring is mechanically fastened to the top layer of subflooring using barbed cleats or staples (fig. 3). In unventilated systems, square-edge parquet blocks are adhered directly to the foam underlayment or to panels laid over the foam.

• **Fixed-sleeper systems** include wood sleepers or metal channels mechanically fastened to the supporting slab.

  Wood sleepers are installed with or without subflooring. Sleepers are side spaced and allow underfloor ventilation (fig. 4). If subflooring is not used, generally sleeper spacing is reduced and thicker strip floor-ing is used. Sleepers are mechanically fastened to the supporting slab through hardboard shims or resilient pads with power-driven steel pins. When fastened through shims, sleepers are set in asphalt mas-tic. Tongue-and-groove, wood, strip flooring is mechanically fastened to the sleepers or subflooring using barbed cleats or staples.

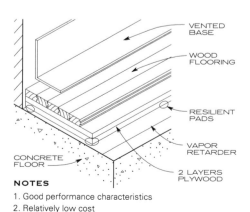

VENTED BASE
WOOD FLOORING
RESILIENT PADS
VAPOR RETARDER
CONCRETE FLOOR
2 LAYERS PLYWOOD

NOTES
1. Good performance characteristics
2. Relatively low cost

Figure 1. Cushioned system

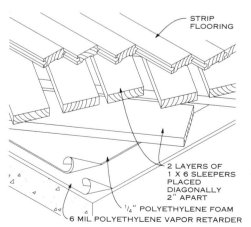

STRIP FLOORING
2 LAYERS OF 1 X 6 SLEEPERS PLACED DIAGONALLY 2" APART
¼" POLYETHYLENE FOAM
6 MIL POLYETHYLENE VAPOR RETARDER

Figure 3. Strips over ventilated sleepers

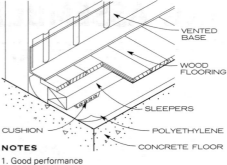

NOTES
1. Good performance
2. Can have dead spots
3. More difficult installation

Figure 4. Sleeper system

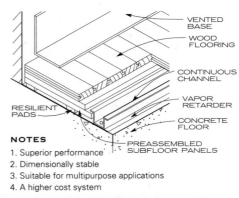

NOTES
1. Superior performance
2. Dimensionally stable
3. Suitable for multipurpose applications
4. A higher cost system

Figure 5. Proprietary channel system

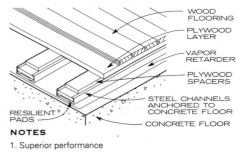

NOTES
1. Superior performance
2. Dimensionally stable
3. Suitable for multipurpose applications
4. A higher cost system

Figure 6. Proprietary floating system

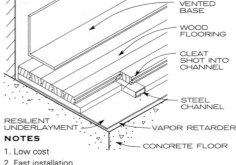

NOTES
1. Low cost
2. Fast installation
3. Dimensionally stable
4. Good multipurpose floor
5. Limited performance characteristics

Figure 7. Nail-in channel system

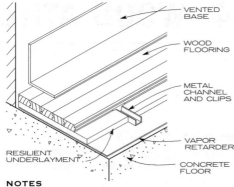

NOTES
1. Dimensionally stable
2. Good multipurpose floor
3. Limited performance characteristics

Figure 8. Channel and clip system

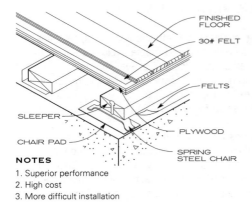

NOTES
1. Superior performance
2. High cost
3. More difficult installation

Figure 9. Spring system

Metal channels are set in grooves of resilient fiberboard or foam underlayment and fastened to the supporting slab with power-driven steel pins (figs. 5, 6). Some metal channels have rigid nailing strips (fig. 7). For channels without nailing strips, tongue-and-groove, wood, strip flooring is mechanically fastened to channels using steel clips (fig. 8). For channels with nailing strips, barbed cleats or staples are used. Metal channel systems have low profiles and do not allow underfloor ventilation.

Other resilient subfloor systems include foam-block and spring-mounted systems (fig. 9).

MAPLE FLOORING SURFACES

The Maple Flooring Manufacturers Association (MFMA) provides technical, installation, and maintenance information for wood flooring. Literature is available free of charge to specifiers.

MFMA Grading Rules for Hard Maple (Acer saccharum) establishes requirements for tongue-and-groove and jointed flooring that is $\frac{25}{32}$-inch (20-mm) thick and thicker. These grading rules also apply to beech (Fagus grandifolia) and birch (Betula alleghaniensis) flooring. A summary of requirements follows:

• **Flooring thickness** is usually $\frac{25}{32}$ inch (20 mm); $\frac{33}{32}$-inch- (26-mm-) thick maple is used for applications subject to extraordinary wear and strain.
• **Face widths** for tongue-and-groove flooring are 1½, 2¼, and 3¼ inches

(38, 57, and 83 mm). Square-edged flooring is called jointed flooring and is available in face widths of 2¼, 3¼, and 3½ inches (57, 82, and 89 mm). Tongue-and-groove flooring is used for blind-nailed strip floor-ing, and jointed flooring is used for adhesively applied parquet strips

- **Edge-grain boards** have annual rings ranging from 30 degrees horizon-tal to 90 degrees vertical to the board face. Flooring is considered edge grain if 75 percent of each piece has these grain characteristics. Unless edge grain is specified, flat-grain boards meet MFMA requirements. See Chapter 09640 for a discussion of grain characteristics.
- **Bundled flooring** is bundled by average length. Bundles may include pieces from 6 inches (152 mm) under to 6 inches (152 mm) over the nominal length of the bundle. No piece may be shorter than 9 inches (229 mm).
- **Nested flooring** is bundled by grade requirements except for those that apply to length. Flooring is random length, bundled end to end continu-ously in nominal 84- or 96-inch- (2130- or 2440-mm-) long bundles. No one piece may be shorter than 9 inches (229 mm). The maximum average number of pieces under 15 inches (381 mm) per bundle varies according to grade; 8 percent is allowed for First Grade, 12 percent for Second & Better, and 42 percent for Third.
- **Color variation** is not considered a grading defect. Maple's heartwood is darker, and its sapwood is lighter. If color consistency is important, con-tact MFMA for additional information.
- **Competition Grade (First Grade)** flooring board faces are practically defect-free.
- **Standard Grade (Second & Better Grade)** flooring board faces may have tight knots and slight imperfections.
- **Multipurpose Grade (Third Grade)** flooring board faces may have knots and defects.
- **Third & Better Grade** flooring is a combination of First, Second, and Third grades.

MOISTURE CONSIDERATIONS

Controlling the moisture content of wood is critical before and after instal-lation. Wood is hygroscopic, meaning it changes dimensionally with the absorption or release of moisture. Swelling and shrinking vary with the wood species and cut.

Manufacturers kiln-dry wood flooring so it will behave predictably. During transit, delivery, and storage, it must be protected from moisture. Before installation, wood flooring must stabilize at (acclimatize to) the temperature and relative humidity of space in which it will be installed. After installa-tion, and even after finishing, fluctuations in environmental conditions cause shrinking and swelling.

Fluctuations in the wood moisture content resulting from concrete-slab moisture-vapor emission or climatic conditions can cause wood to buckle, cup, and crack. Excess moisture can cause adhesive failures. Shrinking and swelling of wood can loosen mechanical fasteners. Underfloor venti-lation prevents moisture build-up below the floor and can reduce the detrimental effects of moisture on the floor surface.

Concrete-slab substrates must be dry and protected from subsurface moisture by appropriate grading and drainage, a capillary water barrier of porous drainage fill, and a membrane vapor retarder. Temperature, relative humidity, and ventilation affect concrete drying time. A slab allowed to dry from only one side generally takes 30 days for every 1 inch (25.4 mm) of thickness to dry adequately.

Wood-flooring installations must accommodate movement. Wood shrinks and swells even when moisture is adequately controlled. Expansion-void requirements vary depending on the flooring assembly and prevailing climate. Manufacturers recommend between 2 and 4 inches

(100 and 50 mm) of expansion space at perimeters of floating assemblies. Fixed assemblies may require less expansion space; large installations may require more. Verify recommendations with manufacturers.

PRODUCT SELECTION CONSIDERATIONS

Many types of wood-flooring assemblies are available for use in areas where athletic activities occur. The type selected for an installation depends on the activity, the project budget, and code requirements. Before selecting an ath-letic-flooring assembly, contact manufacturers for recommendations for specific applications.

Each activity has its own requirements. For example, aerobic exercise requires flooring that absorbs impact, to prevent shin splints, and that returns enough energy to users' legs, to prevent excessive muscle fatigue. These floors must provide enough traction to minimize slipping, while not grabbing shoes and restricting intentional sliding movements. For basket-ball and volleyball, shock absorption and ball bounce are critical characteristics. Floors for roller skating rinks must be stable and durable. Skating rinks often use the most economical grade of maple flooring and are finished with a sealer.

MFMA's *Maple Performance Characteristics Guide* includes a matrix showing the relative importance of general performance characteristics for various activities.

Verify requirements of authorities having jurisdiction before selecting wood, athletic-flooring assemblies. Model codes require fireblocking in concealed sleeper spaces or filling these spaces with an approved noncombustible material. The Uniform Building Code (UBC) allows exceptions to fireblocking requirements in concealed sleeper spaces for gymnasiums at or below grade. If underfloor cavities are fireblocked or filled, underfloor ventilation is elimi-nated, affecting the performance of the finish flooring. Fireblocking or filling cavities may also affect an assembly's shock-absorbing characteristics. Many wood, athletic-flooring installations are on concrete slabs, are not continuous under walls or partitions, and are in discreet buildings separated from other use groups by firewalls. For these installations, authorities having jurisdiction may determine that fireblocking or filling sleeper spaces does not significantly affect the transfer of fire. Therefore, these authorities may allow ventilating assemblies. Contact manufacturers for suggestions on how to fireblock float-ing and resilient-pad-mounted, fixed-sleeper systems and still satisfy performance requirements.

MEASURING ASSEMBLY PERFORMANCE

United States standards currently do not exist for measuring athletic-flooring performance. Some manufacturers reference a German Institute for Standardization (DIN) standard developed at the *Otto-Graf Institut* in Stuttgart. The DIN standard includes test procedures and criteria for the following:

- **Shock absorption or force reduction:** This test requires that a minimum of 53 percent of a load be absorbed by the assembly and that 47 per-cent be returned to the body. However, some manufacturers recommend a minimum of 70 percent shock absorption for aerobic activities, to decrease fatigue. Conversely, high-percentage shock absorption creates a wider depression from impacts, which is undesirable for basketball.
- **Ball bounce:** This test measures the rebound of a ball from the assembly compared to a rigid, concrete floor. A minimum of 90 percent rebound is required. High rebound percentage improves ball control. Channel sys-tems and anchored systems generally provide high ball bounce.
- **Vertical and area deflection:** This test measures the depression (trough or shock wave) created by an athlete landing on the floor. The shock is measured at 20 inches (500 mm) from the point of impact

and cannot exceed 15 percent of the load. Excessive area deflection or shock causes improper ball bounce and may accelerate fatigue in nearby athletes.

- **Surface friction:** This test measures a floor's sliding behavior as the quotient of vertical force applied by a shoe to the horizontal force needed to move the shoe across the floor. To pass, this coefficient of friction must be between 0.5 and 0.7. If the coefficient of friction is high, athletes' feet may tend to stick on the floor, causing strain to feet and leg muscles and ligaments. Floor finish and maintenance procedures affect surface friction.
- **Rolling load:** This test measures the flooring assembly's capability to withstand the effects of a 300-lb (136-kg) load placed on a rolling cart with a single wheel in the center. It is used to predict the assembly's behavior when subjected to loads imposed by items such as portable equipment and telescoping bleachers.

Not all assemblies are DIN-certified. Requiring DIN certification may result in a proprietary specification. Before requiring DIN certification, determine which characteristics are important for an installation. Although assemblies may not meet all requirements of the standard, they may meet the criteria important for the installation. Some manufacturers rate performance characteristics of assemblies such as shock absorption and ball bounce according to the DIN standard, although the assembly is not certified.

APPLICATION CONSIDERATIONS

Wood-preservative treatment can be specified to deter termites and other insects and to prevent mold, mildew, staining, and decay fungi. MFMA states that flooring and wood subfloor components may be treated with "Woodlife F" or its equivalent when specified. "Woodlife" is a registered trademark of Kop-Coat, Inc. It is a clear, penetrating, water-repellent wood preservative in which the active ingredient is 0.5% 3-iodo-2-propynl butyl carbamate. It can be applied by immersion, flood coat, spray, or brush. MFMA members generally use the immersion method. Except for fixed, wood sleepers set in asphalt mastic and plywood, preservative treatment is optional for wood components. Preservative treatment is always required for fixed, wood sleepers set in asphalt mastic. Plywood is generally not preservative treated.

MFMA does not recommend pressure treating wood subfloor components. According to MFMA and manufacturers, pressure treating lumber changes its cell structure and makes it more absorptive. Additionally, salts in the impregnated preservatives retain absorbed moisture for long periods. The eventual release of absorbed moisture by pressure-treated lumber adversely affects the floor and finish. MFMA also cautions that preservatives containing creosote can bleed and stain the floor surface.

Subfloor reinforcement may be required at locations subject to rolling loads, such as under telescoping or portable bleachers. Show these areas on the drawings and include requirements in the specifications.

Consider fastening methods and the effects of activities occurring on the assembly. Demanding activities may cause finish flooring to work loose from the resilient subfloor system.

Coordinate requirements for anchoring gym equipment. Equipment anchors must extend through the athletic-flooring assembly into the supporting slab.

Local VOC restrictions may dictate adhesive and finish system selections. Verify requirements of authorities having jurisdiction.

Excessive wear of finishes can result in areas where game-line and marker paint buildup is heavy. Game lines should not overlap. Where game lines cross, the minor game line should break at the intersection.

FINISH SYSTEMS

MFMA authorizes an independent testing agency to test floor-finish products for sports and other surfaces. Test results provide floor-finish comparison and selection data. Contact MFMA to obtain its current *Floor Finish List*. This publication groups finishes by type and lists products, manufacturers, and addresses. The following product groups and descriptions are listed:

- **Group 1, Sealers:** Provide good penetration with slight surface film. Intended for an economical first coating. Include urethane-oil, epoxyester, and oleoresinous types.
- **Group 2, Heavy Duty Finishes:** Provide adequate penetration and some surface-film buildup. Include urethane-oil and epoxy-ester types.
- **Group 3, Gymnasium Type (Surface) Finishes:** Provide little penetration and good surface-film buildup. Intended for maximum service under heavy traffic. Include urethane-oil, epoxy-ester, and oleoresinous types.
- **Group 4, Moisture Cured Urethane Finishes:** No products are currently listed.
- **Group 5, Water-Based Finishes:** Nonflammable and low odor. Provide adequate penetration and surface-film buildup. Include water-based polyurethanes and oleoresinous type. MFMA notes that the use of water-based finishes has occasionally produced a side-bonding effect, which may result in localized excessive cracks between boards. MFMA recommends consulting an MFMA contractor and the manufacturer to obtain procedures for sealing and finishing maple, strip flooring with water-based products.

Besides MFMA, contact flooring and finish manufacturers for recommendations.

SPECIFYING METHODS

Generic specifications are feasible for wood, athletic-flooring assemblies and finish types common to several manufacturers. However, naming the specific products that are acceptable is a more precise specification method. Some manufacturers may have more than one product that meets generic requirements. Also, some assemblies are unique to a manufacturer or are patented and, therefore, result in proprietary specifications.

REFERENCES

Publication dates cited here were current at the time of this writing. Publications are revised periodically, and revisions may have occurred before this book was published.

Maple Flooring Manufacturers Association

MFMA Floor Finish List #15, 1996.

MFMA Grading Rules for Hard Maple (Acer saccharum), 1995.

Maple Performance Characteristics Guide, 1995.

09651 RESILIENT FLOOR TILE

This chapter discusses *solid vinyl, rubber, and vinyl composition floor tile.*

This chapter does not discuss *static-control resilient tile flooring or sheet vinyl floor coverings; they are discussed in other chapters.*

GENERAL COMMENTS

Floor coverings are prominent interior finishes that typically receive significant wear and abuse and affect the safety and comfort of building occupants. Floor coverings are normally subject to abrasion, water, dirt, chemicals, and cleaning agents. Because their performance requirements vary substantially from one area to another, several different resilient floor covering types are often required for a project. When selecting products, consider the following:

- Amount and type of daily pedestrian traffic
- Abrasiveness of local soils
- Vehicular traffic (carts, wheelchairs, etc.)
- Exposure to reagents, stains, and temperatures that can stain, soften, or otherwise damage floor coverings
- Exposure to UV light (fading potential)
- Exposure to uses or equipment that might cause in-service damage such as cuts, tears, punctures, permanent surface indentations, and gouges
- Anticipated type and frequency of maintenance and its effect on appearance, sanitation, and slip resistance
- Appearance expectations
- Expectations for the comfort of building occupants

The best way to specify resilient floor tile is by naming acceptable products. Color and other aesthetic characteristics are not easily specified by descriptive methods or by referencing standards. Generic specifications may be feasible for products and colors common to several manufacturers, but subtle differences in appearance among products often cannot be precisely categorized. For competitive pricing, naming several acceptable products with a similar appearance establishes a cost baseline. If products are not named, bids invariably reflect the least-expensive products that comply with requirements but not necessarily those that produce the desired visual effect.

Obtain current literature and samples from manufacturers to select products for a project. Use samples to evaluate the appearance and finish of products. Review manufacturers' literature for information on durability, ease of maintenance, resilience, load limits, and recommendations for suitable environments for product installation.

Consider seamless installations for solid vinyl or rubber floor tile in areas subject to wetting. Although resilient floor tile resists moisture, installations may fail if the bond between the floor tile and the substrate is weakened or destroyed by moisture on the surface seeping through the joints between units. Heat welding or chemically bonding seams eliminates these joints. Although sheet products are usually specified for seamless installations, large-size tiles can be heat welded or chemically bonded. If a seamless tile installation is required, verify availability and installation methods with manufacturers.

SOLID VINYL FLOOR TILE

ASTM F 1700, *Specification for Solid Vinyl Floor Tile,* replaced the Federal Specification FS SS-T-312B, which manufacturers' product literature still may reference. The standard describes solid vinyl floor tile as "composed of binder, filler and pigments compounded with suitable lubricants and processing aids. The binder consists of one or more polymers or copolymers of vinyl chloride, other modifying resins, plasticizers and stabilizers." It prescribes the minimum binder content for each of three classes below and states that "polymers or copolymers of vinyl chloride comprise at least 60 percent of the weight of the binder. Any copolymer of vinyl chloride used shall contain at least 85 percent vinyl chloride." The standard classifies solid vinyl floor tile as follows:

- **Class I, Monolithic Vinyl Tile:** Type A, Smooth Surface; and Type B, Embossed Surface.
- **Class II, Surface-Decorated Vinyl Tile:** Type A, Smooth Surface; and Type B, Embossed Surface.
- **Class III, Printed Film Vinyl Tile:** Type A, Smooth Surface; and Type B, Embossed Surface.

RUBBER FLOOR TILE

ASTM F 1344, *Specification for Rubber Floor Tile,* describes products as "manufactured of a vulcanized compound of natural rubber or synthetic rubber or both with pigments, fillers, and plasticizers." No requirements are specified for the minimum rubber and plasticizer content. Wearing surfaces may be smooth, textured, or molded. The standard classifies rubber floor tile as follows:

- **Class I — Homogeneous Rubber Tile,** with surface coloring or mottling uniform throughout the tile thickness. This class is subdivided into subclass A, for solid-color tiles, and subclass B, for mottled tiles.
- **Class II — Laminated Rubber Tile,** with surface coloring or mottling extending throughout the thickness of the wear layer. This class is subdivided into subclass A, for solid-color wear-layer tiles, and subclass B, for mottled wear-layer tiles.

The minimum hardness for rubber tile to comply with ASTM F 1344 is 85 when measured using a Shore, Type A durometer according to ASTM D 2240, *Test Method for Rubber Property—Durometer Hardness.* Softer products are available and have a history of satisfactory in-service performance. Some manufacturers recommend softer products for installations that require extreme resistance to cuts, punctures, and tears, or that are subject to heavy traffic.

VINYL COMPOSITION TILE (VCT)

ASTM F 1066, *Specification for Vinyl Composition Floor Tile,* describes VCT as "composed of binder, fillers, and pigments. The binder shall consist of one or more resins of poly(vinyl chloride) or vinyl chloride copolymers, or both, compounded with suitable plasticizers and stabilizers.

Other suitable polymeric resins may be incorporated as a part of the binder." No requirements are specified for minimum vinyl-resin and plasticizer content. ASTM F 1066 no longer classifies products by composition because all products are now nonasbestos formulated. The standard includes the following three classes:

- **Class 1,** solid-color tiles.
- **Class 2,** through-pattern tiles. The standard defines through-pattern tile as having the colors appearing on the surface extend throughout the thickness of the tile. The appearance of the pattern created by these colors may or may not change throughout the tile's thickness.
- **Class 3,** surface-pattern tiles.

PRODUCT CHARACTERISTICS

Static-Load Resistance

VCT does not resist indentation from static loads as well as vinyl or rubber floor coverings. Not all manufacturers include static-load limits in their product literature or the test method used to determine the limit. Some VCT manufacturers list a static-load limit of 75 psi (517.5 kPa). Some solid vinyl floor tile manufacturers list limits of 125 to 700 psi (862.5 to 4830 kPa), and some rubber floor tile manufacturers list limits of 50 to 600 psi (345 to 4140 kPa).

Resiliency

VCT is less resilient than vinyl or rubber floor coverings because of its lower indentation resistance. The relative importance of the resiliency for floor coverings should be evaluated based on expectations for the comfort of building occupants and requirements for floor covering performance when subject to foot traffic, static loads, and rolling loads.

Chemical Resistance

VCT and solid vinyl floor tile resist alkalis, acids, alcohols, oils, greases, and aliphatic hydrocarbons but can soften when exposed to ketones, esters, and chlorinated and aromatic hydrocarbons. For products to comply with ASTM F 1066 (VCT) and ASTM F 1700 (solid vinyl floor tile), they are exposed to only a limited number of chemicals that are meant to represent those commonly found in domestic, commercial, and institutional use. ASTM F 1344 (rubber floor tile) only requires that pigments be of good quality, insoluble in water, and resistant to alkalis, cleaning agents, and light. Most manufacturers publish tables indicating the effects of many reagents and stains on their products. Ask manufacturers or qualified testing agencies to test any known reagents or stains that are not listed in product literature and that will contact the floor tile.

Cigarette-Burn Resistance

Solid vinyl floor tile and VCT are less resistant than rubber floor tile to damage from burning cigarettes. Depending on the degree of damage, it may be possible to remove scorches and stains with abrasive cleaners or scraping. Contact manufacturers for information on cigarette-burn resistance of specific products.

Light Stability

Exposure to UV light may cause resilient floor coverings to fade, shrink, and blister. In general, resilient floor coverings are unsuitable for exterior installations. Rubber floor coverings are not recommended for areas subject to direct sunlight through glass. Consult manufacturers for recommendations if resilient floor coverings are being considered for use in passive solar applications.

WARRANTIES

Manufacturers' warranties vary. Selecting acceptable products establishes warranty requirements. For descriptive specifications, consider including requirements for a special warranty in the floor-covering specification.

FIRE-TEST-RESPONSE CHARACTERISTICS

In most building codes, resilient floor coverings are classified as "traditional" flooring materials and are exempt from fire-test-response requirements. However, under some circumstances and in some jurisdictions, floor covering materials are required to meet certain fire-test-response criteria. Verify requirements for each project.

The National Fire Protection Association (NFPA) publication NFPA 101, *Life Safety Code,* requires that floor covering materials in exits and accesses to exits meet critical radiant flux (CRF) limitations in certain occupancies. Local jurisdictions may impose other restrictions. Before specifying requirements for CRF or for other fire-test-response characteristics for resilient floor coverings, verify applicable requirements of authorities having jurisdiction.

CRF is established by the radiant panel test in ASTM E 648 or NFPA 253. Both standards describe essentially the same test method. The test was designed to provide a measure of a floor covering's tendency to spread flames when the floor covering is located in a corridor and exposed to the flame and hot gases from a room fire. The higher the CRF value, the more resistant the material is to flame spread. Consequently, the NFPA 101, Class I requirement of 0.45 W/sq. cm is more stringent than the Class II requirement of 0.22 W/sq. cm.

The appendix to NFPA 101 states, "It has not been found necessary or practical to regulate interior floor finishes on the basis of smoke development." However, local authorities and building owners may impose such restrictions. For floor coverings in medical facilities, some states and federal agencies may still require a specific optical density of smoke-generated value of 450 or less according to ASTM E 662 or NFPA 258. Both standards describe essentially the same test method.

The traditional test for flame-spread and smoke-developed indexes, ASTM E 84, tests specimens that are placed in an upside-down position on the ceiling of the test tunnel. Because this test procedure has little to do with the conditions likely to be encountered by resilient products in a real fire, the usefulness of the ratings is probably limited. When resilient products are tested according to ASTM E 84, many manufacturers report only the flame-spread index determined by this test method and the specific optical density of smoke according to ASTM E 662 or NFPA 258.

SLIP RESISTANCE

The Americans with Disabilities Act (ADA), *Accessibility Guidelines for Buildings and Facilities (ADAAG)* does not include static coefficient of friction requirements for walking surfaces. It includes recommendations in Appendix A4.5 that are advisory but not mandatory. The appendix encourages builders and designers to specify materials for floor surfaces that have static coefficient of friction values of not less than 0.6 for level surfaces and 0.8 for ramped surfaces, but does not indicate the test required to make the measurement. To determine these values, the United States Architectural & Transportation Barriers Compliance Board (Access Board) used results from tests of surfacing materials with the NBS-Brungraber tester using a silastic sensor material. This machine operates on a similar principle to the James Machine required by ASTM D 2047; however, the James Machine uses a leather sensor. Results from testing the same floor covering with the two test machines differ and cannot be compared.

A consensus standard for measuring slip resistance has not been developed by the resilient floor covering industry. ASTM Committee F-6 on Resilient Floor Coverings is currently studying the issue and researching available test methods. Despite the lack of consensus within the industry, some manufacturers are publishing static coefficient of friction values for their products. Generally, the values are based on testing according to ASTM D 2047 using the James Machine.

CONCRETE SLABS AND MOISTURE PROBLEMS

Moisture transmitted through concrete slabs can cause resilient floor covering failures.

- **Subsurface-water migration** through slabs-on-grade results from leaks, hydrostatic pressure, and capillary action. Leaks can be repaired. Hydrostatic pressure and capillary action can be prevented by proper grading and appropriate passive or mechanical drainage measures.
- **Moisture-vapor transmission** through slabs always occurs to some degree and is affected by temperature, relative humidity, and concrete quality. Vapor emissions initially occur during concrete curing and drying. After drying, moisture vapor transmits through slabs-on-grade because of pressure differences. Above-grade slabs can absorb moisture from the air below and later reemit it.

Good-quality concrete that is fully cured and dry has low permeability; therefore, it minimizes moisture-vapor emission and its effects. When concrete slabs are tested according to ASTM F 1869, *Test Method for Measuring Moisture Vapor Emission Rate of Concrete Subfloor Using Anhydrous Calcium Chloride*, 3 lb of water/1000 sq. ft. (1.36 kg of water/92.9 sq. m) of slab in a 24-hour period is generally accepted in the resilient floor covering industry as a safe maximum moisture-emission level. Some manufacturers' installation instructions state that up to 5 lb of water/1000 sq. ft (2.27 kg of water/92.9 sq. m) in 24 hours is acceptable.

To avoid resilient floor covering failures caused by moisture problems from concrete slabs, subsurface-water migration through slabs-on-grade must be eliminated and moisture-vapor transmission through slabs must be minimized. Consider conditions affecting moisture and incorporate appropriate preventive measures into the contract documents. ASTM F 710, *Practice for Preparing Concrete Floors to Receive Resilient Flooring*, Appendix X1, includes specific recommendations for concrete slab design to prevent resilient floor covering failures.

MAINTENANCE PROCEDURES

Routine maintenance procedures for resilient floor tile, which are the responsibility of the owner, include sweeping or dust mopping frequently and cleaning floors by damp mopping periodically with a diluted neutral-detergent solution. For VCT and solid vinyl floor tile, mopping is sometimes combined with light scrubbing with a floor machine followed by spray buffing. Dry buffing is recommended for some solid vinyl products and is generally recommended for rubber tile. Manufacturers' recommendations vary, however, and must be verified. Floor machines used for buffing should be operated by well-trained personnel to avoid damaging the floor.

ENVIRONMENTAL CONSIDERATIONS

Plastics in resilient floor coverings generally raise environmental questions. Historically, processes used to manufacture PVC adversely affected the environment. To protect the environment, PVC production activities now occur in closed vessels. Incorporating PVC during resilient floor covering manufacturing processes poses minimal risk to the environment and human health.

Plasticizers are used to make resilient floor coverings flexible. Research shows no evidence of adverse human health effects from plasticizers when they are used in these products. Two plasticizers commonly used in resilient floor covering products are considered safe for use in toys and medical products.

During resilient floor covering manufacturing processes, most of the scrap is recycled for use in the production process. Rubber floor tile manufactured from postconsumer recycled rubber is available, and some VCT products contain postconsumer recycled vinyl. For products advertised as having recycled content, contact manufacturers to determine percentages of postconsumer and industrial waste used in manufacturing processes.

Resilient floor coverings are durable; however, disposal of products after their useful life should be considered. When discarded products are placed in landfills, plasticizers may leach. Thermoset rubber remains inert when dumped in landfills and can be incinerated for energy recovery. Because VCT formulations have a high percentage of filler (typically products are more than 80 percent limestone), these products are basically inert when disposed of in landfills.

When selecting installation adhesives, manufacturers and installers must comply with VOC restrictions of authorities having jurisdiction or they are criminally liable; therefore, specifying compliance with local law is unnecessary. However, if a project requires more stringent restrictions on VOC content than required by law, consult manufacturers for recommendations and include appropriate requirements in the specifications. Water-based adhesives are available for many types of installations.

REFERENCES

Publication dates cited here were current at the time of this writing. Publications are revised periodically, and revisions may have occurred before this book was published.

ASTM International

ASTM D 2047-93: Test Method for Static Coefficient of Friction of Polish-Coated Floor Surfaces as Measured by the James Machine

ASTM D 2240-97: Test Method for Rubber Property—Durometer Hardness

ASTM E 84-99: Test Method for Surface Burning Characteristics of Building Materials

ASTM E 648-99: Test Method for Critical Radiant Flux of Floor-Covering Systems Using a Radiant Heat Energy Source

ASTM E 662-97: Test Method for Specific Optical Density of Smoke Generated by Solid Materials

ASTM F 710-98: Practice for Preparing Concrete Floors to Receive Resilient Flooring

ASTM F 1066-99: Specification for Vinyl Composition Floor Tile

ASTM F 1344-93: Specification for Rubber Floor Tile

ASTM F 1700-99: Specification for Solid Vinyl Floor Tile

ASTM F 1869-98: Test Method for Measuring Moisture Vapor Emission Rate of Concrete Subfloor Using Anhydrous Calcium Chloride

National Fire Protection Association

NFPA 253-95: Method of Test for Critical Radiant Flux of Floor Covering Systems Using a Radiant Heat Energy Source

NFPA 258-97: Research Test Method for Determining Smoke Generation of Solid Materials

United States Architectural & Transportation Barriers Compliance Board

ADAAG: Accessibility Guidelines for Buildings and Facilities, adopted in 1991; continual revisions.

09652 SHEET VINYL FLOOR COVERINGS

This chapter discusses sheet vinyl floor coverings, with and without backings, for commercial projects.

This chapter does not discuss static-control sheet vinyl floor coverings or resilient wall base and accessories; they are included in other chapters.

GENERAL COMMENTS

Sheet vinyl floor coverings are available in a variety of wear-layer compositions and constructions. The best way to specify these products is by naming acceptable products. Color and other aesthetic characteristics are not easily specified by descriptive methods or by referencing standards. Generic specifications may be feasible for products and colors common to several manufacturers, but subtle differences in appearance among products often cannot be precisely categorized. For competitive pricing, naming several acceptable products with a similar appearance establishes a cost baseline. If products are not named, bids invariably reflect the least-expensive products that comply with requirements but not necessarily those that produce the desired visual effect.

Obtain current literature and samples from manufacturers to select products for a project. Use samples to evaluate the characteristics of products, including construction, backings, appearance, and finish. Review manufacturers' literature for information on durability, ease of maintenance, resilience, load limits, and recommendations for suitable environments for product installation. Generally, products without backings are manufactured to suit the needs of commercial and light-commercial applications, while products with backings are manufactured for commercial, light-commercial, and residential applications.

Consider seamless installations for floor coverings in areas requiring more aseptic installations or that are subject to wetting. Although sheet vinyl floor coverings resist moisture, installations may fail if the bond between the floor covering and the substrate is weakened or destroyed by moisture on the surface seeping through seams. Heat welding or chemical bonding eliminates open joints at seams. Generally, manufacturers, installers, and end users prefer the appearance and performance of heat-welded seams over chemically bonded seams. Some manufacturers also offer alternative, proprietary seamless installation techniques.

Integral flash cove bases can be installed in standard and seamless installations with heat-welding bead or chemical-bonding compound. In seamless installations, an integral flash cove base eliminates the open joints where floor coverings meet walls.

- **Cove strips** form a radius at the joint between the floor and the wall surface, to support floor covering that is turned up the wall.
- **Cove base cap strips,** available in metal, vinyl, or rubber, conceal the edge of floor covering that is turned up the wall. Metal and rubber cap strips are available with a square edge. Vinyl cap strips have either a square or a tapered top edge. Vinyl and rubber cap strips are easier to install than metal cap strips. It is easier to scribe floor covering to fit metal cap strips than to fit either vinyl or rubber cap strips.

- **Metal cove base corners** provide additional support for the floor covering at inside and outside corners. Not all manufacturers' installation instructions require using metal cove base corners.

PRODUCT STANDARDS

ASTM F 1303, *Specification for Sheet Vinyl Floor Covering with Backing,* and ASTM F 1913, *Specification for Vinyl Sheet Floor Covering without Backing,* describe floor covering products. ASTM F 1913 is a new standard. Historically, manufacturers of products without backings have referenced ASTM F 1303 and classified backings as nonfoamed plastics, or stated that products complied with the exception of requirements for backings. Because ASTM F 1913 is new, manufacturers' literature may still reference ASTM F 1303 for products without backings.

Performance requirements in the standards for products with and without backings include testing criteria for flexibility, residual indentation, and resistance to chemicals, heat, light, and static loads. Flexibility testing evaluates the performance of floor coverings during installation; other tests evaluate them during in-service use.

ASTM F 1303 categorizes products with backings by wear-layer binder content and thickness and by backing material. Wear layers are transparent, translucent, or opaque. Transparent and translucent materials typically have a background pattern that is printed or otherwise prepared. Surfaces are smooth, embossed, or otherwise textured.

- **Type** designates the wear-layer binder content. Type I products have wear-layer binder contents of not less than 90 percent; Type II products have wear-layer binder contents of not less than 34 percent.

  The wear-layer binder, according to the standard, consists "of one or more vinyl resins, plasticizers and stabilizers. Each resin shall be polyvinyl chloride or a copolymer of vinyl chloride not less than 85 percent of which is vinyl chloride. The vinyl resin(s) shall be not less than 60 percent by weight of the binder." The top layer(s) may be non-PVC layer(s) with an average minimum total thickness of 0.0004 inch (0.01 mm). Thinner top layers may be used but cannot be counted to classify the grade. These non-PVC top layers may constitute up to 49 percent of the wear layer and are not removable by normal maintenance procedures.

Table 1
ASTM F 1303 WEAR-LAYER THICKNESS

Type	Grade	Thickness
I	1	0.020 inch (0.51 mm)
	2	0.014 inch (0.36 mm)
	3	0.010 inch (0.25 mm)
II	1	0.050 inch (1.27 mm)
	2	0.030 inch (0.76 mm)
	3	0.020 inch (0.51 mm)

- **Grade** designates wear-layer thicknesses (listed in Table 1). Typical application recommendations for each grade are listed in the standard. Grade 1 sheet vinyl floor coverings are for commercial, light-commercial, and residential applications; Grade 2, for light-commercial and residential applications; and Grade 3, for residential applications only.
- **Class** designates backing material. Class A backings are nonasbestos, fibrous formulations; Class B, nonfoamed plastic; and Class C, foamed plastic. If these materials act as interlayers, they are not considered backings. For example, some products contain a glass-fiber interlayer with foamed-plastic backing; others have a glass-fiber-mesh reinforcement located in the center of the sheet.

ASTM F 1913, for products without backings, describes a PVC-pattern portion of the wear layer and optional, clear, specialty performance top layer(s), which may be PVC or non-PVC. Specialty performance top layers must have an average minimum total thickness of 0.0004 inch (0.01mm) and are not removable by normal maintenance procedures. Thinner top layers may be used but cannot be counted as part of the specialty performance top layer.

- **The minimum binder content** for the PVC-pattern portion of the wear layer is 50 percent. According to the standard, the binder consists "of one or more vinyl resins, plasticizers and stabilizers. Each resin shall be polyvinyl chloride or a copolymer of vinyl chloride not less than 85 percent of which is vinyl chloride. The vinyl resin(s) shall be not less than 60 percent by weight of the binder."
- **The wear layer and total thickness** of the product are the same. The total thickness is the sum of the PVC-pattern portion of the wear layer and the specialty performance top layer(s). The minimum total thickness average is 0.075 inch (1.9 mm).

WARRANTIES

Manufacturers' warranties vary. Selecting acceptable products establishes warranty requirements. For descriptive specifications, consider including requirements for a special warranty in the floor-covering specification.

FIRE-TEST-RESPONSE CHARACTERISTICS

In most building codes, sheet vinyl floor coverings are classified as a "traditional" flooring material and are exempt from fire-test-response requirements. However, under some circumstances and in some jurisdictions, floor-covering materials are required to meet certain fire-test-response criteria. Verify requirements for each project.

The National Fire Protection Association (NFPA) publication NFPA 101, *Life Safety Code,* requires that floor covering materials in exits and accesses to exits meet critical radiant flux (CRF) limitations in certain occupancies. Local jurisdictions may impose other restrictions. Before specifying requirements for CRF or for other fire-test-response characteristics for sheet vinyl floor coverings, verify applicable requirements of authorities having jurisdiction.

CRF is established by the radiant panel test in ASTM E 648 or NFPA 253. Both standards describe essentially the same test method. The test was designed to provide a measure of a floor covering's tendency to spread flames when the floor covering is located in a corridor and exposed to the flame and hot gases from a room fire. The higher the CRF value, the more resistant the material is to flame spread. Consequently, the NFPA 101, Class I requirement of 0.45 W/sq. cm is more stringent than the Class II requirement of 0.22 W/sq. cm.

The appendix to NFPA 101 states, "It has not been found necessary or practical to regulate interior floor finishes on the basis of smoke development." However, local authorities and building owners may impose such restrictions. For floor coverings in medical facilities, some states and federal agencies may still require a specific optical density of smoke generated value of 450 or less according to ASTM E 662 or NFPA 258. Both standards describe essentially the same test method.

The traditional test for flame-spread and smoke-developed indexes, ASTM E 84, tests specimens that are placed in an upside-down position on the ceiling of the test tunnel. Because this test procedure has little to do with the conditions likely to be encountered by sheet vinyl floor coverings in a real fire, the usefulness of the ratings is probably limited. When resilient products are tested according to ASTM E 84, many manufacturers report only the flame-spread index determined by this test method and the specific optical density of smoke according to ASTM E 662 or NFPA 258.

SLIP RESISTANCE

The Americans with Disabilities Act (ADA), *Accessibility Guidelines for Buildings and Facilities (ADAAG)* does not include static coefficient of friction requirements for walking surfaces. It includes recommendations in Appendix A4.5 that are advisory but not mandatory. The appendix encourages builders and designers to specify materials for flooring surfaces that have static coefficient of friction values of not less than 0.6 for level surfaces and 0.8 for ramped surfaces, but does not indicate the test required to make the measurement. To determine these values, the United States Architectural & Transportation Barriers Compliance Board (Access Board) used results from tests of surfacing materials with the NBS-Brungraber tester using a silastic sensor material. This machine operates on a similar principle to the James Machine required by ASTM D 2047; however, the James Machine uses a leather sensor. Results from testing the same floor covering with the two test machines differ and cannot be compared.

A consensus standard for measuring slip resistance has not been developed by the resilient floor covering industry. ASTM Committee F-6 on Resilient Floor Coverings is currently studying the issue and researching available test methods. Despite the lack of consensus within the industry, some manufacturers are publishing static coefficient of friction values for their products. Generally, the values are based on testing according to ASTM D 2047 using the James Machine.

CONCRETE SLABS AND MOISTURE PROBLEMS

Moisture transmitted through concrete slabs can cause sheet vinyl floor covering failures.

- **Subsurface-water migration** through slabs-on-grade results from leaks, hydrostatic pressure, and capillary action. Leaks can be repaired. Hydrostatic pressure and capillary action can be prevented by proper grading and appropriate passive or mechanical drainage measures.
- **Moisture-vapor transmission** through slabs always occurs to some degree and is affected by temperature, relative humidity, and concrete quality. Vapor emissions initially occur during concrete curing and drying. After drying, moisture vapor transmits through slabs-on-grade because of pressure differences. Above-grade slabs can absorb moisture from the air below and later reemit it.

Good-quality concrete that is fully cured and dry has low permeability; therefore, it minimizes moisture-vapor emission and its effects. When concrete slabs are tested according to ASTM F 1869, *Test Method for Measuring Moisture Vapor Emission Rate of Concrete Subfloor Using*

Anhydrous Calcium Chloride, 3 lb of water/1000 sq. ft. (1.36 kg of water/92.9 sq. m) of slab in a 24-hour period is generally accepted in the resilient floor covering industry as a safe maximum moisture-emission level. Some manufacturers' installation instructions state that up to 5 lb of water/1000 sq. ft (2.27 kg of water/92.9 sq. m) in 24 hours is acceptable.

To avoid sheet vinyl floor covering failures caused by moisture problems from concrete slabs, subsurface-water migration through slabs-on-grade must be eliminated and moisture-vapor transmission through slabs must be minimized. Consider conditions affecting moisture and incorporate appropriate preventive measures into the contract documents. ASTM F 710, *Practice for Preparing Concrete Floors to Receive Resilient Flooring,* Appendix X1, includes specific recommendations for concrete slab design to prevent resilient floor covering failures.

ENVIRONMENTAL CONSIDERATIONS

Plastics in sheet vinyl floor coverings generally raise environmental questions. Historically, processes used to manufacture PVC adversely affected the environment. To protect the environment, PVC production activities now occur in closed vessels. Incorporating PVC during resilient floor covering manufacturing processes poses minimal risk to the environment and human health.

Plasticizers are used to make vinyl flooring flexible. Research shows no evidence of adverse human health effects from plasticizers when they are used in vinyl floor coverings. Two plasticizers commonly used in resilient floor covering products are considered safe for use in toys and medical products.

During the floor covering manufacturing process, most of the scrap is recycled for use in the production process.

Sheet vinyl floor coverings are durable; however, disposal of products after their useful life should be considered. When discarded products are placed in landfills, plasticizers may leach.

When selecting installation adhesives, manufacturers and installers must comply with VOC restrictions of authorities having jurisdiction or they are criminally liable; therefore, specifying compliance with local law is unnec-essary. However, if a project requires more stringent restrictions on VOC content than required by law, consult manufacturers for recommendations and include appropriate requirements in the specifications. Water-based adhesives are available for many types of installations.

REFERENCES

Publication dates cited here were current at the time of this writing. Publications are revised periodically, and revisions may have occurred before this book was published.

ASTM International

ASTM D 2047-93: Test Method for Static Coefficient of Friction of Polish-Coated Floor Surfaces as Measured by the James Machine

ASTM E 84-99: Test Method for Surface-Burning Characteristics of Building Materials

ASTM E 648-99: Test Method for Critical Radiant Flux of Floor-Covering Systems Using a Radiant Heat Energy Source

ASTM E 662-97: Test Method for Specific Optical Density of Smoke Generated by Solid Materials

ASTM F 710-98: Practice for Preparing Concrete Floors to Receive Resilient Flooring

ASTM F 1303-99: Specification for Sheet Vinyl Floor Covering with Backing

ASTM F 1869-98: Test Method for Measuring Moisture Vapor Emission Rate of Concrete Subfloor Using Anhydrous Calcium Chloride

ASTM F 1913-98: Specification for Vinyl Sheet Floor Covering without Backing

National Fire Protection Association

NFPA 253-95: Method of Test for Critical Radiant Flux of Floor Covering Systems Using a Radiant Heat Energy Source

NFPA 258-97: Research Test Method for Determining Smoke Generation of Solid Materials

United States Architectural & Transportation Barriers Compliance Board

ADAAG: Accessibility Guidelines for Buildings and Facilities, adopted in 1991; continual revisions.

09653 RESILIENT WALL BASE AND ACCESSORIES

This chapter discusses rubber and vinyl wall base, stair treads, and accessories for use with resilient flooring and carpet.

This chapter does not discuss resilient floor coverings; they are covered in other chapters.

GENERAL COMMENTS

The best way to specify resilient wall base and accessories is by naming acceptable products. Color and other aesthetic characteristics are not easily specified by descriptive methods or by referencing standards. Generic specifications may be feasible for products and colors common to several manufacturers, but subtle differences in appearance among products often cannot be precisely categorized. For competitive pricing, naming several acceptable products with a similar appearance establishes a cost baseline. If products are not named, bids invariably reflect the least-expensive products that comply with requirements but not necessarily those that produce the desired visual effect.

Obtain current literature and samples from manufacturers to select products for a project. Use samples to evaluate the appearance, method of manufacture, and finish of products.

RESILIENT WALL BASE

Historically, resilient wall base was made from vulcanized thermoset rubber or vinyl. Newer product formulations include thermoplastic rubber. The polymeric binders of these products contain rubber and plastic; the plastic is often vinyl. Vulcanization cross-links the rubber in the mix but has no effect on the plastic; therefore, the binder remains thermoplastic. The development of thermoplastic rubber products confounded the development of an ASTM standard for resilient wall base for more than a decade. The old Federal Specification, FS SS-W-40, only categorized products as rubber or vinyl; it did not address thermoplastic rubber products.

- **Rubber** is defined in ASTM D 1566 as a material capable of recovering from large deformations quickly and forcibly and that can be, or already is, modified to a state in which it is insoluble in boiling solvent.
- **Vulcanization** is defined in ASTM D 1566 as an irreversible process during which a rubber compound, through a change in its chemical structure, becomes less plastic and more resistant to swelling by organic liquids while elastic properties are conferred, improved, or extended over a greater temperature range.
- **Vinyl** is the common name for plastics with binders consisting primarily of *poly(vinyl chloride)* polymers or various copolymers of vinyl chloride with minority percentages of other monomers. Poly(vinyl chloride) is defined in ASTM D 883 as being prepared by the polymerization of vinyl chloride as the sole monomer.
- **Thermoplastic,** when used as an adjective, is defined in ASTM D 883 as describing a material capable of being repeatedly softened by heating and hardened by cooling through a temperature range characteristic of the plastic and that in the softened state can be shaped by molding or extrusion.

Differences in performance characteristics of thermoplastic rubber products from those of vulcanized thermoset rubber products have not been objectively determined. Also, whether rubber products of either category are better than vinyl may depend on the application. Vinyl may shrink when exposed to UV light, and rubber is prone to fading. To evaluate manufacturers' products, consider surveying installations that have been in service for a reasonable time period.

ASTM F 1861, *Specification for Resilient Wall Base,* replaces FS SS-W-40. It includes resilient wall base made from vulcanized thermoset rubber, thermoplastic rubber, and vinyl. Material designations and definitions in the standard are as follows:

- **Type TS — Rubber, Vulcanized Thermoset:** The polymeric binder of this compound satisfies the definition of rubber and has been vulcanized as defined in ASTM D 1566.
- **Type TP — Rubber, Thermoplastic:** The polymeric binder of this compound satisfies the definition of rubber but remains thermoplastic as defined in ASTM D 883. (ASTM D 883 references the definition of rubber in ASTM D 1566.)
- **Type TV — Vinyl, Thermoplastic:** The polymeric of this compound satisfies the definition of poly(vinyl chloride) in ASTM D 883 and ASTM D 1755 and remains thermoplastic as defined in ASTM D 883. (ASTM D 1755 references the definition of vinyl in ASTM D 883.)

Manufacturing methods are classified as Group 1, solid (homogeneous), and Group 2, layered (having multiple layers). Solid products must have a uniform color throughout their thickness and are formed by extrusion, coextrusion, molding, and similar processes. Layered products have a separate wear layer that may differ in color from the substrate. The wear layer is applied to the substrate by coextrusion or is laminated to the substrate after extrusion. Manufacturers' product literature typically does not include descriptions of manufacturing methods. Evaluate manufacturing methods and their suitability for specific applications using current product samples.

Styles are classified as Style A, straight; Style B, cove; and Style C, butt-to. Straight base is often used with carpeting, and cove base is often used with resilient floor coverings. Butt-to base allows a tight, flush fit to floor covering that is the same thickness as the extended, square-edged toe. Some

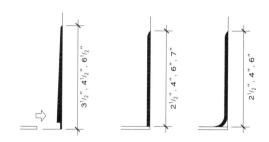

Figure 1. Resilient wall base styles

manufacturers offer proprietary styles with unique profiles and features such as lights (fig. 1).

Finish characteristics vary. Some manufacturers describe their products as having *satin, matte,* or *low-luster finishes* but do not provide objective measures, such as gloss levels, to define the terms.

Premolded inside and outside corners are available from some manufacturers. Whether premolded or job-formed corners produce the best appearance depends on a designer's preference and an installer's skill. Premolded corners may differ in texture and color from straight sections because they are produced separately and may use different manufacturing techniques. Premolded corners generally have 2¼- to 3-inch- (57- to 76-mm-) long returns; however, longer returns are available from some manufacturers. Return lengths are not always indicated in manufacturers' product literature.

Straight sections are available in both cut lengths and coils. For projects with long walls, using resilient wall base in coil form minimizes the number of joints and may reduce installation costs; otherwise, consider leaving the choice to the installer.

RESILIENT STAIR ACCESSORIES

Stair treads, risers, and stringers are formed from materials similar to wall base: vulcanized thermoset rubber, thermoplastic rubber, and vinyl. FS RR-T-650 remains the standard to reference for rubber and vinyl treads; it includes specifications for metallic and nonmetallic treads. An ASTM resilient tread standard is being developed but when it will be adopted is unknown.

FS RR-T-650 classifies rubber treads as "Composition A" and vinyl treads as "Composition B." No differentiation is made between vulcanized thermoset and thermoplastic rubbers. Type designates the top surface design of tread: Type 1 is for smooth surfaces, and Type 2 is for designed surfaces in which the pattern is limited to not more than 50 percent of the tread's overall thickness. Specific dimensions are given for width and placement of abrasive strips in rubber treads, based on requirements for slip resistance or access for the visually impaired.

The intended use of treads is important and should be specified according to FS RR-T-650. Indicate the intended use on the drawings by showing stair construction and location, or include this information in the specifications.

Product patterns and profiles vary. Although specifiers can broadly describe patterns by referencing types in FS RR-T-650, it is best to name products or show profiles and top surface patterns on the drawings (figs. 2-4). Rubber treads with raised discs or other raised shapes that match tiles are avail-

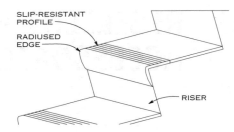

Figure 4. Treads and risers

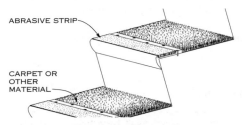

Figure 5. Abrasive edges

able from some manufacturers. Matching landing materials are available from some manufacturers.

Contrasting colors and abrasive strips at the leading edge of treads may be required by OSHA and authorities having jurisdiction for transportation facilities and certain other applications (fig. 5). The State of California's Disabled Access Regulations include slip-resistance and visibility requirements. Nosing styles must comply with access requirements for people with disabilities; verify requirements of authorities having jurisdiction.

RESILIENT MOLDING ACCESSORIES

Resilient molding accessories are available in vinyl and rubber and in various shapes and sizes . The only practical method of specifying these products is by product name or by referring to details on the drawings (figs. 6-7).

WARRANTIES

Manufacturers' warranties vary. Selecting acceptable products establishes warranty requirements. For descriptive specifications, consider including requirements for a special warranty in the specifications.

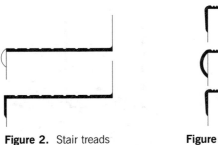

Figure 2. Stair treads

Figure 3. Stair nosings

Figure 6. Reducers

Figure 7. Thresholds, saddles, and feature strip

FIRE-TEST-RESPONSE CHARACTERISTICS

Resilient accessories are generally exempt from fire-test-response requirements in most building codes. However, under some circumstances and in some jurisdictions, floor-covering materials are required to meet certain fire-test-response criteria; for example, resilient stair accessories installed in means of egress. Verify requirements for each project.

The National Fire Protection Association (NFPA) publication NFPA 101, *Life Safety Code,* requires that floor covering materials in exits and accesses to exits meet critical radiant flux (CRF) limitations in certain occupancies. Local jurisdictions may impose other restrictions. Before specifying requirements for CRF or for other fire-test-response characteristics for resilient stair accessories, verify applicable requirements of authorities having jurisdiction.

CRF is established by the radiant panel test in ASTM E 648 or NFPA 253. Both standards describe essentially the same test method. The test was designed to provide a measure of a floor covering's tendency to spread flames when the floor covering is located in a corridor and exposed to the flame and hot gases from a room fire. The higher the CRF value, the more resistant the material is to flame spread. Consequently, the NFPA 101, Class I requirement of 0.45 W/sq. cm is more stringent than the Class II requirement of 0.22 W/sq. cm.

The appendix to NFPA 101 states, "It has not been found necessary or practical to regulate interior floor finishes on the basis of smoke development." However, local authorities and building owners may impose such restrictions. For floor coverings in medical facilities, some states and federal agencies may still require a specific optical density of smoke generated value of 450 or less according to ASTM E 662 or NFPA 258. Both standards describe essentially the same test method.

The traditional test for flame-spread and smoke-developed indexes, ASTM E 84, tests specimens that are placed in an upside-down position on the ceiling of the test tunnel. Because this test procedure has little to do with the conditions likely to be encountered by resilient products in a real fire, the usefulness of the ratings is probably limited. When resilient products are tested according to ASTM E 84, many manufacturers report only the flame-spread index determined by this test method and the specific optical density of smoke according to ASTM E 662 or NFPA 258.

ENVIRONMENTAL CONSIDERATIONS

Plastics in resilient wall base and accessories generally raise environmental questions. Historically, processes used to manufacture PVC adversely affected the environment. To protect the environment, PVC production activities now occur in closed vessels. Incorporating PVC during resilient wall base and accessory manufacturing processes poses minimal risk to the environment and human health.

Plasticizers are used to make resilient wall base and accessories flexible. Research shows no evidence of adverse human health effects from plasticizers when they are used in these products. Two plasticizers commonly used in resilient products are considered safe for use in toys and medical products.

During wall base and accessory manufacturing processes, most of the scrap is recycled for use in the production process.

Resilient wall base and accessories are durable; however, disposal of products after their useful life should be considered. When discarded products are placed in landfills, plasticizers may leach. Thermoset rubber remains inert when dumped in landfills and can be incinerated for energy recovery.

When selecting installation adhesives, manufacturers and installers must comply with VOC restrictions of authorities having jurisdiction or they are criminally liable; therefore, specifying compliance with local law is unnecessary. However, if a project requires more stringent restrictions on VOC content than required by law, consult manufacturers for recommendations and include appropriate requirements in the specifications. Water-based adhesives are available for many types of installations.

REFERENCES

Publication dates cited here were current at the time of this writing. Publications are revised periodically, and revisions may have occurred before this book was published.

ASTM International

ASTM D 883-96: Terminology Relating to Plastics

ASTM D 1566-98: Terminology Relating to Rubber

ASTM D 1755-92: Specification for Poly(Vinyl Chloride) Resins

ASTM E 84-99: Test Method for Surface-Burning Characteristics of Building Materials

ASTM E 648-99: Test Method for Critical Radiant Flux of Floor-Covering Systems Using a Radiant Heat Energy Source

ASTM E 662-97: Test Method for Specific Optical Density of Smoke Generated by Solid Materials

ASTM F 1861-00: Specification for Resilient Wall Base

Federal Specification

FS RR-T-650E-1994: Treads, Metallic and Nonmetallic, Skid-Resistant

National Fire Protection Association

NFPA 253-95: Method of Test for Critical Radiant Flux of Floor Covering Systems Using a Radiant Heat Energy Source

NFPA 258-97: Research Test Method for Determining Smoke Generation of Solid Materials

09654 **LINOLEUM FLOOR COVERINGS**

This chapter discusses linoleum floor tile and sheet floor coverings.

This chapter does not discuss resilient wall base and accessories installed with linoleum floor coverings; they are covered in another chapter.

GENERAL COMMENTS

Linoleum is a solidified mixture of linoleum cement binder (linseed oil and pine, fossil, or other resins or rosins, or equivalent oxidized oleoresinous binder) and ground cork, wood flour, mineral fillers, and pigments. The mixture is bonded and keyed to a burlap (jute) or other suitable fibrous backing so that the backing is partially embedded in the mixture. Linoleum is used to cover floors, work surfaces, and bulletin boards.

Linoleum was invented in England by Frederick Walton in 1860. Because linseed oil is derived from the flax plant, Walton named the product for the Latin *linum* (meaning flax) and *oleum* (meaning oil). It became increasingly popular until its production peaked in the 1940s. Other resilient flooring products surpassed linoleum's popularity in the 1950s and 1960s. In the 1970s, linoleum production in the United States was discontinued. Since the 1980s, linoleum's popularity has rebounded and has been increasing. Currently, linoleum floor coverings marketed in the United States are imported from Europe.

The best way to specify linoleum floor coverings is by naming acceptable products. Color and other aesthetic characteristics are not easily specified by descriptive methods or by referencing standards. Generic specifications may be feasible for products and colors common to several manufacturers, but subtle differences in appearance among products often cannot be precisely categorized. For competitive pricing, naming several acceptable products with similar appearances establishes a cost baseline. If products are not named, bids invariably reflect the least-expensive products that comply with requirements but not necessarily those that produce the desired visual effect.

Obtain manufacturers' current literature and samples to select products for a project. Use samples to evaluate the appearance and finish of products. Review manufacturers' literature for information on durability, ease of maintenance, resilience, load limits, and recommendations for suitable environments for product installation.

Seamless installations using heat-welding beads are recommended for sheet floor coverings. Large-size tiles can also be heat welded. Welding rods can match or contrast with the floor covering.

PRODUCT CHARACTERISTICS

ASTM F 2034, *Specification for Sheet Linoleum Floor Covering,* was adopted in May 2000. ASTM Committee F-6 is drafting a separate standard for linoleum floor tile, but when it will be adopted is unknown. The Federal Specification for linoleum floor coverings was canceled on February 27, 1989.

To manufacture linoleum, the linoleum cement (linseed oil and rosin) is mixed with ground cork, wood flour, or a combination of ground cork and wood flour, powdered limestone, and pigments. The mixture is calendered onto a fibrous backing and then slowly cured in drying ovens. Tiles are often cut from the same materials used for sheet products.

The backing of most linoleum floor coverings is jute. For dimensional stability, some manufacturers use a synthetic backing on tiles.

Drying room film is a yellow coating that forms on the linoleum's surface during the drying process; it is caused by linseed oil migrating to the surface, and is a natural phenomenon particular to linoleum. The change in appearance is temporary and is not a defect. The film disappears when linoleum is exposed to natural or artificial light through an oxidation process. The time required for drying room film to disappear ranges from several hours to six weeks, depending on the intensity of the light source. The film will disappear even after protective floor polish is applied, although polish may slow the process. If linoleum is covered with building paper, other protective materials, or furnishings, the oxidation process will not occur while the protective materials are in place. The owner should be informed that it is necessary to leave linoleum uncovered until the drying room film disappears.

Stove bar marks are surface deformations caused by the linoleum drying procedure. Linoleum sheet is hung in large loops between poles in drying rooms. Deformations caused by the loops over poles are generally cut out. Deformations caused by the suspended loops between poles are called stove bar marks; if they are not cut out, they usually occur about midway in sheet flooring rolls. Stove bar marks can be eliminated by applying adhesive to both the back side of the flooring at the mark and the subfloor (double sticking) and by placing weights on the flooring in the mark's area during adhesive curing.

Linoleum is naturally antistatic, according to manufacturers' literature. Static-dissipative linoleum that complies with ASTM F 150, *Test Method for Electrical Resistance of Conductive and Static Dissipative Resilient Flooring,* is available. Consult manufacturers to verify products' other electrical properties. See Chapter 09661, Static-Control Resilient Floor Coverings, for more information on static-control floor coverings.

Various thicknesses of linoleum are available. Generally, 0.08-inch- (2.0-mm-) thick linoleum is suitable for residential traffic applications; 0.10 inch (2.5 mm), for moderate commercial traffic; and 0.13 inch (3.2 mm), for heavy commercial traffic. Before selecting a thickness, consult manufacturers for recommendations.

INSTALLATION ACCESSORIES

Integral flash cove bases can be installed in standard and seamless installations with heat-welding beads. In seamless installations, an integral flash cove base eliminates the joints where floor coverings meet walls.

Integral-cove-base accessories include the following:

- **Cove strips** form a radius at the joint between the floor and the wall surface, to support floor covering that is turned up the wall.
- **Cove base cap strips** conceal the edge of floor covering that is turned up the wall. They come in metal, vinyl, or rubber. Metal and rubber cap strips are available with a square top edge. Vinyl cap strips have either a square or a tapered top edge. Vinyl and rubber cap strips are easier to install than metal caps. It is easier to scribe floor covering to fit metal cap strips than to fit either vinyl or rubber cap strips.

WARRANTIES

Manufacturers' warranties vary. Selecting acceptable products establishes warranty requirements. For descriptive specifications, consider including requirements for a special warranty in the floor-covering specification.

FIRE-TEST-RESPONSE CHARACTERISTICS

In most building codes, linoleum floor coverings are classified as "traditional" flooring materials and are exempt from fire-test-response requirements. However, under some circumstances and in some jurisdictions, floor-covering materials are required to meet certain fire-test-response criteria. Verify requirements for each project.

The National Fire Protection Association (NFPA) publication NFPA 101, *Life Safety Code,* requires that floor-covering materials in exits and accesses to exits meet critical radiant flux (CRF) limitations in certain occupancies. Local jurisdictions may impose other restrictions. Before specifying requirements for CRF or for other fire-test-response characteristics for linoleum floor coverings, verify applicable requirements of authorities having jurisdiction.

CRF is established by the radiant panel test described in ASTM E 648 or NFPA 253. Both standards describe essentially the same test method. The test was designed to provide a measure of a floor covering's tendency to spread flames when the floor covering is located in a corridor and exposed to the flame and hot gases from a room fire. The higher the CRF value, the more resistant the material is to flame spread. Consequently, the NFPA 101, Class I requirement of 0.45 W/sq. cm is more stringent than the Class II requirement of 0.22 W/sq. cm.

The appendix to NFPA 101 states, "It has not been found necessary or practical to regulate interior floor finishes on the basis of smoke development." However, local authorities and building owners may impose such restrictions. For floor coverings in medical facilities, some state and federal agencies may still require a specific optical density of smoke generated value of 450 or less according to ASTM E 662 or NFPA 258. Both standards describe essentially the same test method.

The traditional test for flame-spread and smoke-developed indexes, ASTM E 84, examines specimens that are placed in an upside-down position on the ceiling of the test tunnel. Because this test procedure has little to do with the conditions likely to be encountered by linoleum floor coverings in a real fire, the usefulness of the ratings is probably limited. When resilient products are tested according to ASTM E 84, many manufacturers report only the flame-spread index determined by this test method and the specific optical density of smoke according to ASTM E 662 or NFPA 258.

SLIP RESISTANCE

The Americans with Disabilities Act (ADA), *Accessibility Guidelines for Buildings and Facilities (ADAAG)* does not include static coefficient of friction requirements for walking surfaces. It includes recommendations in Appendix A4.5 that are advisory but not mandatory. The appendix encourages builders and designers to specify materials for floor surfaces that have static coefficient of friction values of not less than 0.6 for level surfaces and 0.8 for ramped surfaces but does not indicate the test required to make the measurement. To determine these values, the United States Architectural & Transportation Barriers Compliance Board (Access Board) used results from tests of surfacing materials with the NBS-Brungraber tester using a silastic sensor material. This machine operates on a principle similar to the James Machine required by ASTM D 2047; however, the James Machine uses a leather sensor. Results from testing the same floor covering with the two test machines differ and cannot be compared.

A consensus standard for measuring slip resistance has not been developed by the resilient floor covering industry. ASTM Committee F-6 on Resilient Floor Coverings is currently studying the issue and researching available test methods. Despite the lack of consensus within the industry, some manufacturers publish static coefficient of friction values for their products. Generally, the values are based on testing according to ASTM D 2047 using the James Machine.

CONCRETE SLABS AND MOISTURE PROBLEMS

Linoleum is very sensitive to substrate moisture, and moisture transmitted through concrete slabs can cause linoleum floor covering failures.

- **Subsurface-water migration** through slabs-on-grade results from leaks, hydrostatic pressure, and capillary action. Leaks can be repaired. Hydrostatic pressure and capillary action can be prevented by proper grading and appropriate passive or mechanical drainage measures.
- **Moisture-vapor transmission** through slabs always occurs to some degree and is affected by temperature, relative humidity, and concrete quality. Vapor emissions initially occur during concrete curing and drying. After drying, moisture vapor transmits through slabs-on-grade because of pressure differences. Above-grade slabs can absorb moisture from the air below and later reemit it.

Good-quality concrete that is fully cured and dry has low permeability; therefore, it minimizes moisture-vapor emission and its effects. When concrete slabs are tested according to ASTM F 1869, *Test Method for Measuring Moisture Vapor Emission Rate of Concrete Subfloor Using Anhydrous Calcium Chloride,* 3 lb of water/1000 sq. ft. (1.36 kg of water/92.9 sq. m) of slab in a 24-hour period is generally accepted in the resilient floor covering industry as a safe maximum moisture-emission level. Some manufacturers' installation instructions state that up to 5 lb of water/1000 sq. ft (2.27 kg of water/92.9 sq. m) in 24 hours is acceptable.

To avoid linoleum floor covering failures caused by moisture problems from concrete slabs, subsurface-water migration through slabs-on-grade must be eliminated and moisture-vapor transmission through slabs must be minimized. Consider conditions affecting moisture and incorporate appropriate preventive measures into the contract documents. ASTM F 710, *Practice for Preparing Concrete Floors to Receive Resilient Flooring,* Appendix X1, includes specific recommendations for concrete slab design to prevent resilient floor covering failures.

MAINTENANCE PROCEDURES

Manufacturers caution against using excessive amounts of liquid during maintenance procedures. Maintenance solutions that are abrasive or that measure more than 10 pH may damage linoleum.

Products generally have a factory-applied finish that provides temporary protection during installation. After installation, manufacturers typically recommend an initial application of two or three coats of floor polish to seal the surface. Verify recommendations of manufacturers for the products selected.

ENVIRONMENTAL CONSIDERATIONS

Linoleum is generally considered a "green" building product because it is made from natural, renewable materials; its production has little adverse effect on the environment; it has a long useful life; and when it is removed, it can be incinerated for energy recovery.

REFERENCES

Publication dates cited here were current at the time of this writing. Publications are revised periodically, and revisions may have occurred before this book was published.

ASTM International

ASTM D 2047-93: Test Method for Static Coefficient of Friction of Polish-Coated Floor Surfaces as Measured by the James Machine

ASTM E 84-00: Test Method for Surface-Burning Characteristics of Building Materials

ASTM E 648-99: Test Method for Critical Radiant Flux of Floor-Covering Systems Using a Radiant Heat Energy Source

ASTM E 662-97: Test Method for Specific Optical Density of Smoke Generated by Solid Materials

ASTM F 150-98: Test Method for Electrical Resistance of Conductive and Static Dissipative Resilient Flooring

ASTM F 710-98: Practice for Preparing Concrete Floors to Receive Resilient Flooring

ASTM F 1869-98: Test Method for Measuring Moisture Vapor Emission Rate of Concrete Subfloor Using Anhydrous Calcium Chloride

ASTM F 2034-00: Specification for Sheet Linoleum Floor Covering

National Fire Protection Association

NFPA 253-95: Method of Test for Critical Radiant Flux of Floor Covering Systems Using a Radiant Heat Energy Source

NFPA 258-97: Research Test Method for Determining Smoke Generation of Solid Materials

United States Architectural & Transportation Barriers Compliance Board

ADAAG: Accessibility Guidelines for Buildings and Facilities, adopted in 1991; continual revisions.

09661 STATIC-CONTROL RESILIENT FLOOR COVERINGS

This chapter discusses resilient floor coverings designed to control electrostatic discharge (ESD), including vinyl composition tile (VCT), solid vinyl floor tile, vinyl sheet floor coverings, rubber floor tile, and rubber sheet floor coverings.

This chapter does not discuss standard resilient floor coverings, static-dissipative linoleum floor coverings, or resilient accessories typically installed with floor coverings; these products are discussed in other chapters.

GENERAL COMMENTS

Electrostatic discharge (ESD) must be controlled in electronics manufacturing, computer, and explosive environments. A static-control floor covering system is a basic component of an overall ESD-control program. Depending on the sensitivity of the environment, other products and specific procedures may be required to control electrostatic charges. Generally, static-control footwear must be worn by personnel for the floor covering system to perform properly. In some environments, conductive chair covers, casters, and wrist straps on personnel are used.

For information on ESD, contact the ESD Association, a national nonprofit group with various standards and educational documents and programs. It can be reached at www.esda.org.

Static-control resilient floor covering systems have three components: floor covering products, static-control adhesive, and grounding strips. The systems prevent the accumulation of electrostatic charges generated by individuals and casters on furniture or equipment moving across the floor. They electrically connect personnel and objects and provide a path of moderate electrical conductivity to ground.

Unlike standard resilient floor coverings, static-control resilient floor coverings incorporate conductive elements into the body of the product. Some manufacturers encapsulate carbon as the conductive element in their products; others state that their products are noncarbon-based but do not specifically state what the conductive element is. Static-control adhesive links the conductive elements and provides electrical continuity to the grounding strips.

The type and sensitivity of the environment determine which static-control resilient floor covering systems are appropriate for a project. The owner must provide complete information to the architect about the sensitivity of the environment. Review the owner's requirements for static-control, durability, maintenance, resilience, static-load resistance, and other floor covering characteristics. Manufacturers' literature includes information on these product characteristics and recommendations about the suitability of products for specific conditions.

ELECTRICAL PROPERTIES

Electrical characteristics of static-control resilient floor coverings include electrical resistance, static generation, and static-decay properties. The

owner should determine the criteria for each of these properties that floor covering systems must meet and provide this information to the architect.

Electrical resistance is an inherent property of the material and is measured in ohms. Because resistance and conductance are inverse properties, measuring a material's electrical resistance gives a relative measure of the conductivity of the material. ASTM F 150, *Test Method for Electrical Resistance of Conductive and Static Dissipative Resilient Flooring*, includes electrical-resistance criteria for two categories of static-control resilient floor coverings: static dissipative and conductive.

Static generation is a measurement of the charge produced by movement across the floor. The American Association of Textile Chemists and Colorists (AATCC) publication AATCC-134 test procedure measures in volts the charge produced by an individual wearing specified footwear and moving across the floor in an environment with 20 percent relative humidity at 70°F (21°C).

Static decay is a measurement of the speed with which a charge is dissipated. Most manufacturers reference Federal Standard FED-STD-101C/4046.1. This test method measures in seconds the time required for a 5000-V charge induced on the floor surface to completely dissipate in an environment with less than 15 percent relative humidity at 73°F (23°C).

ELECTRICAL-RESISTANCE TESTING

ASTM F 150 includes test methods similar to the National Fire Protection Association (NFPA) publication NFPA 99, *Health Care Facilities;* Underwriters Laboratories (UL) standard UL 779, *Electrically Conductive Floorings;* and ESD-S7.1, *Resistive Characterization of Materials: Floor Materials.* ASTM F 150 also includes criteria for categorizing static-control resilient floor coverings as static dissipative or conductive and allows the use of either 500- or 100-V dc. NFPA 99 and UL 779 test methods use 500-V dc; ESD-S7.1 uses 100-V dc. In Note 1, ASTM F 150 states that the voltage applied should be determined by the sensitivity of the environment where the floor covering is used; conductive floor coverings used in areas where explosive gases, chemicals, or munitions are used or stored should be tested at 500-V dc. The standard establishes the following electrical-resistance criteria for the two categories of static-control resilient floor covering:

- **Static-Dissipative Resilient Floor Coverings:**

  Laboratory Testing: Average electrical resistance greater than 1,000,000 (1.0×10^6) ohms or 1 megohm and less than or equal to 1,000,000,000 (1.0×10^9) ohms or 1000 megohms when test specimens are tested surface to ground.

  Job-Site Testing: Average electrical resistance no less than 1,000,000 (1.0×10^6) ohms or 1 megohm and less than or equal to 1,000,000,000 (1.0×10^9) ohms or 1000 megohms when installed floor coverings are tested surface to ground.

- **Conductive Resilient Floor Coverings:**

    Laboratory and Job-Site Testing: Average electrical resistance greater than 25,000 (2.5×10^4) ohms and less than 1,000,000 (1.0×10^6) ohms or 1 megohm when test specimens and installed floor coverings are tested surface to surface (point to point).

    Job-Site Testing: Average electrical resistance no less than 25,000 (2.5×10^4) ohms with no single measurement less than 10,000 (1.0×10^4) ohms when installed floor coverings are tested surface to ground.

ESD-S7.1 is based on the needs of the electronics and computer industries. It includes test procedures for determining a floor material's electrical resistance from the floor surface to a groundable point and its resistance from a point to another point on its surface. The most significant difference between the test methods in ESD-S7.1 and those in NFPA 99 and UL 779 is the voltage under which the tests are performed.

NFPA 99 was used historically because it included requirements for conductive floor coverings for use in hospital environments where flammable anesthetic gases were used and stored. Currently, this type of anesthesia is not used in the United States, and the electronics and computer industries have become the primary markets for static-control floor coverings. Consequently, NFPA 99 moved information titled "Flammable Anesthetizing Locations," which includes the test methods for conductive flooring, to Annex 2 in its 1999 edition. The annex is not part of NFPA 99 requirements; it is included for informational purposes only. The annex states that while the NFPA 99 Technical Committee on Anesthesia Services is unaware of any medical facility in the United States currently using flammable anesthetics, other countries still use them and rely on the safety measures described in Annex 2.

UL 779, developed for the United States Department of Defense, includes essentially the same test methods as NFPA 99. Unlike NFPA 99, it requires testing of samples exposed to conditions and agents normally encountered during service.

GROUNDING

Manufacturers' recommendations for the number of ground connections required in a given floor area vary. Ground connections are made by connecting grounding strips embedded in static-control adhesive to ground wires installed by the electrical subcontractor or by connecting grounding strips to exposed steel columns or other convenient, known grounds.

The number of ground connections required varies with the products selected. If more than one product is acceptable, show on the drawings locations for the maximum possible number of ground connections that could be required for the products selected. Consult manufacturers for grounding recommendations to satisfy the project's static-control requirements. Making the final ground connections is usually specified in a section in Division 16, "Electrical."

PRODUCT CHARACTERISTICS

Static-Load Resistance

Vinyl composition tile (VCT) does not resist indentation from static loads as well as vinyl or rubber floor coverings.

Resiliency

VCT is less resilient than vinyl or rubber floor coverings because of its lower indentation resistance. The relative importance of the resiliency of floor coverings should be evaluated based on the requirements for performance when subject to foot traffic, static loads, and rolling loads.

Chemical Resistance

VCT and solid vinyl floor tile resist alkalis, acids, alcohols, oils, greases, and aliphatic hydrocarbons but can soften when exposed to ketones, esters, and chlorinated and aromatic hydrocarbons. For products to comply with ASTM F 1066 (VCT) and ASTM F 1700 (solid vinyl floor tile), they are exposed to only a limited number of chemicals that are meant to represent those commonly found in domestic, commercial, and institutional use. ASTM F 1344 (rubber floor tile) only requires that pigments be of good quality, insoluble in water, and resistant to alkalis, cleaning agents, and light. Most manufacturers publish tables indicating the effects of many reagents and stains on their products. Ask manufacturers or qualified testing agencies to test any known reagents or stains not listed in product literature that will contact the floor covering.

INSTALLATION ACCESSORIES

Static-control adhesive is essential to the performance of static-control resilient floor covering systems. If charges cannot easily pass from the floor covering to the ground points, static will accumulate. To maintain conductive continuity, floor coverings must be installed only with the primary product manufacturer's static-control adhesive.

Grounding strips are usually copper or brass, come in various sizes, and are provided by the floor covering manufacturer.

Integral flash cove bases can be installed in standard and seamless installations with heat-welding bead or chemical-bonding compound. In seamless installations, an integral flash cove base eliminates the joints where floor coverings meet walls. Integral flash cove base accessories include the following:

- **Cove strips** form a radius at the joint between the floor and the wall surface, to support floor covering that is turned up the wall.
- **Cove base cap strips** conceal the edge of floor covering that is turned up the wall. They come in metal, vinyl, or rubber. Metal and rubber cap strips are available with a square edge. Vinyl cap strips have either a square or tapered edge. Vinyl and rubber cap strips are easier to install than metal caps. It is easier to scribe floor covering to fit metal cap strips than to fit either vinyl or rubber caps.
- **Metal cove base corners** provide additional support for floor coverings at inside and outside corners. Not all manufacturers' installation instructions require using metal cove base corners.

WARRANTIES

Manufacturers' warranties vary. Selecting acceptable products establishes warranty requirements. For descriptive specifications, consider including requirements for a special warranty in the floor-covering specification.

FIRE-TEST-RESPONSE CHARACTERISTICS

In most building codes, static-control resilient floor covering is classified as a "traditional" flooring material and is exempt from fire-test-response requirements. However, under some circumstances and in some jurisdictions, floor covering materials are required to meet certain fire-test-response criteria. Verify requirements for each project.

NFPA 101, *Life Safety Code,* requires that floor covering materials in exits and accesses to exits meet critical radiant flux (CRF) limitations in certain occupancies. Local jurisdictions may impose other restrictions. Before specifying requirements for CRF or other fire-test-response characteristics for static-control resilient floor coverings, verify applicable requirements of authorities having jurisdiction.

CRF is established by the radiant panel test in ASTM E 648 or NFPA 253. Both standards describe essentially the same test method. The test was designed to provide a measure of a floor covering's tendency to spread flames when the floor covering is located in a corridor and exposed to the flame and hot gases from a room fire. The higher the CRF value, the more resistant the material is to flame spread. Consequently, the NFPA 101, Class I requirement of 0.45 W/sq. cm is more stringent than the Class II requirement of 0.22 W/sq. cm.

The appendix of NFPA 101 states, "It has not been found necessary or practical to regulate interior floor finishes on the basis of smoke development." However, local authorities and building owners may impose such restrictions. For floor coverings in medical facilities, some states and federal agencies may still require a specific optical density of smoke generated value of 450 or less according to ASTM E 662 or NFPA 258. Both standards describe essentially the same test method.

The traditional test for flame-spread and smoke-developed indexes, ASTM E 84, tests specimens that are placed in an upside-down position on the ceiling of the test tunnel. Because this test procedure has little to do with the conditions likely to be encountered by static-control resilient floor coverings in a real fire, the usefulness of the ratings is probably limited. When resilient products are tested according to ASTM E 84, many manufacturers report only the flame-spread index determined by this test method and report the specific optical density of smoke according to ASTM E 662 or NFPA 258.

SLIP RESISTANCE

The Americans with Disabilities Act (ADA), *Accessibility Guidelines for Buildings and Facilities (ADAAG)* does not include static coefficient of friction requirements for walking surfaces. It includes recommendations in Appendix A4.5 that are advisory but not mandatory. The appendix encourages builders and designers to specify materials for floor surfaces that have static coefficient of friction values of not less than 0.6 for level surfaces and 0.8 for ramped surfaces, but does not indicate the test required to make the measurement. To determine these values, the United States Architectural & Transportation Barriers Compliance Board (Access Board) used results from tests of surfacing materials with the NBS-Brungraber tester using a silastic sensor material. This machine operates on a similar principle to the James Machine required by ASTM D 2047; however, the James Machine uses a leather sensor. Results from testing the same floor covering with the two test machines differ and cannot be compared.

A consensus standard for measuring slip resistance has not been developed by the resilient floor covering industry. ASTM Committee F-6 on Resilient Floor Coverings is currently studying the issue and researching available test methods. Despite the current lack of consensus within the industry, some manufacturers are publishing static coefficient of friction values for their products. Generally, the values are based on testing according to ASTM D 2047 using the James Machine.

CONCRETE SLABS AND MOISTURE PROBLEMS

Moisture transmitted through concrete slabs can cause static-control resilient floor covering failures.

- **Subsurface-water migration** through slabs-on-grade results from leaks, hydrostatic pressure, and capillary action. Leaks can be repaired. Hydrostatic pressure and capillary action can be prevented by proper grading and appropriate passive or mechanical drainage measures.
- **Moisture-vapor transmission** through slabs always occurs to some degree and is affected by temperature, relative humidity, and concrete quality. Vapor emissions initially occur during concrete curing and drying. After drying, moisture vapor transmits through slabs-on-grade because of pressure differences. Above-grade slabs can absorb moisture from the air below and later reemit it.

Good-quality concrete that is fully cured and dry has low permeability; therefore, it minimizes moisture-vapor emission and its effects. When concrete slabs are tested according to ASTM F 1869, *Test Method for Measuring Moisture Vapor Emission Rate of Concrete Subfloor Using Anhydrous Calcium Chloride,* 3 lb of water/1000 sq. ft. (1.36 kg of water/92.9 sq. m) of slab in a 24-hour period is generally accepted in the resilient floor covering industry as a safe maximum moisture-emission level. Some manufacturers' installation instructions state that up to 5 lb of water/1000 sq. ft (2.27 kg of water/92.9 sq. m) in 24 hours is acceptable.

To avoid static-control resilient floor covering failures caused by moisture problems from concrete slabs, subsurface-water migration through slabs-on-grade must be eliminated and moisture-vapor transmission through slabs must be minimized. Consider conditions affecting moisture and incorporate appropriate preventive measures into the contract documents. ASTM F 710, *Practice for Preparing Concrete Floors to Receive Resilient Flooring,* Appendix X1, includes specific recommendations for concrete slab design to prevent resilient floor covering failures.

MAINTENANCE PROCEDURES

Proper maintenance of static-control resilient floor covering, which is the responsibility of the owner, is essential to preserve its electrical properties. Sweeping frequently and cleaning with a diluted neutral-detergent solution followed by a clear-water rinsing are standard recommended procedures. Wax and floor finishes can leave an insulating film that reduces the floor covering's effectiveness for static control. A heavy layer of dirt can also affect the floor covering's static-control performance.

Very few manufacturers recommend floor finishes for their static-control resilient floor coverings. Other manufacturers state that the application of any waxes or polishes impairs their floor system's capability to control static charges.

ENVIRONMENTAL CONSIDERATIONS

The electrical properties of the floor covering system usually are the primary selection criteria for static-control resilient floor coverings. However, manufacturers are addressing environmental concerns. Some low-emissivity vinyl products are available, and at least one manufacturer's product literature emphasizes that rubber products will remain inert when dumped in landfills and can be incinerated for energy recovery. Another produces a static-dissipative floor covering from recycled postconsumer tire rubber. Static-dissipative linoleum is also available; see Chapter 09654, Linoleum Floor Coverings, for a discussion of linoleum's characteristics.

REFERENCES

Publication dates cited here were current at the time of this writing. Publications are revised periodically, and revisions may have occurred before this book was published.

The American Association of Textile Chemists and Colorists

AATCC-134-96: Electrostatic Propensity of Carpets

ASTM International

ASTM D 2047-93: Test Method for Static Coefficient of Friction of Polish-Coated Floor Surfaces as Measured by the James Machine

ASTM E 84-99: Test Method for Surface Burning Characteristics of Building Materials

ASTM E 648-99: Test Method for Critical Radiant Flux of Floor-Covering Systems Using a Radiant Heat Energy Source

ASTM E 662-97: Test Method for Specific Optical Density of Smoke Generated by Solid Materials

ASTM F 150-98: Test Method for Electrical Resistance of Conductive and Static Dissipative Resilient Flooring

ASTM F 710-98: Practice for Preparing Concrete Floors to Receive Resilient Flooring

ASTM F 1066-99: Specification for Vinyl Composition Floor Tile

ASTM F 1344-93: Specification for Rubber Floor Tile

ASTM F 1700-99: Specification for Solid Vinyl Floor Tile

ASTM F 1869-98: Test Method for Measuring Moisture Vapor Emission Rate of Concrete Subfloor Using Anhydrous Calcium Chloride

The ESD Association, Inc.

ESD-S7.1-1994: Resistive Characterization of Materials: Floor Materials

Federal Standard

FED-STD-101C/4046.1-82: Electrostatic Properties of Materials

National Fire Protection Association

NFPA 99-99: Health Care Facilities

NFPA 253-95: Method of Test for Critical Radiant Flux of Floor Covering Systems Using a Radiant Heat Energy Source

NFPA 258-97: Research Test Method for Determining Smoke Generation of Solid Materials

Underwriters Laboratories Inc.

UL 779-95 (Rev. 97): Electrically Conductive Floorings

United States Architectural & Transportation Barriers Compliance Board

ADAAG: Accessibility Guidelines for Buildings and Facilities, adopted in 1991; continual revisions.

WEB SITES

The ESD Association, Inc.: www.esda.org

ESD Journal: www.esdjournal.com

09671 RESINOUS FLOORING

This chapter discusses *decorative, general-use, and high-performance or special-application resinous flooring systems applied as self-leveling slurries or troweled or screeded mortars.*

The chapter does not discuss *thin-set, resinous terrazzo or special coatings.*

PRODUCT CHARACTERISTICS

Resinous flooring systems provide a nonporous, seamless surface (fig. 1). They are used in new construction and restoration projects over rigid substrates including concrete, terrazzo, ceramic and quarry tile, and wood. Depending on the resinous flooring system, components may include primers, waterproofing membranes, or flexible reinforcing membranes applied to the substrate; and sealing or finish coats applied to the primary flooring material. The primary flooring material is often called the *body coat(s)*. When properly formulated and applied, resinous flooring systems have excellent bond and mechanical strength and resist abrasion and physical impact.

In lieu of the term *resinous flooring,* some manufacturers use *polymer flooring*. The Construction Specifications Institute's (CSI's) 1995 *MasterFormat* includes "Resinous Flooring" as a suggested Level Four section title, but it can be replaced by *polymer flooring*.

Many resinous flooring systems are available for commercial, industrial, and institutional applications. Manufacturers publish guides indicating appropriate applications for their systems. Resinous flooring can be classified in three basic categories: decorative systems, general-use commercial or industrial systems, and high-performance or special-application systems.

Flooring systems in each category can be applied as a self-leveling slurry or as a troweled or screeded mortar. Self-leveling systems are available with or without broadcast aggregates. They have lower filler-to-binder ratios and use finer gradations of aggregate fillers than trowelable systems. Self-leveling systems that conform to the substrate's contour may reflect surface irregularities and will flow if surfaces are not level. Troweled mortars are generally thicker and may conceal substrate irregularities better than self-leveling systems. The system's thickness generally does not affect its chemical resistance. Thicker systems are typically more impact- and thermal-shock-resistant. Self-leveling systems provide wearing surfaces that are free of trowel marks; troweled systems are subject to troweling irregularities. To fill voids, grout (resurfacer) coats are often applied to broadcast slurry systems and troweled systems. Troweled mortar systems can be sanded after installing the body coat and the grout coat to provide a better mechanical bond between coats (intercoat adhesion); this helps minimize troweling imperfections.

Decorative systems usually consist of decorative aggregates in a clear-epoxy-resin matrix. They are used in commercial, industrial, and institutional applications. Often, ceramic-coated silica, commonly called *colored quartz,* is the decorative aggregate used. Systems using marble, granite, dyed stone, pigmented silica, or vinyl flakes are also available and advertised by some manufacturers.

Colored-quartz aggregate systems are typically available in $\frac{1}{16}$- to $\frac{1}{4}$-inch (1.6- to 6.4-mm) thicknesses when applied as slurry with broadcast aggregates; however, $\frac{1}{8}$ inch (3.2 mm) is generally the minimum thickness recommended. Colored-quartz aggregate systems are $\frac{3}{16}$ inch (4.8 mm) thick or thicker when troweled or screeded. Colored-quartz aggregates provide finely textured surfaces in various standard and custom color mixes. Systems generally have sealing or finish coats that improve cleanability and chemical resistance and provide a gloss or matte finish. Some manufacturers offer flexible epoxy systems with urethane topcoats for exterior applications. Colored-quartz aggregate systems provide wearing surfaces that are easily maintained, sanitary, durable, and slip-resistant. Manufacturers' literature recommends them for many applications including locker rooms, food-processing areas, toilet rooms, and animal holding areas.

General-use commercial and industrial systems usually consist of pigmented resins and natural silica aggregates or clear resins and pigmented aggregates. The polymer resin is generally epoxy. Systems are typically $\frac{1}{16}$ inch (1.6 mm) thick when applied as slurry without broadcast aggregates, $\frac{1}{16}$ to $\frac{1}{4}$ inch (1.6 to 6.4 mm) thick when applied as slurry with broadcast aggregates, and $\frac{3}{16}$ inch (4.8 mm) thick or thicker when troweled or screeded. General-use systems are cost-effective and provide a range of performance properties, including a wearing surface that resists abrasion, impact, and most common chemicals. They are easily maintained, sani-

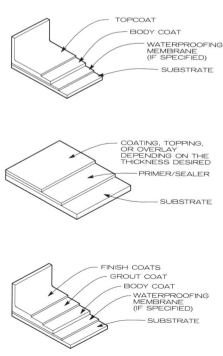

Figure 1. Resinous flooring systems

tary, and available in various slip-resistant textures. Typically, general-use, epoxy-resin systems should not be exposed to high temperatures that will soften the resin or be used in areas subject to hot-water or steam cleaning; consult manufacturers for recommendations.

High-performance or special-application systems are formulated to withstand the effects of particular environments, including corrosive chemicals, acids, solvents, extreme thermal cycles, and exposure to high temperatures; or to provide other specialized physical properties, including static-dissipative or conductive performance and fast curing times. Manufacturers offer epoxy, epoxy-novolac, urethane, and vinyl-ester systems for applications subject to severe chemical or environmental exposures. Although epoxy resins generally provide electric insulation, formulations that are static-dissipative and conductive are available. Methyl methacrylate (MMA) systems provide fast curing times. Decorative MMA systems are available. Some manufacturers state that polyacrylate or acrylic systems can be installed in areas subject to a higher rate of water-vapor transmission through concrete slabs than other resinous systems because they are breathable and allow water vapor to pass through them. For a breathable system, all system components must be permeable.

When high-performance or special-application systems are required, the owner should provide performance criteria. Based on the performance criteria and application considerations, manufacturers will recommend appropriate resinous flooring systems.

Formulations of 100 percent solids contain only reactive ingredients; they do not contain solvents or nonreactive diluents. These formulations provide full chemical-cross-linking of components in the cured mixture.

Chemical Resistance

Resinous flooring systems are generally chemical-resistant; however, the chemicals they resist and the degree of resistance provided differ among formulations. If necessary, manufacturers can adjust formulations to meet specific criteria.

Generally, epoxy resins are resistant to alkalis, fats, oils, solvents, and gases, and have fair resistance to some oxidizing agents and acids. Finish coats of urethane or other compatible materials can be applied to epoxy body coats to enhance chemical resistance. Manufacturers offer epoxy-novolac, urethane, and vinyl-ester systems for applications subject to severe chemical exposure or specific aggressive chemicals.

To select appropriate resinous flooring systems, it is important to determine the chemical-resistance properties required. The owner should compile a list of chemicals and reagents, including strengths, to which the floor will be exposed, and identify the expected frequency and duration of exposure.

Manufacturers publish tables indicating the effects of chemicals and reagents on their systems. Manufacturers' literature cautions that chemical resistance is affected by environmental conditions, including barometric pressure and temperature, and the effects of combined chemicals. Before selecting systems, consult manufacturers for recommendations. Ask manufacturers or a qualified testing agency to test products for the effects of chemicals or reagents that are not listed in product literature and that will contact the flooring.

The test methods used to determine chemical resistance vary among manufacturers, and often the procedure used is not listed in product literature. Three standard tests are listed below. Manufacturers often modify these standard test methods in developing their own testing programs for different levels of exposure, such as prolonged exposure or splash and spills. Verify the test methods required by the owner and used by manufacturers selected.

ASTM D 543, *Practices for Evaluating the Resistance of Plastics to Chemical Reagents,* replaces FED-STD-406, Method 7011. Procedure A in this standard requires the immersion of specimens in reagents for seven days. Reagents' effects are determined by reporting changes in the specimens' weight, dimensions, appearance, and strength properties. The standard includes a list of reagents and a list of liquids encountered in military service environments.

ASTM C 267, *Test Method for Chemical Resistance of Mortars, Grouts, and Monolithic Surfacings,* determines reagents' rate of attack by examining specimens after 1, 7, 14, 28, 56, and 84 days of immersion. Reagents' effects are determined by reporting changes in specimens' weight, appearance, and compressive strength and changes in the test media's (reagents') appearance.

ASTM D 1308, *Test Method for Effect of Household Chemicals on Clear and Pigmented Organic Finishes,* describes spot tests and a 50 percent immersion test; it does not prescribe specific testing time intervals. The chemical resistance is determined by reporting specimen surface alterations, such as discoloration, change in gloss, blistering, softening, swelling, loss of adhesion, or special phenomena. The standard includes a suggested list of reagents.

Antimicrobial Additives

Antimicrobial additives can be included in epoxy systems to enhance their capability to inhibit microbial growth. Some manufacturers also advertise antimicrobial additives for urethane and MMA systems. Antimicrobial additives inhibit the reproductive capabilities of microorganisms and help decrease odors. If a sanitary environment is critical, consult manufacturers for recommendations, results of toxicity tests, EPA registration numbers for additives, lists of tested organisms, and additives' effects on the flooring systems' long-term appearance.

Waterproofing Membranes

Properly applied resinous flooring systems are waterproof; however, waterproofing membranes are generally recommended to protect against cracks or other imperfections. Depending on the flexibility of the resinous system, cracks may occur from substrate shrinkage or structural movement. Waterproofing membranes should be considered for installations that are subject to chemicals and wetting and that are located over occupied spaces. Waterproofing membranes are generally not required over slabs-on-grade, except for special applications where secondary containment is important.

The waterproofing membrane must be physically and chemically compatible with other system components and should be a product formulated specifically for this purpose by the resinous flooring manufacturer. For some systems, waterproofing membranes act as the primer. Waterproofing membranes may affect other physical properties of the system; for example, a flexible waterproofing membrane used with a rigid body coat may reduce a system's impact or thermal-shock resistance. Before specifying a waterproofing membrane, consult manufacturers for recommendations.

Flexible Reinforcing Membranes

Manufacturers offer flexible reinforcing membranes or substrate crack-isolation systems to help prevent cracks from reflecting through the resinous flooring. Fiberglass scrim reinforcement can be installed in the membrane to maximize tensile strength. Some manufacturers' literature recommends applying the membrane and cloth reinforcement at cracks only. Other manufacturers' literature includes recommendations for applying the membrane over the entire substrate surface. Manufacturers often use the same material for waterproofing membranes as for reinforcing membranes.

Sealing or Finish Coats

Sealing or finish coats are generally applied by squeegee or roller. Most systems have a topcoat to seal the system; however, systems without topcoats are available. Sealing or finish coats are available for gloss and matte finishes. Manufacturers' recommendations for materials and number of coats required differ. Urethane finish coats are used often because of their resistance to chemicals; abrasion; jet fuel, hydraulic fluid, and similar hydrocarbons; and ultraviolet rays.

FIRE-TEST-RESPONSE CHARACTERISTICS

When flammability is reported, manufacturers' literature generally states that resinous flooring is self-extinguishing when tested according to ASTM D 635, *Test Method for Rate of Burning and/or Extent and Time of Burning of Self-Supporting Plastics in a Horizontal Position.* Some manufacturers report critical radiant flux (CRF) values according to ASTM E 648, *Test Method for Critical Radiant Flux of Floor Covering Systems Using a Radiant Heat Energy Source.*

The National Fire Protection Association (NFPA) publication NFPA 101, *Life Safety Code,* requires that floor covering materials in exits and access to exits meet CRF limitations in certain occupancies. Authorities having jurisdiction, and the owner, may impose other restrictions. Before specifying requirements for fire-test-response characteristics for resinous flooring, verify requirements of authorities having jurisdiction and the owner.

APPLICATION CONSIDERATIONS

A trained, experienced installer is essential to a successful resinous flooring system. The installer must know how to prepare substrates, including how to treat cracks, joints, and penetrations; how to mix and apply the system components within each component's working time; and how to broadcast aggregate properly or trowel to minimize surface imperfections. Most manufacturers provide some way to ensure that installers are competent; either by approving, training, or certifying them, or by having a manufacturer's representative on-site during the application. Requiring a single-source warranty for installation and materials from the manufacturer may ensure quality but will eliminate some manufacturers. Alternatively, a special warranty signed by the installer and manufacturer can be required. With the consent of the owner, some designers compile a list of preapproved installers before bidding.

Select systems with physical properties that will withstand the mechanical and chemical abuses and thermal-shock cycles to which the installation will be subjected. Mechanical abuse results from abrasion during use, abrasive maintenance procedures, and impacts. Chemical abuse results from cleaning and disinfectants, reagents used in commercial and industrial processes, and urine and feces. Thermal shock results from commercial and industrial operations and processes, and maintenance procedures. Consult manufacturers to determine which of their systems are most suitable for a given application.

Testing procedures to determine physical properties differ among manufacturers, making direct comparisons among products difficult. Two

current general standards for resinous flooring are Military Specification MIL-D-3134, *Deck Covering Materials;* and ASTM C 722, *Standard Specification for Chemical-Resistant Resin Monolithic Surfacings.* Manufacturers' literature rarely states that products fully comply with either standard, although the products may comply.

MIL-D-3134 is a Navy specification intended as a procurement document for coverings on shipboard interior decks. Manufacturers' literature often references this standard when reporting certain physical properties, especially impact resistance and indentation. Architectural specifications usually do not require resinous flooring complying with MIL-D-3134 because full compliance is rarely cited in manufacturers' literature and may not be applicable to architectural applications.

ASTM C 722 establishes minimum physical properties for epoxy and polyester or vinyl-ester flooring when products are tested according to specific ASTM test methods. Manufacturers' literature often references these test methods when reporting physical properties; the data generally indicate that minimum requirements established by ASTM C 722 are exceeded. ASTM C 722 requires that the chemical resistance of formulations be determined according to ASTM C 267, but ASTM C 722 does not establish chemical-resistance requirements. Instead of specifying resinous flooring complying with ASTM C 722, listing the specific physical properties according to the test methods required by ASTM C 722 in the resinous flooring specification more precisely establishes requirements.

Select surface finishes based on appearance, slip-resistance, and maintenance requirements. A heavily textured surface provides slip resistance for floors subject to wetting; however, it is more difficult to keep clean.

Installations in occupied buildings may require formulations that minimize odors during application and curing or formulations with fast curing times.

Substrate conditions and preparation are critical. Generally, a clean, dry, neutral substrate is required; however, moisture-tolerant formulations are available. Consult manufacturers for recommendations for specific substrates.

Concrete Substrates

Before applying resinous flooring, concrete substrates are roughened to ensure that surfaces are clean and free of laitance, oil, grease, curing compounds, or other materials incompatible with the resins, and to enhance adhesion of the flooring system. Substrates are roughened by abrasive blasting (shot blasting), mechanical scarifying, or acid etching. Shot blasting is generally considered the best method for preparing concrete slabs; however, it requires open, accessible areas. Sometimes, both shot blasting and chemical etching are necessary. Manufacturers' preparation procedures differ; consult manufacturers for recommendations.

Moisture from hydrostatic pressure, capillary action, and vapor transmission can cause adhesion failure of resinous systems installed on slabs-on-grade. For slabs-on-grade, capillary water barriers (drainage fill), vapor retarders, and effective measures to prevent hydrostatic pressure are required. See Chapter 09651, Resilient Tile Flooring, for a discussion of concrete slabs and moisture problems.

Uneven surfaces can be built up with resinous patching and fill material, or existing concrete slabs can be sloped to drains using patching and fill material. Manufacturers generally use patching materials formulated from the same resin as the body coat(s) or acrylics. Do not use cementitious or gypsum underlayments on concrete slabs to receive resinous flooring; the resinous flooring system should be applied directly to the concrete substrate to form a mechanical bond.

REFERENCES

Publication dates cited here were current at the time of this writing. Publications are revised periodically, and revisions may have occurred before this book was published.

ASTM International

ASTM C 267-82 (reapproved 1990): Test Method for Chemical Resistance of Mortars, Grouts, and Monolithic Surfacings

ASTM C 722-94: Specification for Chemical-Resistant Resin Monolithic Surfacings

ASTM D 543-95: Practices for Evaluating the Resistance of Plastics to Chemical Reagents

ASTM D 635-91: Test Method for Rate of Burning and/or Extent and Time of Burning of Self Supporting Plastics in a Horizontal Position

ASTM D 1308-87 (reapproved 1993): Test Method for Effect of Household Chemicals on Clear and Pigmented Organic Finishes

ASTM E 648-95: Test Method for Critical Radiant Flux of Floor Covering Systems Using a Radiant Heat Energy Source

Military Specification

MIL-D-3134J (Navy), 5 Oct. 1988 (with Amendment 1, 12 Sept. 1989): Deck Covering Materials

09680 CARPET

**This chapter discusses** tufted, fusion-bonded, and woven carpet, as well as carpet cushion for commercial installations.

**This chapter does not discuss** resilient wall base and accessories; they are discussed in Chapter 09653, Resilient Wall Base and Accessories.

PRODUCT SELECTION CONSIDERATIONS

Consider the following product characteristics when selecting a carpet:

- Face-fiber type
- Fiber treatments
- Carpet construction
- Carpet backing
- Carpet cushion, if any
- Installation method

CARPET FIBER

Carpet face-fiber types commonly used in commercial installations are nylon, polypropylene, wool, and wool blends.

- **Nylon** is the most durable man-made fiber. It is the most popular fiber for commercial carpet, constituting 85 percent of that market. Nylon can hold bright-colored dyes, with some limitations. It has good fade resistance and cleans easily, and it is resilient and resistant to crushing. Nylon is high in static electricity build-up; however, many manufacturers now produce nylon carpet fiber with an antistatic guarantee for the life of the carpet.
- **Polypropylene** (trade name Olefin) has an excellent resistance to soil. It has good fade resistance when stabilized, but colors tend to be dull. It has a low moisture-absorption rate and high chemical resistance.
- **Wool fibers** are enormously elastic and yet have such memory that they can be stretched to 30 percent without rupture and still recover their original dimensions. Deeper, richer colors are available with wool fibers. The outer layers of fibers shed water while water vapor passes through the fibers' microscopic pores, making wool a suitable carpet for areas subject to climatic extremes. Wool and wool blends are not used as frequently as synthetic fibers in commercial installations. However, they are popular for hospitality or entertainment areas, such as hotel lobbies or casinos, because wool shows less damage from cigarette burns than synthetic fibers do.

Fiber treatments include stain-resisting, antistatic, and antimicrobial treatments.

- **Antistatic treatments** are available from most manufacturers. However, the treatments may be water soluble and lose effectiveness after repeated washings. Topical antistatic finishes generally do not ensure reliable electrostatic-discharge control under all conditions.
- **Antimicrobial treatments** should not contain halogens, heavy metals, and phenols. They should have a low solubility in water so they can withstand repeated cleaning. Antimicrobials that inhibit the growth of gram-positive (staph) and gram-negative (_E. coli_) bacteria and mold can help prevent cross infection in healthcare facilities.

CARPET CONSTRUCTION

Carpet construction variables include face construction, pile characteristics, density, gauge or pitch, total weight, face weight, tuft density, and yarn count.

Face construction describes the method used to attach yarn to the backing. The five types of carpet face construction are tufted, fusion bonded, needle punched, knitted, and woven.

- **Tufted goods** account for as much as 95 percent of the broadloom carpet produced in this country (fig. 1). This fast and inexpensive construction is similar to sewing, but a tufting machine sews many rows at a time. Hundreds of needles stitch simultaneously through a backing material. The back is then coated with latex to secure the tufts, and a secondary backing material is adhered for dimensional stability.
- **Fusion-bonded goods** dominate the carpet tile market in the United States (fig. 2). The backing is not penetrated by a needle, as in tufting and needle punching. A yarn bundle is sandwiched between and implanted into adhesive substrates and fused, commonly with heat. A blade is then run between the substrates, producing two carpet pieces. Because of the production process, a cut pile is the only option for fusion-bonded goods.
- **Needle-punched carpets** are formed by hundreds of barbed needles punching through webs or blankets of fiber to mesh them together permanently (fig. 3). The result is an extremely dense sheet, without pile, of considerable weight and thickness.
- **Knitted carpets** are produced on a machine similar to that for textile knitting (fig. 4). They use more face yarn than tufting.

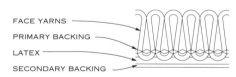

Figure 1. Tufted construction

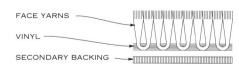

Figure 2. Fusion bonded construction

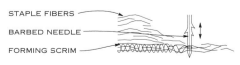

Figure 3. Needlepunched construction

PILE YARNS
WEFT SHOTS
WARP CHAIN
STUFFER YARNS
SECONDARY BACKING

Figure 4. Knitted construction

- **Woven carpets** are made using the original carpet-construction method; they still serve a limited and specialized market. The manufacturing process is slower and more expensive than that used for other carpet types; however, woven carpet is longer wearing and more dimensionally stable. Traditional variations of woven carpets include velvet, Wilton, and Axminster. More recently, Karaloc woven carpets have been introduced.

  Velvet carpet (no relationship to the construction or texture of velvet textiles) requires the simplest loom (fig. 5). However, this limits pattern types to tweeds and stripes. Various textures are available, including plush, frieze, loop-pile, multilevel-loop, and cut-and-loop styles. Velvet is often considered a form of Wilton weave

  Wilton, named after the town in England where it was developed, is similar to velvet but is known for its intricate patterns (fig. 6). The Wilton loom has a jacquard-pattern mechanism that controls all face yarns, producing both simple and complex patterns with accuracy. Perforated pattern cards selectively control the feeding of different yarns onto the pile surface, burying others. Consequently, Wiltons are generally the most dense of the three common weave types. A Wilton loom can accommodate a limited number of colors in a single pattern.

  Axminster is the most complex loom, with patterns available in an almost limitless number of colors. Each tuft is individually inserted into the pile by a mechanical pattern device that selects different colored yarns from prearranged spools (fig. 7). Axminsters (also named after a town in England) are known for their pattern intricacy and color.

  Karaloc loom was developed by Karastan Rug Mills. Patterning is limited compared to Axminsters and velvets. Combined cut-and-loop piles are possible with the Karaloc weave. Like the velvets, Karaloc is often considered a form of Wilton weave.

FACE YARNS
WEFT SHOTS
STUFFER YARNS
WARP YARNS

Figure 5. Velvet construction

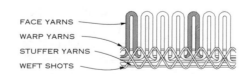
FACE YARNS
WARP YARNS
STUFFER YARNS
WEFT SHOTS

Figure 6. Wilton construction

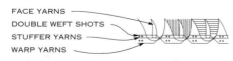
FACE YARNS
DOUBLE WEFT SHOTS
STUFFER YARNS
WARP YARNS

Figure 7. Axminster construction

Pile characteristics include the following:

- **Level-loop pile:** Level loops of yarn form the carpet surface. Low, level-loop construction is usually selected for heavy-use areas. The texture wears well but shows dirt and lint easily.
- **Cut pile:** Low, cut-pile carpet presents a plush surface. Low, dense-plush carpets stand upright to form an even surface.
- **Level tip shear:** Cut-and-loop construction that shows a random pattern. The sheared design shows shading where it is cut.
- **Multilevel loop:** Yarns are looped at several levels.
- **Random shear:** Similar to a multilevel loop except that the highest level of loop is cut.
- **Frieze or twist:** Plush yarns are twisted and heat set to increase resilience and durability. These carpets wear well.
- **Sculptured or carved:** Plush yarns are sheared at different levels to create a sculptured effect.

Density, or average pile, is the weight of pile yarn in a unit volume of carpet expressed in ounces per cubic yard. Density is determined by the following formula:

$$D \text{ (oz./cu. yd.)} = \frac{36 \times W \text{ (oz./sq. yd.)}}{T \text{ (inches)}}$$

$$D = \text{Density}$$
$$W = \text{Pile yarn weight}$$
$$T = \text{Pile thickness}$$

A density of more than 7,000 is suitable for high-wear installations such as an airport. A density of 6,000 is appropriate for bank lobbies or other areas subject to moderate wear. For private offices and areas subject to low wear, a density of 4,000 is adequate.

The metric conversion for density determined by the formula above is as follows:

$$D \text{ (oz./cu. yd.)} \div 26\ 944.67 = \text{g/cu. cm}$$

Pile height refers to the distance from the top of the backing to the top of the yarn. In multilevel construction, an average pile height is used.

Rows or wires are terms used for woven carpet to indicate the number of pile yarn tufts per 1 inch (25.4 mm) of carpet lengthwise. The terms tufts and stitches are used in fusion bonding and tufting, respectively.

Gauge is the number of ends of surface yarn counting across the width of tufted carpet. For example, a ⅛ gauge equals 8 ends per 1 inch (25.4 mm). Gauge is similar to pitch for woven carpet.

Pitch is the number of ends of surface yarn in 27 inches (686 mm) of width of woven carpet. For tufted carpet, the term *gauge* is used.

Total weight includes both the face and backing weight. A heavy face weight is a better indicator of quality than a heavy total weight.

Face weight is measured in ounces per square yard. It is also called yarn weight because it is a measurement of the weight of actual surface yarn or yarn exposed to wear.

Tuft density is the total tufts per 1 linear inch (25.4 linear mm), or as follows:

$$\text{ENDS} \times \text{TUFTS} = \text{TUFT DENSITY}$$

Yarn count refers to yarn thickness and describes fineness or coarseness of carpet.

- **Tufted and fusion-bonded carpets** use woolen and denier count systems. Woolen count is the number of running yards in 1 oz. (28 g) of finished yarn and includes the number of plies. For example, a 3/60 count means 60 yd. (55 m) of 3-ply yarn per 1 oz. (28 g). Denier is a count system that uses metric measures and is used by the synthetic-fiber industry. This method measures weight in grams per 9,000 m of yarn. For example, 1115/3 yarn count means that 9,000 m of 3-ply yarn weighs 1,115 g. The higher the denier, the larger the yarn.
- **Woven wool carpets** use four different count methods: TEX count, metric, dewsbury, and cotton. The method used depends on where the carpet is manufactured. The TEX count method is often used in Australia and New Zealand. It measures yarn count in grams per kilometer. The metric system is used throughout Western Europe and measures yarn count in kilometers per kilogram. The dewsbury system measures yard lengths per ounce, and the cotton system measures 840 yd. lengths per pound; these count systems are often used in the United Kingdom and the United States.

CARPET BACKING

Primary backing is a component of tufted carpet consisting of woven or nonwoven fabric, into which tufting needles insert pile yarn tufts. It is the carrier fabric for pile yarn. It should not be confused with secondary backing, which is a reinforcing fabric laminated to the back of tufted carpet. Most primary backings are polypropylene, although jute is sometimes used.

Secondary backing is woven or nonwoven fabric reinforcement laminated to the back of tufted carpet, usually with latex adhesive. The term is also used in the broader sense to include attached cushions and other polymeric coatings chosen for a project. There is no secondary backing for woven carpet.

CARPET CUSHION CHARACTERISTICS

Carpet-cushion types are fiber, rubber, and polyurethane foam. Carpet cushion classifications are given in Table 1 at the end of this chapter.

- **Fiber cushions** consist of rubberized natural fibers, such as hair and jute, or synthetic fibers, such as nylon, polyester, and polypropylene. Hair and jute blends should be mothproofed and sterilized. They are primarily used in above-grade installations due to their propensity to absorb moisture. Fiber cushions must be mildew-resistant.
- **Rubber cushions** include flat rubber, rippled waffle, textured flat rubber, and reinforced rubber. Flat rubber, rippled waffle, and textured flat rubber can be made from either natural or synthetic materials. Flat rubber cushion has a flat finished appearance on both sides. Rippled waffle rubber cushion is manufactured to give the appearance of bubbles on the surface and usually contains nonwoven or paper scrim on the top side. Textured flat rubber cushion is produced with a fine-textured appearance on the bottom and a nonwoven or paper backing on the top. Some rubber carpet cushions can dry out and crumble.
- **Polyurethane-foam cushions** include grafted prime, densified, bonded, and mechanically frothed polyurethane. Foam is unaffected by moisture and will not oxidize, crumble, or deteriorate. Grafted prime polyurethane-foam cushion is formulated with added reinforcement for increased load-bearing capacity. Densified polyurethane-foam cushion is formulated with elongated air cells for flexibility. Bonded polyurethane foam, sometimes called rebond, is manufactured by grinding scraps of polyurethane foam and binding them together with an adhesive. Mechanically frothed polyurethane-foam cushion consists of polyurethane chemicals and a reinforcing filler mixed with air.

The Carpet Cushion Council's (CCC) minimum recommended criteria for commercial installations are listed in Table 2 at the end of this chapter. In general, carpet cushion for heavy-traffic areas should be thin and of high density (high load-carrying capacity), or carpet should be installed by the direct-glue-down method without a cushion. In light-traffic areas, a low-density cushion should be used.

CARPET INSTALLATION

The Floor Covering Installation Board (FCIB) is an independent organization endorsed by the Carpet and Rug Institute (CRI) and the Floor Covering Installation Contractors Association. FCIB promotes the professionalism of carpet installers by requiring the following of its certified members:

- Business and liability insurance coverage
- Installation supervision by on-site managers with at least five years' supervisory experience
- Industry standards CRI 104, *Standard for Installation of Commercial Carpet,* and CRI's *How to Specify Commercial Carpet Installation* compliance, or manufacturer's specifications compliance when they exceed CRI 104
- Use of experienced, skilled, and trained installers who participate in continuous training programs and refresher courses every two years

Carpet installation methods include stretch-in, direct-glue-down, and double-glue-down. Preapplied adhesives and hook-and-loop systems are also offered by a few manufacturers. Guidelines for proper carpet installation are contained in CRI 104. This standard includes the installation of carpet tiles, carpet on stairs, and outdoor carpet and synthetic turf.

Stretch-in installations are most commonly used for woven wool carpets but can also be used for tufted broadloom carpets (fig. 8). This method requires fastening the carpet under tension onto tackless strips attached to the subfloor at the perimeter of the room. It also requires a separate cushion to avoid a trampoline effect of the taut carpet. A power stretcher is used to stretch and firmly hook the carpet onto the tackless strip. Tufted carpet with a synthetic secondary backing should be stretched 1 to 1½ percent in width and length. Tufted carpet with a jute secondary backing should be stretched drum tight. Woven carpets should be stretched according to the manufacturer's recommendations. Consider a stretch-in installation for applications that require the following:

- Patterned carpet, to make matching easier
- High noise reduction coefficient (NRC) values
- Low carpet-removal costs
- Maximum life of the carpet

Direct-glue-down installation adheres carpet directly to the subfloor without an underlying carpet cushion (fig. 9). The main advantage of a direct-glue-down installation is that it generally eliminates carpet buckling under traffic. Consider direct-glue-down installations for applications that require the following:

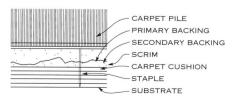

Figure 8. Stretch-in installation

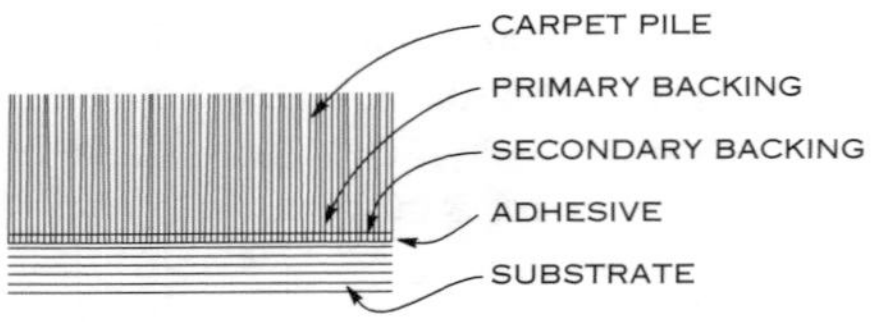

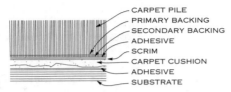

Figure 9. Direct-glue-down installation

Figure 10. Double-glue-down installation

- Capability to withstand rolling traffic or carpet installation on ramps, for example, in hospitals, retail stores, or banks.
- Low installed costs. Carpet cushion costs are eliminated and labor costs are typically low.
- Access to underfloor wire and cable.
- Resistance to the effects of temperature and humidity changes to minimize carpet buckling in spaces not served by conditioned air for extended periods, for example, in schools, churches, or theaters.

Double-glue-down installation, sometimes called *double-stick*, involves gluing carpet with an attached cushion to the subfloor, or gluing carpet cushion to the subfloor with a release adhesive and then gluing carpet to the cushion with a permanent adhesive (fig. 10). Consider double-glue-down installations when the stability of a direct-glue-down installation and the comfort of a carpet cushion are required.

Preapplied adhesive system installations require special subfloor preparation; consult the carpet manufacturer for recommendations. These systems are manufactured with pressure-sensitive adhesives applied to polyurethane or PVC-attached cushion backings.

Hook-and-loop installation systems use hooked tape that is applied to the subfloor and looped fabric that covers the entire underside of the carpet. Intricate designs using various carpet types can be achieved with a hook-and-loop installation. These systems are also practical for installations requiring broadloom goods and access to underfloor systems. Hook-and-loop systems are licensed to a few carpet mills; they are not available from all carpet manufacturers. These systems require specific installation practices, including a special tool for carpet removal. Consult carpet manufacturers for installation requirements.

For glue-down installations, adhesives must be compatible with carpet backing and cushion, if any, and must be properly applied. For direct-glue-down installations, the notch depth of the trowel used to apply adhesives must be deep enough to allow the adhesive to penetrate the carpet backing. PVC and polyurethane carpet backings may require special adhesives. Consult carpet manufacturers to determine the appropriate adhesives for glue-down installations. Two basic adhesive types are permanent and release. The release adhesives hold the carpet or cushion in place during its life but provide for a residue-free removal when replacement is required.

APPEARANCE VARIATIONS OF INSTALLED CARPET

Shading, pile reversal, **and** *pooling* **or** *watermarking* are terms used to describe variations in appearance of installed carpet. Although these words are often used interchangeably, they have different meanings.

Shading is a function of the pile, not a true color difference. It describes a change in a carpet's appearance caused by variations in the direction and orientation of tufts. Tufts laying away from the viewer usually appear shinier or lighter, while tufts laying toward the viewer appear darker. Shading is the feature, not the defect, that causes carpet to show vacuum-cleaner marks and footprints.

Pile reversal is isolated bands of shading, usually appearing across the width of the carpet. It can be caused by rolling carpet too tightly or loosely while it is still hot from a coating operation or by improper storage and folding. A mixture of moisture, heat, and mechanical action, typically applied with a hot-water extraction carpet cleaner, often corrects this problem. Pile reversal is identified by the following characteristics:

- It does not continue across seams.
- It runs across the full carpet width.
- It repeats every 36 to 48 inches (914 to 1220 mm), indicating roll crush.
- It can be corrected by heat and moisture.

Watermarking is also called *pooling* or *permanent shading.* Watermarking can detract from the appearance of carpets. It generally affects cut-pile carpets, although loop and combination cut-and-loop pile carpets also can have this problem. Fiber types, both natural and synthetic, in tufted, woven, or fusion-bonded constructions have exhibited watermarking. Watermarking appears more obvious in solid or dark colors and in large areas. Watermarking is not a manufacturing defect, and exact causes for this phenomenon are unknown. Before selecting and specifying cut-pile carpets, consider notifying the owner in writing that watermarking may occur and that there is no known remedy. Watermarking is characterized by the following:

- It is site-specific.
- It often crosses seams.
- It follows no predictable pattern.
- It is not correctable.

FIRE-TEST-RESPONSE CHARACTERISTICS

Flame spread is measured using the Flooring Radiant Panel Test described in ASTM E 648. This test measures a floor covering's tendency to spread flames when the floor covering is located in a corridor and subjected to flames and hot gases from a room fire. The critical radiant flux (CRF) determined by this test is the minimum energy, in watts per square centimeter, necessary to sustain flame in the floor covering. The higher the CRF value, the more resistant the material is to flame spread. The National Fire Protection Association (NFPA) publication NFPA 101, *Life Safety Code,* requires that floor covering materials in exits and in access to exits meet CRF limitations in certain occupancies. Model codes include CRF limitations for flooring materials judged an unusual hazard, such as carpets, where these materials are installed in exits, passageways, and corridors.

Flammability characteristics are determined by testing according to 16 (Code of Federal Regulations) CFR 1630, the methenamine pill (a tablet that is ignited) test. The rating system is pass or fail. This test measures a carpet's capability to promulgate a flame from a small source, such as a match or cigarette, and spread the flame across the floor to ignite furniture, draperies, or wall coverings. Because by law all carpet marketed in the United States must pass this test, this requirement does not need to be reiterated in specifications.

OTHER CONSIDERATIONS

Reflectance ratings of carpets may be required by the lighting designer or electrical engineer to design interior lighting properly.

Sound absorption characteristics may be important for certain carpet installations. Sound absorption is rated by Noise Reduction Coefficient (NRC) and tested by methods defined in ASTM C 423. NRC rates the effectiveness of sound absorption.

Electrostatic discharge characteristics of carpets may be important for installations housing computer or electronic equipment. Static builds when two dissimilar materials are in contact (e.g., walking in shoes across a carpeted floor). Electrons migrate from one material to another and, when separated, each retains an electrical charge. The normal threshold of human sensitivity to electrostatic discharge is commonly accepted as 3.5 kV. Consult electronic equipment manufacturers to determine the exact levels of electrostatic-discharge control necessary. Three factors to consider in electrostatic-discharge control are static generation (static electricity levels), static dissipation (carpet's conductivity or electrical resistance), and static decay time (time it takes electric charge to dissipate). Of these factors, static generation is the only one typically specified for general commercial environments. It is impossible to achieve a permanent kilovolt rating by treating carpet fibers; conductive fibers, such as carbon-loaded nylon, must be incorporated into pile and be in direct contact with a conductive backing. In highly electrostatic-discharge-sensitive environments, such as plants for assembling electronic components, floor covering alone cannot provide sufficient electrostatic-discharge protection and must be augmented by other means, such as conductive shoes and furniture.

Consider colorfastness of carpets. *Crocking* is the rubbing off of dye as a result of insufficient dye penetration or fixation, the use of improper dyes or dyeing methods, or the insufficient washing and treatment after the dyeing operation. The American Association of Textile Chemists and Colorists (AATCC) publication AATCC-165 is the determining test method for both wet and dry crocking.

CONCRETE SUBFLOOR PREPARATION

For glue-down installations, concrete subfloors may require extensive preparation to ensure proper adhesion. Testing for alkalinity and moisture is required. A pH range of 5 to 9 is generally satisfactory; a reading above 9 usually requires corrective measures. Consult the adhesive manufacturer for testing and corrective procedures. As a general guideline, CRI recommends an acceptable moisture emission rate of 3 lb/1000 sq. ft.

(1.36 kg/92.9 sq. m) per 24 hours or less according to an anhydrous-calcium-chloride test. Carpet with porous backings can usually be installed successfully when moisture emission rates are 3 to 5 lb (1.36 to 2.25 kg); however, the risk of moisture-related problems increases. Consult the carpet manufacturer to determine acceptable moisture emission rates for its products. See 09651, Resilient Tile Flooring, for a detailed discussion of moisture problems associated with concrete subfloors.

SLIP RESISTANCE

The carpet industry has not developed a consensus standard for testing slip resistance. According to the Americans with Disabilities Act (ADA), *Accessibility Guidelines for Buildings and Facilities (ADAAG),* builders and designers are encouraged to specify securely attached carpet with a firm cushion or no cushion; a maximum pile thickness of ½ inch (13 mm); and a face construction of level loop, textured loop, level cut, or level cut/uncut pile. Exposed carpet edges must be fastened to the floor surface and have trim along the entire length of the exposed edge.

REFERENCES

Publication dates cited here were current at the time of this writing. Publications are revised periodically, and revisions may have occurred before this book was published.

American Association of Textile Chemists and Colorists

AATCC-24-94: Resistance of Textiles to Insects

AATCC-165-93: Colorfastness to Crocking: Carpets-AATCC Crockmeter Method

ASTM International

ASTM C 423-90a: Test Method for Sound Absorption and Sound Absorption Coefficients by the Reverberation Room Method

ASTM D 3574-95: Test Methods for Flexible Cellular Materials-Slab, Bonded, and Molded Urethane Foams

ASTM D 3676-96a: Specification for Rubber Cellular Cushion Used for Carpet or Rug Underlay

ASTM E 648-97: Test Method for Critical Radiant Flux of Floor-Covering Systems Using a Radiant Heat Energy Source

Carpet and Rug Institute

CRI 104-96: Standard for Installation of Commercial Carpet

How to Specify Commercial Carpet Installation, 1994.

Carpet Cushion Council

Commercial Carpet Cushion Guidelines, 1997.

United States Architectural & Transportation Barriers Compliance Board

ADAAG: Accessibility Guidelines for Buildings and Facilities, adopted in 1991; continual revisions.

Table 1
CLASSIFICATION OF CARPET CUSHION*

Types of Cushion	Class I Moderate Traffic	Class II Heavy Traffic	Class III Extra-Heavy Traffic
Commercial Application	*Office Buildings:* Executive or private offices, conference rooms *Healthcare:* Executive, administration *Schools:* Administration *Airports:* Administration *Retail:* Windows and display areas *Banks:* Executive areas *Hotels/Motels:* Sleeping rooms *Libraries/Museums:* Administration	*Office Buildings:* Clerical areas, corridors (moderate traffic) *Healthcare:* Patients' rooms, lounges *Schools:* Dormitories, classrooms *Retail:* Minor aisles, boutiques, specialties *Banks:* Lobbies, corridors (moderate traffic) *Hotels/Motels:* Corridors *Libraries/Museums:* Public areas (moderate traffic) *Convention Centers:* Auditoriums	*Office Buildings:* Corridors (heavy traffic), cafeterias *Healthcare:* Lobbies, corridors, nurses' stations *Schools:* Corridors, cafeterias *Airports:* Corridors, public areas, ticketing areas *Retail:* Major aisles, checkouts, supermarkets *Banks:* Corridors (heavy traffic), teller windows *Hotels/Motels:* Lobbies and public areas *Libraries/Museums:* Public areas *Convention Centers:* Corridors and lobbies *Country Clubs:* Locker rooms, pro shops, dining areas *Restaurants:* Dining areas and lobbies
Fiber			
Rubberized Hair	Wt: 40 oz./sq. yd. Th: .27" D = 12.3	Wt: 40 oz./sq. yd. Th: .3125" D = 12.3	Wt: 50 oz./sq. yd. Th: .375" D = 11.1
Rubberized Jute	Wt: 32 oz./sq. yd. Th: .25" D = 12.3	Wt: 40 oz./sq. yd. Th: .25" D = 12.3	Wt: 40 oz./sq. yd. Th: .34" D = 11.1
Synthetic Fibers	Wt: 22 oz./sq. yd. Th: .25" D = 7.3	Wt: 28 oz./sq. yd. Th: .3125" D = 7.3	Wt: 36 oz./sq. yd. Th: .35" D = 8.0
Resinated Recycled Textile Fiber	Wt: 24 oz./sq. yd. Th: .25" D = 7.3	Wt: 30 oz./sq. yd. Th: .30" D = 7.3	Wt: 38 oz./sq. yd. Th: .375" D = 8.0
Sponge Rubber			
Flat Rubber	Wt. 62 oz./sq. yd. Th: .150" CR @ 25% = 3.0 psi min. D = 21	Wt. 62 oz./sq. yd. Th: .150" CR @ 25% = 3.0 psi min. D = 21	Wt. 62 oz./sq. yd. Th: .150" CR @ 25% = 4.0 psi min. D = 26
Rippled Waffle	Wt. 56 oz./sq. yd. Th: .270" CR @ 25% = 0.7 psi min. D = 15	Not recommended for use in this class.	Not recommended for use in this class.
Textured Flat Rubber	Wt. 56 oz./sq. yd. Th: .220" CR @ 25% = 1.0 psi min. D = 18	Wt. 64 oz./sq. yd. Th: .235" CR @ 25% = 1.5 psi min. D = 22	Wt. 80 oz./sq. yd. Th: .250" CR @ 25% = 1.75 psi min. D = 26
Reinforced Rubber	Wt. 64 oz./sq. yd. Th: .235" CR @ 25% = 2.0 psi min. CR @ 65% = 50.0 psi min. D = 22	Wt. 64 oz./sq. yd. Th: .235" CR @ 25% = 2.0 psi min. CR @ 65% = 50.0 psi min. D = 22	Wt. 54 oz./sq. yd. Th: .200" CR @ 25% = 2.0 psi min. CR @ 65% = 50.0 psi min. D = 22
Polyurethane Foam			
Grafted Prime	D = 2.7 Th: .25" CFD @ 65% = 2.5 psi min.	D = 3.2 Th: .25" CFD @ 65% = 3.5 psi min.	D = 4.0 Th: .25" CFD @ 65% = 5.0 psi min.
Densified	D = 2.7 Th: .25" CFD @ 65% = 2.4 psi min.	D = 3.5 Th: .25" CFD @ 65% = 3.3 psi min.	D = 4.5 Th: .25" CFD @ 65% = 4.8 psi min.
Bonded	D = 5.0 Th: .375" CFD @ 65% = 5.0 psi min.	D = 6.5 Th: .25" CFD @ 65% = 10.0 psi min.	D = 8.0 Th: .25" CFD @ 65% = 8.0 psi min.
Mechanically Frothed	D = 13.0 Th: .30" CFD @ 65% = 9.7 psi min.	D = 15.0 Th: .223" CFD @ 65% = 49.9 psi min.	D = 19.0 Th: .183" CFD @ 65% = 30.5 psi min.

Legend:
CFD = Compression Force Deflection as measured by ASTM D 3574
CR = Compression Resistance in pounds per square inch as measured by ASTM D 3676
D = Density in pounds per cubic foot
min. = Minimum
Th = Thickness
Wt. = Weight

Note: All thicknesses, weights, and densities allow a 5 percent manufacturing tolerance.

*Source: Carpet Cushion Council, Commercial Carpet Cushion Guidelines, 1997.

Table 2
MINIMUM CRITERIA FOR DESIGNING WOVEN WOOL CARPET*

	Medium Duty			Heavy Duty			Extra-Heavy Duty		
	Axminster	Karaloc	Wilton/ Velvet	Axminster	Axminster (189 pitch)	Karaloc	Luxury Karaloc	Axminster	Velvet
Pile	Cut	Loop or cut loop	Loop	Cut	Cut	Loop or cut loop	Loop or cut loop	Cut	Cut loop or loop tip sheared
Fiber	80% wool, 20% nylon	100% pure new wool	100% pure new wool	80% wool, 20% nylon	80% wool, 20% nylon	100% pure new wool	100% pure new wool	80% wool, 20% nylon	100% pure wool
Pitch	184	270	216	7 per inch (25.4 mm)	7 per inch (25.4 mm)	270	270	189	216
Rows	10 per inch (10 per 25.4 mm)	10 per inch (10 per 25.4 mm)	9.5 per inch (9.5 per 25.4 mm)	9 per inch (9 per 25.4 mm)	9 per inch (9 per 25.4 mm)	10 per inch (10 per 25.4 mm)	10 per inch (10 per 25.4 mm)	11 per inch (11 per 25.4 mm)	10 per inch (10 per 25.4 mm)
Pile Height	0.275 inch (6.98 mm)	0.25 inch (6.35 mm)	0.25 inch (6.35 mm)	0.28 inch (7.11 mm)	0.3125 inch (8 mm)	0.25 inch (6.35 mm)	0.375 inch (9.525 mm)	0.25 inch (6.35 mm)	0.25 inch (6.35 mm)
Surface Pile Weight	27 oz./sq. yd. (915 g/sq. m)	34 oz./sq. yd. (1152 g/sq. m)	30 oz./sq. yd. (1017 g/sq. m)	29 oz./sq. yd. (983 g/sq. m)	35 oz./sq. yd. (1186 g/sq. m)	37 oz./sq. yd. (1254 g/sq. m)	56 oz./sq. yd. (1898 g/sq. m)	37 oz./sq. yd. (1254 g/sq. m)	40 oz./sq. yd. (1356 g/sq. m)
Total Pile Weight	37.5 oz./sq. yd. (1271 g/sq. m)	48 oz./sq. yd. (1627 g/sq. m)	45 oz./sq. yd. (1525 g/sq. m)	40 oz./sq. yd. (1356 g/sq. m)	46 oz./sq. yd. (1559 g/sq. m)	53 oz./sq. yd. (1797 g/sq. m)	71 oz./sq. yd. (2407 g/sq. m)	50.1 oz./sq. yd. (1698 g/sq. m)	55 oz./sq. yd. (1864 g/sq. m)
Yarn Count									
TEX	R 600 TEX/2	R 590 TEX/2	R 688 TEX/2	R 720 TEX/2	R 776 TEX/2	R 645 TEX/2	R 645 TEX/2	R 805 TEX/3	R 1722 TEX 3/2
Metric Resultant	1.66	1.59	1.45	1.39	1.3	1.55	1.55	1.24	0.58
Dewsbury (yd./oz.)	2/52	2/52.5	2/45	2/43	2/40	2/48	2/48	3/38	2/3/36
Cotton	1.98/2 cotton 0.99 resultant	2/2/2 cotton 1.00 resultant	1.72/2 cotton 0.86 resultant	1.64/2 cotton 0.82 resultant	1.52/2 cotton 0.76 resultant	1.82 cotton 0.91 resultant	1.82 cotton 0.91 resultant	2.2/3 cotton 0.73 resultant	2/3/2 cotton 0.33 resultant
Backing									
Chain	Cotton/polyester	Polypropylene/ polyester	N/A	Polyester and cotton	Cotton/polyester or synthetic	Polypropylene/ polyester	Polypropylene	Polyester/cotton or polypropylene	Cotton/polyester
Stuffer	Cotton/polyester	Polypropylene/ polyester	N/A	Polyester and cotton	Cotton/polyester or synthetic	Polypropylene/ polyester	Polypropylene	Polyester/cotton or polypropylene	Fiberglass or polypropylene
Weft	Jute or polypropylene	Jute or polypropylene	Jute or polypropylene	Jute or polypropylene	Jute or polypropylene	Jute or polypropylene	Jute or polypropylene	Jute or polypropylene	Polypropylene
Warp	N/A	N/A	Cotton/polyester	N/A	N/A	N/A	N/A	N/A	N/A

*The minimum criteria listed in this table was developed by the Wool Bureau for specifiers' use in working with a woven wool carpet manufacturer, and apply to all wool carpet: Backcoating is 12-oz./sq. yd. (407-g/sq. m) latex with antistatic treatment, yarn twist is 4.5 twists per inch (TWI) single and 3 TWI folded, and carpet is resistant to insects per AATCC-24.

09681 CARPET TILE

This chapter discusses carpet tile for commercial installations.

This chapter does not discuss resilient wall base and accessories or metal accessories installed with carpet tile.

CARPET TILE CHARACTERISTICS

For a complete discussion that applies to both carpet and carpet tile, see Chapter 09680, Carpet, which covers carpet materials and fabrication, installation methods, testing, and similar subjects. This chapter discusses only subjects pertinent to carpet tile installations.

Face construction for carpet tile is limited to three types: fusion-bonded, tufted, and needle-punched (figs. 1-3). Fusion-bonded goods dominate the carpet tile market in the United States. See Chapter 09680, Carpet, for a discussion on tufted and needle-punched face construction.

Fusion-bonded construction is where a yarn bundle is sandwiched between and implanted into adhesive substrates and fused, commonly with heat. A blade is then run between the substrates, producing two carpet pieces. This process produces a dense carpet.

Variations in shading may be noticeable between tiles because of the lay of the pile. The terms used to describe the different pile characteristics are *tops and bottoms* or *lefts and rights,* referring to the location of the carpet tile substrate before the final cut. Unacceptable color variations may be

prevented by separating fusion-bonded carpet tiles into tiles of like-pile characteristics.

CARPET TILE INSTALLATION

Three installation methods for carpet tile are glue-down, partial glue-down, and free-lay.

- **Glue-down, also called *full-spread,* installation** anchors every tile to the floor with releasable adhesive. This installation type is recommended in areas where heavy rolling loads are anticipated.
- **Partial glue-down installation** periodically anchors tiles with an adhesive. The adhesively anchored tiles retain the placement of the remaining carpet tiles, which are free-lay installed. This method is often used for carpet tiles with moderate dimensional stability and moderate weight and mass.
- **Free-lay installation** is appropriate for dimensionally stable carpet tiles with heavy backings. These carpet tiles are installed without an adhesive.

The Floor Covering Installation Board (FCIB) is an independent organization endorsed by the Carpet and Rug Institute (CRI) and the Floor Covering Installation Contractors Association. FCIB promotes the professionalism of carpet installers by requiring the following of its certified members:

- Business and liability insurance coverage
- Installation supervision by on-site managers with at least five years' supervisory experience
- Industry standards CRI 104, *Standard for Installation of Commercial Carpet,* and CRI's *How to Specify Commercial Carpet Installation* compliance, or manufacturer's specifications compliance when they exceed CRI 104
- Use of experienced, skilled, and trained installers who participate in continuous training programs and refresher courses every two years

APPLICATION CONSIDERATIONS

Flat, wire cable installations are allowed only where floors are covered with carpet tile according to the National Fire Protection Association (NFPA) publication NFPA 70, *National Electrical Code.*

REFERENCES

Publication dates cited here were current at the time of this writing. Publications are revised periodically, and revisions may have occurred before this book was published.

Carpet and Rug Institute

CRI 104-96: Standard for Installation of Commercial Carpet

How to Specify Commercial Carpet Installation, 1994.

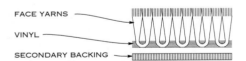

Figure 1. Fusion bonded construction

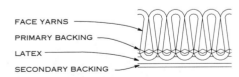

Figure 2. Tufted construction

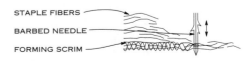

Figure 3. Needlepunched construction

09720 WALL COVERINGS

This chapter discusses vinyl, woven glass-fiber, textile, and heavy-duty synthetic textile wall coverings and wallpaper.

This chapter does not discuss wood-veneer wall coverings, stretched-fabric wall coverings, or rigid vinyl sheet wall protection systems. It also does not discuss wall coverings with flocked, foil, Mylar, cork, grass, bamboo, or reed visible layers.

GENERAL COMMENTS

The visible, decorative layer of a wall covering is colored, textured, patterned, or any combination of the three; is usually thin; and is often selected for visual appearance and effect, durability, and maintenance characteristics. Other characteristics of wall coverings may include acoustical absorption, fire resistance, impact resistance, scratch resistance, moisture resistance, antimicrobial properties, and light reflectivity. Wall coverings also may be used to hide damaged wall and ceiling surfaces. The visible layer may consist of dyed or woven colors and patterns, or it may be ink printed using various methods such as gravure, flexography, surface printing, and screen-printing. For vinyl wall coverings, an intermediate layer, sometimes called the *ground,* provides background color, opacity, and the surface to receive the printed decorative layer. A protective polymer coating applied to or a protective film applied over the visible layer may enhance performance. The wall covering may cover the substrate directly, or a backing or wall liner may overlay the substrate.

Wall coverings are often selected as an alternative to paint in applications where increased durability is required or the appearance of a texture or pattern is desired. Depending on the pattern, texture, and reflectance, wall coverings can hide dirt and damage more readily than flat, monochromatic-painted surfaces. There are several types of wall coverings: vinyl, woven glass-fiber, textile, and wallpaper (fig. 1). Vinyl wall coverings dominate the commercial market because of their superior strength, low maintenance, cleanability, and affordable cost. Wallpapers are more commonly used in residential projects but are occasionally used for their special, decorative effect in low-wear areas such as hotel ballrooms. Textiles must be backed or otherwise treated for use as wall coverings and are unsuitable for high-wear applications. Heavy-duty synthetic textile wall

coverings may be used for heavy-wear areas where a textile appearance is desirable. Woven glass-fiber wall coverings, common in Europe, are gaining in popularity in the United States because of their fire resistance, strength, and permeability.

Because of differences in manufacturing processes, the available coverage from a roll of wall covering produced in the United States using inch-pound (IP) measures is not equivalent to that produced in countries using metric (SI) measures. For example, the U.S. inch-pound wallpaper roll is 27 inches (686 mm) wide by 27 feet (8.23 m) long per double roll, or 60 sq. ft. (5.57 sq. m). The European metric roll measures 20½ inches wide by 33 feet (52 mm by 10 m) long per double roll, or 56 sq. ft (5.20 sq. m). A lineal yard of wall covering is any width by the length of 36 inches (914 mm).

Wall coverings, especially textile wall coverings and wallpapers, are often available from distributor/converters who are not fiber, fabric, or wallpaper manufacturers. Distributor/converters are reliable sources, often of multiple brand names, in a national market.

Natural and synthetic polymers in resin and fiber forms are the basic materials of wall coverings. Natural polymers are animal (protein), plant (carbohydrate/cellulosic), or mineral (petroleum- or gas-based) types. Synthetic fibers are modified plant or mineral types. Polymers are molecular chains made up of repeating units. The properties of natural polymers are limited by their form in the natural state. Synthetic polymers are more versatile. They can be modified or designed to have molecular structures that impart properties for desired end uses such as resistance to flame spread, antistatic capability, greater durability, UV-light resistance, and color stability.

Wall-covering backings may consist of woven and nonwoven fabrics, coatings (textiles), or papers. Acrylic or other polymer-saturated backings are stronger and have better tearing resistance than untreated backings. Backings may be required for strength, dimensional stability, improved bonding, peelability, stippability, or substrate hiding ability.

Stain resistance to reagents that are more severe than those tested for by industry standards may be critical to a project. Examples of reagents not

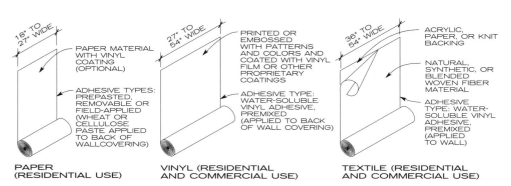

Figure 1. Wall covering materials

listed in the standards are ballpoint pen ink, betadine, lipstick, markers, mustard, shoe polish, and bleach (a common disinfecting agent). Not all water-based dyes and inks used for wall coverings can withstand cleaning and disinfecting by all cleaning or disinfecting agents without color loss. Specifying a protective coating can enhance stain resistance, improve cleanability, and protect dyes and inks. ASTM D 1308, *Test Method for Effect of Household Chemicals on Clear and Pigmented Organic Finishes,* "covers determination of the effect of household chemicals on clear and pigmented organic finishes, resulting in any objectionable alteration in the surface, such as discoloration, change in gloss, blistering, softening, swelling, loss of adhesion, or special phenomena." This test is required by ASTM F 793, *Classification of Wallcovering by Durability Characteristics,* for Categories III through VI, with more stringent exposures for Categories V and VI. Chemical Fabrics & Film Association, Inc. (CFFA) standard test method CFFA 141, *Stain Resistance,* is also based on ASTM D 1308. ASTM D 1308 could be used to evaluate stain resistance to any additional reagents such as ballpoint pen ink, lipstick, markers, and bleach. Consult manufacturers if enhanced stain resistance is needed for a project or if dyed or printed wall coverings are anticipated to need frequent disinfecting or cleaning with alkaline or other harsh products.

Acrylic and other proprietary water-based coatings delay the penetration of common stains but do not prevent them. These wall coverings require prompt cleaning, or stains will migrate through the finish and permanently stain them. Water-based acrylic coatings can be cleaned with mild detergent and, sometimes, alcohol. Do not use solvent-based products on vinyl wall coverings. Acrylics have only fair resistance to deterioration by UV light, potentially allowing wall coverings to deteriorate and colors to fade with time and exposure.

WALL-COVERING CLASSIFICATION

ASTM F 793 classifies most wall coverings by durability (serviceability in use). This standard establishes tests for abrasion resistance, blocking resistance (capability to resist adhesion or sticking between two surfaces of a wall covering), breaking strength, coating adhesion, cold-cracking resistance (resistance to the cracking of coated or decorative surfaces when folded during exposure to low temperatures), colorfastness, crocking resistance (resistance to the transfer of color from the wall-covering surface when rubbed), heat-aging resistance, stain resistance, tear resistance, maximum flame spread, maximum shrinkage, maximum smoke development, scrubbability, and washability. This standard is not used to classify glass-fiber wall coverings because the required paint coating contributes to the performance and is unique to each application. Although not all manufacturers classify their products by this standard in its entirety, a knowledge of the performance categories in the standard helps the design professional to understand the range of wall coverings available and their relative strengths and limitations. The standard identifies six categories, as follows:

- **Category I, Decorative Only:** "Wallcovering manufactured for decorative purposes that can be hung without damage according to the manufacturer's instructions." Category I wall coverings are not tested. Wallpaper and other primarily residential wall coverings fall into this category.
- **Category II, Decorative with Medium Serviceability:** "Wallcovering primarily decorative but more washable and colorfast than Category I wallcovering." In addition to the testing required for minimum washability and colorfastness, Category II wall coverings are tested for maximum flame spread and smoke development. Category II wall coverings are also primarily for residential use.
- **Category III, Decorative with High Serviceability:** "Wallcovering manufactured for medium use, where abrasion resistance, stain resistance, scrubbability, and increased colorfastness are necessary." In addition to

the testing required for Category II wall coverings, Category III wall coverings are tested for minimum scrubbability, stain resistance, and crocking resistance. They meet more stringent requirements for colorfastness than Category II wall coverings. Category III wall coverings are also primarily for residential use.

- **Category IV, Type I Commercial Serviceability:** "Wallcovering manufactured for use where higher abrasion resistance, stain resistance, and scrubbability are necessary in heavy consumer and light commercial use." In addition to the testing required for Category III wall coverings, Category IV wall coverings are tested for maximum shrinkage and minimum abrasion resistance, breaking strength, tear resistance, blocking resistance, coating adhesion, cold-cracking resistance, and heat-aging resistance. All test methods listed in the standard apply to Category III wall coverings, but the wall coverings meet more stringent requirements for colorfastness and scrubbability than Category III wall coverings and meet Type I performance criteria as defined by Federal Specification FS CCC-W-408C. Category IV, Type I wall coverings are generally appropriate for private offices, hotel rooms, and areas not subject to unusual abrasion or heavy traffic.
- **Category V, Type II Commercial Serviceability:** "Wallcovering manufactured for use where better wearing qualities are required and exposure to wear is greater than normal." These wall coverings are tested according to more stringent requirements for scrubbability, abrasion resistance, stain resistance, tear resistance, and coating adhesion than Category IV wall coverings and meet Type II performance criteria as defined by FS CCC-W-408C. Category V, Type II wall coverings are considered appropriate for public areas such as lounges, dining rooms, public corridors, and classrooms.
- **Category VI, Type III Commercial Serviceability:** "Wallcoverings manufactured for use in heavy-traffic areas." Category VI wall coverings are tested for the highest scrubbability, abrasion resistance, breaking strength, tear resistance, coating adhesion, and maximum shrinkage and meet Type III performance criteria as defined by FS CCC-W-408C. Category VI, Type III wall coverings are commonly used in high-traffic service corridors where carts may bump into the walls.

Peelability, strippability, and mildew-resistance definitions and test methods are also included in ASTM F 793 but are characteristics that are not required for classification. *Peelable wall covering* is defined as "a wallcovering from which the decorative surface may be dry-peeled from the substrate, leaving a continuous layer of the substrate on the wall, when the wallcovering has been installed and peeled in accordance with the manufacturer's instructions." This definition by itself does not make it clear that the substrate is not the surface of the wall as it existed before installing the wall covering but the surface of the wall covering that remains after removal of the decorative surface. This decorative surface is explained elsewhere in ASTM F 793 as a "discrete self-supporting film" that, when removed by a dry method, leaves "a surface that may be removed in the conventional manner or left on the wall for rehanging." *Strippable wall covering* is defined as "a wallcovering that can be dry-stripped from the wall after having been installed and stripped in accordance with the manufacturer's instructions, leaving a minimum of product residue on the wall and without damage to the wall surface." *Mildew-resistant wall covering* is defined as "a wallcovering that has been treated to deter the growth of fungi (mildew) on the decorative surface" and is tested per ASTM G 21 for a rating of 0 or 1. FS CCC-W-408D also determines criteria for mildew resistance per ASTM G 21 for a rating of 0 or 1.

CFFA-W-101-B for vinyl wall covering has no criteria for mildew resistance. However, CFFA's *Standard Test Methods Chemical Coated Fabrics and Film* does include testing protocols for mildew resistance (CFFA-120), which is based on ASTM G 21, and bacterial resistance (CFFA-300), which is based on AATCC Test Method 147. Bacterial exposure is to staphylococcus aureus, Klebsiella pneumoniae, Salmonella choleraesuis, and Pseudomonas aeruginosa. CFFA's *Standard Test Methods,* including these and other test methods, is available at www.chemicalfabricsand-film.com. According to this test method, the specifier or the manufacturer sets the pass/fail criteria for this test. If resistance to bacterial contamination is required for a project, establish requirements, including criteria for pass/fail judgment, in the wall covering specification.

A definition and test method for flammability are also in ASTM F 793. Testing for flame-spread and smoke-developed indexes are per the National Fire Protection Association (NFPA) publication NFPA 101, *Life Safety Code,* which references NFPA 255, *Standard Method of Test of Surface Burning Characteristics of Building Materials.* ASTM E 84 is similar to NFPA 255.

WALL-COVERING CHARACTERISTICS

Organic wall-covering materials such as cotton, wool, paper, primers, and many adhesives are susceptible to mold and mildew. Wall coverings, primers, and adhesives usually contain fungicides to resist mold and mildew growth; however, fungicides will not eliminate mold and mildew. To control mold and mildew, it is usually necessary to eliminate the moisture necessary for growth. Sources of moisture are varied but include differences in vapor pressure (diffusion), air-transported moisture due to infiltration and exfiltration (leakage), and leakage through wall assemblies that are improperly designed or constructed. If moisture is present in or on wall assemblies, a means of drying is needed to eliminate moisture.

Mold and mildew on wall coverings is a common problem in humid, coastal regions, often occurring when moisture penetrates an outside wall and is trapped behind nonbreathable wall coverings. A nonbreathable wall covering acts essentially as a vapor retarder and represents a potential surface against which condensation could occur if the thermal and vapor-flow characteristics of the wall assembly result in the dew point's occurrence within the wall assembly behind the wall covering. Drastic changes in interior temperature and humidity conditioning, such as school or hotel rooms that are not conditioned when vacant, can also cause condensation on the backside of nonbreathable wall coverings. There are several ways, used singly or in combination, to reduce the likelihood of mold and mildew, including the following:

- Consider airflow and vapor retarders in exterior walls to keep wall assemblies dry. It is best to analyze the entire wall assembly for each project beforehand and calculate the dew points throughout the assembly to ensure that condensation during both heating and cooling cycles will not occur.
- Avoid multiple layers of wall coverings. Existing wall coverings, backings, or adhesives may be contaminated and they may be vapor retarders. Applying a second layer of wall covering creates the potential for multiple vapor retarders with resultant problems.
- Require hydrophobic construction materials with a low moisture content to ensure that the area is enclosed, dry, and conditioned before interior finish operations begin.
- Provide positive air pressure to reduce moisture infiltration.
- Exhaust high-moisture areas (e.g., shower rooms) directly to the outside.
- Balance HVAC systems for ventilation, and maintain constant temperature and low humidity.
- Use vapor-permeable wall coverings that are breathable and have been tested for permeability. Wallpapers, woven glass-fiber wall coverings, and perforated-vinyl wall coverings (microvented) tend to be more permeable than nonperforated, fabric- or paper-backed vinyl wall coverings. Use vapor-permeable wall coverings on exterior walls, particularly where cool inside temperatures will cause condensation of warm, moist air on the wall coverings or on substrates forming the interior construction of the exterior wall. In spaces where the generation of high humidity will allow moisture to accumulate on wall-covering surfaces, use vapor-retarding wall coverings that can be wiped off or dried by evaporation.
- Use vapor-permeable, non-oil-based primers/sealers. Oil-based primers/sealers create a nonporous surface, which, along with vapor-impermeable wall coverings, tend to trap moisture, prolong drying, and may result in adhesion problems and mold and mildew contamination.

Antimicrobial is a generic term used to describe compounds that act as bactericides and fungicides. A broad-spectrum antimicrobial biocide treatment is formulated to be effective against a variety of bacteria, fungi, and yeasts. Selection of wall coverings with long-term biological resistance may be critical in hospitals, nursing homes, child-care facilities, hotel rooms, food preparation areas, mass transportation facilities, and other facilities where health and sanitation are important.

Pattern selection affects room aesthetics. The perceived spatial characteristics of a room can be altered by a wall covering's color and pattern through optical illusion. For example, light colors seem to expand spaces; strong, dark colors seem to contract them. Disproportionate spaces can be visually altered. For example, vertical stripes add height to a room. Pattern repeat and size should be balanced with room scale. Patterned or textured wall coverings can be used to disguise imperfect wall surfaces. Overall random print patterns help camouflage walls that are out of square. Wall coverings with random match or small horizontally aligned patterns require less material and minimize waste.

Pattern matching is required for wall coverings with a repeating pattern. The repeat is the vertical distance between match points of a repetitive design. There are no standards regulating pattern-match tolerances. A common variation from level is ⅛ inch (3 mm) between two 8-foot (2.4-m) strips at midpoint over a 27-inch- (686-mm-) wide wall-covering strip. Many manufacturers feel that ⅜-inch (9.5-mm) variation from level in a 54-inch- (1372-mm-) wide strip is acceptable. When selecting a straight-across or drop-match patterned wall covering, the pattern match should be specified at eye height. The repeat is the distance and direction between one point on a pattern design to the next identical point. The following are examples of pattern matching:

- **Drop match:** The pattern repeat runs diagonally across the wall. Drop match is also called *offset match.* If the pattern runs diagonally across the wall so that every other strip is the same along the ceiling line, the term used is *half-drop match:* every other strip is the same at the ceiling line and the design elements run diagonally. Two-way diagonals form a diamond grid effect. For half-drop match, the beginning of the vertical design is repeated with every odd-numbered strip. Multiple drop match is similar to half-drop match except that it takes four or more strips to repeat the first strip.
- **Random match:** Patterns that do not have specific match points, for example, textures, are called *random match.* These wall coverings often look better if the strips are reversed, alternating the top and bottom of successive strips. Stripes, all-over textures, and grasscloths are usually random matches.
- **Straight-across match:** The same elements of the design in each strip are aligned at an equal distance from the ceiling line. The repeat is horizontal.

FIRE-TEST-RESPONSE CHARACTERISTICS

Rate of flame spread, ease of ignition, heat release, smoke, and toxicity are the relevant fire-test-response characteristics that may apply to wall coverings and may be a concern to authorities having jurisdiction.

The standard fire tests for surface-burning characteristics are applicable to all wall finishes including wall coverings. ASTM E 84, called the *Steiner Tunnel Test,* is the oldest test used for interior finishes. A sample is placed in a 25-foot- (7.6-m-) long furnace. One end of a 24-foot- (7.3-m-) long sample is exposed to a 4½-inch (114-mm) flame and a draft for 10 minutes. The flame spread of the test specimen is then measured. Test results can vary considerably depending on the mounting method. Wall coverings are tested with the adhesive to be used in the installation and on the substrate to be used, or on one that is similar. The chemical formulation of the adhesive can significantly affect test results. According to NFPA 101, thin materials less than ½8 inch (0.09 cm) thick are "exempt from tests simulating actual installation if they meet the requirements of Class A interior wall or ceiling finish when tested using inorganic reinforced cement board as the substrate material." Some wall coverings, such as woven glass-fiber, have inherently low surface-burning characteristics. Others require treatment to reduce flame-spread and smoke-developed indexes to a level that satisfies code requirements. Textile and paper wall coverings can be treated to reduce flammability. The smoke-developed index is also reported according to ASTM E 84. There is little fuel contribution because of the material's thinness. ASTM E 84 is similar to both NFPA 255 and Underwriters Laboratories (UL) standard UL 723, *Test for Surface Burning Characteristics of Building Materials.* International Conference of Building Officials' (ICBO's) Uniform Building Code (UBC) Standard 8-1, *Test Method for Surface-Burning Characteristics of Building Materials,* is based on an earlier edition of ASTM E 84 and requires, rather than suggests, the use of gypsum board as the tested substrate, if that is the project's intended substrate. This required use of gypsum board may make the test method more stringent and the resulting rating less favorable. Some wall coverings are tested, labeled, and listed by UL for compliance with UL 723 or another accredited, independent testing and inspecting agency.

Room fire-growth contribution may be required by authorities having jurisdiction for textile wall or ceiling coverings. NFPA 265, *Methods of Fire Tests for Evaluating Room Fire Growth Contribution of Textile Wall Coverings,* called the *Room Corner Test,* evaluates flammability and flashover characteristics of textile wall coverings. It includes full-scale tests that simulate a room with corners and is representative of the actual wall covering used, including the substrate and the adhesive. Method A uses a corner test exposure with specimens mounted on two walls of the test compartment. Method B uses the same compartment but with specimens on three walls. For either method, the same procedure is followed. A large burner exposes the textile wall covering to a flame source of 40 kW, which is then increased to 150 kW. The test report includes the flame spread on the wall covering at 15-second intervals during the test, the time of flashover, and the time at which flames extend out of the test compartment doorway. The heat generated and the products of combustion are monitored. NFPA 265 includes a method for measuring smoke developed but does not set limits or indexes. The UBC Standard 8-2, *Test Method for Evaluating Room Fire Growth Contribution of Textile Wall Covering,* is similar to NFPA 265. The Uniform Building Code and the Standard Building Code allow textiles on walls only to pass the requirements for either the Steiner Tunnel Test or the room fire-growth contribution test per the test methods stated in each. The BOCA National Building Code and the International Building Code contain similar requirements for textile wall coverings except that if Steiner Tunnel Test criteria are used, sprinklers must also be specified. Although this test method is intended for textiles, vinyl wall coverings can be evaluated according to room fire-growth contribution testing.

The physical and chemical characteristics of wall-covering materials can impact burning behavior. Because a wall covering is a thin layer of material over a large surface area, it tends to ignite easier and burn faster compared to a dense, thick material with a limited surface area. Materials with raised surface fibers, such as pile fabrics, wall carpets, and flocked wallpapers, have more exposed surface area than materials without raised surface fibers. Many fabrics made from thermoplastic, synthetic fibers such as polyester, nylon, polypropylene and PVC, may soften, distort, melt, shrink away, and fail to ignite when exposed to heat from small flame sources. Nonthermoplastic fiber and mixed thermoplastic and nonthermoplastic fiber fabrics may be more susceptible to ignition unless treated. Natural cellulosics may respond to flame with a protective char layer. Many synthetics have the potential to give off significant heat and emit harmful gases when ignited, causing them to burn to a greater extent than natural materials.

Critical fabric variables affecting flammability include weight, weave or construction, denier, air porosity, and degree of openness. Heavy, tightly woven fabrics are more resistant to ignition than light, sheer fabrics made from the same polymers and materials.

Orientation can also influence burning behavior. The general assumption is that fire spreads faster vertically than horizontally. Loose layers of or cavities in vertically applied materials, such as fabric draperies, create a stack effect that can significantly contribute to fires. This is one reason why wall coverings are required to be tested fully adhered, and why model building codes refer to materials that are "applied directly to the surface of walls or ceilings."

Expanded vinyl wall coverings are governed by special requirements of authorities having jurisdiction. They are defined by The BOCA National Building Code as "Wall covering consisting of a woven textile backing, an expanded vinyl base coat layer, and a nonexpanded vinyl skin coat. The expanded base coat layer is a homogeneous vinyl layer which contains a blowing agent. During processing, the blowing agent decomposes which causes this layer to expand by forming closed cells. The total thickness of the wall covering is approximately 0.055 to 0.070 inch (1.4 to 1.8 mm)." Expanded vinyl wall or ceiling coverings are required by NFPA 101 to be tested per NFPA 265 or NFPA 286, *Methods of Fire Tests for Evaluating Contribution of Wall and Ceiling Interior Finish to Room Fire Growth.* NFPA 286 "addressed those concerns associated with interior finishes that do not remain in place during testing to NFPA 265 test protocols." There are differences in burner placement and fuel flow between the two test methods. NFPA 286 also sets limits for smoke development. If expanded vinyl wall coverings are required for a project, specify requirements to comply with authorities having jurisdiction.

Many chemical treatments now exist that reduce flammability and the tendency of both natural and synthetic polymers and fibers to smolder. Unfortunately, some of these treatments also produce undesirable side effects such as changed or impaired appearance, color change, increased stiffness of the material, tackiness or brittleness at elevated temperatures, and increased hygroscopic tendencies. Inherently and permanently flame-resistant coatings, fabrics, and fibers are available that are made from polymer resins formulated with flame-retardants in their molecular structure. A few fibers and fabrics, such as glass and asbestos, are noncombustible. Of course, asbestos fabric is no longer desirable or available because of health concerns. Because inks and dyes, soil- and stain-resistance treatments, backings, and adhesives may adversely affect the flammability characteristics of wall coverings, verify that test reports include all relevant treatments and backings and that testing is by the adhered method.

Low combustion toxicity may be critical for a project or may be required by authorities having jurisdiction. For example, New York State requires toxicity testing according to the University of Pittsburgh Protocol Test Method for Building Materials. New York City requires more stringent testing based on the same test method.

Early fire warning is a recent innovation for vinyl wall coverings that are designed to react to heat by releasing a vapor that will activate ionization-type smoke detectors before a fire ignites.

Because of increased fire hazard, wall coverings, except borders, may not be recommended by manufacturers or permitted by authorities having jurisdiction to be installed over existing wall coverings. Wall coverings that are not fully adhered or that become delaminated also present an increased fire hazard.

VINYL WALL COVERINGS

Vinyl formulations consist of plastic resins (mostly or entirely of PVC) with plasticisers, stabilizers, and other additives such as pigments, flame-retardants, smoke suppressors, and biocides. Resins impart physical properties to the finished product. Stabilizers prevent the resins from degradation during manufacture and over the lifetime of the product. Pigments provide color and opacity. Embossing provides texture.

Vinyl wall covering for commercial and institutional use is usually produced in 27-inch- (686-mm-) or 54-inch- (1372-mm-) wide rolls; wider rolls predominate in commercial installations. Occasionally, other widths such as 36 or 48 inches (914 or 1219 mm) are encountered.

Vinyl wall coverings are tested for flame resistance. They offer enhanced strength, durability, stain resistance, and washability when compared to wallpapers and fabrics and are available in several categories when classified per ASTM F 793. Unlike other wall coverings, they can be disinfected. Paper-backed vinyl wall coverings, consisting of heavy paper substrate coated with vinyl, are often peelable. When dry-peeled of the decorative layer and the ground, the paper backing remains on the wall and can be used as a liner for hanging new wall coverings. If they are Category III wall coverings, paper-backed vinyl wall coverings may be suitable for commercial use. Woven and nonwoven fabric-backed vinyl wall coverings are stronger and more durable than paper-backed types. Typically, the vinyl-layer thickness ranges from 2 to 35 mils (0.05 to 0.8 mm). Woven fabric backing is about 10 mils (0.25 mm) thick; nonwoven fabric backing is about 6 mils (0.15 mm) thick. Vinyl wall coverings meeting Category IV, Type I; Category V, Type II; or Category VI, Type III criteria are usually fabric backed. Fabric-backed vinyl wall coverings are usually strippable and unpasted. When dry-stripped, the decorative layer, ground, and fabric backing are removed, leaving the substrate surface ready for receiving new wall covering. Vinyl wall coverings are susceptible to deterioration caused by UV-light exposure and plasticizer migration; both decrease wall coverings' longevity and detract from appearance.

Two standards pertaining specifically to commercial and institutional vinyl wall coverings are FS CCC-W-408 and CFFA-W-101. FS CCC-W-408 is superseded by later versions FS CCC-W-408A, FS CCC-W-408B, FS CCC-W-408C, and, currently, FS CCC-W-408D. The amendments resulted in what could be considered a less-stringent standard. For example, a weight requirement does not exist in the later versions. The earlier, A, version may be referenced by manufacturers. FS CCC-W-408A sets criteria for abrasion resistance, crocking resistance, colorfastness, cold-cracking resistance, heat-aging resistance, hydrostatic resistance, maximum flame spread, maximum shrinkage, and maximum smoke development. Later versions of FS CCC-W-408 set additional criteria for blocking resistance, breaking strength, coating adhesion, scrubbability, stain resistance, tear resistance, and washability; hydrostatic resistance has been deleted. These later versions of FS CCC-W-408 set criteria that are harmonized with those set in ASTM F 793. CFFA-W-101-B has replaced CFFA-W-101-A. The Federal Specifications define Types I, II, and III in terms of performance (light, medium, and heavy duty); in CFFA-W-101, Types I, II, and III are defined in terms of total weight, coating weight, and performance. The performance criteria of CFFA-W-101-B are harmonized with both ASTM F 793 and later versions of FS CCC-W-408. Only ASTM F 793 includes residential wall-covering categories. Only CFFA-W-101 has two classes for flame-spread and smoke-developed indexes and sets requirements for length and width. A description, based on information from all the standards and other sources, of the three types of vinyl wall covering is as follows:

- **Type I – Light Duty:** Usually has nonwoven or scrim backing. According to CFFA-W-101-B, the total weight of the vinyl wall covering is between 7 and 13 oz./sq. yd. (0.237 and 0.442 kg/sq. m), and the coating weighs between 5 and 7 oz./sq. yd. (0.17 and 0.237 kg/sq. m). These wall coverings offer moderate resistance to abrasion and wear. Appropriate uses are offices and hotel rooms in areas not subject to unusual abrasion or heavy traffic. In a note appended to the Federal Specifications, the nonmandatory recommendation for intended use states, "for ceilings and as a covering for areas not subjected to abrasion."
- **Type II – Medium Duty:** Usually has an osnaburg, drill, or nonwoven backing. According to CFFA-W-101-B, the total weight of the vinyl wall covering is between 13 and 22 oz./sq. yd. (0.442 and 0.748 kg/sq. m), and the coating weighs between 7 and 12 oz./sq. yd. (0.237 and 0.407 kg/sq. m). These are the most widely used vinyl wall coverings. They offer good resistance to more than ordinary traffic and abrasion. Appropriate uses are lounges, dining rooms, public corridors, and classrooms. In a note appended to the Federal Specifications, the nonmandatory recommendation for intended use states "for general use in areas of average traffic and scuffing."
- **Type III – Heavy Duty:** Usually has a drill fabric backing. According to CFFA-W-101-B, the total weight of the vinyl wall covering is 22 oz./sq. yd. (0.748 kg/sq. m) or more, and the coating weighs 12 oz./sq. yd. (0.407 kg/sq. m). These heavyweight materials have become increasingly rare because of their high cost and the improved performance of Type II wall coverings, but they offer resistance to hard use. Orders may require long lead-times and a minimum square-yard amount. In a note appended to the Federal Specifications, the nonmandatory recommendation for intended use states "for use primarily as wainscot or lower protection for areas of heavy traffic by moveable equipment or rough abrasion such as exist in hospitals."

Selecting a backing depends on the intended use and expected performance of vinyl wall coverings. Paper backing may be selected for use on walls in residences, low-abuse slow-traffic areas, and where cost implications are critical. Fabric backing may be selected for use on walls in nonresidential settings, for high-abuse high-traffic areas, and where wall coverings are heavy or embossed. Backings provide strength and improve bond. Heavy backing materials are stronger than lightweight materials. Paper and nonwoven backings are more dimensionally stable than woven backings. Nonwoven backings are smooth so that more intricate designs, similar to those found on wallpaper, can be applied to the decorative surface without the skrim backing telegraphing through. Polycotton is a blend of polyester and cotton. Fabric backings are summarized in Table 1 and listed according to type and in order of relative strength.

Plasticizing agents used in manufacturing vinyl wall coverings can absorb some stains through a wicking process. Stain resistance may be improved by applying an impervious coating, such as a thin sheet of polyvinyl fluoride (PVF) that is factory laminated (bonded with adhesive) to vinyl wall covering. PVF film is inert, chemically resistant, and mold and mildew resistant. Its slippery surface resists dirt and can be described as self-cleaning. If cleaning is necessary, PVF-coated wall covering is easily cleaned. Common stains cannot penetrate PVF laminate films, although some stains leave a ghosting residue because they can subdue the grain detail of the glossy surface luster. Although PVF film is inherently flexible

Table 1
COMMON VINYL WALL-COVERING FABRIC-BACKING MATERIALS

Type	Backing Material	Common Composition	Description	Typical Weight of Backing oz/sq. yd. (g/sq. m)
I	Scrim (very loose, open weave similar to cheesecloth)	Polycotton	Lightweight	1.0/1.5 (33.9/50.8)
	Nonwoven (paperlike)	Polyester cellulose	Lightweight	1.0/2.5 (33.97)
II	Osnaburg (loose, open weave)	Polycotton	Medium weight	2.0/3.0 (67.8/101.7)
	Nonwoven	Polyester cellulose	Medium weight	2.0/3.5 (67.8/118.6)
III	Drill (denser, firmer weave similar to twill)	Polycotton	Heavyweight	2.5/3.0 (84.7/101.7)

and contains no plasticizers, wall coverings are stiffer after PVF coating. UV-light-blocking PVF film can protect wall coverings from UV-light degradation. PVF film is available colored and nearly colorless and transparent; color and gloss are retained over extended periods. PVF typically outperforms other surface coating options including acrylics, urethanes, and polyvinylidene fluoride.

Dry-erasable wall coverings are a new innovation that consist of a vinyl wall covering overlayed by a transparent or light-colored polymer coating or laminated film that functions as a writing surface and can be marked on with dry-erase markers. Lightweight and fully erasable, these wall coverings can be used in lieu of markerboards. The polymer coating or laminated film also protects the underlying layers of wall coverings from staining and everyday use. Dry-erasable wall coverings are generally available in light-colored, 48- to 62-inch- (1219- to 1575-mm-) wide strips. A range of glosses, patterns, and metallic finish designs are available. Magnetic wall coverings attract magnets. Like conventional markerboards, they can also be used as projection screens, and permanent special graphics can be easily incorporated into the strips. Custom colors and special graphics are possible.

WOVEN GLASS-FIBER WALL COVERINGS

Developed in Scandinavia, woven glass-fiber wall coverings are widely used in Europe because of their inherent flame resistance and their capability to reinforce crumbling substrates. These wall coverings can support deteriorating wall surfaces and can be applied over wood paneling, concrete masonry, brick, stucco, and tile without the extensive preparation required for a typical wall-covering application. They are highly resistant to abrasion and, if torn or damaged, can be patched. They are also chemically resistant. Depending on the coating system used, woven glass-fiber wall coverings can be made soil- and stain-resistant, vapor-permeable, and they can be easily cleaned, disinfected, and decontaminated. Unlike some textiles, woven glass-fiber wall coverings are dimensionally stable; they will not shrink or stretch. They have an extend life cycle, which is estimated by manufacturers to be 30 years or more. Available in a variety of woven textures and patterns, woven glass-fiber wall coverings are typically produced in 1-m-wide rolls. Some manufacturers may provide 3-m-wide rolls for a railroaded-type, one-seam application.

Glass-fiber wall coverings must be coated. Coatings lend additional surface durability and decorative finishes. Common coatings include latex, alkyds, multicolored coatings, or hand-painted faux finishes. Epoxy coatings can be applied for heavy-wear applications. Depending on the product, glass-fiber wall coverings can be repainted numerous times.

Woven glass-fiber wall coverings are handled and installed in a manner similar to vinyl wall coverings. However, the dimensional stability of the woven pattern can be affected if the wall covering is wetted during installation. A dry-hang installation method is used, which means the adhesive is applied to the wall surface, not to the back of the wall-covering strip. The significant difference between the two wall coverings is that woven glass-fiber covering cannot be stripped like vinyl. It becomes a permanent, durable substrate.

Because woven glass-fiber wall coverings are breathable and inherently mold- and mildew-resistant, they are often considered for use in humid, coastal regions where moisture infiltration is a concern. Mildew-resistant paints should be specified. Latex paint should be selected as the coating if permeability is a concern.

TEXTILE WALL COVERINGS

Textile wall coverings can be manufactured from natural fibers such as cotton, flax, silk, and wool; synthetic fibers such as rayon, polyester, and polypropylene; or both natural and synthetic fiber blends. Four synthetic fibers, rayon, acetate, triacetate and lyocell, are derived from modified cellulosic fibers obtained from wood pulp. All other synthetic fibers are chemically based. Fabrics can be designed to maximize their performance and enhance their aesthetic qualities by blending different fibers to take advantage of the best characteristics of each fiber.

Fabrics made from natural fibers may show irregular weaving and color effects as part of the design and manufacturing processes, which should be considered when selecting fabrics with these characteristics. If a monolithic appearance is required, synthetic fabrics may be more reliable.

Textile wall coverings are produced in a variety of widths and lengths. The number of square feet (meters) on a roll and the length of yardage in a bolt should be verified.

Fabric treatments are available to modify fabric performance. Fabrics can be treated for flame and ignition retardance, abrasion resistance, and soil resistance. Textile wall coverings can be vinyl coated. Some treatments can affect appearance, discolor textiles, and alter the feel of the fabric. Fabrics may shrink during finishing processes. To evaluate a fabric sample, all proposed finishes should be applied to the sample to determine their effect on the fabric's color, stiffness, drapability, texture, and dimensional stability.

Textile wall coverings are frequently laminated to a backing to enhance dimensional stability, improve hanging qualities, improve bond, and prevent the adhesive from migrating through to the surface. These backings are typically latex acrylic coatings. Other backings, including paper and knits, are possible. Depending on the fabric's characteristics, the wall covering may have to be trimmed before installation instead of overlapping and double cutting.

Acoustically absorbent wall coverings are available for vertical application to walls but are significantly more effective at absorbing sound when used in combination with acoustically absorbent cores made principally of insulations and backings than when applied directly to wall surfaces. A wall covering's acoustical absorption depends on its extent, location, porosity, and texture. Acoustical fabrics, perforated vinyls, wall panels, and operable walls are tested for a noise reduction coefficient and frequently used to control noise in auditoriums, corridors, elevator lobbies, gymnasiums, offices, meeting rooms, restaurants, schools, and theaters. Acoustically absorbent wall coverings and fabrics are predominantly made of synthetic polyester fibers and olefin (polypropylene) fibers. They are often Velcro-compatible.

Unprotected textile wall coverings may be sinks for odors, may attract and hold dirt, and may be difficult to clean.

HEAVY-DUTY SYNTHETIC TEXTILE WALL COVERINGS

Heavy-duty synthetic textile wall coverings combine the look and texture of a textile with the stain and abrasion resistance of a vinyl. High-performance synthetic yarns are tightly woven into textiles and applied to paper or acrylic backings. These wall coverings are produced in 54-inch- (1372-mm-) or 60-inch- (1524-mm-) wide rolls in bolts of continuous yardage as needed.

Abrasion-resistance ratings for heavy-duty synthetic textile wall coverings exceed those for heavy-duty vinyl wall coverings. Tear and breaking strengths are unmatched by vinyl. These wall coverings may stand up under cleaning with harsh chemicals.

To prevent seaming problems, care must be exercised during installation of these wall coverings; double cutting is usually not possible because of their thickness. Many manufacturers recommend changing the cutting blade after each cut and cutting the wall covering on the back.

WALLPAPERS

Wallpapers are the most common wall coverings for residential applications. Typically, residential wall coverings range from 20½ to 28 inches (521 to 711 mm) wide. A single roll yields 27 to 30 sq. ft. (2.5 to 2.8 sq. m). Single rolls are packaged and sold in double-roll quantities. Double rolls have 56 to 58 sq. ft. (5.2 to 5.4 sq. m) and are approximately 11 yd. (10 m) long. After the number of single rolls needed for a space is determined, the wallpaper is ordered in multiples of two or three only. Suppliers often charge additional costs called *cut charges* for ordering less than double- or triple-roll quantities. Because wallpapers are produced in several widths and lengths, verify the number of square feet (square meters) on a roll.

Both sidewalls and borders are popular. Sidewall is the term used by the wallpaper industry to describe a wide-width wall covering that covers the field or major surface of a wall. Murals are a type of sidewall. Borders are produced in narrower sheets and are intended to be applied to the top of a wall or above the wall molding as a complement to the painted or sidewall-covered surface. Borders come in spools or segments and are normally shipped in 15-foot (4.6-m) increments.

Wallpaper designs are printed by a variety of methods including rotogravure, flexography, surface, rotary screen, and hand-produced silkscreen. Imported wallpapers with silk-screened designs and hand-blocked prints are also available. Acrylic or other polymer-coated or -saturated wallpapers are stronger and have better tearing resistance than untreated wallpapers. Renewed interest in wallpapers made from natural biobased,

renewable, sustainably harvested materials and recycled materials may result in increased use.

Vinyl-coated papers, consisting of a paper substrate coated with acrylic/vinyl or solid PVC with a total thickness of 2 to 5 mils (0.05 to 0.13 mm), are scrubbable and peelable or strippable, but are not suited for commercial applications. These types of wallpapers now predominate the market; the manufacture of untreated, paper-only wallpapers has diminished. Because vinyl-coated papers are more resistant than untreated wallpapers to moisture and soiling, they can be used in residential kitchens, bathrooms, and laundry rooms.

WALL-COVERING INSTALLATION CONSIDERATIONS

A dye lot, also called a *production run,* is a particular batch of wall covering that is dyed or printed at the same time. To ensure uniformity of color, printing, shading, and overall appearance, all rolls of wall covering should be from the same dye lot and should be installed in sequence numbers. If mixed runs are unavoidable in large spaces, use only one run for each wall. The industry standard for uniformity of textile and vinyl wall coverings requires the installer to install three panels or strips and inspect for correctness of materials and application. If satisfactory, the installer is instructed to continue work by the manufacturer. If not satisfactory, the installer is instructed to stop work and contact the manufacturer's representative. Generally, manufacturers assume no responsibility for the installation of material beyond three panels or strips. Fabrics that are suitable for wall coverings may be labeled "suitable for vertical application."

Adhesives are formulated for specific applications of substrate and wall covering. They may vary in materials, formulation, mix requirements, antimicrobial and antifungal resistance, VOCs, wet tack, effective use time, strippability, and ease of application. Traditional adhesives are based on natural organic polymers (starches, dextrins, and caseins); clay may be added as a filler to increase the solids content and the wet-tack or initial adhesion between the substrate and wall covering. Today, synthetic polymers are frequently substituted for natural organic polymers. Adhesives may be available in solid, liquid, emulsion, hot-melt, or pressure-sensitive formulations. Most wall-covering adhesives in use today are water-based. These mixtures of natural and synthetic polymers contain trace amounts of organic solvents or none; VOC emission potential is minimal. Consult the wall-covering manufacturer and, if possible, the actual adhesive manufacturer to determine the most suitable adhesive for the substrate and wall covering concerned. If vapor permeability is critical, verify that the recommended adhesive does not act as a vapor retarder.

Cellulose-based pastes are the least tacky adhesives and are nonstaining. They are furnished as a dry powder. Cellulose-based adhesives are used to install murals, delicate wallpapers, and uncoated wallpapers. Wheat-based pastes are similar to cellulose-based pastes.

Clay-based adhesives with maximum wet tack were developed to hold heavy wall coverings such as fabric-backed heavy commercial vinyls, Mylars, foils, and wall liners. Dry-hang applications, in which adhesives are applied to the wall rather than the wall covering, often use clay-based adhesives.

Newer adhesives for wall coverings are lightweight and clear drying. They are strippable, require less cleanup, and have extended effective use time compared to clay-based adhesives. Strippable wall coverings and adhesives save installation time and reduce many of the problems caused by improperly prepared substrates. These products leave dull, transparent films when dry, eliminating the appearance of paste residue inherent with the traditional opaque adhesives that have clay filler. Fabrics, vinyls, and wallpapers are often hung with clear adhesives. Complete removal of wall-covering adhesives is essential for proper paint application later. Adhesive residue can ruin an otherwise suitable paint application.

Prepasted adhesives are convenient, do not require proportioning or mixing, require less cleanup, and are used frequently in residential wallpaper installations and less frequently in commercial wall-covering installations. Seam splitting and seam lifting are reduced. Water is the common activator for prepasted adhesives. Prepaste activators are an alternative to water. These mold- and mildew-resistant adhesives, made specifically for prepasted wallpapers, may be permitted by manufacturers.

Prepaste activators provide for a continuous, more even distribution of adhesive; activate the factory-applied adhesive faster than water; increase slip; provide extra holding power at the seam; and extend effective use time to provide a longer time to match patterns. *Slip* is the characteristic of an adhesive that allows sliding and repositioning of the wall covering (not fabric) during installation. Prepaste activators are applied to the back of the prepasted wall covering. The need for water is eliminated.

Vinyl-over-vinyl adhesives are for installations of Mylars, foils, and wall liners, and for installations directly over existing wall coverings without adhesion-promoting primers. Vinyl-over-vinyl adhesives are also used for installing borders on vinyl wall coverings and for woven glass-fiber wall coverings. Once cured, vinyl-over-vinyl adhesives are permanent and should be cleaned up before curing. Note that hanging vinyl wall covering over existing vinyl or other wall covering may significantly increase flammability, smoke generation, and toxicity in the event of a fire and may not comply with requirements of authorities having jurisdiction. Also, note that installing vinyl wall covering over existing wall covering means acceptance of an unknown and possibly inadequate substrate because the original substrate preparation and adhesive now must support a greater weight than originally anticipated; the potential for adhesion failure and delamination is unknown.

Seam adhesives provide a strong bond for tightly adhering problem seams and repairing loose seams. They are water-resistant and permanent.

Backings affect adhesive choice. Wall coverings with paper backings need adhesives with significant water content for relaxing. Those with woven backings need moderately wet adhesives, and those with nonwoven backings need less-moist adhesives.

Two methods for hanging wall coverings are dry and wet hanging. For dry hanging, adhesive is applied to the wall or wall liner, and the wall covering is applied over the suitably tacky adhesive; for wet hanging, adhesive is applied to the back of the wall covering, which is then applied directly to the substrate.

Substrate preparation is critical to wall-covering application; procedures depend on the nature of the substrate. Wall coverings require flat substrates that are clean, smooth, dry, structurally sound, and free of flaking or unsound coatings, oils, grease, stains, mold, and mildew. Fresh plaster must be allowed to cure for 90 days or more before priming. Wall irregularities should be filled and sanded before priming and sealing the wall surface to prevent irregularities from telegraphing through the wall covering. Stains or mildew should be removed before priming and sealing to prevent them from bleeding through the wall covering. Gloss and semi-gloss paint must be sanded to dull the surface and primed to seal and promote adhesion. Walls stripped of old wall covering should be sanded or cleaned with an adhesive remover to provide sound substrate and dis-

courage the development of mold and mildew. For best results, after peeling the removable layer of existing peelable wall covering, remove the paper backing by wetting the surface with liquid remover and scraping off with a broad knife.

When water-based adhesives cure, wall coverings may contract; if the wall surface is not sound, the adhesive bond between the wall covering or the liner and substrate may fail. For example, wet wallpaper can swell anywhere from $\frac{1}{8}$ to $\frac{3}{8}$ inch (3 to 9.5 mm) or more during booking. *Booking* is the term applied to the technique of folding the top and bottom of a wallpaper strip to the center, paste side to paste side, so the wallpaper can "relax" for several minutes and can assume its final dimension from absorbing the water or paste. For booking time, refer to the manufacturer's written instructions. If hung over an unprimed surface, wallpaper tends to pull back to its original size as it dries, creating gaps at the seams. Over a primed surface, paste adheres evenly to the primer, wallpaper contraction is controlled, and seams stay tightly butted.

Substrate primers and sealers are acrylic-based or alkyd oil-based coatings that are formulated for two purposes. Sealers are intended to seal porous substrates so adhesives are not absorbed into the wall and nothing can bleed through the sealer to the wall covering. Primers are applied to increase bonding on hard, glossy, slick, slippery, or nonporous surfaces. They are formulated to have uniform porosity for maximum bonding of the wall covering to the substrate and to provide the correct amount of slip to allow the wall covering to be positioned or slid in-place. Primer/sealers combine these two functions. When applied over latex paint, primer/sealers may penetrate and rebind the existing paint to the substrate. Pigmented primer/sealers may also be used to mask contrasting colors or areas of light and dark on the substrate and may be required under transparent or light-colored wall coverings. Strippable wall coverings are applied over sealed and primed wall or wall liner substrates to improve strippability. Alkyd oil-based products are becoming difficult to formulate for maximum performance and compliance with regulatory requirements limiting VOCs. Oil-based products may not be vapor-permeable, resulting in potential adhesion problems and moisture development. If vapor permeability is critical, verify that the recommended primer/sealer does not act as a vapor retarder.

Wall liners, sometimes called *lining paper,* may be recommended to ensure a smooth surface and better bond where substrates cannot be properly prepared. They are nonwoven, paperlike, synthetic sheets. Wall liners cannot mask the texture of an existing wall covering, but they can bridge small gaps like those in masonry and wood paneling. They are applied horizontally over grooved paneling, vertically on concrete block. Wall liners may also be used in lieu of primer/sealers to mask contrasting colors or areas of light and dark on the substrate.

Two basic seaming techniques are double cutting and butting. The seaming method used depends on the thickness of the wall covering, how easily it ravels, whether a pattern must be matched, and the ease of removing adhesive without damaging the wall covering.

- **Double cutting:** Consecutive strips are overlapped about 2 inches (50 mm). Both sheets are cut through, and the residual strips are removed. The adhesive is cleaned from the surface of the wall covering. Double cutting is appropriate for nonpatterned wall coverings and those with damaged edges.
- **Butting:** The edges of consecutive strips are butted tightly together without being trimmed. Butting is appropriate for pretrimmed, deeply embossed, or dark-colored material where removing adhesive from the surface may be difficult.

Pattern and seam placement may be critical. To be aesthetically pleasing in intended spaces, large, complicated, dominant pattern repeats may need careful placement to establish a starting point. These wall coverings are frequently hung with dominant pattern repeats centered at eye level in the central area of the space; but this placement must be balanced with the wall covering's appearance around critical features such as ceiling line, chair rails, door/window headers and soffits, and so on. Where critical features occur, avoid partial design elements and strive for overall symmetry. Shop drawings, if required in the wall covering specification, should indicate pattern placement, seams, and termination points.

Seam edges of strips are sometimes taped using low-adhesive tape to keep the face of seams clean according to the wall-covering manufacturer's recommendation. After the wall covering is adhered, the tape is removed.

Textured or random-matched patterned wall coverings may require reverse hanging of alternate strips for color uniformity among strips. Reverse hanging is achieved by hanging every other strip upside down.

Textiles are generally designed to be hung straight up and nonreversed. Strips of pile fabrics must be hung straight up to avoid color differences caused by pile directional changes. Some natural-fiber textile wall coverings may show some shade or weave variations from strip to strip, which may be an inherent quality of these materials. Acrylic-backed or unbacked textiles are best dry-hung; paper-backed textiles may be either dry-hung or wet-hung if permitted by the manufacturer.

A few wall coverings may not be hung vertically as panels from the ceiling to the floor. Instead, they may be applied in strips running horizontally across the wall. This method is called *railroading*. Railroading has the advantages of fewer seams, neater and stronger wrapped outside corners, faster and economical installation, and visual continuity. Disadvantages are horizontal seams and visual discrepancies on out-of-plumb walls at corners. Wall coverings hung above and below chair rails may be best applied using railroading. Hanging wall coverings vertically as panels from the ceiling to the floor has the advantages of neater inside corners, of being adaptable to high walls, and of less waste for ceilings under 8 feet (2.4 m); disadvantages are potential seam problems.

ENVIRONMENTAL CONSIDERATIONS

The American Institute of Architects' *Environmental Resource Guide (ERG)* includes an application report for fabric, paper, and vinyl wall coverings that features comparative environmental performances and recommendations for architects. The guide also includes a material report for paper and vinyl wall coverings that highlights concerns for waste generation, natural resource depletion, energy consumption, and indoor air quality. Materials used in the manufacture of wall coverings and adhesives are obtained by mining, logging, and petroleum drilling and refining, with subsequent stress on the environment. Often the processes of manufacturing wall coverings and component materials are energy-intensive and require significant water use and disposal of byproduct waste. According to the ERG, "Materials in the life cycle of wall coverings become at least partially regulated in practically all stages."

Indoor air or environmental quality is often cited as a concern for wall coverings, especially vinyl wall coverings. Conflicting studies are summarized in the ERG. Wall coverings, backings, inks, adhesives, and protective coatings, films, and treatments may all be sources capable of emitting VOCs, but emissions reportedly dissipate quickly to trace levels. Water-based adhesives and inks decrease VOC emissions compared to solvent-based products. The Environmental Protection Agency (EPA) has published its *Guidelines for Low-Emitting Materials,* based on recommendations for maximum allowable levels of emission of total volatile organic compounds (TVOCs), which can be used to determine low-emitting materials and products. Wall materials are allowed to emit TVOCs of 0.4 mg/h per sq. m. according to EPA guidelines. Another possible guideline has been developed by Washington State's Department of General Administration for state buildings and incorporated into the State's specifications. For any material or product, including construction materials, interior finishes, and furnishings, TVOCs are limited to a maximum of 0.5 mg/cu. m, formaldehyde to a maximum 0.05 ppm, and total respirable particles to 0.05 mg/cu. m. Products are tested for emissions using environmental chamber tests. Contact manufacturers to verify compliance with requirements of authorities having jurisdiction.

Wall coverings can also be a significant sink for odors and VOCs depending on their extent, porosity, and texture. Textile wall coverings may be especially susceptible to retaining odors and VOCs.

The wall-covering industry has made an effort to reduce and eliminate heavy metals, such as lead, cadmium, and mercury, used as pigments, stabilizers, and biocides. Manufacturers are beginning to offer wall coverings that are allegedly environmentally preferable. Characteristics may include water-based inks, colorants, and adhesives; low heavy-metal and toxic-substance content; low VOCs; and no PVCs or chlorine. If environmental issues are a critical concern, each of these environmentally preferable wall coverings should be individually evaluated for the presence or absence of these special characteristics, in addition to traditional concerns for performance and appearance.

Scotchgard protector is being voluntarily phased out for fabric, carpets, leather, and upholstery by its manufacturer, 3M, following negotiations with the EPA. Scotchgard is based on perfluorooctanyl sulfonate (PFOS) chemistry. PFOSs are now thought to accumulate in human and animal tissues (bioaccumulation) and to be persistent in the environment. These two tendencies could potentially pose a risk to human health and the environment over the long term.

Wall coverings made from natural fibers and recycled-content natural and synthetic fibers are available. Although natural fibers are recyclable, renewable, and biodegradable, they may lack durability and other performance characteristics. They often must be chemically treated for resistance to insects, fungi, fire, and stains. Some of these chemical treatments involve potentially toxic and carcinogenic substances. Fibers made from polyethylene terephthalate (PET) bottles are currently the most common recycled-content textiles available.

Recyclability and disposal may be an issue, especially with products such as wall coverings that are frequently replaced for aesthetic reasons before their functional life cycle is complete.

REFERENCES

Publication dates cited here were current at the time of this writing. Publications are revised periodically, and revisions may have occurred before this book was published.

The American Association of Textile Chemists and Colorists

AATCC 147-1998: Antibacterial Activity Assessment of Textile Materials: Parallel Streak Method

The American Institute of Architects

Environmental Resource Guide, 1996 (1997 and 1998 supplements).

ASTM International

ASTM D 1308-87 (reapproved 1998): Test Method for Effect of Household Chemicals on Clear and Pigmented Organic Finishes

ASTM E 84-00a: Test Method for Surface-Burning Characteristics of Building Materials

ASTM F 793-93 (reapproved 1998): Classification of Wallcovering by Durability Characteristics

ASTM G 21-96: Practice for Determining Resistance of Synthetic Polymeric Materials to Fungi

Chemical Fabrics & Film Association, Inc.

Standard Test Methods Chemical Coated Fabrics and Film, 2000.

CFFA-W-101-B-95: Quality Standard for Vinyl-Coated Fabric Wallcovering

Federal Specification

FS CCC-W-408D-94: Wall Covering, Vinyl Coated

International Conference of Building Officials

UBC Standard 8-1-1997: Test Method for Surface-Burning Characteristics of Building Materials

UBC Standard 8-2-1997: Test Method for Evaluating Room Fire Growth Contribution of Textile Wall Covering

National Fire Protection Association

NFPA 255-00: Method of Test of Surface Burning Characteristics of Building Materials

NFPA 265-98: Methods for Evaluating Room Fire Growth Contribution of Textile Wall Coverings

NFPA 286-00: Methods of Fire Tests for Evaluating Contribution of Wall and Ceiling Interior Finish to Room Fire Growth

WEB SITES

American Association of Textile Chemists and Colorists: www.aatcc.org

The Association for Contract Textiles: www.contract-textiles.com

Chemical Fabrics & Film Association, Inc.: www.chemicalfabricsandfilm.com

Wallcoverings Association: www.wallcoverings.org

This chapter discusses flexible wood-veneer wall covering.

WOOD-VENEER WALL COVERING CHARACTERISTICS

Wood veneer for wall covering is very thin and is bonded to a backing material. The thinness makes rare and exotic woods less expensive than solid-wood or plywood-veneer paneling. The veneer slices are adhered to a woven scrim or nonwoven, paperlike backing to reinforce the wood surface, making the wall covering flexible only in the direction of the grain. The veneer is available prefinished and unfinished. Care should be taken if unfinished wood-veneer wall covering is selected. The veneer is so thin that sanding is not recommended as part of a finishing operation (fig. 1).

Some wood-veneer wall coverings are installed in the same way as vinyl wall coverings, using the same adhesives. Rely on the manufacturer for specific advice and, if possible, the actual adhesive.

Wall liners, sometimes called *lining paper,* may be recommended where substrates cannot be properly prepared. They are nonwoven, paperlike, synthetic sheets. Wall liners cannot mask the texture of an existing wall covering but can bridge gaps and small holes.

VENEER CUTTING OR SAWING

The Architectural Woodwork Institute's (AWI's) *Architectural Woodwork Quality Standards* and the Woodwork Institute of California's (WIC's) *Manual of Millwork* contain reference material and illustrations of veneer conditions. Both publications are helpful in understanding veneer sawing, veneer matching, veneer sheet matching, and custom-veneer sets.

There are five slicing methods: rotary, flat, quarter, rift, and half-round.

- **Rotary cut:** The full log is mounted in a lathe and turned against a fixed cutting blade. The blade follows the annual growth rings, producing a bold and constantly changing grain pattern. Since the grain is nonrepetitive, it cannot be used for sequence- or blueprint-matched patterns. Typical wood species used with rotary-cut veneers are stock softwoods, birch, and red oak.
- **Flat cut (plain slicing):** The blade slices parallel to a line through the center of the log. Individual pieces are kept in order, allowing a natural grain progression when assembled as veneer faces.
- **Quarter cut:** The blade cuts at a 45-degree angle to a line parallel through the center of the log. The cut is perpendicular to the growth rings of the tree. The resulting effect is striped or straight-grained.
- **Rift cut:** The log is cut into quarters and mounted off center in the cutting lathe. This accentuates the vertical grain and reduces the flake effect occurring in quarter slicing. Rift cut is restricted to red or white oak.

Comb grain: A selection of rift-cut material distinguished by a tight and straight grain along the entire length of the veneer.

- **Half-round cut:** Half the log is mounted off center in the cutting lathe. The cut is slightly across the growth rings, creating modified characteristics of both rotary and plain slicing. Wood species typically used are American red and white oak. Half-round sliced veneer is seldom used for sequence- or blueprint-matched paneling.

VENEER MATCHING

There are four types of veneer matches, as follows:

- **Book match:** The most commonly used match in the industry. It requires turning over every other veneer sheet so adjacent pieces produce a mirror image. Book matching is used with rotary-cut, plain-sliced, quarter-cut, rift-cut, or comb-grain veneers.
- **Slip match:** Veneer sheets are placed in sequence, repeating the grain figure. Slip matching is used with quarter-cut, rift-cut, and comb-grain veneers.
- **Random match:** Veneer sheets are random, producing a boardlike appearance.
- **End match:** Veneer sheets are book matched in length as well as horizontally. A mirror image is created end to end.

VENEER SHEET MATCHING

There are three styles of veneer sheet matching, as follows:

- **Running match:** Veneer sheets of many maximum-width veneer pieces.
- **Balance match:** Veneer sheets of equal-width veneer pieces. Balance matching is commonly used for sequence- or blueprint-matched sheets.
- **Center match:** Veneer sheets of an even number of equal-width veneer pieces, symmetric about a centerline veneer joint.

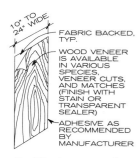

10" TO 24" WIDE
FABRIC BACKED, TYP.
WOOD VENEER IS AVAILABLE IN VARIOUS SPECIES, VENEER CUTS, AND MATCHES (FINISH WITH STAIN OR TRANSPARENT SEALER)
ADHESIVE AS RECOMMENDED BY MANUFACTURER

Figure 1. Wood-veneer wall covering

CUSTOM-VENEER SETS

Custom-veneer sets come in two styles:

- **Sequence-matched veneer sheet sets:** Sequence-numbered sets are for a specific installation. Sequence matching requires veneers cut from one log of an adequate number for the area of the room, including trim.
- **Blueprint-matched veneer sheet and component sets:** Veneered components are exact size and for a specific location. They are continuous on the faces of doors, casework, and other components.

REFERENCES

Publication dates cited here were current at the time of this writing. Publications are revised periodically, and revisions may have occurred before this book was published.

Architectural Woodwork Institute
Architectural Woodwork Quality Standards, 1993.

Woodwork Institute of California
Manual of Millwork, 1992.

09751 INTERIOR STONE FACING

This chapter discusses dimension stone used for interior wall and column facing, trim, window stools, and countertops.

This chapter does not discuss dimension stone flooring, dimension stone tiles used for interior wall facing and countertops, stone masonry veneer used as interior stone facing, or composite stone panels used as interior stone facing. Dimension stone flooring is covered in Chapter 09638, Stone Paving and Flooring; and dimension stone tile, in Chapter 09385, Dimension Stone Tile.

GENERAL COMMENTS

Selecting dimension stone for interior facing is based on color, finish, and to some extent, resistance to soiling and abuse, rather than on structural strength or weather resistance as with exterior stonework. Consequently, the visual qualities (color and finish) of stone for a specific project are usually best determined by selecting from available choices offered by a reputable source. Local fabricators and suppliers are usually helpful in finding suitable varieties.

Because stone is a natural material that varies greatly in appearance, view several samples that show the expected range of variation for each type during the selection process. Be sure to use recently quarried samples because stone produced by a quarry may change over time as the quarrying operations move from one area of the quarry to another. Also be aware that despite all these efforts, the stone furnished for the project may still look slightly different from the samples used in the selection process; stone is a naturally variable material. In general, do not rely on mockups for confirming stone selection; by the time the project is far enough along for a mockup to be constructed, all the stone has usually been purchased and fabrication is well under way.

Selecting the blocks or slabs for use on the project is a method for providing additional control over the final appearance of the stonework. This procedure can be expensive because it usually requires traveling to the quarry or the distributor; for large projects or those requiring the finest appearance, it can be worth the expense. Blocks are usually selected at the quarry, but slabs may often be selected at a distributor's or even a fabricator's yard, which may involve less travel expense. Before specifying this procedure, determine where selection will take place and the costs involved.

Interior stone paneling may be installed over gypsum board construction or over masonry and concrete walls. Although interior stone anchoring systems are not subject to the extreme environmental conditions that exterior dimension stone anchors are, supports and anchors must be compatible with the stone and the substrate (figs. 1, 2).

CHARACTERISTICS OF DIMENSION STONE

Chapter 09638 contains definitions of the various stone groups and information about the classifications of the groups and the standards applicable to each group. Review Chapter 09638 before specifying interior stone facing.

GRANITE

Many granite varieties are so colorful and dramatically figured that their beauty would be almost wasted on the exterior of many buildings. These granites and many others lend themselves well to interior stone facing for impressive spaces in many types of buildings. Granite can be used on interior walls with any of several finishes, from a mirror polish to a highly textured thermal finish. Because granite is much harder than marble, it requires more time and effort to fabricate and finish. For this reason, even the least-expensive varieties of granite are more expensive than the least-expensive varieties of marble. However, the rare, highly decorative varieties of both marble and granite are more expensive than the least-expensive varieties of either.

LIMESTONE

Oolitic limestone is not widely used for interior facing because it typically has a textured surface that collects dirt and is difficult to clean. It has been used in the past for interior facing above a wainscot of marble or granite and has even been imitated as an interior finish: Grand Central Station in New York City has precast plaster panels, made to imitate French limestone, above a polished-marble wainscot.

Dolomitic limestone is more widely used for interior facing and is often polished like marble. It is also used with a smooth honed finish, a textured sandblasted finish, or a split-face finish. Dolomitic limestone is generally not as porous as oolitic limestone, which makes it easier to clean and keep clean when used on the interior. Dolomitic limestone is available in shades of gray and tan, as well as more colorful blue-grays, pinks, creams, and even yellows.

MARBLE

Many varieties of marble that are unsuitable for exterior cladding can be safely used for interior facing where their beauty will be more noticeable. When used on the exterior, marble is vulnerable to scratching and attack by acids and does not keep a high polish. When used for interior facing, marble can retain a bright polish and the intensity of color that accompanies the polish, which enable it to be seen at its best (fig. 3).

The more fragile varieties of marble can be suitably reinforced and repaired for use as interior facing; however, these treatments would not be sufficient to enable its use on the exterior. Dry seams in marble can be glued together (called sticking), voids can be filled (called waxing), and weak areas can be reinforced with metal rods glued into the back of the panel (called rodding). Often, slabs of fragile marble varieties are reinforced with a layer of glass-fiber-reinforced plastic before they are polished and further fabricated.

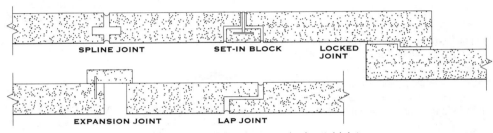

Figure 1. Typical interior stone corner details

CORNER BUTT

RABBETED CORNER

CORNER L

QUIRK MITER

CORNER BLOCK

SLIP CORNER

SPLINE JOINT

SET-IN BLOCK

LOCKED JOINT

EXPANSION JOINT

LAP JOINT

Figure 2. Typical interior stone horizontal joints

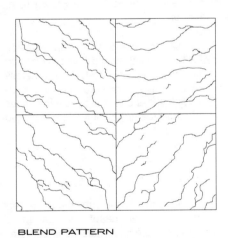

BLEND PATTERN

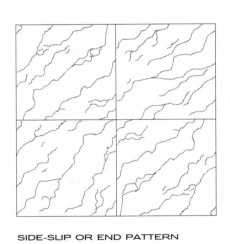

SIDE-SLIP OR END PATTERN

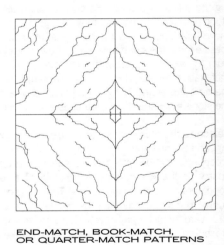

END-MATCH, BOOK-MATCH, OR QUARTER-MATCH PATTERNS

Figure 3. Marble wall facing patterns

Most of the highly decorative varieties of marble are imported from Italy, the center of the world's marble trade, because of the many beautiful varieties found there. However, some figured varieties are found in the United States, such as the colorful onyx marbles from New Mexico. A range of colors and patterns can also be found in Mexico.

The green varieties of marble, which are usually serpentine and not really marble, are very attractive. When using serpentine, be aware that it is sensitive to water and prone to warping if it becomes wet; therefore, instead of mortar or plaster, use setting materials that do not contain water, such as water-cleanable epoxy adhesives.

GREENSTONE

Because greenstone generally does not take a high polish, it is useful for interior stone facing where a honed or cleft finish is suitable. Although no longer quarried in the United States (it was once quarried in Virginia), it is available from England and Europe.

INSTALLATION METHODS

The traditional method for installing interior stone facing is to use wire-tie anchors and plaster or mortar spots, with the wire ties anchored to gypsum board construction or in masonry backup (figs. 4-8). In gypsum board construction, wire ties are embedded in plaster-filled metal boxes or inserted through the gypsum board and fastened to the wall framing. In masonry backup, the wire ties are embedded in the support wall, typically concrete masonry units, in voids filled with mortar or plaster. Details of these methods can be found in the Marble Institute of America's (MIA's) *Dimensional Stone-Design Manual IV.* The wire-tie method should not be used for stone paneling more than 96 inches (2400 mm) high without intermediate horizontal support for vertical stone loads. One disadvantage of the wire-tie method is that for fire-rated gypsum board walls an additional row of studs and another layer of gypsum board must be added if wire ties are not allowed to penetrate the fire-rated wall. Also, it is difficult to engineer the wire-tie system to provide seismic restraint for the stone panels.

Mechanical anchoring systems are available that may be fastened directly to the backup wall, eliminating the need for additional studding and gypsum board and providing verifiable seismic restraint. Anchor systems, similar to those used for exterior work over masonry or metal framing, may be fastened to metal studs through gypsum board. Exterior anchors may also be used with metal channel struts that eliminate the need to coordinate stud location with anchor locations. This type of anchor may still require plaster-setting spots.

Vertical loads imposed by interior stone facing require that metal-stud sizes and thicknesses be designed accordingly. Lateral loads are typically not a concern for interior stone facing less than 25 feet (7.6 m) high except in areas of high seismic activity. In areas of seismic risk, a review of code requirements will be needed to determine whether structural design of the stone anchoring system is necessary.

The installation method can be selected by the architect, or the choice can be left to the Iinstaller if certain requirements for performance and visual effects are met. If the installation method is not specified and detailed on the drawings, investigate available anchoring systems and allow adequate setting space. Although the selection of both the installation method and the setting-space dimension can be left to the Iinstaller, it is usually best to at least decide on the setting-space dimension for coordinating with other materials that contact the stonework.

Latex additives used in grout have become more and more popular because they can produce a more durable joint installation, especially if minor movement is expected. For stone joints, the stone industry is now referencing the same American National Standards Institute (ANSI) standards developed for tile grouting materials.

Joint size will depend on the finish selected and on whether joints are to be coordinated with exterior stone joints or floor joints. If joints are coordinated with other stone joints, the other application usually determines the joint size. In the past, highly polished or finely honed interior stone facing was installed with 1/16-inch- (1.5-mm-) wide joints, but larger joints are

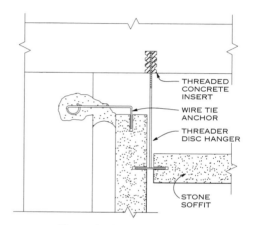

Figure 4. Soffit detail at wall

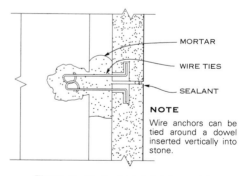

Figure 5. Vertical joint detail — plain

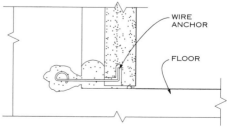

Figure 6. Base detail

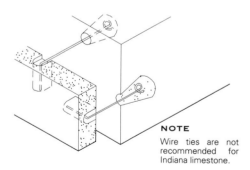

Figure 7. Simple wire anchor connection

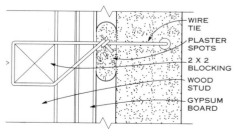

Figure 8. Stone panel on wood studs

more typically used now. Larger joints provide more allowance for inaccuracy in fabricating the stone and in backup and adjoining construction. A joint ⅛ inch (3 mm) wide is certainly adequate for polished or honed stone. For stone with a highly textured finish, such as thermal-finished granite or natural-cleft slate, a joint width of approximately ¼ to ⅜ inch (6 to 10 mm) is appropriate because it will minimize the appearance of lipping and will be in scale with the texture. When different textures are combined, it is best to select one joint size, usually the largest required by the different textures.

Dry-set grouts are mixtures of portland cement and water-retentive additives, are unsanded, and are suitable for joints up to ⅛ inch (3 mm) wide. For larger joints, a sanded grout, such as a commercial portland cement grout, must be used because the sand will reduce shrinkage and help minimize cracking. Sanded grouts should be avoided for polished stone because the sand will scratch the stone as the grout smears are wiped from the surface. This problem is more severe with marble, which is much softer than sand, than it is with granite, which is about as hard as sand.

STONE COUNTERTOPS

Specifying stone countertops requires considering the practicalities involved. Marble is easily etched by the mildest acids, such as fruit juice and soft drinks. Scratches are glaringly evident on a highly polished countertop, and an imperfect polish is usually not tolerated so close to eye level. Therefore, marble tops should generally not be used in kitchens; however, if used, they should have a honed finish, which helps to hide scratches and is more easily repaired than a polished finish. A honed finish can often be repaired by hand sanding with 600-grit wet or dry emery paper used wet over a resilient backing.

Serpentine tends to warp if it gets wet and probably should not be used in bathrooms. Highly figured varieties of marble, because of the potential weakness of the natural seams, should be continuously supported. All stone countertops should be rigidly supported because most stone cannot tolerate much deflection, and people are prone to stepping on countertops to change light bulbs and so on.

Granite for countertops should be selected with closer scrutiny than granite for interior facing. Some granites show pitting at the crystals of some minor constituents, particularly mica, due to that mineral's softness and prominent cleavage. Although this slight pitting may be acceptable for exterior cladding or for interior facing, it is usually not acceptable for a highly polished countertop. Although granite is very hard and resists scratching, that same hardness makes it difficult to polish out scratches, so a honed finish may be desirable even for granite countertops.

Seams are another consideration; they may be unavoidable in kitchen countertops and larger toilet-room vanities. Consult stone sources to determine the sizes of available material before deciding what seams are necessary. Avoid mitered seams and seams located near cutouts; and show seam locations on the drawings. Bonded seams will be practical only where the countertop is straight or small and will require more highly skilled craftspeople at additional cost.

REFERENCES

Publication dates cited here were current at the time of this writing. Publications are revised periodically, and revisions may have occurred before this book was published.

Marble Institute of America
Dimensional Stone-Design Manual IV, 1991.

WEB SITES

Canadian Stone Association: www.stone.ca

Indiana Limestone Institute of America, Inc.: www.iliai.com

Italian Trade Commission: www.marblefromitaly.com

National Building Granite Quarries Association, Inc.: www.nbgqa.com

Stone World and *Contemporary Stone & Tile Design*: www.stoneworld.com

This chapter discusses custom-fabricated, back-mounted, fabric-wrapped panels for ceilings and walls, in which the fabric is not adhered to the core material.

This chapter does not discuss textile wall coverings, spline-mounted acoustical panels, prefabricated acoustical wall panels, and freestanding acoustic panels. Prefabricated acoustical wall panels are discussed in Chapter 09841, Acoustical Wall Panels. Site-upholstered systems for ceilings and walls are discussed in Chapter 09772, Stretched-Fabric Wall Systems.

PRODUCT SELECTION CONSIDERATIONS

Fabric-wrapped panels can provide the appearance and performance of stretched-fabric wall systems for less expense and with less installation time. Stretched-fabric wall systems are site fabricated and custom fit; consider them where walls or ceilings are out of square. Some manufacturers provide curved, fabric-wrapped panels to specified radii. Multiple core materials can be laminated together to provide desired performance characteristics.

Fabric-wrapped panels are selected primarily for their tackability or nailability or for an upholstered wall or ceiling appearance, not for their acoustical performance. Tackable surfaces are often required in conference and presentation rooms and other office settings to display material to be reviewed or discussed. Nailable panels are often used in museums or art galleries where the luxurious look of a fabric wall and the capability to mount heavy paintings or pieces of wall sculpture is required.

PANEL CORE-MATERIAL AND EDGE SELECTION CONSIDERATIONS

Core-material selection affects a panel's appearance, acoustics, and function. Common applications with corresponding core materials include the following (figs. 1, 2):

- **Acoustical, absorptive** — polyester batting, fiberglass board or blanket, mineral-fiber board
- **Tackable** — mineral-fiber board or fiberglass board
- **Nailable** — plywood or wood board nailing strips or particleboard panel
- **Acoustical, reflective** — particleboard

Mineral-fiber board is a dimensionally stable composite of inorganic mineral fibers. It can be microperforated where an absorptive acoustic surface is required. It is more durable and impact resistant than fiberglass. Mineral-fiber board comes with a sanded or coated finish. The sanded-finish fiberboard is gray and retains a tighter thickness tolerance. The nonwashable, white latex coating reduces read-through when used with light-colored or transparent fabrics. Pressed, recycled paper products are not appropriate for use as a core material. They tend to absorb moisture and do not have the required dimensional stability.

Fiberglass board is lightweight, easy to handle, and resists damage from moisture. Densities range from an acoustically absorptive panel with fair tackability to acoustically reflective panels. Tackable, acoustic fiberglass is a lighter, battlike sheet that has a finish face of thin, rigid fiberglass mesh. It heals well and is recommended for tackable applications.

Particleboard is the most dimensionally stable, nailable substrate for fabric-wrapped panels. Plywood is not recommended for use as a core material because of its tendency to warp, but can be used as nailable strips in panels of other core materials.

Core materials can be combined. If the area of the nailable surface is known and limited, grounds or blocking can be placed in the wall behind the fabric-wrapped panel and the nail can be driven through the panel into the supporting surface. A nailable surface can also be provided by inserting a plywood or particleboard nailing strip into a panel with a non-nailable core material. If this method is selected, verify that the fabric is opaque enough to prevent the blocking from telegraphing through to the finish face of the panel.

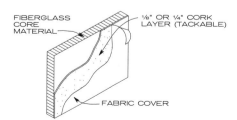

Figure 1. Acoustical/tackable panel

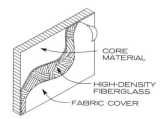

Figure 2. High-impact panel

Panel edges are formed by plastic or aluminum extrusions or by chemical hardening. Extruded panel frames can be infilled with any core material; chemically hardened edges are applied only to fiberglass-board cores.

PANEL FABRIC SELECTION CONSIDERATIONS

Proper fabric selection is critical to the success of a fabric-wrapped panel. Fabrics are stretched over the panel frame and core material, then securely bonded to the panel edges or back. Manufacturers provide a limited selection of fabrics—mostly woven polyesters and perforated vinyls.

C.O.M. fabrics must be approved by the panel manufacturer because of the importance of the dimensional stability of a fabric to the appearance and performance of a fabric-wrapped panel. The term *C.O.M.* indicates that the manufacturer of the primary product does not procure the material, it is supplied to the manufacturer for incorporation into the primary product by the customer (the entity directly purchasing the primary product). Mockup panels should be specified to verify that C.O.M. fabrics appear and perform as required. An acrylic backing can be applied to lightweight or loose-woven fabrics to add body and stability. However, the backing thickness may affect the crispness of the panel edge definition. When selecting a fabric, consider the following:

- **Opacity:** Substrate or core material should not read through the fabric face.
- **Color:** Light-colored fabrics installed adjacent to HVAC return grilles show soil more readily than dark-colored fabrics.
- **Resilience:** Nonbacked fabrics ease stretching and do not impair acoustic transparency.
- **Self-healing quality:** Particularly important if finish surface is tackable or if face-nailed wood system is specified.
- **Flame resistance:** Flame spread index of 25 or less.

Fiber and weave are the two factors that determine fabric stability. Fabrics that contain more than 25 percent silk, rayon, nylon, or acetate may not perform well on fabric-wrapped panels. These fibers are hydrophilic-readily absorbing and retaining moisture—which can cause sagging and

distortion. Modacrylics and polyesters are hydrophobic—they tend not to absorb and hold moisture. Hydrophobic fibers are preferred for fabric-wrapped panels because they are highly stable. Satin, certain taffetas, and basket weaves are unbalanced in construction and can be difficult to stretch evenly over a panel. An acrylic backing can be used to stabilize some fabrics. However, the system's acoustic properties will be altered with fabric backings. Table 1 indicates various fabrics and their percentages of moisture regain.

If a performance warranty is required, it should extend at least two years after installation. This ensures two full HVAC cycle changes from air conditioning to heat. The fabric is most likely to absorb or release moisture during these cycle changes, which causes the fabric to sag or puddle.

PANEL INSTALLATION

The five methods of installing fabric-wrapped panels are magnetic strips, hook-and-loop tape (Velcro), "Z" clips, impaling clips, and adhesive. Consider the distance each attachment method extends panels from the wall and the attachment method's affect on panel intersections with doors, windows, and millwork and panel intersections at inside and outside corners.

Magnetic strips can be adhered to the back of the panels and to the wall. This method allows the installer more flexibility in aligning and adjusting the panels in the field. Installation is quick with this method but the panels are susceptible to removal and vandalism. Consider the danger of inadvertent exposure of magnetic media to the magnetic strips.

Hook-and-loop tape allows an installation tolerance similar to magnetic strips. Typically, 2-by-2-inch (50-by-50-mm) or 2-by-4-inch (50-by-100-mm) patches of loop tape are adhered to the back of the panel (fig. 3). Same-size or larger patches of hook tape are attached to the wall. Mechanical fasteners should be used to secure the hook tape to the wall; self-adhesive provided on the back of tape may not be strong enough to hold panels in place. The shear strength of this tape is about 15 lb/sq. in. (10 546 kg/sq. m). Hook-and-loop tape can be used to hold panels attached by adhesive in place while the adhesive is setting.

"Z" clips require a reveal between the top of panels and the ceiling-typically about ¾ inch (20 mm)—so panels can be lifted and then lowered into place over the "Z" track fastened to the wall. Because the panel can be

Table 1
PERCENTAGE OF MOISTURE REGAIN OF SELECTED FIBERS

Fiber	Percentage	
Wool	13.6 - 16.0	Hydrophilic (absorbs moisture)
Rayon	10.7 - 16.0	
Silk	11.0	
Linen	10.0 - 12.0	
Cotton	8.5	
Acetate	6.0	
Ramie	6.0	
Nylon 6	3.5 - 5.0	
Aramid	3.5	
Modacrylic	2.5 - 4.0	
Acrylic	1.0 - 2.5	
Polyester	0.4 - 0.8	
Vinyon	0.5	Hydrophobic (does not readily absorb moisture)
Olefin	0.0	
Glass	0.0	

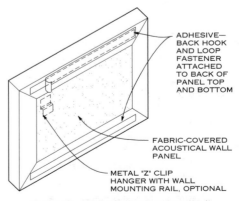

ADHESIVE—BACK HOOK AND LOOP FASTENER ATTACHED TO BACK OF PANEL TOP AND BOTTOM

FABRIC-COVERED ACOUSTICAL WALL PANEL

METAL "Z" CLIP HANGER WITH WALL MOUNTING RAIL, OPTIONAL

Figure 3. Wall panel mounting detail

lifted off, not pried like other mounting methods, "Z" clips are best suited for installations that will change or for panels that will be recovered or replaced often. A "Z" clip at the panel top may be used with a strip of hook-and-loop tape at the bottom.

Impaling clips have small, sharp projections with barbed tips on to which the fabric-wrapped panel is pressed.

Adhesive is the most permanent of the mounting methods. It requires damaging the panel to remove it. A leveling angle or some other method of supporting the panel while the adhesive is setting up is required.

ACOUSTIC PERFORMANCE

Noise Reduction Coefficient (NRC) is the average of the sound-absorption coefficients at the frequency bands of 250, 500, 1000, and 2000 Hz expressed to the nearest multiple of 0.05. NRC expresses sound-absorption capability. The higher the NRC, the more efficiently the material absorbs sound. Since NRC is an average, a given panel's performance varies depending on the frequency band. NRC is affected by the core material, the face fabric, the treatments applied to the face fabric, and the panel mounting method. If specific NRC values are required, see Chapter 09841.

09772 STRETCHED-FABRIC WALL SYSTEMS

This chapter discusses concealed-fastener, site-assembled, site-upholstered systems for ceilings and walls.

This chapter does not discuss textile wall coverings, prefabricated fabric-wrapped panels, acoustical wall panels, and freestanding acoustical panels. Prefabricated fabric-wrapped panels are covered in Chapter 09771, Fabric-Wrapped Panels.

PRODUCT CHARACTERISTICS

Stretched-fabric systems provide the luxurious look of an upholstered wall or ceiling. Unlike textile wall coverings, stretched-fabric wall systems add depth and acoustic absorptiveness to a wall surface. Stretched-fabric wall systems, unlike fabric-wrapped panels, are site-assembled systems, can be custom fit where walls or ceilings are out of square, and can provide a more monolithic appearance by incorporating sewn seams or wide-width fabrics installed lengthwise (railroaded). Other unique applications for stretched-fabric systems include curved panels and fabric-covered doors and speakers.

Fabric-wrapped panels are less expensive and easier to install than stretched-fabric systems, especially in areas that are too high to easily reach. However, fabric-wrapped panels require longer fabrication and delivery lead times and provide a less-tight fit than stretched-fabric systems. Fabric-wrapped panels can also be damaged during shipping and handling.

PRODUCT SELECTION CONSIDERATIONS

Stretched-fabric wall systems include high-, medium-, and low-tension systems. High-tension systems consist of fabric stapled to the back of wood frames (fig. 1). Medium-tension systems crimp the fabric and hold it mechanically in the jaws of a hinged track (fig. 2). Low-tension systems hold the fabric in place with adhesive until the fabric is tucked into a slot in a profiled track. Edge details (fig. 3) for all three systems include beveled, radiused, eased, and squared profiles.

High-tension wood systems provide a crisp, well-defined panel edge and are the most expensive systems to install. The fabric is wrapped around a wood frame and attached to the back, making fabric removal and replacement difficult. Select a self-healing fabric when specifying a wood system because the wood is blind-nailed in place through the face of the fabric. Wood systems require clearance at ceilings and panel edges for lifting and lowering the upper half of the panel into place.

Medium- and low-tension systems can provide much thinner panels than wood systems. The fabric can often be removed for cleaning or replacing without dismantling the entire system. These systems use aluminum or plastic extrusion frames, which hold the fabric taut and rely on the strength of the frame's edge crimp under tension. They are the least-expensive and quickest systems to install.

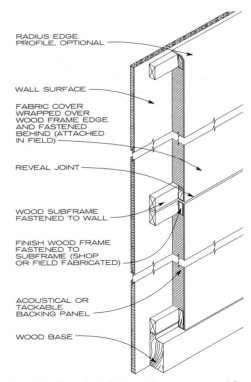

RADIUS EDGE PROFILE, OPTIONAL

WALL SURFACE

FABRIC COVER WRAPPED OVER WOOD FRAME EDGE AND FASTENED BEHIND (ATTACHED IN FIELD)

REVEAL JOINT

WOOD SUBFRAME FASTENED TO WALL

FINISH WOOD FRAME FASTENED TO SUBFRAME (SHOP OR FIELD FABRICATED)

ACOUSTICAL OR TACKABLE BACKING PANEL

WOOD BASE

Figure 1. Stretched-fabric wall system—wood frame

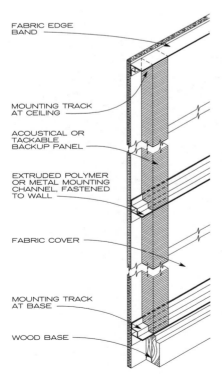

FABRIC EDGE BAND

MOUNTING TRACK AT CEILING

ACOUSTICAL OR TACKABLE BACKUP PANEL

EXTRUDED POLYMER OR METAL MOUNTING CHANNEL, FASTENED TO WALL

FABRIC COVER

MOUNTING TRACK AT BASE

WOOD BASE

Figure 2. Stretched-fabric wall system—track

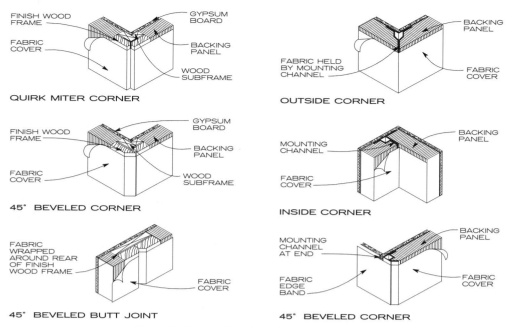

Figure 3. Stretched-fabric wall system edge details

FABRIC SELECTION CONSIDERATIONS

Proper fabric selection is critical to the success of a stretched-fabric wall system. Not all fabrics will provide the look or performance desired. When selecting a fabric, consider the following:

- **Opacity:** Substrate or core material should not read through the fabric face.
- **Color:** Light-colored fabrics installed adjacent to HVAC return grilles show soil more readily than dark-colored fabrics.
- **Resilience:** Nonbacked fabrics ease stretching and do not impair acoustic transparency.
- **Self-healing quality:** Particularly important if finish surface is tackable or if face-nailed wood system is specified.
- **Flame resistance:** Flame spread index of 25 or less.

Dimensional stability is an important characteristic of a fabric selected for use in a stretched-fabric wall system. Fiber and weave are the two factors that determine stability.

Fibers should not be hydrophilic—readily absorbing and retaining moisture—which can cause sagging and distortion. Modacrylics and polyesters are hydrophobic-they tend not to absorb and hold moisture. Because they are highly stable fibers, they are better choices for stretched-fabric wall systems. Other fabrics that perform well are cotton, linen, and olefin. The table on page 208 indicates various fabrics and their percentages of moisture regain.

Highly stable weaves such as jacquards and damasks are recommended for stretched-fabric wall systems. Unbalanced weaves such as satin, certain taffetas, and basket weaves can be poor choices for stretched-fabric wall systems.

Some fabrics can be modified for application in a stretched-fabric system. For example, a knit or acrylic backing can add dimensional stability, and a transparent fabric can be lined with muslin. However, these treatments alter the acoustic absorptiveness of the fabric. Exercise care when combining fabric treatments. Verify the appropriateness of the fabric selected with the system manufacturer.

Warranties are sometimes required for stretched-fabric systems. They should extend at least two years after installation and include restretching the fabric. This ensures two full HVAC cycle changes from air conditioning to heat. The fabric is most likely to absorb or release moisture during these cycle changes, which can cause the fabric to sag or puddle.

Fabric manufacturers may stipulate that if fabric is cut from a bolt, the bolt is not returnable. The specifications should include the requirement that the fabric be examined before installation begins.

CORE-MATERIAL CONSIDERATIONS

Core-material selection affects the appearance, acoustics, and function of the stretched-fabric system. Common applications with corresponding core materials are listed below:

- **Acoustical, absorptive** — polyester batting, fiberglass board or blanket, mineral-fiber board
- **Tackable** — mineral-fiber board or fiberglass board
- **Nailable** — plywood or wood board nailing strips or particleboard panel
- **Acoustical, reflective** — particleboard

Mineral-fiber board is a dimensionally stable composite of inorganic mineral fibers. It can be microperforated where an absorptive acoustic surface is required. It is more durable and impact-resistant than fiberglass. Mineral-fiber board comes with a sanded or coated finish. The sanded-finish fiberboard is gray and retains a tighter thickness tolerance. The nonwashable, white latex coating reduces read-through when used with light-colored or transparent fabrics. Pressed, recycled paper products are not appropriate for use as a core material. They tend to absorb moisture and do not have the required dimensional stability.

Fiberglass board is lightweight, easy to handle, and resists damage from moisture. Densities range from an acoustically absorptive panel with fair tackability to acoustically reflective panels. Tackable, acoustic fiberglass is a lighter, battlike sheet that has a finish face of thin, rigid fiberglass mesh. It heals well and is recommended for tackable applications.

Particleboard is the most dimensionally stable, nailable substrate for stretched-fabric wall systems. Plywood is not recommended for use as a core material because of its tendency to warp, but can be used as nailable strips in panels of other core materials.

Core materials can be combined. If the area of nailable surface is known and limited, grounds or blocking can be placed in the wall behind the stretched-fabric wall system, and the nail can be driven through the panel into the supporting surface. A nailable surface can also be achieved by inserting a plywood or particleboard nailing strip into a panel with a non-nailable core material. If this method is selected, verify that the fabric is opaque enough to prevent the blocking from telegraphing through to the finish face of the panel.

ACOUSTIC PERFORMANCE

Noise Reduction Coefficient (NRC) is the average of the sound-absorption coefficients at the frequency bands of 250, 500, 1000, and 2000 Hz expressed to the nearest multiple of 0.05. NRC expresses sound-absorption capability. The higher the NRC, the more efficiently the material absorbs sound. Since NRC is an average, a given panel's performance varies depending on the frequency band. NRC is affected by the core material, the face fabric, and the treatments applied to the face fabric.

09841 ACOUSTICAL WALL PANELS

This chapter discusses *shop-fabricated acoustical panels that are wall mounted, as opposed to freestanding or ceiling baffles. Both spline-mounted and back-mounted units are included.*

This chapter does not discuss *field-fabricated panels for walls or fabric wall systems or coverings; these are discussed in Chapter 09771, Fabric-Wrapped Panels, Chapter 09772, Stretched-Fabric Wall Systems, and Chapter 09720, Wall Coverings. Also not included in this chapter are: tackable panels with single-ply cores of little or no sound-absorptive capabilities and two-ply core panels with face ply of cork; panels with foil backing; unframed panels attached to wall with exposed moldings or trim; panels with custom edges and corners; curved, sculpted, or custom panels; low-frequency sound-absorptive panels; sound-reflective nonabsorptive panels; perforated-metal acoustical panels; diffusers; and baffles. Panels of similar or identical construction to those described in this chapter may also be suitable for lay-in ceiling panels.*

able in this regard as manufacturers of back-mounted, edge-framed panels. The term *C.O.M.* indicates that the manufacturer of the primary product does not procure the material, it is supplied to the manufacturer for incorporation into the primary product by the customer (the entity directly purchasing the primary product). Impact-resistant and tackable cementitious- and mineral-fiber board core panels are available from manufacturers of these panels. Optional impact-resistant or special tackable core layers bonded to the primary core are available for spline-mounted units with glass-fiber board cores.

Back-mounted panels must be fabricated to size in the factory because of their edge construction. However, they are available in a wider variety of sizes than spline-mounted units. They also lend themselves to a wider choice of fabrics, provided these fabrics comply with certain requirements,

MOUNTING METHODS

Mounting methods are spline mounting and back mounting. Spline mounting (fig. 1) involves attaching a metal or plastic spline to the substrate that engages the kerfed edge of the panel. Spline-mounted panels are installed alternately with splines and sequentially from one edge of the substrate to the other. Back mounting involves using adhesive, metal clips and bar hangers (fig. 2), impaling (stik) clips, hook-and-loop (Velcro) strips (fig. 3), magnetic devices, adhesive tape strips, or a combination thereof, on the back of a panel as the way to attach to the substrate.

Spline-mounted wall panels, although commonly limited to one or two modular widths and to heights of 96, 108, or 120 inches (2438, 2743, or 3048 mm), can readily be reduced in height in the field to fit existing conditions. A few manufacturers make panels in a greater range of sizes, and some make panels in custom sizes. Spline-mounted wall panels are permanently aligned and comparatively tamperproof, and may cost less than back-mounted panels. It may be possible to achieve a monolithic appearance with products that are faced with a fabric whose texture and pattern contribute to making visible joints and splines between abutting panels almost invisible. Although C.O.M., owner-furnished fabrics, or special fabrics may be accommodated for projects where substantial quantities are involved, some manufacturers of spline-mounted panels are not as flex-

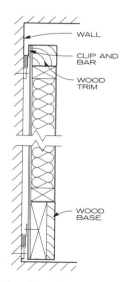

Figure 2. Acoustical wall panel metal clip and bar mounting

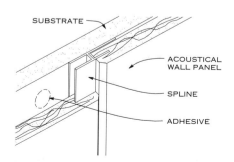

Figure 1. Acoustical wall panel spline mounting

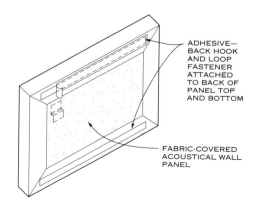

Figure 3. Acoustical wall panel hook and loop mounting

as discussed below. Available with these products are tackable and impact-resistant core-face layers that may decrease panel core sound absorption compared to panels without core-face layers. Back-mounted panels are generally easier to demount than spline-mounted units, making the former easier to replace if damaged. Options available with back-mounted panels include the following:

- Core-face layers, consisting of high-density, molded glass-fiber board; acoustically transparent (perforated), copolymer face sheet; or cork to make the panels impact resistant, tackable, or both.
- Framing consisting of metal, wood, and plastic, or resin or nonresin chemical hardening of the core material.
- Bull-nosed, chamfered, mitered, and custom edge configurations; and square, round, and custom corners.

PRODUCT CHARACTERISTICS

Acoustical wall panels, consisting of a core and decorative facing material, provide one option for acoustical control of building environments (fig. 4). Other benefits may result from acoustical wall panel installations that protect walls, such as in gymnasiums; that hide wall imperfections in existing spaces; that improve thermal properties of spaces; or that add visual interest to walls with display capability and color and texture variation. Trims and moldings (fig. 5), such as reveals, chair rails, and easel ledges, may be used to enhance design and function of wall panel installations. While panels may be needed first for their essential sound-absorptive acoustical performance characteristics, other characteristics, such as impact resistance, may be necessary for panels to function in some environments. Acoustical wall panels are fabricated from diverse materials, with many combinations of characteristics, for a variety of applications, at a range of costs. Characteristics needed may be obtained from a single acoustical panel core material or from a composite core consisting of assembled or bonded layers of materials, which function together to achieve desired performance.

Standard core materials for spline-mounted acoustical panels are cementitious-fiberboard, glass-fiberboard, and mineral-fiberboard. For back-mounted units, the core is often glass-fiberboard. Although a few panels are formed from high-density, molded glass-fiberboard with tackable and impact-resistant properties, this material is more commonly bonded to one of the standard core materials in a ⅛-inch (3-mm) tackable and impact-resistant layer. Glass-fiberboard used to fabricate a standard acoustical wall panel core, when purchased from the glass-fiberboard manufacturer, usually has a density that varies from 6 to 7 lb/cu. ft. (96 to 112 kg/cu. m). Individual acoustical wall panel manufacturers report a density of 6, 7, and 6 to 7 lb/cu. ft. (96, 112, and 96 to 112 kg/cu. m) for the same core material.

Tackable surfaces can be obtained with single-core cementitious- or mineral-fiberboard, or molded-glass construction, or by adding a tackable, molded glass-fiberboard layer to the primary acoustical core to form a composite core. Generally, the higher the density of the molded glass-fiberboard, the greater the tackability and service life of the panel. Tackable panels with cork-face layers are no longer available.

Impact resistance may be inherent to single-core materials such as cementitious- and rigid mineral-fiberboard and high-density, molded glass-fiberboard, or may be obtained with an added protective layer of molded

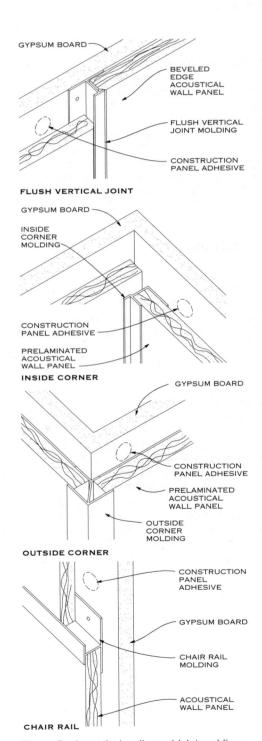

Figure 5. Acoustical wall panel joint moldings

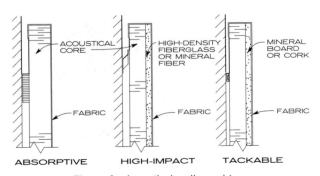

Figure 4. Acoustical wall panel types

glass-fiberboard or acoustically transparent (perforated), copolymer sheet over a standard glass-fiberboard core. Other glass-fiberboard cores, specifically formulated for impact resistance, are available from a few manufacturers.

Standard facing materials include both synthetic fabrics, either woven or nonwoven, and perforated or inherently acoustical vinyls. Usually, in their literature, panel manufacturers do not include information about the composition and construction of their standard fabric finishes. Most panel manufacturers will, however, provide any technical data required on their standard fabric finishes. For optimum effectiveness, fabrics for acoustical wall panels should be acoustically transparent, dimensionally stable, opaque, aesthetically attractive, self-healing if tackable, and have surface-burning characteristics that comply with authorities having jurisdiction. Facing materials can be stretched over or bonded to the core face. For most manufacturers, standard facing materials consist of perforated or inherently acoustically transparent vinyl or fabric constructed with polyester yarn.

Fabrics made from hygroscopic man-made fibers such as nylon and rayon, and natural fibers, such as silk, wool, and linen, absorb and retain moisture and become dimensionally unstable. When ambient conditions change or in humid conditions, fabrics made from hygroscopic fibers tend to sag or otherwise distort. An acrylic backing can be used to stabilize some fabrics but is not recommended by some panel manufacturers. Fabrics woven with a balanced weave are dimensionally stable and are preferred for acoustical wall panel facings. Fabric backings and very tight weaves can negatively affect the acoustical properties of the panel.

Polyester fabrics are stable if exposed to changes in temperature and humidity conditions, are available in many colors, and are affordable. They can be attractively woven in a balanced, nondirectional weave for dimensional stability, and can be tightly stretched over panels for a smooth appearance.

Vinyls are durable, and easy to clean and maintain. However, perforated vinyls may tear and be less resilient to abrasive materials and some chemicals. Some manufacturers' maintenance and cleaning instructions caution that perforated vinyl is a delicate material. For acoustical purposes, vinyl fabrics may be scrim-backed and microperforated, typically for 18 percent open area; or they may be manufactured inherently acoustically transparent with voids in the finished vinyl coatings.

PRODUCT SELECTION CONSIDERATIONS

Owner-furnished facing materials and C.O.M. must be acceptable to the panel manufacturer for the materials' fabrication and acoustical performance characteristics and to authorities having jurisdiction for the materials' fire-test-response characteristics. C.O.M. fabrics are those purchased by a source other than the primary product manufacturer—in this case, other than the acoustical wall panel manufacturer—and supplied to the primary product manufacturer for application. An example use of C.O.M. would be to specify a custom fabric to be obtained by the contractor from a fabric manufacturer for application to the panel manufacturer's acoustical core. If testing of the fabric separately, or testing of panel assemblies complete with proposed facing material, is required by authorities having jurisdiction to obtain such approval, and the tests have not already been performed by the fabric and panel manufacturers, then the testing and its costs can either be made the responsibility of the contractor or be paid for separately by the owner. Manufacturers might also agree to test C.O.M. or owner-furnished fabrics in a humidity chamber for suitability for incorporation into its panels.

Facing materials suitable for acoustical wall panels are those of upholstery-weight fabric or vinyl, with the exceptions being some silks, wools, nylons, metallics, rayons, and acetates. It is always advisable to submit proposed facing materials for evaluation and approval by the wall panel manufacturers. This should be done during the contract document preparation phase or before. To do otherwise may result in unanticipated extra costs during construction, either for testing or for other reasons such as delays caused by the need to find and furnish a suitable alternative material because the original choice is unsatisfactory.

Unmounted fabrics for wall coverings may be available from panel manufacturers in limited quantities. Ensure that these fabrics are suitable for the use intended, particularly for fire-test-response characteristics and installation procedures.

Other types of facing materials available for acoustical wall panels include the familiar painted finishes that are also used to finish acoustical ceiling panels and tiles and to smooth acoustically transparent coatings that mimic the appearance of finished gypsum board and plaster assemblies.

FIRE-TEST-RESPONSE CHARACTERISTICS

Published fire-test-response characteristics of acoustical wall panels can cause confusion if they are not based on tests of assembled units consisting of the same materials and constructed in a manner representative of actual products. Some manufacturers advertise their products as having certain surface-burning characteristics when they are tested as panel assemblies complete with fabric. Other manufacturers are less explicit and only indicate, when expressly questioned, that advertised characteristics of their products represent an interpretation based on results obtained by testing the core and facing material separately. Since the standard test method for measuring flame-spread and smoke-developed characteristics cannot be performed satisfactorily on unbacked fabrics, any manufacturers' claims that their untested panel assemblies perform as well as components tested individually should be challenged if a backing material differs from the core material of the finished product.

Where panels have not been tested with fabrics attached, determine if an interpretation is acceptable to authorities having jurisdiction, using other testing procedures such as those described in the National Fire Protection Association (NFPA) publication NFPA 701, *Methods of Fire Tests for Flame Propagation of Textiles and Films;* Southern Building Code Congress International (SBCCI) SSTD 9, *Test Method for Evaluating Fire Growth Contribution of Textile Wall Covering;* or Uniform Building Code (UBC) Standard 8-2, *Test Method for Evaluating Room Fire Growth Contribution of Textile Wall Covering.* However, these test methods do not provide a result that equates directly to flame spread, and will require an interpretation by the fire marshal, building official, or both. Such an interpretation of panels where the fabric is not adhesively attached to the core might be based on evaluating the surface-burning characteristics of the core, including the frame, as an interior wall finish and evaluating the flame resistance of the facing material as an interior hanging or decoration. For panels where the fabric is adhesively attached to the core, the adhesive could affect fire performance, and determining this requires testing the panel assembly.

Surface-burning characteristics of a fabric may be significantly different when stretched or bonded over an acoustical core. Flame-spread and smoke-developed values increase when panels are tested as an assembly when compared to the sum of values for their component parts. Since an acoustical core must be permeable to air to absorb sound, the panel including the finish is also permeable to flame. Flame penetrating the panel usually results in greater reported values for surface-burning characteristics.

Some manufacturers test their products in their own laboratories; others use independent testing and inspecting agencies. For each project, determine the requirements of authorities having jurisdiction for how products are judged and what is considered satisfactory evidence for proving compliance, relative not only to fire-test-response performance but also to testing procedures and testing and inspecting agencies. This information should be shared with manufacturers for the purposes of determining whether they can provide complying products, and should also be used to develop specification requirements.

ACOUSTICAL PROPERTIES

Noise Reduction Coefficient (NRC) is the average of the sound-absorption coefficients at the frequency bands of 250, 500, 1000, and 2000 Hz expressed to the nearest integral multiple of 0.05. The sound-absorption coefficient of a surface in a specified frequency band is the fraction of randomly incident sound energy absorbed or otherwise not reflected; the unit of measurement is either the inch-pound sabin per square foot or the metric sabin per square meter. A test specimen is in a Type A mounting if it is laid directly on the reverberation room floor. Some manufacturers also publish NRC values for other mounting types. For details of mounting types and Acoustical and Board Products Manufacturers Association equivalents, see ASTM E 795. The higher the NRC, the more efficiently the mounted panel absorbs sound. Since the NRC is an average, a given panel's performance varies, depending on the frequency band. If design requirements call for sound absorption in a particular frequency band, consult the manufacturer's test data for the sound-absorption coefficient in that particular band; and consider consulting an acoustical expert.

Rather than the single value reported per ASTM C 423, the Acoustical Wall Panel Committee of the Ceiling and Interior Systems Construction Association recommends specifying a range of values, 0.05 above and 0.05 below the selected performance value for NRC, to promote fairness among manufacturers and to select realistic performance levels for products. For example, a selected performance value of 0.70 would be expressed as NRC 0.65-0.75. Most manufacturers of acoustical wall panels use the same or similar sources for components, such as core and facings, and fabricate panels that have the same or similar construction. Inconsistencies in properties of these component products, while within manufacturing tolerances for the product, may affect an individual panel's tested acoustical performance. Some manufacturers allege that test conditions are not reliable enough to prevent test value differences, even for retesting the same test sample, and that rounding test values up or down per ASTM C 423 unfairly accentuates minor test value differences into major performance level distinctions. Also, those manufacturers with the greatest resources or the most perseverance could have panels tested and retested to ensure that results are rounded up. In response to these concerns, it could be argued that the mathematics involved in arriving at reported values per ASTM E 423, including averaging, rounding off, and statistical analysis for confidence limits, removes any bias from the test method. Design requirements will determine if specifying strict compliance with a single NRC value is necessary to meet stringent acoustical requirements, or if specifying a range of NRC values or a minimum value will result in satisfactory sound absorption at a more competitive cost.

INSTALLATION CONSIDERATIONS

Lighting design and conditions can be important to the appearance of acoustical wall panels. If panels are subject to stronger light from one direction than another, such as when natural light is stronger than interior lighting or if panels are brightly lit from above, visual imperfections in the panel core can telegraph through some fabric or vinyl facings. If critical lighting cannot be avoided, acoustical wall panels may be specially fabricated to minimize visual defects. A high-density, molded, glass-fiberboard face layer may be bonded to a glass-fiberboard core to provide a smoother, flat surface before covering with fabric or vinyl facing. Stretchable fabric, such as 100 percent woven polyester, may also be stretched across rather than bonded to the panel face and laminated to edges and back only. Because fabric facing does not directly contact the panel core, imperfections are not as readily telegraphed through the fabric.

ENERGY CONSIDERATIONS

Wall panels can also serve as thermal insulation, and most manufacturers publish insulation values for their products. To be truly effective, the panels need to cover the entire wall and be butted tightly together. Back-mounted panels have the disadvantage of not fitting tightly to the wall on which they are mounted. This allows air to circulate behind the panel and effectively destroy any insulating value. Moisture-vapor control could also become a problem if the wall to which the panel is attached is not well insulated and adding panels moves the dew point into the panel thickness. Condensation could then form on the wall surface behind the panel.

AIR-QUALITY CONSIDERATIONS

The absorptive nature of acoustical wall panels acts to absorb more than sound. Panels exposed to odors absorb, retain, and outgas odors over time. Natural fibers and porous fabric construction may enhance odor absorption. Since indoor air quality is a growing concern, outgassing unpleasant or possibly hazardous gases can be a problem; for example, if tobacco smoke is absorbed by acoustical wall panels in a space or building intended to be a smoke-free environment and the odor lingers. Detectable odors are not easily eliminated from acoustical wall panels, so the panels may need to be replaced.

REFERENCES

ASTM International

ASTM C 423-90a: Test Method for Sound Absorption and Sound Absorption Coefficients by the Reverberation Room Method

ASTM E 795-93: Practices for Mounting Test Specimens during Sound Absorption Tests

National Fire Protection Association

NFPA 701-99: Methods of Fire Tests for Flame Propagation of Textiles and Films

Southern Building Code Congress International

SBCCI SSTD 9-88: Test Method for Evaluating Fire Growth Contribution of Textile Wall Covering

International Conference of Building Officials

UBC Standard 8-2-1997: Test Method for Evaluating Room Fire Growth Contribution of Textile Wall Covering

09910 **PAINTING**

This chapter discusses different types of generically similar paint products in these two categories:

- Consumer line products
- Professional line products

The information includes general surface preparation, material preparation, and application procedures for interior and exterior painting.

This chapter does not discuss special coatings such as cementitious, elastomeric, intumescent, high-performance, and high-temperature-resistant coatings; these are discussed in other chapters. It also does not cover traffic-marking paints.

DEFINITIONS

ASTM D 16 defines the term *paint* simply as "a pigmented coating." *Paint Handbook,* by Guy E. Weismantel, defines paint as "a decorative, protective, or otherwise functional coating applied to a substrate. This substrate may be another coat of paint." In its broadest sense, therefore, paint includes organic coating materials such as fillers, primers, sealers, emulsions, enamels, lacquers, stains, sealers, varnishes, and other materials in a complete paint system, whether used as prime, intermediate, or finish coats.

Paint and enamel are the two most common pigmented paint materials. Other frequently used paint materials are stains, varnishes, and lacquers.

- **Paint** is easy to apply by brush, roller, or spray. It is most often used on large areas, such as walls and ceilings, but may also be used on small surfaces. It usually has a flat or low-luster sheen.
- **Enamel** is fast drying and levels out easily to a smooth, hard finish. It has a higher percentage of liquid binder than paint and is more durable. Enamel is commonly used on small areas and smooth substrates. An enamel is a type of paint distinguished for its semigloss or high-gloss sheen, although it sometimes has an eggshell sheen.
- **Stains** are pigmented compositions that change the color of a surface; they are generally used on wood surfaces. They protect by penetrating the surface, and they leave practically no surface film. The industry also classifies bleaching agents and clear, unpigmented materials as stains.
- **Varnishes** are homogenous mixtures of resins, drying oils, driers, and solvents that dry by a combination of evaporation, oxidation, and polymerization to give a transparent or translucent film that allows the substrate to show through.
- **Lacquers** are quick-drying, film-forming solutions that may be clear or pigmented. These finishes are based on nitrocellulose or acrylic resins and are used on automobiles or furniture. However, the industry classifies any coating that dries by evaporation of solvents as lacquer.

Ingredients used in coating formulas fall under one of four general categories, depending on the purpose or function of the particular ingredient in the blend of materials. These categories—pigments, solvents, vehicles, and additives—are defined here and discussed more fully later in this chapter.

- **Pigments** are insoluble, solid particles of uniform size that are used in the coating formula to provide the desired opacity, color, and gloss. They also contribute to film adhesion and serve to protect the substrate.

   Prime pigment, sometimes referred to as the *hiding pigment,* is the chemical ingredient chiefly responsible for providing opacity to a coating. The prime pigment is usually the major constituent of the pigment and is often the most costly chemical in the formula.

   Extender pigments have low hiding power and add strength to the film, control viscosity, and reduce settling and gloss. They are also often used to reduce the amount of prime pigment in the coating formula and the cost of the coating.

- **Solvent** is the volatile liquid that dissolves the binder or film former in the vehicle portion of a coating. It dissolves the binder in solvent-based coatings, separates the binder droplets in emulsion-based coatings, and is responsible for the coating's application properties and cure rate.
- **Vehicle** is the liquid portion of a coating that carries the ingredients that will remain on the surface after the solvent has cured. It provides adhesion and contains the binder that gives the coating film continuity.

   Binder is a nonvolatile, film-forming ingredient that binds pigment particles together. The term *binder* is synonymous with the term *film former.* The names for most generic types of coatings are based on the type of resin or binder used in their formulas.

- **Additives** are ingredients in the paint that modify properties of the vehicle or pigment or both. They either provide properties needed in the coating that are not found in the other ingredients or improve essential properties the other ingredients do not provide adequately.
- **Solids** is the term used to describe the nonvolatile ingredients in a coating. They are the paint ingredients that do not evaporate and remain on the surface when the solvent cures. Pigments combine with the binder to form the coating's solids.

Several other terms have a special meaning when used with paint; they are defined here and will be used later in this chapter. They are known and understood throughout the coatings industry but may not be familiar to a construction specifier.

- **Architectural coatings** are paint materials used in painting buildings, for both interior and exterior applications.
- **Consumer paint lines** are paints that are usually sold to consumers though normal retail outlets such as company paint stores and independent dealers. Other terms used to describe over-the-counter paint materials are *carriage trade* and *trade sale materials.*

- **Hiding** describes the opacity of a coating, that is, its capability to cover or hide the substrate.
- **Industrial coatings** are coatings used primarily for industrial maintenance. Many industrial coatings are termed high-performance coatings.
- **Natural finish** describes an interior unpigmented wood finish consisting generally of several coats of varnish over a filler coat and a sanding sealer. This term is also occasionally used to describe a paste-wax finish over a filler and a sanding sealer.
- **Professional coating** is the term used to identify a type of coating specially manufactured primarily for professional painters. Occasionally they are identical to a manufacturer's consumer paint lines but are marketed differently.
- **Thinner** is a volatile organic liquid used to reduce viscosity of a coating material.

PRODUCT CHARACTERISTICS

Most paint products contain some ingredients from each of the four categories identified in the definitions given above. However, some products, such as clear coatings that do not contain pigments, omit certain types of ingredients because of the intended use or nature of the coating. Each ingredient category in a paint product usually consists of several chemicals. Although the amount of some chemicals in the formula may be extremely small, each chemical is selected because it imparts a specific quality to the end product or serves a special purpose.

Pigments

Pigments are important ingredients that provide paint with essential characteristics such as opacity, gloss, and color. They also provide resistance to corrosion, weather, and abrasion, and protect substrates from damage. Some pigments contribute to film hardness and improve the paint's capability to adhere to the substrate. In most paints, the pigment is a blend of a prime pigment and several extender pigments.

Prime pigments function the mainly to conceal the substrate. This function is known as *opacity* or, more simply, as the coating's *hiding power,* and is usually provided by a white pigment. The rutile form of titanium dioxide is currently the most commonly used white pigment, although zinc oxide is occasionally used in exterior coatings because it improves color retention. Even though titanium dioxide is expensive, the use of other white pigments is declining rapidly.

Extender pigments are added to formulas because they add special properties to the paint. Extender pigments are commonly used to fill space and lower the gloss level in the film of flat and low-luster paints. Calcium carbonate and various forms of silicas and silicates are the extender pigments most often used for these purposes. Other extender pigments are sometimes added to give a paint improved viscosity, control the flow, and improve brushability. Some extender pigments are used to provide a coating with unique characteristics such as fire retardance or electrical conductance.

Pigment Characteristics

The most important pigment characteristics are as follows:

- **Opacity:** A paint's capability to hide the surface is determined by the pigment's index of refraction, which is the measure of its capability to bend light rays. White and yellow pigments have the lowest indices of refraction; black has the highest. White pigments, mainly titanium dioxide, have excellent hiding characteristics. However, because they are expensive, some manufacturers increase the amount of less-expensive extender pigments in their formulations. "Dry hiding" is the practice of adding extender pigments to a paint material solely to reduce product cost. This increases the paint's opacity and lessens the amount of expensive white pigment needed. Although not a recommended practice, applicators can accomplish the same thing by shading, that is, adding dark components such as lampblack to an inexpensive paint. Both dry hiding and shading should be avoided.
- **Color** is the quality most often associated with pigment. In scientific terms, it is the capability of a material to absorb certain wavelengths of visible light and to reflect others. Many chemicals, far too numerous to identify individually in this chapter, are used as sources of color pigments in paint formulas and for tinting to a specific color. Color pigments differ in both properties and costs because they are derived by different processes. Thus, although it is possible to generate a specific color by using a combination of different color pigments, the results may differ in other important properties, depending on the pigment used. One important property of color pigments in paint is resistance to fading from exposure to light, heat, and chemicals. Manufacturers carefully test color pigments over long periods of time under various exposures to determine their characteristics.
- **Gloss:** Pigments also control the degree of a coating's surface gloss (sheen). The total amount of pigment in paint formulas determines the product's gloss level. High levels of pigment produce a flat, rough finish; lower pigment levels increase a paint's gloss (sheen) level. Furthermore, the larger the pigment particle size, the flatter the finish of the dry film. Large pigment particles produce a rougher texture, which causes the surface to become subdued and lose some of its reflectance. Adding non-opaque extender pigments such as calcium carbonate, aluminum silicate (clay), magnesium silicate, and silica to the paint formula will reduce gloss level and may not have a significant impact on the cost to produce the product.

Pigment-Volume Concentration Ratio

An important factor to consider when evaluating paint is the relationship of the total amount of pigment compared to the amount of binder. The pigment-volume concentration ratio expresses the volume relationship of the pigment to the binder in dried paint film and indicates how well the material will perform. Up to a point, adding extender pigments can reinforce and improve the film-forming properties of the binder. However, when the ratio reaches a point called the *critical pigment-volume concentration (CPVC) ratio,* the dry film properties of the paint change significantly. The CPVC ratio is the point at which the formula contains enough binder to coat the pigment particles completely and fill the voids between them. When the CPVC ratio is exceeded, film properties begin to deteriorate and the coating begins to lose many of its desired qualities. For example, the finished paint film may be porous as a result of too much pigment in the formula and will succumb to the effects of exposure to the weather faster than usual and become less washable. Deliberately exceeding the CPVC ratio is called *overpigmentation* and occurs as a result of an attempt to reduce product cost by dry hiding.

Gloss Ranges

The standard procedure for measuring specular gloss is contained in ASTM D 523. The 1999 edition of the National Paint and Coatings Association's (NPCA) *Glossary of Terms* suggests certain gloss ranges to provide a method for categorizing coatings according to their specular gloss; the ranges are, in declining order, high gloss, semigloss, eggshell, and flat. The term satin, which is not included in the current edition of the

Glossary of Terms, was used in previous NPCA publications to describe products at the lower end of the semigloss range.

- **High-gloss enamels,** occasionally called *full-gloss enamels,* usually measure more than 70 when tested according to ASTM D 523. They contain few, if any, extender pigments in the formula. These products are extremely durable and produce the maximum degree of washability possible in a coating. High-gloss enamels are used on interior and exterior wood trim and moldings and on small metal surfaces. High-gloss enamels are seldom used on large surfaces such as walls or ceilings because light reflecting off of these materials can lead to eyestrain. However, they may be used on walls and ceilings for sanitary purposes because high-gloss surfaces discourage buildup of dirt and bacteria and are easier to clean; nonetheless, they should be used sparingly.
- **Semigloss enamels** fall within a range of 35 to 70 when tested according to ASTM D 523. They contain less film former and more pigment than high-gloss materials. Semigloss enamels offer a compromise between the appearance of an eggshell finish and the performance of high gloss. They are often used on trim, moldings, and interior doors, and are occasionally used on large surfaces such as walls and ceilings of kitchens and other rooms that require a high degree of cleanliness and are cleaned frequently but where use of a high-gloss material is unacceptable.
- **Eggshell finish** is between flat and semigloss, although visually it is almost indistinguishable from flat paint. This finish measures between 20 and 35 when tested according to ASTM D 523. Eggshell paints have more resin and less prime and extender pigments than flat paints. They usually outlast flat paints in service and survive more washes. They are suitable where a flat paint may be used and a high sheen is not required but where cleanliness is important and occasional maintenance washing may be expected.
- **Flat paints** are also called *lusterless, low gloss,* or *dull.* They measure below 15 when tested according to ASTM D 523. The flat finish comes from a high pigment content and a low amount of binder. Low gloss minimizes surface imperfections, while sacrificing some washability and durability, and is usually the sheen of choice for large surfaces such as walls and ceilings where repeated washing is not expected.

Flat Enamel

Flat enamel is a type of architectural coating that couples the hard, resistant scrubbability of an enamel with a flat, dull finish. Such a coating has all the advantages of an enamel. It uses a synthetic silica or similar flattening agent to reduce or eliminate the reflectivity of the enamel. The principal use of flat enamel is in areas that require frequent scrubbing and cleaning but where glare must be avoided. Although flat enamels were once popular, their use has declined significantly in recent years, and not all manufacturers offer them; those that do usually include them only with their professional coating lines. Specifiers are encouraged to contact individual manufacturers for information and availability when choosing to use flat enamels on a project.

Solvents

Solvents are low-viscosity, volatile liquids that improve a coating's application properties. They are not part of the paint film. Although some solventless coatings have been developed, most liquid coatings cannot be applied without solvents, which perform several important functions. They dissolve the film former in solution-type coatings or separate film-former droplets in emulsion coatings. Solvents also reduce the solution to the proper viscosity for good application. By controlling the rate of evaporation, paint solvents also control the time necessary for paint to set up. Manufacturers carefully select appropriate solvents for each coating. If an applicator does not precisely follow the manufacturer's recommendations on thinning, changing solvent makeup could have an adverse effect on the coating's properties.

- **Solvent types** are usually either hydrocarbon or oxygenated. A third type, terpene, usually containing turpentine or pine oil, is seldom used today. Hydrocarbon-type solvents are usually derived during the process of refining petroleum and contain only hydrogen and carbon atoms in their molecules. They are among the most common solvents used in coatings today, but their use is expected to diminish as environmental regulations become more stringent. Oxygenated-type solvents are manufactured by several processes and contain oxygen atoms as well as hydrogen and carbon atoms; typical examples of oxygenated solvents used in coatings are alcohols, esters, ketones, and glycol ethels. Oxygenated solvents are usually expensive and have not been used frequently in the past; this is expected to change dramatically in the future as stricter air pollution controls are enacted.
- **Evaporation rate** of the solvent must be carefully controlled to ensure proper film formation and provide good application properties. A proper blend of solvents will avoid an improper evaporation rate and ensure proper film formation. Unfortunately, many states have enacted air pollution regulations that limit the rate at which coating solvents can be released into the atmosphere. These issues are discussed at length later in this chapter.

Paint Vehicles

The liquid portion of a paint that carries the film-forming ingredients remaining on the substrate after the paint has dried is called the *vehicle.* The vehicle contains all liquids in the paint formula, including the binder and the solvent, and the additives needed by these liquids. In addition to its primary function of carrying film-forming ingredients to the surface to be coated, the vehicle also gives the paint film continuity and adhesion to the substrate.

- **The type of binder** in the paint formula is the characteristic used to describe most coatings. The binder, which is either dissolved in a solvent or emulsified in water, may be a drying oil, a dry resin, a plasticizer, or a combination of these elements. Most binders are a combination of resins, plasticizers, and drying oils. Although there are other types, the binders in most architectural coatings used today are either oxidizing or emulsion types. Oxidizing types are based on drying oils that react with oxygen in the air and cure by solvent evaporation. Emulsion types are water-based products and cure by water evaporation. The performance characteristics of the coating depend primarily on the type of binder used in the coating.

    Alkyd paints usually consist of alkyd resins that dry by oxidation as the binder. They are available as clear or pigmented coatings in many colors and in flat, semigloss, and high-gloss finishes. They are easy to apply and may be used over most surfaces except alkaline types such as fresh concrete, masonry, or plaster. Alkyd resins provide good color and gloss retention in both interior and exterior applications not exposed to corrosive environments. Alkyds were formerly the most common enamels in general use; however, environmental concerns about their method of curing (solvent evaporation) have significantly reduced sales.

    Latex paints (water-reducible architectural coatings) are based on aqueous emulsions of three basic polymers: polyvinyl acetate, polyacrylic, and polystyrene butadiene. The most common types of latex paints used today are based on acrylic polymers. Latex paints dry by evaporation of water, followed by coalescence of the polymer particles, to form tough, insoluble films. They have little odor, are easy to apply, and dry rapidly. Many applicators prefer them to oils or alkyds because, being water-based, they are easy to clean up after application. Interior latex paints are used as primer or finish coats on plaster or gypsum board surfaces and are recommended for use on gypsum board because they do not raise the nap. Exterior latex paints are applied to concrete, masonry, and plaster or over primed wood surfaces. They are nonflammable, economical, have good color retention, and are as durable in normal environments as oil paints but require careful surface preparation. Latex paints are probably the most widely used paint types available today.

Oil paints usually have linseed oil as the binder, although soybean oils, tung oils, and various other oils are used in products when their special properties are needed. Oil-based paints once dominated the coatings industry, but the use of these products has been declining steadily for many years; latex paints now command a greater share of the market because they dry faster and are easier to clean up. Oil-based paints are used primarily on exterior wood and metal because they dry too slowly for interior use and are sensitive to alkaline masonry. Linseed oil provides good surface wetting, so oil paints can be used on metal that has been only hand cleaned; however, linseed-oil-based paint yellows in interior finishes and has only fair weather resistance. Oil-based paints are not hard or resistant to abrasion, chemicals, or strong solvents; however, in normal environments, they provide a very durable coating. Oil-based primers are excellent over hand-cleaned, steel surfaces. Like alkyd paints, concerns about their method of curing (solvent evaporation) are expected to significantly affect sales.

Vinyl paints, as used in the coatings industry, usually refer to solvent-thinned PVC resins and their copolymers. Lacquers based on modified PVC resins are used on steel where durability under adverse environments is required. Although vinyls are moderate in cost, they are low in solids and require a high degree of surface preparation to obtain a satisfactory bond. Their low solids content requires application of more coats to achieve an adequate dry film thickness. Therefore, the total cost of paints containing vinyl resins is higher when compared to most paints because of the labor needed for additional coats. Strong solvents present in paints containing vinyls create an odor. Vinyl resin-based paints can be used on metals or masonry but are not recommended for wood. They have excellent resistance to chemicals, corrosive environments, and water, yet are susceptible to strong solvents.

- **Combination binders** may provide different performance characteristics than those of the individual binders themselves. The resulting combination often retains the best characteristics of each binder and results in a superior product.

Oil-alkyd combination binders consist of linseed-oil binders modified with alkyd resins to reduce drying time, improve hardness and gloss retention, and reduce fading. They are commonly used in trim enamels that are applied to exterior windows and doors that require these qualities. Oil-alkyd combination binders are also often used as primers on structural steel when faster-drying finishes are required. If used on structural steel, better surface preparation is required than for straight oil paints.

Phenolic-alkyd binders combine the resistance properties and hardness of phenolics with the color and color retention of alkyds. They are produced by blending phenolic varnish with the alkyd vehicle or by adding phenolic resin during the processing of alkyd resin. They are used over ferrous metal in moderately severe chemical atmospheres that are neither strongly acid nor strongly alkaline.

Vinyl-alkyd resins offer a compromise between the excellent durability and resistance of vinyls with lower cost, higher film build, easy handling, adhesion, and the color retention of alkyds. The vinyl-alkyd resin combination is excellent when used over structural steel in marine and moderately severe corrosive environments.

Additives

Many binders, such as PVC resins, would not work without the added plasticizers to increase the flexibility and adhesion of the film formers. Some additives also improve a paint formula's properties, such as adjusting drying speed, increasing abrasion resistance, or making the material easier to apply. Air driers added to oil-based paints speed drying time. Certain additives serve as catalysts for oxidizing binders. Other types of additives include wetting agents, antisettling or antiskinning agents, ultraviolet-screening agents, fungicides, and preservatives.

Paint Systems

The discussion thus far has been restricted to the various ingredients that go into individual paint products. A single coat of paint, however, rarely does everything needed. A specific paint system is usually selected because of the properties necessary for the end use required. A paint system usually consists of a shop- or field-applied primer and one or more topcoats. Sometimes, the same material is used as both primer and topcoat. A block filler is necessary on porous concrete masonry and may be necessary over rough concrete surfaces. A sealer should be used over porous substrates to prevent the primer or finish coat from being absorbed into the substrate. Knot sealers are required over knots in previously uncoated wood because the knots react differently from the rest of the material and "bleed" often, ruining the finish.

A paint system must be considered as a unit. It is not advisable to choose a coating without considering the surface over which it is to be applied or the coating that may be applied over it. Specifiers should select a system that ensures complete compatibility of the different components, especially if the topcoat is an enamel. Most paint manufacturers select the different components of their recommended systems to ensure complete compatibility. It is always advisable to use the primer recommended by the manufacturer for a given system, and not to accept a substitute material by the same or another manufacturer, particularly when coating metal surfaces that are subject to severe or unusual environmental conditions. A substitution suggested by a contractor may be an excellent product but may be inappropriate for the situation. This area is one where cost should never be a factor in product selection.

Primers are applied directly to bare substrates to improve adhesion of subsequent coats. They link the substrate to subsequent coats that protect both the primer and substrate. Primers play an important part in protecting the substrate, particularly rust-inhibitive primers applied on ferrous metals. Some paints, such as high-binder-content latex paints, are self-priming on some types of substrates and do not require the use of a separate primer. The type of primer to be used in any situation depends on the substrate, the finish coat, and the type of protection required.

- **Primer sealers** seal substrates such as wood or masonry from the suction action caused by substrate porosity. If they are not applied to such surfaces, subsequent coatings may be sucked into the substrate, which destroys paint-film continuity and makes paint application difficult. Some wood primers prevent natural wood dyes from migrating to the surface and leaving unsightly stains. Sealers are also used on alkaline substrates such as concrete, masonry, and plaster to prevent alkali burn of subsequent coats.
- **Corrosion-resistant primers** are required for ferrous and nonferrous metals to provide extra protection against deterioration. Corrosion-inhibiting pigments are added to metal primers for this purpose. Corrosion-resist-

ant primers are applied to metals to retard corrosion; however, these primers are not durable and must be protected by a topcoat or another protective covering. Recent developments in corrosion-resistant paints have lead to the introduction of direct-to-metal coatings, which are offered by many manufacturers. Some of these products act as both primer and finish coat.

Several rust-inhibitive pigments, including red lead, zinc chromate, and barium metaborate, were extensively used in metal primers in recent years to provide corrosion resistance. Use of these substances in paint is currently under attack for several reasons. Lead is known to cause mental retardation, particularly in children, and its use is now prohibited by the federal government. Zinc chromate has been identified as a carcinogen, and its use is now heavily restricted. Most paint manufacturers are finding substitutes for these chemicals and withdrawing products containing them from the market.

Enamel undercoaters dry to a smooth, hard finish. When sanded, they form the best surface for applying enamel topcoats. They provide good film build to smooth out surface imperfections and have good enamel holdout capabilities and sealing properties. They leave a tight, nonabsorbent surface that the enamel finish coat will not penetrate.

Fillers are materials used to fill and repair porous substrates before applying a subsequent paint material.

• **Concrete block fillers** are used over porous masonry materials to fill open pores and provide a smooth surface for later coats. Apply block fillers with a brush or roller because spray application rarely fills all pores and seldom provides adequate coverage. If an initial application of a block filler must be spray-applied, the second filler coat, if required, should be applied with a brush or roller. Concrete block fillers will not fill large surface voids or bridge wide cracks, nor will they conceal mortar joints sufficiently to create a plasterlike surface. Normally, large imperfections in a concrete masonry block wall must be repaired by responsible trade, not the painter.
• **Wood fillers** are applied to open-grain hardwoods such as elm, hickory, oak, and walnut because of the large pores characteristic of these woods. If the wood is to be stained, apply a wood filler about 24 hours after staining; the filler is usually colored with a small amount of the stain to avoid emphasizing the open-grain condition in the finish. For a natural finish, apply an uncolored wood filler directly to the wood before applying subsequent finish material. If the design intent is to accent the grain pattern, adding a light stain to the filler will provide the needed accent.

Finish coats, also called *topcoats,* are the paint system's principal protective barrier against the deleterious effects of exposure to the environment. Products intended to be used as finish coats contain ingredients that provide resistance to weather, chemicals, dirt, scrubbing, and staining. Finish coats also produce the coating's desired finished appearance, color, gloss, and opacity not supplied by the primer. In some situations, particularly with high-performance coating systems, the primer's major purpose is to protect the substrate; in such cases, one of the finish coat's main functions is to protect the primer from degradation due to exposure to the environment.

Transparent finish is a term used to describe a clear, unpigmented finish over wood. Varnish and lacquer are commonly referred to as *transparent finishes* without regard to the specific differences between the two materials. Lacquers are seldom used as field-applied finishes in building construction; they are used on furniture and certain shop-applied finishes. Use of the term *transparent finish* in this chapter is limited to field-applied varnishes. Stains and oil finishes may be part of a transparent finish system when they are applied over unfinished wood before applying final coats of varnish. Transparent finishes protect the substrate yet allow the natural surface of the material to show through the finish. They are primarily used on exposed interior wood surfaces, such as flush panel doors, paneling, or built-in storage units, and they are occasionally used to protect the finish of exposed metals. Some varnishes may darken or otherwise affect the natural color of the substrate. To see the result of applying a transparent finish to a given substrate, apply transparent finishes to samples of the materials to be used. The number of coats to be applied will depend on the effect desired and the durability required; however, applying fewer than three coats is not recommended.

Varnishes, unlike paints or enamels, are normally single-element coatings that consist solely of a binder; as a result, they are usually high-gloss materials. Varnishes are solvent solutions of oil-modified alkyds or other oleoresinous resins that dry by oxidation to produce transparent finishes. The resin imparts some desirable properties to the material, such as hardness or fast drying. The ratio of oil to resin is called the *oil length,* or the number of gallons of oil per 100 lb (45.36 kg) of resin. Varnishes are classified as *short-oil varnishes* if they contain less than 15 gal. (56.8 L) of oil, *medium-oil varnishes* if they contain between 15 and 30 gal. (56.8 and 113.5 L), or *long-oil varnishes* if they contain more than 30 gal. (113.5 L). Short-oil varnishes dry more rapidly than long-oil varnishes and form a harder film; however, long-oil varnishes have greater elasticity and exterior durability.

• **Interior varnishes** are usually based on linseed oil combined with other resins. Manufacturers offer many versions of the same basic varnish type, modified to suit specific applications. Alkyd-resin varnishes are the most common for general-purpose applications. Polyurethane varnishes are used for abrasion resistance and flexibility. Epoxy-ester varnishes are available for applications requiring a greater resistance to acids and alkalis. Increasing environmental concerns are forcing paint manufacturers to search for water-based alternatives to linseed-oil-based materials. Some manufacturers now offer water-based varnish products because of these environmental concerns; all manufacturers are expected to have satisfactory products available within a few years.
• **Exterior varnishes** do not perform well as long-lasting exterior finishes; however, they are sometimes used in exterior applications. Exterior durability in a varnish requires a long-oil-type resin. The most durable varnishes for exterior exposure are combinations of tung oil with 100 percent phenolic resin. The phenolic resins yield varnishes of dark color. Modified phenolic resins form varnishes with good water and alkali resistance. Other resins are available and are often used; however, they do not have the overall good characteristics of phenolics. In well-protected exterior applications, either alkyd- or polyurethane-based varnishes may be used.
• **Spar varnish** is a clear varnish intended for exterior use in marine environments. It is occasionally used in other applications; however, it has limited durability on exterior exposures.
• **Flat varnish** dries to a low-gloss, transparent finish, in contrast to most varnishes, which dry to a high-gloss finish. Flat varnishes are made by adding transparent flatting pigments to the resin to provide lower-gloss, mattelike material.
• **Clear sealers** are varnishes that have been thinned with solvents to penetrate and seal the substrate rather than form a film. Clear sealers are used to prevent grain raising in wood and to seal porous plywood surfaces before painting.

Oil stains consist of color pigments dispersed in a drying oil, such as linseed oil, that has been thinned to a low consistency for maximum penetration into wood surfaces. These stains are generously applied to sanded, interior wood surfaces and are allowed to penetrate and dry; excess material is then wiped off. Only the stain in the wood pores remains; it is left as is or may be rubbed with a light oil finish or receive a clear finish such as varnish or paste wax.

PRODUCT SELECTION

Reasons for painting vary, but those most common are to provide color or decoration, to conceal imperfections, and to protect the substrate. Many consumers say their reason for repainting a space is because the space looked dingy and needed to be brightened. Because a fresh coat of paint usually freshens the appearance of a surface, this is probably the most obvious reason for painting. However, paint also hides minor surface imperfections and improves the appearance of a rough, uneven surface;

this is a second but equally important reason for painting. Perhaps the least obvious but, in some respects, the most important reason for painting is to protect a substrate. Protecting surfaces from weather, moisture, abrasion, graffiti, chemicals, and any number or combination of other destructive agents is very important. With the many coating types available, protective qualities in formulations provide not only protection but also pleasing decorative effects.

See Table 1 for a listing of generic types of products and their properties.

Table 1
PAINTS AND COATINGS: PROPERTIES

TYPE	PRINCIPAL BINDER	BASE/CURE	TYPICAL USES	COMPARATIVE COST RANGE	IN-SERVICE LIFE RANGE IN YEARS	GLOSS RETENTION	STAIN RESISTANCE	WEATHER RESISTANCE	ABRASION IMPACT RESISTANCE	FLEXIBILITY
Clear	Acrylic, methyl methacrylate copolymer	solvent; water	Waterproofing and surface sealer against dirt retention, graffiti; for vertical surfaces of concrete, masonry, stucco; may be pigmented.	moderate to high	5 to 10	excellent to good	fair	excellent to good	good	good
	Alkyd, spar varnish	solvent	For interior and protected exterior wood surfaces. Also as vehicle for aluminum pigmented coatings.	moderate	up to 1 exterior	fair to good	poor	poor	fair	good
	Phenolic, spar varnish	solvent	Exterior wood surfaces subject to moisture. May be used in marine environments. Also vehicle for aluminum pigment.	moderate to high	up to 2 exterior	fair to good	fair	good	good	good
	Silicone	solvent	Waterproofing and surface sealer against dirt retention for vertical surfaces of concrete, masonry, stucco.	moderate	5 to 7	flat	fair	good	penetrating coating	
	Urethane, one-part	moist cure[1]	Surfaces subject to chemical attack; abrasion, graffiti, heavy or concentrated traffic, such as gymnasium floors.	moderate to high	up to 15	excellent to good	good to excellent	good to excellent	good to excellent	excellent
Stain	Acrylic	solvent; water	Pigmented translucent or semi-opaque exterior surface sealers; solvent based for masonry, concrete; water based for wood.	moderate to low	3 to 5	flat finish	not a factor	good to fair	penetrating coatings— resistance same as for substrate	
	Alkyd	solvent; water	Pigmented exterior or interior surface sealer for wood surfaces such as shingles, does not impart sheen to surface.	moderate	3 to 5	flat finish		fair		
	Oil	solvent	Pigmented exterior or interior surface sealer for wood such as shingles, trim, opaque or semitransparent.	moderate	3 to 5	fair		fair		
Opaque	Acrylic	water	For exterior/interior vertical surfaces of wood, masonry, plaster, gypsum board, metals. Good color retention. Permeable to vapor.	moderate to low	5 to 8	good to fair	fair	good	good to fair	good to excellent
	Acrylic, epoxy modified, two-part	water	High performance coating for interior vertical surfaces subject to graffiti, stains, heavy scrubbing. May be used in food preparation areas.	high	10 to 15	good	good	good to excellent	good to excellent	good to excellent
	Alkyd	solvent; water	For exterior/interior vertical and horizontal surfaces, such as wood, metals, masonry. Poor permeability to vapor.	moderate	5 to 8	good to excellent	fair	fair to good	fair to good	fair to good
	Chlorinated rubber	solvent	Swimming pool coatings. Corrosion protection; isolating dissimilar metals.	high to very high	up to 10	fair	fair	good	fair to good	good
	Chlorosulfonated polyethylene	solvent	Protective coating for tanks, piping, valves, elastomeric roofing membranes.	very high	up to 15	not applicable	fair	excellent	fair to good	excellent
	Epoxy, two-part; epoxy ester, one part	solvent cure; solvent	Moisture/alkali resistant. Two-part for nondecorative interior uses highly resistant to chemicals. Esters in wide choice of colors.	high to very high	15 to 20; up to 10	poor to good	excellent for two-part	good to excellent	excellent	good to excellent
	Phenolic	solvent	Chemical- and moisture-resistant coatings. May be used over alkaline surfaces.	moderate to high	up to 10	fair	fair	good to excellent	good to excellent	good
	Polychloroprene	solvent[2]	Marketed as "Neoprene"; resistant to chemicals, moisture, ultraviolet radiation. Also used as roofing membrane; generally covered with Hypalon.	very high	up to 25	not applicable	good	excellent	excellent	good
	Polyester	solvent	Limited application in field; over cementitious surfaces, metal, plywood for exterior exposures.	high	up to 15	good to excellent	good to excellent	good to excellent	good	good to excellent
	Silicone	solvent	Surfaces with temperatures up to 1200°F. Often with aluminum pigments. Corrosion and solvent resistant.	very high	varies	not applicable, special purpose coating			good	good
	Silicone; modified acrylic, alkyd, epoxy	solvent	High-performance exterior coatings. Industrial siding, curtain walls, when shop-applied baked-on.	high to very high	15 to 20	good to excellent	good	good to excellent	good to excellent	good
	Styrene, butadiene	water	Interior coating for gypsum board, plaster, masonry. Limited exterior use over cementitious substrate, as filler over rough porous surfaces.	moderate to low	4 to 6	poor to fair	fair	poor	fair	good
	Urethane, one or two part	moist or chemical cure[3]	Heavy-duty wall and floor coatings. Resistance to stains, chemicals, graffiti, scrubbing, solvents, impact, abrasion.	high to very high	15 to 20	excellent	good to excellent	good to excellent	good to excellent	excellent
	Vinyl, polyvinyl chloride-acetate	solvent	Residential metal siding and trim, gutters, leaders, baseboard heating covers, when shop-applied, baked-on.	high	up to 15	good	fair	good	good	good to excellent
	Vinyl, polyvinylidiene chloride	water	Metal and concrete surfaces in contact with dry and wet food, potable water, wastewater, jet and diesel fuels.	high	up to 10	good	fair	good	good	good
	Vinyl, polyvinyl acetate	water	Exterior and interior vertical surfaces, such as masonry, concrete, wood, plaster, gypsum board, metals. Permeable to vapor.	moderate to low	5 to 8	good to fair	fair	good	good to fair	good
	Bituminous, coal tar pitch, asphalt: emulsions, cutbacks	solvent	Waterproofing of metals, concrete, masonry, portland cement plaster, piping when below grade or immersed.	low	10 to 15 protected	not a factor		good	poor	fair
	Cement	water	Leveling coat over porous masonry or concrete not subject to abrasion or scrubbing. Cement and oil used as primers for metal surfaces.	low	varies	flat finish	poor	poor for color	good	poor

[1] Solvent-based, oil-modified urethane is also available; for use on interior/exterior vertical and horizontal wood surfaces. Cost is moderate.

[2] May be obtained as water-reducible coating; use as field-applied coating very limited; generally used as tank linings.

[3] Solvent base, oil-modified urethane is also available; for use on vertical and horizontal surfaces. Cost is moderate, but durability is lower than for other types.

Paint Composition

Many different chemicals are used to make paint and because paint is a combination of different chemicals, no two paint products are identical in chemical content or perform in exactly the same manner. Each chemical used in a paint formula is selected because it imparts specific qualities to the film or serves a particular function during curing or application. Paint products intended for different purposes may contain the same basic resins and pigments in their formula, but the amount of each ingredient will differ and some ingredients will be in one product but not included in the other.

Coating technology is a constantly evolving process. Each year the coatings industry discovers new materials, finds new uses for old materials, and adds refinements to existing product formulations. Each paint manufacturer uses these discoveries to make new products or improve the performance of existing products. Each coating, by nature of its own unique formulation, has attributes and characteristics that enable it to perform well on particular surfaces under certain conditions. Some coating materials, however, will not perform well in certain applications if conditions are not appropriate. Specifiers should be aware of limitations on the use of any paint material when preparing their project specifications, or they could specify a product inappropriately.

Proprietary Formulas

Each manufacturer carefully selects the ingredients used in each of its paint formulas with a specific purpose in mind. They then blend these ingredients in multiple combinations and proportions to produce the qualities they desire. This blending is what makes each paint manufacturer's products unique. The formulas are carefully guarded corporate property, are not freely disclosed, and are subject to constant refinement as coating technology introduces new materials to improve the product lines. Most manufacturers provide a variety of products that perform similar tasks but do so using different chemical formulations. They also make products that, although similar generically in chemical content to other products in their lines, are designed to appeal to other market segments and therefore are manufactured or packaged differently. This marketing has led to an overwhelming number of products that appear to be similar but are actually different in composition and performance characteristics.

Paint Selection

Selecting the right paint for a given situation can be bewildering. Even experienced design professionals find preparing project specifications for paints and coatings frustrating because of the many factors they must evaluate before they begin work. From among a large number of available products, they must first choose a specific generic product type for each substrate to be painted. Then, from among the large number of manufacturers competing for a share of the market, they must select one or more manufacturers to supply the paint systems required. The large number of options available for material selection and among manufacturing companies places specifiers in a difficult position when selecting manufacturers and products. Furthermore, local environmental regulations in some areas of the United States restrict the types of paint materials that can be applied in those areas. These regulations usually result in problems and confusion because they are not uniform and differ from one part of the country to another.

Reference Standards

For most building products and systems, specifiers have measurable technical criteria available for product evaluation from many sources, such as manufacturing associations and professional and technical societies. Unfortunately, this is not the true of the coatings industry. Although there is no shortage of material standards for the various chemical ingredients that go into a paint formula, there are few useful standards that establish measurable criteria for evaluating paints and coatings. The lack of performance standards for comparing material quality leaves specifiers with no way to compare one product to another or to evaluate products based on realistic performance expectations.

Federal specifications were the primary reference standards for paints and coatings for many years. Unfortunately, their usefulness as quality standards for paints is questionable. The major complaint about federal specifications was that they often did little more than establish minimum content requirements for ingredients, which most major manufacturers far exceeded. Another major complaint was that they contained too many requirements that were unnecessary and did nothing to establish realistic quality levels. Some older federal specifications failed to provide useful measurable criteria for product evaluation. In many cases, when a minimum quality level was established, it was minimal at best. The most prevalent complaint in recent years is that many federal specifications either have been canceled altogether or have not been updated in more than 10 years. This lack of action is not acceptable in an industry where manufacturers continually introduce new products while the federal government is establishing environmental regulations that affect paint content.

Efforts are presently under way by several groups within the federal government to update the older federal specifications and develop new ones for some of the more commonly used new product types. New federal specifications that replace the older documents carry an A-A designation and are called *commercial item descriptions*. However, it is difficult to tell the difference between the new documents and the ones they replace because much of the content is similar. Although the replacement efforts are commendable, they have met with strong resistance from paint manufacturers who feel that the requirements are too restrictive in some cases and not strong enough in others. Some industry analysts claim that there are too many requirements of questionable value in both the old and new federal specifications that could result in disqualification of an otherwise excellent product for inconsequential reasons. Most manufacturers assert that their products comply with the performance requirements but not the compositional requirements of most federal specifications.

All paint manufacturers could make products that comply with minimum federal specifications requirements; however, few want to do so. With rare exceptions, products of reputable paint manufacturers exceed minimum performance requirements in federal specifications. If a paint manufacturer's product literature references federal specifications (many ignore them altogether), the literature usually states that the product complies with the performance intent of federal specifications but not with the stipulated formulation requirements. As a result, it is usually impractical at the present time for architects to reference federal specifications as the basis of quality in a specification for anything other than federal government work.

ASTM does not offer standard specifications that are viable alternatives to federal specifications as a standard for performance. Although ASTM has published more than 700 standards on paint materials alone, most of them specify test procedures and similar requirements for the various chemicals used in a paint formula. Using ASTM standards to establish a quality level is impractical because most paint formulas consist of a large number of chemicals, many of which are present in only trace amounts. Furthermore, the standards that establish test procedures do not set minimum performance criteria, which is critical.

Painting and Decorating Contractors of America (PDCA) once published the *Architectural Specification Manual-Painting, Repainting, Wallcovering and Gypsum Wallboard Finishing* in an effort to establish a basis for the evaluation of paint products. The publication, which is now out of print, failed to set minimum performance criteria. Last published in 1986, it is now out of date, has too few participants, and depends too much on the manufacturers' own proprietary standards to be a useful tool.

Master Painters Institute (MPI) efforts are perhaps the most encouraging new developments for reference standards. MPI, which is headquartered in British Columbia, is trying to establish realistic minimal quality standards for paints and coatings. To date, the work of this organization has been promising and should lead to the establishment of useful measurable criteria for paints and coatings that can be tested and evaluated and ultimately used as a basis of comparison to establish minimum acceptable quality levels.

Measuring Paint Quality

Measuring paint quality is extremely difficult because of the many factors to evaluate. At a minimum, consumers are most concerned with color retention and ease of maintenance; but they also want to know how long the product will last in service, because the cost of repainting after a few years can be an economic burden. Applicators are concerned with the ease of application and how the material flows off the brush. They are also concerned with a product's hiding capability because this may determine the number of coats they will be required to apply. The specifier is concerned with the coating's capability to protect the substrate from degradation or damage and how well it will perform. Everyone involved is concerned with cost. A high-quality paint should satisfy all these concerns.

Volume Solids

Some industry analysts suggest using the percentage of volume solids as the sole basis on which to evaluate paint quality. In their view, the higher the percentage of volume solids, the better the quality of the paint. A high percentage of volume solids is an important consideration but is not by itself an adequate measure of quality because it fails to address many of the concerns raised in the preceding paragraph. Many factors other than volume solids need to be considered in determining quality. For example, the type and quality of the raw materials in an individual paint formula are equally important because they ultimately determine the coating's longevity.

Ratio of Vehicle Solids to Pigment

Other industry analysts suggest that the greater the ratio of vehicle solids to pigment, the better a paint's capability to withstand repeated washing and cleaning efforts. They suggest that the ratio of vehicle volume solids to pigment solids is more useful in measuring paint quality than other criteria. In some circumstances, endurance of the coating is the ultimate criterion for paint quality, but other qualities are also important.

Testing

Test results demonstrating a product's performance are a far better gage of a paint's quality than an evaluation of its material composition. ASTM offers many test procedures that provide a basis for rating performance characteristics of a paint, including tests for scrubbability, stain removal, hiding power, adhesion, and other properties. Test results for such qualities are usually difficult to obtain and evaluate. In the absence of established uniform performance criteria for evaluation, paint manufacturers are naturally reluctant to provide testing for every product in every possible project situation. Because independent testing of paint products is expensive, few owners are willing to absorb these costs on a project-to-project basis.

Multiple Product Lines

To be competitive at any price level, most manufacturers produce a high-quality, premium line of paint and one or more lines of lesser quality at a lower price. Most manufacturers offer several product lines with the same

binder that is designed to serve the same purpose. However, their top-quality line often contains significantly more binder than their less-expensive lines, and their less-expensive lines contain more low-priced extender pigments than their premium line. This deviation demonstrates that these formulations can have different percentages of volume solids yet provide the performance desired in the product. If performance is the criterion used to judge paint quality, then a difference in the percentages of volume solids between two products is immaterial.

Evaluating Raw Materials

To some extent, paint quality can be measured by evaluating the raw materials used in a paint product. Coating performance can be improved by adjusting the formula. Consider, for example, titanium dioxide, the prime pigment used in most architectural coatings. It is a superior white pigment because of its excellent hiding power, but it is expensive. Less costly chemicals can be used as prime pigments but do not perform as well; some yellow over time with exposure to sunlight. A manufacturer could substitute less-expensive extender pigments for some or all of the titanium dioxide in the paint formula and lower the product cost without substantially reducing the percent of volume solids in the material. This action may not affect the paint's hiding capability but it may produce unwanted side effects, and the product may not last as long in actual service. Although the percentages of volume solids are similar, the raw materials are not as high in quality and the product will not perform as well overall.

Performance Criteria

The coatings industry should develop realistic, meaningful, measurable, performance criteria for architectural coatings. Because ASTM currently publishes test procedures for scrubbability, the coatings industry could establish baseline criteria for each gloss level for scrubbability, such as a minimum number of cycles to failure. The coatings industry could also agree on a narrower definition of the gloss levels. Criteria for other characteristics such as abrasion resistance, gloss retention, dry opacity, and mildew resistance could also be established by industry consensus.

Types of Coatings

Each paint manufacturer offers *consumer paint lines* and *professional coatings,* the two paint categories given at the beginning of this chapter, for different market segments. Although these terms are well known in the paint and coatings industry, they are not defined in any known source of definitions on paints or coatings, including ASTM D 16 and MPI's *Master Painter's Glossary*. It is reasonable to assume that most paint manufacturers distribute both types of products. Table 2 provides a comparison of the differences between consumer paint lines and professional coatings.

Consumer paint lines are available at hardware stores, paint stores, home-improvement centers, and similar retail outlets. Many local and regional paint manufacturers sell their products in company-owned stores that offer selected specialty products that are nationally distributed. Most national companies distribute their products through company-owned stores or franchised outlets that may or may not be part of a national chain.

- **Colors:** Most manufacturers offer a wider choice of standard colors in their consumer paint lines than they do in their professional coatings. However, many paint products can be tinted and offered in numerous colors. Most paint stores can match any color desired; therefore, the number of colors available should not be a determining factor when selecting between consumer paint lines and professional coatings.
- **Packaging:** Consumer paint lines are usually available in quarts or gallons and occasionally in pints. Some products are also available in 4- and 5-gal. (15.1- and 18.9-L) containers.

Table 2
COMPARISON OF CONSUMER PAINT LINES AND PROFESSIONAL-COATING MATERIALS

Attribute	Consumer Paint Lines	Professional Coatings
Product Availability	Hardware stores Home-improvement centers Local paint stores	Some local paint stores Manufacturers' warehouses Regional distribution centers
Colors Available	Wide choice of standard colors	Limited number of standard colors
Packaging Method	Quarts and 1-gal. (3.8-L) cans Occasionally, 5-gal. (18.9-L) cans	1- and 5-gal. (3.8- and 18.9-L) cans Occasionally, 55-gal. (208-L) drums
Cost	Varies, but generally more expensive than professional coatings	Generally less expensive than consumer lines
Application Methods	Brush or roller	Brush, roller, spray, painter's mitten, etc.
Ease of Use	Easy to apply by anyone	For professional application only
Material Quality	Varies among products	Varies among products

- **Cost:** Consumer paint lines are usually more expensive than comparable professional materials because of the way they are marketed. However, they are often available at sale prices and are usually available to professional painters in volume discounts. In small quantities, the cost difference between the two product lines is usually insignificant.
- **Ease of use:** Manufacturers make their consumer paint lines easy to apply with brush or roller. Both the average consumer and the journeyman painter can apply them right out of the can. They produce excellent results if applied with reasonable care, even if applied by inexperienced applicators.
- **Material quality:** The quality level of consumer paint lines varies among products. However, all paint manufacturers intend these materials to be used by anyone. No manufacturer wants the reputation of offering an inferior product, so the products are almost always excellent.

Professional coatings are usually available only to professional painters at a manufacturer's warehouse or regional distribution center. They are rarely sold to consumers and are generally not available in retail outlets. On special order, a manufacturer might deliver these products to a local paint store for a professional painter to pick up. Professional coatings are frequently, but not always, identified by the abbreviation "Pro," for professional, in the name of the product or by a phrase similar to "for professional application only" in manufacturers' literature.

- **Colors:** Although the number and variety of colors available for professional coatings are fewer than for consumer paint lines, coatings can be tinted to almost any color. As with consumer paint lines, color should not be a factor in selecting one material over another.
- **Packaging:** Professional coatings are available in 1- and 5-gal. (3.8- and 18.9-L) cans. For spray application or on large projects, they may also be available in 55-gal. (208-L) drums.
- **Cost:** Professional coatings are generally, but not always, less expensive than consumer paint lines. Some manufacturers offer exactly the same paint formula under different names in different containers at different prices for different market segments. Other manufacturers offer two distinct lines.
- **Ease of use:** Manufacturers make professional coatings specifically for use by professional applicators. Some products are formulated for spray application; others may be applied by any conventional method such as brush, roller, or painter's mitten. If used by an experienced painter, they will provide satisfactory results.
- **Material quality:** As with consumer paint lines, quality varies among products. Some manufacturers offer their professional-coating lines in several different quality levels for different application methods. For example, some manufacturers offer professional-coating lines that are suitable only for spray application.

There are differences between consumer paint lines and their professional-coating counterparts but quality is not necessarily one of them. Reputable paint manufacturers make every effort to produce quality materials in both lines. Some large national paint manufacturers make several varieties of each line of material and sell them under different brand names at different price levels. Usually there are variations in the chemical composition of each brand they offer; as a result, the level of quality each brand represents is different. This way, the manufacturer has a product line available at a price that will satisfy every situation. The following subsections discuss in greater detail some of the more important differences between consumer paint lines and professional coatings.

Product Formulation

One significant difference between consumer paint lines and professional coatings is their chemical content, primarily because they are formulated for different users. The amount of certain ingredients in professional coatings may be significantly different from the amount of the same chemicals in similar quality levels of consumer paint lines. Because they are intended for use by anyone, paint manufacturers design their consumer paint lines to be as close to foolproof as possible. They use the best ingredients in their consumer paint lines because this provides a highly workable product. Thus, both the average consumer and the professional painter can apply a consumer paint line easily and achieve the desired results with minimum effort. Conversely, because they know that professional coatings will be used only by skilled applicators, paint manufacturers can use larger amounts of less costly ingredients in these materials, which lowers the cost to produce the product but does not necessarily mean a loss in coating performance or overall quality. Manufacturers are confident that a skilled applicator will achieve the desired result even if using a less-expensive material.

Field Modification of Paint Material

Usually, an experienced applicator will achieve proper coverage with less material than the average consumer. Most paint companies manufacture their consumer paint lines to be ready for use without modification, regardless of the experience of the applicator. As a result, there is seldom a need to add anything to the paint material once the can is opened, but this is not necessarily true of professional coatings. Many experienced applicators will modify the paint in the can for better and faster application, depending on job conditions. There are many legitimate reasons why a professional painter might do this; for example, in hot or humid weather, an applicator might need to modify the paint composition so the paint will flow more easily off the brush, to speed or otherwise improve the application rate.

There are risks associated with modifying paint composition in the field. It must be done judiciously or it could lead to problems. If the material is improperly modified, initial results might appear satisfactory, but the coating might not perform as expected. For example, an additive designed to improve flow might decrease the dry film thickness and shorten the expected life of the product. Another additive designed to improve product opacity might lead to premature yellowing. In some states, particularly those with strict environmental laws, certain additives are illegal if, as is often the case, the modification results in an increase in the amount of VOCs the material releases into the atmosphere. The owner could legitimately raise serious questions if the applicator's main reason for modifying the paint formula is to provide additional profit; this creates a conflict between an owner's legitimate performance expectations and a painting contractor's desire to maximize profits.

Cost

One major difference between consumer paint lines and professional coatings is product cost. Most consumer lines use high-quality materials exclusively, and product cost is high as a result. However, professional-coating lines often reduce the amount of the prime ingredients in the formula, particularly the prime pigment, and substitute less costly materials, thereby reducing the product cost. Because manufacturers formulate, package, and distribute these products differently, professional coatings are frequently less expensive per gallon than comparable consumer paint lines produced by the same manufacturer. This cost difference is insignificant on projects where small quantities of materials are required but could become a major factor on a large project.

Coating Performance

Architects and owners want paint products that give the best overall performance in a long-lasting, trouble-free coating. High levels of both the top-quality prime pigments and volume solids typically produce coatings that have a long service life, with superior overall performance, and that are problem-free. Both consumer paint lines and professional coatings can produce excellent overall coating performance. However, most paint manufacturers provide higher levels of prime pigments in their consumer paint lines than in their professional coatings, which an examination of the label analysis of comparable paint products will usually show. Because these pigments provide superior performance, this means that consumer paint lines will often outperform a comparable professional-coating product.

Extender Pigments

Extender pigments, such as silicas, silicates, and calcium carbonate, are important paint components and are often used in architectural coatings to adjust the gloss level. They may also be used to augment the hiding qualities of the prime pigment in the material. Consumer paint lines generally contain less extender pigment than professional coatings and rely less on them for dry hiding. In some cases, the main reason for using certain extender pigments in consumer paint lines is to lower the gloss level of the paint. Using extender pigments in large quantities can have an adverse effect on a coating. Large quantities of extender pigments can lessen a coating's scrub and stain resistance. Furthermore, they contribute little to color and hiding when compared to the prime pigment materials used in high-quality products.

Solids Content

Most paint manufacturers make consumer paint lines with a higher percentage of volume solids than their professional coatings because of the way the coatings are used. This way the manufacturers try to ensure excellent product performance without having to depend on the skill of an applicator. Higher volume solids result in a greater dry film thickness; this means better overall protection for the substrate. A thicker dry film also provides better hiding and durability; in short, it provides better overall performance for the product, no matter how inexperienced an applicator. In the case of latex

paint, this means more solids and less water in the can. High-quality latex paints usually have between 30 and 40 percent solids by volume. For a lesser-quality paint, this percentage might be between 20 and 30.

Level of Quality

Consumer paint lines generally contain larger amounts of high-quality materials than comparable professional coatings; as a result, they can be expected to adhere to the substrate better. They are also less likely to become brittle with age, so they have better resistance to paint failures, such as cracking and blistering, and fewer flaking problems. These paints are more durable, have better color retention, are more chalk-resistant, and have other advantages over paints that use lower-quality raw materials. Many industry analysts believe that because consumer paint lines contain higher-quality materials than professional coatings they are often higher-quality products. For manufacturers, who use the best materials to make high-quality products for both markets, the difference in quality between the two product lines is marginal; for those who substitute lower-quality raw materials, however, the difference in overall quality can be substantial.

Life-Cycle Cost Analysis

For many owners, the better overall performance of high-quality paint translates into reduced maintenance costs. High-quality consumer paint lines may be priced higher than comparable professional-coating materials, but their superior performance often makes them a better value overall. If maintenance costs are a prime consideration, owners usually find that using a better product reduces costs in the long term. Normally, a higher-quality, higher-priced, paint will outlast lower-quality products by several years. A superior paint material may last twice as long in service as an ordinary paint product because of the high-quality materials it contains. Because the cost of material is much lower than the cost of the labor to apply it, owners often prefer using a higher-cost material to ensure a longer-lasting finish and lower, total life-cycle cost.

Availability

Consumer paint lines are usually more readily available than professional coatings. Some smaller, local paint companies make all their products available through a branch distribution network that includes company-owned stores or authorized dealers. Most larger regional and national companies supply consumer paint lines to retail outlets such as paint stores, home-improvement centers, and hardware stores but distribute professional coatings only through regional distribution centers or selected dealers. Product availability is an important consideration for many owners if periodic recoating by their own personnel is a probability and on-site storage for paint is limited. In such cases, the ease of obtaining paint from local sources may be the determining factor in specifying paint products.

Manufacturing Cost

High-quality paint, whether a consumer line or a professional coating, is expensive to make. High-quality pigments such as titanium dioxide, special additives to improve performance or ease of application, complex and combination binders, and other high-quality ingredients cost more than ordinary ingredients. Furthermore, anything that increases a paint's solids level also adds to the cost of the product. Consumer paint lines typically use larger amounts of expensive ingredients than a comparable professional-coating material. As a result, they are also usually more expensive.

Both consumer paint lines and professional coatings produce satisfactory results if applied properly. If initial construction cost is the overriding concern, professional coatings are the obvious choice. However, if an owner wants the utmost in performance, consumer paint lines often have an advantage because of the quality of the ingredients. Specifiers should expect problems if their paint specification includes professional coatings from one or more manufacturers competing with consumer paint lines from others. A manufacturer whose consumer paint lines are specified in competition with a competitor's professional coating is usually at a price disadvantage because of the potential cost difference between the two product lines. When possible, specifiers should make every effort to specify products of the same type.

SURFACE PREPARATION

Substrate Condition

Proper preparation of the substrate before applying a coating is extremely important. This point cannot be stressed often enough or strongly enough. Most paint manufacturers stress that proper preparation of the substrate is more important than any other factor, including the skill of an applicator; most applicators will add that it is also more important than the quality of the coating material. Many applicators with years of experience in correcting the effects of poor surface preparation often attest to the truth of these statements. A coating's ultimate performance will be only as good as its associated surface preparation. More coating failures are the direct result of poor or inadequate surface preparation than any other single element, including contamination of the coating material. Carefully following the paint manufacturer's recommendations for minimum surface acceptability and the recommendations of recognized trade associations, such as SSPC: The Society for Protective Coatings, will prove beneficial.

General Recommendations

In general, paints adhere best when the substrate is clean, dry, and slightly rough. Surfaces to be painted must be free of dirt, oil and grease, rust, mill scale, efflorescence, laitance, and other surface imperfections, which are only a few of the many imperfections that would make the difference between a successful application and a coating failure. Concrete, masonry, plaster, and similar surfaces must be permitted to cure properly before application; it may be advisable to test such surfaces with a moisture meter to ensure surface dryness before beginning paint application. Some surfaces, such as exterior portland cement plaster (stucco), could require an extensive curing time of several months before it is advisable to begin coating operations. Glossy surfaces must be sanded or roughened to permit the coating to adhere. Proper and complete surface preparation means the difference between coating success and failure and extends the service life of the paint.

Specifiers should carefully review a project's critical areas and surfaces to be painted before beginning to write their painting specifications. If more stringent surface preparation is necessary in areas or on substrates that are crucial to the success of a project, it is better to specify it in advance than to pay extra to have the work performed at a later stage in a project. This way, everyone involved knows what is expected and how to prepare the substrates.

Metal Preparation

Ferrous-metal surfaces should be thoroughly clean and dry before application begins. Metal pretreatments do not contribute to metal protection as do primers or topcoats. However, they are recommended in systems where metal protection is important. Apply pretreatments after cleaning to improve adhesion and the effectiveness of applied paint. Wash primer is a form of cold phosphatizing and is most efficient for field application. Wash primers develop extremely good adhesion to blast-cleaned or pickled steel, and they are effective in promoting coating adhesion to galvanized or stainless steel and aluminum.

Wood Preparation

Knot sealers should be applied over knots and resinous areas of wood being painted to prevent bleed- through or telegraphing on the finished surface.

Substrate Examination

A critical examination of the substrate by the applicator before beginning any coating procedure is an essential element of good surface preparation. Applicators should also be advised not to proceed with application on a surface that is not properly prepared and that they assume responsibility for the surface condition once coating operations begin. These requirements are reasonable because the applicator is probably better qualified than anyone else to recognize problems with the substrate that could lead to coating failure.

APPLICATION

Good paint application depends on a successful combination of many factors, the most important being a combination of proper surface preparation, the use of the correct material for the substrate, and the skill and experience of the applicator. Environmental conditions prevailing at the time of application also contribute to the success of a coating application. Other factors also contribute to a successful coating application, but these are the most critical.

Surface preparation was discussed earlier in this chapter, but its importance cannot be stressed enough.

Material selection is critical. A paint application will not be successful if the applicator uses the wrong combination of materials. Compatibility of materials that make up a paint system and the quality of materials applied are important factors in successful coating application. Manufacturers recommend specific products for each part of a coating system; these recommendations should be followed to avoid incompatibility of coating materials.

The applicator's skill and experience often determines the success or failure of a coating application. Manufacturers' product literature for some coating materials clearly calls for application by a professional familiar with both the product and certain application techniques, which is usually the case with materials that require using special equipment for application or to ensure the applicator's safety. Such materials are not for the do-it-yourself market. In these situations, there is no substitute for the skill and experience of the applicator. Experienced applicators develop a feeling for materials they commonly use; they know when special care is needed and how to apply material to avoid damaging adjacent areas.

Environmental conditions during application can have a major effect on the success of a coating application. Slight changes in environmental conditions during application or curing may cause unexpected coating failure. Temperature and relative humidity are the ambient conditions that have the greatest effect on application, but other climatic conditions such as wind and rain also adversely affect coating application, particularly exterior application. Dampness and frost slow drying time and cause poor adhesion and blistering of paint film. Some materials cure more slowly under certain environmental conditions than others. It does not pay to attempt to shorten the time a coating needs to cure properly under adverse conditions because this can lead to disastrous results. Applying topcoats over inadequately cured primers usually contributes to coating failure because the topcoat might not adhere properly or, in some cases, might lift the primer.

Temperatures prevailing during application can either hasten or retard paint drying time and film adhesion. The most important temperatures to consider when applying paint are surface, ambient, and material temperatures. In most cases, it is prudent to wait until the proper surface temperature is reached before beginning the application process. It is more difficult to compensate for a low surface temperature than for a low air temperature, even though surface temperature is usually a direct result of the prevailing ambient temperature. Some material surfaces gain or lose heat slower than others; therefore, they are slower to recover from the effects of a sudden change in ambient temperature than others. This reduction can cause a delay in beginning a coating application. Low ambient and material temperatures may cause a paint to thicken, which makes it more difficult to apply and increases drying time. High ambient and material temperatures do the opposite; paint viscosity is lower at higher temperatures, which may result in inadequate film thickness and paint that sets too rapidly.

ENVIRONMENTAL CONSIDERATIONS

Environmental Regulations

On September 13, 1999, after many years of delay and controversy, the first national regulation imposing limits on the amount of VOCs contained in paints and other construction products went into effect. The regulations limit the maximum amount of VOCs in flat interior and exterior architectural coatings to 250 g/L and in nonflat interior or exterior coatings to 380 g/L. Although these regulations impose national limits on VOC content, state and local governments may impose harsher limits if their particular situations are serious enough to warrant such action. Enactment and enforcement of these national regulations are a welcome relief from the confusion that has been characteristic of this issue for more than 30 years. The following discussion is provided to help specifiers understand the reasoning behind the promulgation of these regulations.

Background

Restrictions on the amount of VOCs in paints and coatings developed out of concern about deteriorating air quality in some parts of the United States. Severe air pollution, particularly a phenomenon known as *smog,* had become an irritant to many who live in large metropolitan areas. Smog is a brownish haze that often hangs over large cities and the surrounding countryside. It forms as a result of complex reactions involving mainly nitrogen oxides, ozone, and hydrocarbons. Smog causes eye irritation and respiratory system problems for many people and is one agent of the depletion of the earth's ozone layer. The newly imposed regulations concern the coatings industry because many coating formulas contain hydrocarbons and photochemically reactive solvents, which mix with nitrous oxides that are primarily created by automobile exhaust and form ground-level ozone, a major component of smog.

Rule 66

The first action to improve air quality that involved paints and coatings took place in California in 1966 when the Los Angeles County Air Pollution Control Board published the *1966 Code of the Los Angeles County Air Pollution Control Board,* commonly known as *Rule 66.* This regulation defined photochemically reactive solvents. It also established the first limits on the amount of VOCs permissible in paints and coatings in the Los Angeles area. It was very effective and quickly became the model for other localities and states that were concerned with improving air quality in their area.

In April 1971, in response to continuing complaints about deteriorating air quality in cities, the federal government published a list of air-quality standards. These standards set upper limits on the amount of pollutants in the atmosphere in cities that regularly experienced high levels of air pollution. The government required each state to develop and implement plans to achieve the standards. Within a short time, 22 states and the District of Columbia enacted air pollution regulations on solvent emissions. In addition to California, strict clean air laws were soon in effect in Arizona, Kentucky, New Jersey, New York, and Texas. These regulations were subject to constant changes and additions and were far from uniform. To further confuse the situation, many localities, including separate counties and cities, had enacted their own regulations that were often more restrictive than either federal or state regulations.

For some time after Rule 66 was originally published, the paint and coatings industry assumed that if a coating complied with Rule 66, it would meet requirements enacted by any state or local government. Unfortunately, this was not always the case; most states modified Rule 66 to suit their own particular situation. Furthermore, Rule 66 was soon superseded. About 10 years after Rule 66 was first issued, several California air pollution control districts adopted new and stricter regulations.

Because of the lack of uniformity in the various regulations, everyone involved with coatings agreed that nationwide standards for VOCs would be preferable to the prevailing situation with different requirements and levels of enforcement in different parts of the United States. In July 1992, the Environmental Protection Agency (EPA) announced the beginning of a regulatory negotiation (reg/neg) process. The EPA was responding to a congressional mandate of 1990 to develop an approach that would reduce the level of VOCs available to form ground-level ozone while taking into consideration a number of factors such as economic feasibility, health concerns, environmental issues, and energy impact.

For more than two years, the EPA actively pursued the reg/neg process hoping to gain a national consensus for its proposed regulations. Participants in the process included NPCA, PDCA, and other concerned members of the coatings industry; labor unions; state and local governments; and environmental advocates. Achieving a national consensus via this process was in the national interest because such a consensus would avoid much of the opposition and legal challenges that promulgation of any regulation issued by the EPA would be expected to generate.

As the process unfolded, it became clear to everyone concerned that regulating coatings would not be easy. Myriad scientific, technical, economic, and political issues quickly emerged. A series of meetings was held from 1992 until the spring of 1994. Participants were divided into separate interest groups, called caucuses, to study the proposed regulations. These caucuses included state and local governments, environmental advocates, large paint manufacturers (known as the *industry caucus*), regional paint manufacturers, labor unions, applicators, and consumer groups. Unfortunately, the participants were unable to agree on issues as each group defended its own parochial agenda. The announced goal for issuing the regulations, January 1994, came and went with no agreement in sight. Finally, in June 1994, the EPA issued a set of draft proposals. In August 1994, the industry caucus issued a set of counterproposals. The convener of the process then reluctantly notified participants that the process had been concluded without achieving its goal of a national consensus.

The process failed mainly because the participants were unable to agree on key issues and chose to gloss over many important considerations in the hope of reaching a consensus. Unfortunately, the national good was largely ignored in the process as the various caucuses and special interest groups promoted their own interests. Each group accused the others of being unable or unwilling to see beyond their own parochial concerns.

Once the reg/neg process broke down, the EPA was free to pursue any rule it believed was responsive to the congressional mandate. Accordingly, it began the process of drafting regulations with a goal of issuing them early in 1995, with implementation expected sometime in 1996. The cancellation of the reg/neg process prompted several states to move ahead on their own to develop their own rules. The coatings industry expected the regulations to be similar to the last EPA proposal. This process would involve two stages of reductions, one effective in 1996 and the second in the year 2000. The total reduction levels would be set at about 30 percent. The EPA was also expected to propose an exceedance-fee mechanism that would allow manufacturers to produce coatings that exceed the VOC limits; some environmentalists labeled this a "pay-to-pollute" provision.

Meanwhile, NPCA was actively promoting a different set of regulations and threatened a court challenge or other action if the proposed rules were implemented. NPCA was promoting an overall VOC reduction of only 20 percent and elimination of the exceedance-fee mechanism. It advocated those limits as within the reach of current coating technology. NPCA defended the possibility of legal challenges because it felt the EPA deviated from the congressional mandate that calls for an "approach," not "regulations."

All this left the coatings industry in a state of confusion. Everyone had expected the EPA to promulgate the new regulations before the end of 1995; that did not happen. Instead, in June 1996, the EPA issued a new proposal based on input from industry groups, including NPCA as well as environmentalists, and asked for comments. Drafting the final regulation began on receipt of the comments. It took more than a year to complete. The final rule was published on September 13, 1998, and became effective September 13, 1999. Although many environmentalists feel the regulations are not as strong as they should be, most industry analysts feel that the regulations accepted the reality of the current state of technology.

These regulations, modest as they are, are actually a welcome relief from the confusion of the past 30 years. The lack of any uniformity in separate state and local regulations probably hampered progress toward the development of environmentally friendly materials. The greatest problem for manufacturers and their research chemists, in the view of so many conflicting regulations, was that it was impossible to determine what level of restrictions was realistic. Currently, most manufacturers have a full line of products that can comply with the national regulations.

Unfortunately, the enactment of these new regulations will not totally end the problem. Some states, particularly California, have previously enacted regulations that are more restrictive than the new ones. The new regulations do not rescind these laws. Furthermore, the California South Coast Air Quality Management District in and around Los Angeles has decided to proceed with a major revision to the limits now in effect. Meanwhile, another group, on the East Coast, is attempting to enact lower VOC levels than those proposed by the EPA. It is too early to predict what, if any, effect these attempts to impose more restrictive VOC levels will have on the EPA regulations.

Given the action taken in the Los Angeles area and on the East Coast, specifiers should contact the local or regional EPA office for current information or interpretation of regulations for unusual circumstances. It is likely that the VOC issue has not been settled for all time, even though it will probably be less contentious in the future.

SAFETY AND HEALTH HAZARDS

Safety Hazards

Paints and coatings often contain some flammable solvents. When specifying the application of coatings in an enclosed space, solvent vapor buildup in the space could become great enough to reach a low explosive limit. If this occurs, there is always the danger that a spark or another source of ignition could cause a dangerous explosion. Work in enclosed spaces is safe if adequate ventilation is provided. The air must be changed often enough to dilute solvent-vapor concentration below the lower explosive limit. Adequate ventilation is necessary when using spray equipment, regardless of the flash point of the organic solvents in the coating.

Health Hazards

Health hazards include inhaling solvent vapors and physical contact with liquid solvents. In most circumstances, breathing small or moderate amounts of solvent vapors for brief periods of time will not produce an injury. However, long-term exposure to large amounts of solvent vapors is unsafe. Some individuals experience discomfort when exposed to vapors of certain types of coatings. Proper and adequate ventilation will solve most problems. Adequate ventilation is important, particularly on work in existing occupied buildings. Read precautionary information printed on the label of each paint container to understand the nature of the coating and the health and safety requirements of the material.

FIELD QUALITY CONTROL

Substrate Examination

The most important field quality-control measure that painting specifications should require is that the applicator examine the substrate before beginning the application. If the substrate is not in proper condition to receive the coating materials specified, the applicator has an obligation to refuse to begin work on the substrate. In effect, the applicator has the final word on acceptability of the surface preparation. It is not advisable to permit someone other than the applicator to decide whether or not to proceed with the application. Doing so is not in the best interest of the project because it eliminates the best control the specifier has for achieving a good coating application.

Material Testing Provisions

There are many opportunities for paint materials to be altered or contaminated from the time they are formulated to the time they are applied on the job site. Specifying that an independent testing agency test paint materials for compliance with requirements in the painting specification is the best way to ensure that the product applied is the same quality as the material specified. Whether the owner invokes these procedures or not, just establishing these requirements may deter overzealous thinning of materials and extended coverage during application. It also may deter requests to substitute lower-quality paint materials for those specified.

Listing salient characteristics is essential if testing of paint materials by an independent testing agency is anticipated. Specifications must identify those characteristics that are considered important and will be involved in material testing. For projects involving government agencies, including salient characteristics in the specifications is often necessary and may be required. The owner should determine which characteristics are important, what is acceptable, and what will constitute a failure.

Several characteristics could be considered critical to the performance of a coating material and can be tested according to established test methods; these include, among others, abrasion resistance, accelerated weathering, alkali resistance, color retention, dry opacity, flexibility, and mildew resistance. Another important item to consider is an analysis for content of the material actually delivered to the site as compared to the product's published label analysis; this also yields information about the volume solids of the product and the theoretical dry film thickness.

Essential information about a product's performance characteristics for most of the items listed above is rarely included in the manufacturer's product literature. Unfortunately, statements such as "this product can be expected to stand up against repeated washing" are fairly typical of the type of information to be found in product literature. This kind of statement is of little value when attempting to compare products for compliance with specified requirements, particularly when there are established test methods that form the basis of comparison. It is difficult to understand the reluctance of manufacturers to include pertinent information on such important characteristics in their product literature, particularly when this is the type of information most architects and owners need to know.

REFERENCES

Publication dates cited here were current at the time of this writing. Publications are revised periodically, and revisions may have occurred before this book was published.

ASTM International

ASTM D 16-96a: Definitions of Terms Relating to Paint, Varnish, Lacquer, and Related Products

ASTM D 523-89 (reapproved 1999): Test Method for Specular Gloss

Master Painters Institute

Master Painter's Glossary, 1997.

BOOK

Weismantel, Guy E., ed. *Paint Handbook,* New York: McGraw-Hill, 1981.

WEB SITE

Master Painters Institute: www.paintinfo.com

09931 EXTERIOR WOOD STAINS

This chapter discusses general surface preparation, material preparation, and application procedures for exterior wood stains.

This chapter does not discuss interior stains.

PRODUCT EVALUATIONS

Exterior wood stains have been manufactured for more than 100 years. In the past 50 years, they have become increasingly popular as an alternative to paint. Buildings of all types in every part of the United States use wood stain. Residential construction is the major market for wood stain; however, exterior wood stain has been used effectively on churches, motels, small office buildings, neighborhood shopping centers, and similar commercial establishments. As use of redwood, cedar, and similar wood increases in commercial applications, so does the use of wood stain.

Wood stains differ from other coatings because their major ingredients—oil and pigment—deeply penetrate the substrate and strengthen the wood fibers. They add color and provide a breathing ultraviolet-resistant finish; but, unlike paint, they do not form a closed surface film. Paint hides the grain and texture of wood. Many owners want to use stains rather than paint because they prefer seeing wood grain and texture. Stains may also contain water repellents and preservatives to protect the wood from decay, rot, mildew, water damage, and similar deleterious effects. Related products include pigmented bleaching agents, clear wood finishes, preservatives, and exterior wood restoring agents, all of which are also widely used and contribute to the diversity of exterior wood finishes.

Table 1 lists various coatings, including stains, for use on exterior wood.

PRODUCT SELECTION

Selection Considerations

Selecting the proper stain for a particular application requires evaluating many elements, including the types of stains available, the variety of wood, and the nature and function of the substrate receiving the stain. Consideration must also be given to correcting problems with surfaces, such as mildew or extractive bleeding; if such problems are not corrected, the application could become unsightly within a short time. Each of these elements is important and should be thoroughly evaluated before deciding on the stain type.

Semitransparent Stains

Semitransparent stains are lightly pigmented. They add color but do not obscure the grain of the wood. For best results with semitransparent stains, the wood should be porous. Most semitransparent stains are oil- or oil/alkyd-based products, but acrylic- and water-based products are becoming more widely available as stain manufacturers try to produce environmentally friendly products. Although most products are intended for exterior application only, some brands are acceptable for limited interior use on paneling and cabinets. For health and environmental reasons, consult the stain manufacturer before applying any exterior stains indoors.

- **Application:** Manufacturers recommend applying semitransparent stains to new wood or over previously stained semitransparent stain of a similar or lighter color. These stains may be applied to rough wood, such as shingles and shakes, and on smooth, rough-sawn, or textured siding. They may also be applied to unstained or previously stained weathered surfaces. One coat may cover sufficiently when applied to rough wood or to decks and fences, but most manufacturers recommend two coats to ensure adequate coverage and better absorption. Two coats are usually recommended over smooth-surface wood such as clapboard siding.
- **Fences and decks:** Most manufacturers recommend semitransparent stains for application on wood decks, fences, and lawn furniture. One coat is usually sufficient when semitransparent stain is applied to decks and fences, but two coats ensure adequate coverage and better absorption.
- **Limitations:** Do not apply semitransparent stain over previously painted wood, primed hardboard siding, or medium-density overlaid plywood.

Semisolid-Color Stains

Semisolid-color stains are available from few manufacturers that distribute products nationally. Because these stains are linseed-oil based, and most manufacturers are concentrating their research efforts on developing water-borne alternatives to oil/alkyd-based stains, it is possible that no regional manufacturers offer them. They are richly pigmented, deep-penetrating, oil-based stains that provide long-lasting wood protection. Semisolid-color stains have greater hiding power than semitransparent stains, and the flat finish highlights the natural beauty of the wood's texture. They are ideal where hiding coverage is desired and penetrating wood protection is needed. They are also outstanding as a one-coat finish for recoating previously semitransparent stained surfaces.

Solid-Color Stains

Solid-color stains are heavily pigmented and have exceptional hiding power. They cover like paint and conceal the grain. Solid-color stains are available in an oil, oil/alkyd, or acrylic-latex base. They can be applied to a greater variety of surfaces than semitransparent or semisolid types because of their hiding power. They are often used to coat surfaces previously stained with semitransparent or semisolid stains. Unlike other types, solid-color stains can be used on previously painted surfaces and medium-density overlaid plywood. They should not be used on horizontal surfaces such as decks and patio furniture.

- **Application:** Follow the manufacturer's recommendations for the number of coats required to cover a surface with a solid-color stain; pay

Table 1
COATINGS FOR EXTERIOR WOOD: TYPES AND USES

SUBSTRATE		COATING SYSTEM TOPCOAT; TYPE AND BASE		PRINCIPAL BINDER	COATING GLOSS	COLOR RETENTION	SUBSTRATE SURFACE CONDITION	NOTES TO DESIGNER OR SPECIFIER
Wood Dry, Vertical	SIDING, vertical/horizontal • recommended moisture content not over 12% • protected from moisture or limited occasional exposure to water Typical components: • veneered plywood siding • MDO plywood siding • hardboard siding • redwood siding • cedar siding, shingles, and shakes	clear; solvent	topcoat	phenolic, tung oil	gloss semigloss	poor	dry only	1. Clear coatings are not recommended for plywood. 2. Light color stains have shorter durability than heavily pigmented ones. 3. PVA is used on yellow pine and red cedar. 4. Acrylic is resistant to ultraviolet rays, thus doesn't become brittle or yellowed. 5. No coating for wet wood has been recommended; wood should be dry before any coating is applied. 6. Opaque stains hide surface imperfections and will last longer but will also hide the wood grain. 7. Wood requires primer to equalize absorption; hardboards require filler to smooth out grain. 8. Always use oil-based primer under any coating on cedar and redwood. 9. Backprime and edge seal wood in locations subject to occasional moisture penetration or to water vapor migration and/or condensation. Unless properly sealed, only permeable coatings such as acrylic should be used; even then, they may peel. 10. Clear phenolic coatings may be protected with alkyd-type clear coatings for better color retention. 11. All knots and pitch streaks should be sealed with shellac and all nails set and nail holes filled. 12. Even galvanized, ferrous metal nails may corrode and stain water-based coatings because such coatings allow water vapor to penetrate to the nails, increasing the possibility of rusting. 13. Alkyds may react with chemicals in previous coatings. 14. Clear finishes for trim and doors may be pigmented to stain the wood, or a staining primer may be used. 15. Extensive surface preparation, when required, applies to both previously coated and uncoated surfaces but principally to previously coated ones.
			primer	self-priming, topcoat, or shellac			dry only	
		stain; water, or solvent	topcoat	alkyd, oil base, self-priming (solvent)	flat	fair	dry only	
		opaque; solvent	topcoat	alkyd	gloss semigloss	good	dry only	
			primer	alkyd, oil base			dry only	
		opaque; water	topcoat	acrylic	semigloss flat	excellent	may be damp	
			primer	alkyd, oil base acrylic, emulsion			dry only	
	TRIM • recommended moisture content not over 12% • occasional exposure to moisture or water Typical components: • shutters • doors • accent areas of limited size • railings	clear; solvent	topcoat	urethane, one part oil modified	gloss semigloss	fair	dry only	
			primer	self-priming			dry only	
		stain; solvent	topcoat	none recommended				
		opaque; water or solvent	topcoat	alkyd, oil base (solvent)	gloss semigloss	good	dry only	
			primer	alkyd, oil base			dry only	

particular attention to special requirements for certain types of wood, such as cypress. One coat is usually sufficient to cover wood, but two coats are recommended when making a radical color change. Two coats are also recommended for certain wood such as southern yellow pine. If coating new or bare wood with a light-colored stain, a primer may be required. A primer may also be required when an acrylic-latex material is used, particularly if the substrate is cedar, redwood, or Douglas fir. The primer protects against discoloration from extractive bleeding.

Bleaching Agents

Bleaching agents are special stain-related products that accelerate the natural weathering process on raw wood. Bleaching agents are usually linseed-oil-based products that produce a uniform driftwood-gray color that closely resembles the color achieved by most wood after several years of exposure to the elements. These products are usually lightly tinted with a light-gray pigment for initial color. After exposure to the elements for six months to a year, the wood develops a natural gray color.

- **Application:** Use bleaching agents only on raw uncoated wood, either smooth or rough, on siding, trim, fences, shingles, and shakes. One coat is usually adequate over rough wood surfaces. Most manufacturers recommend a second coat over smooth wood surfaces, such as clapboard, after the first coat has thoroughly dried. Apply bleaching agents with a brush or roller.
- **Dipping:** Some, but not all, stain manufacturers recommend dipping to

apply bleaching agents to wood shingles and shakes because this produces the most uniform color.
- **Limitations:** Do not use bleaching agents for interior work or on creosote-treated wood surfaces that have been painted, stained, or sealed.

Clear Wood Finishes

Clear wood finishes provide a transparent finish that allows the natural color of the wood to show. They contain a water repellent for protection against mildew, rot, and decay. A wood preservative and a mildewcide may also be added for additional protection. They are often used as a primer before painting or staining to help stabilize the wood and guard against warping or splitting. Clear wood finishes are not recommended for interior use.

- **Application:** Apply clear wood finishes and preservatives with a brush or brush pad to work the material into the surface of the wood. Two coats are usually recommended, unless applying as a primer under paint or another stain. These materials may also be applied by dipping for three to five minutes to achieve a uniform finish.

Wood Varieties

The wood substrate determines the type of stain that will be used on a project. Some manufacturers do not recommend using certain products on some wood species. Some wood species require more coats than others; some require primers under certain stains; some contain natural materials that bleed and discolor but do not otherwise damage the wood surface; others must be kiln-dried before staining. Wood that has weathered, even for a short time, shows signs of surface deterioration and needs some treatment before stain can be applied successfully. Some types of plywood that have been processed to remove the soft wood grain are difficult for a stain to penetrate.

- **Redwood and cedar:** These wood species are most closely associated with the use of wood stain; however, they contain natural water-soluble colorings that bleed, show through, and discolor some coatings. Such discoloration is not harmful and can be removed with a mild detergent wash. Using oil-based stains protects these woods against bleeding. If solid-color stains are used, some manufacturers recommend using a primer. Most solid-color stains cover redwood and cedar in a single application, although a primer is often required under a solid-color latex stain. If using semitransparent stains or certain bleaching agents over redwood and cedar, two coats may be required to achieve ideal results.
- **Cypress, spruce, and pine:** These species should be kiln-dried before stain is applied. Even when staining kiln-dried wood, oil-based coatings take a long time to dry; therefore, application of two thin coats is advised. If using a latex-based stain on southern yellow pine, apply two coats.
- **Fir and hemlock:** Almost any oil-based stain is appropriate for these woods. Some manufacturers recommend using an undercoat when the finish coat is a latex-based, solid-color stain. One coat is enough if using a solid-color stain. Two coats are required for semitransparent applications.
- **Mahogany:** Several manufacturers indicate that many mahogany varieties are difficult to stain because of the nature of the wood. Most varieties are hard and open-grained and do not take stain well. Furthermore, some varieties from the Philippines are of poor quality and are rarely used for exterior work.
- **Weathered wood:** The surface of unfinished wood exposed to the elements begins to deteriorate after a short time. Surface fibers change to a gray color and lose their adhesion to the fibers below, which can result in a poor finish application if not corrected. Before applying a coating, the weathered surface must be thoroughly cleaned with a chemical cleaning solution or by blasting with high-pressure water. It is essential that all deteriorated wood fibers be removed before stains are applied. Once the surface has been properly prepared, almost any stain may be applied.

Special Applications

Certain applications, as well as some wood species, may directly influence the type of stain to be used.

- **Wood roofs** are subject to more weather-related problems than vertical siding because roofs are directly exposed to sunlight, rain, and snow, and are more difficult to coat successfully. Clear wood finishes protect against major problems such as splitting and warping, and they protect wood shingles and shakes from moisture-related damage and rot. Unfortunately, it is necessary to reapply them at least every two years. Semitransparent stains may also be applied and will achieve similar results. Solid-color stains should not be applied to wood roofing.
- **Wood decks:** Exterior horizontal wood surfaces subject to abrasion, such as wood decks and railings, are difficult to coat. Do not use solid-color stains that form a film on the surface because they soon crack and peel, become abraded by traffic, or are otherwise damaged. Several manufacturers make products specially designed for exterior horizontal surfaces. Others recommend using their semitransparent stains because they penetrate deeply into the wood and do not form a film on the surface.

SURFACE PROBLEMS

Some wood surfaces are more prone than others to problems that affect stain application. Some wood species contain natural elements that may develop surface problems that affect stain application. The most serious problems for stains are mildew, extractive bleeding, and surfactant leaching.

Mildew

Mildew is caused by a fungus that thrives in warm, moist areas. It can occur anywhere conditions are favorable for growth; it is a major problem near seacoasts, lakes, and rivers, and in areas of high humidity. Mildew usually appears on the wood surface as large clusters of small brown or black spots and is easily mistaken for dirt. It grows rapidly through or on any coating applied over it. It must be detected and removed before applying wood stain, particularly when restaining previously stained surfaces. If mildew is not removed, it will continue to grow through the new coating.

- **Preventive measures:** Proper storage and handling of construction materials help prevent mildew from developing on new construction. Most stains contain a mildewcide to help make the wood mildew resistant. If mildew is suspected, it is easy to test a sample by placing a drop of chlorine bleach on the suspect area; if gas bubbles develop and the area lightens, mildew is present.
- **Removal procedures:** Mildew can usually be removed by scrubbing the surface with a solution of 1 cup (0.25 L) of nonammoniated detergent and 1 quart (1 L) of chlorine bleach dissolved in 3 quarts (3 L) of warm water; follow the scrubbing with a clear-water rinse. For heavier mildew, follow the stain manufacturer's written recommendations to avoid damaging the surface.

Extractive Bleeding

Redwood, cedar, Douglas fir, and mahogany contain natural water-soluble materials that migrate to the surface of coatings. This migration is known as extractive bleeding, and the result is a reddish-brown color that is unsightly but does not damage the wood or the durability of the coating.

- **Removal:** Most extractive bleeding can be corrected by rinsing the surface with mild detergent and water. Stubborn problems may require washing with a solution of 1 part denatured alcohol to 1 part water. Extreme cases will require scrubbing with an oxalic-acid solution.
- **Oxalic-Acid-Solution Cleaning:** This procedure can damage plant life and foliage; follow the manufacturer's written recommendations and cautions when using oxalic-acid solutions. After a surface is treated with an oxalic-acid solution, it must be rinsed thoroughly with clear water and allowed to dry before it is stained. Previously stained surfaces may require restaining because this treatment may lighten the color of the previous stain.

Surfactant Leaching

Surfactant leaching, also called watermarking or water spotting, is a term used to describe discoloration caused by moisture. This problem is most evident on dark colors and often occurs at or near uncoated ends of boards exposed to the weather. It can be removed by following the procedures to remove extractive bleeding. Surfactant leaching may occur on dark-colored surfaces covered with latex stain if the surface is exposed to either moisture or the elements before curing thoroughly. Coating the edges of boards will help prevent surfactant leaching.

- **Preventive measures:** Do not apply stain during wet or damp weather; allow the stain enough time to cure properly if weather conditions are conducive to fog, dew, or rain. If surfactant leaching occurs, remove it before recoating or the marks will be transmitted into successive coats.
- **Removing watermarks:** In warm weather, several rinses with clear water will often remove watermarks. Normal washing by subsequent rainfall is also adequate to remove watermarks. If multiple rinses are not effective, the only solution is to recoat after removing the cause of the problem.

APPLICATION CONSIDERATIONS

Material Preparation

As with all coating materials, stains must be thoroughly mixed to ensure the best results and a uniform color. If the stains are not thoroughly mixed, a discernable difference in color may occur. For custom colors that are made by combining two or more standard colors, the contents of all cans of stain must be thoroughly blended before application begins. To ensure color consistency of pigmented stains, one manufacturer recommends the following:

- Pour top oil from a freshly opened can of stain into another container. Mix the contents of the first can using a wide paddle. When the contents of the first can are thoroughly mixed, pour the oil back into the original can and remix. Then pour the contents from one can to the other several times so pigments are thoroughly mixed. Continue the pouring action until no residue remains on the bottom of either can.
- If a project requires more than one batch, blend the contents of all cans, following the procedure described above, and thoroughly intermix them to ensure a uniform color throughout a project. If this procedure is not followed, a discernible difference in color between different parts of a project could result.

These preparation procedures are necessary particularly when two or more standard colors are mixed to produce a custom color. In these circumstances, it is essential to blend the contents of all containers. Without thorough intermixing, a discernable color difference between different areas would be more pronounced than with a stock color. Frequent stirring during application is also necessary because the pigment tends to settle in the bottom of the can.

Application

Wood stains may be applied by brush, roller, or spray, or the wood can be prestained before installation by dipping or machine application. Most manufacturers recommend applying stains with a natural-bristle brush; a brush holds more oil and is better for working the stain into the surface for maximum penetration. Using a long-napped roller is the next best application method.

Spraying is the application method manufacturers prefer least because it results in poor performance. Although it is an efficient delivery method, it may not provide adequate coverage. Furthermore, overspray damage to adjacent buildings and automobiles is expensive to repair. The best advice is not to spray on windy days. If stain is applied by spraying, it should be applied liberally and followed by back-brushing to work the stain into the surface and to even out spray patterns.

Maintaining a wet edge when staining is important.. This practice is important to ensure a uniform finish color and to avoid lap marks. For clear wood finishes, some manufacturers prefer the wet-on-wet method of application, where the second coat is applied immediately after the first coat without permitting the first coat to dry.

Stirring the material occasionally during application is necessary to maintain color consistency.

Pretreating siding with stain before installation is the best application method.

Dipping is frequently used for individual shingles or shakes; machine-prestaining is used for clapboards, beveled siding, and plywood. Dipping is used to apply bleaching agents, clear wood finishes, and semitransparent stains. Unfortunately, manufacturers do not have uniform recommendations for dipping. Some manufacturers suggest partially immersing units and dipping them rapidly in and out of the liquid. Others recommend completely submerging individual units for a short time, then allowing them to drain and dry thoroughly. Regardless of the method, each piece must be allowed to dry while the surface that will be exposed in the finished work is untouched.

Some manufacturers suggest tossing dipped shingles or shakes into a loose pile to avoid stacking, but this method is not recommended. Back-brushing must be used to unify the color and remove striations, runs, and dip marks.

ENVIRONMENTAL CONSIDERATIONS

This discussion addresses only those aspects of federal and state regulations governing VOCs that affect exterior wood stains. For more detailed information about these regulations and the problems they create for the coatings industry, review Chapter 09910, Painting, which provides a detailed history of VOC regulations and recent actions by the Environmental Protection Agency (EPA).

Environmental Regulations

On September 13, 1999, after many years of delay and controversy, the first national regulation imposing limits on VOC content in paints and other construction products went into effect. These regulations limit the amount of VOCs in coatings as follows: flat interior and exterior architectural coatings, a maximum of 250 g/L; in nonflat interior or exterior coatings, a maximum of 380 g/L; in clear and semitransparent stains, a maximum of 550 g/L; and in opaque stains, a maximum of 350 g/L. Although these regulations impose national limits on VOC content, state and local governments may impose harsher limits if their particular situation is serious enough to warrant such action. Enactment and enforcement of national regulations are welcome after the confusion that has been characteristic of this issue for more than 30 years.

Unfortunately, the enactment of these new regulations will not totally end the problem. Some states, have enacted regulations that are more restrictive.

The Future

The EPA is expected to impose even more stringent requirements on wood stain products. For this reason, most stain manufacturers are actively attempting to develop alternative products that will satisfy the desire of owners and architects for the pleasing appearance characteristic of the solvent-based wood stain common today. Many companies now offer solid-color exterior wood stains that are based on acrylic resins and are normally lower in VOC content than their oil- and oil/alkyd-based products; these products have a record of successful service. For semitransparent stains, however, the future is bleaker. A few companies offer acrylic-based semitransparent stains, and reports on the performance of these products is uneven. Several companies admit to working on waterborne products but are not satisfied with the results and will not currently offer them for commercial sale. This unwillingness only indicates that further development is needed before products are offered that will satisfy all requirements.

Recent history indicates that environmental regulations are subject to change and refinement. Informed paint and coating commentators and trade publications expect enactment of even more stringent regulations in the future. The specifier should contact the local or regional EPA office for current information or interpretation of regulations for unusual circumstances.

09945 MULTICOLORED INTERIOR COATINGS

This chapter discusses polychromatic paint.

This chapter does not discuss paint, fire-retardant coatings, high-performance architectural coatings, or industrial coatings.

PRODUCT CHARACTERISTICS

Multicolored interior coatings gained wide acceptance after World War II as a cost-effective alternative to decorative construction and industrial coatings. Because of their excellent hiding capability, multicolored coatings are particularly useful for coating irregular surfaces; they disguise surface imperfections that are difficult to hide with conventional coatings. These coatings are also used for their inherent decorative effect or as a faux stone finish.

Multicolored interior coatings can be more durable than paint, less costly than vinyl wall covering, and easier to maintain than either. Unlike wall covering, they are applied without seams. Touching up and repairing damaged surfaces requires conventional spray equipment. Designed for almost all interior vertical surfaces, multicolored coatings are not recommended for surfaces subject to wear. Consult manufacturers for unusual applications.

Solvent-based multicolored coatings consist of discrete beads of pigment coated with resin and suspended in an aqueous solution that contains a suitable stabilizing agent. This water-based solution keeps the pigment beads from mixing or rupturing prematurely. The coating is always spray applied, and the pigment beads rupture and spatter either at the nozzle of the spray device or on contact with the surface to be coated. Because pigment beads are fragile, the shelf life of solvent-based multicolored coatings is usually limited to six to 18 months.

Water-based, multicolored-coating formulations vary. Some consist of pigment beads suspended in an aqueous solution, similar to solvent-based formulas. Some use three separate containers of paint that are simultaneously spray applied using a separate nozzle for each color.

Water-based formulations have less odor, lower VOCs, and are easier to clean up than traditional solvent-based multicolored coatings. Water-based, multicolored finish coats are applied in the same manner as solvent-based products—with spray equipment. They are appropriate for projects where adjacent spaces are occupied.

PRODUCT SELECTION CONSIDERATIONS

Optional topcoats are available from some manufacturers and are for applications requiring increased wear performance. They improve the multicolored coating's resistance to water, stains, and soil, and are available in low or gloss sheens.

Preformulated color mixtures and custom formulations are available. Custom-formulated coatings are specified by determining the fleck colors, fleck sizes, and color proportions. Custom formulations may cost more.

APPLICATION CONSIDERATIONS

Proper equipment is essential for successfully applying multicolored coatings. A compressor, a pressure tank with dual regulation, and an air spray gun with an internal mix nozzle are required for most multicolored coatings. Using an external nozzle or an airless system will overatomize the coating, producing a solid color. Unlike conventional paint, multicolored coatings should not be agitated or thinned before application.

Multicolored interior coatings are typically applied in two steps with conventional equipment. Generally, the background coat is applied with the air pressure higher than the fluid pressure, atomizing the different-colored particles and producing an almost monochromatic coat. Some manufacturers apply a solid-color background coat with a brush or roller. The pattern coat is spray applied with the air pressure lower than the fluid pressure; this distributes different-colored flecks in proportion to the quantity of beads of each color in the mix.

Larger flecks of color are produced by two methods in solvent-based multicolored coatings: enlarging the pigment beads or lowering the spray-equipment air pressure. Most manufacturers do not offer a range of pigment bead sizes; they vary tonal effects by lowering air pressure.

09960 HIGH-PERFORMANCE COATINGS

This chapter discusses *high-performance coatings for architectural and industrial applications.*

This chapter does not discuss *high-temperature-resistant coatings, which are covered in 09975, High-Temperature-Resistant Coatings, or coatings for immersion service.*

DEFINITIONS

Special Coating

The coatings industry considers any coating material designed for a particular purpose and requiring more than normal skills and techniques for mixing, handling, and application, a special coating. High-performance coatings fit this description because they are designed to resist severe or corrosive environments and other forms of abuse. A special coating system includes prime, intermediate, and finish coats.

Table 1 lists various special coatings including high-performance coatings. Cementitious coatings, elastomeric coatings, high-temperature-resistant coatings, and itumescent paints are additional types of special coatings that are discussed in other chapters.

Environment

The terms *mild, moderate,* and *severe,* as used in this chapter to describe the environmental conditions a high-performance coating is expected to resist, are not precise. Without a standard quantitative measurement to establish their exact meaning, these terms are subject to interpretation. Words such as *aggressive, harsh,* and *corrosive* are frequently used in manufacturers' literature to designate environmental conditions without additional qualification or embellishment. Each manufacturer uses whatever words and phrases it finds most advantageous to describe environmental conditions relative to its products. The definitions in the list below establish meanings for the three environmental levels that are discussed in this chapter.

- **Mild:** Normal outdoor weathering and standard industrial exposures are considered mild environments. A normal industrial setting is one with low to moderate levels of humidity and condensation and little development of mold and mildew. A mild environment has only limited exposure to chemical fumes or mist, and occasional occurrences of chemical spills or splash. Regular cleaning with standard commercial chemical cleaning agents, with only occasional use of stronger chemical cleaning agents, is also characteristic of a mild environment. Metal corrosion will occur in a mild environment, but it is minimal.
- **Moderate:** An atmosphere that can be characterized as corrosive within reasonable limits is considered to be a moderate environment. In an industrial setting, a moderate environment indicates intermittent exposure to high humidity and condensation with occasional development of mold and mildew. Exposure to heavy concentrations of chemical fumes or mist and accidental chemical spills or splash occur occasionally in a moderate environment. Regular use of strong chemicals rather than standard commercial cleaning agents also changes a mild environment into a moderate one. Metal corrosion is common in a moderate environment.

- **Severe:** An aggressively corrosive industrial or predominantly chemical environment with regular exposure to strong chemical fumes, mists, and dust is considered a severe environment. In an industrial setting, a severe environment is one with sustained exposure to high humidity and condensation that results in heavy development of mold and mildew. Frequent spilling and splashing of strong chemicals (acids, alkalis, and solvents) are also characteristic of a severe environment. Metal corrosion can be expected in a severe environment. Immersion conditions, marine environments with sustained exposure to saltwater spray, and arctic environments with long periods of extremely low temperatures are considered severe environments. Use of high-performance coatings is often recommended for these conditions.

RELATED WORK

This chapter discusses only polyamide epoxy, aliphatic polyurethane, and waterborne acrylic high-performance coating systems. These coating systems are designed to protect ordinary building substrates from the effects of highly corrosive atmospheres, such as those found in chemical and industrial plants. These products are also frequently used in buildings where the nature of the occupancy rather than the environment is expected to be the source of heavy abuse; health facilities and educational institutions are examples. Regardless of the coating or environment, consult knowledgeable representatives of the coating manufacturer during the preparation of high-performance coating specifications.

Other generic products, such as polyesters, silicones, and vinyls, and combinations of generic products, such as acrylic epoxies and acrylic polyurethanes, are also used as high-performance coatings. These products have specific properties that may make them more suitable for use in certain situations than other products. When the coating manufacturer recommends their use, they should be considered as viable alternatives.

Highly specialized coating systems include cementitious coatings, elastomeric coatings, high-temperature-resistant coatings, and intumescent paints. These systems are designed for particular uses or exposures and often require application by specially trained applicators. Like high-performance coatings, they fall under the general heading of "special coatings." However, because of the special purpose of these materials, they are discussed separately in other chapters.

Other Specialty Coating Systems

Abrasion-resistant, chemical-resistant, graffiti-resistant, and immersion coatings are also considered to be special coatings because of the unique properties they possess. Before specifying these materials, consult a manufacturer's representative.

GENERAL COMMENTS

Coating technology is constantly evolving. Every year research chemists develop new materials for use by the coatings industry. In turn, manufacturers use these materials to develop new products and adjust existing

Table 1
SPECIAL COATINGS

DEFINITION

Special coatings are adhesive materials that have been developed for specific purposes such as resisting severe or corrosive environments or other forms of abuse. Special skills and techniques are usually required to mix, handle, and apply these materials.

A ìspec ial coating systemî includes applied materials used in prime, intermediate, and finish coats. Factors that influence the choice of a system include

1. Substrates
2. Environmental conditions and surroundings
3. Cost

Prime and finish coats should be specified from the same manufacturer to eliminate many compatibility problems.

Proper substrate preparation, priming, and spread rate thickness are important for successful application of special coatings. Application is made by spray, brush, roller, or trowel.

SURFACE PREPARATION

The major reason coatings fail is poor surface preparation, which impairs adhesion. No coating is better than the surface over which it is applied. Surfaces must be prepared by a method suited to how they will be used and the exposure they will receive, in accordance with manufacturers' recommendations and SSPC: The Society for Protective Coatings.

METAL SURFACES

Before a coating is applied, metal surfaces must be thoroughly cleaned, eliminating all visible deposits of surface dirt, grease, oil, and other deposits. Loose mill scale, rust, paint, and other detrimental foreign matter must also be removed. Grind rough welds and sharp edges, and remove weld spatter.

The SSPC recommends a variety of methods for preparing steel surfaces before application of a coating:

SSPC-SP-1 Solvent Cleaning
SSPC-SP-2 Hand Tool Cleaning
SSPC-SP-3 Power Tool Cleaning
SSPC-SP-5 White Metal Blast Cleaning
SSPC-SP-6 Commercial Blast Cleaning
SSPC-SP-7 Brush-off Blast Cleaning
SSPC-SP-8 Pickling
SSPC-SP-10 Near-White Blast Cleaning

CONCRETE AND MASONRY SURFACES

Coatings adhere best to clean and slightly rough substrates. Grease, dirt, oils, efflorescence, laitance, and other surface deposits must be removed before additional surface preparation begins. Cleaning may be achieved by methods such as mechanical abrasion, abrasive blast, high pressure water wash, or acid etching. If cleaning solutions are applied, they must be completely removed before the coating is applied. Surfaces must be dry. If the surface is very smooth, it must be abraded or roughened slightly.

TYPES OF SPECIAL COATINGS

CEMENTITIOUS COATINGS

Polymer-modified, inorganic coatings can be ideal on concrete and masonry substrates. These coatings are primarily used on vertical surfaces above or below grade, on the exterior or interior, and on new construction or restoration and renovation work for aesthetics, permeability, and moisture resistance. They are also useful for walls subject to positive or negative hydrostatic pressure.

ABRASION-RESISTANT COATINGS

Epoxy or elastomeric seamless coating may be used over substrates of brick, stucco, concrete, block, drywall, and plywood in both interior and exterior applications. These coatings may be weatherproof and resist chemicals. Abrasion resistance may be inherent or achieved through an additional topcoat.

ELASTOMERIC COATINGS

Acrylic polymer coatings may be used over exterior concrete, masonry, and stucco surfaces. These thick, dirt-resistant, membranelike coatings are flexible in a range of temperatures, displaying an ability to follow expansion and contraction of surfaces without rupturing or wrinkling. They are very high-build materials that bridge small cracks and protect against deterioration from moisture penetration of the substrate. Like other special coatings, these typically should not be used to bridge building expansion joints. Acrylic polymer coatings are available in smooth and textured finishes.

HIGH-BUILD GLAZED COATINGS

Acrylic resin, elastomeric, or epoxy coatings may be suitable for use over exterior or interior concrete, block, masonry, plaster, stucco, wood, and metal surfaces in vertical or horizontal applications. Applied in multiple coats or thick single coats, these coatings usually provide resistance to chemicals and abrasion. These high-performance coatings provide good adhesion and hardness, producing a tile-like gloss finish. Some systems may be reinforced with fiberglass mesh between base and seal coats to increase maximum impact resistance.

FIRE-RESISTANT PAINTS

Fire-resistant paints are able to withstand fire and protect the substrate for short periods of time, usually less than one hour. They will not support combustion and do not deteriorate readily under fire conditions. They will reduce or prevent the spread of flame over a combustible surface. In some cases they may be used as one component of a fire-rated assembly. The products of such an assembly are noncombustible, and the coating, which prevents oxygen from reaching the substrate, contains chemicals that inhibit the release of volatile gases necessary for combustion.

To be eligible for listing as a fire-retardant paint, a coating must either reduce the flame spread of the surface to which it is applied by at least 30% or have a flame spread rating of 70 or less as tested under current ASTM E-84 guidelines. Manufacturers may recommend a three- to five-year schedule for reapplying the coating in order to maintain its fire-resistant capability. Fire-resistant paints can be used to coat wood, drywall, plaster, and metal.

INTUMESCENT PAINTS

Intumescent paint is a type of fire-resistant paint that behaves differently than typical such products in a fire condition. When subjected to flame or intense heat, intumescent paints liquefy, allowing escaping gases to form an insulating layer of char, which forms a protective layer around the substrate. Fire-resistant designs have been tested by independent laboratories to establish application requirements and the extent of protection available. Incompatible paints used as a topcoat with intumescent paints may prevent the chemical reactions necessary to form the intumescent char, thereby reducing or negating the fire-resistant property.

GRAFFITI-RESISTANT COATINGS

Graffiti-resistant coatings permit the easy removal of graffiti without damage to the substrate. The system comprises a multicoat base system that increases the hardness of the substrate and a sacrificial, multicoat topcoat system. Cleaners can be nontoxic and do not require sandblasting, solvents, or toxic materials. Additional topcoats can be added after cleaning, if desired, to reinforce the sacrificial protection layer.

COATING SYSTEMS FOR STEEL

Selection of steel coating systems for tanks and piping are primarily governed by substrate and service conditions. Industry specific standards also affect specifications. Water treatment, food processing, energy production, and chemical processing industries have different requirements and standards that should be verified prior to specification. Water tanks in most U.S. jurisdictions must meet very stringent National Sanitary Foundation (NSF) requirements for potable water storage.

EXTERIOR COATING SYSTEM FOR STEEL STORAGE TANKS

Choice of coating for steel storage tank exteriors depends on tank condition and location, the weather during application, and the service conditions. A number of two-part epoxy systems and urethane systems have been formulated to address these concerns. Coatings may possess rust-inhibitive qualities, the ability to cure at low-temperatures, and excellent weathering ability and may offer galvanic protection. Dry-fall ability may be desirable in some instances and is available from alkyd products. Compatible products can be used as metal fillers and to accelerate curing rates. Local regulations regarding the content of volatile organic compounds (VOCs) will influence product selection and application techniques.

INTERIOR COATING SYSTEM FOR STEEL STORAGE TANKS

Choice of coatings for steel storage tank interiors is affected by tank condition and location and service conditions. A number of two-part epoxy systems and phenolic systems have been formulated to address these concerns. These products are designed to provide sustained immersion service in food processing, petrochemical, and water treatment industries for use in freshwater, saltwater, and severe chemical environments. National Sanitation Foundation (NSF) approvals may be necessary in certain applications.

COATING SYSTEM FOR STEEL PIPING

Coatings for steel piping are subject to many of the same conditions as coatings for steel tanks. Coatings for piping used for chemical service must be selected to match the level of chemical exposure expected. Mild exposures may permit the use of an acrylic coating, while aggressive chemical and moisture exposure may require the use of chlorinated rubber coatings. Severe chemical exposures typically require a two-part epoxy system.

The American Society of Mechanical Engineers and ANSI publish standardized color codes for pipe identification. For example, red means fire protection equipment; yellow, dangerous materials; blue, protective materials; green, safe materials; yellow with a black legend or stripe, radioactive materials.

formulations to improve the performance of their existing products. They design each coating for characteristics that enable it to perform properly within a given range of conditions on particular surfaces. One example of this evolution over the last 50 years is the rapid development and increasing use of high-performance coatings for substrate protection in harsh industrial and chemical environments.

Coating Formulas

High-performance coatings must meet the varying requirements of industry and satisfy the environmental requirements that exist under corrosive atmospheric conditions. Most coating manufacturers have developed unique product formulas that include ingredients that provide their coatings with special characteristics. Each ingredient in the formula is selected because it possesses some attribute desired in the coating. Combining several ingredients allows manufacturers to develop products with the particular qualities they want in the end product. Because combining ingredients may result in compromising other highly desirable qualities, manufacturers select their ingredients carefully.

Potential Problems

Some coatings that produce excellent results on metal cannot withstand the attack of lime in masonry. Coatings that perform well in a dry atmosphere may be unable to withstand conditions of extreme condensation. Coatings that provide optimum protection on interior surfaces may react unfavorably when exposed to direct sunlight. Coatings that perform exceptionally well when in contact with ordinary drinking water may break down when submerged in sewage. Coatings that have good alkaline resistance may have a low index of acid resistance, and vice versa.

Coating Characteristics

High-performance coatings are tough, dense, durable, organic coating systems. They achieve a seamless, high-build film and cure to a hard, glazed finish. Coatings for severe and moderate environments are usually based on an epoxy or polyurethane resin; coatings based on waterborne acrylic resins are often used in mild environments. They resist persistent heat and humidity, abrasion, staining, chemicals, and fungal growth. Although they are more expensive than other coatings, they perform effectively for many years without the need to recoat. As a result, life-cycle cost is usually much less than for conventional coatings in similar applications.

Areas of Use

Use high-performance architectural coatings where humidity is high; considerable wear is expected; chemical resistance, particularly to soiling, is needed; and strong detergents are used to maintain sanitary conditions. Typical uses include public halls and stairways, lavatories, locker areas, stall showers, animal pens, and biological laboratories. Food-processing areas, dairies, public buildings, restaurants, schools, and transportation terminals also are sites where these systems can be used to an advantage.

High-performance coating systems should be used only as recommended by the manufacturer because manufacturers formulate their products to be compatible with each other. These coating systems can be applied over properly prepared surfaces such as steel and masonry, including concrete masonry units. They can also be applied over plaster and gypsum wallboard. Because of their high-gloss finish, high-performance coating systems are often used in building interiors as an alternative to ceramic tile.

Dry Film Thickness

The capability of a coating to protect a substrate from the damaging effects of exposure to the environment depends, to a large extent, on the coating thickness. To achieve the ideal dry film thickness for its products, many manufacturers recommend a spreading rate, expressed in square feet per gallon (square meters per liter), for their products.

Occasionally, a substrate specified to be coated with a particular coating will be subjected to an unusually harsh environment in some locations on a project. Increasing the dry film thickness is not the solution to this problem. Some coating systems work best when the film thickness applied to a substrate is minimal. Increasing the amount of material applied to the surface, to increase the film thickness, may be detrimental to coating performance. Consult the manufacturer before increasing the dry film thickness.

COATING SELECTION

Coating Selection Process

When selecting a high-performance coating system, an architect must carefully evaluate many elements. Although several factors need to be considered, the two most important elements to evaluate are the severity of the environment and the actual cost of the coating system, including the cost of maintenance programs necessary to protect the system's integrity. These elements, plus careful analysis of the required level of surface preparation, should narrow the selection to the coating system best suited to the application. An architect should also evaluate the generic composition of the coating even though it usually has less impact on the selection process than the severity of the environment. A generic coating that is desirable for use on a particular substrate because of the severity of the atmosphere may not be compatible with the adjacent coatings and materials; in this situation, a different generic coating that is compatible with the adjacent coatings might be more suitable if it can withstand the environment.

Environmental Conditions

The atmosphere or environment to which a high-performance coating is subjected is the most important item to consider during the selection process. A coating system that cannot withstand severe corrosive environmental conditions is unsuitable where those conditions are known to exist. Conversely, a coating suitable for a harsh chemical environment is inappropriate in a mild environment, unless other conditions dictate its use. Fortunately, coating manufacturers have developed a range of generically diverse products. As a result, specifiers often have a choice of several generically different products suitable for almost any environmental situation. Their task is to select the product that is most appropriate for a particular application.

Classifications

Manufacturers designate their coatings as suitable for service under severe, moderate, or mild conditions. They may also classify their products as suitable for use in chemical or marine exposures. Manufacturers usually further classify coatings as suitable for immersion or nonimmersion service. Some coatings are also classified as suitable for use in highly corrosive environments. One manufacturer indicates that certain coatings are suitable for aggressive environments. Specifiers must determine the precise meaning of these terms before specifying a coating for a given application.

Cost

For many owners, product cost is the most important item to consider when selecting a coating system. Nevertheless, when evaluating high-performance coatings, specifiers should consider the protection achieved at the lowest cost per square foot (square meter) per year, not just the initial cost. If two generically different products provide the same level of protection and are suitable for use in the prevailing environment, most owners will select the system with the less-expensive first cost if all other considerations are equal. However, this is not always the most cost-effective procedure if coating maintenance is expected to be important. In many cases, recommending a high-performance coating system that has a higher initial cost than another system is the best advice a specifier can give an owner.

Coating Maintenance Costs

One cost element often overlooked is the cost of preventive maintenance for coatings. In most cases, regular cleaning and periodic inspection are all that is required to ensure that the coating integrity is intact. Sharp edges, exposed fastener heads, pipe threads, and other surfaces difficult to coat are often the first surfaces to show signs of coating degradation; a minor touchup is all that is required to maintain the integrity of the coating system. However, under adverse conditions, some coating systems may begin to degrade after prolonged exposure to an unexpectedly harsh environment, and recoating may be necessary to maintain the desired level of protection for the substrate. In this case, a lower first cost is often negated by the high cost of maintenance. This situation can be avoided by recognizing the potential problem at the outset and selecting a coating more suitable for the environment.

Coating Compatibility Problems

Specifiers must be vigilant when specifying high-performance coatings to be certain that the various coats that make up the system are compatible. Specifying that prime and finish coats be from the same manufacturer will help eliminate many compatibility problems. However, this presupposes that specifiers will follow the coating manufacturer's recommendations on which primer to use with a particular finish coat material. This also presupposes that applicators will follow the coating manufacturer's recommendations for surface preparation. Specifiers must also closely coordinate various specification sections that include shop-primed materials to ensure that prime coats applied by the manufacturer or fabricator are compatible with the finish coating system required on the particular item.

Solvent Strength

One of the most important factors in coating compatibility is the strength of the solvents in the various materials that make up the system. The purpose of solvents is to reduce the consistency of a coating's solids content so application is possible. Coatings contain various solids (film-forming binders) such as natural or synthetic resins, drying oils, combinations of drying oils and resins, and similar combinations. Different solids require different-strength solvents to reduce them to proper consistency. Some coatings contain weak solvents such as mineral spirits or turpentine. Other coatings require toluol, xylol, ketone, high-flash naphtha, or stronger solvents. The strength of a solvent in any one coating can have a favorable or an unfavorable effect on the entire system.

Coatings containing a mild solvent will not lift or disturb substrate coatings. In some cases, a mild-solvent coating might not form a good bond over a coating that is not softened by a mild solvent. A strong-solvent coating can wrinkle, lift, or destroy coatings that form a dry, hard film by polymerization or oxidation. Strong-solvent coatings partially dissolve lacquer-type coatings without lifting. This permits the merging or blending of coats, providing they are otherwise compatible. Often, coatings furnished in a flat finish can be coated over with a strong-solvent coating without wrinkling or lifting because of the bottom coat's high volume of pigment concentration.

Coating Film

Coatings form a film by changing to a solid state, by evaporation of the solvent alone, or by a combination of solvent evaporation and oxidation or polymerization of the film-forming binder that gradually hardens. Materials used in formulating a coating determine how quickly and to what extent the film becomes hard. How, when, and why a coating achieves a degree of hardness also influence the compatibility of particular coatings. For example, a straight phenolic dries hard in a short period and becomes almost insoluble in its own solvent. If successive coats of straight phenolic are applied with a drying period of one month between coats, the bond between coats will be poor. This occurs even though the same solvent is used in each successive coat. The same phenomenon exists in certain epoxy-resin coatings. These coatings cure by internal polymerization and form a film that is insoluble in its own solvent. The result is delamination, an eventual splitting away of one coat from another. In such cases, special surface preparation or certain solvent modifications to coats that will go over the bottom coat can eliminate the problem.

SURFACE PREPARATION

Substrate Condition

Poor surface preparation is the major factor in most coating failures. A properly prepared surface is critical to good coating performance because no coating is better than the surface over which it is applied. Coatings on ferrous metal quickly deteriorate when the surface contains moisture, dirt, grease, mill scale, rust, concrete dust, or other foreign materials that interfere with good coating performance. These substances constitute a barrier between the substrate and the coating. They usually intensify, then deteriorate and detach from the substrate, taking the coating with them. The subsequent failure should not be blamed on the coating but on the condition of the substrate before application. These failures are expensive to repair and can be avoided by properly preparing the substrate to receive the coating.

Surface-Preparation Requirements

The level of surface preparation required on any given substrate is determined by the nature of the surface, the environmental conditions to which the surface will be subjected, and the type of coating applied. Regardless of the nature of the substrate, the degree of surface preparation required for any substrate is directly proportional to the severity of the corrosive atmospheric elements the surface encounters. For example, ferrous-metal surfaces that will be continuously submerged in saltwater always require more thorough surface preparation than metal surfaces that will only be subjected to occasional exposure to ocean spray.

Steel

SSPC: The Society for Protective Coatings, formerly the Steel Structures Painting Council, has adopted several standards for preparation of steel surfaces. Four of these standards have also been adopted by the National Association of Corrosion Engineers (NACE) and are issued as joint surface-preparation standards. These standards vary in the intensity of the cleaning process and the result required. Basic SSPC surface preparation consists of wiping the substrate with a solvent to remove grease, oil, and other soluble surface contaminants and then using hand tools to remove loose rust, mill scale, and other loose surface contaminants. The highest levels of surface preparation require blasting the surface to white metal with an abrasive or "pickling" in an acid bath for complete removal of rust and mill scale. There are four separate levels of abrasive blasting surface preparation. SSPC's *Steel Structures Painting Manual* describes these blasting levels in detail.

Abrasive Blast Cleaning

The best surface preparation for steel is abrasive blast cleaning. Most coatings, including high-performance coatings, adhere best when steel surfaces to be coated have been thoroughly cleaned and profiled by abrasive blast methods. The following list describes, in declining order of the intensity of the cleaning process, the four SSPC/NACE joint standards for abrasive blast cleaning of steel surfaces:

- **SSPC-SP 5/NACE No. 1, *White Metal Blast Cleaning:*** This standard requires the complete removal of all visible rust, mill scale, paint, and other foreign matter by blast cleaning. It provides the best surface preparation available for steel. SSPC-SP 5/NACE No. 1 is also the most expensive of the various blast cleaning levels and should be used only when the high cost can be justified. It is required for steel exposed to extremely corrosive environments and for steel used in immersion service. The standard strongly suggests that surfaces cleaned to this level should be coated as soon as possible to preserve them against rust-back, which can occur within minutes under certain circumstances. SSPC recommends coating the surface within 24 hours to minimize the problem. Consult a qualified manufacturer's representative to determine if this level of surface preparation is required for unusually harsh environments.
- **SSPC-SP 10/NACE No. 2, *Near-White Blast Cleaning:*** This standard requires cleaning to near-white metal. It requires the complete removal of all rust, mill scale, and other deleterious matter, but permits residual random stain, amounting to less than 5 percent of a unit area of 9 sq. in. (6400 sq. mm) to remain on the surface under certain conditions. SSPC-SP 10/NACE No. 2 is satisfactory for all but the most demanding conditions and can be considerably lower in cost than the SSPC-SP 5/NACE No. 1 level. Nevertheless, it is still a costly level of surface preparation and should only be used when required to satisfy manufacturer's recommendations because of the aggressive nature of the environment. It is usually required for high-humidity conditions and in aggressive chemical, marine, and other highly corrosive environments. This level of surface preparation is recommended for severe exposures by many manufacturers of high-performance coatings.
- **SSPC-SP 6/NACE No. 3, *Commercial Blast Cleaning:*** This standard requires blast cleaning until at least two-thirds of the surface of a unit area of 9 sq. in. (6400 sq. mm) is free of visible rust, mill scale, paint, or other foreign matter. As a result, the surface is far from uniform in color. It is a general-purpose level of surface preparation and is used when a high, but not perfect, level of surface preparation is required. Because it is less demanding than SSPC-SP 10/NACE No. 2, it is much lower in cost. It is the level required by most coating manufacturers for all but the most severe environments.
- **SSPC-SP 7/NACE No. 4, *Brush-off Blast Cleaning:*** This is the least demanding of the four blast cleaning standards. It only requires that the metal be free of all except the most tightly adhering residue of mill scale and coatings. It is not recommended for severe conditions, and its use is generally not recommended by high-performance coating manufacturers.

Concrete

It is as important to properly prepare concrete substrates before applying a high-performance coating as it is to prepare steel. A concrete surface must be dry, clean, and in sound condition before the coating is applied. This means that the surface should not be wet; there should be no dust, dirt, grease, or oil present on the surface; and there should be no laitance or other surface defects that would impair the coating bond. Surface irregularities must also be removed.

- **Surface repair:** The first step in preparing a concrete substrate for coating is to correct surface defects such as mortar spatters, fins, bulges,

holes, and cracks. Surface repair should take place before any other form of surface preparation. This requires removing protrusions higher than $\frac{1}{16}$ inch (1.6 mm) by grinding or using impact tools and filling holes larger than $\frac{1}{8}$ inch (3.2 mm) in diameter with portland cement-based grout, dry-packed mortar, polymer-modified concrete, or other products suitable for repairing the defects. Cracks should be ground to a V-shaped notch before filling. The specific material used to repair concrete will depend on the size of the defect and the strength required in the finished work. To avoid problems, consult the coating manufacturer before undertaking concrete repairs. Some high-performance coating materials will react unfavorably to certain chemicals used in some concrete repair products. Early consultation will avoid compatibility problems.

- **Dryness:** A concrete substrate must be dry before any coating can be applied. Good construction practice requires a 28-day curing period before coating fresh concrete. However, in some situations, the concrete might not be thoroughly dry at the end of this period. If there is any doubt about the suitability of the surface, procedures outlined in ASTM D 4263, *Test Method for Indicating Moisture in Concrete by the Plastic Sheet Method,* may be followed to detect the presence of moisture in the substrate. If, after adequate curing time, tests reveal that the concrete is not dry enough to proceed, determine the reason the concrete is wet or damp. Often the cause of the problem is a hidden source of water that keeps the concrete wet. The best solution to hidden water problems is to find the source and eliminate the problem. However, the sources of water may be difficult to find, and correcting hidden problems of this type can be expensive. In extreme cases, it may be necessary to install extensive drainage systems or even a pumping system to remove unwanted water. Nevertheless, corrective action must be completed before coating can begin.
- **Cleaning concrete:** If the substrate is dry enough to apply a coating, the next step is to make certain the surface is clean enough to begin coating application. This means removing surface contaminants, including dust, dirt, oils, and grease. Broom or vacuum cleaning is usually adequate to remove loose surface dirt and dust. More severe problems may require the use of low- or medium-pressure water washing to remove stubborn dirt and loose debris.
- **Chemical cleaning:** Oil and grease require stronger cleaning procedures. In some cases, using detergents is adequate; however, scrubbing with caustic soda solutions or other chemical measures is often required. If chemicals are used for cleaning, the surface must be thoroughly flushed afterward to remove chemical residue. After chemical cleaning, the pH level of the substrate must be checked to make certain the surface is neutral or slightly alkaline. If it is not, the surface must be neutralized by rinsing with an alkaline solution, then rinsed again with an alkaline solution and rechecked. If chemicals do not work, steam cleaning may be required to remove contaminants. Finally, the surface must be allowed to dry thoroughly before applying coatings.
- **Unsound concrete repairs:** Surface defects must be repaired before coatings can be applied. Grinding or scarifying with power tools, abrasive blasting, and the use of high-pressure water are some techniques used to repair surface irregularities. Acid etching may be required to remove surface defects, such as laitance or efflorescence, in extreme circumstances. These repair techniques require experience and should only be performed by skilled workers.
- **Abrasive blasting:** Laitance, efflorescence, and other non-oil contaminants may be removed by blasting, using many dry and wet abrasives. Abrasive blasting also helps to open holes concealed below the surface and to roughen the surface for improved coating adhesion. After the blasting has been completed, residual dust and debris must be removed and the surface checked for voids and cracks, which must be repaired, as previously described.
- **Acid etching:** Laitance, efflorescence, and other non-oil contaminants may also be removed by acid etching. Because the acid must remain on

the surface for a few minutes, it is best used on horizontal surfaces. Some acids leave a residual salt on the surface, which may cause coating failure. Potential environmental problems exist with the use of these chemicals.

Masonry Surfaces

Concrete masonry units and other open-pored masonry surfaces do not present the best surface for high-performance coatings because the coating cannot bridge the pores and provide an even appearance. Most manufacturers recommend that block fillers compatible with the finish coats be applied to such surfaces. Sanitation or maintenance requirements may dictate using heavy-bodied block fillers.

Concrete and Masonry Surface Preparation Standards

There are few established standards for surface preparation of concrete or masonry substrates, although both SSPC and NACE have recently published joint documents on surface preparation of concrete.

Nonferrous Metals

Nonferrous metals, although not usually requiring sandblasting, do require definite surface preparation. Clean these surfaces with solvents to remove oxidation and oil that are almost always present. The pretreatment used in this system cannot secure a permanent bond unless such interfering materials are removed.

COATING SYSTEMS

General

This discussion describes the generic coating types most typically used in high-performance coating systems. As stated earlier, this chapter covers only those high-performance coating systems that use epoxy, polyurethane, or waterborne acrylic resins. Occasionally, in special circumstances, a high-performance coating system that uses alkyd, phenolic, polyester, or vinyl resins is justified or warranted. Both organic and inorganic zinc-rich coatings are frequently used, particularly as primers where the unique protective qualities of zinc are necessary to protect ferrous metals. Architects should review with a knowledgeable coating manufacturer's representative each project situation that requires the application of high-performance coatings to determine the suitability of a particular generic coating type for the service expected.

Each situation that requires the use of high-performance coatings is unique, and the atmosphere in certain severe environments may be more aggressively corrosive than others. Specifiers should select coating systems to suit the situation that exists for a project.

Epoxy Coatings

Epoxy resins are frequently used because of their excellent adhesion, toughness, and abrasion resistance. They also have good resistance to solvents, water, and chemicals. For these reasons, they have largely replaced alkyd coatings as the material of choice for use over steel and concrete on the interior of a building, for long-life protection of steel and concrete in severely corrosive environments. Epoxy resins are also frequently used as an intermediate coat under a polyurethane topcoat on the exterior of a building in severe environments. Their primary limitation is a tendency to yellow or chalk when exposed to direct sunlight. Epoxy coatings characteristically cure to a tough, slick finish. This can be an advantage if frequent surface cleaning is anticipated. However, where an epoxy is used as a primer or an intermediate coat, the slick film may be a problem because it is often difficult to apply a topcoat over a fully cured coating.

Thorough preparation of substrates, according to manufacturer's instructions for filling, sealing, cleaning, and priming, is important for successful application of epoxy coatings.

From the standpoint of use and composition, epoxies fall into the following three categories:

- Unmodified (unesterified) baking types
- Unmodified (unesterified) air-drying types
- Esterified types suitable for either air-drying or baked finishes

This discussion is restricted to air-drying types for field application. The United States Department of Agriculture permits both amine and polyamine-cured epoxies in food-processing areas because they are nontoxic in the cured state. Epoxy esters use oxidizing oils in esterifying and, as a result, chalk less than straight two-component epoxies. Two-component epoxies are not recommended for decorative finishes subject to exterior exposures because the chalk adheres and will not wash off in rain, as will conventional housepaints.

Amine-cured epoxy resins combine the good properties of a baked film with the convenience of an air-dried coating. Reactive amines are introduced into the vehicle shortly before use. Once the amine hardener has been added, the mixture's pot life is from 8 to 60 hours, depending on the nature of the resin and amine used. Most manufacturers recommend an induction period of from one-half to one hour after mixing and before applying. Reactive organic amines are caustic, volatile, and toxic, and applicators must carefully avoid contact with the skin and provide adequate ventilation during use. Since curing proceeds by direct cross-linking rather than by oxidation, thick coats harden evenly throughout, provided the substrate is porous enough to permit the escape of the solvent. On nonporous surfaces, limit the thickness of each coat to about 2 mils (0.051 mm), with one or two days allowed for curing before overcoating. This will avoid entrapping the solvent that might migrate to the interface and impair adhesion of the topcoat.

Amine-catalyzed, cold-cured epoxy resins have good chemical and solvent resistance, toughness, and durability. They are primarily used in industrial maintenance paints and clear coatings on floors and furniture and may be applied by brush, spray, or flow-coating methods. Special equipment is advised for spray application.

Polyamide-epoxy resins are a blend of reactive polyamide and epoxy resins. The polyamide resin serves as both curing agent and modifier for the epoxy resin. The resulting blend yields coatings with excellent gloss, hardness, flexibility, impact resistance, and abrasion resistance. These resins also have very good resistance to solvents, chemicals, and outdoor weathering. They are superior to straight epoxies in resisting continuous water immersion.

Although polyamide epoxies resemble amine-cured epoxies in their capability to cure at room temperature without requiring oxygen, they have a longer pot life. Some products may be applied as soon as they are mixed, without the induction period amine epoxies require. Polyamide-epoxy coatings show outstanding adhesion to almost any surface, including metal, plastics, glass, wood, and masonry. Their principal uses are in chemical-resistant coatings, weather- and water-resistant finishes, and abrasion- and corrosion-resistant coatings for industrial equipment. Polyamide-cured epoxies have better flexibility, adhesion, weatherability, gloss retention, water resistance, and a slower chalking rate than amine-cured epoxies.

Esterified-epoxy resins cost less and are more soluble and adaptable than unmodified epoxy resins. However, they are not as chemical- or weather-resistant. They chalk rapidly on outdoor exposure, but their ultimate film life is greater than medium-oil-length alkyds, and they are more resistant to mildew and dirt. Epoxy esters offer a useful combination of adhesion, flexibility, toughness, and durability where maximum chemical resistance obtainable with unmodified epoxies is not required. Long-oil epoxy esters are used as floor enamels, trim paints, and general-purpose interior and exterior enamels.

Epoxy-zinc-rich coatings provide a combination of properties of two basic materials. These coatings contain high percentages of zinc dust in an epoxy or polyamide-epoxy vehicle. They are used as primers on steel for underwater structures and other severe marine services where their corrosion-resistant properties justify the higher cost. Zinc-dust content should not be less than 80 percent by weight of total nonvolatile content.

Epoxy emulsion coatings are two-component, water-based systems that display many of the properties of catalyzed, polyamide-epoxy coatings. The main difference is a low-odor characteristic that makes epoxy emulsion coatings ideal for occupied areas.

Polyurethane Coatings

Coating products based on polyurethane resins are regularly used as high-performance coatings. They are extremely versatile and are used for both interior and exterior applications. These products are frequently used over epoxy intermediate coats on exterior applications because of the tendency of epoxy coatings to chalk or yellow. When formulated for optimum performance, polyurethane coatings possess an outstanding combination of properties, including hardness with flexibility, high gloss, and excellent resistance to abrasion and chemicals. Polyurethane products are available as either two-component or single-package materials. Two-component materials are mixed shortly before use and cure by direct cross-linking. Single-package materials cure when exposed as a film to moisture, oxygen, or heat.

- **Moisture-cured polyurethanes** have successfully been used over all common building substrates and excel as high-performance coatings over metal, concrete, and wood surfaces. Moisture-cured polyurethanes are usually packaged in one container. The rate of cure depends on prevailing weather conditions, thus use in arid climates is difficult. The film dries tack-free in about an hour by solvent evaporation and then cures to a cross-linked coating by reaction to atmospheric moisture. Under low-humidity conditions (below 30 percent relative humidity), a long curing time may be required. When fully cured, the film has properties that approach those of two-component systems.
- **Two-component polyurethanes** are among the most versatile high-performance coatings in use today. The finished coating may be hard and rigid or soft and flexible, depending on the resin used. The product is noted for high gloss and color retention and is both chemical- and solvent-resistant. Two-component polyurethanes are catalytic-cured coatings that provide optimum hardness and resistance properties. The pot life of mixed ingredients and the time for the coating to cure depend on the nature and concentration of curing agents and the temperature.
- **Air-cured, single-package polyurethanes** are sometimes called urethane oils because they behave like alkyds. They dry quickly by the oxidation of drying oils and require drying oils to cure within a reasonable time frame. Their performance is similar to conventional alkyd coatings when fully cured. The cured film is hard and abrasion-resistant. However, color retention is poorer than for other coatings of this generic type. These products are difficult to topcoat because the hardness of the film impairs intercoat adhesion and the cured surface must be lightly sanded between coats to provide an adequate bond. They are not frequently used as high-performance coatings.

Waterborne Acrylics

Although studies show that waterborne acrylics often perform as well as epoxies and polyurethanes in harsh, corrosive, and chemical environments, they are primarily used as high-performance coatings in mild and moderate environments. Acrylic polymers are known for their toughness, resistance to ultraviolet light, and superior color retention. They are usually very low VOC materials. Waterborne coatings are also noted for their reduced odor and low toxicity when compared with solvent-based coating materials.

Waterborne coatings are versatile and easily modified for other purposes, depending on the requirements of a particular situation. They are suitable for use over ferrous and nonferrous metals, and concrete, masonry, and wood substrates. Because they have a high moisture-transmission rate, waterborne coatings are useful over wood and concrete surfaces where it is necessary to allow internal moisture to escape through the coating film. They have been used as primers and as high-gloss finishes in direct-to-metal coatings and are frequently used as the coating of choice on offshore oil-drilling platforms because of their toughness, hardness, and superior color retention in harsh environments. Because of their high gloss and color retention, waterborne acrylics are also used as factory- and shop-applied finishes on heavy equipment and as industrial maintenance coatings.

Waterborne acrylics are one-component materials in which the acrylic resin is suspended in water to form an emulsion. They cure by evaporating the water and the subsequent coalescence of the resin particles. Because curing is the result of water evaporation, film formation depends on prevailing ambient conditions, including air movement, temperature, and humidity.

ENVIRONMENTAL CONCERNS

This discussion covers only those aspects of federal and state regulations governing VOCs that impact high-performance coatings. For background information on federal and state regulations that govern VOCs and the problems this concern for the environment creates for the coatings industry, refer to Chapter 09910, Painting, which provides a detailed discussion on the history of VOC regulations and recent Environmental Protection Agency (EPA) actions.

VOC Levels for High-Performance Coatings

EPA regulations set the maximum VOC content of high-performance coatings at 450 g/L or 3.75 lb/gal. Major reasons for higher limits for high-performance coatings than for other coatings are that these coatings have unique characteristics, perform a necessary function, and have few known viable alternatives.

Recent history indicates that existing VOC regulations are subject to change. Specifiers should contact their local EPA office for current information or interpretation of regulations for unusual circumstances.

HEALTH AND SAFETY HAZARDS

Potential health and safety hazards involved in coating applications, particularly during recoating operations in occupied spaces, are major concerns of the coatings industry. These hazards exist because most coatings contain volatile solvents. Some high-performance coatings are of particular concern in these areas. Applicators should consult the manufacturer about special precautions that may be necessary when applying its products.

Safety Hazards

Flammable solvents are present in high percentages in most coatings. When applying coatings in an enclosed space, the danger exists that solvent vapor buildup in the space could become great enough to reach a low explosive limit. Under these circumstances, a spark or source of ignition could produce a dangerous explosion. However, work in such spaces is safe if there is adequate ventilation. This requires that the air in the enclosed space be changed often enough to dilute the solvent vapor concentration below the low explosive limit. Precautions for using spray equipment are also necessary, and adequate ventilation is an absolute necessity and should be in effect regardless of the flash point of solvents in the coating.

Health Hazards

Health hazards include inhaling solvent vapors and physically contacting the liquid solvents. Solvents used in coatings are not toxic if only small or moderate concentrations are inhaled for brief periods, but long-term exposure is unsafe. Some individuals may experience extreme discomfort when exposed to vapors of certain coatings. Proper and adequate ventilation will solve most problems. Some curing agents used in certain coatings are dangerous when their vapors are inhaled or when they come in contact with the skin.

REFERENCES

Publication dates cited here were current at the time of this writing. Publications are revised periodically, and revisions may have occurred before this book was published.

ASTM International

ASTM D 4263-83 (reapproved 1993): Test Method for Indicating Moisture in Concrete by the Plastic Sheet Method

SSPC: The Society for Protective Coatings

SSPC-SP 5/NACE 1 1994: Joint Surface Preparation Standard—White Metal Blast Cleaning

SSPC-SP 6/NACE 3 1994: Joint Surface Preparation Standard—Commercial Blast Cleaning

SSPC-SP 7/NACE 4 1994: Joint Surface Preparation Standard—Brush-Off Blast Cleaning

SSPC-SP 10/NACE No. 2 1994: Joint Surface Preparation Standard—Near-White Blast Cleaning

BOOK

SSPC: The Society for Protective Coatings. Pittsburg, PA: SSPC, *Steel Structures Painting Manual,* vol. II, 7th ed. 1995.

09963 ELASTOMERIC COATINGS

This chapter discusses *elastomeric coatings containing a specially designed acrylic polymer for use on the exterior of masonry, concrete, and stucco structures. These coatings are dirt-resistant, are flexible in a range of temperatures, and are very high-build materials. These coatings also bridge small cracks and protect against deterioration resulting from moisture penetration of the substrate.*

GENERAL COMMENTS

The coatings industry considers any coating material as a special coating if it is formulated to resist exposure to a specific form of abuse such as continuous immersion in saltwater or regular exposure to wind-driven rain. Manufacturers of special coatings have developed unique product formulas with ingredients that provide their coatings with special characteristics that can protect a substrate from the damaging effects of exposure to an aggressive environment. Some special coatings effectively protect several types of substrates from various adverse conditions; other coatings are specially designed to protect a specific substrate against a particular hazard within a narrow range of atmospheric conditions.

This chapter discusses acrylic-based elastomeric coatings specially formulated for use over concrete, masonry, or stucco surfaces exposed to heavy, wind-driven rain. Elastomeric coatings are thick, dirt-resistant, membrane-like coatings that can expand and contract with surfaces over a broad temperature range without rupturing or wrinkling. Their purpose is both aesthetic and protective. Manufacturers do not recommend using these coatings on the interior or over other exterior building materials except for small elements, such as wood trim, that are contiguous to concrete, masonry, or stucco.

Use of Elastomeric Coatings

Elastomeric coatings are designed to cover monolithic concrete, concrete masonry, and portland cement plaster (stucco) surfaces that eventually develop small, thermally driven cracks. Because of their ability to bridge cracks and follow thermally driven building movement without embrittling and cracking, elastomeric coatings effectively prevent water penetration. The high film thickness also disguises surface deficiencies that might otherwise mar the building's appearance. For this reason, they are also used to help restore an attractive appearance to buildings that have surface deterioration problems.

Appearance Considerations

Elastomeric coatings are available in both smooth and textured finishes and in a variety of colors. Because the binder in these coatings is a specially designed acrylic, they resist dirt build-up on the surface. The coatings, therefore, maintain an attractive appearance long after conventional coatings need to be replaced. They are also mildew resistant; this characteristic helps avoid the disfiguring appearance caused by airborne mold and mildew fungus.

Elastomeric coatings are frequently used on the exterior of concrete and masonry buildings in Florida and along the Gulf Coast where they are useful for protection of beachfront properties. Although heavy, wind-driven rains do not occur as frequently in other parts of the United States, architects often specify elastomeric coatings in other regions as well. Architects have found that these coatings are useful for buildings subject to high thermal movement and energy loss, and to help restore the appearance of buildings that have experienced exterior surface degradation. Many manufacturers expect elastomeric coatings to become popular in other parts of the United States because they are flexible and dirt resistant.

Product Selection Criteria

When selecting any coating, architects must consider many elements. This selection process is especially true for elastomeric coatings. Two major considerations include prevailing environmental conditions and actual cost of the coating including projected maintenance costs. These considerations, and careful analysis of required surface preparation, should help determine whether a coating is well suited to the intended application. Each factor must be thoroughly evaluated in determining the final selection. Because surface preparation for these coatings is extremely important, it is discussed separately and in greater depth in this chapter than the other selection considerations.

Environmental Conditions

The climate is always an important factor to consider when selecting exterior coatings. Masonry buildings in the humid coastal areas of Florida and along the Gulf and South Atlantic coasts are prime candidates for elastomeric coatings. The thunderstorms and hurricanes that regularly occur in these areas produce heavy, wind-driven rain that can cause severe damage to buildings unless protective measures, such as application of elastomeric coatings, are taken. Masonry buildings in more northerly climates are also suitable for the application of elastomeric coatings. In these areas, buildings' exterior wall surfaces are subject to wide temperature variations during the year, which cause expansion and contraction that often result in surface cracks. If not properly protected, these cracks provide an easy avenue for water penetration.

Cost

Actual cost is a part of the coating selection. Elastomeric coatings are more expensive than conventional exterior coatings, principally because of the high coating thickness required. Most manufacturers recommend a minimum of two coats with a finished dry film thickness of 7 to 8 mils (0.18 to 0.20 mm) or more per coat to achieve the intended results and resistance to wind-driven rain. To be conclusive, an evaluation of elastomeric coatings must consider the protection achieved at the lowest cost per square foot (square meter) per year, not just initial cost. Actual cost also includes considering requirements for maintenance and expected life of the coating. Obviously, the high initial cost of elastomeric coatings is a deterrent to their extensive use. However, when their flexibility across a broad temperature range, dirt resistance, and resistance to moisture penetration are evaluated along with the material's attractiveness, elastomeric coatings begin to outweigh these cost factors for many owners.

SURFACE PREPARATION

Poor surface preparation is a major cause of coating failure; this is true for elastomeric coatings as well as any other paint or coating system. No coating is better than the surface over which it is applied. If the surface contains dirt, grease, mildew, moisture, concrete dust, or other foreign substances that interfere with good performance, the coating will likely fail. Such deleterious substances create a break between the surface and the coating. They soon deteriorate and fall away from the surface, taking the coating with them. These failures are easily preventable with proper surface preparation and cannot be considered the fault of the coating.

If mildew is present, it must be removed and the surface neutralized before any other surface-preparation work, including crack patching, begins. The manufacturer's written recommendations must be followed closely when using cleaning solutions for mildew removal. Because most solutions are irritating to the eyes and skin, protective goggles and clothing must be worn during cleaning operations. After the cleaning solution is applied and surfaces are scrubbed to remove mildew growth, the surfaces must be thoroughly rinsed with clear water and allowed to dry thoroughly before coatings are applied.

Most manufacturers recommend cleaning masonry surfaces by power washing, water blasting, or scrubbing, and then allowing the surfaces to dry thoroughly before applying coatings. This cleaning removes surface dust, dirt, and similar impediments to good adhesion. If a detergent is used, the surface must be rinsed well with clear water. Because some environmental regulations affect cleaning processes, check local regulations before specifying cleaning procedures.

Crack repair is an important aspect of surface preparation for elastomeric coatings. Failure to repair small cracks may lead to moisture penetration and surface deterioration. Elastomeric coatings bridge hairline surface cracks that do not extend deeply into the substrate. One reason for the popularity of elastomeric coatings is their ability to bridge small cracks and prevent the entrance of moisture. More elaborate repair measures are necessary where cracks are deeper or wider, up to ⅜ inch (9.5 mm). Each manufacturer has its own method to seal and repair cracks and surface defects. Most manufacturers produce a knife or buttering grade of material that can be forced into the crack as a sealant. The manufacturer's written instructions about crack repair must be followed closely. Cracks larger than ⅜ inch (9.5 mm) in width usually suggest structural problems and should be investigated by a structural engineer before proceeding.

Many manufacturers do not recommend priming before applying elastomeric coatings because they feel that the materials are self-priming. However, some manufacturers recommend using primers over highly alkaline surfaces. Because these coatings are part of each manufacturer's proprietary systems, closely following the manufacturer's written recommendations is important.

Masonry surfaces with open pores do not present the best coating surface for conventional paints because the coating cannot bridge the pores and give an even appearance. Most manufacturers suggest using a conventional masonry block filler before applying elastomeric coatings over such surfaces.

Stucco should be thoroughly cured a minimum of 30 days before applying elastomeric coatings. The stucco must be sound and well adhered to the substrate. Because all cementitious surfaces are subject to extensive cracking, they should be thoroughly examined before applying coatings.

PERFORMANCE STANDARDS

For most building products and systems, measurable technical criteria for product evaluation are available from many sources such as manufacturing associations and professional and technical societies such as ASTM. Unfortunately, this is not the case with the coatings industry. Although there is no shortage of material standards for the various chemical ingredients that go into coating formulas, few standards establish measurable criteria for evaluating the performance of paint and coating products. The lack of performance standards for comparing material quality is a serious concern because it leaves specifiers with no way to compare or evaluate products based on realistic performance expectations.

Until recently, the only comprehensive source for generic technical information on paint and coating products was Federal Specifications. Unfortunately, the usefulness of Federal Specifications as quality standards for paints was questionable. Many of these specifications were prescriptive and did little more than establish minimum content requirements for the most basic ingredients in a coating formula. Many of them failed to set performance requirements or did not provide useful criteria for product evaluation. The quality level they established for paint products was minimal at best. Most coating manufacturers paid lip service to the Federal Specifications by indicating in their product literature that they complied with the qualitative requirements in those documents, but not the quantitative requirements. Few manufacturers made products that complied precisely with the Federal Specifications because the quality levels of their product lines far exceeded the minimum levels required by the Federal Specifications.

For various reasons, the Federal Government has decided to review all Federal Specifications and to eliminate or replace them with established consensus standards where they are available. Most Federal Specifications for elastomeric coatings have been canceled by the Federal Government or have not been updated in more than 10 years. Of those that have not been canceled or withdrawn, many are readily not available. This unavailability of standards is not acceptable in an industry where manufacturers introduce new products on an ongoing basis. The withdrawal of Federal Specifications presents a quandary to specifiers who depend on them to provide a minimum level of quality assurance in their project specifications. This dilemma has recently been addressed by the Master Painters Institute (MPI) of British Columbia, Canada.

Previously, the only alternative available for specifiers to use instead of using Federal Specifications to establish quality levels for coating products was ASTM standards and specifications. ASTM has approximately 700 standards on paint and coating materials. Most ASTM standards specify testing procedures and other requirements for the individual chemicals used in paint and coating formulas. However, using ASTM standards to establish a level of quality for a coating product by comparing requirements for each of the individual ingredients in a coating formula is not practical. Most paints and coatings are composed of a large number of carefully selected chemicals. Manufacturers use different ingredients to produce similar results without affecting the quality of a product. Therefore, the number of standards used as references for quality could become prohibitively large and many would not be applicable for all coating products, making comparison difficult, if not impossible.

MPI has developed detailed performance specifications for various paint products and, more important, has tested paint manufacturers' products for compliance with its standards. Paint products that meet MPI standards are listed in its *Approved Product List (APL)*. The United States Navy Facilities Engineering Command (NAVFAC), faced with the loss of acceptable quality standards that comply with Federal Government regulations, has thoroughly investigated MPI standards and determined that its test procedures and standards are appropriate for all paint products used on projects under NAVFAC's jurisdiction. They have also alerted design professionals and contractors that do business with NAVFAC to its requirement that paint products for its projects must be included on MPI's *APL*. The Army, the Air Force, the General Services Administration, the Department of Veterans Affairs, and NASA are following NAVFAC's lead in this matter. It is likely that most other federal agencies will do the same.

A different problem faces design professionals doing business in the private sector. Only some paint manufacturers, primarily located in the western and northwestern United States and Canada, have elected to submit their products to MPI for testing and listing in the *APL*. Because of the limited number of participants in the MPI program, and because most of them do business primarily in Canada and the states on the West Coast, it may not be practical to use the MPI system as an exclusive reference standard for elastomeric coatings.

It is too early to tell if the efforts of MPI will be more widely accepted, but the requirement for products to be listed with MPI before being acceptable to the Federal Government is a powerful incentive. It is also likely that as more architects, engineers, and specifiers become familiar with the MPI system and the *APL,* they will begin to use it in their project specifications for private sector work.

Federal Specification FS TT-C-555 is one exception to the problem with Federal Specifications. FS TT-C-555 establishes basic test procedures for wind-driven rain and moisture-vapor permeability that are essential criteria for elastomeric coatings. Federal Specifications and ASTM performance standards are used as benchmarks for the performance for elastomeric coatings because of the nature of the coatings and the important performance requirements they must meet. MPI and all elastomeric coating manufacturers continue to reference FS TT-C-555 as establishing one of the most important performance requirements for elastomeric coatings.

Specifications often include performance requirements for elastomeric coatings based on MPI 113, *Performance Standard for Exterior, Waterborne, Pigmented Elastomeric Coating.* Many coating manufacturers do not use MPI 113, but their performance standards have long been the basis for specifying elastomeric coatings.

ENVIRONMENTAL CONSIDERATIONS

This discussion addresses only those aspects of federal and state regulations governing VOCs that impact elastomeric coatings. For background information on federal and state regulations that govern VOCs, and the problems that this concern for the environment creates for the coatings industry, refer to Chapter 09910, Painting, which provides a detailed discussion on the history of VOC regulations and recent actions of the Environmental Protection Agency (EPA).

Environmental Regulations

After many years of delay and controversy, the first national regulation imposing limits on the amount of VOCs contained in paints and other construction products was published on September 13, 1998, and became effective September 13, 1999. Enactment and enforcement of these national regulations are a welcome relief from the confusion that has characterized this issue for more than 30 years. Although many environmentalists feel that the regulations are not as strong as they should be, most industry analysts feel that the regulations accept the reality of the current state of technology. The regulations limit the maximum amount of VOCs in flat interior and exterior architectural coatings to 250 g/L, and in nonflat interior or exterior coatings to 380 g/L. Although these regulations impose national limits on VOC content, state and local governments may impose harsher limits if their particular situations are serious enough to warrant such action.

The lack of uniformity in state and local regulations has hampered progress toward development of environmentally friendly materials. With so many conflicting regulations, the greatest problem for manufacturers and their research chemists was that it was impossible to determine what level of restrictions was realistic. Currently, most manufacturers have a full line of products that can comply with the national regulations.

Unfortunately, the enactment of these new regulations does not totally end the problem. Some states, particularly California, had previously enacted regulations that were more restrictive than the new ones. The new regulations do not rescind these laws. Furthermore, the California South Coast Air Quality Management District in and around Los Angeles has decided to proceed with a major revision to the limits now in effect. In this regard, it is important to note that Air Quality Management Districts have regional jurisdiction and do not impose their requirements statewide. Meanwhile, another group on the East Coast is attempting to enact lower VOC levels than those proposed by the EPA. It is too early to predict what, if any, effect these attempts to impose more restrictive VOC levels will have on the EPA regulations.

As a result of the action taken in the Los Angeles area and on the East Coast, specifiers should contact their local EPA offices for current information or interpretation of regulations for unusual circumstances. It is unlikely that the VOC issue has been settled for all time, even though it will probably be less contentious in the future.

Many architects assume that because elastomeric coatings are based on an acrylic resin, all such coatings comply with state and federal VOC regulations, which is not necessarily the case. Use of acrylic resins does not by itself guarantee that a product will be VOC compliant. Because of the many other chemicals used in coating formulas, it is possible to find similar elastomeric coatings in two different formulations: one that complies with current regulations, and one that does not. Fortunately, product information supplied by manufacturers usually lists the VOC levels of their products and, in almost every case, products are within the limits currently imposed by even the most restrictive jurisdictions. However, until such time as these regulations are well established, specifiers should check with their local EPA offices for the latest information about changes in VOC regulations before specifying paints and coatings.

SAFETY AND HEALTH HAZARDS

Safety Hazards

Coatings often contain flammable solvents. If the coatings are applied in an enclosed space, solvent vapor build-up in the space could become great enough to reach a low explosive limit. If this build-up occurs, there is always the danger that a spark or another source of ignition could cause a dangerous explosion. Work in enclosed spaces is safe if adequate ventilation is provided. The air must be changed often enough to dilute solvent-vapor concentration below the lower explosive limit. Specifying adequate ventilation is necessary when using spray equipment, regardless of the flash point of the organic solvents in the coating. Because elastomeric coating products are intended for exterior use, the chance of solvent vapor build-up becoming great enough to present a hazard to applicators is remote.

Health Hazards

Health hazards include the inhaling of solvent vapors and physical contact with liquid solvents. In most circumstances, breathing small or moderate amounts of solvent vapors for brief periods of time will not produce an injury. However, long-term exposure to large amounts of solvent vapors is unsafe. Some individuals experience discomfort when exposed to vapors of certain types of coatings. Proper and adequate ventilation will solve most problems. Read precautionary information printed on the label of each paint container to understand the nature of the coating and the health and safety requirements of the material.

FIELD QUALITY CONTROL

Substrate Examination

The most important field quality-control measure that painting specifications should require is that the applicator examine the substrate before beginning the application. If the substrate is not in proper condition to receive the coating materials specified, the applicator has an obligation to refuse to begin work on the substrate. In effect, the applicator has the final word on acceptability of the surface preparation. It is not advisable to permit someone other than the applicator to decide whether or not to proceed with the application. Doing so is not in the best interest of the project because it eliminates the strongest control the specifier has for achieving a good coating application.

Material Testing Provisions

There are many opportunities for coating materials to be altered or contaminated from the time they are formulated to the time they are applied at the project site. Specifying that an independent testing agency test coating materials for compliance with requirements in the coating specification is the best way to ensure that the product applied is the same quality as the material specified. Whether the owner invokes these procedures or not, just establishing these requirements may deter overzealous thinning of materials and extended coverage during application. It also may deter requests to substitute lower-quality materials for those specified.

Listing salient characteristics is essential if testing of coating materials by an independent testing agency is anticipated. Specifications must identify those characteristics that are considered important and will be involved in material testing. For projects involving government agencies, including salient characteristics in the specifications is often recommended and may

be required. The owner should determine what characteristics are important, what is acceptable, and what constitutes a failure.

Several characteristics could be considered critical to the performance of a coating material and can be tested according to established test methods; these include, among others, abrasion resistance, accelerated weathering, alkali resistance, color retention, dry opacity, flexibility, and mildew resistance. Another important item to consider is an analysis for content of the material actually delivered to the site as compared to the product's published label analysis; this also yields information about the volume solids of the product and the theoretical dry film thickness.

Essential information about a product's performance characteristics for most of the items listed above is rarely included in the manufacturer's product literature. Unfortunately, statements such as "this product can be expected to stand up against repeated washing" are fairly typical of the type of information found in product literature. This kind of statement is of little value when attempting to compare products for compliance with specified requirements, particularly when there are established test methods that form the basis of comparison. It is difficult to understand the reluctance of manufacturers to include pertinent information on such important characteristics in their product literature, particularly when this is the type of information most architects and owners need to know.

REFERENCES

Publication dates cited here were current at the time of this writing. Publications are revised periodically, and revisions may have occurred before this book was published.

Federal Specification

FS TT-C-555B(1): Coating, Textured (for Interior and Exterior Masonry Surfaces)

Master Painters Institute

MPI 113: Performance Standard for Exterior, Waterborne, Pigmented Elastomeric Coating

Approved Product List, 2001.

WEB SITE

Master Painters Institute: www.paintinfo.com

09967 INTUMESCENT PAINTS

This chapter discusses intumescent-type, fire-retardant paints, which can be used on interior combustible and noncombustible substrates.

This chapter does not discuss fire-resistance-rated intumescent mastics, which are usually specified in a Division 7, "Thermal and Moisture Protection," section.

PRODUCT EVALUATION

Intumescent paints will not burn; and when applied to a substrate, they reduce surface flame spread. These paints minimize the effects of an explosion called flashover and reduce the amount of smoke developed in the event of a fire. These coatings provide only minimal fire protection because they are applied in the same manner as conventional paints and achieve only a thin film covering. Intumescent mastics, which are usually trowel applied from ⅛ to ⅜ inch (3.2 to 9.5 mm) thick, provide fire-resistance ratings of 45 minutes' to 2 hours' duration, depending on thickness.

Conventional paints are often blamed for the spread of a fire, when in fact, the final analysis invariably shows that combustible trim or ceiling material caused the fire to spread. Under some conditions, a conventional paint will reduce the rate of flame spread of a combustible substrate. Tests on some conventional coatings actually demonstrate good flame-spread indexes, indicating that the coatings do not contribute to increasing the surface-burning characteristics of the substrate to which they are applied. However, because conventional paints have a very thin paint film, they will not retard combustion of a surface for an extended period.

Code Requirements

Building codes require interior finishes to have specific flame-spread indexes. The flame spread required for finishes of wall and ceiling surfaces for certain areas of a building, such as vertical exits, passageways, and exit-access corridors, are generally lower than what is required elsewhere. Many older buildings, and some new buildings, contain combustible substrates that must be protected with an acceptable fire-retardant coating to comply with local building codes.

Advantages of Intumescent Paints

Most fires in buildings for human occupancy start small but can grow rapidly. Intumescent paints help confine a fire that might otherwise spread and become large to a small area for easier control. As fire progresses and flames spread, the air inside a building becomes intensely heated and toxic gases are formed. When the mixture of toxic gases and superheated air reach a critical stage, oxygen is depleted, and the mixture ignites producing flashover. This soon leads to total combustion of the building. Tests show that using intumescent paints properly can reduce flame spread on combustible and noncombustible surfaces. This decreases smoke development and delays the buildup of toxic gases and superheated air, thereby controlling or eliminating flashover.

Intumescent paints can also allow building occupants more time to evacuate by slowing the rate at which a fire spreads over combustible surfaces. Intumescent paints are often applied over noncombustible surfaces in hospitals and nursing homes to give the staff more time to evacuate occupants who are unable to leave the building without help.

Most building codes recognize the fact that the flame-spread index of interior wall and ceiling surfaces is not generally affected by the application of ordinary paint and wall coverings, unless coatings are applied at a very heavy rate. However, highly flammable finishes such as lacquer, shellac, and some plastic resins are not considered ordinary.

Definitions

Two important terms, *fire-retardant coatings* and *fire-resistive coatings,* are often used with intumescent paints to describe the degree of resistance to fire exhibited by a coating.

- **Fire-retardant coatings** have the capability to slow the normal rate at which flame will travel over a combustible substrate and to delay both ignition and combustion of the substrate. These coatings are noncombustible but do self-destruct when exposed to flames and very high temperatures associated with combustion.
- **Fire-resistive coatings** have the capability to withstand fire and to protect the substrate. They do not support combustion and do not deteriorate readily under fire conditions. Such products are not described in this chapter.

Underwriters Laboratories (UL) divides coatings intended for application on building materials into two categories, fire-retardant coatings and general-purpose coatings, to express the degree of surface-burning characteristics of the coating.

- **Fire-retardant coatings** are intended for application over interior combustible surfaces for the expressed purpose of reducing the surface-burning characteristics.
- **General-purpose coatings** are intended for application over various interior and exterior surfaces.

To be listed as a fire-retardant coating, a product must either reduce the flame spread of Douglas fir and all other tested interior combustible surfaces (having a flame spread of 100 or greater by test) to which it is applied by at least 50 percent or have a flame-spread index of 50 or less, whichever is less.

Paint Function

The purpose of fire-retardant paints is to reduce or prevent the spread of flame over a combustible surface. These products accomplish this through a combination of unique attributes. First, the coating deprives the fire of the oxygen it needs for combustion by preventing air from reaching the substrate. Second, when exposed to the heat of a fire, chemicals in the coating react to protect the substrate. This protection is achieved either by preventing or inhibiting the release of volatile gases necessary for combustion or by forming an insulating foam that prevents heat from raising the temperature of the combustible substrate above the fire point.

Intumescent, fire-retardant paints, when subjected to the heat of a fire, expand and form a thick, charred, foamlike layer of insulating material that protects the substrate from heat and flame. This intumescent char delays ignition of substrates. Intumescent paints are formulated so that when exposed to heat, they liquefy and allow gases of decomposition to create an expansion or bubbling of the coating to form an insulating layer. Intumescent paints should not be top-coated with an incompatible paint that will prevent this chemical reaction, or fire-retardant properties would be lost.

Moisture Sensitivity

The first fire-retardant paints were dry powder and water mixes with poor resistance to humidity and washing. Most gas-forming or intumescent agents are water-soluble. Therefore, the first intumescent paint films were water-sensitive. After aging in the presence of moisture or high humidity, they lost some of their intumescent properties. But because it is necessary to have a high degree of intumescence to produce a coating with a low flame spread when applied to a combustible substrate, newer intumescent paints have overcome this deficiency, and the paint can be expected to function well for several years. However, as with any coating, periodic recoating is necessary to maintain the desired qualities and improve appearance.

Paint Qualities

The paint attributes of commercially available intumescent paints have improved in recent years. The finished appearance of these paints approaches the properties of conventional paints. New intumescent paints are easy to apply and have good decorative appearance and washability. Work on improving intumescent paints is continuing, with improvements anticipated.

Proper surface preparation is probably more important for intumescent paint than for standard paint finishes. Wood surfaces must be clean and dry. Although some manufacturers recommend that steel surfaces be prepared according to SSPC: The Society for Protective Coatings publication SSPC-SP 10/NACE No. 2, *Near-White Blast Cleaning,* this high degree of surface preparation is not always warranted, and SSPC-SP 6/NACE No. 3, *Commercial Blast Cleaning,* may be adequate.

Application

The coating must be evenly applied at the recommended spreading rate, with no holidays, to provide the required level of fire retardancy. As is true of any coating, proper application procedures must be followed to obtain a high-quality coating. The major difference regarding the application of intumescent paint is that poor application procedures could endanger the safety of building occupants.

The spreading rate of intumescent paints is similar to that of corrosion-resisting coatings. Generally, most manufacturers listed in UL indicate that two coats are required. However, some systems indicate compliance with fire-retardant criteria with a single application but at a lesser rate of coverage per gallon. Consult manufacturers' literature for the proper spreading rates for the fire-retardant rating required.

Appearance

Intumescent paints appear the same as many standard paint finishes and are applied in the same manner—by brush, roller, or spray. Due to a lower

spreading rate, the resulting finish is two to four times as thick. This is a more expensive finish. Intumescent paints should be considered as a functional material rather than a decorative one.

Intumescent paints are available in pigmented and clear finishes. Pigmented finishes are available from various manufacturers and are produced in emulsion and solvent systems. Clear finishes are not as readily available, though, several manufacturers do produce quality, clear intumescent coatings.

Maintenance

Normal maintenance of coated surfaces should be followed according to the manufacturer's recommendations. Recoating, to maintain fire-retardant effectiveness, may be required after three to five years, depending on the substrate, area coated, and environmental conditions.

Product Identification

It is not unusual for a manufacturer to market identical products under different names or designations in different parts of the country. This is particularly true of products manufactured for distribution in the western states. Therefore, consult local manufacturers' representatives to ensure the correct local product name or designation before preparing final product specifications.

TEST METHODS

There is considerable confusion between fire endurance as evaluated in ASTM E 119 and flame spread in ASTM E 84. Satisfying requirements for fire endurance does not automatically satisfy flame-spread requirements; there is no relationship between the two. Flame-spread indexes indicate the time it takes a surface flame to spread across a given area. Fire-endurance ratings apply more closely to the performance of walls, columns, floors, and other building members under fire exposure, indicating a period of time before failure occurs, not fire retardancy or combustibility. Both are important in controlling fires.

If test methods other than ASTM E 84 are permitted in code specifications, a change may be needed in numerical requirements for flame spread and smoke developed. Numerical variations have been reported with the same coating when using different test methods.

Building Codes

Except in the most remote areas, building construction is controlled by local building codes. Most building codes are based on model codes or the National Fire Protection Association (NFPA) publication NFPA 101, *Life Safety Code.* Consult local codes for material requirements and acceptable materials. A flame-spread index of 0-25 is generally required in most codes for critical areas such as exits, corridors, flammable storage, and heat-producing rooms.

ENVIRONMENTAL CONCERNS

This discussion covers only those aspects of federal and state regulations governing VOCs that impact intumescent paints. For background information on these regulations, and the problems this concern for the environment creates for the coating industry, refer to Chapter 09910, Painting, which provides a detailed discussion on the history of VOC regulations and recent actions of the Environmental Protection Agency (EPA).

EPA Regulations Regarding Intumescent Paints

EPA regulations set VOC limits on various categories of architectural and industrial maintenance coatings. Limits for fire-retardant/resistive coatings are set at 850 g/L or 7.1 lb/gal. for clear coatings and 450 g/L or 3.8 lb/gal. for opaque coatings. Limits for opaque coatings are the same as for most industrial maintenance coatings but are much less restrictive than architectural coatings because these coatings have unique characteristics, perform a necessary function, and have no viable alternative.

Recent history indicates that existing VOC regulations are subject to change. Specifiers should contact their local EPA office for current information or interpretation of regulations for unusual circumstances.

REFERENCES

Publication dates cited here were current at the time of this writing. Publications are revised periodically, and revisions may have occurred before this book was published.

ASTM International

ASTM E 84-96a: Test Method for Surface-Burning Characteristics of Building Materials

ASTM E 119-95a: Test Methods for Fire Tests of Building Construction and Materials

SSPC: The Society for Protective Coatings

SSPC-SP 6/NACE No. 3 1994: Joint Surface Preparation Standard—Commercial Blast Cleaning

SSPC-SP 10/NACE No. 2 1994: Joint Surface Preparation Standard—Near-White Blast Cleaning

09975 HIGH-TEMPERATURE-RESISTANT COATINGS

This chapter discusses general surface preparation, materials preparation, and application principles for high-temperature-resistant coatings used on the interior and exterior.

This chapter does not discuss other specialty coatings, such as fire-retardant coatings.

GENERAL COMMENTS

Coatings technology is constantly evolving. Every year, research chemists develop new materials for use by the coatings industry. In turn, the coating manufacturers use these materials to develop new products and to adjust existing formulations to improve the performance of their existing products. They design each individual coating for characteristics that enable it to perform properly within a given range of conditions on particular surfaces. One example of this evolution over the last 50 years is the rapid development and increasing use of silicone resins for high-temperature resistance in coatings for steel.

Special Coatings

The coatings industry considers any coating formulated to resist a specific form of abuse, such as regular continuing exposure to very high temperatures, as a special coating. Most coating manufacturers have developed unique product formulas that include ingredients selected to provide their coatings with special characteristics. Each ingredient in the formula is selected because it possesses some attribute desired in the coating. Combining several ingredients in this manner allows manufacturers to develop products with the particular qualities they want in the end product; unfortunately, they often compromise another highly desirable quality in the process.

Chemical Background

Silicones are synthetic, semiorganic chemical compounds consisting of silicon, carbon, hydrogen, and oxygen. Silicon is a nonmetallic element, which, next to oxygen, is the most abundant element on earth. Carbon, also a nonmetallic element, is essential to life and the basis of organic chemistry. Silicon and carbon occupy adjacent places on adjoining rows of the periodic table, which means their actions are similar.

Silicone resins were originally developed during World War II for use as dampening agents for high-flying aircraft. After the war, American industry discovered that these resins had important commercial applications in fields as diverse as adhesives, textile finishes, surface treatment for glass and ceramics, and insulation for electric motors. Initially, the construction industry had few applications for silicone resins. However, as industrial chemists pursued their research, they found new uses for these materials. The market for silicone resins in construction quickly expanded as several companies began using them in sealants and water-repellent coatings for masonry walls.

Silicone-Based Coatings

The coatings industry also found commercial applications for silicone resins after World War II. Coating products using silicone resins are recognized for their outstanding heat resistance, superior water repellency, and excellent weatherability. Few other ingredients possess these qualities to the same extent as these resins. Silicone-modified alkyd resins quickly found a market niche because of their attractive combination of excellent corrosion resistance and weatherability. Today, silicone alkyds are popular coatings for exterior steel structures, such as storage tanks, bridges, and similar items that require a hard, durable, weather-resistant finish. Nevertheless, the most important use of silicone resins in coatings today is as the major component of high-temperature-resistant coatings.

This discussion covers high-temperature-resistant coatings for use over steel surfaces exposed to temperatures that range from 250° to 1200°F (121° to 649°C). Most high-temperature-resistant coatings contain silicone resins as the principal ingredient in the coating formula. However, depending on the maximum temperature anticipated, inorganic, zinc-rich coatings and some coating formulas containing acrylic, alkyd, phenolic, and some epoxy resins as the main ingredient may also be effective in protecting steel substrates from the effects of very high temperatures.

HIGH-TEMPERATURE-RESISTANT COATING SYSTEMS

Some alkyd and phenolic-based coatings protect steel to temperatures in the 200° to 300°F (93° to 149°C) range. Coatings containing inorganic, zinc compounds are effective to temperatures below 787°F (419°C), which is the melting point of metallic zinc. However, coatings containing silicone resins often withstand temperatures in excess of 1000°F (538°C), depending on the coating formula. Furthermore, coatings that combine silicone resins and ceramic frits are useful for protection where steel is exposed to temperatures at or above 1400°F (760°C). Pure 100 percent silicone coatings developed by the National Aeronautics and Space Agency (NASA) have been used on space vehicles subject to temperatures in excess of 2500°F (1371°C) during reentry into the earth's atmosphere.

Characteristics of Silicone Resins

Silicone resins are polymerized resins of organic polysiloxanes that combine excellent chemical resistance with high heat resistance. They are also noted for their excellent color and gloss retention, even when exposed to extremely high temperatures for long periods. They are extremely durable in exterior exposures and they perform well in highly corrosive environments because of their outstanding chemical resistance. However, these resins have poor solvent resistance, and they are soft finishes when air-dried. Chemists can overcome the poor solvent resistance by adding organic resins to the formula. If heat is applied and the coating baked at very high temperatures during the curing process, the resulting film is tough, hard, and extremely durable. Although silicon is one of the most abundant elements on earth, silicone resins are expensive to produce; as a result, coatings based on these resins are expensive.

Silicone-Modified Organic Coatings

The term *silicone-modified organic* refers to organic coating formulas in which silicone resins constitute less than 50 percent of the total formula. Adding silicone resins to organic resins improves both the heat resistance and weatherability performance of the organic coating. The amount of silicone in a silicone-modified organic coating formula usually lies somewhere between 15 and 50 percent. The heat resistance of the coating depends on the percentage of silicone resins in the formula.

Organic-Modified Silicone Coatings

When the amount of silicone resin in a coating formula exceeds 50 percent, the resulting product is termed an *organic-modified silicone*. Adding organic resins enhances the abrasion resistance, hardness, and adhesion qualities of silicone resins. The amount of silicone in these coatings is usually between 51 and 90 percent of the resin content. The higher the silicone content of the coating, the higher the temperature the coating can successfully resist.

Aluminum-Silicone Coatings

Adding leafing aluminum-powder pigments to silicone resins increases the coating's heat resistance substantially. Aluminum-silicone coatings were among the early commercial applications of silicone resins for high-temperature resistance. Aluminum powder has high heat resistance. It is also a durable coating with excellent ability to hide the substrate.

Silicone Ceramic Coatings

The combination of 100 percent silicone with ceramic frits produces a coating that can withstand the assault of temperatures of 1000°F (538°C) and higher. When exposed to prolonged temperatures in this range, the silicone in the resin decomposes, leaving a silica matrix that fuses the frits into a hard, durable, protective coating that adheres tightly to the substrate.

Zinc-Rich Coatings

Zinc-rich primers provide protection to steel exposed to corrosive elements in much the same way as hot-dip galvanizing. Typically, these coatings have high zinc-dust content. They are formulated to provide hard, tough, abrasion-resistant protection to steel with varying degrees of rust inhibition from the galvanic protection provided by the zinc. These coatings are for conditions of high humidity, marine atmospheric exposures, and freshwater immersion. Not all zinc-rich coatings are suitable for acidic or alkaline service without overcoating.

Inorganic, zinc-rich coatings withstand exposure to solvents, oils, and most petroleum products and are resistant to high humidity, splash, and spray. The weathering ability of inorganic, zinc-rich coatings is excellent as the coatings continue to cure during prolonged exposure. These coatings are also highly resistant to prolonged high temperatures below the melting point of zinc. This gives the specifier an alternative to silicone-based coatings where the other qualities of zinc-rich coatings are needed.

COATING SELECTION

Selection Process

Before selecting a high-temperature-resistant coating for a particular application, an architect must carefully evaluate all the information available about the project. Several important factors often combine to determine which high-temperature-resistant coating system is most suitable for a particular situation. Remember that no single high-temperature-resistant coating is suitable for service in all circumstances. Do not assume that a single generic coating will fulfill all the high-temperature-resistance requirements on a project. Nontemperature-related service requirements are often more important in determining the appropriate coating material than the temperature range anticipated.

Coating Selection Considerations

The maximum temperature the substrate is likely to encounter is usually the first factor to consider when selecting a high-temperature-resistant coating; however, for some coating types, the maximum sustained temperature is more important than an occasional high-temperature spike. The prevailing environment at the location where the coating will function is also a major factor in the selection process. The total cost of the coating system, including essential coating maintenance, is often an important factor. Other important considerations include the type of surface preparation required and the compatibility of the high-temperature-resistant coating system with other coatings on the project. Careful evaluation of these factors should narrow the selection to the coating most appropriate for the project situation.

Temperature Ranges

Industrial applications subject metal surfaces of heat-generating equipment, such as smokestacks, boilers, and engines, to temperatures that may range from 200° to 1200°F (93° to 649°C) or higher. Table 1 and the subsequent list divide this broad overall temperature range into seven more convenient ranges that correspond to the effective service temperature ranges of specific generic coating formulations. However, the temperature limits of these ranges are not precise. Because of differences in specific product formulations and the amount of ingredients in a specific product, the coatings developed by some manufacturers may perform better over a wider range than those of their competitors. When the expected maximum service temperature of a metal surface is near the upper limits of a specific coating, factors other than temperature are often the most important selection criteria.

Table 1
TYPICAL HIGH-TEMPERATURE-RESISTANT COATING CAPABILITIES

Temperature Range	Minimum Coating
200°–300°F (93°–149°C)	Acrylic-, alkyd-, epoxy-, or phenolic-resin base coatings
250°–400°F (121°–204°C)	Silicone-modified organic coatings
400°–600°F (204°–316°C)	Aluminum-pigmented, silicone-modified organic coatings or organic-modified silicone coatings
450°–750°F (232°–399°C)	Inorganic, zinc-rich coatings
600°–800°F (316°–427°C)	Organic-modified silicone coatings (black or aluminum)
800°–1000°F (427°–538°C)	Aluminum-silicone coatings (100 percent silicone)
1000°–1200°F (538°–649°C)	Silicone ceramic coatings

- **200°–300°F (93°–149°C):** Some organic coatings based on acrylic, alkyd, epoxy, or phenolic resins protect steel surfaces exposed to temperatures between 200°–300°F (93°–149°C). These coatings are often a good choice because of their modest cost when compared with other organic coatings modified by adding costly silicone resins. These coatings have a fast cure time, good adhesion, and abrasion resistance. However, they may degrade or yellow at the upper limits of this temperature range. If this is a serious concern, silicone-modified organic coatings also perform well in this temperature range.
- **250°–400°F (121°–204°C):** In this temperature range, the coating of choice is a silicone-modified organic coating. Most organic coatings, including alkyds, acrylics, epoxies, phenolics, and polyesters, may be modified by adding silicone resins. Combining silicone resins with an organic resin increases the heat resistance and durability of the material and provides an economic alternative to higher-cost products. Combining these resins is usually achieved by cold blending rather than by copolymerization that may limit the coating's ability to resist some chemicals and solvents. These coatings are available in either an aluminum or a color-pigmented finish material.
- **400°–600°F (204°–316°C):** By adding leafing aluminum pigments to a silicone-modified organic coating, the effective service range of the coatings is extended to about 600°F (316°C). If colored pigments are required, an organic-modified silicone coating, in which the silicone resins comprise between 50 and 90 percent of the total formula, is the only alternative. When color pigments are required, a higher level of silicone is necessary because most color pigments are not as stable as aluminum pigments. The resulting coating is more expensive than a silicone-modified organic coating that contains less silicone in the formula. These coatings require curing at high temperatures for several hours to achieve optimum film properties.
- **450°–750°F (232°–399°C):** The melting point of metallic zinc is 787°F (419°C). Consequently, inorganic, zinc-rich coatings are often used to protect steel from the effects of high temperatures in dry conditions if the maximum temperature will not exceed 750° to 770°F (399° to 410°C). These materials are also often used as a base coat under silicone-based coatings to achieve protection against even higher temperatures. When used alone, inorganic, zinc-rich silicates are an attractive alternative to coatings containing silicone resins because they are less expensive. They should not be used, however, in environments where acid might attack the coating and cause erosion and disintegration of the coating film. Waterborne, inorganic, zinc-rich coatings generally have a low VOC content.
- **600°–800°F (316°–427°C):** Black- or aluminum-pigmented organic-modified silicone coatings are the major coating products in this temperature range. To achieve adequate protection against the ravages of these high temperatures, a very high silicone content is required. For aluminum finishes, a silicone content of 50 to 70 percent is recommended. For a black or colored finish, the silicone content must be at least 70 percent, but a silicone content of 100 percent may be required in some circumstances. Coating formulas based on 100 percent silicone also offer excellent weatherability but do not adhere as well as other coatings, require a longer curing time, and are significantly less resistant to abrasion. For colors other than black, metal-oxide pigments produce the best results. These coatings require curing at high temperatures for several hours to achieve optimum film properties.
- **800°–1000°F (427°–538°C):** In this temperature range, aluminum-pigmented silicone coatings are used because they provide the best prolonged performance at these temperatures. The silicone-resin content of these materials is usually 100 percent. These products dry hard at ambient temperatures. However, these coatings require curing at high temperatures for several hours to achieve optimum film properties.
- **1000°–1200°F (538°–649°C):** One-hundred percent silicone-resin-based coatings with ceramic frits added are usually needed for protecting steel substrates at these very high temperatures. When temperatures in this range are achieved, the silicone resin decomposes, fusing the ceramic frits to the substrate to produce a durable, heat-resistant finish.

Environmental Conditions

The environment in which a coating functions is often the most important factor to consider when selecting a coating. Substrates that require protection from high temperatures are also often exposed to corrosive industrial atmospheres. This hostile environment may be a byproduct of the very forces that generate the high temperatures. Local atmospheric conditions, unrelated to temperature, may also be an important factor when selecting a high-temperature-resistant coating. A coating that cannot withstand corrosive environmental conditions is unsuitable for use where those conditions exist if a different coating performs well in such an environment.

Consider, for example, the factors architects must evaluate when selecting a coating for a boiler exhaust stack in a chemical-processing plant near the ocean. The coating selected must be capable of resisting temperatures that may exceed 700°F (371°C) at times, as well as enduring the corrosive effects of chemical fumes from the processing plant and occasional salt mist or spray from the nearby ocean. If the local authorities having jurisdiction also impose restrictions on the amount of VOCs coatings can contain, there will be other complications. In this example, a waterborne, inorganic, zinc-rich coating would satisfy both the high-temperature and low VOC requirements, but would be totally inappropriate because of exposure to acid fumes from the chemical plant and salt contamination from the ocean. Selecting a pigmented organic-modified silicone coating may be a better choice, even though it may be more expensive and less resistant to abrasion.

Terminology

One major problem architects face when dealing with coating manufacturers is the inconsistent use of terms. Many manufacturers classify their special coatings as suitable for service under severe, moderate, or mild weather and for chemical or marine exposure. They also usually further classify their coatings as suitable for immersion or nonimmersion service. Some coatings are also classified as suitable for use in highly corrosive environments. One manufacturer indicates that certain coatings are suitable for aggressive environments but does not define what *aggressive* means. The specifier must determine the precise meaning of these various terms before specifying a particular coating for a given application.

Coating System Costs

High-temperature-resistant coating systems are usually expensive because of the ingredients in the various products, but the protection they provide makes them well worth the investment when the cost of substrate repair, or possibly even equipment replacement, is considered. Part of the higher material cost of these coatings is a result of the refinement process required to produce the silicone resins on which many of these coatings are based. Because the silicone resins are expensive, most of the commercially available coating systems are combinations of silicone and organic resins. Only a few alternative systems, notably inorganic, zinc-rich coatings, are available. Most of them, however, are deficient in some qualities that make silicone resins attractive for high-temperature service.

For most owners, the total cost of the coating system is an important consideration. Many special coating systems lose some protective qualities over time as the coating is exposed to the elements. The system must be refreshed from time to time to restore these qualities or it will fail to fulfill its intended purpose. The total cost of a special coating system must, therefore, include costs involved in maintaining the system's protective qualities. Architects should try to obtain the required level of protection at the lowest practical cost per square foot (square meter) per year for the entire life of the system; they should not consider only the initial cost of applying the coating. This means they must also consider known maintenance requirements, the expected life of the coating, and the initial coating cost.

Coating System Compatibility

Many coating systems fail because of a lack of compatibility between the primer and the topcoat. Many high-temperature-resistant coating systems are designed for use indoors or in noncorrosive environments. These systems usually consist of two coats of a silicone-based product without a primer. There should not be a compatibility problem in such a system. However, many systems are designed to be used outdoors or in highly corrosive industrial environments. In these situations a primer is often necessary. When a different product is specified for use as a primer, it should also be silicone-based. If it is not, compatibility problems are likely. Following the topcoat manufacturer's recommendations closely for the type of primer required usually forestalls any compatibility problems between the primer and topcoat. The specifier should also follow the manufacturer's recommendations for primer-coating film thickness and curing time.

Product Limitations

Specifying that prime and finish coats on any surface be from the same manufacturer usually eliminates problems with compatibility of primers and topcoats. This presupposes the specifier will follow the manufacturer's recommendations on which primer to use with a particular topcoat. It also presupposes that the applicators will also closely follow the manufacturer's recommendations for surface preparation. Specifiers must also closely coordinate the high-temperature-resistant coatings specification with those specification sections that specify shop-applied prime coats. This will ensure that prime coats applied by the fabricator of shop-primed items that will receive high-temperature-resistant coatings are compatible with the finish coating system required.

SURFACE PREPARATION

Substrate Condition

Poor surface preparation is the major factor in most coating failures. A properly prepared surface is critical to good coating performance because no coating is better than the surface over which it is applied. Coatings on ferrous metal quickly deteriorate when the substrate contains dirt, grease, moisture, mill scale, rust, or other foreign materials that impede good coating performance. Such substances constitute a barrier between the substrate and an applied coating. They usually intensify, then deteriorate rapidly and detach from the substrate surface, taking the coating with them. When this occurs, the failure should not be blamed on the coating, but on the condition of the substrate before coating application. These failures are expensive to repair and can usually be avoided by properly preparing the substrate to receive the protective coatings in the first place.

Surface-Preparation Requirements

The level of surface preparation required on any given substrate is determined by the nature of the surface, the operating conditions to which the surface will be subjected, and the type of coating that will be applied. For example, ferrous-metal surfaces that will be continuously immersed in saltwater will require a more thorough surface preparation than similar metal surfaces that will only be subjected to occasional exposure to ocean spray or the elements. The degree of surface preparation required for any substrate is proportional to the severity of the corrosive atmospheric elements in which it must function.

Steel

SSPC: The Society for Protective Coatings, formerly the Steel Structures Painting Council, has adopted several standards for surface preparation for steel surfaces. Several of these standards have also been adopted by the National Association of Corrosion Engineers (NACE) and are issued as joint surface-preparation standards. These standards vary in the intensity of the cleaning process and in the result required. Basic SSPC surface preparation consists of wiping the substrate with a solvent to remove grease, oil, and other soluble surface contaminants, followed by use of hand tools to remove loose rust, mill scale, and other loose surface contaminants. The highest levels of surface preparation require blasting the surface to white metal with an abrasive, or "pickling" in an acid bath for complete removal of rust and mill scale. There are four separate levels of abrasive-blasting surface preparation. SSPC's *Steel Structures Painting Manual* describes these blasting levels in detail.

Abrasive Blast Cleaning

The best surface preparation for steel exposed to high temperatures is abrasive blast cleaning. Silicone-resin-based coatings adhere best when the steel surfaces to be coated have been thoroughly cleaned and profiled with abrasive blasting. The following list describes the four SSPC/NACE joint standards for abrasive blast cleaning, in declining order of the intensity of the cleaning process:

- **SSPC-SP 5/NACE 1 White Metal Blast Cleaning:** This standard requires complete removal of all visible rust, mill scale, paint, and other foreign matter by blast cleaning. It provides the best surface preparation available for steel. SSPC-SP 5 is also the most expensive of the various blast-cleaning levels and should be used only when the high cost of surface preparation by this method can be justified. SSPC-SP 5 is required for steel exposed to extremely corrosive environments and for steel used in immersion service. The standard strongly suggests that surfaces cleaned to this level should be coated as soon as possible to preserve them against rust back, which can occur within minutes in some circumstances. SSPC recommends coating the surface within 24 hours to minimize the problem. Only a few coating manufacturers require this level of surface preparation for their high-temperature-resistant coatings, and those that do require it for only the highest temperature levels anticipated.
- **SSPC-SP 10/NACE 2 Near-White Blast Cleaning:** This standard requires cleaning to near-white metal cleanliness. It requires complete removal of all rust, mill scale, and other deleterious matter but permits residual random stain, amounting to less than 5 percent of a 9-sq. in. (6400-sq. mm) unit area to remain on the surface in some conditions. SSPC-SP 10 is satisfactory for all but the most demanding conditions and can be considerably lower in cost than the SSPC-SP 5 level. Nevertheless, it is still a costly level of surface preparation and should only be used when required to satisfy manufacturer's recommendations because of the aggressive environment. It is usually required for high-humidity conditions, and in aggressive chemical, marine, and other highly corrosive environments. This level of surface preparation is required by most manufacturers of high-temperature-resistant coatings for the highest temperature exposures.
- **SSPC-SP 6/NACE 3 Commercial Blast Cleaning:** This standard requires blast cleaning until at least two-thirds of the surface of a 9-sq. in. (6400-sq. mm) unit area is free of visible rust, mill scale, paint, or other foreign matter. As a result, the surface is far from uniform in color. SSPC-SP 6 is considered a general-purpose level of surface preparation. It is used when a high, but not perfect, level of surface preparation is required. Because it is less demanding than SSPC-SP 10, it is much lower in cost. It is the level required by most coating manufacturers for all but the highest anticipated temperature levels.
- **SSPC-SP 7/NACE 4 Brush-off Blast Cleaning:** This is the least demanding of the blast-cleaning standards and requires cleaning the metal free of all except the most tightly adhering residue of mill scale and coatings. It is not recommended for severe conditions, and its use is generally not recommended by high-temperature-resistant coating manufacturers.

Coating specifications for high-temperature-resistant coatings should call for completely removing rust, mill scale, and other foreign materials. If all mill scale is not removed, there is a chance of it coming loose later and causing coating failures. In the shop, pickling removes all mill scale and other interfering materials and can be used instead of blast cleaning; however, pickling is usually impractical for high-temperature coating application because of the nature of the items being coated. Cleaned steel provides an excellent bonding surface for most coatings and produces superior, long-lasting results. Immediately priming blast-cleaned steel is an important consideration whether using shop or field abrasive blasting. This deters any chance of rusting, as blast-cleaned steel is susceptible to rustback.

Preparing steel surfaces to receive zinc-rich coatings is more extensive than for other primers. Blasting the base metal is required. For best results, use near-white blast-cleaned steel (SSPC-SP 10), although the degree of required surface preparation varies with the specific coatings. Some coatings must be used only over the best surface preparation; others will tolerate a lesser-prepared surface; and still others will perform satisfactorily, under mild service conditions, over a good mechanically hand-cleaned surface. With this diversity, to obtain the best performance, select the specific coating carefully and follow the coating manufacturer's recommendations.

ENVIRONMENTAL CONCERNS

This discussion addresses only those aspects of federal and state regulations governing VOCs that impact high-temperature-resistant coatings. For background information on federal and state regulations that govern VOCs, and the problems that this concern for the environment creates for the coatings industry, refer to Chapter 09910, Painting, which provides a detailed discussion on the history of VOC regulations and recent actions of the Environmental Protection Agency (EPA).

VOC Levels for High-Temperature-Resistant Coatings

EPA regulations set the maximum VOC content of high-temperature-resistant coatings at 650 g/L or 5.4 lb/gal. One reason for much higher limits for high-temperature-resistant coatings than for other coatings is that these coatings have unique characteristics, perform a necessary function, and have no known viable alternative. Low VOC silicone resins are possible, and research on developing such products is ongoing; however, there is currently no concerted effort to lower the proposed VOC limits for these coatings. For situations where they are appropriate, waterborne, inorganic, zinc-rich coatings are a low-VOC alternative to higher silicone-resin-based coatings. However, their use is generally limited to applications in acid-free environments.

Recent history indicates that existing VOC regulations are subject to change. Prudent specifiers should contact their local office of the EPA for current information or interpretation of regulations for unusual circumstances.

SAFETY HAZARDS

Major concerns of the coatings industry are potential health and safety hazards involved in coating application, particularly during recoating operations in occupied spaces. These hazards exist because most coatings contain volatile solvents. Special coatings are of particular concern in these areas.

Flammable solvents are present in high percentages in most coatings. When applying coatings in an enclosed space, the danger exists that solvent vapor buildup in the space could become great enough to reach a low explosive limit. In these circumstances, a spark or source of ignition could produce a dangerous explosion. However, work in such spaces is safe if there is adequate ventilation. This requires that the air in the enclosed space is changed often enough to dilute the solvent vapor concentration below the low explosive limit. Precautions in using spray equipment are also necessary because of the nature of the work. When using spray equipment, adequate ventilation is an absolute necessity and should be in effect regardless of the flash point of the solvents in the coating.

REFERENCES

Publication dates cited here were current at the time of this writing. Publications are revised periodically, and revisions may have occurred before this book was published.

SSPC: The Society for Protective Coatings

SSPC-SP 5/NACE 1 1994: Joint Surface Preparation Standard—White Metal Blast Cleaning

SSPC-SP 6/NACE 3 1994: Joint Surface Preparation Standard—Commercial Blast Cleaning

SSPC-SP 7/NACE 4 1994: Joint Surface Preparation Standard—Brush-Off Blast Cleaning

SSPC-SP 10/NACE 2 1994: Joint Surface Preparation Standard—Near-White Blast CleaningCoatings

BOOK

SSPC: The Society for Protective Coatings, *Steel Structures Painting Manual,* vol. II., 7th ed., Pittsburg, PA: SSPC, 1995.

09981 CEMENTITIOUS COATINGS

This chapter discusses polymer-modified cementitious coatings to use above or below grade on the exterior or interior over masonry and concrete. After curing, these coatings produce a durable, hard, weather-resistant surface.

GENERAL COMMENTS

Cementitious coatings are prepackaged, dry-powder formulations containing white portland cement and hydrated lime or aggregate that are applied to exterior or interior concrete or masonry surfaces above or below grade. They produce a durable, inexpensive, weather-resistant finish and are suitable for use on new construction or on renovation and restoration work on high- and low-rise building projects. Two types of cementitious coatings in common use are the following:

- **Water-based cementitious coatings:** This variety requires adding potable water to the formula to produce the coating material.
- **Polymer-modified cementitious coatings:** This variety requires mixing two prepackaged components, according to the manufacturer's instructions, to produce the coating.

Water-based cementitious coatings are time-tested products that have been in use for years. The coatings industry, however, regularly discovers new materials and adds them to existing formulations to improve performance. Polymer-modified cementitious coatings are an example of how refinements improve the performance of existing products. Combining liquid polymers and cement results in a product that is stronger and more resilient than the original water-cement coating systems.

PRODUCT CHARACTERISTICS

Suitable Substrates

Cementitious coatings are inorganic coatings with high bond strength and a coefficient of thermal expansion that is similar to that of concrete. This makes them particularly suitable for use over cast-in-place and precast concrete. Brick and concrete masonry block are also acceptable substrates. However, these coatings may be used on any type of masonry substrate, including stucco and porous stone. The high bond strength of these coatings ensures good adhesion to these substrates.

Typical Use

Cementitious coatings are primarily used on vertical surfaces and occasionally used on overhead horizontal surfaces, such as soffits and canopies, and on tank floors. Although they are abrasion-resistant, most manufacturers do not recommend cementitious coatings for traffic-bearing horizontal surfaces, unless the surface receives a suitable protective topping. Consult manufacturers for advice on unusual applications.

Principal Applications

Cementitious coatings are used on almost every type of building. Manufacturers' literature shows applications on public buildings, such as museums and libraries, and on bridges, parking garages, and industrial plants. Other typical applications include silo exteriors, tunnels, waste-water treatment plants, and retaining walls. Cementitious coatings are also used in residential basements to provide a decorative finish for rough, unfinished concrete block walls. They are excellent for building renovations where a fresh, new appearance is required for deteriorating exterior building walls.

Cementitious coatings are useful for walls subject to positive or negative hydrostatic pressure. They are nontoxic when in contact with potable water and are often used to line pools, ponds, and reservoirs; occasionally they are used on submerged structures. Because they resist the damaging action of deicing salts used in winter, they are often used on substrates exposed to these salts.

Exterior Decorative Uses

Cementitious coatings are frequently used as a finish coat on exterior applications where an inexpensive, decorative appearance is required. These coatings are used instead of a mechanical finish over concrete because of the deep texture the coatings provide. This same deep texture also hides or disguises surface defects in architectural concrete and concrete masonry construction.

Advantages

Properly applied cementitious coatings provide a low-cost, low-maintenance, tough, durable finish that is resistant to wind-driven rain, impact damage, and abrasion. Other attributes include the following:

- **Surface-burning characteristics:** Cementitious coatings are noncombustible and do not contribute to flame spread or smoke generation.
- **Fungus-resistant:** Cementitious coatings do not support fungus growth and they resist mildew.
- **Odor:** These coatings have very little odor.
- **Freeze-/thaw-resistant:** They are resistant to the harmful effects of rapid, alternate freeze/thaw temperatures.
- **Ultraviolet degradation:** Cementitious coatings resist ultraviolet light.
- **Toxicity:** They are nontoxic when in contact with potable water.
- **Salt-spray-resistant:** Cementitious coatings are highly resistant to chemical salts.

Radon

Several manufacturers claim that cementitious coatings serve as a barrier to infiltration by radon gas and are useful as part of a total system of radon-abatement systems. One manufacturer claims a 99 percent reduction in radon penetration when using its product.

Composition

Besides white portland cement and hydrated lime or aggregate, most proprietary formulas also include calcium carbonate, titanium-dioxide pigments, and occasionally colored pigments for tinting. The dry-powder coating mix usually consists of 70 to 80 percent white portland cement. Proprietary mixtures typically consist of one part hydrated lime to five parts portland cement; the mix contains hydrated lime for easier brushability. Provided hydrated lime is not used to excess, it also helps the product achieve a hard, weather-resistant coating. Cementitious coatings applied over open-textured masonry surfaces usually include white or light-colored silica sand aggregate to fill the open pores and voids in the surface.

Polymers

Two components are necessary to produce polymer-modified cementitious coatings. For most proprietary products, a special liquid-based acrylic polymer bonding agent is added to the dry-powder portland cement and aggregate blend to produce the cementitious coating. Some companies also require adding potable water to the blend of prepackaged ingredients. Adding acrylic polymers to the portland cement and aggregate blend produces a stuccolike mix that bonds tightly to the substrate.

Other Ingredients

In proprietary formulas, manufacturers usually include calcium chloride to help draw moisture from the air. The presence of airborne moisture promotes proper curing and hardening of cementitious coatings. Proprietary formulas also usually include titanium-dioxide pigments to improve wet opacity. Some manufacturers add up to 1 percent of calcium stearate to improve the coatings' water-repellent characteristics. Color pigments are also often added for different tints.

SURFACE PREPARATION

Substrate Condition

Careful attention to the condition of a substrate that is to receive an applied coating is an important factor in the success of the application. More coating failures are attributable to poor or inadequate surface preparation than to any other factor. Furthermore, complete and proper surface preparation also extends the coating's surface life. For this reason, all cementitious coating manufacturers stress the importance of proper preparation of the substrate scheduled to receive their coatings.

Good surface preparation is particularly important for cementitious coatings because these materials depend on both a chemical and mechanical bond for adhesion to the substrate. A tight bond prevents delamination and subsequent coating failure. Most manufacturers recommend a bond test before application because the coating will fail within a short time if it does not adhere fully to the substrate. Review areas and surfaces to be coated and, if necessary, specify more stringent surface preparation in areas that are critical to the project.

Surface Condition

Cementitious coatings adhere best when a substrate is clean and slightly rough. Surfaces receiving cementitious coatings must be free of surface contaminants such as dirt, oil, grease, efflorescence, and laitance, or a good bond is impossible to achieve. Use abrasive blasting, if necessary, to remove surface contaminants. A wet blast or a high-pressure water wash is an effective method for preparing a surface. In addition, remove residual paint film from previously painted surfaces. Cut out and repair static cracks, voids, honeycombs, and similar defects, using methods and materials recommended by the manufacturer.

Dampening the Substrate

Unlike conventional paints and coatings that must be dry, surfaces receiving cementitious coatings must be uniformly dampened, but not wet, before application. This prevents surface drag and improves surface bond. Manufacturers recommend dampening, but not soaking, surfaces to be coated at least one hour before application. The surface should be redampened, but not soaked, immediately before starting coating operations. If the surface has been cleaned by water blasting as part of the surface preparation, or otherwise thoroughly soaked by heavy rain, it must be permitted to dry completely before applying the coating materials.

Concrete

To prepare a concrete substrate to receive a cementitious coating, it must be thoroughly washed with a detergent to remove form oils, dust, dirt, and similar surface contaminants. Form ties must be removed and the surface patched according to the manufacturer's instructions. New concrete must be allowed to cure long enough to support the material without damage. Most manufacturers recommend allowing new concrete to cure for 2 to 14 days before applying cementitious coatings; however, at least one manufacturer requires 28 days' curing time. If there is any doubt about the surface condition, perform a bond test as recommended by the manufacturer.

Coatings intended to be applied over a sleek or glossy surface, such as glazed tile, or on concrete, where a clear surface sealer has been used, usually require extra care in surface preparation. It may be necessary to etch such surfaces with a muriatic acid solution to remove laitance to provide a clean, rough surface similar to that of smooth or fine-grit sandpaper. This produces a better mechanical bond. If there is any doubt about the surface, consult the coating manufacturer.

Previously Coated Surfaces

It is not necessary to remove an existing cementitious coating material from surfaces to be recoated if the existing material is sound. However, thoroughly cleaning the existing surface before recoating is necessary. If portions of an existing surface delaminate easily, potential problems exist and coating failure is likely. Following manufacturer's recommendations, test the entire substrate for proper bond before applying the coating material. Remove unsound, previously coated areas and patch the substrate before proceeding.

Masonry

Mortar joints in masonry walls must be completely cured and in sound condition before applying the coating. As with concrete, a new substrate must have adequate curing time before starting application, or coating failure is likely. Several manufacturers suggest applying one light trowel coat over uncoated concrete masonry as a block filler before beginning the regular application. This helps disguise masonry joints and evens the surface. Most manufacturers suggest allowing at least 14 days' curing time before proceeding; however, one manufacturer requires a minimum of 28 days' curing time before beginning application.

APPLICATION

Climatic Conditions

Because cementitious coatings contain portland cement, all manufacturers advise against applying them to frozen or frost-filled surfaces. These coatings should not be applied when the temperature is below, or expected to fall below, 40°F (4°C) within 24 hours. They should not be applied when it is raining or when rain is expected before the coating has attained its initial set. In hot, dry, or windy weather, it is usually necessary to frequently apply a light water mist to the coated surface to prevent premature drying.

Application Methods

Many proprietary coatings may be applied by spraying, and some by roller, but designers usually prefer the appearance achieved by brushing the material onto the surface with a masonry or tampico fiber brush. Trowel application is also possible. Most manufacturers suggest two coats over an uncoated surface or one coat over an existing cementitious coating. Some brush-applied products may be recoated within 24 hours. However, to disguise some surface irregularities, such as mortar joints in brick or concrete masonry and on walls subject to high hydrostatic pressures, allow the first coat to cure for five to seven days before recoating. Consult the coating manufacturer for other special situations.

ENVIRONMENTAL CONCERNS

Many architectural coatings have been limited by federal and state regulations governing the amount of VOCs that can be contained in the coatings. These restrictions are an effort to decrease the amount of irritating pollutants some coatings release into the atmosphere. It is expected that the number of states restricting the amount of VOCs will increase over the next few years. However, because cementitious coatings are inorganic or largely inorganic in nature, their use has not been restricted by current federal and state regulations. Nevertheless, before specifying any type of coating in areas where state regulations have been promulgated, check with the local Environmental Protection Agency (EPA) office for the latest information about changes in VOC regulations.

SAFETY AND HEALTH HAZARDS

Coatings usually contain some flammable solvents. This is not usually the case with cementitious coating materials. However, cementitious coatings contain portland cement, which is irritating to the eyes and skin. In some cases, both components are irritants, so manufacturers recommend that extra care be taken to protect the eyes, skin, and respiratory system. Applicators should always wear safety goggles and impervious gloves when handling or mixing the coatings. In some cases, using a respirator during application is recommended. For interior applications, adequate ventilation is always recommended.

ILLUSTRATION ACKNOWLEDGEMENTS

05511
Joseph Iano, Architect; Boston, Massachusetts
Edward Allen, AIA; South Natick, Massachusetts
Rippeteau Architects, P.C.; Washington, D.C.
Erica K. Beach and Annica S. Emilsson, Rippeteau Architects, PC; Washington, D.C.
Charles A. Szoradi, AIA; Washington, D.C.

06402
Richard J. Vitullo, AIA; Oak Leaf Studio; Crownsville, Maryland
Architectural Woodwork Institute; Centreville, Virginia
Chart reprinted with permission from the Hardwood Plywood and Veneer Association
Greg Heuer; Architectural Woodwork Institute; Reston, Virginia
Architectural Woodwork Institute, Architectural Woodwork Quality Standards, 7th ed. (version 1), 1997.
Helmut Guenschel, Inc; Baltimore, Maryland

06420
Richard J. Vitullo, AIA; Oak Leaf Studio; Crownsville, Maryland
Architectural Woodwork Institute; Arlington, Virginia

08110
Daniel F.C. Hayes, AIA; Washington, D.C.
James W. G. Watson, AIA; Ronald A. Spahn and Associates; Cleveland Heights, Ohio
National Fire Association, Quincy, Massachusetts

08211
Daniel F. C. Hayes, AIA; Washington, D.C.
National Fire Protection Association; Quincy, Massachusetts
Richard J. Vitullo, AIA; Oak Leaf Studio; Crownsville, Maryland
Architectural Woodwork Institute; Centreville, Virginia

08212
Jeffrey R. Vandevoort, Talbott Wilson Associates, Inc.; Houston, Texas
Daniel F. C. Hayes, AIA; Washington, D.C.

08311
Daniel F. C. Hayes, AIA; Washington, D.C.

08351
Daniel F. C. Hayes, AIA; Washington, D.C.

08710
Richard J. Vitullo, AIA; Oak Leaf Studio; Crownsville, Maryland
Daniel F.C. Hayes, AIA; Washington, D.C.

09210
James E. Phillips, AIA; Enwright Associates, Inc; Greenville, South Carolina
United States Gypsum Company; Chicago, Illinois
Walter H. Sobel, FAIA & Associates; Chicago, Illinois
The Marmon Mok Partnership; San Antonio, Texas

09220
James E. Phillips, AIA; Enwright Associates, Inc; Greenville, South Carolina
The Marmon Mok Partnership; San Antonio, Texas

09260
Ferdinand R. Scheeler, AIA; Skidmore, Owings & Merrill; Chicago, Illinois
James Lloyd; Kennett Square, Pennsylvania

09271
Reed A. Black; Oehrlein & Associates; Washington, D.C.

09310
The Council of America, Inc.; Princeton, New Jersey
Jess McIlvain, AIA, CCS, CSI; Jess McIlvain and Associates; Bethesda, Maryland

09385
Mark Forma; Leo A. Daly Company; Washington, D.C.

09400
John C. Lunsford, AIA; Varney Sexton Sydnor Architects; Phoenix, Arizona

09511
Keith McCormack, CCS, CSI; RTKL Associates; Baltimore, Maryland
Setter, Leach, & Lindstrom, Inc; Minneapolis, Minnesota
Blythe + Nazdin Architects, Ltd.; Bethesda, Maryland

09512
Setter, Leach, & Lindstrom, Inc; Minneapolis, Minnesota
Blythe + Nazdin Architects, Ltd.; Bethesda, Maryland
Keith McCormack, CCS, CSI; RTKL Associates; Baltimore, Maryland

09513
Setter, Leach, & Lindstrom, Inc; Minneapolis, Minnesota

09514
Setter, Leach, & Lindstrom, Inc; Minneapolis, Minnesota

09547
Keith McCormack, CCS, CSI; RTKL Associates; Baltimore, Maryland
USG Interiors, Inc., Chicago, Illinois
Setter, Leach, & Lindstrom, Inc; Minneapolis, Minnesota

09635
Mark Forma; Leo A. Daly Company; Washington, D.C.

09638
Mark Forma; Leo A. Daly Company; Washington, D.C.
Eric K. Beach; Rippeteau Architects, PC; Washington, D.C.
Building Stone Institute; New York, New York
George M. Whiteside, III, AIA, and James D. Lloyd; Kennet Square, Pennsylvania

09640
Rippeteau Architects, PC; Washington, D.C.
Annica S. Emilsson; Rippeteau Architects, PC; Washington, D.C.

09644
Jim Swords; HOK Sports Facilities Group; Kansas City, Missouri
Connor/AGA Sports Flooring Corporation; Amas, Michigan
Robbins Sports Surfaces; Cincinnati, Ohio
Annica S. Emilsson; Rippeteau Architects, PC; Washington, D.C.
Connor/AGA Sports Flooring Corporation; Amas, Michigan
Robbins Sports Surfaces; Cincinnati, Ohio

09653
Broome, Oringdulph, O'Toole, Rudolf & Associates; Portland, Oregon
Alan S. Glassman, Assoc. AIA, CSI; Armstrong World Industries, Inc.;
   Lancaster, Pennsylvania
Annica S. Emilsson; Rippeteau Architects, PC; Washington, D.C.
Erica K. Beach and Annica S. Emilsson; Rippeteau Architects, PC;
   Washington, D.C.

09671
Chip Baker; Sverdrup Facilities Inc; Arlington, Virginia

09680
Neil Spencer, AIA; North Canton, Ohio

09681
Neil Spencer, AIA; North Canton, Ohio

09720
Richard J. Vitullo, AIA; Oak Leaf Studio; Crownsville, Maryland
Kristie Strasen; Strasen Frost Associates; New York, New York

09751
Mark Forma; Leo A. Daly Company; Washington, D.C.
Building Stone Institute; New York, New York
George M. Whiteside, III, AIA, and James D. Lloyd; Kennet Square,
   Pennsylvania
Alexander Keyes; Darrell Downing Rippeteau, Architect; Washington, D.C.

09771
Richard J. Vitullo, AIA; Oak Leaf Studio; Crownsville, Maryland
Kristie Strasen; Strasen Frost Associates; New York, New York

09772
Richard J. Vitullo, AIA; Oak Leaf Studio; Crownsville, Maryland
Kristie Strasen; Strasen Frost Associates; New York, New York

09841
Rippeteau Architects P.C.; Washington, D.C.
Setter, Leach, & Lindstrom, Inc; Minneapolis, Minnesota
Blythe + Nazdin Architects, Ltd.; Bethesda, Maryland
Michael G. Lawrence, AIA; M Lawrence Architects; Washington, D.C.
Neil Thompson Shade; Acoustical Design Collaborative, Ltd; Falls
   Church, Virginia

09910
James W. Laffy; Washington, D.C.

09931
McCain Murray; Washington, D.C.

09960
Isabel Ramirez and Ted Hallinan; Sverdrup Facilities Inc; Arlington, Virginia

09963
Isabel Ramirez and Ted Hallinan; Sverdrup Facilities Inc; Arlington, Virginia

09967
Isabel Ramirez and Ted Hallinan; Sverdrup Facilities Inc; Arlington, Virginia

09980
Richard J. Vitullo, AIA; Oak Leaf Studio; Crownsville, Maryland
Kristie Strasen; Strasen Frost Associates; New York, New York

09981
Isabel Ramirez and Ted Hallinan; Sverdrup Facilities Inc; Arlington, Virginia

INDEX

263